10,000 Days in Alaska

Book Three
1998-2005

Norman Wilkins

Copies of this book (volume three of three) can be ordered from Amazon or from the publisher. For additional information about the author, go to www.10000daysinalaska.com.

Books by Norman Wilkins:

Volume 1: 10,000 Days In Alaska Book One
Volume 2: 10,000 Days In Alaska Book Two
Volume 3: 10,000 Days In Alaska Book Three

ISBN 10: 1-886352-34-8
ISBN EAN 13: 978-1-886352-34-6

Published by
Cloud 9 Publishing
www.cloud9publ.wordpress.com

Volume one transcribed by Nadia Giordana, Cloud 9 Publishing
Volumes two and three transcribed by Linda Law of Stillwater, Minnesota
Technical advisor, Laura T. Behrendt

Front cover photo: Norman Wilkins taken by Ralph Fuson

All names of persons and places mentioned in this book are real; they have not been changed.

A letter written by Norman Wilkins
May 26, 2002

Dear Nadia and Chuck,

It's so beautiful here this morning. Sun is breaking over the horizon and a pair of swans are sitting on the water down towards the west end of the lake. Early light casts such a pretty yellow over everything. I feel so privileged to be up and catch this time of day. The snow on the mountains to the south is so clean and white, contrasting nicely with the green of the spruce trees at lower elevations.

    Kestrels are nesting in a box here in the yard. Being very territorial, they attack all intruders. As I sit here, a goldeneye duck flies by the window. Just then, a kestrel dives off his perch in a spruce top and hits the duck with his knotted talons, knocking feathers out of its back. Last evening, that same kestrel took after a nosey raven. Each time it dove, the raven would flip over on its back. The kestrel then broke off his attack. Flickers have tried to nest nearby and were driven out. Sylvia really enjoys the flicker activity and didn't want them chased away. She thinks kestrels are messy when they bring in their bloody kills to feed their young.

    Sylvia has her greenhouse started. She put some plants outside to harden them off. A vole must have climbed in the box and cut off every cauliflower. That was bad enough, but the next morning, she found that it had cut off the cabbages! The potatoes are planted. I planted some sweet corn just see what will happen. Sylvia has red, white, and blue pansies in boxes for the Legion Post and will put them out when the danger of frost is past. The lawn came through the winter in the best condition ever.

    Allen Farmer called to tell us a grizzly had been sighted a mile east of Eureka. I grabbed huntin' gear, drove over there, looked all up and down the country, but saw no sign. Later learned mileage was off.

    Late afternoon of the 24th, Sylvia noticed something swimming in the lake. Grabbing the binoculars, it was soon evident that this was nine bull caribou. They were trying to cross the lake south to north and it appeared like they became intimidated by the houses—or perhaps barking dogs. They swam in a confused manner for some time, then exited the lake to the south. Most had horns two feet long and covered with velvet. Those horns will grow lots more over the summer. One of the caribou had lots of white on it, suggesting reindeer blood in its veins. It was neat to see then, for it has been quite some time since we have observed them here.

    We have tickets for a flight to Minnesota leaving August 6th, and returning September 4th. So many people to visit and so little time in which to do it. I would like to spend a few days in Iowa, and you can bet Sylvia wants to see her sister Frances in Chicago. We'll see how things fall together.

Love, Dad and Mom

Thursday, March 8, 2001

"A cow moose with her last year's calf were bedded in the snow 10 yards from kitchen window this morning and stayed there till after we had our breakfast. They were chewing their cuds. Both are getting thin, calf more so. They fed around here today. This afternoon I fired up the snowgo and drove down to lower part of water line and shoveled some more snow away from it."

—Norman Wilkins

The last volume in this series is dedicated to my wife and three daughters. All are talented individuals in their own unique ways—and yes, they do have stories to tell. My wife Sylvia has been amazingly patient, when you consider that living in Alaska was not her first choice; Beverly Volk, the youngest; Theresa Austin, the middle girl; and Nadia Giordana, the eldest, who published this three-volume documentary journal.

Norman Wilkins

FORWORD

10,000 Days In Alaska is a three-volume documentary journal written by Norman Wilkins as he and his wife Ladislava (Sylvia) lived it. Norman recorded daily journal entries throughout the entire 25+ years he and Sylvia spent carving out a life on the Alaskan tundra.

The contents of this book have been transcribed from Norman's notebook-style pages as originally written with the exception of occasional edits and insertions for clarity. We have made every effort to maintain Norman's unique personal style in order to preserve the naturalness of his voice, and the meanings of his words.

Book one covers the first twelve years of their incredible experience, and book two encompasses 1990 through 1997. This is book three; it completes the series, picking up the story in 1998 and ending in 2005 when the Wilkins' left Alaska and moved to Minnesota. All three books are available online and can be ordered wherever books are sold.

Prior to moving to Alaska in 1979, the couple farmed for more than 25 years in Iowa and Minnesota. At the time of this printing, Norman and Sylvia are in their 80s and living in Little Falls, Minnesota to be near their children.

Nadia Giordana, Cloud 9 Publishing

When the time comes for a man to look his maker in the eye,
where better could the meeting be held, than in the wilderness.
—Richard Proenneke

TABLE OF CONTENTS

1998—50th Wedding Anniversary 9

1999—Chronographing bullet speeds 59

2000—Sylvia gets interviewed, and hunt at 5-mile 107

2001—Trip to Fairbanks 155

2002—Hunting Dall sheep 205

2003—A buffalo hunt and two family reunions 255

2004—Selling the remote parcel at Old Boot Lake 303

2005—Leaving Alaska 357

Epilogue—A poetic encounter with wolves 417

Norman Wilkins in front of his trap cabin in 1996. Photo taken by Ralph Fuson.

1998—50th Wedding Anniversary

Thursday, January 1, 1998—partly cloudy, -17° to -7°. We did a few little things around the house. Charlie, Beth, Charlie Jr., Cora and Paul Trowbridge got here mid afternoon. Got settled in and we are visiting and enjoying their company. It's been too long since we've spent any time together.

Friday, January 2, 1998—cloudy and snow in afternoon and evening, -15° to -5°. Charlie, Beth and the kids did some skiing, sledding and rode my snowgo some. Then we all went to Odden's, ate a lot and the musicians played a lot of music. Made homemade ice cream. Plowed snow off our lane.

Saturday, January 3, 1998—mostly sunny, -21° to -5° to -20°. Sun dogs this afternoon and moon dogs tonight. We slept late. This afternoon we went over to Dan and Patti's place, The Point on Lake Louise. Nice visit, pot luck dinner, music and more visiting. Trapper Bob showed up and we visited awhile. Saw two moon dogs.

Sunday, January 4, 1998—mostly sunny, -31° to -19°. After breakfast, Trowbridge family got ready to start for their home. Tom, Lisa, Lauren and Emily Smayda brought Cora by and stayed to visit for a while after Trowbridges left. Not too long after Tom and Lisa left, Jim O. came with our ice cream freezer and a Christmas gift. I gave Jim my gift to him and we signed each others permanent fund applications.

Monday, January 5, 1998—sunny, -36° to -24°. Mailed dividend application and a bunch of letters. Jim and Elaine Manning brought over a nice apple pie. Allen stopped by and visited for awhile.

Tuesday, January 6, 1998—mostly sunny, -47° to -30°. I pulled the snow off the little porch roof over the front door. Carried a bucket of old coffee grounds out to the greenhouse. Sure nice to be outside doing something, even at this temperature.

Wednesday, January 7, 1998—mostly high clouds, -34° to -24°. Split a few pieces of wood and carried it into the basement. Repaired a child's toy. Read some. I don't feel well and am tired.

Thursday, January 8, 1998—partly sunny, -30° to -15°. I took garbage to transfer site. Visited Tom H. Took a jar of cranberries to Mary G. Cal was getting wood. Phillip was helping too. Allen was gone.

Friday, January 9, 1998—most cloudy, -20° to -3°. We went to Glennallen on senior van. Lunch, cash checks and a little shopping. We tried to pump water, but there is ice in the line. Tried to thaw it in place, no luck.

Saturday, January 10, 1998—most cloudy, 0° most of the day. Went to Jim's – loaded water hauling tank, got down to Little Nelchina River to load water in the tank and someone had parked in the way and left their vehicle-so not possible to get water and came back home. After supper, Allen phoned and we went to his place and ate a little pizza, blueberry pie and ice cream. Odden had brought the pie and Mary made the pizza. Visited a while. Charlie T. phoned today.

Sunday, January 11, 1998—partly cloudy, Near 0° most of the day. Made a false start but got one load of water hauled and unloaded into the tanks in basement. Replaced a bulb in turn signal on the truck. Jim, Mary, and Kari were here for supper with us.

Monday, January 12, 1998—mostly cloudy, some fluffy snow in afternoon, -15° to 0°. Did lots of reading. Received CBA information targets etc and a letter from Ed Doonan in answer to some of my rifle shooting of cast bullets.

Tuesday, January 13, 1998—mostly cloudy, -17° to -6°. Skiff of snow. Sorted and packaged some gun sights to take to gun show for trading.

Wednesday, January 14, 1998—mostly sunny, 1" snow in night, -20° to -14°. A wolf walked in on our driveway during the night. It left walking east under the power line. I plowed our snow. Visited Allen. Polished some .223 brass in preparation for making key rings.

Thursday, January 15, 1998—partly cloudy, -24° to -6°. Assembled the cartridge key rings. That work makes my hands hurt. Allen came over to visit after supper and brought ice cream.

Friday, January 16, 1998—mostly cloudy, -13° to -5°. Saw a fox near the house when I looked out the bathroom window in middle of night. It was staring back at me. Jim O. borrowed the water hauling tank. I organized a note book for .308 win reloading and record keeping.

Saturday, January 17, 1998—sunny here, -15° to -3°. Jim O. Tom H and I went to Wasilla. It was cloudy there. Jim got building materials. I sold some old gun parts and bought a clip, and three books. Tom and I did lots of looking. Jim, Tom and I shopped for a few groceries.

Sunday, January 18, 1998—foggy till mid afternoon, then cleared off for a little while and clouded over, -14° to -6°. Filled out an order to LSB. Jim O. brought water tank and visited a while.

Monday, January 19, 1998—mostly cloudy, -9° to 0. Don't feel well today. Hauled a load of water from Little Nelchina River.

Tuesday, January 20, 1998—sunny and beautiful, -15° to -5°. Didn't feel well today again either. Carried in some firewood. Tried switching barrels and actions on two rifles to get an idea for a different stock for one of them.

Wednesday, January 21, 1998—sunny, -20° to -10°. I walked down to well and replaced the light bulb used for heat. Lots of fox track, all over down there. Carried one arm load of wood, Ha! Read a lot.

Thursday, January 22, 1998—sunny. -22° to -7°. Wrote one letter. Drew plans for rifle action wrenches. Allen and Sammy had supper with us. Sent ad to Gun List.

Friday, January 23, 1998—sunny, -19° to -5°. We went to Glennallen on senior van. Paid electric bill and had lunch. CVEA phoned to discuss the electric bill that we think is too high.

Saturday, January 24, 1998—sunny, -20° to -10°. Didn't feel well today. Did some measuring and drawing of a rifle action tool. Ted Mattson and friend are visiting Jim and Mary Odden. They asked us to have supper with them. We had a good visit.

Sunday, January 25, 1998—sunny and very nice, -25° to 2°. Quite a bit of snow slid off north side of house roof. Shoveled it from where we walk. Cal and Mary visited late in morning.

Monday, January 26, 1998—sunny, nice, -14° to 7°. Jim came over and got our water hauling tank. I went to help him a little with some carpentry work. We talked about Charleton Heston, NRA and the "Alaska" movie and how much we are disappointed in that whole mess in the way it disparages hunters. Had a good reloading and gun talk.

Tuesday, January 27, 1998—light snows with very little sun. I helped Jim for a couple hours. Didn't do much.

Wednesday, January 28, 1998—sunny and nice, 3° to 13°. Helped Jim with his water room today. Brought water hauling tank home.

Thursday, January 29, 1998—partly cloudy, ice fog over along Heavenly Ridge, 3° to 14°. Ice crystals falling through the sunlight for a while this afternoon. I hauled a load of water from Little Nelchina River. We pumped it off into our

11

supply tanks. I made a small holder for use in trimming the long necks from .30-06 brass sized down to .308 win. Reamed flash holes, uniformed primer pockets and resized the .308 win cases I have on hand.

Friday, January 30, 1998—cloudy, light snow and fog, 1° to 10°. Sylvia went to Glennallen. I didn't feel well. Tannery phoned that the bear hide is ready. Electric company phoned that the old meter reads okay. Allen visited a couple of times. We went to Manning's for supper (very good) and watched an old movie.

Saturday, January 31, 1998—cloudy, 3" snow, 9° to 24°. Plowed our snow. Took down the two marten boxes. Did some reading, listed the powders I will use to develop loads for the .308 win.

Sunday, February 1, 1998—partly cloudy, 3° to 20°. Frances phoned. Nadia phoned birthday greetings. Sylvia baked a cake and prepared ice cream mix. She made a black bear burger and fries for supper. I cleaned and rearranged the area in the basement where I keep fur skinning and brass cartridge polishing.

Monday, February 2, 1998—partly cloudy, 2° to 16°. Didn't feel well—tired. Made a knife sheath. Sylvia fixed a meal and we took it to Dave and D Johnson at supper time. They have a new daughter Laurel Reann.

Tuesday, February 3, 1998—mostly sunny, 1° to 15°. Did a few little chores. Read a lot. Watched a shooting sports video.

Wednesday, February 4, 1998—cloudy and foggy morning, 1° to 16°. We went with Allen and Roxanne and Sammy to Eureka for breakfast. They had invited Tom and Kim H. and son then we visited at the Farmer home—coffee and cake. Good time.

Thursday, February 5, 1998—sunny, 2° to 15°. Did some target practice. Repaired a holster snap. Did my exercises and walked down to lake and back. Read. Checked my .308 brass in cartridge case gauge. Darrel from Loon Lake phoned.

Friday, February 6, 1998—mostly sunny, -10° to 8°. We went to Glennallen on senior van. Lunch and paying phone bill, a few groceries and cashing of checks completed our business. When we got home Allen had left me a piece of ¼" steel tubing near our door.

Saturday, February 7, 1998—mostly sunny, -14° to 3°. Cleaned the shop vac. Jim O. came and borrowed the water hauling tank. I've got the flu.

Sunday, February 8, 1998—mostly sunny, -16° to 7°. Still sick but feeling better tonight.

Monday, February 9, 1998—mostly sunny, -10° to 7°. Feeling better today. Tried to thread the end of the steel tubing and failed, got cold fingers and came back into the house. Jim and Elaine brought the Sunday paper over. Stayed and visited awhile.

Tuesday, February 10, 1998—most sunny with some flurries and cloudy evening. -10° to 17°. Went to Jim's and got water tank. Lots of work with the ice chisel to get water hole open in river ice. We hauled one load and pumped it into the house. Talked to a guy in Des Moines, Iowa about a couple 105mm empty shells. Allen came over and ate supper with us. Jeff Routt phoned. Jim, Mary and Kari Odden visited.

Wednesday, February 11, 1998—mostly clouds, some quite low, 4° to 18°. I cleaned the oil line sump and the screen at the Toyo stove. Cleaned the snow off the car. Sylvia and I went to visit Cal and Mary. Cal was working on Tom Huddleston's Ski-Doo. They got it fixed. We had pie and coffee and watched a short home movie from Arkansas. I had target practice again today.

Thursday, February 12, 1998—sunny, ice fog early, 0° to 20°. Drove snowgo to Allen's and had coffee. Back home I walked down and up the hill. Later Tom H. visited. No sooner had he left, the snow on garage roof slid off. I helped some of it by jarring the roof. Then I put the plow on the truck and pushed the snow out of the way.

Friday, February 13, 1998—sunny, some fog to the south early, -5° to 13°. We went to Glennallen on senior van. Sylvia did a little shopping for dinner tomorrow. I lubed some bullets and seated them in some cartridges.

Saturday, February 14, 1998—cloudy, most of the day, -12° to +12°. Sun shining under the clouds from the west was beautiful. Sylvia cooked a turkey and trimmings and Odden and Huddleston families, Allen, Samantha, Elaine Manning all were here to share with us. We showed them a National Geographic Special about Four Alaska families that live the remote bush lifestyle.

Sunday, February 15, 1998—cloudy all day with a little snow, -12° to 18°. We rested most of the day. Sylvia slept a lot. I mounted a scope on a rifle I will sell.

Monday, February 16, 1998—sunny all day, some fog early morning, 5° to 15°. Jim borrowed water hauling tank. Visited with Ed and Mark at mailbox. Worked a little on trap line maps.

Tuesday, February 17, 1998—cloudy and fog, -5° to 14°. I shot a mini 14 a little this morning and found that the scope was bad. Tom H. visited till mid afternoon. I did my exercises and walked up and down our hill.

Wednesday, February 18, 1998—mostly sunny, 10° to 20°. Went down to visit Allen but he wasn't home. Took the garbage to transfer site. Didn't do much else. Cal and Mary were here to supper.

Thursday, February 19, 1998—mostly sunny, 0° to 15°. Drove snowgo to Allen's, he wasn't there. Came home then shoveled some snow. Walked down to lake and back to house. We hauled a load of water. Saw two strange dogs down that way.

Friday, February 20, 1998—sunny, clouds in evening, 0° to 12°. Sylvia went to Glennallen on senior van. Did my exercises and walked the hill. Allen visited in evening. Saw a boreal owl in tree.

Saturday, February 21, 1998—sunny, a little snow shower in evening, -2° to 16°. Watched some tapes.

Sunday, February 22, 1998—sunny, -2° to 16°. Went to Jims at noon and helped him get the steel on his water room roof. Water room looks good.

Monday, February 23, 1998—sunny, cloudy in evening, -8° to 15°. Exercised and read. Sylvia doesn't feel well.

Tuesday, February 24, 1998—sunny, -7° to 27°. I changed the light bulb in the well. Shoved a little snow. Tried to find a special piece of aluminum. Phoned our daughter, Nadia (Giordana). Daughter, Beverly Volk called us. Got a letter from grandson, Steve Wilkins.

Wednesday, February 25, 1998—sunny, 0° to 26°. Took the Toyo stove apart and cleaned it. Got one new gasket for it from Jim Manning. Sylvia phoned her nephew John Kaffel and asked how her sister, Fran is doing.

Thursday, February 26, 1998—sunny, 1° to 24°. A few squirrel tracks lately. Harold and Rachel Dimmick visited and lunch with us. They brought a couple packages of ground beef from Hawaii. We sent a package of halibut home with them. We had a nice long visit over soup and a sandwich.

Friday, February 27, 1998—foggy all morning, sunny afternoon, 0° to 19°. Sylvia went to Glennallen. I paid Mannings the $5.00 for the stove gasket. Allen and Samantha visited for a while in afternoon. I gave him a 1" brass full flow valve he can use on his wood splitter. A lynx has walked right by our house some time in the last three days. Wish I could have seen it.

Saturday, February 28, 1998—sunny, -9° to 24°. Henry and Sally came over with an invitation to Britt T and Sven (Norwegians) Wedding. Then stayed and visited all afternoon. We had a good time.

Sunday, March 1, 1998—sunny, -12° to 15°. Walked down to lake. Did exercises. Bought a rifle stock over the phone. Called about a barrel. Talked to a fellow about doing the barrel work.

Monday, March 2, 1998—sunny and breezy late afternoon, -15° to +15°. Called around trying to get best price on airline tickets. Allen and Mark needed 7" sander discs and borrowed a few here. Sent check for rifle barrel.

Tuesday, March 3, 1998—sunny, -18° to 13°. Mailman put my postal money order in Manning's box. Fred Rungee visited this morning and brought some maple syrup. We gave him a package of blueberries. Jim brought the money order over. Sylvia sent a lemon cake for Elaine with Jim when he went home. I shoveled snow from near the steel pile. Dug around in there and found some steel I have been looking for.

Wednesday, March 4, 1998—sunny, -15° to 13°. Went to Allen Farmer's for breakfast. Roxanne showed up later. I washed the picture windows and put a fan light over the cookstove, in hopes of cleaning grease out of the air over the stove. Did some bedding repair on a rifle.

Thursday, March 5, 1998—sunny, -19° to 19°. Snow is shrinking by melting and evaporation. I packaged a rifle scope and will send it off for repair. We went to Little Nelchina River and got a load of water. Just got it unloaded when Patti Billman visited and brought a good number of magazines.

Friday, March 6, 1998—sunny, -10° to 20°. We went to Glennallen on senior van. Ate lunch, shopping, cashed checks and mailed scope to Simmon for repair.

Monday, March 7, 1998—sunny, -10° to 20°. I worked on an action wrench for rifles, after building a warm up fire in the wood shop. Two moose fed on swamp grass at northeast end of our lake.

Sunday, March 8, 1998—sunny, -10° to 21°. Some breeze taking snow our of spruce. Didn't do anything but write a letter today. Saw a moose on lake in evening.

Monday, March 9, 1998—sunny, breezy down on lake, -6° to 20°. Made a rifle action wrench this afternoon. Loraine Hanson (Minnesota) phoned that Harold passed away 6:30 PM their time. I phoned our son Paul to arrange for flowers at the funeral. Phoned Terry Bartley and booked airline tickets to Minnesota for April 15, returning May 13.

Tuesday, March 10, 1998—sunny, some breeze, -10° to 18°. Wrote a letter. Straightened some things around in house. Checked the action wrench for fit in the DGA. Loose but should work.

Wednesday, March 11, 1998—sunny, -7° to 21°. Went to Legion meeting with Bartley this evening. Interesting group of guys.

Thursday, March 12, 1998—sunny, -2° to 26°. We went to Anchorage. Did our shopping. Bought airline tickets to Minnesota. Looked at watches. I'd like to get Sylvia one for our 50th wedding anniversary. Ate in town and again at Nicks Creek (Chili). Saw a bull moose west of Gunsight Mountain Lodge. We aren't getting a signal from satellite dish tonight. Allen came over for a visit.

Friday, March 13, 1998—sunny, 0° to 28°. We went to Glennallen on senior van. Our receiver for the satellite dish won't stay programmed and has to be sent for repairs.

Saturday, March 14, 1998—cloudy, then high clouds and sunny, 8° to 33°. Charlie and Cora arrived before noon. Lots of phone calls. Harold, Rachel, Rusty Arman and Azallia visited then we all went to KROA to help celebrate Britt and Sven wedding. Sam married them at his old cabin site on top of the Nelchina River Bluff then a pot luck and reception and music at KROA.
　　　　After we got to Mendeltna, Sylvia got sick. She stuck it out till after I ate with the other people, then asked to go home. Libby Riddles, Iditarod champ was there and we renewed our friendship. Quite a few other people we had not seen for a while. Mailed the TV dish receiver in to be repaired.

Sunday, March 15, 1998—we didn't get up till 8:00 AM, 8° to 33°. Charlie Trowbridge and I ate breakfast and loaded a few cartridges of his. I cut my thumb and index finger—DUMB. Britt, Sven, Libby stopped by and gave us each a drinking glass. Then later Mary Odden and Kari stopped by with pie. We had made ice cream to go with it. Bruce Bartley must have forgotten to stop and look at traps.

Monday, March 16, 1998—cloudy to partly cloudy, 7° to 36°. Rifle barrel came today. Worked on a rifle stock today. Shoveled snow off the water line below the road. Took a rifle over to Henry Johnson at Nelchina Lodge. He will give it to the gunsmith to fit a barrel on it. Had a nice visit with Henry and Sally. He found Bill Wolfe's address on the internet. Bill is an old friend from when we lived and farmed in Iowa and I wanted to look him up.

Tuesday, March 17, 1998—partly cloudy to cloudy in afternoon and windy most of day, 18° to 40°. Snow moving in this evening. We went to Little Nelchina and got a load of water polished the expander on a rifle die. Modified a .308 gauge. Sharpened the meat grinder plate.

Wednesday, March 18, 1998—partly cloudy, 18° to 41°. Tried again to sharpen the meat grinder cutting parts. Still not good enough. Loaded a few .30-30 for Steve. Rode with Bart to Legion meeting in Glennallen.

Thursday, March 19, 1998—cloudy and partly cloudy, 20° to 35°. I made a rifle barrel vice today. It and the action wrench work perfectly. Cal came and got a 1/2" pipe plug he needed. I visited Sam and left a legion sponsored 'Notice of Van Schedule' to the VA in Anchorage. I forgot the key to garbage gate so I didn't get rid of the garbage.

Friday, March 20, 1998—sunny, 9° to 44°. We went to Glennallen. I picked up the gunstock package from the guy in Pennsylvania. Ate lunch. I'm a little disappointed in the gunstock. It will require some work. I remounted the scope on the rifle. Set up the shooting bench and fired four old cartridges from early 1970s. Headspace with the new barrel looks good. Shots were on the paper. I lubed some cast .308 bullets. Went down to Allen's and borrowed his meat grinder and Sylvia ground some caribou and pork sausage together and packaged it.

Saturday, March 21, 1998—sunny, 15° to 45°. I took the garbage to the transfer site. Returned Allen's meat grinder first. Visited Tom H. also. Shot the new rifle barrel. It shoots very well. Loaded and shot some cast bullets. They shot pretty well. Loaded some more cast bullets with different powders. I'm chronographing these loads. Sure was a nice day.

Sunday, March 22, 1998—sunny, 14° to 40°. Shot some more cast bullets. Walked down to well checking the water lines. They aren't free of ice yet. Bruce and Terry Bartley stopped to visit a little while. Mary O. visited after supper. Granddaughter Laura phoned this afternoon. Cleaned rifle and measured its chamber.

Monday, March 23, 1998—sunny. 18° to 44°. Cleaned up some old bullets. Loaded them in some brass and used them to break in the new barrel. This barrel cleans up nicely.

Tuesday, March 24, 1998—sunny, windy in afternoon, 12° to 42°. Snowy looking in mountains to east and to the west. I brought the cover tarp up here from the well. Loaded 20 more rounds. Ate supper at Harold and Rachel's (Dimmick). Rusty and Corky were there. We had a good visit. They showed us some home videos of Beluga Whale hunting in Cook Inlet, their camp there etc. Enjoyed the movies, interesting.

Wednesday, March 25, 1998—sunny, some breeze in afternoon, 16° to 38°. Wrote some letters. Did some shooting of load development efforts. Nothing outstanding so I cleaned the rifle and loaded four more powders and will try them tomorrow. My brother Jerry's son Mark passed away on this date.

Thursday, March 26, 1998—sunny and some breeze, 21° to 37°. We had Allen, Roxanne, Samantha, Tom & Kim H here to breakfast. Hauled a load of water from Little Nelchina. Saw an eagle near there hunting. Sized and lubed some .30 caliber cast bullets.

Friday, March 27, 1998—partly cloudy, 23° to 38°. We went to Glennallen on senior van. Ate lunch, paid electric bill, visit a couple minutes with Rhynell at her store. The dish receiver was delivered by Fed Ex. With help I got it hooked up.

Saturday, March 28, 1998—mostly sunny, breezy in afternoon, 15° to 37°. Walked the hill. Cast 80+ 120 grain 30 caliber then the handle broke on the mould. Lubed them and boxed them. Snow machines have left tracks all over Heavenly Ridge. Is this adventure or bear hunting? Ralph phoned from Fairbanks. He has his gear all ready to go to Kodiak and hunt brown bear at Dead Mans Cove over on the south east corner of Kodiak Island.

Sunday, March 29, 1998—cloudy with snow on Heavenly Ridge, sunny, cloudy, 12° to 36°. Bob Green called and wanted to buy ten Manning # 9's. He offered $70 each. I wanted $75, but called him back later and left a message saying I would take the $70.00. Reloaded 10 rounds .308 using a different powder. Checked stand pipes in drain field and found ice down at end.

Monday, March 30, 1998—snowed till noon (3"), 20° to 29°. I plowed our yard and lane. Bob Green stopped by and picked up 10 traps. I haven't felt very well today.

Tuesday, March 31, 1998—cloudy, -3° to 23°. Did some reading, some varmint hunting. Tried to spot bear dens on Heavenly Ridge with no luck.

Wednesday, April 1, 1998—partly cloudy, some breeze then cloudy and windy in late evening. 5° to 36°. I did some load development this afternoon. Sylvia fixed baked halibut and had Harold, Rachel, Rusty and Corky Dimmick over to eat supper with us. We had a nice visit.

Thursday, April 2, 1998—sunny, cloudy afternoon, 7° to 35°. Cast more (125 good ones) .30 caliber and put gas check on them. The mould cast good bullets. After the second one and they fell out of mould easily. I honed the top of mould and the sprue cut off and put mould back together. Hope it works even better next time. The fox was back last night and took some food I had left out.

Friday, April 3, 1998—some snow and windy, 24° to 40°. Snow melted when it hit bare places. Some sunny time also. We went to Glennallen and paid phone bill. I cast some more .30 cal. bullets. Had a lot of rejects today. Allen got a "new to him" Ford 1 Ton crew cab and brought it over to show us. He stayed and had hamburgers with us.

Saturday, April 4, 1998—mostly cloudy and windy sometimes, 13° to 38°. Cast some more bullets this afternoon. The fox didn't come through last night.

Sunday, April 5, 1998—partly cloudy, 24° to 41°. Wrote a letter. We visited Gilcreases. David and D Johnson came there just as we were leaving. We stopped by the Little Nelchina River and pumped on a load of water. That water sure makes good coffee.

Monday, April 6, 1998—partly cloudy, 22° to 43°. We went to Anchorage. I bought a 50th anniversary gift (Seiko Gold Nugget watch) for Sylvia. We ate lunch after a little shopping and came home to a letter from Jerry. His son Mark passed away of melanoma cancer March 25th. I called Jerry and offered our condolences. A long talk seemed to lift Jerry's spirits. Prepped some brass to keep my mind busy but to no avail.

Tuesday, April 7, 1998—mostly sunny, windy sometimes, 25° to 41°. Cast a few bullets. Got a few things ready to go to Minnesota. Phoned Ben, Bill Wolfe. and Chad's work place.

Wednesday, April 8, 1998—sunny, 16° to 43°. Did a few small jobs. Then put snowgo away for the summer. Did some more load development work with the .308 Winchester. We ate supper at Mary Odden's tonight. Sealed sand leaks on shooting rear bags.

Thursday, April 9, 1998—sunny and a little breeze, 13° to 41°. More load development today. Shoveled more packed snow from waterline on south side of house. Saw a spruce hen down in the "hole".

Friday, April 10, 1998—cloudy all day, 20° to 39°. We went to lunch in Glennallen. Got to talk to Darrel a few minutes. Allen and Roxanne were having breakfast at the Rendezvous. A fox was checking out our place this morning. I did some pistol practice when we got home. Got some clothes ready to pack.

Saturday, April 11, 1998—mostly sunny, 19° to 41° Fired 60 rounds in load development. The ProChrono gave erratic readings due to a weak battery. Shot my first varmint with this barrel today. My back is really sore. The snow is leaving fast.

Sunday, April 12, 1998—mostly sunny, a little snow this morning, 20° to 41°. Mary visited they bought a 96 Mazda pickup. Cut some .308 win size cleaning patches. We hauled a load of water from Little Nelchina. I had a bunch of bait thawing out on floor of storage shed.

Monday, April 13, 1998—partly cloudy, 9° to 39°. Cleaned ashes from two heaters and scattered them on the garden and the deeper snow around the house. Cast and lubed some bullets. Packed duffle back. Made a bracket for telescope. Chad phoned.

Tuesday, April 14, 1998—sunny, 20° to 46°. Getting ready to go to Minnesota. Shot the .308 some more today. Got some dream catcher hoops ready to sell. Hauled garbage to transfer site. Called Ralph, then he called back. They saw an 8' bear during the hunt at Deadman Bay Kodiak Island. Didn't shoot it, windy storms, snow etc.

Wednesday, April 15, 1998—20°. We finished getting ready for the trip, left home about 10:00 AM. Got gasoline at Eureka and again at Palmer. Stopped by gift shop with some willow hoops. Ate lunch in Anchorage then onto Griffith's. Visited with them and will park our truck with them till we get back. They drove us over to airport. Our plane left on time at 9:45 PM. Along in middle of night the northern lights were at their best and we were seeing them from 37,000 feet up.

Thursday, April 16, 1998—sunny here in Minneapolis and St. Paul, 37° to 55°. We got in at 6:03 Central time. Dragged our luggage out to passenger loading and met Nadia and Chuck and went to their place. We are really tired today. Nadia looked up two web sites for me and ran off some copies of some of the surfing that we did. It was interesting and fun.

Friday, April 17, 1998—partly cloudy here, 32° to 58°. Phoned Northwest Airlines and applied for mileage. In the afternoon we went to Galyan's sporting goods store, a book store and a K-Mart. A good supper and watched a movie on TV. We can't find the movie "Battle of Adobe Walls"

Saturday, April 18, 1998—cloudy, partly cloudy and a shower, 30s to 50s. Made a few phone calls. Chuck and Nadia drove us about 30 miles north sight seeing that part of Minnesota possible area to buy some land. Later did a little shopping and they got barbeque ribs to take home. Watched TV and ate ice cream. Saw two deer in a field.

Sunday, April 19, 1998—cloudy, sunny and some showers, 50s. Laura brought over her Oneida contest recipe dish, Oneida Eggs Benedict, very good. Then we went home with her for the afternoon and got to see Brittany. Chuck drove over later and we went back to Nadia's place. Theresa tried to phone. My sister, Virginia Wink phoned.

Monday, April 20, 1998—partly sunny, 42° to 58°. Nadia and Chuck took us over to Beverly's. We got them breakfast near Bev's. Tyler stayed home from school today. Nice to see them. A guy named Mark Erickson was here and later Clifford Lee stopped by for a couple hrs and swapped hunting stories. Darcy just phoned and will bring great grandson Dylan over to visit. We had a good time. Dylan is a good baby – so happy.

Tuesday, April 21, 1998—sunny with light breeze, 38° to 67°. Did a little shopping at K-Mart, went to a book store. Didn't find one I really wanted. Watched a little TV. Read awhile out on deck in the sun. Vanessa and Scott came over for dinner and we got to visit with them. They stayed to watch a movie.

Wednesday, April 22, 1998—sunny and a warm breeze, 34° to 69°. We caught a bus and went to Fort Snelling area. Mark met us there and we walked to a park on the Mississippi River. Mark and Tyler fished with no luck. Tyler played in the sand and water. We had a picnic lunch. Saw a tug pushing two barges come out of the river locks at the end of a dam. A couple of other boats and a kayak. Two ducks, one rooster pheasant and few crows. Tyler went to a practice soccer game. We had pizza delivered. Mark is here this evening. Tyler won his soccer game.

Thursday, April 23, 1998—sunny and warm breeze, 38° to 71°. Did some reading, shower, took a walk. Theresa phoned that she couldn't come to see us. Then grandson Lee Austin phoned and we visited with him. We walked with Beverly to the grocery store and got some groceries.

Friday, April 24, 1998—sunny and warm, 40° to 76°. Sylvia and I walked over to K-Mart for shopping. I checked out book store. Tyler was in school. Then his dad wanted him this weekend. Bev and Mark walked to park. I have some kind of crud. They saw some animals and birds.

10,000 Days in Alaska Book Three 1998-2005

Saturday, April 25, 1998—sunny, breezy, cloudy and sprinkles in evening, 45° to 70°. Went for a walk. Tyler came home early afternoon. He went with me for a long walk. I walked maybe five miles today.

Sunday, April 26, 1998—cloudy and clear at Staples, 40° to 50°. Nadia and Chuck picked us up at Beverly's and took us to Laura's. There we transferred our luggage to Laura's car. Then Laura drove Nadia and Sylvia and I to Paul and Ruth's at Staples. Steve is off working at a job in Minneapolis. We had a bite to eat then Laura and Nadia went back to Minneapolis. Helen Converse came over to see us here and visited quite a while.

Monday, April 27, 1998—sunny, 30s to 50s. Paul, Steve and I went out to Dower Lake and Steve made a beaver set at a culvert. Paul spotted a pair on honkers there. We messed around here for a while after lunch then visited the local pawn shop and the Ace Hardware. Read and visited after supper.

Tuesday, April 28, 1998—sunny, 32° to 70°s. Steve went to school till noon. Then he and I went to check the beaver set at Dower Lake-nothing. Then in afternoon he drove Sylvia and I out to Loraine Hanson's and we visited all afternoon and we ate supper with Loraine. Came back to Paul's and visited a while and phoned Allen and Lillian Rollins and they drove over and visited for a while. Good to see them. Steve showed us some of his projects. The Rollins are busy and look good. Allen and I exchanged key rings.

Wednesday April 29, 1998—sunny, 40° to 72°. Steve went to school till noon. I phoned a couple people. We went out to check Steve's beaver set and it had a snapping turtle in it. That we took out and he put it back in swamp and remade the set. Saw a few small bass nearby. We cut some birch and willow wands and made a hoop for a beaver pelt. Ruth fixed a good supper and birthday cake for Sylvia. Met Steve's friend Pete. We had a nice visit this evening. Sylvia and I did a little shopping.

Thursday, April 30, 1998—partly cloudy, 40s to 70s. We checked the beaver trap then Paul, Steve, Sylvia and I went to Walker. Fun trip. What with the scenery, crows ducks etc. Steve showed us Reeds Sporting Goods Store and went spent two hours shopping. Didn't buy much but had a good time. Ate lunch at Akely. Found out Leonard Berg had died about five years ago. Visited Loraine on way home. Today is Ruth's birthday.

Friday, May 1, 1998—cloudy, partly cloudy, some light rain, 40s to 60s. Pulled the beaver trap. Fred and Ann Marolf visited in morning and we went to café and treated them to lunch. Had a long visit. My son Paul sold his car. Steven and I went to Verndale to pick him up. He had started to walk back to Staples. We went to Jim Rudbeck's for supper and had a good visit. They have sold their place, cattle and all. We packed tonight to be ready to go back to Minneapolis.

Saturday, May 2, 1998—partly cloudy and nice, afternoon rain in the Twin Cities, 40° to 68°. We got up and got ready to go to Minneapolis. Mike Griffith wanted to see us and came over and visited an hour and a half. We stopped at Randall and Little Falls looking for leather thongs that Steve needs to lace his beaver hide on to the birch hoop. We stopped at Nelson's truck stop in Clearwater and ate. Kind of late and I got quite hungry. We saw a guy lose control of his car and with great luck it didn't roll over or involve anyone else. We ate at Laura and Brittany's. Paul, Ruth and Steve went to a motel. We had chili for supper. My back is very bad. Sylvia put a spray medication on it and Laura gave me a heating pad to lie on and it helped. Brittany is going to put on a "play show" for us.

Sunday, May 3, 1998—sunny, a beautiful day, 44° to 74°. We got all dressed up and Laura drove us to Shoreview for the party to celebrate the 50th anniversary for Sylvia and me. Paul, Ruth and Steven followed us over there. Brittany came with Nadia and Chuck. Vanessa and Scott brought Beverly, Tyler and Mark. Mary Lou came. Theresa and Earl came. Ranette and Janette with daughter and son's wife and two grandchildren were in attendance. Cousin Gladys and Harold Schmidt, Mark and Demitra (Nadia's friends), Mark and Cleo Holtberg (Cleo graduated from Motley High School with Nadia in 1966). Lee Austin, his girl friend and friend, Darcy Austin and our great grandson Dylan. Pete and Delaine Achermann, grandson and his cousin, Al Eckes, Don Sirecek and Denise and a grandson and his friend. (Cousin Mary Helland couldn't find the party). Jerry Wilkins sent a letter. Lorraine Hanson had given us a card, and Jim and Arlene Rudbeck gave us a card earlier. Evelyn Bishop (cousin) sent a letter. Marion and Rae Wilkins sent a card. The young folks cleaned the party room. Then we came to Laura's home. We are tired tonight but we stayed up and visited a while.

Monday, May 4, 1998—beautiful day with a light shower about supper time, 50° to 78°. Brittany stayed home from school and we enjoyed her company. Then just after noon Bud and Gerry Smeltzer knocked on the door. They have driven here from Michigan to visit us while we are in Minnesota. Visited all afternoon. When Laura came home from work, Sylvia and I took them all out to supper.

Tuesday, May 5, 1998—sunny, 45° to 74°. Brittany went to school today. I picked up trash. Fixed toilet seat and towel rack. Sylvia and I took the storm windows off and put the screens on. Bud and Gerry visited an hour and half and left to go back to Michigan. I walked over to Walgreens and shopped a little. Checked out the rental movies with no luck. After work, Laura took us to Britt's school, picked her up there and they went shopping for knitting supplies.

Wednesday, May 6, 1998—sunny and very nice, 45° to 76°. Grubbed out some dandelions. Mowed the back yard. Swept driveway and garage. Went for a short walk and got some gum on my shoes. Saw a mallard drake walking on street and nearby lawns. Some men worked at repair in the south privacy fence.

Thursday, May 7, 1998—cloudy and rainy, 55° to 65°. Dug a few more dandelions. Slow day. Phoned Virginia—she and Don won't be coming to Minneapolis. Laura took us to Brittany's try-out. We got there too late. Brittany spends this weekend with her dad.

Friday, May 8, 1998—clearing and sunny, 50° to 65°. Breezy on the way to Chicago. Stopped at Nadia and Chucks for rolls and coffee. Left most of our luggage there. Laura drove Nadia, Sylvia and I to Fran's house in Lockport Ill. (Chicago). We stopped a few times for rest stops and a sandwich at noon. It is a nice time of year to drive. Shortly after dinner at Fran's, Johnny came over. We looked at pictures of old times in evening.

Saturday, May 9, 1998—high clouds and sunny, 55° to 68°. Walked two houses down to a yard sale. Bought 4 ratchet tie-down straps at a yard sale. Went for a walk around a couple nearby blocks. Sat out on one of Fran's bench's in her yard and got a tick stuck on my right wrist. Laura got it off with alcohol. A while after lunch we all went over to John and Sandy's, Nicole and Jamie. Visited a while. John put on a huge table of specialty foods. Then a meat dish Italian style, pasta, salad etc. Then a fruit custard, fancy cookies and coffee. Lots of story telling, visiting and camaraderie. Later we drove back to Fran's for the night.

Sunday, May 10, 1998—sunny, 55° to 70°. Up early and got on the road about 8:00 AM. Gassed up and found our way out of Chicago. Uneventful but tiring trip. Saw quite a few road kill deer, coon and etc. Got back to Nadia's at 3:30. Rested a while. Chuck had supper ready. Later he, Nadia and I went for a walk and I bought some ice cream. Took a shower.

Monday, May 11, 1998—mostly sunny, 55° to 75°. Chuck gave me a ride to a mall, 2 miles away. I looked for books on way back to their place. Found two books at Goodwill store. Nadia phoned a dental lab and got information for Sylvia about new false teeth. She now has plans to go there early in morning. Chuck and Nadia fixed a good supper. Theresa phoned in evening. Saw some crows today.

Tuesday, May 12, 1998—up early, 55° to 75° to 60°. Nadia took Sylvia to the dentist, who got mouth impressions and built a nice set of dentures that we picked up at 5:30 PM. On the way back to Nadia and Chuck's place we picked up a few groceries. Chuck rented a movie for evening entertainment. Called AK and learned the ice went out on our lake.

Wednesday, May 13, 1998–52° to 72°. Up early, 6:00 AM. After breakfast, Nadia and Chuck took us, bag and baggage, over to Beverly's. Had lunch with her, went to bookstore and to K-Mart where she take bought flower to put on her balcony. We had a taxi take us to the airport. We could have given up our seat on that flight for the next flight, three hours later and they would have given us $400 each. We didn't do it. Uneventful flight to Anchorage. Addie and Betty met us. After visiting an hour with Addie, Denny, Betty and Jerry, we pumped 235 gallons of gas, a few groceries. Got home after 2:00 AM. Saw one moose.

Thursday, May 14, 1998–34° to 52°. Mostly sunny, four hours sleep. Lots of rabbits around here. Kestrels and flickers. Unloaded the gasoline. Filled the car with gas and went to Copper Center to fax longevity papers to Juneau. Picked up some brass. Also my caribou hunt applications. Saw a moose on paving. Very dry around here. Rudbecks visited. Allen visited and had supper with us. Ducks are on our lake.

Friday, May 15, 1998–30° to 46°, partly cloudy. Went to Glennallen to lunch and cashed our checks. Paid electric bill.

Saturday, May 16, 1998–partly cloud, some snowy hail, 31° to 45°. Wrote thank you cards most of the day. Walked down to well and switched off the light bulb and hooked up the small water line. Picked up some spent lead bullets out of area; melted snow berm. Allen brought over a dozen fresh brown eggs and visited.

Sunday, May 17, 1998–mostly sunny, 32° to 50°. I visited Sam with info on VA. He rode back to Nelchina. We visited with Henry and Sally at Nelchina. I shot a snowshoe hare. I made a burn barrel by cutting one end out and adding vent holes. Picked up some bullets that I had shot last winter. Jim Manning borrowed our tiller and a belt broke. Sally came over with some onion sets. Sylvia went back with her and bought some pea inoculant. Phoned Al Eckes and Lorraine Hanson.

Monday, May 18, 1998–sunny to cloudy, 28° to 56°. We picked up Sam and went to Wasilla and did some shopping. Sylvia got her yearly check-up. Saw a moose and some sheep. An ermine was in our yard.

Tuesday, May 19, 1998–sunny, windy, cloudy, 35°to 49°. Cut some willow hoops. Tilled the lower garden. Rode with Bart to VA meeting. Rode home with Jim Manning.

Wednesday, May 20, 1998—partly cloudy, sunny, windy, 31° to 53°. Pulled large water line out of basement. Tightened the lower roof screws on garage. Shot two rabbits and butchered them. When Sylvia got back from Glennallen we planted potatoes, beets, carrots and kohlrabi. Visited Bob Rudbeck for a few minutes. Looked at griz tracks down by lake. Loaded some varmint-fouling loads.

Thursday, May 21, 1998—mostly cloudy, windy noon, very light rain afternoon, 31° to 50°. Sylvia raked spruce cones and I hauled them away. We picked up tarps and blue board from off the septic drain field. An eagle hunts our ridge every day. Kestrels and flickers are nesting. More ducks on our lake, swans still here. I loaded some 44 magnum 300 grain and some .308 varmint loads. Karin had a bowl of beans here before she, Sylvia and some other ladies went to a program at Glacier View School.

Friday, May 22, 1998—cloudy, rain and snow in evening, 32° to 49°. We went to the Little Nelchina School to watch the kids receive their awards. There was a potluck lunch afterwards. Then I went with Bart to the American Legion meeting in Glennallen.

Saturday, May 23, 1998—partly cloudy, sunny, 31° to 54°. Quite a few goldeneyes pairing up on our lake. Walked down to Allen's. Just as he was going over to Manning's to help run cement. I cleaned a plug on car, used the new adhesive to reattach the mirror on windshield. Fixed windshield wiper. Helped Sylvia a little with wire netting for pea vines to climb on. Put away gas water pump. Loaded some .308 Winchester. Tried for a squirrel and missed. Mark identified a circling Super Cub as Don Deering. We don't know why he was here yet. Watered some of our trees and ran water over the septic tank to melt off any ice that might be there. A cow moose swam kitty-corner south across the west end of our lake. A Fish and Game Super Cub crashed a couple miles west of here. A Man and woman walked away from it and out to highway.

Sunday, May 24, 1998—high thin clouds, 33° to 63°. Watered some trees. Shot some targets. Did some small jobs. Installed "tee' for water at garden. Raked the south side of garden for planting. Denny and Joey Eastman visited in the afternoon

Monday, May 25, 1998—cloudy, high thin clouds, 40° to 63°. Cloudy, high thin clouds. Parked snowplow. Took canopy off truck. Watered trees. Re-tightened clamps on "tee" at garden. Loaded a different powder in 5 - .308 Winchester. Loaded a box of .45 ACP. Ralph phoned and is back from trip up the Haul Road to Prudhoe Bay.

Tuesday, May 26, 1998—sunny, 39° to 64°. We picked up our one mile of road trash. There wasn't very much this year. Did some target shooting. Parked snowgo trailer. Watered trees after putting water hose back together. Reloaded some more load development. Allen visited.

Wednesday, May 27, 1998—sunny, high wind, sculptured clouds. We went to Glennallen for lunch. Took garbage to transfer site. They have had some land clearing done. Picked up some brass at mile 149. Did some shooting this afternoon. Cleaned the brass I found. Saw two moose ¾ mile east and one moose 20 milee east.

Thursday, May 28, 1998—partly cloudy, 43° to 68°. Went fishing on Mirror Lake. Only got a little rainbow. Stopped by Little Lake near Cache Creek. Some ducks on lake, beaver den is abandoned. Saw a field sparrow nest with one egg in it. No graylings hit my spinner. Line is bad on this reel. I put new line on at home. Walked down to well. Back hurt all afternoon. Got the screen door down from garage and hung it on arctic entry. We had Bob and Kahren over for a crock pot rabbit supper.

Friday, May 29, 1998—sunny. 47° to 69°. Put more clamps on waterline. Watched ducks feeding on fresh water shrimp. Watered a little of garden. Check the depth in ground of the septic tank. Allen stopped by. Pulled a double spruce over with a come-along and chopped off its roots. Tried to remove and rewind some brass wire off a generator with no luck. Fixed one of Sylvia's cottonwood planters.

Saturday, May 30, 1998—partly cloudy, 47° to 68°. It rained from 26 miles west of Glennallen to town. Windy and dusty in afternoon. The kestrels really "play" in and on the air currents, very acrobatic. We went to Glennallen and Sylvia participated in the health fair. It rained on the way home for about 25-26 miles. Saw a porcupine and shot it. Brenda and Darrel came out to visit us. We looked at photos. Visited and had a good time. Sylvia helped me pull the air compressor out of the basement. A cow moose walked up and down the south side of our lake, keeping in the water. Reloaded some more cast bullets.

Sunday, Mary 31, 1998—mostly cloudy, 39° to 55°. A few drops of rain. I went to Billman's at Snowshoe Lake—no one was there. George wasn't at Odden's house. I checked out the gravel pit at mile 149. No brass. Stopped at mile 146 gravel pit and picked up 4-9 MM Luger brass. Walked around the area and came upon a very old trap set under a large tree, with a very old fox foot in the trap. Did some repairs to my bullet stop and target support. Picked up some spent bullets. Found a clump of gravel containing a lot of iron. Crushed it and panned it for gold. Quite a bit of fine gold in it. Flushed some debris out of the frost proof outside spigot.

Monday, June 1, 1998—partly cloudy and breezy, especially down on lake, 36° to 62°. I shot targets this morning. Started trimming on the spruce trees. Grubbed some volunteer grass out. Reloaded some .308 Winchesters. Visited Cal, Mary, Hannah.

Tuesday, June 2, 1998—partly cloudy, 39° to 60°. The kestrels sure hunt morning and night. I trimmed some more on spruce trees. Put a handle in a small hoe for Sylvia. Cast a couple hundred bullets and installed the last of my .30 caliber gas checks. Herb from Chickaloon came over to look at my two-sided logs. Allen just phoned; they will come over and visit.

Wednesday, June 3, 1998—sunny, 37° to 68°. Shot a squirrel that was trying to get into the kestrel nest. Sylvia went to Glennallen. I wired and mounted a fan in greenhouse. Moved a trailer so we can get at the log pile. Herb and helper will be here to lead them in morning. Lubed some bullets. Lisa and Kahren Rudbeck brought over three rainbow trout for our breakfast. Bob and Jerry Rudbeck flew their planes this evening.

Thursday, June 4, 1998—mostly cloudy, 44° to 66°. Herb and Jeff loaded up my two sided logs and put them up today. I trimmed a little more on the trees while the lead melting pot was heating up. I cast some pure lead bullets as well as some that I didn't quench in water.

Friday, June 5, 1998—cloudy to sunny in afternoon and evening. 37° to 58°. We went to Glennallen, cashed checks, paid phone bill and had lunch. Repacked 2-wheel trailer. Cut 24" steel pipe stakes and re-staked the retaining wall on south side of upper garden. We visited Dan and Patti Billman at Snowshoe Lake.

Saturday, June 6, 1998—sunny and beautiful, a little breeze, 37° to 63°. Tested another reload. Laid around a lot today. Went to Bob and Kahren's supposedly for a shrimp dinner. It was a surprise party for our 50th wedding anniversary. Pretty overwhelming for me. Sylvia handled it very well.

Sunday, June 7, 1998—mostly sunny, 46° to 69°. While glassing Slide Mountain, I got a brief glimpse of two bears, probably blacks. I put some J-B Weld patch on the leak on the car gas tank. Later Kahren and Joey brought over the cards and mementos of 50th wedding anniversary party.

Monday, June 8, 1998—cloudy and real windy and dusty, partly cloudy in evening, 50° to 62°. I worked at inleting the used rifle stock to fit my DFA with safety. Made a loading ramp for the DGA, making the action a single shot and compatible with this stock. We went to Dimmick's for a fresh red salmon supper—very good.

Tuesday, June 9, 1998—partly cloudy, cloudy, a little shower in night and some within sight today, 38° to 58°. Did odd jobs around the place. Mostly worked with the Shilen B.R. rifle stock. Lots of fitting and measuring. Drove the Suzuki 4 x 4 up on a ridge on Slide Mountain and walked around a little and glassed some. No game. One moose track, one old fox track.

Wednesday, June 10, 1998—mostly cloudy and some rain, 39° to 57°. We went to Glennallen and did some shopping. I was disappointed that I wasn't able to find the type of screw I needed.

Thursday, June 11, 1998—partly cloudy, 32° to 57°. Worked on rifle stock. Chopped the dirt out of downed spruce tree roots. Bob and Kahren visited. Sylvia baked a lemon pie and we took it over to Elaine and Jim Manning. Helped Jim off load his camper and hook up to a big trailer.

Friday, June 12, 1998—partly cloudy, 32° to 57°. Went to Glennallen. Got some epoxy and modeling clay. Ate lunch. Saw two caribou, a vixen and three kits. A cow moose and her calves turned around at our outhouse and left. I worked on rifle action screws.

Saturday, June 13, 1998—rained all night and early morning, then cleared up and was a beaut of a day, 37° to 61°. I slept late after calling John in Pennsylvania. I epoxied the pillers in the Shilen stock. Put "Ross for Governor" decals on car and truck. Built a frame for the road signs and put them up. Bob came over about grading the lower road and asked my permission to cross our land between his and Jerry's hanger. Allen visited in late afternoon. I weighed some .308 Winchester brass.

Sunday, June 14, 1998—cloudy and rainy, 41° to 60°. Glass bedded the rifle action today. It went okay—now if it comes out of the stock. The kestrel kills shrews and mice and voles.

Monday, June 15, 1998—rainy, sunny, 40° to 64°. Finished, cleaned up the rifle stock. Cleaned trigger oiled and reinstalled it on rifle action. Checked the air and inflated the tires on the vehicles. Cut up the trees that I pulled over earlier. Made some more stakes for garden. Visited Cal and Mary and Hannah. Gave H. some balloons. Cal gave me some epoxy. I shot two rabbits that were out by wood shed and butchered them. Started getting blocking and jack into basement to put a post in.

Tuesday, June 16, 1998—rainy, partly cloudy, 41° to 65°. Put a little of Cal's epoxy on the gun stock. Reformed 10 -.30-06 brass to .308 Winchester. Prepped the brass and reloaded using cast bullets. After supper we returned

Rachel's book. They were gone but we got to visit with Philip and Arlene Hobson. I took the epoxy back to Cal. We visited for awhile. Jim M. paid me for the logs.

Wednesday, June 17, 1998—partly cloudy, 46° to 66°. We went to lunch and shopping in Glennallen. Dug up some volunteer grass in our yard. Found the rifle bolt handle in gun stock needed some relief. Did that. Went to gravel pit. Relocated a "pit" on a gravel ridge. Didn't find any brass. Missed a shot at a varmint. Found a quarter. Beautiful evening. Ralph phoned, he is coming down Friday.

Thursday, June 18, 1998—sunny, some breeze in evening, 42° to 70°. I made a little improvement on the bed, then went to gravel pit to shoot targets at 100 yards. Really cleaned the rifle. Hoed the potatoes. Checked on well.

Friday, June 19, 1998—sunny, 47° to 68°. Ralph Fuson visited. We went target shooting at water filled pop bottles and milk jugs. Had a lot of fun. He brought me some range brass and I gave him some that I had prepped and polished. Bud and Gay Swecker from Minnesota visited and had supper with us.

Saturday, June 20, 1998—sunny, cloudy and windy, 44° to 63°. Ralph and I went to Copper Center and Klutina River. We didn't see any salmon being caught there. We spent a couple hours there, then headed out for the Gulkana River. We stopped at the shooting range. We found very little brass. Then on to river and parked. Spoons, eggs, etc., upstream from bridge. I saw a couple salmon caught, two that were tied by stringer to a rock. Three rubber rafts floated in. Those fishermen had caught kings and red salmon. We left after while and got home around 6:00 PM. Ate supper, then Allen phoned and wanted to take us to Eureka for a bowl of ice cream. That was fun and a good visit. After we got home Ralph left for Fairbanks. He will take a "snoozer", at Gulkana, then fish for a while and continue on. Ralph fired up a Coleman stove and we had good hot dogs for lunch, washed down with Pepsi.

Sunday, June 21, 1998—cloudy, partly cloudy, then rain, 36° to 59°. Jeff phoned. Shot a rabbit. Polished some brass. Gave 20 brasses and a movie to Jeff when he visited later in afternoon. Cleaned up near reloading bench. Rearranged things. Fooled around with some old brass. Shot a rabbit that hopped into greenhouse (after it came back out). Shot another down in "hole,"—that's three today. Nadia phoned a Father's Day greeting. Allen came over to look at some pipes. Snowing on Heavenly Ridge, rain here.

Monday, June 22, 1998—partly cloudy, 35° to 65°. Loaded some cartridges. Went to gravel pit to shoot. It was windy enough to blow my target down, so I came home and built a better stand. Burned trash. Polished two batch's of brass. Reloaded some more development loads.

Tuesday, June 23, 1998—partly cloudy. I went to gravel pit for a shooting session. Went pretty well. Built a new base for the rear bag. Put some glue on bottom of rear bag so it doesn't slide so easy. Checked truck over.

Wednesday, June 24, 1998—partly cloudy and some breeze, 47° to 68°. We had lunch in Glennallen. I bought a pair of Levis overalls and two wheels for the car at a garage sale. Sylvia paid electric bill and got some groceries and medication for her flu-like symptoms. Put a little dye on rifle stock and put a couple coats of varithane on it (spray type).

Thursday, June 25, 1998—beaut of a day, good breeze, 44° to 71°. Hauled garbage to dump. Measured 100 yard, 200 yard, and 250 yard distances and marked them at Army Trail gravel pit. A griz has been in transfer site garbage. I watered some garden and rhubarb. Planted some potatoes under mulch. Mowed the lawn. Loaded some more brass in search of most accurate load. Sent order to Sinclair.

Friday, June 26, 1998—partly cloudy, 46° to 69°. Loaded Suzuki and some gear on truck in preparation for a day trip into Talkeetna Mountains via Ballanger Pass. Stopped by Cal's, Allen was there. I helped put up the rafters on Allen's camp office. Then came home and did a few little jobs. Reloaded some fouling shots. Sylvia heard some wolves or coyotes howling this evening. A squirrel investigated sounds emulating from kestrel nest box. I shot him off the tree.

Saturday, June 27, 1998—partly cloudy, 51° to 71°. I drove to Ballanger Pass Trailhead. Met Clyde Peck and wife. Later on trail we met again and he told me of a better trail put in by a gold miner. All along Pass Creek there were caribou (from 1 to 60 in a bunch). I shot a few parka squirrels. The birds of prey cleaned them right up. Saw several juvenile bald eagles. Saw one with something clutched in a claw, being followed and harassed by a sparrow-sized bird. Saw a couple good places to mine with small equipment. Really enjoyed my day out in the mountains. Met Dave (father) and son (Cord) while on my way home. Dan Billman visited while I was gone and left some really old ammo to deactivate. I finished that job. I picked up the barricades from our lower road.

Sunday, June 28, 1998—sunny, 48° to 74°. I made some cartridge key rings from Lloyd's brass. Took them to Billman's. Gave him one and sent two to Lloyd. Visited awhile. Made some cartridge holding blocks to use at the range. Sprayed them with Varithane. Watered some garden and rhubarb. Sylvia is still feeling sick. I washed dishes for her. Then Allen phoned and invited us down for ice cream. Sylvia is too sick to go. Visited with Allen for a while. Met

Jacoby's mother, Patti.

Monday, June 29, 1998—sunny and some breeze, 50° to 80°. Sylvia is still under the weather. Picked some radishes and lettuce and gave some to Jim M. and some to Patrick the new man renting from Mannings. Loaded up the shooting gear and went to gravel pit. Shooting didn't go very well as far as groups went, on the targets. I did find some fired brass in pit. I cleaned it and put it away after I got home.

Tuesday, June 30, 1998—sunny, 50° to 80°. I went to Anchorage to the VA outpatient clinic. Saw a Dr. Ferrel, and the lab drew blood samples. X-ray took a lot of pictures of my back. The pharmacy gave me some medications. I shopped for some primers and powders that I had been wanting to try out. Got some groceries. Went to Eagle House for some screws to redo the basement stairs. The road was pretty good. Heavy in Anchorage. Really hot in Anchorage.

Wednesday, July 1, 1998—sunny and breezy in open places, 50° to 74°. I worked on two rifle action screws. Jim Manning and I went riding on our ATV's on the trail on east side of Slide Mountain. We saw fox, wolf and four different sized bear tracks. One of the bears was quite large. We went east at the four corner in the Seismic trails went east a mile then south on Seismic and back to highway. There we turned west and returned to Nelchina. Trip was fun even through somewhat strenuous at times. I washed the machine when I got home.

Thursday, July 2, 1998—cloudy, partly cloudy, cloudy, 49° to 76°. I went to gravel pit for more target shooting. Annealed the necks of some casings. Sylvia and I both have some kind of intestinal flu. After supper I worked on the canvas covers for some loading blocks. The kestrels bring ever larger prey in to feed the young ones. An eagle keeps hunting on our lake.

Friday, July 3, 1998—partly cloudy and some breeze, 49° to 75°. I went to gravel pit and shot the rifle. Some groups were very good. This batch of brass is really stretching (WW). Checked on Charlie's property. Shot a rabbit this morning and ate it tonight. Jeff phoned.

Saturday, July 4, 1998—mostly cloudy, 52° to 70°. Watched early hunting and shooting shows, then slept late. Finished the canvas covered loading blocks; each holds 10 cartridges. I shortened the bench rest stock 3/8". That went well. I worked on and sorted my problem brass. Weeded the upper garden. Reloaded a 100 of .45 ACP.

Sunday, July 5, 1998—cloudy, tried to rain a little, 51° to 65°. We went to Mendeltna Chapel church services and picnic held at Allen and Roxanne Farmers home. Had a good time. Allen brought our water tank home. Saw a kestrel knock a duck out of the air at the kestrel nest. Both flew off. Jeff stopped by for a couple minutes.

Monday, July 6, 1998—cloudy, 48° to 60°. Some rain in the night and showers in the afternoon. This morning I went to gravel pit and shot the 22-250. Shot up some old loadings. Did pretty well. Barely got back home and it rained. Started preparing a lot of brass for neck turning.

Tuesday, July 7, 1998—cloudy, some rain, 45° to 55°. The case neck turner came today but won't work on my Herters. I built a box to hold my new screw driver and all its bits and sockets. Prepared and loaded some 22-250 testing primers on two powders.

Wednesday, July 8, 1998—partly cloudy, a little light rain, 42° to 60°. Loaded 10 more cartridges, then went to gravel pit. Shot some very good targets. Cleaned two barrels when I got home. Went to Harold and Rachel Dimmick's for supper. Visited a while. Stopped by Cal and Mary's on way. Home visited and got two loaves bread and an oil filter for Suzuki. Phoned Sinclair, will send a different neck turner.

Thursday, July 9, 1998—a beautiful sun rise and nice all day, 42° to 68°. I dug down to the outlet on the septic tank to inspect it. It was fine so I covered it up again. After lunch we visited Cal and Mary. Paid him for the oil filter. He gave me a wheel for our car and a pump for the windshield washer. I installed the pump when we got home. I started stocking the range box. Discovered I needed a small box for cleaning aids—so built that and painted it.

Friday, July 10, 1998—partly cloudy, very nice, 45° to 69°. We went to Glennallen to bank, post office, store, paid phone bill, and lunch. Stocked the range box. Mailed package to Sinclair.

Saturday, July 11, 1998—nice rain in night, clearing and partly cloudy later, 45° to 65°. Kahren brought a gold pan engraved with our names and 50th anniversary. She gave Sylvia four halibut ear drums. I did a couple little chores and worked on some shooting bench rest equipment. Went for a ride to Tazlina gravel pit. Visited a little with Dan Billman and Mike Shelton.

Sunday, July 12, 1998—partly cloudy and a few showers, 45° to 65°. Didn't do much today. Sorted some things. Made a study of neck turning brass. Loaded some target rounds with cast bullets. Walked down to the lake. We saw a young bull moose in the shallows on south side of the lake. Then Allen visited in evening. He noticed two beavers swimming down the middle of the lake. He needed a belt buckle and fastener for his belt. He brought ice cream. Good treat for us.

Monday, July 13, 1998—beautiful day with some breeze, 43° to 71°. Got up early and went to gravel pit to shoot. I just couldn't get the scope sighted in for this barrel. Finally gave up and came home. The package from Sinclair was here already! And cost more than expected. Pulled weeds from garden. Turned 28 case necks and resized them.

Tuesday, July 14, 1998—partly cloudy, cloudy and a shower, 48° to 72°. Hauled a little gravel down to the turn around at well. Went over to Bobs to look at his work rebuilding the "mule." I got the scope re-sighted. Neck turned and prepared more brass.

Wednesday, July 15, 1998—hard rain in early morning hours, 48° to 69°. Beautiful day and cloudy in evening. Worked at putting notch's to rest the cleaning rod on the gun cradle on top of my range box. Put roof cement on a part of camper roof. Put some wood preservative on front and arctic porches. Ed Farmer borrowed my post hole drill. Started prepping some .243 Winchester brass. Sylvia baked a rhubarb cake and slow cooked a pot of ham and beans and we asked Harold and Rachel to eat with us. They saw a black bear wearing a collar cross the highway a ways east of Joe Virgin's place. David F. was having fun pulling a water skier behind his boat for hours today on our lake. I took the tarp belonging to Ed, home to him. The wind blew it over on our place last spring.

Thursday, July 16, 1998—some rain in the night, cloudy morning and partly cloudy afternoon, 47° to 65°. Got up real early. Worked on some brass. Went to gravel pit but a shower came, so went home. Later went back to gravel pit and did some target shooting. Didn't get any really good groups. It's so beautiful outside this evening.

Friday, July 17, 1998—some showers, 47° to 64°. I rode the VA Van to Anchorage. Bill Gillam drove. A Kenny Lake man and Cecil A. went to VA Clinic also. My doctor was sick and not there. Saw a licensed practitioner who explained the previous X-rays and blood tests. She scheduled an appointment to do an upper GI.

Saturday, July 18, 1998—lots of rain in night, cloudy morning and partly cloudy in afternoon, 43° to 65°. Up early to watch hunting shows. I made rifle rests and put them on the range box—nice. Transplanted clumps of grass to cut the bank along switch back. Made a case holder fitting a drill chuck for annealing case necks. Works fine. Another brood of ducks hatched. The hen with 7, only has 4 now. The kestrels stick their heads out of the box now. The neighbor dogs carried off the raven carcass from down in the hole. The wrecker operator who was retrieving the truck tractor that left the highway at bottom of caribou, was mauled by a black bear while he worked.

Sunday, July 19, 1998—partly cloudy with a breeze, 46° to 67°. Took garbage to dump. Stopped by gravel pit and got three buckets of gravel. Shot the .338 in practice. When I got home, called Cal and told him of the 500 gallon tank at the dumpster. Then went with him to load it on his pickup. I replaced the gravel at the man door on the garage. Loaded some target loads.

Monday, July 20, 1998—partly cloudy, breezy, 39° to 70°. Went to gravel pit to shoot some more load development, did quite well too. Tried to work on front rifle rest with no luck. Removed and altered the left rear corner of shooting bench, in an effort to shoot in a more comfortable position. Annealed and neck turned some more brass. Took pictures of this process.

Tuesday, July 21, 1998—mostly cloudy, 46° to 64°. We went, up real early, to Anchorage and Wasilla, Palmer. We got some particle board for upstairs closets, groceries my medicine from the VA. It was a long hard trip.

Wednesday, July 22, 1998—cloudy, 46° to 58°. Put a primer on particle board then a coat of latex enamel. The little kestrels are hanging around in some nearby trees. Reloaded some more development loads—trying for the best target load.

Thursday, July 23, 1998—mostly cloudy, 43° to 64°. We started putting the floor down in the closets. The young kestrels are learning to use their wings.

Friday, July 24, 1998—very nice day, 40° to 66°. I rode the VA van to the VA Clinic. There they did an upper GI on me. My doctor was gone so I have to go back next week. We did a little shopping. I rebuilt the sand bag holder on the front rifle rest. Ralph phoned.

Saturday, July 25, 1998—very nice then windy in afternoon and cloudy in evening, 39° to 64°. Went target shooting in morning. Sharpened the blade on Sylvia's mower. I put the three books together, by gluing the backs of pages together. Seems to have worked well. Went to Cal and Mary's. Cal is making progress on his model "A" car. Gave one of the books to Mary to read. Then went to Dimmick's and gave Rachel a book. Sylvia went to Anchorage with Rudbecks to a wedding.

Sunday, July 26, 1998—partly cloudy and rain in evening, 42° to 64°. I put some crushed rock around the well. Cultivated the garden. Corky Dimmick came over and used my acetylene torch to melt a brass fitting out of the muffler of their Honda 4-wheeler. I drilled, tapped two holes on the barrel on the .22 rim fire and mounted an open rear sight there. I had gotten the holes drill true and the rifle shoots very well.

Monday, July 27, 1998—partly cloudy with a few showers moving through, 44° to 64°. We worked on getting the flooring put in upstairs closets. It's looking more like fall weather now.

Tuesday, July 28, 1998—cloudy and showers passing through from west, 45° to 52°. We finished the laying floors in both upstairs closets. Fooled around with the front sight on .22. We went to Bob and Kahren's for supper and visit.

Wednesday, July 29, 1998—partly cloudy and heavy showers passing through the taller mountains to the south, 43° to 56°. Have fresh snow on them. Put up some shelves for Sylvia and two for my closet. We had Allen, Roxanne and Sammy here for watermelon this evening.

Thursday, July 30, 1998—partly cloudy and a beautiful day, 45° to 66°. Looked over our lumber supply. Cleaned the wood shop. Reloaded some brass. Shot the .22 after a while. Shot a squirrel after supper.

Friday, July 31, 1998—very nice today, 43° to 70°. Rode VA van to clinic in Anchorage and saw my doctor. She explained the results of barium and X-rays, also the X-rays of my back. Now she expects to get an appointment with an ear, nose and throat specialist for me. Shot a squirrel this morning.

Saturday, August 1, 1998—partly cloudy, 51° to 70°. I loaded ATV and drove to highway camp and went up Slide Mountain on the trail. Saw tracks of two bears, a couple moose. No caribou. Came home. Allen stopped by with a nice chunk of moose ribs. Lucky him, he got an early moose permit. We went to Dimmick's to celebrate Harold's birthday. Visited with Cal and Mary. Came home and then drove 10 miles up Lake Louise Road looking for a bull caribou with no luck. Got Billman's mail from their mailbox.

Sunday, August 2, 1998—mostly cloudy and a light rain 42° to 60°. Cast some bullets and sorted them. Elaine brought us a salmon and we gave her some lettuce. I shot a rabbit with the .308 and cast bullet. A mature eagle grabbed a duck from lake edge. Allen gave us moose backstrap and heart.

Monday, August 3, 1998—mostly cloudy, 44° to 65°. Took the carburetor apart on ATV and cleaned it in hopes of stopping the fuel bowl from overflowing. So far it looks like success. Went to gravel pit to shoot. These loads did not perform well at all. Transplanted a few clumps of grass on a gravel slope on switch back. Saw a mother spruce hen and little one near switch back. The eagle hunts ducks every day. One hen has eleven ducklings. Ordered rifle barrel.

Tuesday, August 4, 1998—partly cloudy, 48° to 66°. Cut about 100 willow wands and coiled them in buckets to sell as dream catcher rings. Visited Allen after supper. Roxanne is working tonight. Kyle's ankle is better.

Wednesday, August 5, 1998—cloudy all day and rain in evening, 46° to 60°. I shoveled and leveled the fill over septic drain field. Kahren, Joey and Sylvia went currant picking.

Thursday, August 6, 1998—low clouds and sprinkles all day, 44° to 52°. Took garbage to dump. Picked up Billman's mail and put it in safe keeping place. New rifle barrel came today.

Friday, August 7, 1998—cloudy, partly cloudy, cloudy, 36° to 56°. We went to Glennallen on senior van for lunch, shopping and errands. After we got back home, I went target shooting at gravel pit. Rain in evening.

Saturday, August 8, 1998—cloudy till noon, then nice with a westerly breeze, 41° to 59°. Sharpened eight knives for Sylvia. She made kraut today and fixed a swell dinner for Rudbecks (Bob and Kahren). I went to gravel pit and fired 30 rounds at targets.

Sunday, August 9, 1998—cloudy, partly cloudy, and showers, 47° to 57°. I went to gravel pit at Army Trail to check .338 and scope. It just doesn't hold a zero. I'm very disappointed. Picked up some brass there. Dimmicks had us over for barbeque. Michigan Tom was there. He was helping Rusty with replacing a bearing in ATV front wheel. We stopped by Cal and Mary's and left some sweat shirts for her to sell. When phone rang Sylvia jumped out of bed tripped and fell out into hallway. Luckily she wasn't seriously hurt.

Monday, August 10, 1998—partly cloudy, 42° to 58°. Reground the lawn mower blade and balanced it. Checked oil and tires on car. Sylvia sewed a tarp to cover our well this winter. I planted a few small trees. Mailed scope to Leopold.

Tuesday, August 11, 1998—partly cloudy and a little shower in the evening, 39° to 59°. We got up 5:00 AM - left home 6:00 AM went to Anchorage. Doctor appointment was good, in that all that is wrong with my throat is acid reflux. We got our shopping done early. Stopped by Wasilla and Sylvia's doctor office and a little shopping. Only animals we saw were rabbits. Got home 5:45 PM and unloaded groceries.

Wednesday, August 12, 1998—partly cloudy, 42° to 62°. Melted down the wheel weights I brought home and cast them into ingots. Darrel and Brenda visited for a while. Bob R. came over for a couple screws for the carburetor and linkage on the ATV he and Jeremy rebuilt. Started making some .308 win brass from

.30 - .06 brass.

Thursday, August 13, 1998—sunny, 42° to 68°. We filled out our absentee voting ballots. Went to gravel pit target shooting. Not good with this load for cast bullets. Jacketed bullets shot excellent. Decided to go boo hunting tomorrow. Loaded the ATV, but it won't stay running very long. I'm disappointed. Ralph phoned with some questions about his rifles.

Friday, August 14, 1998—sunny and breeze, 42° to 72°. Worked on Suzuki, then went to Cal's. He wasn't sure what was wrong. This evening I phone Suzuki in Wasilla and the mechanic told me the float needle and seat were leaking. Sure enough the motor oil was diluted. Changed oil and filter. Will have to get new needle and seat.

Saturday, August 15, 1998—partly cloudy, 45° to 70°. Talked to Dan Billman and he wanted to go up by Paxson and hunt moose and caribou. Gathered up gear—forgot maps and gloves. He drove his van. It rained some. We saw a cow moose. Talked to a few hunters. The caribou are way back off the road. Dan shot his rifle a few times, sighting it in. Went to mile 52 on Denali Highway turned around and went back, not seeing any game. Ate supper at Tangle Lakes drove the road more and parked at Swede Lake Trail Head for the night. Rainy and foggy. I felt sick to my stomach, tainted food? Slept very poorly. Woke up early.

Sunday, August 16, 1998—rainy and foggy. Up early. Went to Paxson, the Lodge was closed. Went to Meyer's Lake Lodge and it too, was closed. Tried to drive in on Dick Lake Trail. It was slippery and he backed out. Went to Paxson. By now they are open. He got the gas and I got the breakfast. Then we drove down the highway, saw a bull cow and calf caribou across the road. Quickly parked the van in a pull off. Walked around in scrub spruce for a while but with so many leaves on brush we didn't see the caribou. Back out on highway, we saw a bull running in front of a pickup right towards us. These guys jump out with their rifles and we holler don't shoot towards us. That bull got away also. We then drove to Dan's. I loaded my gear over to my pickup, said hi to Patti, and looked at her effort to put out a small peat fire. Came on home. Rested a little after unloading gear and vacuuming the truck. Cleaned the vacuum cleaner. After supper I loaded the Suzuki in the truck and hunt gear. Hope to hunt tomorrow. Allen took us to Eureka for pie and ice cream.

Monday, August 17, 1998—partly cloudy and windy here. I left early and drove to Paxson and up the Denali Highway a ways hunting. No luck. Someone had gotten a paddle horn moose. Saw a huge bodied moose with a small rack and a bigger rack on a trailer. These would be permit moose. Did some walking and couldn't find any fresh tracks. Came back to Glennallen. Visited Darrel and he wanted me to check on some septic tanks at Paul White's Check on the summer thaw level at first well sight. Pulled some weeds.

Tuesday, August 18, 1998—sunny. My knee is very sore. Did a little shovel work. We picked blueberries at several places between here and Gunsight Mountain. Got enough for a pie. Luepold sent my scope back and I mounted it and went to gravel pit and sighted it in at 200 yards.

Wednesday, August 19, 1998—sunny, 28° to 61°. Shoveled some more dirt to shape up the septic drainfield. Went to Legion meeting with Bartley. Picked up my Alaska moose and sheep harvest tickets while I was in town. Saw a young cross fox cross the highway.

Thursday, August 20, 1998—cloudy, 38° to 55°. Got up early and drove west at first light looking for a legal moose to shoot for winter moose. Saw Cal and Mary at Tahneta. Didn't have any luck on the drive. Then Sylvia had "Lady" company. Then Elaine came over with 4 Plumcott's and a book for me to read. We gave her a book to read and a couple large new potatoes and several packages of turnip greens she cooked up to give Jim. In the afternoon we drove the Lake Louis Road, looking for a moose or caribou no luck. We picked about one cup of blueberries. Got gasoline and pop at Dawson's and visited with Leona.

Friday, August 21, 1998—mostly cloudy, 41° to 55°. Sylvia went to Glennallen. I put the camper on truck. Checked out the appliance in camper. Worked on Steve's brass.

Saturday, August, 22, 1998—a shower, cloudy, sunny, 42° to 57°. We are getting the camper stocked. Got a young spruce hen and a squirrel. Worked at preparing 30-30 brass. Phoned Paul. They are doing ok.

Sunday, August 23, 1998—40° to 50s. We finished packing the camper and drove to Valdez. About 30 miles from town it started raining. We drove around town and got re-oriented and familiar with the streets. Did a little shopping. Ate supper. T. J. Huddleston saw our pickup and camper, recognized it and visited with us while we ate. Then we went to Tom Huddleston and visited for a while. Then back to town. We parked at the city pier for the night. Still raining. Some folks are catching a few silvers and herring off the dock.

Monday, August 24, 1998—light rain, 50s. We got up early by two hours. Went to the tour ticket office and validated our trip. The trip started at 9:00 AM and returned at 8:30 PM. We saw hundreds of sea otters some with pups lying on their mom's bellies. Steller sea lions at Hauling Out Beach. A pod of orca or killers whales. One humpback whale, harbor seals, puffins, many kinds of gulls.

A few eagles. The boat captain got us up close and personal at "Meares" Glacier. The icebergs kept us about six miles from Columbia Glacier. We had some snacks and a lunch at Chowder Island. He took us fairly close to ferry terminal. We saw oil tanker, a huge tourist cruise ship, fishing vessels and the big boats that process the catch. Even some oyster farming. It was a very nice day. Todd Huddleston bought our supper. Met Tom's friend Ron? Nice guy. We parked at City Dock again.

Tuesday, August 25, 1998—50s. I got up as it was getting light. Saw the tide was in, so got fishing gear together and fished for herring off the city dock. Caught one but it got off the hook before I could get it the 20 feet up out of the water; finally gave up. We drove over to Allison point. Fishing for silver salmon was very slow. We decided to head for home. Got gas in Glennallen. Stopped by Darrel and Brenda's to plan out a sandhill crane and goose hunt at Delta Junction Farm Project. At home we unloaded camper. Readied the trailer hitch on car. Dug out some weeds and wild roses.

Wednesday, August 26, 1998—partly cloudy, 35° to 52°. I hunted the area mostly south of the gravel pit east of here. Didn't see any moose or caribou. Saw a spruce hen and a wolf den. Took canoe down to lake. Shortened the dock. Put a new end on it and brought the remainder up here. Kahren was picking rose hips nearby and helped lift part of the dock onto the ATV trailer. Sylvia is making cucumber pickles, beet pickles and picked fresh peas. Creamed fresh peas and new potatoes for supper! Good sized flock of ducks flying on lake.

Thursday, August 27, 1998—fog nearby in morning, partly cloudy, 36° to 51°. We worked on water line and winterized it. I mowed the lawn while Sylvia canned carrots. Hunted west to Little Nelchina in morning. Hunted the area just to the east of here this evening; saw a spruce hen. Shot a squirrel today. Allen brought us some fresh salmon.

Friday, August 28, 1998—snow early morning that didn't stay long, 29° to 49°. We went to Glennallen on senior van and paid electric bill and had lunch. Finished cleaning out camper. Called Bart and relayed message to Sam.

Saturday, August 29, 1998—beaut of a day, 33° to 49°. We put up some tripods and support for water line and shortened well stand pipe. Got a squirrel. Drove to Cal's and back just at dark, hunting, saw cow and calf moose.

Sunday, August 30, 1998—nice day, 29° to 56°. We built more tripods for the waterline support. Then Ralph and Jeff stopped by on way to hunt mountain goat. After lunch we dug potatoes and got about 150 pounds. Jerry, Betty Rudbeck brought pickled fish and visited.

Monday, August 31, 1998—Nice day, 34° to 50s. Welded a part of snow plow. Got car ready for trip. Sylvia went to State Fair in Palmer on senior van.

Tuesday, September 1, 1998—nice day. We loaded car with goose hunting gear. Drove to Glennallen. Filled with gas. Went to Darrel and Brenda's. Transferred gear to their motor home. Darrel drove it and Brenda her pickup to Delta. We stopped by shooting range but not much brass there. We saw a cow and calf moose at upper end of Summit Lake, right side of highway, near old pipeline camp. Trip was uneventful till Donkey Dome and a nice big bull moose. Stopped at Brenda's daughter, Robin's home. Darrel and I went out to Holenbeck's and Roy Beavers to visit and look hunt prospects and flight patterns. Roy has killed one griz and he and doc run off three more griz. We went to Tanana River, just off Roy's farm. Walked and explored. Drove over to Holenbeck's and hunted till dark. Darrel got two geese. I did lots of missing. We slept in motor home. Sylvia and I slept down below, and Darrel and Brenda, over the cab. Looked at carcass of Buckley's Bear.

Wednesday, September 2, 1998—frost and warm day. We got up early and went to Hollenbeck's Farm to hunt. Geese and crane flew very well all day. I finally got to hitting a few. Russel H., age 12, stopped by and hunted with us. Nice boy. We got seven birds. Mostly speckle belly geese and a couple sandhill crane. We got back to town after dark.

Thursday, September 3, 1998—frost and then a warm day. Darrel drove the motor home to farm today. We stalked a huge flock with no luck. I shot a Canada and young sandhill crane. No luck for Darrel. He could have shot a crane. We took turns, slept about 1:00 PM. Later with no birds flying we went back to Delta. Robin's husband Mike Smith is a nice guy. He is getting his swamp buggy ready to hunt. We left for home. We got to our place about 2:00 AM.

Friday, September 4, 1998—beaut of a day, 34° to 48°. Unloaded gear. Sylvia washed and prepared birds for freezer. Allen and Sammy visited and had a sandwich and cookies with us. Robin had given us a huge bologna. We gave Allen some. I took garbage to transfer sight. Found some brass in gravel pit. Cleaned one shotgun.

Saturday, September 5, 1998—beaut of a day. 28° to 56°. Rested a lot today. Called Darrel (and he called me), Tom H and Allen. Visited Allen in the afternoon. After supper Sylvia and I road hunted to Gunsight and back. Didn't see any moose to hunt, some on swamp buggies and a caribou on vehicle.

Sunday, September 6, 1998—mostly cloudy, 39° to 53°. Got up late. Rested some. Tried to glass for bear on Slide Mountain—no luck. Watched a couple hunting shows. Ralph and Jeff drove in, fresh from the hunting in the Wrangle Mountains. They each got full curl Dall rams. A real nice hunt and they had a good time. We let them put their meat in our freezers. Sylvia cooked some of the meat for supper. Very, very good. After supper, Jeff, Ralph and I drove our car to Mile 119 looking for moose. Saw a moose two days ago. Jeff's brother Dale and wife Heidi drove out from Wasilla to see the sheep heads. Sat around the table eating sheep meat, cookies and drinking soda pop.

Monday, September 7, 1998—beautiful day, rain in early morning and early afternoon, 38° to 54°. Deciduous tree leaves are very colorful. Jeff, Ralph and I rode our car Molly to Mile 120 and back. Jeff spotted a big cow moose and twin calves. We looked for bears on Slide Mountain—no luck. They went on to meet Dale at "Lions Head." Dale saw a mountain goat there. Sylvia cut and packaged most of Jeff's sheep meat. I did a few little jobs. Tired; napped an hour or so. Steve phoned.

Tuesday, September 8, 1998—very nice day, 34° to 55°. Up early and drove up Lake Louise Road hunting. No luck. Got gas at Dinty Bush's from Steve. Ground a chisel point on one knife. Got a spruce hen. Rested some. Found some brass in gravel pit. Kahren visited after supper gave us some pix of 50th anniversary party. Then I drove to gravel pit at mil 132 and glassed for moose. Saw horns of a bull a long way away. Turned into gravel pit east of Cal's while driving along the west side I saw a pure white wolf. Got to see it as it moved away for about 30-40 yards. Back out to highway and at the old road at west side of Little Nelchina Hill, two moose cows were crossing the highway. Stopped to look at them.

Wednesday, September 9, 1998—very nice today, 28° to 55°. Went to Little Nelchina and hunted moose. No luck. Came home. Visited Ed. Allen came along. Mark showed us his bob cat loader and snow plow for it he is building. Jerry R. brought Ed some meat. Then I went down to help Allen put the tracks together for his ranger. Ed was already there. Allen BBQ some caribou for lunch. We got the tanks together and on machine. Ate supper here and went to gravel pit to see if the bull was still there. It was not! We went to Eureka and glassed another area. Saw two cows and one calf. A 172 Cessna airplane was flying the area making many passes. Didn't see anything along the road on way home. Ordered barrel for rifle.

Thursday, September 10, 1998—pretty nice day, 36° to 54°. Allen, Ed and I decided to go down Squaw Creek to look for a legal bull moose. Sylvia babysat Samantha. We got a really late start. We packed and unloaded at the trailhead. Allen's Ranger ran fine. New cleats on track are okay.

We saw lots of moose and bear tracks on trail. Visited with two hunters a few minutes. We ate lunch and then hunted a small valley with a small stream. There were seven Dall Rams at head of valley. I went up the middle, and they went up the ridges on each side. I scared out a cow moose right away. Others simply evaded me in the tall thick brush and willows. I got quite a ways up the valley when the grass got shoulder high and difficult to walk through. Finally I saw a feasible place to climb out and up on the ridge. Up there Ed came along and we moved to an overlook and watched for moose and ate large sweet blueberries. Ed spotted Allen walking towards our ATVs so we went down there also. We then started back to trail head hunting along the way. One little valley in particular. I saw a marten and a snowshoe rabbit there. Ed spotted a sow silver tip griz with two large silver tip cubs more than two years old. They were running towards Allen and he got off the ridge and back down on road. Somewhat later I got to the road. Allen set up the spotting scope. They saw all three bears but I only saw one 2-year-old. We saw two cows and a calf moose before we got to trailhead. On the way home my car overheated, blew upper radiator hose. Parked it in the school teacher's house yard for the night. Allen brought me home. After supper and a shower I phoned Dan. He plans to fish for halibut the rest of the week. He will try to pick me up a valve and seat for the Suzuki.

Friday, September 11, 1998—mostly cloudy, 37° to 54°. Ed F. drove me to Cal's and he gave me a radiator hose for our car. Back to Steve and Mary Rose's. Put it on and put in antifreeze and drove "Molly" (our vehicle) home. She is functional again. Put a little repair on upper garden fence. Rested some today. After supper Sylvia and I drive the road hunting. Saw two cow moose.

Saturday, September 12, 1998—mostly cloudy and frequent shower, 39° to 52°. Rested today. Started to go look for a moose but it was raining there. Glassed for bears on Slide Mt.—no luck. Repair welded a support for the bed of the trailer that I haul the Suzuki on. Sylvia picked in between showers two gallons cranberries.

Sunday, September 13, 1998—mostly cloudy, 37° to 55°. Birch tree by house dropped a lot of leaves. I got a late start. Went to gravel pit east of Cal's. Went south on trail towards Nelchina River. At drainage area there I saw wolf tracks. Cut two logs on trail and moved them out of trail. Saw marten pooh in trail. Saw fresh moose tracks out near north end of trail. Saw a moose calf bull out the corner of my eye. Stalked the area. Found large moose tracks. Didn't see animal. Sylvia went to Mendeltna Chapel to services and pot luck. (T.J. Huddleston goes to National Guard for six months.) I vacuumed birch leaves. Sylvia picked two quarts of cranberries. Allen visited in evening for awhile.

Monday, September 14, 1998—cloudy and a shower or two, 38° to 48°. Put canoe in lake. Managed to get four ducks. Had gotten four squirrels first thing this morning. After lunch we got a trailer load of rotted straw. Will use it to cover the sewer system. Tamped large gravel in the top of drainfield. Sylvia picked six quarts of cranberries.

Tuesday, September 15, 1998–cloudy, foggy, clearing, partly cloudy, 35° to 48°. Went to a treeless hill west of Eureka. Glassed for moose with no luck. Stopped at DOT station on way home. Ran ATV up the trail north to the fork, Then walked. Saw a few moose tracks, sow and cub track, fox and bear pooh and two spruce hens.

Wednesday, September 16, 1998–cloud-foggy, rain all night, partly cloudy, 37° to 49°. Didn't do anything for a while, then went down to lake and shot two ducks. Cleaned them and drove to Mile 132 and took trail north and east to second lake and walked over a little ridge and overlooked yet another valley. Didn't see a moose or a caribou. Sylvia went to Eagle River with Kahren and Betty. She got home about same time I did. Ralph called with four hunting stories. Ed came over and wants me to hunt a bull moose with him in the morning.

Thursday, September 17, 1998–cloudy, foggy to cloudy, 36° to 45°. Got up early and drove to Little Nelchina. I drove ATV's up on shoulder of Slide Mountain, then walked. I saw two cows (moose) It was nice to go up there and hunt for them. The trail was good. Rested when I got home. Finished loading Steve's 30-30 shells. I need a needle and seat for my Suzuki. Tonight I'm calling around to save a trip to Palmer.

Friday, September 18, 1998–partly cloudy and breezy, 31° to 56°. Lots of phone calls and no luck finding a needle and seat for Suzuki. We went to Glennallen for lunch and cash checks. Back home I took Suzuki carburetor apart. Ralph called–I asked him to try in Fairbanks. He was successful and he and Roma are coming down this evening. Arrival depending on possible success hunting along the way.

Saturday, September 19, 1998–cloudy, partly cloudy, windy and a little rain in evening, 34° to 52°. Ralph and I got up early, put ATV trailer on back of Suzuki. After I put the new needle and seat in carburetor. We drove to Cal's. Parked and drove the trails southwest, south put 11 miles on Suzuki. Found some new trails to explore. Saw wolf, bear, fox, marten sign. Some moose tracks. No moose in flesh. It was a good day to be out hunting. Did enough walking for one day. Jeff phoned after supper.

Sunday, September 20, 1998–partly cloudy, 35° to 53°. Ralph and I got up early and drove to Gunsight Mountain and back looking for a moose–no luck. After breakfast and some visiting, Ralph and Roma visited a couple other neighbors and started for Fairbanks and home and hunted along the way. I went hunting on an old trapline trail. No luck but walked around in a beautiful park like area.

When I got home, Roma had phoned. A moose had crossed the highway in front of them. It had three browtines on both antlers (makes it legal). It was in some thick trees. Ralph whistled at it. That stopped it and he got a perfect shot in—threaded a single bullet between the tree trunks and into the moose's boiler room! It dropped after five or six steps. They wanted me to come and get a share of meat. I got there in time to help put it in meat sacks and carry-slide-pull it out to road and load it in his truck and my car. I got home about 8:30 PM. Sylvia and I hung each piece in garage and took the meat sacks off so it could cool down. Sure tired tonight. Took a hot shower to relax tense muscles. A wonderful day with good friends.

Monday, September 21, 1998—partly cloudy, windy morning, 37° to 54°. Sylvia worked on neck of moose. Hurt my back carrying it to house. Washed the mud off the Suzuki. Trimmed up two quarters of moose and put meat sacks on them. Meat smells good. Went to Cal's and borrowed his meat grinder.

Tuesday, September 22, 1998—partly cloudy, 34° to 47°. We ground Dall sheep and moose meat. Formed it into patties, packaged it and put it in freezer. About 80 pounds of meat. The four signets (swans) are trying to fly.

Wednesday, September 23, 1998—mostly cloudy, 29° to 49°. We cut up and packaged the moose ribs. Tamped the rest of fill over septic drain field. Took garbage to transfer site and a few little jobs. Gave Allen some moose ribs.

Thursday, September 24, 1998—partly cloudy, frost in morning, 29° to 48°. We spread straw over septic drainfield. Put Styrofoam on and covered that with tarps. I did some work on waterline. Kahren brought Moe Liezta over to visit.

Friday, September 25, 1998—cloudy and foggy morning, 34°. Bob R came over to look at shot shells, but I didn't have 2-¾" length he needed. We went to Wasilla and Anchorage. Then drove down Seward and Sterling Highways. We haven't driven here for 16-17 years. After a sandwich supper we found Andy and Connie Boyle's place. Connie and son Arlo were home. We visited with Connie for awhile. It wasn't dark yet, so we drove towards D. Eastman's. Phoned them from Anchor Point. Denny met us out at highway and lead us to their place. We visited a couple hours.

Saturday, September 26, 1998—cloudy and rainy, clearing later. Den and Joey drove us around Homer. Lunch at "Steamer Clams." The bought a tuna fish from a fishing boat. Joey barbequed some it for supper. We stayed with them again tonight. They have a great view of the mountains and Cook Inlet. We watched a movie.

Sunday, September 27, 1998—cloudy and windy. We all went to Homer for breakfast. Then we drove out the "East Road," to Tom Baudette's corner and turned off on the road to Charlie and Beth's place. Drove right to it. Charlie will be in from Cordova on a plane at 4:00 PM. Beth and Cora showed us the damage the moose had done to their garden. Not much left. We all went in their van to airport and met Charlie. After greetings we drove around the spit and some of town. Out to their place, visit and supper. Having a nice time.

Monday, September 28, 1998—some frost in morning, cloudy then nice. Visited with Beth. Charlie got off work mid afternoon. He drove us out east end road quite a ways. Nice sight seeing. Cora showed us her school. After supper, Charlie (son) took his dad to a scout meeting. After they got back, Charlie wanted to talk guns.

Tuesday, September 29, 1998—cloudy and windy here at Homer and much of trip home. Good trip though. We stopped in Anchorage and did some shopping and I picked up my prescriptions at VA clinic. We saw two moose calves 30 and 40 miles west of here. The caribou are on Eureka Summit. We saw quite a few. Allen phoned. There are 15,000 here now. 15-18 on his campground that we saw plus many more along the road. Ralph phoned, he wants to hunt grizzly bear tomorrow.

Wednesday, September 30, 1998—cloudy and some breeze and snow occasionally. 31° to 35°. We unloaded the camper. Carried the front leg of moose in house and Sylvia started cutting and wrapping the meat. I cleaned up around the place putting things away should we get a lot of snow. Took lime and fertilizer down to the garden. Spread it around and tilled it in. Went over the garden twice. Ralph Fuson drove down from Fairbanks. He wants to hunt grizzly bears. Dale Routt got his self ran up a tree by a grizzly that was coming in on his partner was calling like a cow moose in hopes of getting a bull moose to come in. Saw a spruce hen in house yard today.

Thursday, October 1, 1998—clear and sunny, 17° to 39°. Some ice on lake this morning. Sylvia finished cutting and wrapping meat. Ralph and I went up Slide Mountain hunting grizzly. No luck, but we did see a wolverine track, at one place it had dragged its rear end through 1" snow on the ground. It seemed it did so to pull a large moose hair turd out of its rectum. As soon as we reached the top of Slide, we saw caribou. Maybe a thousand in the time we were up there. We walked a half mile or so north and ate some of Ralph's MRE's. Spent a lot of time just watching the caribou herd. Really great to see them like that. Ralph took a swing east and south near some previous bear dens with no luck. We took pictures and walked back to Suzuki and came home to a supper of moose steak and fresh garden peas.

Friday, October 2, 1998—sunny, frost, 14° to 37°. Our lake is mostly frozen over. The swans are trying to get the four signets up and flying. They are doing better though one is much weaker. A few ducks are stopping in to rest. Ralph and I took the camper off the truck. He bought hamburgers at Eureka. On the way there we saw a very large coyote eating something in the road ditch. We went to gravel pit for target shooting and spruce hen hunting. Didn't get any spruce hens. We went to the school house at teacher Mary Rose's request. I spoke on dairy farming and Ralph spoke on the electrician profession. Allen and Sammy visited.

Saturday, October 3, 1998—sunny, 10° to 35°. Today is granddaughter Vanessa's wedding day. Beverly phoned and filled us in on some of the highlights. Ralph and I drove to DOT gravel pit and rode Suzuki up the trail to Slide Mountain. We parked short of the top and walked up. Saw caribou right away. We didn't see any grizzly bears. We walked up the mountain and looked at a place a bear had started a den and quit after a short distance. We continued up to top rim of mountain. Often looking at groups of caribou. All moving and feeding in a north and easterly direction. Some of the herd bulls are magnificent. Their colors and horns are outstanding. They were continuously checking for cows in heat. We didn't see any cows get serviced. Mid afternoon I started back to the Suzuki. Ralph continued east hunting grizzly bear. The trail back down the mountain was easy as all the mud and water is frozen and I traveled over it instead of through the mud.

Sunday, October 4, 1998—mostly cloudy, 18° to 38°. A little snow just before dark. Ralph left for Fairbanks after breakfast. We rested all day. A few ducks on lake.

Monday, October 5, 1998—cloudy, 16° to 36°. The small areas of our lake that are not frozen, got somewhat larger this afternoon. Didn't do much today. Unloaded the Suzuki from pickup. Propped up the front overhang on camper. The ermine that lives in our woodpile gets whiter each day.

Tuesday, October 6, 1998—cloudy and a skiff of snow, 26° to 35°. I put some oil and STP in the transfer case on truck. Drained the gas out of the Suzuki. Cleaned some ice and sand out of water hauling tank.

Wednesday, October 7, 1998—cloudy, 25° to 32°. Hauled ashes to dumpster. Visited Tom H. and then Jim O. Back home I got truck ready to go to Anchorage tomorrow. Picked up Sam Weaver at Bart's and we went to Legion meeting in Glennallen. Bart showed up later. The three of us did not a quorum make so there wasn't any meeting. Sam did pick up a few groceries.

Thursday, October 8, 1998—sunny, 21° to 34°. Didn't sleep well. We went to Anchorage. Tried to sell some willow hoops. No luck. We shopped for a toilet stool, groceries, 220 gallons of gas. Nice drive in and out. Saw caribou between here and Eureka.

Friday, October 9, 1998—sunny, a very nice day, 10° to 33°. We went to Glennallen and cashed checks and paid phone bill. Saw some caribou along the way. I unloaded the load of gasoline. Started on getting the new stool installed by putting several coats of varithane on the seat and lid. Changed the oil and filter on the truck. Measured the fuel oil in the supply tank. Sylvia saw a spruce hen. I saw a snowshoe hare in our yard.

Saturday, October 10, 1998—sunny and very nice, 9° to 33°. We installed the stool in the bathroom. Just a tiny place unfrozen on our lake. Saw a couple spruce hens around the place. One squirrel ran by the house.

Sunday, October 11, 1998—sunny, 8° to 32°. Tom and Lisa Smayda stopped by and we had a real nice visit. Walked down by the lake etc. Phoned Paul and Steve. Lake is frozen over.

Monday, October 12, 1998—sunny, 3° to 31°. Walked down to lake. Cut some limbs off a couple trees that were hanging out. Moved the dock off to one side. Put the new fire pot fan in the heating stove.

Tuesday, October 13, 1998—sunny, high thin cloudy in evening, 7° to 31°. Did a few small jobs. Prepared rifle receiver for shipping. Allen mounted five tires for me and we had a nice visit.

Wednesday, October 14, 1998—cloudy, 15° to 33°. Took a couple tickets to Allen and showed him a couple pictures of a bear den we had found. Show the pix to Ed also. Put the tarp cover over the well house cover. Unloaded tires and wheels from car. Britt and Sven (Norway) sent us a couple little presents.

Thursday, October 15, 1998—cloudy, snow in afternoon, 24° to 29°. 2" snow. Put the canopy on truck. Fuel line on truck was leaking so put a different clamp on it. Readied the truck to plow snow. Phoned Tyler and Steve.

Friday, October 16, 1998—sunny, 13° to 32°. We went to Glennallen to get flu shots. That office was closed. Ate lunch and came home. I did a few little jobs. Sylvia did some laundry.

Saturday, October 17, 1998—Sunny, cloudy in evening, 5° to 31°. Reworked the truck fuel line. Saw a red fox race through the yard this morning. Gathered up some electric wire and tools to install a couple outlets in Sylvia's closet upstairs.

Sunday, October 18, 1998—sunny, 18° to 34°. Didn't feel well today. We did get to Dimmick's for supper with them. Billmans left some magazines here for Sylvia. We stopped by Cal and Mary's and borrowed the meat grinder.

Monday, October 19, 1998—cloudy, 19° to 39°. Did some target shooting. After putting a .22 barrel on the action. Then neck turned some brass and loaded it for hunting. Sylvia ground and packaged sausage meat. Jim, Mary and Kari visited.

Tuesday, October 20, 1998— foggy till noon, cloudy, partly cloudy, 21° to 34°. Put in a couple outlets in Sylvia's closet upstairs. Turned some necks on .22-250 brass. Sylvia finished grinding sausage. While the sun was out, a red fox came up close to house. Probably the one we have seen before.

Wednesday, October 21, 1998—partly cloudy, 16° to 33°. Rifle barrel came today. Jim Odden drove and we went up Lake Louise Road to see what the caribou prospects are. Some hunters had been successful. I returned the meat grinder to Cal. Bart took me to Legion meeting in Glennallen. We were the only ones there. Disappointing. I tried to clean the barrel I got today; It sure is dirty.

Thursday, October 22, 1998—partly cloudy, 10° to 30°. Cut the boards for risers for the stairs going to the basement. We saw the fox cross the west end of lake. Some caribou came out on our lake at 5:45 PM.

Friday, October 23, 1998—snow all day, 20° to 29°. We went to Glennallen. Paid electric bill. Mailed rifle barrel back to John. Had lunch. Put plow on and plowed our snow and at the mailboxes. Repaired light switch on truck and put amber warning light on truck. Shoved snow around arctic entry. Allen visited. Sylvia gave him some eggs pickled in beet juice.

Saturday, October 24, 1998—partly cloudy, 27° to 34°. Snow slide off roof of house and garage. Lots of snow melted. I plowed more snow here and plowed out Dimmick's. Shoveled lots of snow. Dropped off some sausage and magazines at Cal and Mary's.

Sunday, October 25, 1998—cloudy and light snow most of the day, 27° to 38° to 25°. I framed a picture of Darrel. Started the snowgo and packed the trail to water line and well. Jim and Elaine visited with us this afternoon.

Monday, October 26, 1998—cloudy, partly cloudy, 10° to 27°. Removed and replaced a bushing on reloading press. Drew a plan to hold a die in press. Shot a squirrel. Did exercises and walked up and down the hill.

Tuesday, October 27, 1998—sunny, 1° to 26°. Tried to design a die to taper cast bullets. Fox ate yesterday's squirrel. Shot another one today. In late afternoon 13 caribou came out on our lake. I phoned Ed F and Kyle F. Sylvia could hear shots. We didn't see any bull go down. At that same time a coyote came out on west end of lake and spent quite a lot of time out on lake. There is more overflow everyday.

Wednesday, October 28, 1998—fog till noon, sunny, fog in evening, 0° to 20°. Walked down to lake, adjusted water line height. Cleaned some bolts. Watched a prospecting movie. Saw two spruce hens out by the garage.

Thursday, October 29, 1998—sunny, 1° to 11°. Walked down to lake. We sorted through one freezer and rearranged things so we can find things. Allen visited. I went to Pat's for a while this evening. Coyote was on our lake again.

Friday, October 30, 1998—cloudy, sunny, -5° to 12°. We went to Glennallen for lunch and got some groceries. The neighborhood red fox was on the lake this afternoon.

Saturday, October 31, 1998—warmer. Shoveled snow up to well cover.

Sunday, November 1, 1998—cloudy, sunny, partly cloudy, 4° to 17°. I shoveled snow around the well. Put new 100 watt bulb in well. Sylvia tried to pump water and the water line is frozen. We put the 1-½" line into basement. Sylvia fixed a really nice baked salmon dinner. Harold and Rachel came. Jim, Mary and Kari came later. We visited after dinner. Ralph phoned. Rachel got to see our red fox when they went out to get in their van to go home.

Monday, November 2, 1998—partly cloudy, 8° to 24°. Did a lot of work on getting a better grade on water line. Shoveled more snow around the well cover.

Tuesday, November 3, 1998—cloudy till noon then sunny, 4° to 18°. I shoveled more snow around the well. Sorted some bolts. The little red fox walked along south side of the house at a distance of two feet. She then turned off southwest and stopped—looking straight ahead then went down the hill.

Wednesday, November 4, 1998—cloudy, sunny, foggy evening, 0° to 17°. Brought the frozen section of frozen water line up and put it in basement. Went to Glennallen with Sam and Bart for a Legion meeting, but we were the only one's there again.

Thursday, November 5, 1998—cloudy, sunny, cloudy and some fog, 9° to 20°. Drained the water from pipe that had been frozen. Pulled the pipe behind me and walked down the hill and replaced it where it belongs.

Friday, November 6, 1998—sunny, some fog in afternoon and again in evening. We went to Glennallen for lunch, pay phone bill. Went to visit Allen in evening. Cleaned vacuum cleaner.

Saturday, November 7, 1998—cloudy till noon, foggy, 14° to 21°. We pumped water today. Put plywood supports in rocking chair for the cushions. Took down political signs. Searched stock of the maps—couldn't find the one I needed.

Sunday, November 8, 1998—fog, light snow, fog, 9° to 14°. Tried again to remove the barrel from the DGA action with no luck.

Monday, November 9, 1998—fog, sunny, cloudy and fog across the river, -7° to 9°. We pumped water again today. Packaged a barrel and action to send to gunsmith.

Tuesday, November 10, 1998—fog, sunny, cloudy and fog, -13° to -2°. Read some and watched hunting videos.

Wednesday, November 11, 1998—more reading, more videos.

Thursday, November 12, 1998—fog, cloudy and snow all day, 4° to 12°. Jim O. came over to use some penetrating oil I have. The pump quit on snow plow lift. Built a fire in garage. Cleaned the inside of the pump and screen put new oil in and it works fine now.

Friday, November 13, 1998—cloudy, foggy, 2° to 10°. We went to Glennallen to lunch, bank, groceries and post office. Mailed gun barrel.

Saturday, November 14, 1998—cloudy and fog around us, 3° to 13°. Didn't do much today. Pumped water for house.

Sunday, November 15, 1998—cloudy, 11° to 18°. Taped some hunting shows. Sylvia is working on a quilt. Lee Dudley stopped by for a few minutes.

Monday, November 16, 1998—cloudy, foggy, 1° to 13°. We pumped water. I visited Jim Manning. Sylvia did some laundry.

Tuesday, November 17, 1998—fog all day, 1° to 7°. We had Jim and Elaine

Manning and Lee Dudley to lunch with us. We went to Jim and Mary Odden for supper. Had a nice visit. We took Ellie Farmer to her home when we went home.

Wednesday, November 18, 1998—fog and low clouds, 5° to 11°. We pumped water. Five bull caribou and one cow went east on our lake this afternoon. The red fox walked by living room window again this afternoon.

Thursday, November 19, 1998—fog and clouds, 2" snow. I visited Jim O. Plowed our snow. Saw fox. Jim had wolf tracks on airstrip. Paid dump fee.

Friday, November 20, 1998—cloudy and a little snow, 5°(night) to 16° to 24°. We went to Glennallen lunch and a little shopping Pumped water. I put a new fitting in well to direct the returning water away from light bulb. Packed trail to lake with snowgo.

Saturday, November 21, 1998—cloudy and snowed two inches, 20° to 15°. We went to Dan and Patti's skating party at Lake Louise. Got to visit with some old friends and eat some good food.

Sunday, November 22, 1998—sunny, cloudy, 2° to 6°. Snowed two inches in the night. Plowed out snow. The fox left a deposit at the small door of garage. Cast some bullets with new mold.

Monday, November 23, 1998—cloudy, a little snow, -2° to 7°. We went to senior Thanksgiving dinner at the Legion Hall. Sylvia shopped for groceries. I mailed an order for dies and brass.

Tuesday, November 24, 1998—cloudy and lots of fog, -3° to +6°. Light bulb burned out in the well replaced it and pumped water. Redone the gas line on the truck.

Wednesday, November 25, 1998—mostly sunny, -16° to -2°. I made eleven cutting boards. The fox was in front of garage and as it ran north it was springing bounce-like, well up off the snow. Cal phoned. Elaine phoned. Read up on the 7.5 x 54 MAS.

Thursday, November 26, 1998—sunny, cloudy, by noon light snow all afternoon, -5° to +5°. Sylvia baked a turkey and we took it to Odden's for Thanksgiving dinner. Mary fixed lots of other dishes' including carrot pie. They had other guests, Michael and Robin invited also. Homemade ice cream with the pies. We came home about 6:30 PM.

Friday, November 27, 1998—sunny, cloudy in later afternoon, -17° to 0°. We pumped water. Measured the heating oil in storage rank. Saw the fox again today.

Saturday, November 28, 1998—sunny, cloudy, -3° to 15°. Slept late. Ralph phoned. Jon B. visited.

Sunday, November 29, 1998—sunny, partly cloudy, 0° to 5°. Did some reading and watched hunting shows. Jeff Routt and his kids, Kitten, Jarred and Shobie visited and stayed for supper. We had a good visit talking about things of interest to both of us. Then Jim and Mary O. stopped by with a carrot pie and I made some homemade ice cream.

Monday, November 30, 1998—cloudy all day, -1° to 10°. Some snow just to the south of us. Polished brass today after breaking the rounds down to components. Allen visited a couple hours this morning.

Tuesday, December 1, 1998—sunny, -6° to +8°. We pumped water. Read. Sorted some brass. Did a couple small jobs.

Wednesday, December 2, 1998—sunny, cloudy, -11° to +9°. Did a little reading. Watches some hunting movies. Weighed individual brass cases and boxed the weight separately. Went in Legion meeting with Bart. Again only he and I showed up. We did have a good visit.

Thursday, December 3, 1998—cloudy, -4° to +4°. Worked on some more brass.

Friday, December 4, 1998—cloudy, a little snow, -5° to 16°. Went to Glennallen for lunch and some shopping. Pumped water up to house. Worked on brass again.

Saturday, December 5, 1998—cloudy, 1-1/2" snow, 0° to 18°. I plowed our snow and took garbage to transfer site. Stopped by Tim's and picked up my rifle. Back at home I fire formed brass for it. Darrel and Brenda were here for goose dinner and a sled dog movie. The sound of firearm shots doesn't bother the fox.

Sunday, December 6, 1998—cloudy, a little snow, -8° to +6°. Test fired the 1.5 x 54 rifle.

Monday, December 7, 1998—cloudy, 0° to 3°. We went to Manning's for breakfast. Allen, Roxanne and Samantha came also. The fox ran through our yard caring a small sack of someone's garbage and goes around the neighborhood. Allen saw a cross fox here also, three caribou crossing our lake. I'm working hard at cleaning the barrel of the rifle. I made a follower adapter for it to make it a single shot when target shooting. Jim O called to check if it would shoot.

Tuesday, December 8, 1998—partly cloudy, cloudy in evening, -11° to -3°. Pumped water. Worked on the brass-annealing it. Loaded 5 and shot them at a target. Rifle shoots much better. Needs more cleaning though.

Wednesday, December 9, 1998—cloudy, light snow in evening, -5° to +5°. Packed snow on road to well. Went to visit Allen but he was at work. Shoveled snow off wood shed roof. Worked on some more brass. Loaded some and fired all but five rifle shoots. Much better the cleaner I get the barrel. Phoned and asked about Sylvia's Rx.

Thursday, December 10, 1998—cloudy and snow in afternoon, -5° to +7°. Shoveled more snow off a couple roofs. Shot a good group on a target. We took a cutting board I made to Rachel Dimmick and to Mary Gilcrease. I went to school house and made some copies to send to Steve and to Ralph.

Friday, December 11, 1998—cloudy, 3" snow, -10° to +5°. We went to Glennallen on senior van for lunch. Paid phone bill and did a little shopping. Loaded a few cartridges and pulled snow off some roofs. Plowed our snow. Allen and Sammy brought over ice cream and chocolate syrup and we had a nice visit.

Saturday, December 12, 1998—mostly cloudy, 1" snow in night, -5° to +2°. Wrote lots of Christmas cards. Pumped water. Test fired and chronographed some cast bullet loads. Cast some more bullets. Fred Rungee visited. Brought veggies and ice cream. We showed the smoke jumpers training film. Fred being an old smoke jumper enjoyed the film. We had ice cream, a hamburger and gave him a package of sheep steak and moose back strap. Oddens came over this evening for hugs and byes as they leave for Wisconsin in morning.

Sunday, December 13, 1998—mostly sunny, -14° to -4°. Cleaned the rifle. Sylvia has the "crud."

Monday, December 14, 1998—cloudy, -14° to +6°. We pumped water. I shoveled some snow up around the house. Fire lapped that rifle barrel. Sylvia did a load of laundry. Ralph phoned about low hog prices his dad is getting.

Tuesday, December 15, 1998—light snow in night, 0° to 10°. Plowed our snow. Elaine drove off our lane and couldn't get back on. I pulled her car a little and it came back up on the lane. Shot 10 more firelapping bullets in the rifle. Sized and lubed some bullets. Sylvia went to the ladies lunch at Eureka.

Wednesday, December 16, 1998—close to 0° all day. Cleaned and lapped the rifle barrel after 20 shot at target. Visited with Ed and Mark out at mailbox. Rude with Bart to Legion in meeting in evening.

Thursday, December 17, 1998—clear. -28° to -18°. I pulled snow off green house, north side of wood shop and its lean to, front porch roof. Polished the chamber on 7.5 x 55. Steamed a few couple dents on its stock to raise the wood fibers. With pretty good success. Sharpened a pair of scissors.

Friday, December 18, 1998—it was -18° to -7° this morning, 2° this afternoon. We went to Glennallen on senior van, lunch and shopping. We pumped water. I did a lot of leveling of water line. Shoveled snow and packed the trail down to well with the snow.

Saturday, December 19, 1998—mostly cloudy, -8° to 0°. Fired some 7.5 test loads. They were not accurate. Shoveled a little snow. We went to Glennallen. Shopping, post office, visited Darrel and Brenda, then to prime rib dinner at Legion Hall. Christmas party afterwards.

Sunday, December 20, 1998—mostly cloudy. -10° to 0°. Did more load development work. Sylvia baked cookies. We went to Mendeltna Chapel to see the children put on their Christmas program.

Monday, December 21, 1998—lots of thin ice fog, -8° to 0°. We drove to Glennallen senior Christmas party at Legion Hall. Good meal and program put on by home school students. Door prizes and games. I took a rifle to be re-barreled to gunsmith. He will work on a bullet swadging die for me.

Tuesday, December 22, 1998—mostly cloudy, -12° to -3°. With a little modification to the bench I got a backup reloading press mounted. Loaded 20 rounds to check it out. We pumped water and I did some adjustments to lower part of water line. Took the bolt apart of 7.5 x 54 and cleaned its face. Jim and Elaine brought over some Christmas goodies and we gave them some back.

Wednesday, December 23, 1998—mostly cloudy and a little snow, -15° to -1°. Joe Virgin brought us a coffee cake. I cleaned 7.5 x 54 rifle barrel and resized some brass. Kind of a dreary day.

Thursday, December 24, 1998—partly cloudy, windy this evening, 0° to 12°. Light was burned out in the well. I replaced it after taking some goodies around to a few friends. Did some target shooting. The ProChrono got cold at 13th shot and wouldn't register the feet per second. Tom H. phoned and asked us to have Christmas dinner with them this evening. Lots of their relatives were there.

Friday, December 25, 1998—mostly sunny, -13° to -5°. Cleaned rifle twice and tried another load. This one is no good. We went to Allen and Roxanne's to supper. Jim and Elaine visited a while in afternoon before they went to Anchorage to pick up Dan and family.

Saturday, December 26, 1998—mostly sunny, -23° to -16°. We phoned Paul and talked to Ruth. Steve wasn't home, he was at girlfriends home.

Sunday, December 27, 1998—cloudy and some light snow, -25° to 0°. We phoned Laura and Frances. Steve phoned us. We pumped water. I had to do some more shimming of water line to keep it on a grade to drain. It had a big piece of ice just outside the house. We thawed it by running a hose full of hot water through the water line.

Monday, December 28, 1998—it was 0° most of day then started dropping about dark. 2" snow last night and lightly all day. We went to lunch in Glennallen. Did some shopping. Plowed our snow and Manning's driveway. Polished some brass and reload some.

Tuesday, December 29, 1998—partly cloudy, sunny, cloudy, -25° to -16°. I shoveled some snow. Cleaned the ashes out of barrel stove. Read some. Watched a couple TV hunting shows and a gold prospecting show.

Wednesday, December 30, 1998—warming all day to -3° and then -24° this evening. We pumped water today. Everything worked fine. Mannings brought their daughter Loretta, hubby David and their two sons, Kyle and Allen over for a visit in late afternoon. They are from North Carolina. David has been a shooter-hunter and fun to visit with.

Thursday, December 31, 1998—mostly sunny, -17° to -8°. Did some target shooting. Robbie brought over a birthday calendar for us and collected $5.00.

The Wilkins cabin and garage on Scoter Lake.

Norman with marten. Photo taken in 1997.

1999—Chronographing bullet speeds

Friday, January 1, 1999—cloudy, sunny, cloudy again, -24° to -8°. We pumped water. I reloaded a few cartridges for 7.5 x 54.

Saturday, January 2, 1999—mostly cloudy, some light snow, a little sun, 0° to 10°. We got ready and rode with Jim, Mary and Kari to Glennallen. They had a couple things to do. Our video film wasn't ready. We ate lunch, then we went to the Kluti Kaah Hall in Copper Center to an Athabaskan funeral for Morey Secondchief. Today would have been her birthday. She was born 1/2/1910. A fine lady, well liked and loved by many. After the service she was buried beside her husband's grave there in Copper Center. We went back to Glennallen. Oddens did laundry and we did a little shopping. Stopped by the Rendezvous Café for coffee. Then back to Kluti Kaah Hall for a pot luck in Morey's honor. Many people told stories about their experiences with Morey and the love she gave to so many. Lots of food, tea, coffee, pop, cakes. Native dances to skin drums to comfort the family. Mary decided to go home, so we said good-byes to many friends, native and white alike and left before the gift giving of 240 blankets, 34 rifles and some other gifts. We got home just before midnight.

Sunday, January 3, 1999—cloudy and a few flakes of snow, -9° to 14°. We slept a lot today. I did a little target shooting and cleaned rifle.

Monday, January 4, 1999—sunny, -18° to -8°. Sylvia has a "bug" and I don't feel well. Slept a lot today. Did some year end bookkeeping things.

Tuesday, January 5, 1999—sunny, -28° to -18°. We pumped water and it went well at this temperature. I measured the striker protrusion through the bolt face of 7.5 x 54 French rifle.

Wednesday, January 6, 1999—sunny, -31° to -20°. Ed Farmer came over with a box of candy that Sandy had brought back from Virginia, NC.

Thursday, January 7, 1999—sunny all day, -34° to -29° most of day, -21° evening. Worked on some brass and polished the inside of 7.5 x 54 die. I phoned Robert Lengelback (Anchorage) and talked match shooting cast bullets.

Friday, January 8, 1999—sun came through for a while in afternoon with sun dogs, -34° in night and warming to -2° then +3°, and about 1-1/2" granulated snow. We went to Glennallen on senior van. Lunch, shopping, phone bill etc. Back home I plowed our snow. Prepare some 7.5 x 54 brass. Shot then cleaned the rifle.

Saturday, January 9, 1999—mostly cloudy, -17° to -5°. We pumped water. Some ice in line and we ran hot water back down to well in hopes of getting rid of ice. Trimmed and resized some brass. Ralph and Jeff phoned.

Sunday, January 10, 1999—mostly cloudy, -5° to -0°. Cal and Mary visited. Reloaded some 75 x 54.

Monday, January 11, 1999—cloudy (some low), -14° to -3°. We pumped water. Cut some more rifle cleaning patches. Belled the mouths of some cases. Sewed a small canvas pouch. Jim and Elaine Manning visited and brought a tape back.

Tuesday, January 12, 1999—foggy, cloudy, foggy, -8° to 0°. Did some target practice. Shoveled snow off camper and woodshed. Jim came over and welded on his snowplow. We had pie with Mannings. Mark and Henry stopped by and picked up my bullet mold.

Wednesday, January 13, 1999—cloudy, a little light grainy snow, -1° to 16°. Shot a few and reloaded a few rounds. Bulb burned out at well.

Thursday, January 14, 1999—cloudy and 1/2" snow, 4° to 16°. We pumped water. Shot a few targets for load development. Cleaned rifle. Had supper at Allen and Roxanne's; Tom and Kim were there.

Friday, January 15, 1999—cloudy, 10° to 18°. I rode the VA van to VA clinic in Anchorage with John, Jay, Cecil and another lady. Doctor canceled three of my subscriptions. Set up an appointment for another upper GI X-ray. Shopped for some groceries. Saw 18-20 moose on Palmer Hay Flats.

Saturday, January 16, 1999—windy, blowing snow, some sun, 5° to 9°. Late in starting out to go to Wasilla. Got about thirty miles. Blowing snow convinced me to turn around and go back home. Didn't do much today. Loaded a few cartridges. We ate supper at Odden's. Kurt Skoog was there also.

Sunday, January 17, 1999—sunny, -18° to -9°. I didn't feel like driving to Gun Show in Wasilla especially with these temps. We pumped water this afternoon.

Monday, January 18, 1999. sunny, -29° to -13°. Didn't do much of anything today.

Tuesday, January 19, 1999—sunny, -34° to -22°. Breakfast at Tom and Kim's. Tom's sister Mary and her twins were there as well as Allen, Roxanne, Samantha, Jim and Mary Odden. Sylvia went to a Queens luncheon at Tolsona. Lorraine Hanson phoned this morning about a subscription.

Wednesday, January 20, 1999—sunny, -43° to -24°. Didn't do much today.

Thursday, January 21, 1999—sunny, -42° to -25°. Didn't do anything today.

Friday, January 22, 1999—sunny, then cloudy towards evening, -37° to -21°. Saw the fox cross the highway. We pumped water. Ran hot water back down the line and cut some ice out of line. Ron called: Robin Lee is leaving as Director of Senior Services. We talked prospecting also.

Saturday, January 23, 1999—cloudy, 3/4" snow, fog in afternoon, 18° to 28°. Pulled some snow of roofs. Shoveled some and plowed our snow. Did some target shooting and cleaned rifle and polished bore with JB compound. Phoned Nadia and tried to call Theresa and Beverly.

Sunday, January 24, 1999—mostly cloudy and a skiff of snow, 18° to 24°. We pumped water I pulled some snow of house and arctic entry roofs. Reloaded some brass.

Monday, January 25, 1999—17° to -14°. Rifle stock came today. I'm disappointed in it. Dies came for .30 BR will take a little work. Shot a nice group today. Cleaned rifle and loaded some more. Jeff phoned—he found some linotype.

Tuesday, January 26, 1999—low clouds and frost in morning, sunny afternoon, -7° to 3°. Allen, Roxanne and Sammy had breakfast with us. We put a gold panning tape on for Allen—it's his birthday.

Wednesday, January 27, 1999—1/2" snow during night and snowing all day, -10° to 3°. We pumped water today. Tom H. visited in the afternoon. I phoned Larry Rickertsen.

Thursday, January 28, 1999—mostly sunny, -1° to -17°. Plowed our snow. Shoveled some snow. Took garbage to transfer site. Padlock was frozen, got it thawed with some matches. The crank that lowers the lid doesn't work very well. Showed the mail order rifle stock to Jim O. He didn't think much of it. Tom H. visited, he thought it was 50%. Fellow I bought from will only give me $15 for it!!

Friday, January 29, 1999—partly cloudy, cloudy and light snow, -25° to -17°. We went to lunch in Glennallen on senior van. Did a little shopping. Ron drove and wanted to talk gold prospecting. We visited Bart and Rosemary. Bart is recovering from stroke. We pumped water tonight.

Saturday, January 30, 1999—snowed all night and day, 2" clear tonight, -23° to -15° to -22°. Jim and Mary came and got two pool table slates. We ate supper there. Met Ken and Barb from McGrath.

Sunday, January 31, 1999—snowed until noon, then mostly sunny, -26° to -18°. Fox is hanging around here today.

Monday February 1, 1999—cloudy, partly cloudy, -32° to -20°. Pumped water, plowed snow. Took cans to garbage can, smashed pope cans. Mark stopped by with the things Clarence has been working on. Frances phoned birthday greetings.

Tuesday, February 2, 1999—mostly cloudy -25° to -15°. Windy in morning. I remounted my reloading press on bench. Cleaned the barrel Clarence mounted. Nadia phoned birthday greetings.

Wednesday, February 3, 1999—mostly sunny, -43° to -29°. When a vehicle drives past on the highway, it leaves a trail of fog. Sylvia did some laundry. Ralph and Jeff phoned from Fairbanks, -55° this evening there.

Thursday, February 4, 1999—mostly sunny, extremely cold, -49° to -31°. Ice fog in the air. Clouds forming in mountains to south this evening. VA van will not be going to Anchorage tomorrow—too cold.

Friday, February 5, 1999—sunny, cloudy afternoon, snow to south and ice fog in the afternoon, still cold, -37° to -24°. Allen, David and Sammy visited after supper.

Saturday, February 6, 1999—sunny, 1/2" of snow last night, -31° to -13°. We pumped water today. The sun felt warm, even at -16°. Wrote up a plan to hone the two 7 mm br dies out to 30 br. Drew a pattern and cut out leather for a rifle receiver bolt holster. Sylvia baked two pumpkin pies.

Sunday, February 7, 1999—sunny, some snow on south side of river, -40° to -26°. Sewed the holster for rifle bolt. Looks good. Read some, and wrote a letter. Sylvia fixed Canadian honker breast for supper.

Monday, February 8, 1999—sunny, -39° to -17°, a little snow early this morning. Saw smoke from Jim Luce's trap cabin on Botley Creek.

Tuesday, February 9, 1999—sunny, -38° to -18°. We pumped water today. Tom H. visited.

Wednesday, February 10, 1999—sunny, -41° to -20°. Jim M visited. The fox followed him in our lane and it did the same to me on my way back from the mailbox.

Thursday, February 11, 1999—sunny, -44° to 0°. Read a lot today. Elaine phoned, Bart is back in hospital with mini strokes. Ron called with the new changes in his job and senior program.

Friday, February 12, 1999—partly cloudy and light snow in evening, -34° to 0°. Went to Glennallen for lunch and shopping. Paid phone bill and cashed our checks. Snowing in town at 11:00 AM.

Saturday, February 13, 1999—sunny, -7° to +8°. We pumped water. I found both light bulbs burned out at well. Replaced them and packed the trail with the snowgo.

Sunday, February 14, 1999—mostly cloudy, -20° to 3°. Sylvia had a bad allergy cold in night and still today. She rested most of day, but she did make a cake for Valentine's day. I washed a big pile of dishes for her.

Monday, February 15, 1999—mostly sunny, cloudy in evening, 0° to 20°. Shoveled some snow that slid off house roof. Cast some bullets and lubed a few.

Tuesday, February 16, 1999—cloudy, 6° to 21°. We went to Palmer and Wasilla. Renewed my driving license, did some shopping. Got back home 4:30 PM.

Wednesday, February 17, 1999—cloudy, 2° to 17°. We pumped water and I adjusted water line height in two places. Jim and Kari were here to supper.

Thursday, February 18, 1999—cloudy, 8° to 22°. Went with Jim Odden to Gullkana. He was having his plane "Rags" annualed. It took longer than planned. I took a look at the rifle range while I was so close. It has been plowed.

Friday, February 19, 1999—Sunny, -5° to 19°. We went to Glennallen for lunch and a little shopping. Sized, lubed and tapered some cast bullets.

Saturday, February 20, 1999—cloudy, sunny afternoon, -4° to 12°. Formed some 7.5 x 54 brass from military .30-06 brass. Chickadees are feeding on trees here.

Sunday, February 21, 1999—sunny, -7° to 11°. Pumped water. Fire formed the brass. Patti Billman asked us over for caribou soup. Jim Kare and cousin Emily and her husband Doug were there. It had been -27° at Lake Louise this morning.

Monday, February 22, 1999—sunny, clouding over in evening, -23° to 12°. Sylvia fed the fox this morning. I washed some windows and put her quilting hoop together. (Mary O. gave it to her). Checked the volume of a few cartridge cases. Saw a moose out on the lake in evening.

Tuesday, February 23, 1999—mostly sunny, -22° to 9°. Neck-turned some brass. Nice day.

Wednesday, February 24, 1999—sunny, -9° to 14°. Weighed brass. Visited Dimmicks and Gilcreases.

Thursday, February 25, 1999—cloudy, -7° to 10°. Visited Jim M and Elaine this morning. Tried to pump water—line is frozen. Did some work on it.

Friday, February 26, 1999—sunny morning, cloudy and light snow in the afternoon, -16° to 8°. We went to Glennallen on senior van. Lunch and shopping. Paid the electric bill.

Saturday, February 27, 1999—sunny, 0° to 23°. Did some load development with 7.5 x 54. Not much luck. Did a little work on water line. Washed the picture windows. Resized some brass. Ralph phoned and visited awhile.

Sunday, February 28, 1999—snowed 1-1/2 inches today, 2° to 15°. Reloaded the formed mil 30-06 brass. Grandson Steve phoned. Scott Rollins phoned also. Talked to Bart on phone. He is doing better and in physical therapy now.

Monday, March 1, 1999—sunny, 3° to 15°. Plowed our snow. Shovels some snow and pulled some snow off roofs. Did some target practice and then cleaned the rifle. Sylvia went to birthday luncheon for Mary Gilcrease.

Tuesday, March 2, 1999—it was -2° to 21°. Went to lower end of water line. It has lots of ice in it. More load development, target shooting. Went pretty well today. 7-½ lbs linotype came in the mail today.

Wednesday, March 3, 1999—cloudy, sunny afternoon, 9° to 18°. We tried to get water at the Little Nelchina River. I couldn't back the truck up to Cal's hole in ice. Came back home and cast some bullets. Beautiful evening. Allen visited this evening.

Thursday, March 4, 1999—sunny and some breeze, -21° to 10°. Lubed, sized cast bullets and loaded some of them for the 7.5 x 54 load development and target practice.

Friday, March 5, 1999—sunny, -24° to 9°. Made a handle to eject sized bullets out of the Eagan die.

Saturday, March 6, 1999—sunny, -26° to 10°. Went to Allen's. After rounding up a length of 1-½" plastic pipe he pumped me a load of water. Unloading it here at home went okay. Ralph and Jeff phoned.

Sunday, March 7, 1999—sunny, -24° to 13°. Got sick with the trots last night and this morning and again this evening. Watched TV and read today. Ralph phoned. Bart phoned.

Monday, March 8, 1999—sunny, -17° to 5°. We still have a "gut ache." Sent order Redding for bullet seater.

Tuesday, March 9, 1999—sunny, cloudy and then snow about 5:00 PM, -25° to 3°. We saw a couple spruce hens feeding on needles. They were part way down the hill.

Wednesday, March 10, 1999—snow over an inch in the night and most all day, -20° to 5°. Watched GPAA movies and drew plan for a high banker spray bar.

Thursday, March 11, 1999—sunny, 0° to 23°. Plowed our snow. Did some target shooting. Reloaded some more to try tomorrow. Allen had a bowl of beans with us.

Friday, March 12, 1999—sunny, 0° to 30°. We went to Glennallen, lunch and a little shopping. More target practice and reloaded for tomorrow.

Saturday, March 13, 1999—sunny and breezy sometimes, 7° to 31°. Took coffee grounds out to greenhouse. Did some more target shooting and cast more bullets. Saw a squirrel this morning and Sylvia noticed a spruce hen by outhouse.

Sunday, March 14, 1999—cloudy, windy, sunny, cloudy, 9° to 32°. Ralph phoned. He thought Jeff might stop by, so I loaded up some 7.5 x 54 mm for him to shoot. He hasn't shown up here. I pulled some snow off the house roof and the west side of garage roof. Jim Manning visited then we went out and worked a little on his snow blower. He left some magazines here. Mary O. stopped by for a while and borrowed a movie.

Monday, March 15, 1999—sunny, some snow slid off house roof, 11° to 32°. I shoveled snow off woodshed. Cast more bullets. Put gas checks on them, lubed then sized them in the Eagan taper die. Mary O. brought the movie back.

Tuesday, March 16, 1999—mostly sunny, late afternoon gusting winds, 0° to 20°. Shoveled more snow. Loaded some for postal match. Lee Dudley visited for an hour or so.

Wednesday, March 17, 1999—sunny, some breeze, 1° to 21°. I have sized the last batch of bullets too small. Damn! Worked on sizer a little. Pulled some bullets and seated some others. Shot some small ones but they don't group well.

Thursday, March 18, 1999—cloudy, sunny, cloudy, -9° to 22°. Prepared the undersized bullets for re-melt and recasting. Baked a batch of gingersnaps. Found a lead hammer I've been looking for.

Friday, March 19, 1999—cloudy, 18° to 32°. Rode the VA van to clinic in Anchorage. Got appointment for Apr. 15th. Did some grocery shopping. Saw some moose along highway all looked in good shape. Saw Roxanne and Afton at Eureka.

Saturday, March 20, 1999—snow till noon, sunny, cloudy, clearing, 11° to 32°. When I went to mailbox, saw Ed, who is now back home. We visited a while. In the afternoon, Tom, Charlie, and Kindra, Peter, Mark and Derek Huddleston all stopped by. They were out riding their snowgos. Tom bought a new one! We went to Mary Odden's and Kari for supper. Darrel and Brenda were there also. I went to Allen's and got a load of water.

Sunday, March 21, 1999—sunny, 5° to 37°. Stopped by Lucky's and he went with me to a gun show in Palmer. I only bought a cartridge box and a pound of powder for cast bullets. Did a little grocery shopping. Had soup and sandwich with Lucky. Got home early.

Monday, March 22, 1999—sunny, cloudy in evening, 5° to 34°. Tried to take the "noise" out of heater with no luck. Tried to alter 7mm die to .30 cal with no luck. Worked on target stand. Jeff Routt visited a few minutes.

Tuesday, March 23, 1999—sunny, 16° to 42°. Loaded shooting gear in truck and we went to Glennallen shooting range where I shot targets for postal match C.B.A. Military rifle. Visited Darrel and Brenda on our way home. Started snowgo and put a new bulb in the well.

Wednesday, March 24, 1999—sunny, skiff snow, cloudy, 10° to 36°. Visited with Ed a few minutes. Lee D. stopped by and encouraged me to hone seater die to size. I've got over 2/3 of it done. Mary O. visited. I phoned Jim O. in McGrath.

Thursday, March 25, 1999—sunny, 21° to 40°. Lee D. visited, and gave me emory paper. I gave him high speed drills. Loaded some .308 Winchesters and cast some .308 bullets put on G.C. and lubed them.

Friday, March 26, 1999—sunny, 12° to 38°. We went to Glennallen, had lunch and paid electric bill, got a few groceries. I cast lubed and tapered a few bullets.

Saturday, March 27, 1999—sunny, 9° to 37°. Shoveled 260' of snow off the waterline. Got pretty tired. Started honing another die.

Sunday, March 28, 1999—sunny, 6° to 33°. Finished the die by drilling it and then honing it. Sighted in the scope on the rifle I'll use on the next postal match.

Monday, March 29, 1999—sunny, 1° to 33°. Finished shoveling snow off the waterline. Measured the heating oil. We visited Bart and Rosemary for awhile in the afternoon. His son Bruce was there. He has gotten three wolves.

Tuesday, March 30, 1999—sunny, cloudy late afternoon, 0° to 28°. Allen and Roxanne picked us up and we all went to Tom and Kim's for breakfast. Didn't do anything this afternoon.

Wednesday, March 31, 1999—sunny, cloudy and very windy after 2:30 PM, 1° to 31°. Did some target shooting and cleaned the rifles. Took the garbage to transfer site. Phoned Beverly. Darrel called about VA.

Thursday, April 1, 1999—windy and mostly sunny, 26° to 38°. Walked over to visit Jim—they were not home. Loaded a few rounds for target practice. Saw a boreal owl and a squirrel.

Friday, April 2, 1999—sunny, cloudy, windy, and some snow squalls going by this evening, 6° to 31°. We went to Glennallen. Septic field is frozen up. I worked on a path to out house. Steve phoned this evening. He is trapping beaver. School is going good. Will graduate soon. Ralph phoned and we talked reloading. Jeff and Justin stopped by. Talked guns and cartridge feeding problem of a 30-30 savage. Jeff took a few pieces of moose and sheep meat.

Saturday, April 3, 1999—sunny, partly cloudy, 13° to 31°. More load development and reloaded more also. Ralph phoned. Allen and Samantha visited in evening.

Sunday, April 4, 1999—sunny, some breeze, -2° to 32°. Sylvia saw a finch. Didn't do much except haul a load of water with the tank in the pickup. Did some reading.

Monday, April 5, 1999—partly cloudy, 2° to 35°. Hauled a load of water from Allen's. Did some target shooting and loaded more to try. Measured gasoline in overhead tank.

Tuesday, April 6, 1999—cloudy, sunny, 13° to 33°. Lee Dudley visited awhile. Later he stopped by again with a movie and a couple magazines. Went to Sam Weaver and he wasn't home. Phoned him at KROA.

Wednesday, April 7, 1999—mostly sunny, 12° to 26°. Fred Rungee stopped by with ice cream and a bag of oranges. I didn't feel well today. Stopped at Sam Weaver's and he rode in to Glennallen to American Legion meeting with me. Election of offices.

Thursday, April 8, 1999—sunny, -3° to 27°. We went to Palmer and Wasilla and did some shopping and got three drums of gasoline. Roads were dry. Nice trip. Lots of traffic. Unloaded groceries, pumped gas into storage tank. Moved snow plow out where I store drums.

Friday, April 9, 1999—sunny, -2° to 30°. We went to Glennallen for lunch. Paid phone bill. Did some target shooting. Lee D. visited in evening.

Saturday, April 10, 1999—cloudy, sunny, snow and wet, rain-like snow, -3° to 33°. Didn't do much. Reloaded a few pounds. Ruth Looney died today. Saw a boreal owl in a tree on south side of house.

Sunday, April 11, 1999—partly cloudy, 22° to 39°. 3/4" snow. Jim and Elaine brought some magazines to read. Did some target shooting with some success. Granddaughter Vanessa phoned. Nice to talk to her.

Monday, April 12, 1999—sunny, 10° to 41°. Did a few little jobs. We went to Odden's and had supper with them. They leave for Oregon to Mary's mother Ruth's funeral Friday. Then straight to McGrath to work for summer.

Tuesday, April 13, 1999—sunny, cloudy, sunny and windy, 12° to 42°. Visited Ed. Looked at risers at ends of drainfield lines. Shoveled a little snow. Cleaned some gas checks.

Wednesday, April 14, 1999—sunny, 20° to 39°. Went to Anchorage VA. They looked in my stomach, found an ulcer, and gave me medication to treat it for 14 days.

Thursday, April 15, 1999—sunny, snow, sunny, 25° to 41°. Shoveled some snow checked ice in drainfield. Lots of phone calls. Went with Allen to Eureka for pie and ice cream. Ralph was here when we got home.

Friday, April 16, 1999—mostly sunny, 17° to 43°. Ralph and I got snowgos ready to go bear hunting. Jeff was to drive mine out but he didn't show up. Ralph removed one scope and replaced it with a new one. Gave me the rings and bases. He gave me a bunch of brass last night. About 1:00 PM he went out alone hunting along side and around behind Slide Mountain. Saw moose and coyote tracks—no bear sign. I cleaned his new mould blocks. A few planes were flying around—looking for bears? Saw swans flying west while using telescope.

Saturday, April 17, 1999—sunny, 21° to 47°. Ralph went bear hunting again with no luck. This evening we went to Cal's to get a new belt for his machine. My back has been very painful. Even muscles and joints hurt. We hauled a load of water from Allen's. The rabbits are breeding.

Sunday, April 18, 1999—sunny, 23° to 52°. Ralph went bear hunting this morning. Got back about noon when snow started getting soft. No signs of bears. Saw a moose, Jeff came out from Anchorage got here about 11:00 AM. We three have been shooting rifles, chronographing bullet speeds. Cut up a bar of linotype and Ralph and Jeff cast a couple hundred bullets. Sylvia fixed a good moose stew.

Monday, April 19, 1999—sunny, windy sometimes, 35° to 50°. Ralph and Jeff rode snowgos 36 miles today. Didn't see any bears. Ralph cast a bunch of bullets. Sylvia made a pot of chili—very good. We had Allen and Roxanne and Sammy over for supper. Saw a track over on heavenly ridge.

Tuesday, April 20, 1999—partly cloudy, cloudy, 27° to 50°. Ralph hunted again today with no luck. He switched the winter-summer tires on the car for me, when he came in from hunting. I prepped some brass for loading. We got trailer ready for Ralph to use tomorrow.

Wednesday, April 21, 1999—cloudy, light snow, 32° to 42°. Ralph hunted Squaw Creek. Saw 5 moose and 13 Dall sheep, no bears. I visited Ed. Loaded cartridges for postal matches. Lee Dudley visited in the afternoon. We picked up Sam W. and went for pot luck supper and installation of Legion officers.

Thursday, April 22, 1999—cloudy, snow this evening, 18° to 39°. We got shooting gear ready and went to Glennallen rifle range so I could shoot my postal match targets. It just didn't work, due to cold or something. I couldn't get the rifle to shoot to the same place. Stopped by Darrel and Brenda's with some magazine and Reader Digests. We did pick up a lot of brass at range. Got some copies of my military service made. Back at home we fire formed some brass for Ralph. Will shoot them for effect. Saw two robins on our lawn yesterday. Lots of rabbits breeding now. Swans are flying. Large gulls are here. After supper Ralph shot some of his cast bullets. Then we cleaned his rifle. He figured out that 8 of his .308 brass had been fired in a French 7.5 x 54 in Fairbanks and wouldn't go in his .358 Winchester die. Gave them to me and I shot (fire formed) them in my 7.5 x 54 rifle.

Friday, April 23, 1999—mostly sunny some snow showers going by, 23° to 44°. Ralph hunted bears with no luck. Saw fox, coyote, lynx tracks. I cleaned and polished brass. Burned trash. Ralph left early afternoon for home. Ron Beshaw ate his lunch here.

Saturday, April 24, 1999—cloudy, +3 inches of snow, 27° to 41°. I woke up at 4:00 AM with hives. Probably due to the antibiotics I'm taking. I drove myself to Crossroads Medical in Glennallen. Dr Flaming saw me, prescribed an antihistamine. Rested all afternoon. Lee Dudley stopped by with a tool he had made.

Sunday, April 25, 1999—28° to 40°. Pretty sick with hives. Lee D. stopped by with a tube of Benadryl for the itching.

Monday, April 26, 1999—mostly cloudy and snow shower, 21° to 36°. Lee D. stopped by and we talked guns.

Tuesday, April 27, 1999—snowed 3" this morning, 22° to 41°. Sunny in afternoon. Lee Dudley went to Palmer and brought back more Benadryl for me. Very thoughtful of him. The hives are going away.

Wednesday, April 28, 1999—partly cloudy, very nice, 18° to 46°. Pumped old water out of well and hooked up water line. Put snowgo away for this winter. Tom Gray has my rifle about ready.

Thursday, April 29, 1999—mostly sunny. 19° to 49°. Surprise the rifle was in the mail. Looks good. This medical reaction is hard on me. Slept some and rested a lot. Sylvia's birthday Fran and Nadia phoned.

Friday, April 30, 1999—cloudy to partly cloudy in evening, 28° to 46°. We went to lunch in Glennallen on senior van. Dimmicks went also. I am still very sick. The hive is somewhat better. Esophagus is real sore. Digestive tract is upset.

Saturday, May 1, 1999—cloudy, sometimes windy, 10" - 12" snow, 26° to 44°. I'm still pretty sick. Allen plowed our driveway. Steve Mailly, two daughters and son Jonathan, brought Sylvia seeds and plants. Lee Dudley stopped by with some medicine and ate with us and visited.

Sunday, May 2, 1999—some more snow, 19° to 41°. Pretty sick all day. Throat is really sore.

Monday, May 3, 1999—cloudy and windy sometimes, 24° to 42°. A little better today. Jim Manning brought over some magazines. I injected some compressed air into water system tank. Burned trash.

Tuesday, May 4, 1999—mostly cloudy, 2" snow last night, 27° to 47°. In some ways I'm better and other ways still sick. Jim and Elaine brought some yogurt and bananas from town. Nice of them. Phoned Nadia this evening.

Wednesday, May 5, 1999—it snowed hard all day—wet and settled a lot, 29° to 36°. Partly cloudy after supper. Feel a little better today. Have a bronchial cough now. Saw a large owl near our lane. Smaller bird chased it. Saw an eagle flying in snow storm.

Thursday, May 6, 1999—partly cloudy, nice day, 25° to 47°. Plowed our snow off to side. The lift-lower cable broke on plow control. Cut up linotype ingots. Feel better today.

Friday, May 7, 1999—cloudy, 32° to 46°. Went to VA clinic on Glennallen van. Saw Dr. and changed prescription. Did a little grocery shopping.

Saturday, May 8, 1999—mostly sunny, 30° to 48°. Visited Allen. Annealed some case necks. Polished RCBS mould sprue plate. Allen stopped by and I gave him a double pulley he needed. Then we found a trailer jack he could use. Saw a squirrel. A robin is singing its head off.

Sunday, May 9, 1999—sunny and windy, 22° to 50°. Mother's Day. Nadia phoned. Dale Routt and Dave Cabin visited for a while. I cast, sized and lubed some .30 cal bullets. It looks like a hawk owl may be nesting down by the lake.

 Monday, May 10, 1999—mostly cloudy and quite windy, 35° to 48°. Bob and Kahren visited. Bob borrowed a router bit. We went to Cal and Mary's. He gave me a wire that I used to repair my snow plow lift cable this afternoon. We now think it may be kestrels nesting down by lake side.

Tuesday, May 11, 1999—partly cloudy, nice, some breeze, 26° to 52°. Raked some ruts closed. Shoveled gravel in some low spots. Got car ready to go to Anchorage. Cast a couple hundred bullets. Made a wrench for the die adapter on reloading press. Sylvia raked yard and enjoyed it.

Wednesday, May 12, 1999—34° to 54°. We went to Anchorage. Lots of shopping, garden fertilizer, seeds and plants, some groceries, prescription, a sundry of other items. The trip went well. A couple rains for a little while. Sure glad to get back home.

Thursday, May 13, 1999—partly cloudy, one sprinkle of rain, 34° to 55°.

Unloaded lime and fertilizer from car. Cast 200 bullets. Kim and Tom visited in the afternoon. Sylvia worked in greenhouse.

Friday, May 14, 1999—sunny and very nice, 34° to 62°. Shoveled snow from roof slides over winter on north side of house. Hauled garbage. Glass bedded barrel area of .30 BR rifle. Sent card to Steve.

Saturday, May 15, 1999—partly cloudy, 33° to 62°. We drove to Lake Louise and back. Visit with Dan Billman for a little while. Saw one porcupine. We weren't home long and Allen invited us down for desert. I had to re-glass the gun stock due to a large void. This time it turned out very good. Turned off the light in the well. Started removing blue board and straw from over the septic systems.

Sunday, May 16, 1999—partly cloud and a few sprinkles, 35° to 60°. Folded tarps off septic field and put blue board in wood shed. Went to Dan's, he and Tom H. loaded a culvert in my truck and then helped unload it down by our spring. Did lots of other small jobs.

Monday, May 17, 1999—partly cloudy, 37° to 59°. Went to old dump site to look for 3' culvert band. No luck, saw good size black bear tracks. Went also to west old dump site and no band there either. Tilled the little garden. Put 1" water line in operation. Picked up bullets from snow berm. Shot three varmints today. Planted potatoes.

Tuesday, May 18, 1999—mostly sunny and some breeze, 31° to 59°. We planted potatoes in garden. Started shooting the new rifle barrel and sighted in the scope. Parked the snow plow for summer. Took the canopy off the truck.

Wednesday, May 19, 1999—partly cloudy, some breeze, 29° to 56°. Moved snowgo trailer. Put some oil in Suzuki. Cleaned debris from spring. Bart and son Brian visited. Shot a rabbit snowshoe.

Thursday, May 20, 1999—very nice day, 29° to 59°. Worked on culvert for new well. Tarped and tied blue board. Went to BBQ and party for Kendra Huddleston. Ice on our lake is dark and rotten.

Friday, May 21, 1999—partly cloudy, sprinkles in late afternoon, 33° to 54°. I covered our chimney opening to keep the nesting goldeneye ducks out. Patched a hole in the culvert with a bolt, nut and washers. Visited Allen. Lee D. came down to Allen's to visit a while. Moved the slate out by wood shed. Lots of duck on lake which is about 1/3 clear of ice. Kahren visited.

Saturday, May 22, 1999—windy, a sprinkle, partly cloudy, 28° to 56°. Our son

Paul phoned at 6:00 AM. He has appointments for angioplasty then surgery June 8ᵗʰ and 9ᵗʰ. The 9ᵗʰ being his birthday! Sylvia planted more garden. I mopped kitchen floor and beat out a rug. Did some adjusting and focus of a rifle scope. We are going outside to be there for Paul.

Sunday, May 23, 1999—mostly sunny, some breeze on lake, 34° to 58°. Lots of ice left the lake today. Kahren visited a couple times. Bob brought my router bit back. I did some load development with the 30 BR. I went over to Marks to look at the travel section of Sunday paper. Met Reyne's dad Mike. Kahren found us a travel agent in Minneapolis. We'll get our tickets through her.

Monday, May 24, 1999—cloudy sometimes, 36° to 62°. We went to Wasilla for Sylvia's yearly medical exam. She got some antibiotics for sinus infection. Checked on Assay office location. They were long gone. Saw a few skinny moose along highway and one small caribou with 6" horns. Reloaded some more 30 BR. Lots of ducks on lake. Almost all ice gone now. Jerry went flying.

Tuesday, May 25, 1999—cloudy and rain all afternoon, 36° to 49°. Tried to make a tool to push out Berdan primers with no luck.

Wednesday, May 26, 1999—cloudy, light snow, a little sun in evening, in afternoon, 32° to 48°. Reloaded some 44 magnum for Paul. Sylvia visited Elaine. We rode with Bart and Sam to a Legion dinner in Glennallen. Saw three nice caribou bulls along the road with 2' long horns—in velvet, of course.

Thursday, May 27, 1999—partly cloudy with rain, and rain mixed with snow moved through here, missing our place, 29° to 53°. Walked down to lake. Checked oil in car. We went to Glacier View School to watch the graduation of two neighbor kids, David and Robbie Farmer.

Friday, May 28, 1999—29°, we got up early and went to Anchorage. Sylvia shopped for tee shirts, gifts for men and boys in Minnesota. We drove out to Dennis and Adrienne Griffith's, parked the car, phoned a taxi which took us to international airport. Our plane was a half hour late. Nice flight to Minneapolis. We were met by Nadia and Chuck and they took us to their place for the night.

Saturday, May 29, 1999—60° to 80°. Nadia drove us to Beverly's. Sorry that Theresa wasn't able to meet us there. Nadia drove us to Motley. Sylvia shopped at a flea market, then on to Staples. Paul and Ruth were home. Steve was at his girlfriend's home and came over later. Had a lot of visiting to catch up on.

Sunday, May 30, 1999—60° to 80°. We all went to Wadena Armory and a gun show, but didn't buy anything. Saw Al Eckes and one of Vogel boys. When we got back, Paul and Steve did some measuring on a shot gun receiver that needed a stock. I went with Steve back to gun show. He bought a stock that with modification, will probably fit. He brought his girlfriend Lisa over to meet us. She is a nice girl. Raining this evening.

Monday, May 31, 1999—50° to low 60s. Took a shower, visited with Paul this morning. Steve came home at 1:30 PM. He, Paul and I put the stock he bought yesterday on his receiver. Steve went back over to his girl friends about supper time. Looks rainy this evening.

Tuesday, June 1, 1999—mostly cloudy, some sprinkles, 50° to 60°. Asked for linotype at printers—no luck. Steve and Paul took us to cemetery. We left flowers at Mildred Rose (the baby we lost as a newborn) and Anitra Anne's (baby Paul and Ruth lost) graves. I got a tick there at cemetery. We stopped at Lorraine Hanson's and visited. We saw two sandhill cranes out in the fields. Some kind of antihistamine made me sick this evening.

Wednesday, June 2, 1999—partly cloudy, nice day, 48° to low 60s. Loraine came to town and took Sylvia and me to lunch at Motley. Then for a drive stopping at Helen Converse's and Allen and Lillian Rollins. Then back to Staples. We enjoyed the visits and time with Loraine. Ruth and Sylvia went to Brainerd to do some shopping. Steve and Lisa went on a charter trip down to Twin Cities. Paul pulled a bullet back in place on a cartridge. Steve worked on his shotgun project.

Thursday, June 3, 1999—mostly sunny, 60° to 80°. I walked uptown, looked in a few stores. Did lots of reading. Before suppertime Paul, Ruth, Steve and I went 7 miles south of Motley and hauled four picnic tables to Joe Mrazek's place. He hauled two tables. These are to be used for Steve's graduation party.

Friday, June 4, 1999—sunny, thunder lightning, some rain in night, 60° to 80s. Went with Steve and Paul to gunsmith who put a brass bead front sight on his shot gun barrel. Left the hammer there to be fixed. Lots of Ruth's relatives are here for the party. Women have started fixing food for party.

Saturday, June 5, 1999—mostly sunny, 60° to 80s. Lots of Ruth's relatives here. Everyone went to Joe Mrazek's for a big picnic for the graduates in the family. Saw some people we hadn't seen for a long time. Bud and Gay Swecker were there. Awfully hot in afternoon and evening.

Sunday, June 6, 1999—mostly sunny, 60° to 80°. Ruth's relatives left this afternoon. We took one tent down and put it away. Paul, Steve and I went to rifle range. They shot their T/C 44 magnums. One cartridge I loaded must not have had powder in it and bullet lodged in the barrel of Paul's T/C. Jim O.

Phoned: Dan Zappa died in the crash of his plane in Wisconsin. He will be missed.

Monday, June 7, 1999—mostly sunny, some breeze, 60° to 80°. We rode along with Paul and Ruth and Steve to Brainerd. Steve applied at MNDOT for a job. Ate lunch, then shopped and explores a couple of second hand stores and a military surplus store. Sylvia, Paul and I went to grocery store. Saw Joe DeGeest and visited a few minutes. He now lives in back of Dairy Queen in Motley.

Tuesday, June 8, 1999—60s till noon then 80s. Up very early and went to St Cloud to heart clinic. They did the angioplasty procedure on Paul. Only one artery was blocked. His aorta and valve need repair. They will do that tomorrow—big operation. Nadia and Chuck visited Paul this evening. Saw a fairly large flock of geese. Steve took us to Gander Mountain store.

Wednesday, June 9, 1999—60s to 80s, rain in morning and evening. About 8:00 AM to 12:30 was the operation on Paul: bypass and valve and aorta. Recovery was slow and difficult for him as the tubes in his throat would make him want to gag. We left close to 9:00 PM. Long day. Sylvia phoned Loraine Hanson and Helen Converse.

Thursday, June 10, 1999—partly cloudy, 50° to 70°. Up early and went to St Cloud. Paul is better. They moved him to a room in "telemetry" from intensive care. His color is good and he is doing things for himself. Sat up for awhile. Nadia and Chuck visited this evening. Back at Staples we fixed sandwiches for tomorrow and phoned different friends who are concerned for Paul.

Friday, June 11, 1999—partly cloudy, 50° to 70°. Slept a little later and went to St Cloud. Paul is lots better and walks to bathroom. Dr. took out more tubes and pulled the "jump start" wires out. He looks so much better. Allen and Lillian Rollins came over and visited in evening.

Saturday, June 12, 1999—mostly sunny, 50s to 80°. Back to St Cloud Hospital. Paul is walking better. He did two minutes on both the rehab tread mill and bicycle. While Paul was sleeping we went to some yard sales—nothing there for Sylvia or me. Saw a deer while going to St Cloud and one while coming back to Staples.

Sunday, June 13, 1999—sunny, some breeze, 60° to 80°. Paul is even better this morning. He needs to have an echo gram and his blood to thin down a little more and he can go home—great! Nadia and Chuck came to St. Cloud to take us to Minneapolis. We had lunch on the way. Beverly and Tyler were glad to see us. Chuck and Nadia visited, then left. Beverly, Tyler, Sylvia and I went for a walk to a nearby lake. Beverly fixed a great supper including shrimp and baby lobster. Theresa and Earl, Vanessa and Scott ate later and visited and showed Vanessa's wedding pictures. Tyler and I got to watch parts of a couple movies.

Monday, June 14, 1999—partly cloudy, 50° to 70s. Mary Lou Bolton took Bev and us to HHH Terminal at airport. Lots of people. Denny and Joey Eastman were there. Denny was on our flight. Bob and Kahren met Denny, Sylvia and I and a friend of Kahren's at the airport and took us to Griffiths where we got our car. Sylvia shopped for plants and I went to my appointment with Doctor Scott at VA. Got my prescriptions filled. Got some wheel weights and got home about 7:30 PM.

Tuesday, June 15, 1999—sunny, cloudy afternoon and some light rain, 47° to 71°. We worked on lower garden. Put a screen door on arctic entry. Sylvia put a lot of water on lawn and the garden up here. Allen visited in evening.

Wednesday, June 16, 1999—rain in night and most of morning, partly cloudy, 45° to 60°. Brought in a motor with buffer wheel. Polished, buffed tarnished places off some brass. Called Cal and visited. Sorted the brass by head stamp afterward.

Thursday, June 17, 1999—nice day. Did small jobs. Some garden work. Transplanted willows on cut bank.

Friday, June 18, 1999—partly cloudy after a shower in the night, 46° to 66°. We went to Glennallen on senior van. Lunch, shopping, paid phone bill and prescriptions at Crossroads Clinic. I phoned Juneau about our longevity. Sylvia bought flower and cauliflower plants, which she transplanted into garden. I cultivated four rows and cut some willows and piled wood at the spring and cleaned twigs out of well.

Saturday, June 19, 1999—partly cloudy to cloudy, 46° to 67°. I gathered up prospecting gear. Met Ron and Jeremy in Glennallen. We drove two vehicles to near the Thompson Summit on Richardson Highway. Parked and walked in to a couple creeks. Lot of snow where it hasn't melted yet. 20' to 30' deep. Some places it bridges over the creeks. We did some panning with no luck. Lots of parka squirrel holes. The lichens are sure big there.

Sunday, June 20, 1999—rain in night and all day, 40° to 53°. We went to Cal and Mary's to talk about sweatshirt painting. Little Nelchina is running high and muddy and brown. Sylvia cleaned bottom water tank. I cleaned the vacuum filter and burned trash. We saw a moose cross highway near Little Nelchina. Nadia phoned Father's Day greetings. Nice!

Monday, June 21, 1999—beautiful day, 38° to 61°. We went to Glennallen on senior van. Paid bill at clinic. Lunch then a little shopping I hauled generator and tools down to well site and culver. I bent a heavy aluminum sheet and pop riveted it to the culver. Sylvia mowed yard and seeded some weak spots in lawn and put on fertilizer and lime. Jim Manning came over to visit.

Tuesday, June 22, 1999—cloudy, sprinkles, partly cloudy, a breeze down on lake, 43° to 60°. Worked most of day getting ready to pump water from lake with dredge pump. Saw a cow moose and calf wading down the far side of our lake this morning. Looked as if she had her hackles up. Bob R. walked over and visited a little while this morning while I was unloading the dredge at our boat landing.

Wednesday, June 23, 1999—mostly sunny, 45° to 66°. More work getting ready to try developing the spring. We rode with Bart to Legion supper. We see the mother duck leaving the nest a lot this evening.

Thursday, June 24, 1999—partly cloudy, 50° to 70°. Tried to develop the well by dredging the sand and silt out. We couldn't get a good flow of water. No coarse gravel. Sand was fine as dust. Lots of long buried pieces of wood. Brought tools and all back up to storage shed. We went down to Bob and Kahren's after supper. Played a game of cards and had sherbet ice cream, cake and tea. Saw Lisa, NikiNiki's baby.

Friday, June 25, 1999—cloudy and rain all night and most of today, 48° to 68°. We went to Copper Center to a monthly meeting of senior elders. Had a lunch and Sylvia name got drawn for one of the door prizes. Counted 40+ goldeneye drakes on our lake.

Saturday, June 26, 1999—more rain, cloudy to partly cloudy too, 44° to 65°. Worked on left rear wheel hub on Suzuki—bearings are bad. Took our garbage to transfer site. The bears are still doing damage and scattering garbage. I checked both gravel pits for brass with little luck. Did some target shooting with the 44 magnum and made some adjustments to sights and the holster. Went to Harold and Rachel's for supper. Met Carl and Molly. Their relatives, Little Harold's wife and son Harold III were there as well as Carmon and quite a few others. Navajo? from Arizona.

Sunday, June 27, 1999—rainy and cloudy, partly cloudy in late afternoon, 44° to 61°. Slept poorly and so slept late this morning. Worked awhile on Suzuki. Didn't accomplish much. Ralph phoned. I called Steve Donaldson, offering a suggestion for the bear problem at the transfer site.

Monday, June 28, 1999—partly cloudy, 42° to 64°. Up at 6:00 AM, got ready and went to Anchorage Suzuki and got new bearings in left rear hub. Cement and 4" x 10 drain pipes at Eagle Hardware. Some paint and other shopping plus groceries in Wasilla. Got home at 7:00 PM. Unloaded everything. We did see Bob and Kahren at Eagle hardware. Saw Jeff (Chickaloon) and his wife at Carr's groceries in Palmer.

Tuesday, June 29, 1999—partly cloudy with showers, 44° to 60°. Put the Suzuki back together. Put a flag pole together. Needs painting. Sylvia has some kind of crud. Shot a squirrel. Missed a rabbit twice. Returned Jim's ABS cement.

Wednesday, June 30, 1999—partly cloudy, a beaut of a day, 45° to 69°. Painted flag pole. Dug a hole for the base. Mixed in wheel barrow and placed the cement. Put in pole. Tied it off to Suzuki, Pick up and a tree. Used a 4' carpenter's level to plumb the pole. Hoed the volunteer grass from the gravel in yard and planted part of it in the bank on upper part of switch back. The mosquitoes are the worst I've ever seen here.

Thursday, July 1, 1999—sunny and very nice with light breeze, 46° to 72°. We dismantled the stairs to basement. Started painting all the parts. When painting is finished will glue and screw it back together.

Friday, July 2, 1999—sunny, 48° to 80°. East breeze blows smoke here from (Tok?) fire. Cheryl Smith drove senior van. We painted some more on the basement stairs. Flew the new flag from the new flag pole today. Ron and Jeremy Beshaw stopped by to talk gold prospecting.

Saturday, July 3, 1999—sunny, cloudy for a little in afternoon, smoky, 51° to 80°. We reassembled the stairs. Allen called in morning and invited us to church services at his home tomorrow. Shot two squirrels and a rabbit.

Sunday, July 4, 1999—smoky to very smoky at times, 50° to 78°. Fires at Tok, Chicken and the Yukon. We went to services at Allen and Roxanne's this morning. Pot luck afterward. Then we went to Glennallen. Had to watch the parade from 3/8 mile (stuck in traffic line) then took in the Ahtnea Craft Show. Then to shooting range to pick up range brass. Got some. Then to Dry Creek Camp ground to visit Darrel, Brenda, her daughter Robin with new baby Samantha, Robin's husband Mike, Al Smith and girl friend Song were there also. Had more to eat and visiting. Stopped by Tom and Kim Huddleston's. They are having their house raised 10 feet in the air. They plan to build a garage etc. underneath the house.

Monday, July 5, 1999—smoky all day, 49° to 73°. Measured the water line that needs drain pipe to cover it. 400 ft. Bob R. gave us walkie-talkies to use. Will save lots of walking and or hollering when one is at lake and the other at house. Put three drain pipes underground on south side of house. These to put our waterlines and wash machine drain line in. Got it all done and covered up.

Tuesday, July 6, 1999—smoky and windy, 42° to 71°. Stiff and sore today. Did some measuring of water line. Pulled some weeds in garden. Took some lettuce and radishes to Jim and Elaine. Looked for my larger gold nugget again. Rearranged the flag pole pulley and rope.

Wednesday, July 7, 1999—not so smoky with pretty good breeze, 49° to 74°. Mosquitoes are bad. Got out the chain saw and cut 6, 9' poles. Pulled 10' culvert up to garage. With a two ton come-a-long and log chains I pulled a 4' diameter x 4' long culvert out of its hole. Then pulled it up the hill and I put it out back of wood shed. Cut 3' off the 3' diameter culvert and put the 7' piece with the other 4' culvert. Ed needed some fix all. Luckily I had some. We visited Allen and Roxanne in evening.

Thursday, July 8, 1999—partly cloudy, some smoke, 50° to 66°. Started raining 2:00 PM. We hauled a bunch of gear, pipe, tools etc. down to well. Put 3' culvert in it and started bucketing the sand out. We were tired and ready to quit when the rain started. Bugs were real bad. Sylvia didn't feel like cooking supper so we went to Eureka and ate. Roxanne and Ellie were working there. We visited Cal and Mary on way home.

Friday, July 9, 1999—cloudy, partly cloudy, cloudy, 46° to 65°. Pretty nice day. We went to Glennallen on senior van. Got some pipe fittings and plastic waterline. Went to the bank after lunch. Sylvia got a few groceries. The driver went past our driveway three miles before I got her to understand she had gone too far. We got some more sand out of well. I couldn't get the 3' culvert deeper in the well. We hauled some equipment back up here to storage. I put the new plastic line in as an extension of the laundry washer drain line. Had to shoot a nuisance rabbit today.

Saturday, July 10, 1999—beautiful day, 48° to 68°. We removed the 3' culvert from inside the 4' culvert. Then bucketed more sand out from bottom. Pumped the murky water out a few times then chlorinated the well. Nick Rudbeck came over and talked awhile. Put the plumbing back together at the well. Shot another flower eating rabbit.

Sunday, July 11, 1999—rainy all day, 48° to 62°. Took hydraulic jack to Tom's. Fastened up two water lines in basement. Made 10, .338 Winchester magnum out of .300 Winchester magnum brass.

Monday, July 12, 1999—cloudy, breezy, sunny, 46° to 66°. We cut two clumps of tall alders and loaded the slash on truck and hauled it off, then sharpened chain saw. Changed oil and filter in car. Back-flushed the car heater. Lost a ¼ drive

3/8 socket. Sylvia mowed the lawn and helped with the slash.

Tuesday, July 13, 1999—partly cloudy and some breeze, 42° to 70°. We cut and loaded a big clump of alders and I hauled the slash off. Hand cut a lot of fire weed. Weeded and hoed half the garden. We are fertilizing the cauliflower in an effort to perk it up. Corky Dimmick visited. Kahren brought strawberries to Sylvia. Found 3/8 socket.

Wednesday, July 14, 1999—beautiful day, 47° to 76°. Cut and hauled the rest of willows. Cut trees, willows on lower part of waterline.

Thursday, July 15, 1999—nice day, some breeze, 53° to 76°. Talked to Ed about TGI beams. We got the septic tank pumped today. Raked and burned the twigs and leaves. Trimmed a big spruce and cut it up for stove wood. Sharpened the saw again. Got the three logs at the other spring back up on the road. Sylvia baby sat Lisa NikiNiki's baby.

Friday, July 16, 1999—beautiful day, good breeze on lake, 52° to 63°. We went to Glennallen after Ron and Jeremy visited. Ate lunch, shopped a little, paid phone bill and got some stamps. Sylvia fertilized the garden. I raised the water line to grade where it crosses the lower trail.

Saturday, July 17, 1999—mostly cloudy with rain for an hour in afternoon, 48° to 59°. Dark, and looks like rain at 7:00 PM. Went to Tom Huddleston's to help him put walls up under his double wide mobile home. Only worked 4 hrs or so. Cleaned a revolver. Bob and Kahren visited in late afternoon.

Sunday, July 18, 1999—sunny, cloudy afternoon and rain in evening, 37° to 61°. I went down to lower trail and shoveled fill in around the pipe crossing the trail. Then went to gravel pit and practiced off hand shooting with the .338 Winchester. I was fire-forming brass from .300 win shells then went on to Tom's and worked there till about six in the evening. We got the OSB up, the door frames for the garage part up, then put up the two glue lam beams.

Monday, July 19, 1999—mostly cloudy, 42° to 59°. We went to Glennallen on senior van for lunch. Went to Tom's and worked for him about three hours. Got home about 5:00 PM or before. Got truck ready to go to Anchorage tomorrow. Mike Zimbicki from MI stopped by. He has spent a little time at Tolsona Lake and Chuck's old place.

Tuesday, July 20, 1999—partly cloudy, 47° to 66°. We got up early and left for Anchorage at 7:00 AM. Traffic was light all day. We got 4" drain pipe for water line enclosure and some paint for house, Alaska flag, groceries etc. among other things. Trip went well. Tired.

Wednesday, July 21, 1999—partly cloudy and occasional showers, 42° to 64°. I went to Tom's and helped him a little. Back home I started shoveling the gravel away from the lower end of drain field lines. I intend to wash the lines out. I thought tonight was Legion social evening. We went to Glennallen and no one at the hall—I got the evening wrong.

Thursday, July 22, 1999—partly cloudy, 42° to 64°. Shoveled more gravel. Unloaded the drain pipe. Cut up stacked several wheel barrows of wood. Visited with Bob, later he came over to borrow a hole saw.

Friday, July 23, 1999—partly cloudy, 44° to 67°. Hauled 10, 5-gallon buckets of sand and put it in low place near well. Saw Ed at sand pit and Chuck put a loader bucket full in my truck and I hauled it by 5-gallon bucket in trailer behind the ATV, down the hill to well. Hauled wood blocks back up and put them in wood shed. I mowed the boat landing area and road to it. Mowed all the grass around the out buildings. Took our garbage to transfer site after supper. Did some offhand shooting with.338 magnum and the 45 ACP.

Saturday, July 24, 1999—started raining in night and rained lightly all day, 47° to 56°. I split the larger green spruce blocks. Cut up the rest of the willow and spruce and ricked it up in wood shed. Sylvia went to Anchorage with Kahren yesterday morning.

Sunday, July 25, 1999—cloudy all day, 46° to 56°. Started raining 5:00 PM. I pillar bedded the wood stock for the .308 Winchester. It went slow but not too bad. Hope the barrel comes out of the stock. Cut down some more willows. Got two squirrels. Mark Brockman came over and borrowed some catalogs. Sylvia got back about 7:00 PM.

Monday, July 26, 1999—partly cloudy, a couple of showers, 45° to 62°. Hauled a load of brush over to Ed's for his land fill. I had to re-do the rifle stock bedding job as I had three small voids in it. Took the barrel out of stock in evening and put trigger back in the receiver. With Ed's help we borrowed his pipe rack and built an extension made of 2 x 4's on front bumper. Harold and Rachel stopped by with a bag of onions and lots of bananas. We think a duck is nesting in the box to the south. Saw an eagle swoop down behind the trees at edge of the lake. It flew off as though it may have had something in its beak.

Tuesday, July 27, 1999—cloudy and lots of rain, 44° to 55°. We went to Glennallen, had lunch and got TJIs, insulation etc at lumberyard. The pipe rack and extension hauled 6 - 28' TJIS's very well. I fixed a chip out place in that rifle stock.

Wednesday, July 28, 1999—mostly sunny, 40° to 64°. Bob helped unload the TJI's. I painted Thompson's water deal on them, also both of the steps to house. We took turnip greens over to Jim and Elaine. I put the Alaska flag on flag pole. Did a few other jobs.

Thursday, July 29, 1999—cloudy and showers, 45° to 61°. We built "pocket" like things to fit one TJI to another for continuity in the water line support. Hen duck surely appears to be brooding eggs. A pair of kestrels was driving off a raven from their nesting area. I didn't walk over to see if the young kestrels were out and just learning to fly and thus were at risk. Scraped more old finish from rifle stock.

Friday, July 30, 1999—partly cloudy, 44° to 59°. Went to Glennallen for lunch. Harold and Rachel went also. It's Harold's birthday. Got some screws for waterline support. Picked up my moose and sheep harvest tickets. Saw a cow moose along side the highway. Saw a mature bald eagle in a tree a short distance from highway. This afternoon I put the "pockets" on 5 of the TJI's. Then we went to supper at Harold and Rachel's. Stopped by Allen and Roxanne's campground to see how their project is coming along. Visited Cal and Mary G. I finished scraping with glass the old finish off the rifle stock.

Saturday, July 31, 1999—wonderful sunny day, 41° to 72°. Bugs bad. We went to breakfast with Allen and Roxanne at Eureka. Then worked on waterline. Cutting roots and digging out the base for the upper starting point of suspension TJI's. We got three tripods up today. Saw a family of kestrels learning to fly over in Allen's driveway.

Sunday, August 1, 1999—sunny and hot, 49° to 76°. We got the rest of TJI's up plus a lot of other work done on waterline. After supper I sanded the rifle stock. Really stiff and sore tonight.

Monday, August 2, 1999—sunny, 51° to 82°. Changed two tripods and made one new one. We got all the lower line insulated and the drain pipe that will protect it on the line. Went to Glennallen after more insulation. We went to Jim and Elaine's to supper. We sure got hot and tired today.

Tuesday, August 3, 1999—sunny, some breeze, 43° to 78°. Worked on waterline all day (9 hrs) mostly all done up the hill to garden. Put a clear coat on the rifle stock. Tom, Lisa, Lauren and Emily Smayda visited for a nice long time this evening. So good to see them again. The girls are pretty young ladies now. Lisa and Tom look good too.

Wednesday, August 4, 1999—sunny, some breeze in morning, windy in afternoon and evening, 53° to 72°. Worked on waterline again today, though not so many hours. We got all the way up the hill with insulation and cover pipe. We are sure stiff and sore.

Thursday, August 5, 1999—sunny, a breeze and some clouds, 45° to 71°. I burned four tanks of gas in chain saw. Cut brush all along water line. Trimmed branches off some trees. Cut rose bushes and willow from three sides of garden. Cut up the logs at a switch back and stacked them in woodshed. Then picked up wood, dunnage and blocks along waterline and stacked it in woodshed. Hauled up the wood board "trough" that we used to lay waterline in. Sylvia froze turnip greens and mowed lawn.

Friday, August 6, 1999—sunny, partly cloudy in evening, good breeze, 40° to 75°. We went to Glennallen on senior van, had lunch, cashed ckecks, did a little shopping. Visited with Ron Harold and Rachel. Smoothed the ground under the waterline down as far as the garden. Too hot to do that work so piled some willow brush. Got a drink of water and some lemonade, then the raked the strips of grass clippings on lawn. Raked the saw dust and duff from under a spruce tree. Loaded some .308 Winchesters to break in the new barrel.

Saturday, August 7, 1999—mostly sunny and breezy, 48° to 68°. Put water line to grade across front of garden. Built a box to protect it at garden gate. The sod and plants that I dug out we replanted on bare gravel cut in hillside. Went to gravel pit target shooting for three hours this afternoon. Got two squirrels this evening. We connected the 1-½" water pipe in two places today.

Sunday, August 8, 1999—mostly sunny and some breeze, 48° to 67°. We worked on waterline transplanted and put dirt plugs in gravel cut on a switch back. Pulled two stumps and one clump of willow out of ground near garden. Allen and Kyle came over. They needed a pair of sling swivels and visited awhile. Sylvia and I readjusted the anchor chains for waterline and gave it more slack. Allen came back and needed the use of a couple screw drivers. I dismantled the old line troughs after supper. With new battery screwdriver.

Monday, August 9, 1999—mostly sunny, some showers going by, 47° to 63°. Made some strap iron archest to hold waterline in place on the hill. Made the parts for garden gate. Rounded up feat to go hunting. Serviced ATV and loaded it in pick up. Elaine came over to pick up her box of groceries. I took it over and carried it in the house. The M.S. makes things like that difficult for her.

Tuesday, August 10, 1999—mostly sunny, 45° to 69°. Got up early. Went to trail head to go over Ballanger Pass. I was going down pass creek and the ATV was making a bad strange noise from the transmission. I turned around in trail and came back. We did see a parka squirrel. Back at truck Al and Faye were there. They plan to camp with Allen and his family at Five Mile Cabin. Back home I washed the ATV, built a garden gate for Sylvia. Built some steel hoop like stakes to hold the culvert in place.

Wednesday, August 11, 1999—partly cloudy, 44° to 67°. We took the Suzuki to Anchorage and had it checked out. They think the noise in tranny is because I have improper oil in it. Motorcycle oil is the one to use. We did a little shopping and got home early in afternoon. After supper we went to Allen's to visit about their Dall sheep hunt. David and Kyle each got a sheep. David's is 9 yr and Kyle's 6 yr. Real nice trophies. Allen gave us a piece of backstrap. Their hunt was a good one. I bought motorcycle oil in Suzuki store and put it in ATV when I got home.

Thursday, August 12, 1999—mostly cloudy, sprinkles and then rain, 45° to 60°. Worked on the truck. Then shoveled some gravel and dirt. Worked on light in the well. Started cutting off two tundra humps that are crowding the ATV trail to the well. Harold says caribou are on Lake Louise Road. Darrel phoned and wants to set up goose and sandhill crane hunting. Tom ? from Michigan flew into Eureka and visited at Dimmick's. He is on his way to Nome for a month or so to prospect for gold.

Friday, August 13, 1999—rain and fog all night, 48° to 64°. Cleared off a little at 6:00 PM so got up ate breakfast and drove the Lake Louise Road hunting caribou. Rusty Dimmick got a small one. I stopped by Billman's three times and got to visit with them on last try. Got gas a "Dinty Bushes." I didn't see a caribou. Saw a few above average to small sets of bull antlers. Got back home mid afternoon. Bob R. had covered our waterline. A car can be driven over this now. I finished cutting off the humps of tundra. We hear that Lonnie ? a friend from Utah got 50 oz of gold just a little east of Nome.

Saturday, August 14, 1999—partly cloudy, cloudy and a shower, 37° to 62°. Up early and went to trail head and over Ballanger Pass. Saw some ice on puddle near Pass Creek. The miners have really improved the road around the gorge. A yearling? ewe wanted to cross Alfred Creek ahead of me but changed its mind. Saw two small groups of ewes and lambs. Plus some other sheep. My spotting scope doesn't have good definition. The creeks are high due to rain. I decided not to try crossing Alfred Creek and went back to Fossil Creek, walking up it a little ways. Saw a wrecked ATV trailer and a ATV trail in a place new to me. Ate some sandwich then went up Alfred Creek a ways. Floods have made travel difficult so I came back to Junction with Pass Creek and went up it to Ballanger Pass. Visited with four people on machines there. Down the pass trail and near the bottom met two more riders. Ed and Chuck Farmer in Ed's Blazer 4 x 4. Washed ATV at home. Watered the potatoes growing in the straw.

Sunday, August 15, 1999—cloudy and very light showers, 43° to 55°. Checked the septic drain field and put "57" in tank. Removed the skid plate from Suzuki and discovered that the exhaust pipe had come unbolted. The one nut was loose and lying on skid plate. Got it all back together. Moe and friend got turned around mistakenly tried to go down our switchback road and got stuck trying to back up hill. I drove it out and showed them how to get to Rudbeck's.

Monday, August 16, 1999—mostly cloudy, 46° to 58°. Worked on ATV front skid plate. Shoveled on and off three loads of gravel from ATV trailer. I put it on area of the humps I removed from trail to well. The area was slick black mud. Didn't sleep well last night so I took a one hour nap this afternoon. Sylvia and Kahren went to Glennallen to get mammary exams and go berry picking near Chitna.

Tuesday, August 17, 1999—sunny and very nice, 42° to 67°. Jacked up and leveled the wood shop. Now the door closes properly. Cut weeds and wild roses near the greenhouse south side. Repaired the ground wire of left handle bar heater on the Suzuki. Allen, David came over to dig up and move our septic tank. We found that the baffle going into the tank was plugged solid with goo. We cut a hole in other end of tank and found that baffle to be relatively clean. Two swans have come back to our lake. They didn't bring any little ones with them. I hauled garbage to transfer site. Met Dave Johnson and Gary ? in gravel pit sighting in Gary's rifle.

Wednesday, August 18, 1999—sunny and very nice, 39° to 69°. I shoveled gravel back in around the end of drain lines. Repaired lid on septic tank. Cut and fit Styrofoam to cover the top of tank. Pushed a scraper through drain line from basement to septic tank. Rested awhile, Allen came over with Sammy, David and Jamie and had supper with us. After supper, David loaded and Allen hauled four loads gravel. Sylvia and I put down Styrofoam and weighted it with a few shovels of sand-gravel to hold it in place when Allen spread s and g over it with his CAT.

Thursday, August 19, 1999—sunny, 46° to 66°. Did some small jobs this morning. Then dug out some big willow stumps with Allen's dozer. Then moved some dirt down the hill to the first switch back. Went to lower road cleared a turnaround near waterline then improved the turn off the road to trail to lake. About then Allen started hauling fill for our septic system. I moved and spread it. After supper we loaded the willow stumps and Allen hauled them to Ed's place. Very tired and ribs hurt.

Friday, August 20, 1999—partly cloudy, breezy afternoon and evening, 38° to 57°. I smoothed up the road down to the switch back and spread clay over the gravel there. Smoothed the fill over the drain field. Jacked up and put more blocking around outside perimeter of wood shop. Cut the aspen saplings on south side of greenhouse. Allen hauled seven more loads and I spread them with his dozer. Sylvia went to the ladies luncheon and party at Eureka. I took two huge plastic bags of old Styrofoam to transfer site. Stopped at gravel pit and picked up 13-30.06 brass.

Saturday, August 21, 1999—partly cloudy, breeze from east, 40° to 60°. We cut 16 trees east of house. Piled some and cut some in blocks and put them in the woodshed. Using Allen's dozer I pushed the stumps out and into the deeper areas and pushed tundra and gravel over them landscaping and blending the area. Allen started hauling gravel about supper time. Had spaghetti with us and hauled seven loads and I pushed them in on top of the limbs, roots, stumps etc.

Sunday, August 22, 1999—partly cloudy and windy in afternoon and evening, 36° to 59°. Did some more landscaping. Chopped some roots. Re-riveted chainsaw chain and sharpened it. Mixed some bar oil. Changed the oil filter on Suzuki. We visited Cal and Mary. Kahren gave Sylvia salmon fillets.

Monday, August 23, 1999—partly cloudy and some sprinkles, 35° to 59°. Shoveled and raked the dozing on lower road. Shoveled and raked the dozing up here by the house. Cut up most of the logs and ricked the wood in woodshed. Chainsaw quit about 10 small sticks from getting job finished. Used axe to cut and then I pulled a bunch of roots. Carried some off. Couldn't fix chainsaw. Bob R called. He saw some caribou on top of Slide Mountain, maybe six nice bulls. Nice of him. Kahren visited a couple times. Once with salmon from Bartley's.

Tuesday, August 24, 1999—mostly cloudy, hard rain in afternoon and evening, 41° to 54°. Drove ATV up Slide Mountain. Not much for tracks down lower. Walked over toward the lake, saw a small cow and calf caribou. Later another pair. While I was eating lunch and glassing the valley and slope on the other side I observed two very nice bulls and others I couldn't be sure of. All were much too far away for me to pack back to the Suzuki. Nice to be up there. Hailed and rained hard on the way home. After supper it rained hard right after supper and stopped us from driving up Lake Louise Road to hunt boo. Shortly after that Allen drove over and visited a while and told me about recent boo tracks crossing the road and about a black bear along the highway.

Wednesday, August 25, 1999—rain in night and showers today, 47° to 53°. We drove up Lake Louise Road. Saw three caribou, one a nice bull, but too far away for me to kill. Got some gas at Steve Dawson's. Saw Chuck F. He had seen 5 boo near the gravel pit at mile one. By the time we got there they were gone. Came home ate lunch. Loaded Suzuki and went to trail just east of Dimmick's. Drove about a mile down it. No boo but Sylvia picked enough blueberries for three pies and two bowls of fresh berries.

Thursday, August 26, 1999—partly cloudy, 42° to 51°. In the morning, hunted three miles of Army Trail. Saw a moose kill and where a bear had passed a lot of plastic bags and wrappers. Worked on chainsaws. Got one running. Other one needs a fuel line. Went to Cal's but he doesn't have the right part. Allen hauled more fill this evening—it's looking good. At dark we had a piece of blueberry pie, coffee and visited awhile.

Friday, August 27, 1999—partly cloudy and showers, 41° to 55°. Went to VA Anchorage for check up and renew prescriptions. Did a little grocery shopping. Cal Datta rode back with us on van. Rudbecks got silver salmon in Valdez plus some red salmon out of a fish wheel. They gave us four fillets and borrowed one of our pressure canners.

Saturday, August 28, 1999—mostly cloudy, some breeze, 39° to 57°. Raked and leveled lots of the fill. Worked on chainsaws. Allen visited and we had lunch. I went to gravel pit for some off hand shooting at water filled gallon jugs.

Sunday, August 29, 1999—sunny, 29° to 61°. Chopped and carried roots off cleared area—finished raking same. Lee came over and we chronographed some loads and did some target shooting. Started gathering gear to go goose hunting. Jim and Mary Odden visited in evening.

Monday, August 30, 1999—partly cloudy, 37° to 61°. Loaded most of goose hunting gear in car. Drove Suzuki up Slide Mountain. Walked around a little. Didn't see a single caribou much less a moose. Saw a small den. Jerry R. must have his cub flying satisfactorily again.

Tuesday, August 31, 1999—29° to 60°. Loaded goose hunting gear in car and went to Glennallen. Did some shopping, ate lunch, went to rifle range to pick up brass. Then to Darrel's and load into the motor home. He and I went to Delta Jct. Farmers are all charging $100 to $200. We drove around a while, saw few birds, cow and calf moose. Camped at Clearwater.

Wednesday, September 1, 1999—36° to 60°. Went to see Alaska F & G at Delta. Talked to Dave ?. He answered all questions and offered his observation on goose and sandhill crane hunting in that area. We went to Fort Greely and got a permit to drive one their roads and possibly hunt birds. Too windy to hunt. We left for Glennallen about 8:00 PM. We saw a couple cows with twin calf moose. I got home and to bed at 1:00 AM.

Thursday, September 2, 1999—partly cloudy, 32° to 60°. Unloaded the car and put all the gear away. Then Harold Dimmick phoned. Someone saw a bull caribou on Old Man Creek trail. I loaded Suzuki and went to take a look. Saw bear pooh in trail, and two or three caribou tracks. One three-man swamp buggy (Ford) seemed to go everywhere I wanted to go. Didn't see any caribou. Visited Allen in evening. Pat, Russ, and another guy were there.

Friday, September 3, 1999—partly cloudy, 41° to 52°. We went to Glennallen on senior van to lunch shopping, bank. Back home I put a different fuel line on Allen's chainsaw. Repaired muffler on my XL12 and washed the Suzuki. Raked the cat tracks from the driveway. Bob R. flew in and left again. Allen, David and Robby are putting up community pavilion. Talked to them when I took garbage to transfer site.

Saturday, September 4, 1999—mostly sunny, 31° to 55°. Cut up four trees that had been dozed out for our road down to lake. Hauled them up and stacked wood in shed. Took ATV winch control switch apart and cleaned contacts. It was a bugger to reassemble. My winch problem is in motor its self. Disassembled the carburetor on XL12 chainsaw. Didn't see anything wrong and it still doesn't run right.

Sunday, September 5, 1999—partly cloud and nice, cloudy in evening, 34° to 54°. Problem was not ignition. Ignition quits when chainsaw get warmed up. Didn't get much wood cut. New chain was too long so I shortened it. Cut some brush around here. David borrowed my power tin shears.

Monday, September 6, 1999—sunny, cloudy in evening, 36° to 55°. We worked on the basement stair area, trimming it out. Sylvia painted till the paint in a quart can was gone. I worked on the XL12 chainsaw. Its problem was I hadn't reassembled the carburetor correctly. It now runs great. It was a nice day for Rudbecks to be flying.

Tuesday, September 7, 1999—cloudy, sunny, partly cloudy, 40° to 54°. Couple light showers, hail on Eureka Summit. We went to lunch Glennallen. Shopped for chainsaw spark plug materials and paint for stairs and stair hand rails. Made some parts when we got home. Harold and Rachel Dimmick brought Rachel's sister Ruth and her husband Walter Outwater from Nome, AK. We sure enjoyed visiting with them this evening.

Wednesday, September 8, 1999—partly cloudy, sprinkles, 39° to 54°. We made two handrails for the stairs and one post and painted them. Worked on chainsaw. Took Elaine and Jim's produce over to them. Rudbeck group, Bob & Kahren, Denny G. + Kruski got three moose out at their camp.

Thursday, September 9, 1999—very nice day, 37° to 55°. We dug the potatoes (30 gallons) 6, 5-gallon buckets. Put a few buckets gravel in yard. Removed the water piping for garden and lawn from main waterline. Did some shooting at gravel pit. Phoned son Paul. Cal thought he had a coil for chainsaw but no luck when I got there. He showed me his latest building projects. I road hunted for moose going to and from his place.

Friday, September 10, 1999—sunny, breeze in afternoon, 27° to 57°. We went to Glennallen on senior van. Sylvia cashed her check. Saw a nice caribou bull at mile 150. Piled some wood. Split a few chunks. Took the coil off a chainsaw.

Saturday, September 11, 1999—sunny, 30° to 57°. We went to Valley Timber in Palmer and got a coil for 240 Homelite chainsaw. Some shopping at Wal-Mart in Wasilla, lunch, groceries & gas and Bishops attic in Palmer. There we saw Art and Bonnie Wikle. Harold and Rachel at filling station. Sheep on Sheep Mountain. Back home I put coil on saw and it seems to run ok. Split and stacked some wood. Made three file handles.

Sunday, September 12, 1999—partly cloudy, cloudy and rain in evening, 36° to 58°. Chopped some roots and shoveled and leveled a short strip on back side of wood shed. Split more wood and restacked it. Went down by lake. We put up the hand rail on basement stairs. Allen visited in morning and gave us some moose tenderloin. Sylvia gave him eggs pickled in beet juice. I gave him an electric tin shears.

Monday, September 13, 1999—mostly sunny, 37° to 57°. Went road hunting and glassing from Mile 133 gravel pit. No luck. Stopped by Cal and Mary's. He decided we would drive Oil Well Road and to Lake Louise. We didn't see any game. Back home I split and piled wood. Reyne and son Adam came over to claim Adams toy pistol that I had found in gravel pit. I drove to the land for sale on way to Little Nelchina. Allen had suggested hunting there. I found an old Ford yellow state pickup there. Just as I was driving away I saw movement coming from mountain to parking area. I just came on home. Split and stacked some more wood.

Tuesday, September 14, 1999—mostly cloudy, 31° to 48°. Split and stacked the wood I had up to shed. Took a nap after lunch. Called Allen. He had just gotten home. Didn't mention hunting. Took truck and saws down to lower road and to dock area on lake. cut up a blown down spruce and loaded it on truck. Small saw threw chain off. Cut up a dozed out tree. Loaded it. Unloaded in woodshed.

Wednesday, September 15, 1999—rain all day, 37° to 48°. Split the 11 wet pieces of stove wood and a few little jobs. Got Cal to go with me road hunting to Gunsight and back. We got back to about 1 to ¾ mile from his place when he saw a legal bull moose (3 brow tines). Its horns measured only 41". Very tall and long. Cal hopped out of my truck and shot it. I saw first bullet hit it in the boiler room. Cal did shoot two other shots as bull moved off to south. We think it had pushed some cows across the highway north and he was waiting for us to go by then he would join them across the road. I started skinning and Cal took my pickup and went to get help. He brought his son in law Ron and three friends back. Ron was a lot of help. His friends held the lights. Ron had brought a generator. I drove my pickup through the ditch and willows to moose. Shot a moose when it was almost dark, (around 9:00 PM) and finished hanging it in our garage at midnight. We had two visitors while skinning. Allen Farmer. Also someone phoned troopers we had shot a baby moose! Of course troopers had to investigate. He found our moose to be legal.

Thursday, September 16, 1999—cloudy, partly cloudy, and windy, 33° to 46°. Cut up some down trees and hauled to wood shed. Cal cut horns out of moose skull. Horns measured 41" on my tape. Sylvia has picked five gallons of cranberries. This wind and temp very good for moose meat.

Friday, September 17, 1999—cloudy and rain, clearing and wind in afternoon and evening, 40° to 52°. Cal came to cut up moose ribs and some hamburger. Lee Dudley was here and we had coffee. Cal and I worked on meat. A little ermine is attracted by smell of blood and fresh meat. Four golden eagles flew by. I didn't do much today. Sylvia went to Queens luncheon.

Saturday, September 18, 1999—cloudy then sunny, lots more snow on Mountains to the south. 38° to 49°. I hauled a load of brush over to Ed's fill. Visited Allen, Lucky is helping him with the "office." Loaded the Suzuki and went to 133 mile pull out. Drove Suzuki then down blueberry picking trail to its end at a drainage to north, about 2.2 miles. Didn't see any animals but did spot what may be a cabin with the roof fallen in about a mile and a ½ to south west. Saw a jeep and three ATVs over on the Crooked Creek Trail. Stopped by Cal and Mary's store and at the house Ron and Evelyn are building. Ron and Jeremy stopped by on their way home from the GPAA gathering down near Seward. They got there a day early. When no one showed up this morning they left for Glennallen. I split some more wood.

Sunday, September 19, 1999—cloudy, sunny and nice, 31° to 50°. Split a little wood. Sharpened both chain saws. Tom and Lisa Smayda visited and picked cranberries and had supper with us. I cleaned up birch leaves off lawn. Had a nice visit with Tom and Lisa.

Monday, September 20, 1999—partly cloudy, 31° to 57°. I got up late and went to trailhead for Ballanger Pass. Trail was frozen. From an overlook of Wood Creek area I couldn't see any sheep and none were down on Alfred Creek. I did see four sheep over in another drainage. On way back home a moose was being butchered after being hit by a car. Washed the Suzuki as it was very muddy. Sylvia picked more cranberries. Looks rainy this evening. Allen and Roxanne visited in evening.

Tuesday, September 21, 1999—partly cloudy, cloudy in evening and breezy, 33° to 47°. Cal came over and we cut off the neck and the brisket of moose. I did some target shooting at gravel pit. Brought up a wooden box from well to use cutting meat. Sylvia picked berries and took some over to Elaine.

Wednesday, September 22, 1999—mostly cloudy, 32° to 46°. Too much breeze to wax house and garage roofs. Started getting wood from the upper dozing at the "hole". Got about ¼ cord cut and stacked in wood shed. Lee Dudley visited then Tom H. and Kim and Charley drove in with a new Ford 150 ext cab pickup.

Thursday, September 23, 1999—mostly cloudy and a shower in evening, 32° to 51°. I visited Lee Dudley at his place. Then visited with Steve Mailly. Sylvia went to KROA with Bob and Kahren. Allen called and wanted to bring up some fried halibut. Roxanne and Samantha came with him. I scurried around setting table, ice tea etc. Sylvia came home shortly after we got started eating. Charlie Trowbridge phoned and visited for an hour.

Friday, September 24, 1999—cloudy and showers, some sun in evening, 30° to 40°. Cal came over and got one of the front moose legs. We went to Elder-Senior Meeting in Copper Center. Did a little shopping. Got a letter from Bob Burns of Iowa City, Iowa (an old friend). Sure is beautiful outside this evening. More snow and lower on the mountains. Scott Hollenbeck phoned. I could come up and hunt geese and sandhill cranes.

Saturday, September 25, 1999—snow and snowing several inches, lots of it melted off this afternoon, 30° to 41°. Cal came over and we cut up moose meat. While Sylvia wrapped meat I went down to the well and put a different light fixture in there. We went to a 30th wedding anniversary party for Joey and Denny Eastman. Lots of fun. Bart Bartley rode home with us. Tonight the swans were calling and flying down the valley by the light of a partly cloudy moon. A neat experience to hear.

Sunday, September 26, 1999—partly cloudy, 25° to 39°. We cut and packaged one front leg and one hind leg of moose. Some breeze down on lake this evening. Reloaded some pest loads and plinking for the .223 Remington.

Monday, September 27, 1999—partly cloudy, 26°. Finished loading goose hunting gear and started for Glennallen. Did a little shopping and gas then went to Darrel's. Loaded my stuff over to their motor home. We got ready to go and we left for Delta Junction. The mountains with sun and clouds were beautiful. We got gas and buns at grocery store and went out to Barley Project. Saw some sharp tail grouse. I spotted a sandhill crane. Darrel stalked it but didn't shoot. We stopped at the Wrigley Farm and got permission to hunt. Went on to Scott H. and got permission. I gave him some ammo and BDV camouflage. We drove over to west side of farm. Saw sharp tails and I shot one. We picked up Scott's decoys and moved them to some large round bales for him. Put out our decoys. While I was getting ammo and gun ready Darrel saw a single crane and another group of six. We didn't see any others. He parked the camper at the irrigation pump.

Tuesday, September 28, 1999—snowing 3-1/2" accumulation, 30°+. No birds flying. In the afternoon, we picked up our decoys and drove over to Scott's game farm. Saw his buffalo and Ruby's reindeer. A large herd of wild buffalo was nearby. We saw a large flock of Canada geese on one of Shultz's fields. Ran into Scott on road. Visited a little, then we drove over to Wrigley Farm. No geese there though we did see a small flock of cranes nearer to Delta. We got gas and started for home. The roads were pretty good for the most part. Dry, wet, snow covered, ice etc. Saw beaver on Summit Lake and cow and two moose calves farther on. The light on the mountains was beautiful. No supper, and I got hungry. I don't like so much sugar—too many snacks. Got home about 10:00 PM and unloaded gear. Sylvia made me an egg sandwich.

Wednesday, September 29, 1999—a little snow and mostly cloudy, 27° to 40°. Put gear away. Checked out the right rear brake on truck. Grease seal is leaking. Grease looks bad. Drum needs turning. Put license tag on snowgo trailer. As we were to leave for halibut dinner at Legion Hall the alternator belt on car broke. We took the truck instead. Back home I adjusted the headlights higher.

Thursday, September 30, 1999—light snow, cloudy and calm, 28° to 35°. Six swans and two ducks on our lake. Pulled both rear wheels and brake drums off truck. Cleaned them up. Measured the brake shoes. Ralph called back for measurements and will bring new ones out with him from Wasilla. I took the broken alternator belt off the fan on the car. Ralph got here late afternoon. Sylvia fixed moose back strap for supper. Ralph and I had some hunting stories to exchange.

Friday, October 1, 1999—cloudy all day, 30° to 41°. Ralph and I worked on truck brakes. He did most of the work. The seals he brought out didn't fit. We phoned NAPA in Glennallen. They were to send them with Sylvia when she came in to pick up the fan belt, alternator for car. They failed to give them to her and Ralph drove clear to Glennallen to get them. We got the job done and the brakes tested out ok. Then we went to moose kill site - nothing left but the hide. Allen and Kyle were near there getting firewood.

Saturday, October 2, 1999—nice day, 32° to 47°. Ralph had breakfast with us and left for Fairbanks. I forgot to give him some of our fresh moose meat. Laura phoned—they have bought a new house. Polished some brass. Hauled garbage to transfer site. The bear(s) leave lots of droppings full of berries at site. Saw two spruce hens in our lane.

Sunday, October 3, 1999—snow and slush was frozen to everything this morning, 30° to 44°. After the mess thawed loose on car, I got it in garage and put studded winter tires on it. Added antifreeze, tranny oil and power steering oil and windshield washer fluid. Checked the truck tires and added air. Changed oil and filter. Checked and added the other fluids. Adjusted bright beams on car.

Monday, October 4, 1999—mostly cloudy, 35° to 44°. I wanted to go look at the "pyramid" but the clouds were low and threatening and it had been raining in that area. I tried twice. Jim and Elaine are driving to North Carolina, they left at noon today. After supper I burned two brush and rotted wood piles.

Tuesday, October 5, 1999—two to three inches of snow in the night and wind, 30° to 40°. Sun came out in the afternoon and melted most of it. As snow melted from spruce boughs the sun shone on it like diamonds. Swans feed all the time, six just flew over to Lower Twin Lake. We heated the dent in Sears "cargo", with hair driers and I pushed the dent out. I straightened out the trap-snowgo storage area.

Wednesday, October 6, 1999—mostly cloudy and light snow, 30° to 37°. Burned another pile of brush. Started the snowgo. Washed the kitchen stove hood and filter. Went to Legion meeting. Saw a large cow moose and calf near Marci White's place. The alternator on the car quit and the battery went dead at the Ranch House Lodge, which is closed now. Just at that time Burt's son Don came home. Let me use the phone and call Allen. He came and brought me home. I put the charger on a spare battery for the night.

Thursday, October 7, 1999—cloudy and light snow that melted off today, 30° to 36°. Did a little adjustment on water line. Allen came over after he got off work and we went to Tolsona Creek (Ranch House). Put my spare alternator on the car, jump started it. We stopped at a place near Mendeltna Chapel where a pickup and trailer loaded with construction materials rolled over last summer. We picked up maybe $50.00 of odds and ends. Sure am grateful to have Allen's help. I gave him three large traps that I don't use.

Friday, October 8, 1999—cloudy and light snow that melted off in afternoon,

28° to 34°. We went to Glennallen on senior van, lunched and paid phone bill. In the afternoon I helped Allen get out some wood and move some equipment. We took Allen, Roxanne and Kim to dinner at Eureka.

Saturday, October 9, 1999—sunny, pretty day, 19° to 36°. I cut up two wheel barrow loads of wood from the hole. About 40 plus swans left our lake today. Jerry's plane taking off scared the last of them off. Tried to call grandson Tyler. Our lake started freezing over.

Sunday, October 10, 1999—very nice day, 16° to 38°. I repaired and adjusted two kitchen cabinet drawers. We had five spruce hens in our yard and I took a picture of them. We visited Cal and Mary G. Their daughter, Evelyn gave us a food sealer. Phoned birthday greetings to grandson Steve. He wasn't home. Talked to Paul.

Monday, October 11, 1999—cloudy, 13° to 32°. Went to Glennallen on senior van. Lunch tickets at Mechanic's Warehouse. Got home at 1:00 PM went to Allen's campground. He was working there. He wants to get wood tomorrow. Phoned Lucky Beaudoin to get a phone number for muffler shop. Made appointment. Our lake is frozen over. Four swans left this morning. I repaired and put the wood hauling rack on truck.

Tuesday, October 12, 1999—snow, cloudy all day. 23° to 31°. Went to Allen and Roxanne's for biscuits and gravy. Then Allen, Kyle and I went to wood lot and cut the piles of trees into logs and firewood. A load on Allen's plow truck and a smaller load on my truck. Went to Joe Virgin's to unload it and no one home. Walked around here checking that all was ready for winter. Swept snow off car. Parked wood for Joe in garage, smells good.

Wednesday, October 13, 1999—snowing all the way to Palmer, 27° to 33°. We shopped Palmer and Wasilla. Got back to Lucky and Mary's about 9:00 PM. They got home about 10:30 PM. We visited till 12:00 AM then to bed.

Thursday, October 14, 1999—clear when we got back home, 21° to 27°. We shopped in Anchorage after having a new tailpipe put on car. We got almost everything we went to town for. A military convoy had some vehicles go in ditch mile 134, 1st curve east. Another went over the big fill east of Cal's looked bad. We unloaded and put away all our purchase except for meat items. This is out on arctic entry.

Friday, October 15, 1999—cloudy, 9° to 21°. We went to Glennallen on the van. I got some differential oil for the truck. We put it in this afternoon and greased the truck.

Saturday, October 16, 1999–cloudy, some snow, 16° to 28°. Toyo stove quit working–fooled with it all morning. Built a fire in barrel stove and burned a lot of trash from basement, mostly cardboard.

Sunday, October 17, 1999–cloudy, a little snow, 16° to 30°. Took two sheets plywood down to well. It is to support the water line at that end. Had to chain up the truck to get back up the hill. Packed the snow on our driveway with truck. Put a new filter on fuel oil storage tank. It had rust and ice in it. Sylvia put up the bird feeder.

Monday, October 18, 1999–cloudy, a little rain at suppertime, 28° to 38°. Melted and slid wet snow off house and east side of garage. This snow I had to shovel and carry to north end of garage, for I didn't want to walk over that ridge all winter. I loaded up wolf traps and snares and drags and took them down to Allen. I don't need them and he can have them. He has done so much for us. While there we had ice cream and cookies.

Tuesday, October 19, 1999–mostly cloudy, some breeze, 26° to 39°. Cleaned out some old trapping stuff. Dropped off two old batteries at Grizzly Towing. Took garbage to transfer site. Pulled snow off arctic entry roof.

Wednesday, October 20, 1999–sunny, 21° to 33°. Worked on supports for plywood the waterline rests on down by the well. Walked up and down the hill three times. Checked the wiring for a low temperature light. It's ok. The duplex outlet up at house has failed. Skim of ice on water in well. We went to dinner at Legion Post in Glennallen. Should have done some shopping for outlet and pipe clamps but didn't go early enough.

Thursday, October 21, 1999–cloudy, light snow in evening, 14° to 30°. Worked on the outlet for the wire to light in well. Put snowplow on truck. Drained gas from ATV and jacked the weight off the tires. Toyo stove quit again. I changed filters. Saw Jim O's airplane "Rags" fly past our place.

Friday, October 22, 1999–cloudy, skiff of snow, 21° to 27°. We went to Glennallen for lunch. Tried to get electric wire for light in well with no luck. Sorted and boxed my trap that I have left.

Saturday, October 23, 1999–beautiful day, 20° to 30°. Left home before daylight for Palmer. The car had a coat of ice as well as the road for the first 35 mile and slowly got better. Was good at Palmer. Went to old RR station, rented a table at a trap swap. Sold a few traps. Visited a little with a few people, Bob? and Al Dubard. Left about 3:30 PM and went to Wasilla and bought electrical wire rolls 2-250', shopped a little groceries and came home, roads were mostly dry, wet from Sheet Mt to home.

Sunday, October 24, 1999—cloudy and some fog, 3° to 23°. Called Jim O. this morning and visited. We got the 2 rolls wire soldered together and spliced. Sylvia held the spool stand and I strung it down to the well. I rolled up 200' of old wire. Hooked up at well and a plug at house. We now have a 100 watt bulb heating our well. Did a couple other little chores.

Monday, October 25, 1999—sunny most of day, 14° to 27°. Cloudy and looking like snow just before dark. I helped Allen build his water house at camp ground. Got two walls up and rafters and purlins. Roxanne and Sammy brought lunch about 1:30 - 2:00 PM. Kind of a fun day.

Tuesday, October 26, 1999—cloudy, sunny most of day, just a skiff of snow, 12° to 28°. Allen came over about 11:00 AM and went to his campground to work on the water room. Got the steel roof on and plywood on sides. He and Roxanne took Sylvia and me to Eureka for a late lunch. When Allen brought me home I gave him a throttle cable for his band saw mill. At supper time Fred Rungee stopped by and ate with us. He brought fresh veggies. We had a good story telling session.

Wednesday, October 27, 1999—mostly sunny, 5° to 23°. Tried to make a Styrofoam air block for wood chute. Changed the filter on the heating oil tank. Checked light bulb in well and adjusted height of suspended water line. Put some wood in basement. Oddens visited. Ralph phoned.

Thursday, October 28, 1999—pretty nice day, 5° to 19°. Finished the "plug" for the wood chute. Put a 100 watt bulb in well. Magpies are pulling insulation from garage walls. We saw a red fox in yard this afternoon. Theresa phoned collect. She is doing okay. Beverly phoned also. Helped Allen after supper work on his sawmill.

Friday, October 29, 1999—cloudy and skiff of snow, 9° to 19°. We went to Glennallen on senior van. Got heating oil conditioner and filter, copper tubing for Sylvia's crafts and paid electric bill. Then lunch and meeting of the elders. Back home I installed the filter and conditioner and trimmed a large number of lower limbs from yard and lane trees. Put a quart of oil in car.

Saturday, October 30, 1999—mostly sunny, 5° to 16°. Loaded all the limbs trimmed yesterday in truck and hauled them to Ed's and put them on his hillside. Tested the fuel oil line and it is frozen. I had enough line here to run another one by piecing it together. Had a few problems. But we did get it done and the oil heater works now.

Sunday, October 31, 1999—cloudy, light snow all day, 2° to 13°. Covered the oil line with boards then snow. Put a tarp over ATV in shed. Took gun boot off ATV. Helped Sylvia with one of her craft projects. Cal and Mary visited in the afternoon. Lauri brought her three kids and a nephew for Halloween treats. Later Oddens, Huddleston kids, Brockmans and Farmer kids all came for treats.

Monday, November 1, 1999—snowed all night ending about noon with six inches total. 7° to 16°. I plowed our snow and Manning's driveway. Fixed a loose wire on plow light and replaced a fuse.

Tuesday, November 2, 1999—snow in night and flurries today—got about three inches, 5° to 14°. Shoveled some and raked snow off two lean-tos. Started snowgo and packed trail to well. Built a little roof over bird feeder. Sylvia ground hamburger and packaged it. Swept snow off Molly car.

Wednesday, November 3, 1999—skiff snow, sunny and cloudy before dark, -6° to 9°. Plowed Manning driveway and our place. Cleared off some roofs, put antifreeze in "Molly" car. Shoveled some snow up to house foundation. Took garbage to transfer site. It hasn't been plowed yet. We visited Jim and Mary O. in evening.

Thursday, November 4, 1999—cloudy all day, -2° to +3°. Plowed some more at Mannings. Shoveled the snow off their deck and steps. Shoveled the snow off our woodshed. We pumped water and I walked down to well and back. We returned Cal's meat grinder. I put some stop leak in car radiator. The heater seems to be leaking. Started reading "Alaska Wolf Man" by Jim Reardon. Saw the fox at our picture window this afternoon.

Friday, November 5, 1999—cloudy and skiff (1/2") of snow, 1° to 13°. We went to Glennallen for lunch and shopping. Got a fuel oil filter and 20 amp buss fuses. Jim and Elaine got home, picked up their mail and left us two pounds of raw peanuts. Ralph phoned with a recent hunting story. Dale Routt and friend and client saw a small bear carcass. Next day as they got close to carcass a red fox ran by and friend arrowed it. Dale grabbed his friend's arm and put hand over his mouth and whispered "there is a big bear." The big bear walked to the dead fox and this guy arrowed the bear. Blood ran from its mouth and in 5 seconds it keeled over dead. Skull will be #33 in Pope & Young record book. Dale had been ready with his rifle as back up.

Saturday, November 6, 1999—very nice day, 8° to 20°. Didn't do much all day. Waited for Theresa to phone. Went to Odden's and checked on their house. Shortly thereafter Theresa phoned. She was at Don and Evelyn's at Brainerd. Earl was deer hunting. Sylvia cooked some moose steak in a crock pot. Allen, Roxanne, David and Sammy helped us eat it. Roxanne brought a gingerbread cake and lemon topping. Very good. I am reading Frank Glasier's, The Alaska

10,000 Days in Alaska Book Three 1998-2005

Wolfman by Jim Reardon.

Sunday, November 7, 1999—sunny, -2° to 12°. Did not do much today. Read some. Bob and Kahren came over and visited in late afternoon. Phoned Beverly.

Monday, November 8, 1999—sunny, -1° to 15°. We went to Glennallen. Mailed a package of bullets to Ralph. Had lunch and Sylvia got a little groceries. We saw a cross fox that had been killed on highway, ravens had eaten much of it. I checked Odden's house and put some more stop leak in my car radiator.

Tuesday, November 9, 1999—sunny, -7° to 15°. Bob and Kahren were here to breakfast. Did some reading. Put out some crumbs for birds.

Wednesday, November 10, 1999—mostly sunny, 7° to 15°. We pumped water. I covered the well with a plastic tarp. Packed the trail with snowgo. Checked Odden's house. The stop leak has repaired the car heater. I did some target shooting with 30 BR. Jim and Elaine had supper with us.

Thursday, November 11, 1999—cloudy, 3° to 10°. Veterans Day. Shoveled snow up around the well. Chinked a place in garage wall where the birds had pulled it out. Shot the Mini-Mauser, got a very small group, (.30) Kahren came up and borrowed a pair of Sylvia's GI mukluks. Bob showed up later. Read some more. Another rat pushup on the lake.

Friday, November 12, 1999—cloudy and skiff of snow, 4° to 9°. We went to Glennallen for lunch and a little shopping. Did a little target shooting later. Kahren brought Sylvia's GI Mukluks back and visited awhile. Cleaned two rifles and 40 brass after supper. Northern lights were out.

Saturday, November 13, 1999—mostly cloudy, 5° to 20°. Reloaded some .30 BR. We went to Billman's skating party. Got to visit some old friends and acquaintances. Good pot luck supper. Put together a stone grinder we have and ground some bird seed finer for little birds.

Sunday, November 14, 1999—sunny. 8° to 23°. Shot targets with 30 BR. Some were very good. Cleaned the rifle. Did some reading. Tried to phone Paul, no luck.

Monday, November 15, 1999—mostly sunny, cloudy late afternoon, 4° to 17°. Went to Jim Odden's, Kari O. wanted an interview about WW2. Then went to help Allen cut and haul firewood. He had one load when I got there and we got a load on my truck and cut and moved a lot of sawmill logs. He and Roxanne took me to Eureka for a bite to eat.

Tuesday, November 16, 1999—snowy, most of day, 8° to 16°. Snow—not much accumulation. Went to Little Nelchina and next pull out west and tried to call a varmint in with no luck. Went on to Eureka and had propane bottle filled. Cast some bullets and a little target practice in afternoon.

Wednesday, November 17, 1999—mostly sunny, 7° to 14°. Skiff snow in night. I plowed out snow today and cast bullets in the afternoon. We went to Thanksgiving dinner at the Legion in the evening. Jim M. brought over a gasket for Toyo stove.

Thursday, November 18, 1999—mostly clear all night and turned cloudy before daylight, -5°. The clouds got quite low today almost foggy. Phoned about switching vehicle insurance carriers. Sorted some cast bullets. Put gas checks on them and lubed them.

Friday, November 19, 1999—mostly cloudy, 4° to 14°. Snowy looking this evening. We went to senior Thanksgiving dinner at Kluti Kaah Hall in Copper Center. Sylvia did a little shopping.

Saturday, November 20, 1999—sunny, -3° to 15°. Moon is nearly full. Pumped water today. Made a wood handle and glued it on the lever that ejects cast bullets from the taper die. Cleaned the filters for room air purifier and the shop vac. We went to "Harvest Party" at school house.

Sunday, November 21, 1999—mostly sunny, -7° to +7°. Read a lot. Put gas checks on and lubed some bullets. Made a box to put the next batch in.

Monday, November 22, 1999—beautiful day, -11° to 4°. Clouding over in evening. Helped Allen for a couple hours hauling logs. We visited Bob and Kahren in afternoon. Sided and lubed some rifle bullets in evening.

Tuesday, November 23, 1999—lots of fog today, 2° to 7°. I did some target shooting. Cleaned a couple guns. Took garbage to transfer site. Checked front driveshaft on truck. Hooked the second TV antenna up. The two of them gave us a picture that is pretty good. Cleaned some brass. The bore cleaner that I mixed up seems to work well.

Wednesday, November 24, 1999—cloudy to partly cloudy, ½ inch of snow, 1° to 13°. Cleaned another rifle barrel. Gave Allen a starter rope for his chainsaw. Jim M. brought over magazines to read.

Thursday, November 25, 1999—cloudy and low clouds and ice fog, 7° to 14°. Sorted magazines, put some in large manila envelopes. We went to Odden's for

Thanksgiving dinner, baked chicken, pork and prime rib. Very good. John, Coleen, Axel and Erik Odden, Jim's cousin Emily and Doug, Brenda and Darrel were there. Nadia phoned. Ralph phoned. Beverly wasn't at home when we tried to call her.

Friday, November 26, 1999—partly cloudy, low clouds and some fog this morning, -5° to +5°. We both have some kind of post nasal drip and sore throat. Honey, vinegar and vinegar gargles and salt water snuffed up the nose seems to help. Supposedly this is a viral bug. Made a stopper for rifle barrel and poured the bore full of "Ed's Red" to soak.

Saturday, November 27, 1999—cloudy and ice fog, -18° to -10°. We went to Darrel and Brenda's. Her sons Ron and Dave, Robin and husband Mike, and Robin's son Robert were there. Had a nice visit and great meal. Brenda says Darrel is in a lot of pain now.

Sunday, November 28, 1999—cloudy, some fog, -16° to -9°. Drew some plans for a different forend rifle rest. Found some scrap steel in the pile to make it. We pumped water today. Had to replace the light bulb in the well. Shoveled more snow up around the well house.

Monday, November 29, 1999—cloudy and some fog, -25° to -5°. I have a bad head cold. Didn't do much of anything today. Slept a couple hours.

Tuesday, November 30, 1999—cloudy and fog, -13° to -3°. Still have bad head cold. Tried to work up a plan to make use of the "yard sale" tripod incorporating it in a different front rifle rest. Fishers delivered gasoline.

Wednesday, December 1, 1999—light snow till noon, 10° to 12° to about 2° in evening, then sunny till about 3:00 PM, then partly cloudy. Kahren was out skiing on our lake. My cold is better this evening.

Thursday, December 2, 1999—partly cloudy, -8° to 0°. Cold still hangs on. Did some reading. Kahren went skiing again today.

Friday, December 3, 1999—mostly cloudy, skiff of snow, -9° to +9°. We went to lunch and shop in Glennallen. Paid electric and gasoline bills. My cold hangs on.

Saturday, December 4, 1999—quite foggy, -8° to +7°. Built a fire in garage stove, but then didn't feel well enough to work. Read some, slept a little. Corky and Russ Dimmick visited a while in the afternoon.

Sunday, December 5, 1999—sunny, very nice day, -5° to +5°. Still have the cold. Rested all day. Phoned Nadia, and a guy in NC about a rifle rest.

Monday, December 6, 1999—sunny, -18° to -8°. We went to Glennallen. Lunch, Post Office, shopping, and bank. I'm adapting a tripod to a shooting rest. Ralph and Jeff phoned from Fairbanks. Ralph got a 59 1/4" bull moose. Jeff gave it a shot also. They had a great hunt and a great trophy.

Tuesday, December 7, 1999—sunny morning, cloudy afternoon, -23° to -10°. We pumped water today. I've been soaking a rifle barrel in cleaner. It is not cleaning up very fast. Elaine brought over some magazines to ready. Patty Billman has some magazines for me to read.

Wednesday, December 8, 1999—some sun, cloudy and ice fog, -22° to -4°. Cleaned rifle bore again. Talked to insurance agent and changed carriers. Sylvia is pretty sick.

Thursday, December 9, 1999—low clouds, -15° to -2°. Sylvia is still sick. Made out more Christmas cards. Called "Dish Network" and Sylvia's Dr's office to talk to the accountant there. Had to leave a message.

Friday, December 10, 1999—cloudy, snow in evening, -13° to -5°. Tried to check the strength of antifreeze in car. Couldn't get a good reading. Bob and Kahren stopped for 10 min or so. Allen came over after supper. He hit a moose with his crew cab and totaled it. He Roxanne and Sammy didn't get hurt.

Saturday, December 11, 1999—cloudy, skiffs of snow and frost, -12° to -3°. We pumped water today. I did some pistol practice today. Polished the empty brass.

Sunday, December 12, 1999—cloudy, skiff of snow, -10° to 5°. We went to Darrel and Brenda's for a nice visit and supper. Shopped a little in Glennallen.

Monday, December 13, 1999—cloudy, skiff snow and lots of frost, -12° to 1°. I heated up the garage and cut out and bent to shape the main frame for a new front rifle rest. Did lots of hacksaw work. Borrowed a drill from Allen. He is down to one vehicle now.

Tuesday, December 14, 1999—cloudy, skiff snow and frost, -20° to -3°. Worked on the "rise" for the rifle rest. Finished it and started the base for the rest top.

Wednesday, December 15, 1999—partly cloudy, -26° to 9°. Worked on rifle rest. Took Allen's drill home. We went to supper at Jim and Mary Odden's. Had a nice visit.

Thursday, December 16, 1999—most cloudy and lots of frost in air, -28° to -18°. Jim Manning brought over a Xmas card, banana bread and magazines to read. Worked on rifle rest awhile today.

Friday, December 17, 1999—partly cloudy, frost and ice fog, -30° to -15°. I kept the fire going all day in garage even though we went to Christmas party for seniors at Kluti Kaah Hall in Copper Center. Singing by a couple ladies and by ladies (from Kenny Lake) and small children sang hymns and Christmas songs. A fine Xmas meal then present exchange and a cake walk for donated presents. We did a little shopping and paid phone bills. Visited with different people.

Saturday, December 18, 1999—partly cloudy to cloudy, -28° to -10°. Worked on rifle rest. Jim and Mary Odden stopped by with a Christmas wreath. Allen left guns for safe keeping while he is on vacation. We rode to Legion Christmas dinner and party with Bart and Rosemary.

Sunday, December 19, 1999—cloudy, snow in night, sunny turning cloudy and some snow in afternoon, -10° to 8°. Clear and moon light tonight. I finished up rifle rest for the most part--unless I modify it. We pumped water, plowed snow and then had to replace the bulb in the well. Went to Odden's to supper. Kurt Skoog was there. We looked at Jim's pictures of his float trip down the Grand Canyon on Colorado River.

Monday, December 20, 1999—cloudy, 5° to 20°. Snow in afternoon, some wind last night. Switched barrels on a rifle. Loaded up some target loads. Got to shoot 10 rounds before snow started.

Tuesday, December 21, 1999—warmed up in night to 33° and by evening 38°. About 2" snow then rain this afternoon. Shoveled some snow. Cast some .30 cal bullets. Pulled snow off greenhouse roof and the car. No mail delivery. Supposedly the highway has been blocked near Hick's Creek with snow. Very bad driving conditions near Glennallen. Very few vehicles traveling.

Wednesday, December 22, 1999—what a storm! 32° to 45°. Snow, mostly rain all night. Winds were very strong 40-45 MPH, the strongest gusts. Rain all morning. Mostly snow in afternoon and evening. Both garage door and man door were frozen shut. Salted them and they thawed out. Cast some more bullets. Pumped water. Tough walking in 6" slush up and down our hill. Joe Virgin brought a coffee roll and we sent cookies home with him. Kim H brought caramel corn and took home cookies. Lots of TV dishes aren't working. Slides have closed roads. Snow each side of us is 12" and getting deeper.
      Lots of vehicles have gone into the ditches. Semi-trucks are chained up.

Road is so slick the wrecker couldn't pull a pickup out of ditch. Three avalanches at Thompson Pass and wiped out a CCI phone line. Some radio stations antenna out of commission. Dimmick's, TV antenna got blown around. They are snowed in.

Thursday, December 23, 1999—got just a skiff of snow, 32° in night to 17° morning and 9° in evening. Took a cookie plate over to the Mannings. Had a cup of cocoa with Elaine. Jim came home bringing Mary Gilcrease to do Elaine's housework. I then helped him adjust his garage door track. I examined and sorted the 400 bullets I just cast this week. We went to Odden's. Got to see Smayda's there. Had a nice time. Nice out tonight.

Friday, December 24, 1999—mostly cloudy, -7° to +5°. Cleaned the frozen slush off the car the best I could. Robert Banfill from near Tazlina Lodge called and asked me to plow his snow. Tough plowing 30" snow, packed and dense. Got it done, though. A package came by UPS. We think from Nadia. Allen Farmer phoned from Virginia to see how things were here.

Saturday, December 25, 1999—cloudy, 5" snow in night, -8° to +7°. We called most of the kids and Laura and Bob Burns. Sylvia's new sewing machine is on the fritz. Tried to help her with it but no luck. Put gas checks on and lubed the 400 recently cast bullets. Plowed our snow. Visited with Ed F. We went to Odden's for supper. Bart and Rosemary came later for coffee and desert. Jim had made the supper Norwegian style, complete with fruit soup and steamed pudding, lefse and lutefisk etc. Everything was very good. We had an enjoyable evening.

Sunday, December 26, 1999—got three inches of snow, some rain and windy sometimes. 0° then warming to 32° to 36°. Plowed our snow. Went to Allen's campground. Lots of snow with a frozen snow berm across the entry. Tried to push it, didn't get much done and gave up. Dropped off a card and goodies at Cal and Mary's. Brought the things they gave us home. Plowed the driveway down to Allen's house. Ed hasn't plowed since Allen left. Dale and Heidi stopped in with Jeff 3 kids. Dale and some really good bear hunting pictures of the hunt on Kodiak. Our electric service was off 3-4 hours this afternoon. Broken wire 11 miles east.

Monday, December 27, 1999—clear overhead, 35° to 14°. Cloudy in mountains to the south. Cleaned snow off the car and re-parked it, then plowed the snow in that area. Shoveled the snow off the roof of the camper. We pumped water today. I packed the road to well with the snowgo. Jim Odden borrowed our water hauling tank. Phoned Allen a couple time (answered only once) about snowplowing his campground. Our new telephone redial button is stuck and puts the phone out of commission. We got out the old rotary phone.

Tuesday, December 28, 1999—14° to 20°. Got up 6:30 AM and decided to go to Wasilla. We drove in snowy, loose snow and ice ruts for 50-60 miles. Exchanged a broke telephone and sewing machine for machines we hope will work. Bought a vacuum packing (packaging) machine. Groceries, drug prescriptions a shirt etc. Ate lunch. The roads were better on the drive home. We always unload our shopping and put it away when we get home. I'm real shaky this evening.

Wednesday, December 29, 1999—sunny, -22° to -16°. Went to Allen's campground and plowed driveway and turnaround. Tore up a tire chain. Got stuck twice. Hauled our garbage to transfer site. Filled both truck and car with gas. No mail delivery today for some reason.

Thursday, December 30, 1999—sunny, -36° to -16°. Read some. Wrote to Bob Burns. Intend to check on Allen's house later this evening. Fixed the fire for the night.

Friday, December 31, 1999—a skiff of snow as it warmed, -39° to -34° then warms up to -20° by evening. Went to Allen's when I got up and fixed the fire there. It will last all day. Wrote some letters. Put out some bird food. A Moose cow and calf were walking west on our lake.

Norman and Sylvia in their greenhouse

Norman Wilkins

Sylvia Wilkins sitting on front step of their Scoter Lake log home.

2000—Sylvia gets interviewed, and hunt at 5-mile

Saturday, January 1, 2000—sunny, -13° to -10° all day. Temperature dropped after sunset. Ron Beshaw phoned. Jeff and Dale Routt stopped by. We shot Dale's new 416 Rigby. Gave Jeff some dies and cast bullets. Allen phoned from VA and visited. Dale saw six moose today, one near us and 5, 8 miles east.

Sunday, January 2, 2000—sunny, -34° to -26°. Slept a lot today. Did some reading and watched TV.

Monday, January 3, 2000—partly cloudy, -34° to -6°. I went to Palmer driving the "Molly" car. Picked up Allen, Roxanne and family at her dad's (Lucky and Mary's) and visited a little while. Took them to grocery shop. Then we drove home after a light lunch. Roads were rough a third of the way. As Allen was unloading at this house he gave me a special ham and some sausage from Virginia. Glad to be home again this evening.

Tuesday, January 4, 2000—mostly cloudy, 1" snow, -17° to -10°. Jim and Elaine visited in the afternoon. Brought some magazines to read. I paid Jim $6.25 for a gasket for stove. Allen stopped by for a visit. Sylvia put out crackers, Italian salami, and Italian cheese.

Wednesday, January 5, 2000—partly cloudy, -29° to -17°. Went for a walk and read for a while. Bart phoned, ask me to go with him to Legion meeting. He had a couple of errands so we left home extra early.

Thursday, January 6, 2000—mostly cloudy, -4° to 0°. We pumped water today. I did some reading. Theresa phoned with a new number.

Friday, January 7, 2000—cloudy all day, -0°. Threatening snow from mountains to the south. We rode the senior van. Paid phone bill and did some shopping, had lunch, and went to Post Office. There was a bad accident on Glen Highway today.

Saturday, January 8, 2000—cloudy all day, 10° to 8°, got 1-1/2" of snow in the night. Cleaned snow off some roofs, and plowed our snow. Called Theresa and helped Sylvia a little. She is cooking the Virginia ham Allen and Roxanne gave us. Allen, Roxanne Farmer, Elli and Sammy, Jim and Mary and Kari Odden were all here for supper and we had a nice visit with them this evening.

Sunday, January 9, 2000—cloudy and skiff of snow, -9° to +9°and 0° almost all day. Read some today. The two older Brockman boys, Luke and Nicki brought a thermos of coffee over that their mother Reyne couldn't get open. Nice boys.

Monday, January 10, 2000—mostly cloudy, ice fog in morning, -10° to -5°. Fired up the snowgo and packed the trail to the well. Shoveled snow down by the well. Took a ham hock and some ham over to Allen.

Tuesday, January 11, 2000—clear with ice fog in the air, -27° to -18°. Frost on tree trunks, buildings, anything exposed to the air. Vehicle insurance policy and bill came today, so I put a check in mail. Mark Brockman phoned and asked if I would plow for them if it snows while they are on vacation.

Wednesday, January 12, 2000—mostly cloudy, -34° to -20°. Walked down to lake and back, did some reading. Nadia phoned. We got lots of calls today.

Thursday, January 13, 2000—sunny, -34° to 20°. Walked down by lake. Saw tracks of four ptarmigan out by mailbox. They feed on the willow buds near there. A mouse browsed along the north side of our place. It came out in our driveway, making its way to the west. Small birds visit the feeder everyday. A skim of ice is forming on the water in our well.

Friday, January 14, 2000—cloudy, -33° to -15°. I put two 100 watt bulbs in our well to keep it warmer. Sylvia went to the neighborhood Queens luncheon at Eureka.

Saturday, January 15, 2000—light snow in the night, and all day—one inch. Temp started out at -16° but got up to 0°. We pumped water. Most of the ice in well is thawed now. Pulled the snow off greenhouse roof. Repackaged Sylvia's new mixer prior to returning it. Allen visited for a while this afternoon.

Sunday, January 16, 2000—sunny, cloudy in evening, -24° to -15°. Read, watched TV. Ralph phoned. I called Dale. Dale called in evening about a rifle he saw at show. A moose crossed our suspended water line—stepped right over it, doing no damage. Phoned Jay Gandy.

Monday, January 17, 2000—sunny morning and cloudy along in afternoon and evening. -23° to -7°. Emptied the last of the oil from a 5-gallon bucket into some one-quart containers. Read some and more TV.

Tuesday, January 18, 2000—clear to cloudy this evening, -10° to +10°. Walked down to well and took out one bulb. Shoveled snow off storage shed and woodshed. Wrote some letters.

Wednesday, January 19, 2000—clear and cloudy later in the afternoon, 0° to 14°. Plowed our snow. Moved the car. Allen borrowed our water tank and hauled a load of water for Mark Brockman. Then Jim Odden filled his holding tank with it. I cast 200, .30 caliber Grom wheel weight lead.

Thursday, January 20, 2000—mostly cloudy, 11° to 23°. We pumped water today. Worked at leveling plywood under the waterline at well. Shoveled a little snow. Cast about 250 .30 cal bullets today. Went to supper at Odden's. Had a very nice evening. Jim talked about hunting in Africa.

Friday, January 21, 2000—cloudy and some fog, 13° to 19°. The senior van was late this morning. Sylvia did a little shopping. Harold, Rachel, Ed and B and a volunteer road the van. We had a substitute driver today.

Saturday, January 22, 2000—sunny to clouding over in the afternoon, 1° to 20°. I lubed and put gas checks on most of the recently cast bullets.

Sunday, January 23, 2000—sunny, cloudy later, 5° to 14°. Electricity went off about 3:00 PM and came back on about 8:00 PM. Called Nadia this morning. Lynda (Burns) phoned this afternoon.

Monday, January 24, 2000—windy and cloudy, 30° to 20°. Snow in late afternoon. Lee Dudley stopped by in morning. Jeff Routt came in a little while later. He brought some lead. I had some bullets cast for him.

Tuesday, January 25, 2000—snow in the night and all morning, about 6+ inches. Temp went from 9° to 29°. Plowed our snow, Mannings, Mark Brockman's, and Harold Dimmick's.

Wednesday, January 26, 2000—got three inches of snow and windy all day, 2° in night, 16° to 24° in the day. Pumped water today. I packed trail to the well with snowgo. Shoveled snow off camper. Raked some snow off roofs. Plowed our snow. Went to Allen's for supper today, it's his birthday. Plowed some of his driveway.

Thursday, January 27, 2000—three more inches of snow, 22° all day. Plowed our snow, and shoveled some. Changed filter at fuel oil tank. The truck has a antifreeze leak somewhere. Block heater?

Friday, January 28, 2000—mostly sunny, cloudy in later afternoon, 7° to 23°. We went to Glennallen on senior van—driver Myra. Our oil burner is on the fritz. I put a small jag of wood in basement to heat until oil burner is fixed.

Saturday, January 29, 2000—sunny, 1° to 14°. Delivered Elaine's mail and plowed their driveway of snow. Drained the fuel oil sump on the heater. Jeff dropped of his copy of "Handbook for Shooters and Reloaders" by Parker O. Ackley.

Sunday, January 30, 2000—snow all day, maybe 5 inches. A kind of granulated snow, probably full of moisture. Temp, -2° to 13°. I'm reading one of Jeff's books "Handbook of Shooters and Reloaders." I like it a lot. Plan on going out after the Super Bowl game is over and plow our snow. Darrel and Brenda stopped in. Darrel saw Ambulance and rescue people at Knik River. Steve Berge died.

Monday, January 31, 2000—cloudy this morning, sunny afternoon, then clouded over, 6° to 21°. Many storms, avalanches in Alaska for several days now. Helen Lee is having some kind of spell again. We went to Glennallen on senior van. Sylvia shopped. Saw Ralph Fuson in town. Back home I plowed some more snow. Did some target shooting with the MAS 7.5 x 54. Put some wood in basement. Worked on the fuel oil line from storage tank to heater. The trouble may have been an air lock that prevented enough fuel from getting to burner.

Tuesday, February 1, 2000—mostly sunny, 7° to 22°. Did some target shooting and adjusted the front sight on French 7.5 x 54. Started reloading some more. Jim looked at our heater and Elaine baked a birthday cake and brought it over. Sylvia had baked a cherry cake and we all had a couple pieces of cake. Sylvia took me out to supper at Eureka this evening. Just as we came home Allen and Roxanne followed us in and wished me Happy Birthday. Nadia and my sister Virginia both called with greetings. Good to hear from them. Theresa phoned birthday wishes later in the evening.

Wednesday, February 2, 2000—windy, turbulent, 29° to 34°, lots of snow. I did get a chance to do some target shooting in between strong winds this morning. Plowed some of our snow. Put more wood in basement. The oil burner didn't run all night. Ground and fashioned a tool bit to work on the French 7.5 x 54 front sight protector. Reloaded some more rounds. Would like to get it sighted in.

Thursday, February 3, 2000—mostly sunny, clouded over in afternoon and evening, 29° to 22°. Plowed our snow. Packed snow down to well with snowgo. We pumped water. Did some more shooting and adjusting of rifle sights. More snow slide off house roof and I have to shovel it from where we walk. Odden's phoned me and advised me they were going flying over Old Boot Lake and Blue Lake and my old trap cabin. Mary called again when they got back. Saw snowgo tracks on Blue Lake.

Friday, February 4, 2000—partly cloudy, 11° to 24°. Went to lunch and shopping in Glennallen. Went to supper at Odden's. Henry and Sally Johnson, Sam Weaver and Kurt Skoog were also there.

Saturday, February 5, 2000—cloudy and fog just above our elevation, especially at

Eureka Summit. 16° to 25°. We don't feel well today. I saw David and Allen, then T J Huddleston out at mailbox. Then Don Culp stopped by and visited. I read for a while this afternoon.

Sunday, February 6, 2000—cloudy all day, 21° to 27°. Did some reading. Sorted and looked over some brass. three moose were around the lake today. Kahren R. phoned. Jim Manning stopped by. I phoned Bart.

Monday, February 7, 2000—cloudy, very foggy, 24° to 29°. We got ready to receive Linda Burns and husband, Kurt Curtiss and their Eagle River friends, Lloyd and Shirley (not sure of their last name). They got here about 3:30 PM and stayed an hour or so. Jim M and I made plans to work on oil heater.

Tuesday, February 8, 2000—ice fog and cloudy, 20° to 27°. Jim M came over and worked on our stove. We need a new part. Jim cleaned the fire pot and exchanger. I cleaned the tube that introduces fuel to pot. Used a drill bit to get some tar like gunk out of tube. More target shooting. Got a good target. Loaded more and cleaned rifle.

Wednesday, February 9, 2000—low clouds and fog skiff of snow, 18° to 26°. Sun shone through across the river for a few moments. I glued two knee patches on a pair of 55-yr-old US Navy deck overalls. Swept the snow off the car. Jim came over and got his box of tools. Needed to work on a stove for church. Cal and Mary visited for a little while. Elaine borrowed some super glue.

Thursday, February 10, 2000—sunny and very nice, 3° to 22°. Shoveled the snow off the north side of wood shed, and read some more.

Friday, February 11, 2000—cloudy, fog, and frost, -1° to 12°. Went to Glennallen on senior van. Lunch and shopping, mailed scope to be repaired. Borrowed some raisins from Elaine. The part to repair our oil burner came today. Jim is gone driving the school activities bus. We pumped water and put wood in the basement.

Saturday, February 12, 2000—sunny, 1° to 17°. Studied cast bullet targets and regulation books. Constructed a target to copy. Did some reading. Bart and Rosemary took us to Legion Hall for installation of new officers and a good dinner.

Sunday, February 13, 2000—sunny and some ice fog, -4° to 14°. We went to Darrel and Brenda's for a birthday dinner for Darrel (he turns 52 tomorrow). Took a rifle along in case of a chance at a wolf, fox, coyote etc. Checked out the shooting range—no brass. It has the snow plowed. We had a fun visit with Darrel and Brenda. We got back home before dark. Fred Rungee showed up about 8:00 PM with ice cream, lettuce and a red cabbage. We ate the ice cream, visited. He stayed overnight and had breakfast with us.

Monday, February 14, 2000—sunny after the fog lifted, -6° to 10°. Jim Manning came over after Fred left. He put the heater back together. It works okay now. We got a propane delivery today. I shoveled the snow off both lean-tos and the storage shed. Tried to walk out to pickup canopy to clean snow off it but the snow is too deep to walk through. Phoned about airline tickets to Mpls/St Paul.

Tuesday, February 15, 2000—foggy, sunny, -2° to 10°. We went to Wasilla, prescriptions, shopping, lunch, made Sylvia's appointment with her doctor. We bought plane tickets to Minneapolis, Minnesota. At about Mile 90 on the Glenn Highway, on the way home, a moose had blocked the road. It had its ears laid back and hackles raised. Very angry. It would run at and strike with its front feet at vehicles. When a vehicle would sneak by, it would either kick the vehicle (if its back was turned at the time) or if looking at the vehicle as it tried to go by, the moose would strike with its front feet, striking the car sometimes, then chasing the vehicle. When we got our chance, we got by it before it could do anything—but it sure looked at us like it wanted to get some licks in. Though this was our first experience like this, it is not unheard of. Some moose get ornery when snow is deep and browse is in short supply.

Wednesday, February 16, 2000—sunny, partly cloudy, -14° to 9°. We went to mile 130 of the Glenn Highway and took pictures of Sylvia holding up a shovel in front of the snow piled there. Henry drove up in the big end loader he was using to pile the snow. Mark was using a dozer. Allen, a grader with ice blade. We visited Cal and Mary on way home.

Thursday, February 17, 2000—partly cloudy, cloudy in afternoon, -3° to 18. Looks snowy. Pumped water. Shoveled some snow off waterline. The birds sure go after everything we put out for them. Jim Odden borrowed the water hauling tank. Allen Farmer and the Odden family visited in evening.

Friday, February 18, 2000—foggy, cloudy and looking like snow this evening, 10° to 19°. We went to Glennallen to lunch. Cal called about snow plow troubles he has. He got it figured out. We saw a very large moose on our lake.

Saturday, February 19, 2000—cloudy, sunny, cloudy, 17° to 31°. A fitting at kitchen sink broke and I had to repair it. A dog came along and stole the "fat ball" we had out for the birds, so I replaced that. Did some target shooting with the French 7.5 x 54. Got one good target and cleaned the barrel. Lee Dudley returned a book he had borrowed. We had a good visit.

Sunday, February 20, 2000—cloudy, sunny, cloudy in evening, 11° to 27°. Sick today. A dog got into garbage can. Put out feed and grease for birds. Red poll, junko, grosbeak, gray jay and woodpecker. Slept some. Re-cleaned the French 7.5 x 54. Couple kids out on snowgos on the lake.

Monday, February 21, 2000—mostly sunny, 6° to 23°. Still sick with head cold. Read some. Reloaded some jacketed bullets impregnated with a fine grit in hopes of smoothing the bore of the 7.5 x 54 MAS rifle.

Tuesday, February 22, 2000—sunny, 4° to 24°. Feeling better today. Two moose hung around our place eating brush. Took pictures of them. Did a lot of reading. We went to Odden's for supper.

Wednesday, February 23, 2000—cloudy and light fluffy snow (one inch), 6° to 17°. Moose walked out to our lane this afternoon. Put some oil in car. Shot 5 firelapping rounds down the barrel of the 7.5 x 54 MAS. Looked again for my misplaced dinosaur fossilized footprint with no luck. Cleaned the rifle bore.

Thursday, February 24, 2000—cloudy and then sunny in afternoon, clouds in evening, -3° to 10°. Wrote four long letters today. Cleaned snow from a roof and part wood shed (overhang). Plowed our snow.

Friday, February 25, 2000—fog, breezy, sunny, clouding over in evening, -6° to 12°. Went to senior meeting at Legion Hall in Glennallen. Nice day.

Saturday, February 26, 2000—sunny, -4° to 18°. Bruce B. stopped by and picked up some old moose bones. I made a Plexiglas cover for the bowl of Sylvia's electric mixer. Using a different powder, I shot some more targets. Jim Odden flew out to McGrath for another season of work.

Sunday, February 27, 2000—sunny, -11° to +11°. Reloaded some more experimental loads. One didn't work out, one shows promise. Ralph Fuson phoned, we may see him tomorrow evening.

Monday, February 28, 2000—sunny, then cloudy in afternoon, 3° to 24°. We went to lunch and some shopping. At home we pumped water. I check Odden's house, then did some target shooting and reloading. Ralph is down this way from Fairbanks–is having supper with us and will stay the night. We plan to hunt tomorrow.

Tuesday, February 29, 2000—mostly sunny, 5° to 25°. Got up at 6:00 AM. Ralph drove us up the Lake Louise Road. We saw three ptarmigan and lynx tracks about mile 1-½. Back home for breakfast then we shot some cast bullet loads. He shot his rifle on a couple targets. He went on to work. I reloaded brass and shot those without much luck. I will abandon the use of that powder for cast bullet loads. Manning's Subaru died at the mailbox. Jim got it going. We will go to Allen and Roxanne's to visit.

Wednesday, March 1, 2000—sunny, 0° to 26°. Reloaded some brass after annealing it. Smashed a container of tin cans. We do not have to pay by volume to get rid of our garbage. Jim and Elaine were here for supper this evening.

Thursday, March 2, 2000—partly cloudy, skiff snow, -5° to 22°. Checked Jim's place. Read newspapers. Practiced target shooting. Cleaned rifle. Tumble cleaned some brass.

Friday, March 3, 2000—partly cloudy, 10° to 28°. We went to lunch in Glennallen. Did a little shopping. Mary Gilcrease is coming along now and really enjoys the outing. I cast 400, .30 cal bullets when I got back home. It took two hours to cast them.

Saturday, March 4, 2000—mostly sunny, 8° to 32°. Checked Jim's place. Cast some more bullets, put gas checks on them and lubed them.

Sunday, March 5, 2000—nice sunny day, cloudy in evening, 0° to 26°. Jim Odden phoned. Ralph phoned. I cast some more 30 - 180 sp. Put out some bird food. Burned paper in stove.

Monday, March 6, 2000—sunny, -2° to 26°. Jim brought our spare blower for the Toyo stove home. All clean and ready to work. I checked Odden's place. Loaded some brass and did some target shooting.

Tuesday, March 7, 2000—sunny, a little light breeze, -5° to 23°. Did some more target shooting. The French 7.5 x 54 is not going to be a competitive rifle in postal competition. Checked the fuel levels in gasoline and heating oil. Made some "For Sale" notices for our belt pulley attachment for a D47U CAT.

Wednesday, March 8, 2000—sunny, -4° to 25°. Sore back today. Bushnell company returned my scope repaired. I put rings on it that fit the 700 REM and will use it with .308 sporter barrel. Put the same quick release rings on my varmint scope for use on same rifle receiver and different barrel.

Thursday, March 9, 2000—sunny, -7° to 24°. Checked Jim's place. The newspaper is being left every other day. Sorted my .308 Winchester brass. Got another scope ready to be sent for repair. My back is bad again today.

Friday, March 10, 2000—it's -7° to 22°. We went to lunch in Glennallen, mailed another scope off to Simmons to be repaired, cashed our checks, and put gas in the car to go to Palmer tomorrow. Phoned Lucky that we expected to see them Saturday. Checked Odden's.

Saturday, March 11, 2000—cloudy, sunny, -6° to 16°. We got up early and went to Palmer. Visited Lucky and Mary. Went to gun show and had a good time. Got some copies made. Exchanged vac sealer and shopped for groceries.

Sunday, March 12, 2000—sunny, cloudy, 7° to 26°. Slept late. Checked Odden's place. Ricked some of his wood. Sorted out some of the copies I made in Palmer and got them organized. We went to Steve and Karen Mailly's for supper. Lee Dudley was there too.

Monday, March 13, 2000—cloudy, partly cloudy in afternoon, 10° to 27°. We pumped water today. Did a couple little chores. The quick detach rings I mounted on a rifle do not allow centering the scope.

Tuesday, March 14, 2000—partly cloudy, 6° to 27°. Did a lot of barrel changing and shooting to check the scope and mounts out. Checked Odden's place. Cut up and stacked under roof some of his wood pile.

Wednesday, March 15, 2000—mostly cloudy, 1° to 29°. I don't feel very well today. George Perkins phoned that he will be two weeks late to house sit for Odden's. We had a gasoline delivery today. Allen visited in evening.

Thursday, March 16, 2000—mostly sunny, very nice, 9° to 31°. Went to Odden's. Checked hose. Finished cutting up and stacking the wood in Jim's shed. Cleaned two rifle barrels. Pumped water.

Friday, March 17, 2000—mostly sunny, 9° to 35°. We went to Glennallen. Lunch, shopping. Copies made and mailed large envelope. Visited Dimmicks before we got home (last week they rolled their car over and got hurt a little). Called Darrel Gerry, he will try to contact Shooter News about my subscription since I can't contact them by mail or phone.

Saturday, March 18, 2000—partly cloudy, 20° to 39°. Checked Odden's place. Delivered Elaine's food, bank and mail to her. Visited Henry and Sally Johnson at Nelchina Lodge. Shot the rifle and cleaned it. Bart and Rosemary took Sylvia and I, and Bob and Kahren, to the Legion corned beef and cabbage supper.

Sunday, March 19, 2000—cloudy, 4° to 30°. Very windy and blowing snow on south side of house. Did some research and no luck. Lee Dudley stopped by and I showed him a short tape of making Osage Orange long bows and knapping arrowheads out of flint. Sylvia asked Bob Kahren and Lisa Niki Niki and baby over for a spaghetti supper. Bruce Bartley, and a friend (with son Jay) stopped by on their way home from wolf trapline. They had caught a nice female. I took pictures of it. Bruce shot a wolf on the Tyone River a couple weeks ago. The electric bulb burned out in the well. The power was off for a few minutes after 8:00 PM.

Monday, March 20, 2000—partly cloudy, nice day, 17° to 36°. Put a new bulb in the well. Lubed some bullets and reloaded some brass. My joints sure hurt today.

Tuesday, March 21, 2000—cloudy, partly cloudy, 8° to 34°. Checked Odden's place. Got the summer tires out of storage for the car. Did a few little chores. Did some pistol practice. Prepped the brass for reloading. Helped Jim Manning clean and replace the carburetor on his electric generator.

Wednesday, March 22, 2000—sunny and very nice, 1° to 35°. Repaired the carpet sweeper. Lubed some more .45 ACP bullets and loaded 100 of them. Cleaned a little snow from off the truck.

Thursday, March 23, 2000—cloudy, sunny, cloudy, 7° to 34°. Checked Odden's place. Removed the winter tires from car and put on the summer tires—sure took the sap out of me. We pumped water today. Allen visited in the evening.

Friday, March 24, 2000—cloudy and light snow, 13° to 32°. Went to lunch in Glennallen, paid electric bill. Did target practice, cleaned rifle. Phoned Dan B and Denny B.

Saturday, March 25, 2000—cloudy, sunny, cloudy. 16° to 36°. Checked Odden's place. Target shooting. Harold, Rachel, and John Dimmick were here for supper.

Sunday, March 26, 2000—cloudy and some light snow, 16° to 35°. Charlie Trowbridge dropped in about 10:30 AM and stayed till about 4:30 PM today. We had lots of visiting to do. He used my skis to go down to his storage shed. We drove around a little and saw Sam and got to visit with him awhile.

Monday, March 27, 2000—partly cloudy and a nice day, 13° to 33°. Checked Odden's place. Haven't felt well today. Rested and slept. Did some repair on some kitchen drawer runners. Bob Burns (old friend from Iowa) phoned.

Tuesday, March 28, 2000—partly cloudy, -9° to 27°. Sylvia and I both don't feel well, some kind of cold in our eyes. The census taker was here. I cleaned and oiled a couple bullet molds.

Wednesday, March 29, 2000—partly cloudy, windy in afternoon, 4° to 37°. Dust blowing dirt off the river bank across the west end of our lake. Checked Odden's house. Took coffee grounds out to greenhouse. Measured our heating oil in the tank and ordered 100 gallons. Cleaned and oiled the rest of my bullet molds. Bob and Kahren brought over a carpet sweeper they aren't using. Snow coming from south. Visited Allen—he gave me a rifle stock.

Thursday, March 30, 2000—cloudy, sunny then windy, partly cloudy, 22° to 41°. Pumped water today. Shoveled a little snow. Did a little target shooting. Electricity went off. Fooled with micrometer trying to adjust it so all the zeros line up at "0" setting with no luck. Built a fire in the heater. When we found out we were the only place without power, I checked around and found our main breaker had "tripped." Turned electricity back on.

Friday, March 31, 2000—partly cloudy, nice day. Went to Glennallen, paid ahead on phone bill and had lunch. Got a loaf of bread. Cast a batch of .22 cal. bullets. Put gas checks on them and put one coat of lube on them. Baked a batch of molasses cookies, had to make them without nutmeg. That changed the taste.

Saturday, April 1, 2000—cloudy, partly cloudy, 13° to 38°. Snow slide off garage roof. We went to the Point Lodge for lunch with Dan and Patti Billman. Their lodge was participating in the Lake Louise snowgo Poker Run. Then we went to Harold and Rachel Dimmick's for supper. Phillip Arlene and Corky were there also.

Sunday, April 2, 2000—cloudy and a skiff of snow, 20° to 33°. Tired today. We went to Allen and Roxanne's for dinner after they got home from church. Allen and I made plans to go fishing tomorrow morning. Karen brought over a couple magazines and a book "Danger Stalks the Land."

Monday, April 3, 2000—got an inch of snow then sunny, 23° to 42°. Allen took me fishing this morning. He caught one rainbow. No luck for me. We used Tom Huddleston's snowgos. Checked Odden's. Read papers. Did some odd jobs and target shooting. Went to Bob and Kahren's for a sunfish supper. Bart was there. Jim Manning, with chest pains, went to Glennallen Clinic, then Anchorage Hospital. They will do a triple bypass on his heart tomorrow morning.

Tuesday, April 4, 2000—three inches of snow, 28° to 43°. Jim came through the operation okay. George Perkins called and won't be here till next week to take care of Odden's house. I plowed our snow. My back is pretty bad. Cal Gilcrease visited.

Wednesday, April 5, 2000—got four inches of snow today, 22° to 33°. Plowed our snow and Manning's place. Started getting things ready for our trip to Minnesota. Bob Rudbeck drove Bart, Sam and I to Legion meeting in Glennallen. We saw a moose feeding on brush just east of Sam's place.

Thursday, April 6, 2000—cloudy and snow flurries, 10° to 28°. Hauled garbage to transfer site. It hadn't been plowed. Checked Odden's. Got some things ready for trip. Took five guns to Allen's to keep for me while we are gone. Got stuck on Allen's hill. We had to sand it before I could drive up it. When I was going to his place a small lynx was sitting in his driveway. It ran as I got closer. Ralph phoned this evening.

Friday, April 7, 2000—cloudy and snowing, 12° to 30s. Went to bank in Palmer, prescription in Wasilla, made copies in Anchorage. Went to VA. Had lunch. Spent evening and night at Griffith's.

Saturday, April 8, 2000—warm here at Dennis and Adrienne's this morning. A bite of breakfast. Dennis drove us to the airport. We saw lots of Canadian honkers on the way. Everything went well at airport. Quite a lot of the time we had a good view of mountains, forest, farms. Had a 100 mph tail wind. Plane did 678 mph at one time. Got to Mpls/St Paul one hour early. At 4:15 PM Nadia and Chuck met us and drove us to their place.

Sunday, April 9, 2000—sunny and windy here at Nadia's. Nadia copied and enhanced some quilt patterns for Sylvia. We went for a ride and Chuck and Nadia showed us a house they would like to buy. Quite large by our standards, built into a steep hillside. I helped Chuck replace a screw in the right rear fender well on his car. We phoned Linda Burns-Curtiss and told her when we would be coming to Iowa.

Monday, April 10, 2000—partly cloudy, cloudy and a little wind, 32° to 40°. We went to bank and checked the safe deposit box. Looked at a lot of old pictures. Went to grocery store for a steak supper tonight. Beverly phoned. Theresa phoned that they wouldn't be able to come over this evening.

Tuesday, April 11, 2000—some snow last night and flurries today with sunshine sometimes, 30° to 43°. Walked a couple miles today. Darcy phoned and Theresa phoned. Earl is sick.

Wednesday, April 12, 2000—cloudy, partly cloudy, snow, 32° to 34°. Walked over to Office Max and had a couple photos copied. One with Dad, Mom and possibly me, Grandpa and Grandma Wilkins. One with Uncle Ernie and a deer (doe) he had killed. Nice walk. Theresa phoned.

Thursday, April 13, 2000—mostly sunny, Minnesota was 32° to 60° in Iowa. We

118

got up early and went to Marion Iowa. Got "lost" two times. Phoned Kirt Curtess (Linda's husband) and got directions. They showed us their wood carving shop. Drove us to the Amana Colonies and showed us around there. Then to the "Ox Yoke" restaurant. There we met Bob Burns and sons Mike, Steve and Tony. Bob treated us to a great dinner and some great reminiscing. Came back here to Linda and Kirt's place. Tony brought over some of his carvings and played the guitar. Kirt and Linda gave us a grizzly bear figure that they had carved when they were in Alaska last February.

Friday, April 14, 2000—sunny and wind from south, 45° to 65°. Tony and his son came over. Visited a while then went out, took everyone to breakfast. Back at their place, Kirt and Linda set up Sylvia and Nadia to carve cottonwood bark into facial-head features of an old man. Kirt and Linda gave them a lesson on carving by taking them through each progressive step. Their carvings turned out very well. Really pleased Sylvia and Nadia. They sure had fun. Then we went across Cedar Rapids to Linwood Cemetery. There we found Dad's grave. Took pictures of me at the headstone. Then back to their house for a few moments then drove back to Mpls-St Paul to Nadia's place. Ordered pizza for supper.

Saturday, April 15, 2000—raw and chilly, cloudy, rain, cloudy, 35°. Went to the christening of great grandson Devin Jacob Woods (Darcy's son). Theresa went with us. We had a difficult time finding her house both coming and going. Also the church was hard to find. The ceremony was nice. Met Jason Woods' immediate family. Went to the reception after christening. That was easier to find.

Sunday, April 16, 2000—rain, ice and snow, 30° to 33°. Up early, got ready and went to Paul, Ruth and Steve's at Staples. Chuck wanted to get back to Mpls-St Paul. We visited here. Steve showed us a couple guns he had worked on.

Monday, April 17, 2000—cloudy, some light, snow, 30° to 34°. Went with Steve to Brainerd in the afternoon. He did some shopping. I couldn't find any long johns. We checked out the pawn shops and the hardware store's used gun rack in the morning. Lorraine Hanson visited us in late afternoon for a while.

Tuesday, April 18, 2000—cloudy, 48° misting rain, clearing in the afternoon and warmer. Walked up town. Sat around back at Paul's watching TV. Lorraine Hanson picked us up 1:00 PM and took us to lunch. Drove us around the area then to outlying and east to 64 and south to Harry and Neva McCoy's. Visited there. Then visited Fred and Ann Marolf. Back to Lorraine's new home for spaghetti supper. Then she drove us back to Paul's. Phoned Billmans. Patti gave me their address. Phoned Rollins, Steve drove us over and we have a nice visit with Allen, Lillian, Andy and Scott.

Wednesday, April 19, 2000—cloudy, sometimes rainy, 38° to 46°. Steve and I went to Randall (Red Wing shoe store) and looked at shoes, but didn't buy any. After lunch Steve, Paul and I went to Wadena to Bill's guns. He had a couple Romanian .22 Cal rifles but priced too high. We checked out the two hardware stores with no luck. Sylvia and I went through a lot of old farm receipts and papers. Pete, a friend of Steve's brought over a rusty rifle for Steve to cleanup.

Thursday, April 20, 2000—cloudy, sunny, 36° to 52°. Checked prices of comic books. Lorraine Hanson visited. Called Peter Achermann. He brought Clayton Geary to Tower pizza and Sylvia and I ate pizza with them. Sylvia did a little shopping at drug store. Then Steve drove his folks and us out south and west of Staples and looked at a house for sale. Saw ducks and quite a few deer.

Friday, April 21, 2000—cloudy, sunny and real nice, 40° to 65°. Steve and I went to hardware store and he bought some muritic acid to remove the bluing from Peter's rifle. He did it when we got back to house. Paul's boss visited. Walked a lot today. In the afternoon, we went to Swan Valley cemetery to Mildred's grave and grave of Paul and Ruth's daughter, Anitra. We watched pulp wood harvesting operation for a little while. Randy Hanson, Kevin Brown.

Saturday, April 22, 2000—sunny and nice breeze, 40° to 65°. We got ready and Steve drove his folks and us to Laura and Brads cabin on Eagle Lake, six miles from Emily. It's a really nice place and very new. Laura fixed good food, and we had a good time visiting and soaking up sunshine. Watched a movie before bedtime. Played games with great granddaughter Brittany who is nine years old. Saw large flock of big white bird with black wings.

Sunday, April 23, 2000—sunny and breeze, 50° to 70°. Spent a nice morning here at the lake home. A couple squirrels in the Norway pines. Laura took us on a little walk to see a "nest" in a tree which we identified as a "witch's broom". They drove us to their place in Rogers, Minnesota. They have a new, large, beautiful home. Nadia and Chuck came over and we ate a nice ham dinner. Read newspapers and watched some TV. It was Nadia's birthday.

Monday, April 24, 2000—sunny, some breeze, 50° to 70°. Took a walk. Watched Brittany roller blade. Loafed around the house. Chuck came over and drove Laura, Britt, and us to Nadia's place of employment. There we switched cars and left with Nadia for Beverly and Tyler's when she got off work. We stopped for supper at a buffet style place. At Bev's we all visited a while then Chuck and Nadia went home. Gave papers and pix to Beverly.

Tuesday, April 25, 2000—sunny, 50s to 75°. Walked over three miles. Read some magazines. I noticed that for some reason, I have double vision at over 25 feet today.

Wednesday, April 26, 2000—sunny and breeze, 50°s to 75°. Read, watched TV, watched Tyler play computer combat games. Tyler, Sylvia and I went to K-Mart and did a little shopping. Bev fixed supper and Sylvia made a cheesecake.

Thursday, April 27, 2000—cloudy, sunny, cloudy and sprinkles in evening, 60° to 75°. Loafed around the apartment. Walked over to mall and bought two pair glasses @ $1.00 each. Vanessa and Scott came over to visit. Bev fixed steak for supper and ice cream and cake. Vanessa brought her cat.

Friday, April 28, 2000—sunny and nice breeze, 57° to 73°. Walked over to Lyndale and circled back. Sylvia cleaned the refrigerator-freezer. Bev went to work and Tyler went to school. Planes taking off make lots of noise. Sylvia saw four geese fly over. I saw a crow and heard others.

Saturday, April 29, 2000—sunny, some breeze, 50° to 65°. About noon Beverly and I walked over to a HUD house for sale. Believing its price was $55,000 it looked fairly good. Back home it came up on computer, $110,000. What a disappointment. Tyler is having trouble with getting good info off that web site. We then walked a long way to an antique store and thrift store. We rode the bus back to Lyndale and the K-Mart. Back at home, we rested. After a while Tyler tried to bring up some properties, with incomplete results. It's Sylvia's birthday. Bev and I gave her cards and Nadia phoned. Tyler had a friend stay over.

Sunday, April 30, 2000—sunny, cloudy in evening, 50° to 70°. Went to grocery store for Sunday paper, rolls and bananas. Later Sylvia, Beverly and I shopped for groceries. She and Sylvia went to K-Mart later. I read newspaper. Really sleepy this evening.

Monday, May 1, 2000—sunny and nice, 46° to 70°. Walked around looking for a pair of shoes. Returned a K-Mart shopping cart. Crab apple blossoms are emerging.

Tuesday, May 2, 2000—sunny, some breeze very nice, 45° to 74°. Tried on the shoes at Red Wing store and the left one didn't fit. A repairman fixed a screen for Bev's apartment. I tightened up two of her plant stands. We went to Kentucky Fried Chicken for supper. Tyler's Dad, Kevin Volk, took him to soccer practice.

Wednesday, May 3, 2000—sunny and windy, 55° to 83°. Cloudy towards evening. Walked to hardware store and got two small bolts for Bev's plant stand. Theresa, Earl and Lee came over 1:30 PM and stayed till 7:30 PM. We had a good visit. They brought us a sundae and had supper here. We took pictures with flowering crab apple tree background.

Thursday, May 4, 2000—sunny and some breeze, 60° to 88°. Sylvia went shopping. Didn't do much today. Read some and watched TV, and sat out on the deck. After supper, Scott Beckett (Beverly's daughter Vanessa's husband) came and got Beverly and us, took us to their home and showed us around. We watched their wedding video, looked at pictures and had a piece of cake Vanessa had made.

Friday, May 5, 2000—sunny, cloudy, windy, sunny and calmer in evening, 67° to 89°. We started packing for the trip home. Theresa phoned. Nadia stopped by after work and had supper with us.

Saturday, May 6, 2000—mostly sunny and a pretty good breeze, 68° to 89°. Finished our packing. Showered for the trip. Bev phoned cab company. Visited with Beverly when she got up. We had an easy time at the ticket counter (no crowd). We were 1-½ hours early. The plane took off on time. Continued with flight to Anchorage. Just out of Mpls/St Paul we had thin clouds and could see fields and lakes. Then mostly cloudy till Alberta and BC. I saw lots of pure wilderness. The sight of that kind of country makes my heart beat fast. Somewhat later were a few roads and a pipeline. Ice on the rivers and lakes. Saw a small 15-18 house village. Very few buildings in the deep Rockies. Saw a winter cat trail (mining supplies?). Cloudy closer to AK. Saw a dense snow storm, Tazlina Lake, Nelchina Glacier, Lake Louise etc. Couldn't make out our Nelchina. Good landing at Anchorage. Adrienne and Dennis picked us up at airport. We off-loaded our luggage in our "Molly" car and left for home. Stopped in Palmer and got a few groceries. Got home and unloaded just before midnight. Nice to be home. Quite a bit of snow here. We have had a low of 2° to a high of 57° while we were gone.

Sunday, May 7, 2000—mostly sunny, some breeze, 29° to 49°. Saw eagle hunting in trees across lake four swans on lake. Raven's are flying a lot. A kestrel, gull, marsh hawk. Roxanne phoned that two hummingbird tried to get to blooming pansies through window glass!! Very unusual sight. Shut off the light in well. Polished some brass, Paul's, mine (Steve gave me).

Monday, May 8, 2000—mostly sunny, 26° to 52°. Phoned some neighbors and visited. Sylvia did a little in green house. We are resting up. We see snowshoe hares, ravens, raptor hawks. Shot one squirrel with pistol. Started reading a month's mail.

Tuesday, May 9, 2000—sunny, cloudy in evening, 30° to 46°. Wrote a couple letters. Sent off film to be developed. Put oil in car motor. Picked up and folded two traps. Started ATV. Cal and Mary visited. Put snowgo away. Plus did a few other jobs.

Wednesday, May 10, 2000—mostly sunny and a little windy, 27° to 42°. Shot a couple rabbits and a squirrel. Checked out the vac booster on truck and it isn't operating right. Haven't felt well today. Patti Billman visited in the evening. Ralph phoned, told about him and Jeff hunting bears.

Thursday, May 11, 2000—sunny, 22° to 51°. We went to Palmer, Wasilla, and Anchorage. Visited Lucky and Mary Beaudoin. Sylvia's doctor appointment was messed up, we have to go in Monday. I got a prescription filled at VA. We shopped K-Mart, Costco, Boondockers. Had a nice lunch at North Slope Café, and got cottonwood bark at the Sutton sawmill (for Sylvia's carvings).

Friday, May 12, 2000—partly cloudy, 29° to 48°. Allen visited in morning before we went to Glennallen on senior van. Paid telephone and electric bills. Had lunch and senior meeting. Got back home and senior van tranny quit. Ron called a wrecker to come and take it to Copper Center. Bought a salmon fishing rod and reel at a yard sale. It took 2-½ hours to clean it and get the reel working. Cost $12.50 for outfit and life vest.

Saturday, May 13, 2000—partly cloudy, 26° to 51°. Did some work on both the car and truck. Went to pick up trash from our mile of highway and someone had already picked it. Went to gravel pit. Saw two moose there. Something drove the flickers from nest box—kestrels? Worked some more on rod and reel. Removed snowplow from truck and parked it for the summer. Ed Farmer came over and looked at the vacuum assist on my truck.

Sunday, May 14, 2000—snowed all night and off and on all day (4+ inches), 28° to 36°. Some of snow melts when it lands. Took Sylvia to breakfast at Eureka. Brockman family was there, Denny Eastman's and Scott? and Bart Bartley. I accidentally left my lights on and ran the battery down. Lee Dudley came along and gave me a jump. Sam Weaver was with him. Later Lee stopped by to visit. Nadia gave Sylvia a Mothers Day call.

Monday, May 15, 2000—snow all night, 30° to 46°. All the new snow was melted off when we got back from Wasilla. Sylvia had her yearly visit with doctor. I didn't have an appointment to get my eyes tested so didn't get to have it done. We did some other shopping. Saw one yearling moose calf.

Tuesday, May 16, 2000—partly cloudy, nice, 36° to 51°. Checked car over. Shoveled snow north of house. Repaired a set of jumper cables. Visited Allen and Roxanne.

Wednesday, May 17, 2000—mostly sunny, 29° to 54°. Repaired the ladder for garage roof. Picked up some bullets that could be seen as snow berm recedes. Straightened up storage shed. Evaluated my old hip boots.

Thursday, May 18, 2000—partly cloudy, 32° to 55°. Our lake ice is melting quite fast. I put chicken wire netting over house and garage chimneys to keep ducks out. Put garage roof ladder back up there. Shot one rabbit. Tilled the small garden up by the house. Tore up my back doing it. Reloaded some 44 magnum brass with 300 grain cast bullets. Lubed some more bullets. Burned some lawn rakings and some brush. Henry phoned, he has kidney problems. "Bud" Smeltzer is making improvement. There are quite a few goldeneyes on our lake. Allen phoned and invited me to shoot some trap with him and Lucky. I declined because of my back.

Friday, May 19, 2000—mostly cloudy, 33° to 49°. Light rain, a shower of hail. My back is really sore. Rested a lot. Did put gas checks on some cast bullets and lube them. We went to Ellie Farmer's promotion exercise from 8th grade. Roxanne and Allen ask us to a family get together at the Rendezvous Café afterward. We saw two caribou bulls on our way home—horns about 16-18" long and in velvet.

Saturday, May 20, 2000—partly cloudy, small snow storm, 31° to 56°. Cast some 44 caliber bullets. Felt real bad at noon. BP and pulse was okay. Took a one hour nap. Got ready and picked Bart and Rosemary up and went to a supper the girl scouts put on at the Legion Hall. Very good. Snow, hail and rain on the way home. Saw a porcupine and shot it with 44 magnum. Gave Lucky some moose burgers. Visited Allen. Sylvia's package of wood carving tools came today.

Sunday, May 21, 2000—partly cloudy, 28° to 47°. Shot a rabbit this morning. Did some things for Sylvia's carving. Rebuilt the door on a lean-to. About half the ice is out on our lake.

Monday, May 22, 2000—mostly cloudy, 30° to 47°. We removed the temporary fuel line to Toyo stove. Hooked up the regular fuel line. I closed some ruts in the mud out by camper. Walked down to lake. Carried one sheet of plywood up to road. Put a 3/8" wide band saw blade on saw. Saw a little ermine with its summer coat.

Tuesday, May 23, 2000—mostly cloudy with sleet and rain showers, 33° to 49°. Started building a sharpening mandrel for Sylvia's wood carving tools. The lake ice is deteriorating rapidly. Kahren visited.

Wednesday, May 24, 2000—partly cloudy, scattered snow, rain showers, 32° to 46°. Up early and hunted porkies on Lake Louise Road and got one before breakfast. Got another porkie on the way over to Cal and Mary's for a visit. Saw his nice street rod. Visited Dimmicks, who are getting ready to hunt seals. Attached a new cord to an electric motor. Saw three wood cocks on Lake Louise Road.

After supper we saw Mark Brockman take his father-in-law, Mike across the lake in a small boat with a trolling motor. After landing, the father-in-law stalked over to a trail through the trees. There he saw the object of the hunt. A very large black bear lying down facing him. It rose up on its front feet for a better look and we saw the smoke come from the hunter's rifle and later the "report" of the shot. Both men walked into the trees. Shortly we saw the bear appear near the lake's shore. Then in a moment or two, we heard another shot. After a while the men got in the boat and came back across the lake. A while later they went back across the lake. Apparently they tried to track the bear then returned to this side of the lake. Allen says they think both shots missed the bear. Later in the evening, they went back across the lake and killed a smaller black bear with an 18 3/8" skull measurement.

Thursday, May 25, 2000—mostly cloudy, 29° to 48°. Some rain and snow showers blowing by. Did quite a bit on the tool-knife sharpener. Went to gravel pit to shoot and someone was already there. Did shoot a porcupine. There are lots of them. Cal stopped by and had a bite of supper with us.

Friday, May 26, 2000—snowing hard when I got up. 31° to 48°. Jeff Routt phoned and we had a good visit. Melted off later in the day. Went to lunch in Glennallen. Couldn't get any parts for the sharpener in town. Visited Mark and got the bear hunting story. Darrel phoned in evening. A porcupine walked through the house yard and I killed it with 44 magnum.

Saturday, May 27, 2000—mostly sunny, cloudy evening, 30° to 53°. Visited Allen in the morning. Went to gravel pit and shot one gallon jugs of water with .338 magnum offhand at varying yardages. Visited Bart Bartley. Set out a few little spruce trees, sprinkling in a few cranberry bushes. Picked up cast bullets that have melted out of snow berm. Polished some brass. The vacuum assist that Cal left me has a broken part. Bob Burns phoned.

Sunday, May 28, 2000—partly cloudy, 31° to 54°. Positioned the motor on the sharpener. Read some. Sylvia got home about 5:30 PM. We visited Elaine M, Rosemary B, and Mary G were there. Elaine is doing well.

Monday, May 29, 2000—partly cloudy, nice, 33° to 59°. We went to Legion Memorial Service at Glennallen. Very moving and glad we went. A prayer, a three-volley salute and taps at cemetery. A wreath cast on the waters of Moose Creek to signify those lost at sea in combat. Had lunch. They use native rifle men at Copper Center Cemetery so Sylvia and I went home. I pulled my old wire rope out of the brush. I'm giving it and cable clamps to Jay Gandy. Walked down to lake. Saw raven in area of the black bear kill. Ducks are breeding. An eagle hunts them. We saw a half dozen caribou along the highway today. Reloaded some .338 magnum cartridges.

Tuesday, May 30, 2000—partly cloudy, 29° to 59°. Saw young eagles chasing ducks. Tested soil in garden for PH "acidity." Went to lunch at Glennallen. Picked up some range brass. Visited Darrel and Brenda. Had my eyes tested by optometrist Grand Humphreys OD. He ordered glasses for me. Cleaned some brass when I got home. Ralph phoned.

Wednesday, May 31, 2000—cloudy and some showers, 33° to 57°. We put lime on lawn and fertilizer on lawn and garden. Allen, Kyle, and Nicki came over to till our garden. Allen did most of it. Sylvia and I put the T's in water line for garden and green house. I pushed a stiff wire 35' into basement and pulled the electric wire that heats the well in winter, in through the under ground pipe that contains the waterlines. Sure sore in lots of joints this evening. Allen, Kyle and Sammy came over and took a motor I had here home to put on Kyle's "Tote Goat," ATV. Three caribou towards east end of our lake.

Thursday, June 1, 2000—partly cloudy, rain showers going by, 39° to 57°. We left for Palmer, Wasilla and Sylvia's doctor appointment. Her thyroid isn't working right and needs a prescription. We saw two moose on the way in. Didn't get everything I needed in town, nice to be home again. Went to gravel pit for .338 magnum target practice.

Friday, June 2, 2000—partly cloudy and couple sprinkles, 38° to 62°. We went to lunch and shopping in Glennallen. Saw moose and caribou both ways. Sylvia and I planted potatoes. I raked the gardens smooth. Then worked on the wiring for light bulb for water well. Then modified the sharpener for Sylvia's tools. We went to Allen and Roxanne's for supper. All their kids were there.

Saturday, June 3, 2000—mostly sunny, very nice, 38° to 60s. Contact centered some rubber to bottom of the tool sharpener. Made a short cover for part of water line. Hauled garden tiller up to house. Put Stabil in snowgo fuel tank. Ralph got here mid afternoon. We went shooting at gravel pit. He put a new starter on his pickup after supper. Jeff Routt got here about 9:30 PM. We all had a good visit they stayed overnight here. Saw caribou bulls.

Sunday, June 4, 2000—sunny, 38° to 72°. We drove down Oil Well Road looking for a bear. No luck. Got back home. Had a late breakfast then we did a lot more target shooting and sighting in of rifles. Ralph and Jeff left mid afternoon. We saw two caribou bulls.

Monday, June 5, 2000—sunny, with breeze, 39° to 74°. I visited Lee Dudley. Made a "strop" for sharpening tools.

Tuesday, June 6, 2000—sunny, partly cloudy and windy, 48° to 77°. Went to gravel pit and shot targets for postal matches. Prepared some pistol brass for reloading. Coiled some 5/8" wire rope on a cable spool. Robins are carrying bugs in their beaks now.

Wednesday, June 7, 2000—partly cloudy, 39° to 70°. Started trimming and cutting up stove wood down in "hole." Starter rope pulled out and had to take recoil apart and retie knot in rope. Didn't feel well all day. Picked up Bart and went to Legion meeting. Gave some 130+ feet of 5/8" cable to Jay for his fish wheel.

Thursday, June 8, 2000—mostly sunny, 41° to 64°. Breezy morning and quiet by evening. Went to Glennallen. Ordered arbor adapter, mailed postal targets. Picked up my new glasses. Visited Darrel and Brenda. Cut up more wood in "hole." Chopped some grass and raked it out of gravel. Visited Allen and Roxanne. Kahren stopped by.

Friday, June 9, 2000—went to Glennallen, lunch, bank. Cut up some wood. Visited Allen and Roxanne.

Saturday, June 10, 2000—mostly sunny, some breeze, 39° to 72°. Lots of "no see ums" (tiny biting insects). Installed a buzzer to warn me if I leave car lights on. Finished cutting up the wood down in hole. Went to Cal's and got another vacuum brake assist. Cow moose walked east along lake, 10:00 PM.

Sunday, June 11, 2000—sunny, some breeze, 36° to 70°. Put the vacuum brake assist on the pickup. Got some wood up out of hole. David F. borrowed 4 foot level. Cast some .45 bullets and loaded brass for Jeff.

Monday, June 12, 2000—sunny and good breeze to blow bugs away, 39° to 72°. Worked on truck. Cast bullets and lubed them. Carried 4 armloads of wood up out of hole and used wheelbarrow to run them over to woodshed and stacked it. We went to Bob and Kahren Rudbeck's to a birthday party for Lisa NikiNiki's daughter, Grace.

Tuesday, June 13, 2000—shower in night, sunny and a good breeze today, 40° to 70°. Put another wheelbarrow of wood in the shed. We went to lunch in Glennallen then to Sylvia's eye doctor appointment. Road crews are still working on repairs. Worked on truck, couldn't get brakes to work. Ed and Chuck came over, found the problem, fixed it and brakes seem real good. Quite a relief for me. I'm grateful to them.

Wednesday, June 14, 2000—mostly cloudy and sprinkles in evening, 43° to 68°. Put another wheel barrow load of wood in shed. Burned a bunch of trash. Cast and lubed more bullets. Made up a tow rope for car. Checked alternator on car.

Thursday, June 15, 2000—cloudy and rainy till evening then clear and nice, 40° to 62°. Put more wood in shed. Wrote three letters and cast more bullets. Went to three gravel pits in evening. Only 4 brass, 1 pair sunglasses. No bears or varmints.

Friday, June 16, 2000—partly cloudy and a few showers, 39° to 55°. I got the last of the wood from the "hole" and in wood shed. Went to Glennallen shopping and lunch. Jim Manning and I went to TV repeater site on Tolsona Ridge. I had bought some electronic contacts cleanser in hopes of improving the area AK TV reception. Tried to bleed the truck brakes with no luck. Lubed more cast bullets.

Saturday, June 17, 2000—rain most of night and more today, 39° to 57°. We left for Gary Griffith's wedding in Anchorage at 9:00 AM. We did some shopping. Attended the wedding, then more shopping including an alternator for car. Got back home about 9:30 PM.

Sunday, June 18, 2000—partly cloudy, 40° to 61°. Put new alternator on car. Loaded some fishing gear and drove to Lake Louise but it was too windy to fish for lake trout. Visited Dan and Patti. Nadia, Bev and Theresa have phoned Father's Day greeting. Jim Manning came over to borrow a teaspoon of cayenne pepper. Beaut of an evening.

Monday, June 19, 2000—partly cloudy, windy in afternoon, 37° to 60°. Mowed our lawn. Hauled a few buckets of gravel and put around our well. Fussed with the truck brakes to no avail. Don't feel well. Nadia phoned Father's Day greetings.

Tuesday, June 20, 2000—partly cloudy, cloudy breezy, and partly cloudy, 37° to 58°. Started out to go fishing at Ryan Lake but it was too windy, so I visited Lee Dudley. Then we rode his swamp buggy out to Steve Mailly's. Visited then with Steve. Worked on truck. Finished cutting up wood alongside the switch back road. Hauled a few buckets of gravel. Saw a moose cow and calf at southeast corner of lake.

Wednesday, June 21, 2000—mostly cloudy, cloudy and rain in afternoon, 37° to 57°. Worked on truck brakes. They are fixed—haven't tested them yet. Couldn't get left rear wheel cylinder out. Got them "bled." My back has been real bad today. Sylvia has the crud. Cow and calf moose walked through our yard.

Thursday, June 22, 2000—partly cloudy, mostly sunny, 40° to 64°. Put some fertilizer on lawn. Cut and made a cardboard box to fit pool table light. Cleaned up ashes from burning brush last fall. Worked on Paul and Steve's brass. Moose cow and calf walked by the house again.

Friday, June 23, 2000—mostly sunny, one small shower, 45° to 72°. We went to senior meeting in Copper Center. Pd electric and got arbor adapter at Walt's. Finished putting arbor sharpening together. Made another strop for sharpening carving tools. Allen and Kyle came over for throttle cable. Mine not correct. Took some magazines to Mailly's. Met Karen's father Harvey and his wife (name?). Went fishing in Ryan Lake. Caught one small trout and released it.

Saturday, June 24, 2000—sunny, windy all afternoon, 42° to 72°. Did a few little jobs. Put Oakum in some house logs. Loaded brass for Paul. Allen visited in evening and I put some shoe goop repair on his shoe.

Sunday, June 25, 2000—sunny and breeze getting strong in evening, 44° to 75°. Melted down wheel weights and got 80 pounds of clean lead. Put a little more Oakum on house walls.

Monday, June 26, 2000—partly cloudy, some breeze, 47° to 74°. Made a measuring device firewood bundles. Lee Dudley visited. Put more Oakum in house logs. Returned a book and magazine to Kahren. Joie borrowed my canoe.

Tuesday, June 27, 2000—partly cloudy in the morning, clouded up and rained in the afternoon breeze also partly cloudy in evening, 51° to 73°. Did some caulking of house with Oakum. Lee Dudley stopped by for a few minutes. Didn't feel well today. Went down to Allen and Roxanne's. She tried to make an anniversary card and ran out of color ink in the copier. Had a nice visit anyway.

Wednesday, June 28, 2000—mostly cloudy, 50° to 62°. We have 1-3/4" rain. I planted a few trees and grass clumps on the cut bank along the switch bank road to lake. We went to Legion meeting at Glennallen and supper. Helped Jim Manning unload lumber.

Thursday, June 29, 2000—mostly cloudy, 49° to 62°. Sore back. Finished with Oakum on house. Sharpened Sylvia's carving knives on the arbor I built.

Friday, June 30, 2000—partly cloudy, couple light showers, 48° to 68°. We went to Glennallen for lunch and shopping. Sylvia mowed lawn, I wired a switch on the carving tool sharpener for her tools. A goldeneye drake is flying around looking in the duck nest near the house. A bohemian wax wing sits in the top of a tall spruce. Two flickers show interest in the next box. Jim Manning phoned, needed help unloading some plywood.

Saturday, July 1, 2000—partly cloudy, 48° to 70°. Some smoke in air. We had a garage sale, but didn't have many buyers, only two. Sylvia is sick with a flu of some kind. Chinked part of garage logs with Oakum.

Sunday, July 2, 2000—partly cloudy, 46° to 70°. Put more Oakum in walls of garage. Lee Penwell stopped by. After supper Charlie Trowbridge came over. We went down to his storage shed and hauled a few things he wants to take to Homer up here to Charlie's car. We had a good visit before bedtime.

Monday, July 3, 2000—mostly sunny, 42° to 73°. We rode the senior van to Copper Center, switched vans and went on to Chitna, picking up more seniors on the way. We ate our picnic lunch at the Native meeting Hall. Shopped at Chitna store and started home. Saw a moose feeding in Two Mile Lake. Got home around 7:30 PM, and went over to Henry and Sally's at Nelchina. (Charlie Trowbridge had left us a note that he was at their place.) Sam was over there also. Visited a while and came home. Then Charlie and I drove ATV to Charlie's storage shed, picked up more things he needs in Homer and loaded the same in his car. I cut some limbs from around two nest boxes as ducks are showing interest. Roxanne and Sammy came over and she visited awhile. Then Charlie and I visited a couple hours—until 12:20 AM.

Tuesday, July 4, 2000—sunny, 51° to 73°. Got to Glennallen too late to see the parade. Only one couple came to our garage sale this afternoon–no sales. Cut some weeds and brush and trimmed more limbs off two spruce trees and hauled them off. Cut larger entrance holes in two nesting boxes to accommodate some bigger ducks that were trying to find a nesting site. Did some reading and studying on scout rifle. Allen brought us watermelon.

Wednesday, July 5, 2000—extremely beautiful sunrise, 46° to 66°. Then rain showers off and on all day. Did a little caulking on garage. Got a letter from James McLellan and Bob Burns phoned.

Thursday, July 6, 2000—partly cloudy to almost clear in afternoon, 46° to 71° and lots of smoke from Tanana and Denali forest fires. A young kestrel survived crashing into one of our house windows. Fixed a box for Darrel and Brenda's presents. Sylvia mowed the yard and fertilized garden. Cleaned up garage and put things back in order. Started making a hand rail for the arctic entry.

Friday, July 7, 2000—sunny, 48° to 76°. Went to Glennallen, bank, Post Office, shopping, hardware store, and lunch. A moose walked through our yard. Reworked arctic entry steps. Started building a pipe hand rail to assist Elaine when she visits us.

Saturday, July 8, 2000—mostly sunny, some breeze, 48° to 75°. Jim Manning and I cleared some downed trees from the trail up on Slide Mountain.

Sunday, July 9, 2000—mostly sunny, breeze and very nice, 48° to 76°. Did more work on the railing for the arctic entry steps. Patched some holes in a pair of Helly-Hanson rain pants. Had to scrub them first.

Monday, July 10, 2000—cloudy sprinkles here, 47° to 66° and rain in Glennallen—I went there and cleaned the ceremonial rifles at Legion Post. They need lots of work. Got pipe and fittings for another railing at arctic entry. Stopped at Darrel's. Saw Brenda at work. We ate supper with Jim and Elaine. The older neighborhood kids are swimming and water skiing on our lake this evening using wet suits.

Tuesday, July 11, 2000—mostly cloudy and a little rain, 48° to 66°, and the bugs are bad. Visited Cal and Mary. Cleaned two legion rifles. Worked on the two railings and got one installed at arctic entry.

Wednesday, July 12, 2000—mostly cloudy, rain in night, 59° to 69°. Lots of smoke from the forest fires. Looked rainy most of day. Found a rain soaked note book in yard. Mowed dock area at lake, also in front of garden and woodshed. Sharpened mower blade. Finished the second railing for arctic entry.

Thursday, July 13, 2000—mostly cloudy, rain in night, 46° to 58°. Kyle won't need to borrow the tiller so I cleaned it and put it in shed. Fit some cartridges to rifle chamber. Stiff and sore today. Henry and Sally took us to the Carriage House at Gakona for dinner tonight. Very good and lots of good conversation. Very enjoyable evening. Saw a spruce hen along the road.

Friday, July 14, 2000—mostly cloudy, a little rain, 45° to 68°. Went to Glennallen. Paid phone bill, had lunch. I served on the rifle squad for a memorial service for Sam Yates. Put a little more Oakum in garage walls. Shot a pesky squirrel.

Saturday, July 15, 2000—mostly sunny, 45° to 69°. Took ATV to 133 mile pull-out. Drove ATV back to Old Man Creek on the blueberry picking trail. Had a 60-power telescope along and got a good look at two separate land features I had been curious about since last fall. Both turned to be outcroppings of rock.

Talked to Allen on way home. Rested, then we picked up Bart and Rosemary and went to Legion dinner. George, I think his name was, rode with us back as far as his place on Tolsona Creek. Saw an eagle attempting to catch a duck.

Sunday, July 16, 2000—mostly cloudy and sprinkles, 45° to 58°. Called Dale and talked to Jeff and Ralph also. Called Dave J. with the name of AK Tannery. Shoveled some gravel. Went with Jim to Tolsona Ridge to try to fix TV transmission. Spent a lot of time today looking for a quart of penetrating oil that I have misplaced.

Monday, July 17, 2000—sunny and nice breeze, fewer bugs, 43° to 66°. Chinked garage logs with Oakum. Visited Allen in evening.

Tuesday, July 18, 2000—partly cloudy, sprinkles, 44° to 61°. Finished chinking the west side of garage. Shot some targets. Kahren brought her grandson over and asked to use the Slide Mountain trail.

Wednesday, July 19, 2000—partly cloudy, sprinkles, 44° to 61°. It's 12:00 AM midnight and the sun is shining north of Slide Mountain, reflected down off clouds and has cast a golden glow on south side of lake.

Thursday, July 20, 2000—sunny and breezy, 43° to 65°. Finished chinking. Brought some reject gravel home and filled two low places in driveway. Picked up some brass and polished it. Polished some 7 mm Remington magnum and a few bullets. Nadia phoned.

Friday, July 21, 2000—partly cloudy, 43° to 63°. Rode VA van to Anchorage for a check up and refill of prescriptions. Got a few groceries. We expect Ralph and Jeff this evening. They arrived about 9:30 and stayed the night. We talked till 1:00 AM.

Saturday, July 22, 2000—partly cloudy and some morning fog, 44° to 58°. We chronographed several kinds of .22 caliber ammo, and shot some targets. Then went to gravel pit and did a bunch of target practice. Ralph and Jeff ate supper with us and then went over to Manning's to electric wire their new addition. They brought lots of food. Beautiful evening.

Sunday, July 23, 2000—partly cloudy, few showers going by, 47° to 68°. Ralph and Jeff took us to breakfast at Eureka. Allen, Roxanne, Lucky, Tom, and Charlie came into the café later. On way home, I showed Ralph and Jeff the band saw mill that Allen built. The guys went back to town and I loaded some 45 ACP using the bullets Ralph gave me. Weeded a little in garden and moved some dirt up the grade in garden. Lee Dudley stopped by and visited.

Monday, July 24, 2000—partly cloudy, shower in evening, 46° to 67°. We went to Palmer and got some more cottonwood bark for Sylvia. Went to the avalanche area on old Glenn Highway—no luck there. Did a little shopping and tried to sell hoops at a craft store. No luck.

Tuesday, July 25, 2000—partly cloudy, sometimes looking like rain, 44° to 67°. We took the three upstairs windows out to the garage. Striped paint, Sylvia put on primer coat, I painted the hardware. A black bear got into our garbage mid morning while we were working. Took garbage to transfer site. Reloaded some 30 br for target practice.

Wednesday, July 26, 2000—partly cloudy and showers in between, 46° to 64°. Cal came over and we loaded some cartridges for him. The bear was back last night. He turned over the burn barrel and scattered the ashes.

Thursday, July 27, 2000—nice day with shower in evening, 45° to 65°. Did a few welding jobs. Started building a shooting bench (cut out the parts).

Friday, July 28, 2000—partly cloudy and windy in the afternoon, 44° to 59°. Cut out parts for another shooting bench. Got one put together, and second one is started. Then wind got strong and three spruce trees growing together at east end of house acted like they would blow over onto the house, so I put a long rope and chains from high in the tree, and with the pick-up, pulled three tree clumps over in a safe direction. Cut down a lot of tall grass fire wood. Our new phone quit working. Found two more sets of bear tracks here.

Saturday, July 29, 2000—partly cloudy and windy all afternoon, 37° to 63° with winds gusting to 30 MPH. Trimmed the trees that I took down yesterday. Hauled the trimmings to Ed Farmer. Cut into blocks and split and stacked the wood in shed. Helped Allen with his pavilion roof for a while, then went back to Allen's campground for a picnic supper and visiting in the evening.

Sunday, July 30, 2000—mostly sunny, 37° to 61°. Finished the second shooting bench. Got the ATV ready for a trip over Ballanger Pass. Kahren brought Sylvia back mid afternoon. Soon after, Roxanne phoned and asked us to come over and shoot some clay pigeons. Bob had a couple shotguns and shells, Allen had a thrower. Almost everyone shot quite well. Lots of fun. The kids enjoyed shooting. Kim fired one shot—her first ever. We had a picnic plate and sat around the fire and visited.

Monday, July 31, 2000—sunny and nice with breeze, 36° to 67°. Loaded some gear, rifle and Suzuki in pickup and drove to Ballanger Pass Trailhead. Trail was dry and in very good shape. Shot some parka squirrels. There are many of them, and will make easy fox food. Drove and walked a ways on Fossil Creek. Saw some caribou tracks along Pass Creek and Alfred Creek. The water is fairly low. Saw a young ptarmigan, huge eagle, young magpies. Noticed some changes in the creeks. Very good trip. Ralph phoned. Jeff phoned. Ron brought over some maps from Glennallen when I wasn't here. Saw some Dall sheep (too far away to see if they were rams or ewes) over west of Wood Creek.

Tuesday, August 1, 2000—sunny, light breeze, 43° to 66°. Pulled over two stumps, lots chopping and chain saw work. Cut seven stove blocks out of them, then split and stacked the wood. Re-hung the newly painted upstairs windows.

Wednesday, August 2, 2000—partly cloudy, 37° to 64°. Burned the remainder of the stumps in the yard all day. Cut a lot of fire weed with the hand scythe. Went to Legion Post meeting with Bart.

Thursday, August 3, 2000—mostly sunny and a little breeze, 41° to 70°, and the mosquitoes are bad. I walked over to the Nelchina River bank. It is running lots of water. Finished burning out the stumps. Put subsoil in holes and covered them with topsoil, grass seed, and water.

Friday, August 4, 2000—mostly cloudy and light showers. Went for lunch and to do some shopping in Glennallen. Drained and flushed our water heater. Pulled pig weeds out by the burn barrel.

Saturday, August 5, 2000—partly cloudy day, cloudy in the evening, 45° to 65°. Pulled pig weed, and cut weeds with hand scythe. Hoed Kahren's two rows of vegetables.

Sunday, August 6, 2000—mostly cloudy, little rain shower, 46° to 61°. Got some camp gear ready. Made a spatula handle. Reworked rifle carrier on pack frame. Bob Rudbeck came over to have some wood turned on my lathe.

Monday, August 7, 2000—mostly sunny, scattered showers. Pulled a few weeds, sighted in rifle. Went with Jim Manning to Glennallen and got moose and sheep harvest permits. Gathered some more hunting gear. Borrowed some rug doctor. Visited Cal and Mary Gilcrease.

Tuesday, August 8, 2000—mostly sunny, 43° to 63°. Continued getting ready to go hunting—putting air in tires, etc. Carried food and gear to garage. Charlie Trowbridge came about 4:00 PM (after supper) and we loaded the trailer and Suzuki so we will be ready to go in the morning.

Wednesday, August 9, 2000—partly cloudy, 43° to 60°. Charlie and I took our time leaving for Squaw Creek Trailhead. Unloaded ATV and trailer. Two BLM ladies who were mapping, documenting camp sites, cabins etc. by GPS, started out ahead of us. We met up with them several times. I got discouraged with the trail and was concerned about getting back out. We turned around to go back and shortly met Allen Farmer and his sons, David and Kyle. Went on to a camp site on the creek leading to the sheep hunting area we wanted. Good supper and visiting.

On the way in, we saw griz, moose, caribou and sheep tracks. Also saw a guide, wrangler, and hunter riding one horse and rest mules. Saw a few sheep high on the mountains. At the campground, we put up our tent and the boys built a small fire. We had supper and a nice visit. Allen and Charlie walked up on the upper bench and glassed ewes and lambs.

Thursday, August 10, 2000—nice day, a few afternoon showers. Up early, breakfast and walked up creek. I was last in line and spotted a pair of horns from a 5-yr-old ram. We rested awhile at the first fork in creek. Allen and boys went to the right. Charlie and I took the left fork. We jumped 15 ptarmigan right away. Saw miscellaneous sheep bones and tufts of hair. Charlie spotted what was left of a tiny moose calf, some rabbit feet, and lots of interesting rocks. I picked up quartz with crystals and two sheep bones. Saw three eagles, no sheep. On the way back to camp, we jumped a nice caribou bull. At camp Allen wanted to go back out to "5 mile cabin". He used my tire pump for a flat tire. We broke camp and got about a mile from 5 mile, when Allen spotted a Toklat sow griz with two big cubs (2 yr old?) running hard, chasing a cow moose. She ran that cow 1-½ miles while we watched. From camp, we saw five running rams, and a couple ewes with lambs. Also saw a tent and two hunters way up, near the top of the mountain in a cirque. Charlie fixed supper again, and we slept in the cabin.

Friday, August 11, 2000—partly cloudy, 37° to 67°. Allen and I walked across Squaw Creek and up on a low ridge to an old trail. Glassed for sheep, saw 11, none legal. Ate breakfast. Loaded up gear, pumped Allen's flat tire back up, and drove out to trailhead. Got ATV high centered a few times in mud holes. Stopped to glass the mountains. At trailhead, loaded ATV in pick-up and ATV trailer on my snowgo trailer and returned home. Unloaded ATV trailer. Unpacked and put most of the stuff away. Hung tent to dry. One tent pole needed repair, fixed it. Ralph phoned to see how the hunt went. Sylvia had an interview with a reporter for the "Senior Voice" of AK newspaper. She enjoyed it and felt it went well. Charlie and I started getting ready for a hunt tomorrow.

Saturday, August 12, 2000—very nice day, 47° to 67°. Charlie and I drove to trailhead and went over Ballanger Pass and down Pass Creek to Alfred Creek. Saw four hunters. Got to creek a lower end of gorge. We walked north gaining altitude all the time and reached the board and tar paper cabin. The sluice is gone, someone may have burned it in the stove. We saw three sheep on the way there. Charlie climbed higher, but did not find sheep. Found some rock specimens, and we did see three sheep south, across Alfred Creek. We walked back to ATV and drove out. Along Pass Creek, we saw a really nice crossfox. A mile from trailhead we met a nice young couple hunting ptarmigan. Unloaded gear at home and had supper.

Sunday, August 13, 2000–sunny, partly cloudy and windy, rain, 44° to 69°. We went to Mendeltna service on the lawn at Allen and Roxanne's campground. Potluck afterwards. Got to visit with lots of folks. Tired today. Ian Mailly phoned for rifle advice.

Monday, August 14, 2000–sunny, cloudy, then high north wind in evening, 47° to 61°. Washed Suzuki and trailer. Replaced a repair patch on tent. Repaired tent bag. Soaked inside of sheep horn with Clorox solution. Worked on car also. Rotated two front tires. The wind blew the diving platform across the lake and the boys pulled it back to this side.

Tuesday, August 15, 2000–cloudy, 34° to 47°. Worked on the little loading dock. Picked blueberries in the afternoon–Kahren went with us. Checked some rifle loads for accuracy at gravel pit.

Wednesday, August 16, 2000–sunny, 38° to 60°. Worked on kitchen door lock. Went to gravel pit and practiced with the .308 Winchester and cast bullets. Pulled weeds in garden, hilled beets.

Thursday, August 17, 2000–sunny, clouds in evening, 33° to 64°. Scrubbed sheep horns with bleach. Test scrubbed two logs in garage wall and did a couple other small jobs. We took Kahren with us and picked blueberries along the site road.

Friday, August 18, 2000–cloudy and rain, 47° to 52°. Had lunch and went to Post Office in Glennallen. The van had a flat tire on the way home. Ron changed it.

Saturday, August 19, 2000–partly cloudy with numerous showers, 38° to 55°. Had a flat tire on car, but couldn't plug the hole. Polished some brass. Phoned Harold D. He phoned back. Tried to call Theresa.

Sunday, August 20, 2000–partly cloudy, 33° to 58°. Hauled some gravel and rebuilt loading dock and area. Did some small jobs. Worked on 06 brass in evening.

Monday, August 21, 2000–partly cloudy, a shower here, 37° to 55°. Repaired hi lift jack, and windshield wiper on truck. Then we went to Site Road mile 118.

No luck fishing, so I helped Sylvia pick blueberries. About 2:00 PM we could see dark clouds and rain showers all around so we headed home. Drove through intense hail and rain in a couple showers. Planted four small trees after supper. Trimmed 06 brass. Allen brought over his "sawzal" for me to use.

Tuesday, August 22, 2000—cloudy and rain, snow on Slide Mountain which melted off with rain in the afternoon, 36° to 46°. We went to vote in Glennallen. Then lunch and shopping. Started wiring in a light fixture over the basement stairs.

Wednesday, August 23, 2000—mostly sunny, very nice, 31° to 56°. Finished wiring the light for basement stairs. Chopped a little brush from garden fence. Allen is going to fix that tire for me.

Thursday, August 24, 2000—most cloudy, but very nice, 34° to 54°. Went to gravel pit to shoot and forgot the ammo, so came back and worked on hi lift jack and cleaned handyman jack. Changed oil and filter in car. Replaced a board on snowgo trailer and put Thompson's water seal on all the wood. Some years ago I forced open our safe. Today I fixed the damage. Allen and David brought over the "O" ring for me. Jim Manning borrowed our Shop Vac. Rain shower at bedtime.

Friday, August, 25, 2000—mostly sunny, 38° to 50°. We went to Copper Center (Kluti Kaah) to senior elders meeting and lunch. Had moose nose soup, roast, mashed taters etc. Did some shopping. Later, brought safe into basement. Sorted and filed the important papers. Laura and Brittany phoned. Nice long call.

Saturday, August 26, 2000—sunny, frost on everything, 28° to 54°. Ground froze on top. Wanted to target shoot in gravel pit but someone camping there. Cut a lot of brush. Split big stump in three pieces, loaded it and brush on pickup. Build a frame and tarp to cover Sylvia's peas. She canned the beets today. Sharpened the chain saw, adjusted its carburetor.

Sunday, August 27, 2000—cloudy, light rain most of day, 38° to 51°. Read a lot, watched TV. Kahren came over with a nice piece of silver salmon and we ate some for supper.

Monday, August 28, 2000—mostly sunny, very nice, 41° to 56°. Sylvia went to state fair on senior van. I went to Glennallen and had CMP disclaimer notarized. Mailed CMP application. Had lunch at Rendezvous café. Picked up brass at rifle range. Visited Darrel and Brenda. Cleaned brass at home and sorted it.

Tuesday, August 29, 2000—cloudy and rain on west side of the pass, 34° to 57°. We went to Wasilla. Exchanged faulty telephone at Wal-Mart and shopped there. Exchanged a pair of shoes at Fred Meyer store. Did some other shopping. Got home in good time.

Wednesday, August 30, 2000—cloudy, partly cloudy in evening, windy in morning, 31° to 51°. I made a bore guide for cleaning 03A3 and similar .30 – 06 rifles. Back hurts, joints also. Sharpened buck knife.

Thursday, August 31, 2000—beautiful day, 31° to 50s. Worked at getting gear ready to go goose hunting with Allen and Kyle. Allen got off work at 2:00 PM. He and Kyle got to our place about 4:30. Sylvia sewed some buttons on a shirt for him. Kyle got some 5-minute epoxy at Dave Johnson's and got his glasses repaired. We parked at the trailhead near Tex Smith Lake. Trail has lots of water in it. We got through all of it. Stopped at our preferred campsite. Larry Phyfe and Claire White and friends were camped there. We continued on to high knob just west of Seismic Junction. Saw black bear tracks in trail and a small, recently "moose rubbed" spruce tree, with fresh velvet hanging on it. We got camp set up with a few minutes of daylight left. From here, we can see Alaska Range, Wrangles, Chugach and Talkeetna Mountains, Tazlina Lake, Lake Louise and Susitna, Crosswind and Fish Lake with a multitude of small lakes all around.

Friday, September 1, 2000—cloudy and light rain on tent, mid 30s to 50°. Woke up early, but we dislike getting up and out in the rain. Allen and Kyle sleep on his "otter" rig. We do get going and walk east on a sharp ridge glassing for game. Moose must be three browtine or 50-inch spread or spike fork. Allen's caribou must be a bull. Allen saw two cow caribou. Back at camp we breakfast, then try to find the bull moose who rubbed his velvet off. We went separate ways. I got turned around but figured it out and came out on Seismic—albeit a half mile from my intended spot. Allen and Kyle got to walking in circles and came out on a different seismic but not a long ways from where we had parked the ATV's. I talked to Larry Phyfe, glassed for moose and back in camp for a nap. Got re-hydrated and rested up. We ate supper and walked towards a new area after parking ATV's. Crossed two ridges and to top of the third. No moose sign there. Much rain moving towards us. That and concern for fog prompted us to go back to ATVs and ultimately, to camp. Built a fire and dried some clothes in a light sprinkle, then to bed.

Saturday, September 2, 2000—no frost, rain in night and breezy, cool this morning and still breezy. Allen is discouraged at the lack of moose sign. We decide to go home. Sure enough, sun comes out and would have dried the bottom end of my damp sleeping bag. We load up. Stop and visit with campers on our way back out. Everything goes well. Load onto trucks and trailers at highway. Stop at KROA for a hamburger and on home. Unload gear, hang tent and sleeping bag to dry.

Sunday, September 3, 2000—mostly cloudy, low clouds and fog, light rain, 35° to 51°. Put truck and ATV in garage and ATV trailer under roof. My back is very bad—all night and all day today. Tired and took a couple naps. Read and watched TV. Cleaned three Garand clips. Shortened binocular strap.

Monday, September 4, 2000—partly cloudy, some showers, 39° to 52°. Did a few odd jobs. Repair boots and grease them. Read and research. Back is sore, but better. Allen visited, then we drove to mile 121 looking for moose, saw two cows.

Tuesday, September 5, 2000—partly cloudy, fog early, 30° to 52°. Sylvia had a doctor appointment in Wasilla. We did a little shopping. Watched for a legal moose to shoot, both going and coming, with no luck.

Wednesday, September 6, 2000—cloudy, rainy all day, 39° to 49°. Back hurts. Legs hurt. Didn't do anything today.

Thursday, September 7, 2000—rain till noon, sun came out about 2:00 PM, partly cloudy and windy in evening, 35° to 50°. New snow on mountains all around us. Very, very white and bright. Visited Ed this morning. He gave me four storage cans. I gave him a lead on airplane and adjusted the pilot light on a cook stove of his. Hauled some sand to be used for storing carrots.

Friday, September 8, 2000—snowing at 6:00 AM till noon, mostly cloudy afternoon, 32° to 45°. Snow melted. We went to Glennallen on senior van. Had lunch, paid telephone bill, cashed checks and did a little shopping. Back home Jim borrowed our shop vac. We dug two rows of potatoes, 4+ 5-gallon buckets, washed them and put them out to dry off in the basement. Fairly nice this evening.

Saturday, September 9, 2000—sunny and nice, 26° to 50°. We dug the last two rows of potatoes and got 5 buckets. Pulled all the carrots, washed everything on the lawn with hose. Carried everything into basement. Sylvia bedded carrots in damp sand. Spuds are drying off. Folded tent. Painted three ammo cans.

Sunday, September 10, 2000—mostly cloudy, variable breeze, sprinkle in evening, 32.9° to 43°. Started building a mini sluice for Ron Beshaw. Took down the tarp for frost shelter from over the garden peas.

Monday, September 11, 2000—cloudy, then sunny and nice, partly cloudy in evening, 32° to 52°. Drove to mile 133 and back early this morning and didn't see a moose. Worked on mini sluice and annealed some 30-06 mil brass. Took garden and green house "T's" out of water line. Cleaned 3006 primer pockets.

Tuesday, September 12, 2000—mostly cloudy and showers all around us, 32° to 48°. Road hunted real early. Visited Cal. Sprayed wax on house and garage roof. Went up Slide Mountain on ATV. No luck glassing for moose. Moved three large diameter logs and 3 small diameter logs into a hole in trail. After supper we drove the road west again, road hunting with no luck.

Wednesday, September 13, 2000—partly cloudy, 27° to 46°. Didn't feel well. Took a couple naps. Did a few little things. Sylvia picked first of cranberries. Ralph Fuson drove in about 4:00 PM with pizza for supper. Then we went to mile 124 and tried to call in a bull moose—no luck but we did get a howling response from a coyote. A swan flew low over us giving a low one syllable call.

Thursday, September 14, 2000—mostly cloudy, some sun, 33° to 50°. Tried to call moose near Tahneta Lake. No luck. Hunted on way home to breakfast. Drove to Lake Louise Road, then down Oil Well Road to Mendeltna Creek. Walked the creek a little ways and came upon a salmon that a bear had caught and only ate a tiny bit of the head. Jumped a hen mallard. Couldn't shoot, as creek was too high to wade and retrieve duck. Called moose there after eating lunch. No luck but did hear something circle down wind of us and then leave. We drove 2-3 miles back toward Lake Louise Road and called again at another place with no luck. Then shortly, we met Jim Luce and his wife on road. We saw a nice meat bull caribou near Odden's and near the creek. Back home we ate supper, then went back to Tahneta to call moose again. Saw a beaver, two flying swans, no luck calling moose. After it was quite dark, I spotted a moose along the road on the way home. It ran away before we got a good look at it. It's been a great day.

Friday, September 15, 2000—partly sunny, 34° to 47°. Tried calling moose in two places. Ralph heard a cow respond once. Then went to Lake Louise Lodge and Ralph bought hamburgers. Didn't see any game on the road. He did some wiring for Mannings in afternoon. Kyle brought over a moose calling tape for us to watch and had supper with us. After supper we went west of Eureka, parked in a gravel pit, walked over a hill and called from there. Saw a cow moose, no bulls. Moved to another place and didn't get a response. Saw a moose feeding in ditch when coming home in dark.

Saturday, September 16, 2000—cloudy, 33° to 45°. Early morning called moose—no luck. We shot rifles over the chronograph for load information. Ralph went over to Mannings and helped them. After supper we drove over 30 mile highway one way—no moose. Some hunter were parked where we have been parking to go call moose so we moved east near Mendeltna in a gravel pit and did some calls and hope for a legal moose to be there in morning. Early this morning the light was reflecting off the Chugach ice field on the bottom of the clouds, a kind of blue tint.

Sunday, September 17, 2000—cloudy and snow showers, 35° to 41°. Ralph and I went to Mendeltna gravel pit and called but no moose came in. After breakfast, we waited for Dale and Heidi to show up. A while after they got here, Jeff stopped in. Had a good visit about hunting, guns, shooting, taxidermy etc. Dale brought a tanned lynx hide to Ralph. He wants a life size mount with a ptarmigan in its mouth. I got some copies made at Mannings from a book of Ralph's. He went back to Fairbanks. I washed ATV.

Monday, September 18, 2000—sunny, very nice, 24° to 41°. Rested by putting together a mini sluice I am building for Ron Beshaw. In the afternoon, I walked west a mile down a ridge towards the river hunting moose. There was a moose on the ridge ahead of me, though all I saw of it was a fresh pile of pellets. Never saw the moose. Found a bungee cord along the road. A spruce hen picked gravel in our lane both morning and evening. Both Cal and Kahren brought plants to Sylvia to care for. Lake was glass smooth this afternoon and evening.

Tuesday, September 19, 2000—sunny, a little ice on east end of our lake, 22° to 49°. Slept late. Went to gravel pit and hunted south and east. Called for moose—no luck. I did find a box of 12-gauge steel shot shells. Back home, hauled two ATV trailer loads gravel in to fill low spots in the trail to well. Ate supper at Allen and Roxanne's.

Wednesday, September 20, 2000—mostly sunny, 23° to 49°. Put away most of big game hunting gear swept out the storage shed. Hauled ashes and garbage to transfer site.

Thursday, September 21, 2000—sunny, with clouds developing in evening. Mounted snow plow and pushed some dirt-gravel into a low place out at beginning of our lane. Leveled it off and drove on it to pack it. Denny Eastman stopped to visit. Moved some dirt in lower garden and raked the potato patch. Large grey owl flew by house.

Friday, September 22, 2000—sunny, cloudy evening, 39° to 59°. Gave Ron a mini sluice. Went to senior meeting and lunch. Paid electric bill. Shopped some groceries. Raked some spruce cones, burned trash. Allen came over with two dozen fresh eggs and visited. An eagle flew by south windows. Then Bob and Kahren came over to get some CAWL tickets. They gave Sylvia some green tomatoes. They are leaving to hunt geese in Saskatchewan Monday morning.

Saturday, September 23, 2000—rain started 5:30 AM and rained all day, 35° to

40s.

Sunday, September 24, 2000—little rain, cloudy all day, 36° to 42°. Didn't do much today. Write, read and TV. Kahren sent some jars up to Sylvia.

Monday, September 25, 2000—cloudy all day and sprinkles of rain, 35° to 51°. Did exercises and walked down to the lake and back. Wrote three letters. Carried gun, shells and gear down to canoe and went out to try for a duck. No luck, they are really wild. Organized some of my M1 Garand notes. Went over to Jims and made some copies and visited.

Tuesday, September 26, 2000—snowed four inches last night, 32° to 40°. Lots of it melted today. May get more tonight. It slid off both house and garage roofs. I shoveled it from east side because I walk there. Twisted my left hip joint doing it. Looked for ducks on our side of lake with no luck. Did a few chores. Cleaned snow off the car. Recessed the striker plate for the door going upstairs. Works fine now. Did my exercises.

Wednesday, September 27, 2000—6" snow last night and today and still snowing hard, 29° to 32°. I phoned CMP about my rifle order. I must now join AK CMP Association and send in a photocopy of my card. So I made arrangements to join. Removed summer tires off the car and put winter tires on. Brought truck tires and rims over to car. Moved burn barrel, covered ATV with tarp in shed. Walked down to lake, no ducks nearby. Swans flying down the valley.

Thursday, September 28, 2000—got ten more inches of wet snow, 28° to 34°. Plowed snow here and some at Manning's. Shoveled some here and off camper. Put air in car tires, thawed ice off windows and covered windshield with piece of tarp. Did enough work today. Sylvia cooked a nice meal and asked Jim and Elaine over to eat with us. Nadia phoned to talk to Sylvia about the article that was in "Senior Voice."

Friday, September 29, 2000—sunny, 15° to 33°. There is a thin layer of ice on three quarters of the lake. The swans and their signet are still here as well as a few ducks. I shot a rabbit for meat today. We went to Glennallen for lunch. Got stamps at Post Office.

Saturday, September 30, 2000—partly cloudy, 21° to 36°. Shoveled snow off north side of wood shed. Shot two spruce hens for meat. Another pair of swans with a signet is on our lake. A small flock of swans stopped to rest a while. Read some. We took a gift to TJ Huddleston and Tonya's wedding reception. Had a nice dinner and visited with people we know.

Sunday, October 1, 2000—sunny today, 10° to 30°. Walked down to the lake—

no ducks. Cleaned snow off top of well. Henry Johnson visited. He wants me to look after their house and fish-well etc., while they see Sally's mother and Bud in Michigan. He went flying this evening. Must have been very pretty up that high.

Monday, October 2, 2000—sunny, 2° to 27°. Plowed some snow, then removed plow from truck. Started snowgo. Shoveled snow. Checked oil, and gassed truck. Turned on 100 watt bulb in well. Two swans and signets have left, one pair and signet still here. Lake is frozen over. Signet tries to flap its wings. Parents call and encourage it by example.

Tuesday, October 3, 2000—sunny, 1° to 29°. Sylvia and I both do not feel well. Got a nice call from Beverly and nice letter from Paul. Checked Henry and Sally's house. The drama here is the two swans trying to get the signet to fly. It flaps its wings and runs on the ice but doesn't get air borne. They all must be hungry. Sit on the ice a lot. A few swans flying south drop in on them from time to time.

Wednesday, October 4, 2000—partly cloudy, 10° to 30°. Some time mid afternoon the swan family left the lake. We did not get to see them leave. Target practice with 30 br. Very good. We had supper with Jim and Elaine Manning.

Thursday, October 5, 2000—cloudy, 22° to 30°. 2-1/2" snow last night and snowing this evening. Checked Henry's house. Packed snow down in our driveway and dooryard. Put a jack under the Suzuki frame to take its weight off its tires. Skiff of snow.

Friday, October 6, 2000—cloudy mostly, 16° to 41°. Snow melted off highway. Went to Glennallen on senior van. Lunch, Post Office, and bank. Made copies at Manning's. Swans are still on our lake. Note: Receivec Alaska competition shooter organization card.

Saturday, October 7, 2000—cloudy, rain and snow showers, 27° to 33°. Went to Henry Heinz's funeral as one of the riflemen for 21 gun salute. Visited Darrel and Brenda.

Sunday, October 8, 2000—mostly sunny, 22° to 41°. Swans are still here. Checked Henry and Sally's place. We had Darrel and Brenda here for supper and a nice visit.

Monday, October 9, 2000—cloudy, 26° to 34°. We went to Eureka with Allen and Roxanne for breakfast. Helped Allen install a double outhouse at Grizzly Towing. He wanted to pay me, but I declined.

Tuesday, October 10, 2000—light snow here, 17° to 28°. Snow quit in Anchorage. We got tires for truck and lots of grocery shopping. The truck was nearly packed with stuff. Ran into snow about 50 miles from home. Not too bad. Winds gusting to 65 mph in Palmer. Lots of dust. Checked Henry's place. A pulley came off the lodge furnace blower. We got everything unloaded and mostly put away this evening.

Wednesday, October 11, 2000—got 3-1/2 inches of snow, cloudy and flurries in evening, 23° to 32°. Went over to the lodge and put the pulley back on the furnace squirrel cage blower. Did some correspondence and house chores. Joe brought out gasoline.

Thursday, October 12, 2000—got two inches of snow, plowed snow here and at Henry's, 23° to 30°. Henry's place is all okay. Allen is going to mount my new truck tires. Loaded 45 ACP + .223 Remington for target practice.

Friday, October 13, 2000—cloudy, low overhead, 21° to 32°. We went to Glennallen on senior van. Paid phone bill, lunch, shopping. Theresa called. Lee is to be father of a son. We went to Mendeltna, Nelchina Corp for Fall meeting at Mendeltna Chapel.

Saturday, October 14, 2000—cloudy, partly cloudy, 33° to 41 °. Shoveled snow. Checked Henry's. Reloaded .223. Called Frances (Sylvia's sister) and then called Virginia (my sister).

Sunday, October 15, 2000—very little sun, cloudy and dusting of snow, 16° to 33°. Took ashes from stove in basement. Jim Manning brought shop vac back.

Monday, October 16, 2000—fog, sunny most of day, 18° to 34°. Checked Henry's house. Put in new bulb to heat well. Carried out stove ashes. Reloaded some 45 ACP. Put fuel conditioner in heating oil. Allen came over and we put the new tires on truck. He painted the rims for me.

Tuesday, October 17, 2000—sunny, 19° to 35°. Checked Henry's place. Put away used tires. Fit chains to the new tires. Cast some bullets and loaded some target loads.

Wednesday, October 18, 2000—partly cloudy, 8° to 32°. Allen came over for some starting fluid for his backhoe. I cast some .452 bullets. Sunset on snow covered mountains on east side of Tazlina Lake is very, very beautiful.

Thursday, October 19, 2000—sunny, 4° to 26°. Checked Henry's place. Tried to make a muzzle guide for rifle cleaning rods—not successful. Saw a coyote on our lake.

Friday, October 20, 2000—partly cloudy, 4° to 28°. Went to lunch in Glennallen. Brought Legion rifles home and cleaned them.

Saturday, October 21, 2000—frosty, 5° to 25°. Checked Henry and Sally's. Dropped rifles off at Legion Post. Went to Friends of NRA evening fundraiser and steak dinner. This is for local shooting facilities and child education. Visited with folks I knew and met new people. Got home late, 11:00 PM.

Sunday, October 22, 2000—cloudy, partly cloudy, 6° to 26°. Didn't sleep well and slept late. Watched TV and phoned Paul, Steve, Nadia. Laura phoned and we all talked for over an hour.

Monday, October 23, 2000—mostly cloudy, 14° to 28°. Light snow in the morning. Allen, Roxanne and Mary Hanna were here to breakfast. Smashed tin cans. Beverly phoned, we talked for a long time.

Tuesday, October 24, 2000—partly cloudy, 7° to 24°. Plugged the hole where the voles were getting into our arctic entry.

Wednesday, October 25, 2000—partly cloudy, 10° to 33°. Helped Jim carry a water tank out of his basement. Nice visit, coffee and roll. FedEx brought my M1 Garand. I worked at cleaning it of cosmoline. Went back over to Jim's and made some copies.

Thursday, October 26, 2000—partly cloudy, 16° to 31°. Shot the M1 Garand and chronographed those loads. Henry and Sally visited for three hours, mostly about her step dad, Bud Smettzer and our friend also. Beverly phoned. Lee's girlfriend went to hospital to have a baby.

Friday, October 27, 2000—fog, sunny, 14° to 28°. We went to Glennallen shopping and lunch. Reloaded more .30-06 and shot a few to evaluate them.

Saturday, October 28, 2000—sunny, -2° to 19°. Plowed a little snow in case Henry brings some gravel. Did more load development. Pulled bullets dumped powder and re-loaded T3 cases. Really worked at cleaning the rifle barrel. It shoots better.

Sunday, October 29, 2000—fog, then light snow all day, 0° to 12°. Harold and Rachel Dimmick were here for breakfast. Worked a little on the Garand. Watched rodeo.

Monday, October 30, 2000—snow in night and snow all day (5 to 6 inches), 8°

to 17°. Went with Jim and Elaine Manning to Kluti Kaah Hall in Copper Center. Jim is teaching the 55 Alive Class. Saw a fox near Glennallen. Grandson Lee Austen's baby was born. Zachariah Taylor Lee. Blue eyes. 5:19 PM 7# 3oz 20 1/2" long.

Tuesday, October 31, 2000—cloudy and a little snow, 17° to 23°. Rode with Jim and Elaine to 55 Alive Class. Trick or treat kids were here. Lee phoned about the birth of his son.

Wednesday, November 1, 2000—partly cloudy, 14° to 21°. We went to Wasilla to have Sylvia's blood work done. Did some grocery shopping. Saw three moose at Allen's campground. Two of them standing on hind legs fighting, ears laid back with hackles up. Three more a few miles west. Rode to Legion meeting with Bart, saw one moose. One semi had left the road into a deep ditch and didn't roll over. Two huge wreckers got it back on highway.

Thursday, November 2, 2000—cloudy, mist, and light snow, 13° to 17°. Drained sediment from heating oil tank sediment glass. Looked at fuel nozzle. When stove still didn't work, I called Jim Manning. He found the blower motor was working too hard. I had a replacement part on hand. Put some firewood in basement.

Friday, November 3, 2000—sunny, 9° to 26°. Made a copy at Jim's. Saw a lynx track along his lane. Went to Glennallen on senior van. Bank, Post Office, and lunch.

Saturday, November 4, 2000—low clouds, and frost-snow in air sometimes, -1° to 18°. Didn't do much of anything today except write a letter.

Sunday, November 5, 2000—mostly cloudy, 3° to 12°. Tried to burn a brush pile with poor results.

Monday, November 6, 2000—mostly sunny, -3° to 10°. Built a fire in woodshop and started turning two 105 Howitzer projectiles for Legion post on the lathe. Ate dinner with Jim and Elaine Manning.

Tuesday, November 7, 2000—mostly sunny, -1° to 12°. Gave up trying to use spruce in the lathe. Did some target practice with the M1 Garand. Ian Mailly stopped by to talk trapping. Gave him some supplies. Bev phoned. We are avidly watching election results. I plowed Bartley's driveway.

Wednesday, November 8, 2000—mostly sunny, -4° to 8°. Brought Sylvia's cottonwood bark in to basement. Made some copies of wolf trapping "how to," for Ian Mailly. Cal and Mary Gilcrease visited.

Thursday, November 9, 2000—cloudy, 2° to 15°. Shoveled snow off trailer and trailer storage. Put new bulb in well. Allen visited in evening. Packed snow to well with snowgo.

Friday, November 10, 2000—partly cloudy, 12° to 26°. Did some target shooting. Tumbled some brass. No senior van today.

Saturday, November 11, 2000—partly cloudy, 17° to 35°. One inch of snow in night. Worked on some brass. Reloaded 12 rounds. Shot 6 over the ProChrono gear. Brenda Gerry invited us to dinner 11/19.

Sunday, November 12, 2000—sunny, 10° to 25°. Plowed snow. Pulled, shoveled snow off roofs. Put Alaska Trapper magazines in order. Allen and Samantha visited. Finished cleaning MI.

Monday, November 13, 2000—sunny, cloudy and windy by 3:00 PM, 3° to 32°. Had a steak and eggs breakfast at Allen and Roxanne's. Got our flu shots. Visited Jim Odden and had coffee. Target practice this afternoon. Started cleaning pistol.

Tuesday, November 14, 2000—partly cloudy, 16° to 31°. Shoveled snow up around house. Built fire in woodshop. Painted target template. Swadged some primer pockets. Finished cleaning pistol. Lee Dudley visited in afternoon.

Wednesday, November 15, 2000—sunny till noon, cloudy and snow around us, 2° to 18°. Sylvia put out bird feed today. Did some little jobs. Failed another attempt to remove Berdan primers. Copied some 6" bulls-eye targets.

Thursday, November 16, 2000—low clouds, 12° to 18°. Sylvia went with neighbor ladies to Palmer Wasilla. Had battery cable problems and will get home late. Cal called to tell me about vehicle trouble Eagle River. Re-crowned muzzle on barrel on MI. Didn't do much.

Friday, November 17, 2000—partly cloudy, 1° to 21°. We went to Thanksgiving dinner and monthly meeting for seniors at Rendezvous Café. Paid phone bill and Sylvia cashed her Social Security check.

Saturday, November 18, 2000—partly cloudy, 13° to 32°. Cut down a birch tree and cut three lengths of 20" to turn 105 Howitzer "projectiles" on the lathe. Trouble is the wood will be green. Bart and Rosemary invited us to go with them to Ducks Unlimited dinner at the "Carriage House" in Gakona. I won a nice back pack in a drawing. We got back home at 2:00 AM. Had ribs at legion then ate New York broil at Carriage.

Sunday, November 19, 2000—cloudy, 20° to 36°. Jim Odden phoned and we will ride with him to Darrel and Brenda's for a Thanksgiving dinner. Dug around in my steel pipe pile and found some pipe Henry Johnson needs. Nice dinner at Gerry's. Lots of Brenda's family were there. Ron made a deep-fried turkey—very good. We had a nice visit.

Monday, November 20, 2000—cloudy and a few snow flakes, 18° to 32°. Watched the Florida Supreme court session to hear vote question. Henry didn't come over. Did a rough turn of green birch. Only one is satisfactory.

Tuesday, November 21, 2000—mostly cloudy, 22° to 26°. Low clouds and some fog on each side of us. Sharpened Sylvia's wood carving tools, and my lathe tools. Phoned Fred Marolf, Bob Burns and daughter Linda, and Lorraine Hanson.

Wednesday, November 22, 2000—cloudy, 12° to 26°. Looked in lumber wood storage again for projectile suitable pieces with no luck. Put new "O" ring on cleaning rod guide.

Thursday, November 23, 2000—cloudy and freezing fog, 10° to 23°. I cut another birch and brought a piece in the house to dry. We went to Jim and Mary Odden's to Thanksgiving dinner. Jim's mother, Lois, Brother John, wife Colleen, sons Alex and Eric, friends Francis and Joey, and another man were there for dinner.

Friday, November 24, 2000—partly cloudy, 6° to 18°. Sylvia spotted two bull moose (still had their horns) walking west on south side of our lake. We went to Odden's at 5:30 PM, listened to music and visited. Ate lefse, lutefisk and side pork, pie and ice cream. More visiting.

Saturday, November 25, 2000—sunny, -3° to 10°. Turned some birch wood on lathe.

Sunday, November 26, 2000—fog in morning, mostly sunny afternoon, -4° to 5°. Watched election controversy. Cleaned some brass. Did some target shooting.

Monday, November 27, 2000—mostly sunny, -3° to +8°. Tazlina, fog along mountains. We pumped water. Counted the seconds it took for water to return down hill. Measured heating oil depth. Allen, Roxanne, Samantha visited in afternoon.

Tuesday, November 28, 2000—cloudy, sunny, very nice, cloudy, -5° to +7°. LS & B package came. Soldered .22 rifle clip. Fred Rungee stopped by in afternoon and stayed to have supper with us. Great visit.

Wednesday, November 29, 2000—mostly sunny, 5° to 13°. Built a fire in wood shop. Then we had Jim and Elaine over to have breakfast with us. Visited quite a while. Then Henry brought back the rest of a piece of borrowed pipe. It got too late to turn the birch on the lathe. VA cancelled my Friday appointment.

Thursday, November 30, 2000—cloudy, and 1-1/2 inches of snow, -2° to 9°. Built a fire in woodshop stove and worked some more on the birch "projectiles." Cal came over and worked on parts for his street rod using my drill press.

Friday, December 1, 2000—mostly sunny, some snow in night, -5° to 8°. Plowed our snow. Kept a fire in woodshop today. We went to Glennallen on senior van. Had lunch, paid bills, and a little shopping. Went over to Elaine Manning's to read Nel-Mel Corp past meetings with partial results. Jim stopped by, borrowed my varmint call. Bev phoned. I phoned Jim Odden about shooting range.

Saturday, December 2, 2000—partly cloudy, -12° to -5°. Worked some more on 105 Howitzer case. Paint, primed it. Jim, Mary, and Kari Odden; Allen, Roxanne (7 months pregnant), Kyle, Ellie and Sammy were here for a bean soup supper and pumpkin pie. Jeff phoned.

Sunday, December 3, 2000—mostly sunny, cloudy evening, -11° to -3°. Made a template of 105 Howitzer projectile that I turned on wood lathe. Did some primer painting. Jeff Routt had supper with us.

Monday, December 4, 2000—cloudy, -12° to 2°. Put more primer on projectile.

Tuesday, December 5, 2000—cloudy and three inches of snow, 3° to 16°. Plowed our snow, Bartley's drive and place, Sam's parking place. Shoveled camper roof, trailer, and wood shed roof.

Wednesday, December 6, 2000—sunny, 7° to 24°. Returned books to Mannings and they gave me three more to read. Went to Legion meeting in Glennallen with Bartley. Karl Bengston gave me some birch wood. Bought two cans paint.

Thursday, December 7, 2000—cloudy, 12° to 21°. Worked on piece of birch, got it rough turned. Will dry it now. Presidential election drags on.

Friday, December 8, 2000—cloudy, some fog, 5° to 22°. Went to Glennallen on senior van. Lunch, paid phone bill. Did some shopping. Resized 14 GI cartridges-had dents. Went down to well, replaced light bulb. Small water line must have come apart. I hooked up the large line and Sylvia pumped water.

Saturday, December 9, 2000—foggy till afternoon, then low cloudy and a little snow, 10° to 15°. Watched the election saga on TV, some other shows. Read. Tried to use chronograph and broke a wire and re-soldered it. Allen and Kyle came over. I will watch their place while they are vacationing.

Sunday, December 10, 2000—cloudy, snow in evening, 7° to 10° to 12° in evening. Target practice and chronographed some. Brass got wet and dried it. Entered feet per second and other pertinent stats. Supper with Oddens. Ralph phoned, he got a female lynx.

Monday, December 11, 2000—cloudy, 3° to 13°. Visited Cal in afternoon. Mary was working. Cal showed up the recent work on his "street rod." Primed some brass.

Tuesday, December 12, 2000—cloudy, with a beautiful colorful sunrise, 8° to 15°. Sylvia went to ladies Christmas party at Eureka. Got the vehicle insurance squared away. Put glue in the checks in the birch wood. Dried too fast. Checked Allen's house.

Wednesday, December 13, 2000—sunny, -4° to 14°. Built a fire in woodshop stove. Carved a birch wood spoon. The glued birch wood is still drying. Joe didn't leave heating oil. Reloaded 84 30-06.

Thursday, December 14, 2000—sunny, -15° to -8°. Splendid sunrise. Checked Allen's house. Turned another birch "projectile" on lathe. Primed and painted both projectiles. Printed the one shell case that I have here.

Friday, December 15, 2000—clouded over and warmed up some, -21° to -3°. Built a fire in wood shop. Went to senior Christmas party at Kluti Kaah Hall in Copper Center. Picked up shell casing at Ed Knoebel's. Wire brushed it and primer coated it when I got home. Will spray paint it before going to bed. Had a nice visit with Cal and Mary, Al Taylor, Lincoln and Ann Smith.

Saturday, December 16, 2000—cloudy, -11° to -6°. Finished painting and assembled the 105 Howitzer shells. Went to Dimmick's, fed and watered their dog. Gave Mary Gilcrease a wooden spoon I carved. Visited with her and Cal. Came home and made another. Bart brought a poinsettia over for Sylvia. Checked Allen's house for heat.

Sunday, December 17, 2000—cloudy, -16° to 3°. Made another birch spoon today. Jim and Elaine brought a Mel-Nel letter and visited in afternoon. Darrel Gerry phoned. Ian Mailly visited about trapping in evening.

Monday, December 18, 2000—partly cloudy, -9° to 21°. Packed the snow on trail to well with snowgo. Checked Allen's house. Heated wood shop and made another birch spoon. Allen phoned from south Mexico this evening.

Tuesday, December 19, 2000—partly cloudy, 3° to 12°. Beautiful sunset. Vanessa and Scott's Christmas package to us arrived this morning. Did some target practice. Made another birch wood spoon. Turned a piece of birch down for drying. Will attempt a rolling pin later. Checked Jim Odden's house. Cleaned rifle.

Wednesday, December 20, 2000—partly cloudy, -3° to 5°. Did some target practice. Made two more wood spoons. Cleaned rifle. Called Darcy with birthday greetings.

Thursday, December 21, 2000—cloudy and skiff snow, 5° to 20°. Went to check Dimmick's house. Fed and watered the dog. It had one hind leg entangled in its tether. Leg had started to swell. Pushed some snow there. Visited Cal and Mary. Checked Allen's house and then Odden's house. Back home I tried to find the break in the larger 1-1/2" water line. Appears to be where line goes under the lower trail.

Friday, December 22, 2000—partly cloudy, ½ inch of snow, foggy in Glennallen, -5° to 15°. Rode senior van in and had lunch and did some shopping. Joe Phillips delivered fuel oil.

Saturday, December 23, 2000—cloudy, one inch of snow, -11° to 3°. Plowed our snow and Bartley's driveway. Fed and watered Dimmick's dog. Visited Cal and Mary. Checked Odden's place. Checked the lower end of our water line—froze in corrugated line. Phoned Paul and Steve. Nadia phoned, so did Jeff R. We went to Legion supper.

Sunday, December 24, 2000—cloudy, -10° to 0°. Allen had breakfast with us. Got to see pix of their Mexico vacation. Jeff Routt called in a fox this morning. Ralph and Roma Fuson celebrated their 25th wedding anniversary in Montana. Bob Burns phoned. We called Theresa.

Monday, December 25, 2000—cloudy, -13° to -3°. Put a new light bulb in our well. Went to Odden's and found the electricity off. Had a hell of a time getting a fire gong in the heater. Made several trips back and forth. Their telephone battery was low. We had Jim and Elaine Manning over to eat a Christmas goose dinner with us. Jim phoned me back just after 5:00 PM. Built a fire at Jim's—tough stove to fire. More phone calls to Wisconsin and from CVEA. Billmans stopped at Odden's as I was leaving after fixing the fire for overnight.

Tuesday, December 26, 2000—mostly sunny, -13° to -5°. Up early built fire in Odden's heater. Waited for CVEA employees to re-set hi line breaker. Jim's furnace now heats the house. Bob Rudbeck phoned to get senator, congressman phone numbers. Harold Dimmick phoned.

Wednesday, December 27, 2000—cloudy, -10° to 12°. Package from Nadia arrived. Phoned Nadia and senators.

Thursday, December 28, 2000—mostly cloudy, some fog to south, -11° to 10°. Took our garbage to transfer site. Grizzly towing. Visited with Chris Lee, Dudley and Trooper Dupre. Allen phoned and asked if we needed water. Phoned Congressman Young.

Friday, December 29, 2000—1/2 inch of snow, cloudy, 10° to 16°. Went to lunch in Glennallen on senior van.

Saturday, December 30, 2000—cloudy, one inch of snow, 7° to 25°. We went to Eureka for coffee with Bart, Rosemary, Denny, Joey, Carol, Jim and Elaine. Talked to Lee Dudley a few minutes. Came home and made another wood spoon. Phoned Bev and Tyler, Theresa and Earl. Then went to Bartley's and played cards with Carol, Denny, Joey and Emily.

Sunday, December 31, 2000—low clouds and fog, 19° to 23°. I haven't felt well today. Made one spoon. Took a couple naps. We went to Allen and Roxanne's for supper—very good. The boys gave us each a glass mug from Mexico. We watched some TV, then came home.

Left to right: Sally Johnson, Norman Wilkins, Phil Petrie Sr., Phil Petrie Jr.,
Photo courtesy of Henry Johnson, Nelchina Lodge.

Middle left: an eagle in flight at Scoter Lake

2001—Trip to Fairbanks

Monday, January 1, 2001—cloudy, 5° to 6° and falling in evening. Got a load of water at Allen's. Unloaded it at home without a hitch. Cleaned snow off the car. Put a little oil, Heet and anti-freeze in car. Also a shovel and two coolers. Started and ran it a little while. Jeff and his kids Krysten, Jarret and Shobie were here while I was down at Allen's getting water. Darrel Gerry phoned holiday greetings. Ron Beshaw phoned—his dog had gotten into a trap on a nearby trail.

Tuesday, January 2, 2001—lightly snowing when we got up and left for Wasilla, 0° to 12°. Saw three moose on the way to town. Sylvia saw an eagle. Shopped at Wal-Mart and Carrs-Safeway. Got gasoline. Asked bank to send statements back home before 5:00 PM and unloaded groceries. Sandy F. sent homemade candy over with her son Chuck. Ron's dog is much better.

Wednesday, January 3, 2001—one inch of snow, cloudy, 8° to 18°. Put repaired tire on car. Added one quart oil. Lee Dudley visited in the afternoon. Rode to Legion meeting with Bart, there were five of us there. Ian Mailly returned a marten stretcher he had borrowed.

Thursday, January 4, 2001—sunny, 3° to 14°. Plowed our snow. Fed the birds. Did a couple other jobs. Jim Manning brought back a replacement onion for one he had borrowed.

Friday, January 5, 2001—sunny, -3° to 10° to 17°. Rode senior van to Glennallen. Had lunch, cashed our checks. Ian Mailly brought two of his marten skins over. He is doing a fine job putting them up. We talked a lot about a trail—directions so he can find it. His enthusiasm is a joy to see. Gave him a hand-carved birch spoon to take home to his mother.

Saturday, January 6, 2001—cloudy and light snow, -6° to 12°. Snow weight tipped over a small tree here. Allen and Kyle visited just as we were finishing supper and had ice cream with us.

Sunday, January 7, 2001—snow all night and day, 5". 22° to 32°. Took starter off truck and looked at it. It is worn out. Put it back and plowed our snow. Racked snow off half the wood shop and the over hang on woodshed.

Monday, January 8, 2001—cloudy, 20° to 30°. Pulled snow rake snow off several roofs. Looked over my old 350 Chevy starters, made a box for one of them. Lee Dudley visited and we talked reloading.

Tuesday, January 9, 2001—cloudy, 2° to 24°. Allen, Roxanne and David had breakfast with us. Shoveled snow off storage shed roof, a trailer and camper.

Removed ice frozen in bottom of water hauling tank. Jim Manning came over for his mail. I sent a starter core with him. Ralph told me Dave Bruss has caught 77 lynx, 2 wolverines, and 1 wolf.

Wednesday, January 10, 2001—skiff snow and cloudy, 7° to 12°. Made a prototype wrench for holding M1 gas cylinder when removing the gas plug when cleaning the cylinder. Laid out the wrench its self. Jeff called. I called Allen needing a 13/16 drill bit. Jeff called again with some questions about his new rifle. Jim Odden called and talked awhile. He will be home the 23rd.

Thursday, January 11, 2001—cloudy, light snow, frost all day, 1° to 9°. Allen phoned. I finished making the wrench for M1 looks good. Propane was delivered today. Allen and I hauled water to his campground and to our house.

Friday, January 12, 2001—cloudy, four to five inches of snow in the night, 3° to 21°. Plowed our snow, and some for Mannings. Cleaned snow off Jim Odden's airplane. Went to Glennallen for lunch on senior van. Sylvia mailed the sweater she knitted for Beverly. Jeff Routt came out in the afternoon. He and I shot my MI. I shot the smallest group so far 2-7/8" with a flyer. Jeff shot his .375 Ackley. I fired one round. We loaded six more, tried to chronograph them but it got too dark. Jeff brought a great KFC supper. Polished some brass for Jeff in evening.

Saturday, January 13, 2001—cloudy, foggy, one hour sun, 7° to 16°. Jeff had breakfast with us and went to Gakona to pick up his kids. Put out some bird feed. Found a "lost" piece of -06 brass. Did a lot of reading Jim Manning brought over our starter for truck.

Sunday, January 14, 2001—cloudy, snow, windy rain, 4° to 34°. Put the new starter on truck. It needs a shim under it. Jeff stopped by for his things. Tom H. visited. Snow slid off house roof and two-thirds of the east half of the garage roof. Pulled some snow off garage with snow rake, also arctic entry off, then pushed it into a pile with plow. Cleaned snow off car.

Monday, January 15, 2001—snow, rain and snow all night to 1:00 PM, at least ten inches, 23° to 33°. Snow broke limbs off birch trees and broke 12' -14' tops out of spruce trees near house. Did some shoveling and lots of snow plowing. Plowed snow at Mannings, Bartley's driveway at the highway, and the school yard. Cleaned snow off Jim Odden's airplane, Rags. Lee is on senior run again. Bev phoned.

Tuesday, January 16, 2001—clear, 9° to 16°. Shoveled snow off woodshed and camper. Moose cow and calf are feeding here. There were two spruce tree limbs almost touching our high line wires. I cut them off at the tree trunk with my 10-

gauge shotgun, "moose dick." Worked great! Spent quite a while today making a special "take up" washer to position the gas cylinder correctly on the MI. Cleaned its bore, greased the action. Cleaned and oiled the 10-gauge. Allen and David came over to get guns stored here.

Wednesday, January 17, 2001—partly cloudy, cloudy, 6° to 14°. Packed the trail to the well with snowgo. Put one shim under pickup starter motor. Took old starter over to Jim. He came over to listen for starter noise. Removed the overhead smoke fan from above the cook stove. It just doesn't do its job.

Thursday, January 18, 2001—cloudy and some breeze, 7° to 29°. Did some M1 06 target practice. Cleaned the rifle. I put a 4" strap on the spruce tree leaning over the house. Attached a chain to pickup and jerked the tree shaking its load of snow off, hoping the tree will straighten up. Another birch with a large broken branch. Cow moose still walking around here. Bev called, she had gotten the sweater that Sylvia made and sent her. She talked of Lee also.

Friday, January 19, 2001—sunny, 25° to 32°. We went to Glennallen on senior van. Lunch and a little shopping.

Saturday, January 20, 2001—cloudy, clear and cloudy and fog, 7° to 27°. Tired today. Fooled with M1 a while. Read some. Tried to call Barry Wilkins. Got a letter from my brother, Jerry Wilkins wanting info for birth certificate.

Sunday, January 21, 2001—mostly clear, -1° to 13°. Worked on a little genealogy to send to Barry Wilkins including identifying people in a photo including his grandfather Eddie. We went to Allen and Roxanne's to supper and watched a movie. Sylvia did our laundry there.

Monday, January 22, 2001—mostly cloudy, 0° to 14°. Mailed picture to Barry Wilkins. Tested some 9-Volt batteries, charged one. Lee D. visited and we talked squib loads and taper crimping.

Tuesday, January 23, 2001—partly cloudy, 5° to 16°. Did some cast bullets research for Lee Dudley. Sorted catalogs, and read for a while. Light bulb in well burned out.

Wednesday, January 24, 2001—sunny, 0° to 20°. Put a new light bulb in this well. Pulled three broken spruce tops across the yard with snowgo. Trimmed them with axe and piled the limbs. Plowed the scattered twigs over to the side. Loaded and shot some .30 caliber squib loads. Linda Langanbaugh phoned that her brother Bob Burns passed away at noon in Iowa. We phoned Nadia this evening to order flowers for Bob's funeral.

Thursday, January 25, 2001—sunny, 1° to 17°. Carried the small tree top across the yard. Smashed the tin cans. Loaded nine more squib loads. Tired today. Jim and Mary Odden are back home, visited a while. They gave Sylvia some quilting material and me two shirts.

Friday, January 26, 2001—cloudy, strong breeze, and gusty, fine snow, 3° to 29°. We went to Glennallen seniors meeting and some shopping. Jeff saw a Northern Hawk Owl at end of our lane sitting in an aspen tree. He stopped by while we were gone. Allen's birthday.

Saturday, January 27, 2001—partly cloudy, cloudy and snow, 17° to 28°. Off hand target practice. Did some load development w .308 squib loads. 45.7 grain ball. Allen hauled us a load of water. Sylvia gave him a pie for his birthday (lemon).

Sunday, January 28, 2001—mostly sunny, 10° to 24°. Plowed two inches of snow. Pulled snow off arctic entry, one side woodshop and over hang on woodshop. Talked with Jeff about tanning a fox. My brother Jerry called and talked a while. Ralph called, but I was outside. Sylvia spotted a cow and calf moose on our lake.

Monday, January 29, 2001—cloudy, frost, and light snow in the air, 3° to 13°. I pulled snow off greenhouse roof. Practiced off hand rifle practice. Read some. Ate supper with the Mannings. Returned their Foxfire books.

Tuesday, January 30, 2001—cloudy, low fog, flakes of snow and frost, -2° to 6°. Mary Odden called, arranging a supper. Jim Odden called to talk about establishing a shooting range.

Wednesday, January 31, 2001—1-1/2 inches snow fell, cloudy, sunny, cloudy, 2° to 15°. Plowed the snow. My appointment was cancelled at VA clinic. The pharmacy will extend my prescription until 3/16/01. Called Mary Odden so she can plan the supper accordingly. Talked to Jim a few minutes. Shot load lot #9 over the chronograph. Trying to get a good load developed. Checked out income against the IRS guidelines and we don't have to file this year.

Thursday, February 1, 2001—cloudy, sunny, very nice, 6° to 21°. Oddens, Elaine M, Nadia, Theresa, and Allen all called birthday greetings. Oddens stopped by late afternoon with carrot cake. Great!

Friday, February 2, 2001—sunny, -6° to 14°. We went to Glennallen, had lunch, paid phone bill and shopped. Went to post office. Mary Gilcrease gave me a birthday pie.

Saturday, February 3, 2001—sunny, -11° to 8°. Sylvia made a cake and we took it to Cal Gilcrease and visited a while. Then came home and went to Odden's for supper, a birthday party for me. Very nice. Huddleston family, Farmers, Oddens, and John Johnson, the well driller were there, and Darrel and Brenda. Samantha gave me some things she colored. The group gave me a back-scratcher of caribou horn that is a facsimile of grizzly front paw.

Sunday, February 4, 2001—sunny, -17° to 8°. Cleaned the gas cylinder on the M1. Cleaned P90. Checked its recoil spring for pounds of resistance 10 lbs. Did the same with Sig 220 20 lbs. Jeff phoned.

Monday, February 5, 2001—sunny, -7° to 15°. Packed the trail to our well with snowgo. Put some gas in it. Pulled snow off the two lean-tos. Didn't feel well today. A squirrel was trying to get at bird feed.

Tuesday, February 6, 2001—sunny, cloudy and light snow in evening, 2° to 22°. Repaired a hinge on snowplow extension on the left side. Hawk owl watched our bird feeder.

Wednesday, February 7, 2001—snowing lightly all day, two inches, 13° to 22°. David Adkins died last night. Cut a batch of .30 caliber cleaning patches. Allen and David visited in evening.

Thursday, February 8, 2001—sunny, full moon, -3° to 16°. Moose cow walked by bird feeder and browsed on hillside. I plowed our snow and pulled snow off storage trailer. Deprimed and swadged the primer pockets on some military 06 brass. Ed Farmer visited in evening.

Friday, February 9, 2001—sunny, got ½ inch of snow, -3° to 22°. We went to Glennallen, lunch, bank, shopping. Polished military 06 brass reamed the primer pockets. Phoned Tom Smayda.

Saturday, February 10, 2001—sunny, sun dogs, -8° to 10°. Dan Billman came over. He needed a ground cable and a solenoid for his snowplow. We visited for awhile. I annealed the 06 brass. Phoned Tom Smayda about funeral. Cleaned downstairs windows.

Sunday, February 11, 2001—skiff snow, mostly sunny, -7° to 17°. Resized and trimmed and measured 06 brass. Put primer in them. Jeff Routt phoned. Allen brought us a load of water. Jim, Mary, Kari came and picked us up and we all went to KROA and visited with Vern Adkins who is back here from Florida for the funeral of his son David. Sun dogs were out today.

Monday, February 12, 2001—cloudy, 4" snow most all day, 8° to 23°. Didn't feel well all day. Cal got his plow truck stuck and called me to come and get him out. I went right down. It came out easily. Plowed our snow here at home after supper.

Tuesday, February 13, 2001—sunny, beaut of a day, 1° to 22°. Plowed a little snow here, mailbox and some at Mannings. Used the corporation copier for targets and order form from CMP. We went to the viewing and celebration of life for David Adkins at Glennallen. Northern lights are out tonight.

Wednesday, February 14, 2001—sunny, -10° to 10°. We went to the funeral for David and the reception afterward. Lots of people there. Denny, Joie and Emily drove up from Homer. Mailed off the order to CMP for gas cylinder lock nut for M1.

Thursday, February 15, 2001—partly sunny, -9° to 12°. Did a little target practice with M1. First target very good. Jim Odden flew by our place this morning.

Friday, February 16, 2001—sunny, sun dogs in the afternoon, -8° to 19°. We went to Glennallen for lunch and shopping. Cleaned rifle.

Saturday, February 17, 2001—sunny, -8° to 21°. Called and wished Beverly Happy Birthday. Got to talk to Tyler for a while. Darrel and Brenda, Jim, Mary, and Kari were all here for a roast moose supper. Had a nice visit. Mary read an essay about my trap line. Darrel brought the time schedule (7:00 PM) for space station and the space shuttle for our viewing. Very impressive.

Sunday, February 18, 2001—sunny, cloudy in evening, -3° to 11°. Did research in old American Rifleman magazine. Someone phoned from Eureka wanting a trailer tongue welded. Hope they find someone else to do it, but I will if need be. Missed seeing space station.

Saturday, February 19, 2001—sunny, -10° to 18°. Went to Eureka for breakfast, Allen and Roxanne went with us. Nice visit too. Measured and ordered heating oil and gasoline. Read some. Wrote order to Nosler for bullet sample and cap. 6:47 PM, saw the space station briefly as it passed Juniper and Saturn and streaked to horizon and out of sight.

Sunday, February 20, 2001—sunny, cloudy evening, -4° to 26°. Read a lot. Made a support for a propane torch while annealing cartridge cases.

Monday, February 21, 2001—cloudy, sunny, 10° to 30°. Jim Odden brought us some potatoes and milk etc. They are going to McGrath for eight months. He had breakfast with us. I went over to see Ed Farmer and his new CAT backhoe and loader. Rick and Charlete came there to see it also. Joe delivered heating oil and gasoline. He has a new Arctic Cat snowgo.

Tuesday, February 22, 2001—sunny, -2° to 22°. Jim Odden had breakfast with us and a nice visit. A cow moose walked along lawn on south side of our house while we were eating. Got a picture. I did some target practice in the afternoon. The bore in the rifle seemed smoother when I ran a patch in it. Had supper with Jim and Elaine. They had Bart and Rosemary there also.

Wednesday, February 23, 2001—sunny, fog in view, -7° to 14°. We went to the monthly senior meeting at Kluti Kaah Hall. Kay Branch presented information about assisted living programs in Alaska. We had lunch and birthday cake. I annealed some more rifle brass. Jeff phoned.

Thursday, February 24, 2001—sunny, -14° to 12°. Jeff phoned—won't be coming out. Loaded 35 cast bullets for M1 and shot them on targets. Cleaned rifle. Went to Bartley's for a potluck and cards in evening. Taped a movie for Fred Rungee. Stars are bright tonight.

Friday, February 25, 2001—sunny and light snow late afternoon, -18° to 8°. Read for a while, shot a squirrel. Cut and pasted up a Charlie Mayse story for copying. Saw a moose crossing lake.

Saturday, February 26, 2001—sunny, 1-1/2 to 2 inches of snow in the night, cloudy and windy, 3° to 20°. Plowed our snow and Manning's lane. Snow slid off house and I shoveled some of it. Real sick with a sinus cold. Allen brought us a load of water. Cal and Allen visited a while. Sylvia took a blanket she had made to a baby shower for Roxanne Farmer.

Sunday, February 27, 2001—we got four inches of heavy wet snow, 27° to 37°. Plowed all of ours, mailboxes and some of Manning's. Did a lot of shoveling, cleaned 16" of snow off the car. Raked snow off some of the roof. Made copies at Manning's. Packed trail to the well with snowgo. Had to dig the wet snow from under carriage of snowgo.

Monday, February 28, 2001—sunny, cloudy mid afternoon, 21° to 34°. Still sick. Chronographed seven load development targets. Two look good. Checked Odden house.

Thursday, March 1, 2001—partly cloudy, 2° to 24°. Still sick. Did my exercises. Reorganized my data for M1 Garand and reloading for it and put it in a note ring book binder. Reloaded 35 more cartridges for long development and practice.

Friday, March 2, 2001—sunny, still sick, 3° to 23°. Sylvia went on senior van to

Glennallen. Read and cleaned house a little bit.

Saturday, March 3, 2001—sunny, -12° to 19°. Shoveled snow off 100 feet of the waterline. Put a new bulb in the well light. Feel better today. Target practice this afternoon.

Sunday, March 4, 2001—sunny, -15° to 17°. Did a few chores and put out bird seed. Finished reading another book. Phoned grandson a Lee Happy Birthday greeting. Loaded and shot five rounds—checking on barrel fouling. Started cleaning rifle.

Monday, March 5, 2001—mostly sunny, 0° to 26°. Read a lot today. Re-hung the bathroom towel holder.

Tuesday, March 6, 2001—sunny, cloudy, and light snow in afternoon, -2° to 24°. Built a four round clip for Garand. Smashed our tin cans.

Wednesday, March 7, 2001—sunny, cloudy, sunny, 15° to 30°. Checked Odden House. Lee Dudley visited. We had a good discussion of shooting and reloading. Theresa called.

Thursday, March 8, 2001—cloudy, sunny, cloudy, 2° to 28°. A cow moose with her last year's calf were bedded in the snow 10 yards from kitchen window this morning and stayed there till after we had our breakfast. They were chewing their cuds. Both are getting thin, calf more so. They fed around here today. This afternoon I fired up the snowgo and drove down to lower part of water line and shoveled some more snow away from it. Beverly phoned this evening.

Friday, March 9, 2001—cloudy, 20° to 35°. We went to Glennallen for lunch shopping and cash checks. Shoveled more snow away from waterline. M1 cylinder lock arrived—order took 23 days to get here.

Saturday, March 10, 2001—cloudy, sunny, 17° to 38°. Went to Palmer to a gun show at fairgrounds. Saw a few people I knew. Then ran into Dale and Jeff Routt. We had a bite of lunch and walked around looking at guns and accoutrements. I enjoyed being with them talking guns and hunting etc. Got some groceries and came home. We went to Tom and Kim Huddleston's for supper and movie of their trip.

Sunday, March 11, 2001—sunny, cloudy in evening, 17° to 39°. Didn't feel well today. Called Dale Routt and asked him to buy me a cartridge belt and bayonet for M1 Garand. Sent a check for the belt. Went to the well and checked small waterlines, it looked OK. We tried to pump water and it was thawed out—plenty of water now.

Monday, March 12, 2001—partly cloudy, 10° to 33°. Oiled two rifle slings. Lee Dudley visited. I took a check over to Elaine as a pledge of $15.00 15 hours in a rocking chair during a fundraising for an ambulance here in the valley. Beverly phoned.

Tuesday, March 13, 2001—sunny, 18° to 33°. Saw a squirrel near bird feeder. Did a little target shooting. Mark Brockman brought over a newspaper article about moose hunting prospects for the fall.

Wednesday, March 14, 2001—cloudy, partly cloudy, 7° to 30°. Cleaned some carrots, will give them away as we have so many.

Thursday, March 15, 2001—sunny, 23° to 39°. We pumped water from our well. Did a little work on water line. We went to supper at Steve and Karen Mailly and family. Lee Dudley was there. Had nice visit and enjoyed the kids. Checked on Odden house.

Friday, March 16, 2001—partly cloudy, 13° to 24°. I rode the VA van to the clinic in Anchorage. Got a check up and prescription refilled. Rudbecks plan on coming over this evening.

Saturday, March 17, 2001—mostly cloudy, -12° to 30°. Called Jim Odden about shooting range. He called back. Got car ready for trip to the Legion post "Paddy" Irish Dinner. We ate a lot of good food and visited with other folks. Saw a moose feeding at about 155 mile.

Sunday, March 18, 2001—sunny, windy in Glennallen, -12° to 16°. Jeff called and talked awhile. Read a lot. Went to Darrel and Brenda's for supper. Darrel did some research for shooting range insurance on his computer for me. Saw a boreal owl on way home.

Monday, March 19, 2001—sunny, -19° to 15°. Jane Wineagar (NRA) called to make appointment to talk about organizing a shooting range. Allen had breakfast with us this morning. Read a lot today.

Tuesday, March 20, 2001—sunny and some breeze from the east, -19° to 14°. Visited with Jim and Elaine for a couple hours. Read and located a movie for D Johnson.

Wednesday, March 21, 2001—sunny, -19° to 15°. Kahren brought a Bible with large type for Sylvia. Bob Rudbeck needed some old newspapers. Charlie Trowbridge phoned. He plans to visit us a few days.

Thursday, March 22, 2001—sunny, -18° to 11°. Up at 5:00 AM. Charlie and I got to see the International Space Station go by in its orbit. We also saw many flashes of light-sparkles etc unexplained to us. Not of or from the space station? Charlie, after breakfast, got his gear and left to camp with his friend Scottie who is building a cabin on the Nelchina River, a short distance from here. Saw the moose calf bedded down in the "hole" to the west on our property.

Friday, March 23, 2001—sunny, -18° to 12°. Went to Glennallen. Paid electric bill, shopping and lunch. Steve called again today. I called Paul this evening. Reading the Zane Grey book Charlie gave me. Got up 30 minutes late to see the space station. Elaine Manning called to say they did see it.

Saturday, March 24, 2001—sunny, light snow in afternoon and evening, -13° to 13°. Tried to glue a shoe and it didn't work. Read a lot. NRA field representative, Jane Wineagar and her helper dropped by to talk about establishing a shooting range on our community park area. Prospects of this happening look bleak. Lots of hurdles. Charlie stopped by a few minutes. Jim and Elaine took notes on our meeting and will report at Nel-Mel spring meeting.

Sunday, March 25, 2001—1" snow, sunny afternoon, 5° to 26°. Dale phoned, he won't be out today. Jeff stopped by with his custom 375 Ackley improved, nice rifle for big bears. Dale phoned from Anchorage he found some bayonets for me. Henry invited us to his retirement party. Charlie, Scott Meyer and Kate bull visited in evening. Charlie is staying the night. Nice visit.

Monday, March 26, 2001—3" snow, 13° to 25°. Charlie Allen and Roxanne were here for breakfast. Downy woodpecker is here every day. Plowed our snow this evening. Ralph called this afternoon and I called Dale this evening.

Tuesday, March 27, 2001—sunny, 11° to 34°. Plowed snow from our mailboxes. Checked Odden house. Went to Grizzly Towing and talked to Chris about shooting range, Tolsona Ridge TV transmitter, politics, and a myriad of other issues. Dee and son Clinton stopped by to borrow a movie and had tea, cocoa and visited. Her battery went dead and I jump started her vehicle with our car. Saw marten tracks at Odden house. Glassed for bears on Heavenly Ridge.

Wednesday, March 28, 2001—sunny, 14° to 38°. Some snow slid of garage roof and I shoveled that. Sylvia re-hemmed the Alaska flag. Did some reading and research. Went to Allen's and brought Kindra H over to our place till her sister could come and get her after work. Jim Odden called me back. Steve Donaldson brought over some Nel-Mel papers regarding the recreation property.

Thursday, March 29, 2001—sunny, 8° to 37°. Worked some on shooting range materials. Jim M. brought over a paper. Robert and Kahren were here for supper.

Friday, March 30, 2001—partly cloudy. 20° to 37°. We went to Glennallen to the senior's monthly meeting. Some shopping in town. Lunch at Kluti Kaah Hall.

Saturday, March 31, 2001—cloudy, snowy across river, sunny till evening then cloudy, 17° to 33°. Pulled out burn barrel and burned paper. Went to Henry's retirement party. Had a good time, saw people we know. Tom and Lisa Smayda will be staying overnight here. Dale, Jeff left my M1 bayonet and WW II ammo belt here while we were at KROA and Henry's party.

Sunday, April 1, 2001—sunny, -2° to 28°. Tom and Lisa had breakfast with us. Real nice visit. They left at 10:00 AM for their home in Palmer. My back is really bad. Let Dale know the belt and bayonet got here. Jeff phoned and I told him also. I taped an Alaska grizzly hunting trip to show them. Started cleaning the eyelets on ammo belt.

Monday, April 2, 2001—sunny, 9° to 35°. Back is very bad. Rested a lot. Kahren brought over some "Aleve" to try.

Tuesday, April 3, 2001—sunny, windy in the afternoon, 18° to 42°. Phoned State Lands Office and two insurance companies in regards to a shooting range. Bob and Kahren came over in the afternoon and got involved about the range. Drucilla and Bruce Dickerson visited. Dru wanted to copy an apron Lisa Smayda made.

Wednesday, April 4, 2001—cloudy, 12° to 38°. Called Doug Rhodes about their shooting club. Wrote some reports on my shooting range findings. Jim gave us some magazines. Theresa called to tell us a car had struck her side of their car, ambulance to emergency room for x-rays and back home this evening. She is stiff and sore.

Thursday, April 5, 2001—cloudy, then sunny, some breeze, 19° to 38°. Finished writing up papers for shooting range. Proposal to be voted on tomorrow evening. Bob R. stopped by. Went over to Mannings and copied some more receipts for making bore cleaner for guns. Really nice outside today. Evening is beautiful.

Friday, April 6, 2001—cloudy, partly cloudy, 4° to 36°. Went to Glennallen. Lunch, bank, shopping, paid phone bill. Bob and Kahren came over. Bob doesn't want a rifle range on our recreation site. We went to Nel-Mel Corp Spring meeting. I presented the pros and cons about the shooting range. There was a long discussion and many questions. The show of hands was overwhelmingly in favor of pursuing the possibility of developing the range. There were two dissenting votes. A few people who came up and complimented me on my presentation. Jim Miller said he would take adult gun instruction in Glennallen. Great! We took Allen home after the meeting. Roxanne is close to having the baby.

Saturday, April 7, 2001—sunny, very nice, 16° to 38°. Burned catalogs, magazines. Put water in car radiator. Jeff phoned. Jim Odden phoned. We went to Bob and Kahren's for supper. Addy Griffith was there with grandson Jesse. Lisa NikiNiki and Dave. Grace was there.

Sunday, April 8, 2001—Sunny and very nice, 14° to 40°. Slept late called and talked to Paul and Steve. Steve had another pickup sideswipe his pickup. The driver was going the wrong way on a two-way highway. Foggy night. Jeff R stopped by and gave me an ammo bandolier from 1950s with 6 M1 clips and 41 blank 30-06 cartridges. A mature bald eagle swooped down on something near the bird feeder. It missed whatever was its intended prey. Finished polishing the blank 30-06 brass. Removed rust from 6, M1 clips the best I could.

Monday, April 9, 2001—cloudy, 7° to 33°. Made some phone calls relative to shooting range. Jane Winegar phoned to talk about the range effort was going. Re wrote some notes. Did a little research. Kahren called-her computer isn't receiving email. Roxanne had her baby about 1:00 AM this morning. She and baby are fine and will stay a few days at Lucky and Mary's in Palmer.

Tuesday, April 10, 2001—mostly sunny, snow is shrinking, 17° to 42°. Took a garbage can to transfer site. Visited with Lee Dudley and Chris (Grizzly Towing). We get key there. Talked about the shooting range and possible development. He has copies of the minutes since he has been on the board. It is hard to get away from the store. I checked and added some oil in the truck. Needs no coolant. Parked the snow plow out in yard.

Wednesday, April 11, 2001—cloudy, light snow, clearing and sunny, 30° to 44°. Allen invited us down for lunch and to meet their new baby son, name is Reed. Sylvia held him a lot. I went for a short walk on highway. Carried her cucumber planters down into basement.

Thursday, April 12, 2001—cloudy, some breeze, 25° to 40°. Replaced burned out bulb in well. Brought up the tarp cover for well. Wrote one shooting club by-law. Cleaned bore on M1. Oiled its leather sling.

Friday, April 13, 2001—sunny, breezy, 30° to 41°. We went to Glennallen. Lunch, post office and shopping. Joe (Puddin) drove today. Back home I put the summer tires on car and store the studded ones.

Saturday, April 14, 2001—cloudy, snow to south in evening, 15° to 41°. We went over to Mannings for brunch. Peg and Joe Virgin there also.

Sunday, April 15, 2001—sunny, 20° to 44°. Went to Easter Service at Mendeltna Chapel. Theresa phoned—she has better news this call. My brother Marion called. He and Ken may come up late July, early August. Allen and Roxanne invited us down to their place for lunch. Then we went with them west of Gunsight Lodge to watch young people snowboard and ride snowmobile on the slopes and in rock quarry. Put on quite a show. On way back, near Gunsight Lodge, a snowgo had driven onto highway and was struck by a car. Appeared very serious. Person wrapped in blankets. Snowgo demolished. Went to Bartley's for dinner and a game of cards. Lots of people there.

Monday, April 16, 2001—cloudy and snow flurries, partly cloudy, 22° to 40°. Removed new snow tires and put old tires on the truck for the summer. Ice has torn up the right rear tail light wiring. Worked on it a while today—what a mess! Scattered a five gallon bucket of ashes over the snow on the garden in hopes of accelerating the snow melt.

Tuesday, April 17, 2001—sunny, 21° to 43°. Jeff, Dale and Ralph are on Kodiak Island hunting great brown bear. Called Cal Gilcrease hoping I could get parts off an old car at his place to fix our car rear light. He thinks snow is too deep. Did my exercises and walked two miles along highway. Snow is melting.

Wednesday, April 18, 2001—sunny, very nice, 15° to 46°. Snow sure melted today. Did a 2-½ mile walk. Filled a rut in the yard. Sylvia made lasagna for Allen Farmer family. Theresa and Bev both phoned. Put the telescope on Heavenly Ridge—no bear tracks.

Thursday, April 19, 2001—sunny, 22° to 47°. Put away the winter tire and rims. Moved snowgo to summer storage. Kahren visited.

Friday, April 20, 2001—sunny, 19° to 46°. We went to Glennallen on senior van. Lunch and shopping. Sylvia saw a lynx three miles southeast of Glennallen. I saw a yearling eagle. Rosemary gave us a dozen eggs. We gave Ron two bottles of some ginger ale extract. Dust is in the air this afternoon.

Saturday, April 21, 2001—sunny, really nice, 18° to 45°. Burned some trash and filled some ruts in the lane. We rode with Bart and Rosemary and Sam to Legion supper in Glennallen. Good turnout there. Sylvia had the lucky number in the drawing and won half the cash in the pot. She gave it back to Legion.

Sunday, April 22, 2001—sunny, 17° to 44°. Walked 2-½ miles this morning. Sylvia is really busy with the greenhouse. We sorted through the chest freezer. Went to Darrel and Brenda's for dinner today. Stopped by the shooting range at Gulkana—I picked up some brass. SD Big Jim let little Rosemary Bartley load and take the garbage to transfer site.

Monday, April 23, 2001—sunny, 23° to 46°. Checked oil in front differential of truck. Did some chores.

Tuesday, April 24, 2001—cloudy, snow showers, partly cloudy, 30° to 45°. We went to Palmer, Wasilla, Eagle River, and Anchorage checking on possible water well. Shopping. Got fitted for a hearing aid. Left about 7:00 AM and got home about 5:30 PM. Marion phoned with dates he and Ken will be here.

Wednesday, April 25, 2001—sunny, 26° to 46°. Took my walk today. Drove Henry over to Tom's to get the big loader. Henry brought us some gravel for a wet spot. Joe Philips delivered some heating oil.

Thursday, April 26, 2001—partly cloudy, 28° to 43°. Cast some bullets today for use in Postal Matches. Gas checked and lubed them. Witched for water. Found a couple wide streams. Kahren visited late afternoon.

Friday, April 27, 2001—sunny and really nice, some breeze, 28° to 48°. We went to senior monthly meeting. Lunch and cake. Paid electric bill. Went on my walk when we got home. Saw 55 swans flying west at an altitude of about 1000 feet. Soon after that I saw three large moose. They looked to be in excellent shape. Went over and talked with Mark B about shooting range and other things. Ralph phoned while I was gone.

Saturday, April 28, 2001—sunny, 29° to 49°. Tracks of a large moose walked between house and garage. Put up two short metal poles for Sylvia to hang dresses on in upstairs closet. Cast 200+ .30 caliber bullets. Allen, Roxanne, Samantha and David ate supper with us.

Sunday, April 29, 2001—sunny, breezy, 21° to 45°. Picked up aluminum cans on my walk this morning. Found a pliers holster, bungee, and a piece of steel, some of Brockman's mail. Greased and lubed some bullets. Put some ashes on snow around the house.

Monday, April 30, 2001—sunny, 24° to 47°. Bob Rudbeck came over to use table saw. I made a birch spoon.

Tuesday, May 1, 2001—windy from west, 28° to 45°. Did my walk. Worked on 105 Howitzer mounting bolts. Filled some low places in our driveway. Allen welded wires to bolts for a project.

Wednesday, May 2, 2001—windy, partly cloudy, cloudy and snow flurries, 17° to 43°. Shoveled and leveled the bank run sand gravel Henry brought us. Got about half of it done. I had just quit when I heard loud footsteps. A cow moose and last year's calf walked by at 10'. Her hackles were up—ears vertical. I made it a point not to make eye contact. She was very thin, no belly, maybe not PG. Calf was thin also. Glad she didn't chase me. Installed the mounting bolts on 105 Howitzer shells. Now ready to mount them on the arctic entry, one on each side of the door of Legion Post 27. Cal Gilcrease visited an hour or so. Light snow this evening.

Thursday, May 3, 2001—partly cloudy and windy in the afternoon, 25° to 40°. Did my walk. Moose was hit and killed a half mile east of us last night. Kahren was out walking too. Raked out some ruts and shoveled some gravel.

Friday, May 4, 2001—cloudy, 25° to 42°. Went to Glennallen on senior van. Lunch, bank, telephone, shopping. Made another wood birch spoon. Henry Johnson brought over a new answering machine for our phone. Very generous of him. We went to Cal and Mary's to pick up sweatshirts we had there.

Saturday, May 5, 2001—mostly sunny, some breeze, 19° to 42°. Decided not to attend the NRA teaching adults to be instructors of shooting. It was at Tazlina. Would have cost $40.00 for gas for two trips. Am disappointed, would have liked it. Laura phoned about vacation plans. I found a cheap knife-tool, a bungee cord and a 7/16-1/2" open end wrench while on my walk this morning. Took a look at Allen and Ed's logs. Swans are on our lake. Five caribou went east on south side of our lake. Shoveled some gravel while the water was heating to dye some traps. Put some stop-leak on some pipe threads near the fuel filter on the gasoline storage tank. Sylvia asked Mannings over for supper and gave them a birch spoon for their daughter Loretta. Elaine wanted a spoon for another friend.

Sunday, May 6, 2001—partly cloudy, 26° to 46°. Finished dyeing the traps. A snowshoe rabbit eats the grass as the snow melts back. We went to a party for Ian Mailly who is graduating high school. Very nice young man. We gave him some traps.

Monday, May 7, 2001—cloudy, snow flurries, 28° to 44°. Did my walk. Bob and Kahren Rudbeck were walking also. Allen Farmer picked up the moose hide. Mannings left on vacation. I loaded a barrel of aluminum and changed oil and filter in truck. Joe Virgin brought me a Sunday paper with article about Sandhill cranes in Alaska. Three swans on our lake.

Tuesday, May 8, 2001—rain and snow overnight, one inch on the ground. We left 7:00 AM. Shopped at Costco, K-Mart, Wal-Mart. Sold the aluminum cans for enough money for lunch at Royal Fork. Got some grass seed and fertilizer for garden and lawn. Had the hearing aid fitted at Costco. Sylvia got her prescription. Nice evening.

Wednesday, May 9, 2001—snow in night and morning, nicer in afternoon, 26° to 45°. Knees were not up to a walk today. Did some small jobs. Sylvia saw a marten go through by the woodshed. Saw a kestrel and a boreal owl. Rode with Bart to the Legion meeting in Glennallen.

Thursday, May 10, 2001—cloudy, partly cloudy, 26° to 45°. Took my walk, found a 12V 4 amp battery. Cal came over and used the table saw. Had cake and coffee and visited awhile. Put charger on battery. It took a charge, will test later to see it if holds a charge. Dimmicks asked us over to have halibut chunks and clam chowder. Reyne Brockman brought her mother over to visit.

Friday, May 11, 2001—sunny, 28° to 48°. Went to Glennallen on senior bus. Lunch, bank and shopping. Did a few odd jobs.

Saturday, May 12, 2001—sunny, very nice, 23° to 50°. Found a couple goodies on my walk. Did some odd jobs. Varithaned the 105 Howitzer shells. Cleaned up some spruce trimmings. Hung up the awning I found. Shoveled some snow off the lawn.

Sunday, May 13, 2001—sunny, breeze from west, 23° to 54°. I have three coats of varithane on the cannon shells. Walked down to well and the lake. Removed light bulb from well. Frost is down about 8-9" in garden. Reloaded some .30 caliber pest loads. We went over to Brockman's. Party for Luke's confirmation. Robins are here. Coyote howled. Ten swan flew off out lake leaving four here. Ducks on open place at west end.

Monday, May 14, 2001—sunny and some breeze, 28° to 58°. Did a three mile walk. Cut up four broken off tree tops. Burned trash. Straightened up TGI waterline supports. Burned some lawn raking. Lots of robins.

Tuesday, May 15, 2001—partly cloudy morning, cloudy afternoon and a few sprinkles, 34° to 54°. Raked some lawn. Put lime and fertilizer on garden and we worked it in soil, in rows ready to plant. Virginia sent me a program—obituary of our dad's funeral (from years ago).

Wednesday, May 16, 2001—snow, rain, cloudy till noon, partly cloudy afternoon and very nice, 33° to 50°. Shoveled snow away from north side of house so the grass can get sun and air. Went for a walk. Jeff came along, we came back here to visit and look at the pictures of his bear hunt and kill. He had lunch with us. I made two birch wood spatulas.

Thursday, May 17, 2001—cloudy, rain and west snow, 33° to 56°. Depth was 324 feet. Doused for water. We defrosted and repaired shelves in upright freezer. Kahren visited. Wanted package mailed tomorrow. Sylvia gave her cucumber plants. Jeff phoned. I called Dan Billman. Jeff got a small black bear boar this evening.

Friday, May 18, 2001—snow, rain mostly cloudy, 32° to 43°. We went to Glennallen on senior van for lunch. Did a little shopping. Sylvia mailed a package for Kahren. A thin yearling cow moose almost ran in front of the van. We saw three caribou. Lots of ducks on the quarter of our lake that is thawed out. Visited an hour this evening. Robbie is driving his boat on the lake.

Saturday, May 19, 2001—sunny and nice, 35° to 57°. Snow is going fast. 4/5 of our lake is ice free now. Lots of ducks. We went to Cal and Mary's after my walk and got the bulb holders for right rear lights on car. Bob and Kahren were here for coffee and cake. Sylvia helped with the wire colors and I wired the bulb holders into the car rear lights - works fine. Went to Bart's with the Rudbecks and then we all rode with Bart and Rosemary to prime rib dinner and installation of officers at Legion Post. We saw four caribou on highway on the way home.

Sunday, May 20, 2001—sunny and breeze, 29° to 54°. Parked snowgo trailer. Phoned Linda Burns Kurtis. Checked the well. Witched for water. Raked some lawn and lots little jobs. Went for a walk. Ann and Lincoln Smith stopped by.

Monday, May 21, 2001—partly cloudy, cloudy, windy, 33° to 47°. Went to Lake Louise Road to varmint hunt. Construction crew there so came back home. Picked up brass at two gravel pits. Found a rusty socket tool on highway. Finished raking the yard. Bev phoned.

Tuesday, May 22, 2001—mostly cloudy and light showers, 31° to 46°. Took my walk this morning. Found a bolt and a rope. Saw a very large moose track. Twenty-one caribou spent mid-day hours loafing around on the grassy point out into our lake. Last evening a bald eagle made several tries for a duck on the water with a raven harassing him all the time. Eagle wound up in the water and had a heck of a time getting airborne. Seeded some bare spots in lawn that voles had eaten bare. Wheelbarrow sand then top soil and seeded a small extension to the lawn near the arctic entry.

Wednesday, May 23, 2001—mostly cloudy, snow flurries in the morning, 34° to

48°. Seeded a little more grass. Hundreds of scoters and Goldeneye ducks were on our lake this morning and all day. Nine swans here. Two males fought over the female. We went to a picnic at the school house. Teacher and kids put on an end of year program.

Thursday, May 24, 2001—partly cloudy, couple sprinkles, 30° to 52°. Went for my walk. Swans are courting on lake. Lots of ducks have left. Raked and leveled some gravel. Put on snowplow and leveled more of it. Tested a solenoid on snowplow. Parked snowplow for summer. Picked up more bullets. Carried up another broken off spruce tree top.

Friday, May 25, 2001—mostly sunny, 32° to 47°. Sylvia went to Anchorage for the weekend with Kahren. I went to monthly senior meeting at Kluti Kaah Hall in Copper Center.

Saturday, May 26, 2001—partly cloudy, 36° to 49°. Went for walk early. Did some small jobs. Happened to be in the house as Dan Billman phoned and ask me to accompany him to Wasilla to pickup building supplies and air plane parts. Lots of visiting, ate twice, met some new people. He plans to restore a Stinson Gull Wing plane from scratch. We saw some caribou and moose. Got home 10:00 PM.

Sunday, May 27, 2001—partly cloudy till noon then cloudy and windy, 46° to 57°. Put a 10' telephone cross arm in for a post to support garden windbreak. Cleaned up a winter damaged birch. Started auger motor. Sylvia and Kahren got back about 6:00 PM. Sure bought a lot of yard sale stuff. File cabinets, new Bissell rug washer.

Monday, May 28, 2001—partly cloudy, 43° to 56°. We went to American Legion Post 27 Glennallen to honor fallen veterans of past wars. It is always a moving experience. I served on firing squad again this year. A service at Glennallen cemetery and placing flags and wreaths. A service at Moose Creek and placing a wreath so as to float down creek to honor those lost at sea. Saw caribou both going and coming back home.

Tuesday, May 29, 2001—partly cloudy and showers in evening, 37° to 58°. Went for a three mile walk. Touched up paint on arctic entry railings for steps. Cleaned out and burned 30 lbs magazines. Sylvia brought home two, double filing cabinets and I rearranged things and stacked the two cabinets and set our old one beside them. Sylvia planted garden. We visited Allen and Roxanne in evening. Got to hold Reed for awhile.

Wednesday, May 30, 2001—partly cloudy and a couple shower came in from west and north over Slide Mountain, 41° to 56°. Finished burning magazines.

Leveled more gravel over by camper and storage shed. Scattered some gravel I had pushed up with snow last winter. Picked up some more bullets. Re-raked some lawn on north side of house. Kahren called and told me of speckle belly geese resting on their beach. Took a couple pictures. Jerry Rudbeck got his plane out and flew around for an hour or so and did a few touch-and-gos.

Thursday, May 31, 2001—partly cloudy, cloudy and some little rain, 39° to 56°. Did two, half-mile walks. Repaired the 1-1/2" water line. It had frozen and split last winter. The speckle belly geese are still hanging out at Kahren Rudbecks. Cal and Mary stopped by, visited and borrowed my hand cart and a nylon strap load binder.

Friday, June 1, 2001—rainy night and morning, partly cloudy afternoon, 39° to 63°. We went to Glennallen for lunch and a little shopping. Loafed in the afternoon then went to Glacier View School in evening. Mary Hannah Luna graduated from 8th grade and Shawn Ti Wright graduated 12th grade, David Farmer's girlfriend. Cal and Mary Gilcrease are Mary Hannah's grandparents. We saw three moose this evening.

Saturday, June 2, 2001—mostly sunny, very nice, 38° to 67°. Went to visit Lee Dudley. Then finished placing the gravel out by the woodshed. Worked on waterline grade above the culvert at trail. Rolled up some old electric wire. Put on arctic entry screen door. Cal brought back the hand cart. We went to Allen and Roxanne's for supper.

Sunday, June 3, 2001—mostly sunny, 40° to 69°. Cooler breeze toward evening. Walked two miles. Put in water manifolds at garden and at top of hill for irrigation garden and lawn. Opened gold screw crate and put some marvel mystery oil in on piston top. Turned motor over a few times. Tried to witch water at the earlier place with no luck. Did a few other small jobs.

Monday, June 4, 2001—cloudy, sunny, cloudy, couple little showers, 42° to 62°. We went to Glennallen and I cleaned the Legion Post rifles used in Memorial Day ceremonies. We had lunch with the seniors at Rendezvous Café. Jeff Routt visited late afternoon and had supper with us. He had bought a used .22 cal bolt rifle with scope. We got it sighted in. It shoots very well. Cleaned it too. Had lots of fun.

Tuesday, June 5, 2001—rain till 1:00 PM, then sunny, 43° to 58°. Nice rain. Made a couple birch spoons. Poked around looking at some of our "stuff." Hoed some grass. Ralph called. He won $2800.00 worth of DeWalt tools at AIH in Fairbanks.

Wednesday, June 6, 2001—cloudy, sunny, cloudy and light rain, 44° to 64°.

Went for my walk before breakfast. Cleaned up some plowed up gravel. Seeded a patch of grass. Hoed the volunteer grass on north side of house. Transplanted some of it on the cut bank. Allen visited early evening. Saw an evening grosbeak in spruce tree—bright yellow.

Thursday, June 7, 2001—rainy all morning, 38° to 57°. Filled two little low places in our lane. Mike and Marsha Achermann from Motley, Minnesota are visiting us. Nice to get caught up happenings from down that way. After supper we did a tour around the place. Marsha talked to Roma in Fairbanks.

Friday, June 8, 2001—partly cloudy and a shower, 42° to 63°. Visited with Mike and Marsha till senior van came. They left for Fairbanks and we went to Glennallen. Lunch and pay phone bill and got some flowers for Kahren. After supper drove to Bart's. Someone had just hit a caribou and smashed front of their SUV. Probably killed the caribou. Rode with Bart to Legion meeting in Glennallen. Sylvia joined the Ladies Auxiliary. Beautiful evening.

Saturday, June 9, 2001—sunny and nice breeze, 38° to 69°. Called my son Paul with birthday greetings. Up at 5:00 AM and went for walk, then a nap. Did some odd jobs. Went to gravel pit to look for bear tracks. None. Found a few pieces brass. We took some food to Rusty D. John was there also. Stopped by Cal and Mary's. Someone is doing some vandalism at Marks property and tried to start a piece of DOT equipment. Checked the boo carcass about 11:00 PM. Lots of traffic. Trooper wrote someone a ticket near caribou carcass.

Sunday, June 10, 2001—sunny some breeze, clouding up in evening, 43° to 73°! Up 5:00 AM and went to check boo carcass. Then called Allen. He had removed 3/qts and the hide. Reloaded ammo for three postal matches. Cal and Mary came over and got a load of water.

Monday, June 11, 2001—cloudy, sunny, cloudy and windy, 48° to 69°. Went for a walk. Gathered targets and shooting gear. Went to gravel pit to set up postal shoot targets. Sylvia watched the clock to time shots. Did poorly. Back home. Cleaned rifles and put gear away.

Tuesday, June 12, 2001—partly cloudy with shower and small hail in evening, 43° to 62°. Went to pick up Kyle Farmer to go hunt his dad's black bear station. Allen asked me to accompany Kyle as he had to work. We didn't stay long. Went down to their place at noon and Kyle and I went back to watch the station. I even took a nap on the tundra. I had been awake for a few moments when a small, two-yr-old black bear showed up. It was on the bait, with its back to us. Kyle got up, used a tree for a rest. Kyle's 100 yard shoot to the neck dropped the bear instantly. He prepared to shoot again but this was not necessary. We walked down and made sure the bear wasn't playing possum, then picture taking and congratulations time. We went home and got Sylvia's kid sled to pull it out to where we could load it in truck. This idea didn't work as bear and sled kept tipping over. The back home and loaded my ATV and with it hauled the bear out, loaded both on truck and went to Kyle's place. Put a tarp on garage floor and unloaded the bear. I skinned all four feet out which is the hardest part of skinning job. Was getting tired so went home to supper. Rained and hailed this evening. Allen came over later and we put out more bait.

Wednesday, June 13, 2001—mostly cloudy with afternoon showers, 42° to 51°. Serviced the car and truck. Sylvia vacuum packed the bear meat. Loaded the burn barrel on truck and garbage. Went over to Henry's to see all the work he has done. Kahren came over to get some chicken wire netting for her beans to climb on. Later she brought over some fresh lake trout.

Thursday, June 14, 2001—mostly cloudy, some light rain, 43° to 63°. Took some meat scraps down to road kill boo. The bears have eaten it up. Changed out the #8 spark plug on the car. Cal and Mary came just as I was finishing. Cal needed to borrow the hand cart again. We had cinnamon toast and coffee. Planted some grass seed on the cut banks on the switch back road that goes down to lake. Hauled the garbage and ashes to transfer site. Had a hell of a time dumping the 55-gallon drum again. My right boot (shoe), the sole, is coming loose. I'm trying to fix it with shoe goo. Before supper a cow moose was wading east in the lake eating emerging water lilies. We had lake trout for supper that Kahren brought over last night.

Friday, June 15, 2001—sunny, nice breeze. Went to Glennallen on senior van. Lunch, post office, groceries, cabbage and flower plants. Went to yard sale. Al Smith had a black bear on his porch this morning. He shot the bear in the tail with a .410 shotgun. Ed gave me some blanks. Rigged the tarp hanging in front of the snowgo. Gold screw to be pulled up and tied off with a rope. We went to Cal and Mary's for supper. Nothing is on the carcass in the gravel pit.

Saturday, June 16, 2001—sunny, 44° to 70°. Mosquitoes are getting worse. Went for walk before breakfast. Mowed scattered patches of grass. Made four birch wood spoons and spatulas. We went to Legion Post for a spaghetti supper.

Sunday, June 17, 2001—sunny, 50° to 76°. Mowed lawn and down by lake. Plug fouled, cleaned it. Carried four buckets of Nome concentrates and Gold wheel up out of basement and out to garage to load on truck for trip to Fairbanks. Panned one sample. Consolidated others. Started packing for trip. Nadia phoned Father Day greetings. Bev called earlier in week.

Monday, June 18, 2001—partly cloudy, thunder shower after supper, 48° to 70°.

Worked a little with gold stuff. Cut a couple winter-ravaged trees along the lane. Cut a lot of alder, willow, and the tundra roses alongside the greenhouse. Checked oil and water in the car. Put fertilizer on the lawn after supper. Ralph called late, couldn't contact his friend Steve about claims.

Tuesday, June 19, 2001—partly cloudy, 50° to 70s. Near Isabell Pass and again near Fairbanks sprinkled rain. We loaded Molly car for trip to Fairbanks. Forgot camera and binoculars. Shopped in Glennallen. Got hugs from Brenda. Sylvia fixed sandwiches for lunch near Donley Dome. We've seen some moose. Got gas in Delta Junction. Went to shooting range and picked up about 100 pistol brass. More moose and one calf on way to Fairbanks. Also cranes and geese. Stopped by Legion Post 57 to ask directions and for recommendation of a place to eat dinner, which was a good 7 ounce New York Steak Sylvia bought for my Father's Day present. Called John Odden. He drove to the restaurant and we followed him to pick up his dip net salmon. Then onto his place. John, Coleen, Axel and Eric ate supper. John filleted five salmon. Colleen had filleted 24 salmon while John was at work. They vacuum sealed a lot of them before we went to bed. John has built a place high on a mountain with a great view.

Wednesday, June 20, 2001—sunny and breezy, 50° to 78°. Called Dan Walsh, left message. He phoned back and gave me an appointment for 1:30 PM to bring my Nome concentrates. Coleen had to pick up Axel at summer school. We followed in our car. She showed us where the Mineral Research Laboratory is located. Got a one time use camera at K-Mart. Put gas in Molly. Got lost on campus. Had a helluva time finding MRL lab. It took two hours to run the concentrate samples. Very poor valves. Not worth running over concentrate table. Got maybe $10 worth of gold. Dan was patient with the futile effort. We found our way out of Fairbanks and to John's place without too much trouble, where we had BBQ salmon for supper—excellent. Had a nice visit this evening.

Thursday, June 21, 2001—partly cloudy, 50° to 76°. Smoke from two forest fires can be seen. We left John and Colleen's about noon then followed the map John had drawn to get to Fort Knox Mine where John works. After orientation and our pictures taken with a 23# bar of gold worth $84,000, John drove us to the overlook at the pit. We watched the operation. While doing this I got a picture of blasting a large area of rock loose so huge loaders could load large ore trucks that hauled the rock to be processed at the mill. After the "all clear signal," we drove drown into the pit. John looked at a vein in the rock. We watched ore trucks being loaded with 150 ton of rock. Repairs were being made on a CAT 5230 clamshell hoe while a CAT 994 loader filled ore trucks with flour buckets of blasted rock. Then he took us to the ball milling plant and it multitude of different operations extracting and processing of the gold. We were very impressed with the whole operation. John, as geologist works in a different department and explores for more gold reserves. Got turned around twice on way back to town and John got us straightened out twice!! Watch some hand panners working a tailing pile open to recreational. Ate supper at same place on Cushman Street. Luckily Sylvia had the complete phone number for Ralph and Roma. He came over soon as I called and led us to the apt. they are living in. Roma took Sylvia over to the house they have just bought. Ralph and I went over later. The lady living there is having a yard sale. Then we went to a nearby shooting range. Found some brass for Ralph. Back to their place. Fixed a leak in the flapper in the toilet water closet.

Friday, June 22, 2001—sunny, 50s to 70s. Smoke from forest fires is in air. We helped Roma. Ralph is at work. She bought a new mattress set and a waterfall, "garden type" for their new home. When Ralph came home from work we went for a ride after supper. Had a ice cream cone, saw Roma's favorite trout fishing hole. Went to shooting range and picked up some brass Ralph uses. Had a good time.

Saturday, June 23, 2001—partly cloudy and some breeze, 50s to 80°. Pancakes with Montana huckleberries for breakfast. We loaded a picnic lunch in the cooler. Ralph drove his pick up and Roma drove their car and Sylvia. I rode with Ralph. Out the Steese Highway to Montana Creek at about 80 miles or so. Then we all got in his pickup and Ralph drove us over a mountain and down to a creek to see two California Gold dredgers he had met a few days earlier. We watched them dredge for a while. When they shut down and talked about dredging gold and showed us some "pickers" in the upper part of their sluice box. Ralph gave them a Pepsi each. Lots of mosquitoes. Then we drove back out to Steese Highway. Ate our sandwiches. The ladies drove back to town and worked in the garden in the new home. Sylvia dug some wild iris to bring home with us. Ralph showed me, stopped by his friends trap cabin. He took a "snoozer." Then we backtracked six miles and walked north on a trail that passed under the Davidson ditch waterline. It was put in the early 1900s not in use now. He showed me some Iron Pyrite - hoped it was gold. Saw marten sets and a bear track. Drove back to Fairbanks. Saw one of Ralph's favorite gun stores. Back at his house we found Sylvia had bought "Chinese" food for supper. I finished reading a hunting book that I had started. Read the Sunday paper. Ralph went and got some ice cream. I took a shower. Pretty hot tonight. Roma put a fan in our room. House cooled down about 3:00 AM.

Sunday, June 24, 2001—sunny, breezy, 50s to 80°. Got up 6:00 AM and got ready to go to Harding Lake, which is on the way home. Ate some melon for breakfast, said goodbye. Got onto the Parks Highway, saw my mistake, turned around went back and got on the Richardson Highway. Stopped for gas near Harding Lake. Then drove into Harding Lake campground. Driving slow and looking, we spotted their pickup and camper. Brenda and her son, Roger were up and outside. Darrel got up after while. Robin, Samantha, Robert and Mike got up. After while Mike took his boat down to the launch ramp, rest of us walked. The young people all went across the lake to a house another son Ron was at. Brenda, Darrel, Sylvia and I went back to camping area. Soon Sylvia and I started for home. Picked up some brass at Delta Junction. Had a hamburger, got gasoline and drove to Delta River. Car got hot so put in some water. Stopped a range near Glennallen and picked up a few pieces brass. Back to home-sweet-home. Unloaded car. Brought my journal up to date. Mosquitoes are persistent. Smoky here. Ralph phoned to be sure we were home safe. Tried to phone Charlie Trowbridge with no luck.

Monday, June 25, 2001—partly cloudy, 44° to 74°. Lots smoke in the air. Did a little work on car. Polished brass and put it away. Loaded some brush on the truck and unloaded it on brush pile.

Tuesday, June 26, 2001—partly cloudy, lot of smoke in the air and a couple drops of rain, 49° to 72°. Went for a walk. Mosquitoes are very bad. Loaded and hauled more brush. Hauled the stove wood to wood shed and split and piled it. Visited Allen, Roxanne, Reed, Kyle, Ellie.

Wednesday, June 27, 2001—partly cloudy, 49° to 72°. Smoky. Sorted through and selected lumber to build shipping style display case for the M1 Garand. Used a screw in anchor, cable and clamps to hold the north side of upper garden fence vertical. Saw a snowshoe rabbit again tonight.

Thursday, June 28, 2001—mostly sunny, some breeze, 46° to 73°. Made some more pieces for M1 display case. Wood bottom, sides and ends are assembled. Bob R. gave me wood to make a 2" x 6" x 15 1/2" piece with.

Friday, June 29, 2001—partly cloudy, showers in the area, 46° to 68°. Went to monthly senior meeting at Kluti Kaah Hall in Copper Center. Paid electric bill and did a little shopping. Ducks were really flying this morning. Saw a robin land on picture window sill and catch a mosquito catcher. Sylvia got a couple huckleberry plants. Sent order off to Grizzly Imports for repairs.

Saturday, June 30, 2001—partly cloudy w showers in the afternoon and evening, 48° to 68°. Went for walk very early—no mosquitoes then, but plenty of them later. Changed the oil in lawn mower. Stopped at Brockman's when after the mail. He and Luke and Nickie were putting sheeting the rafters. Fooled around in wood shop a little. No phone call from Fairbanks.

Sunday, July 1, 2001—one inch rain last night, clearing in morning and nice day, with good breeze in evening, 46° to 68°. We went to church services baptism of 12 people at Allen and Roxanne Farmers. Pot luck dinner afterwards. Lots of people. Charlie Trowbridge called from Tok, Alaska. We invited them to our home. They then drove on over to Farmers in time to eat and visit with lots of people they know. Afterwards they came to our place. Their son Paul asked to drive the 4-wheeler. Did a good job for a four-yr-old. Both his dad and I rode with him. Charlie Jr. watched "October Sky" a movie of a book he had just read. I gave him some books as he is an avid reader. Charlie Sr. is talking to Jerry Rudbeck about ground rules for driving over Charlie's land. Mary Odden is here for a few days and visited a while this evening.

Monday, July 2, 2001—sunny, 48° to 73°. Trowbridge family and Dennis and Jody Eastman were here fot breakfast. Lots of visiting and story telling. Denny took Paul and Charlie Sr. for a short ride in his airplane. Lincoln Smith and wife Ann visited a short while. Charlie and family went to Odden's house to play music with Mary. Came back about 3:30 PM. I put water soaked towels on lid of the box I'm building-clamped it to tweak the twist out of it. Looks good this evening. Let Paul drive the ATV after supper. Charlie then borrowed it and trailer to do down to their storage shed on their land.

Tuesday, July 3, 2001—partly cloudy, cloudy evening, 46° to 75°. We had a late breakfast. Then went over to the Trowbridge property to find the northwest corner. Charlie wanted to look over the possibility of putting a road in to South Road to access that part. Beth didn't seem to want a road there. Back at our place they got their gear together and left soon after noon. I worked on the box for a while. Then took a movie over to Cal and he gave me another one. Helped Henry get a pump hooked up to a supply tank. For house water while pulling his water pump, a little later the pump motor lodged in well and pipe broke off the motor. They quit for today and I came home to find Patti Billman and Mary Odden visiting here.

Wednesday, July 4, 2001—tried to rain this morning and trying again this evening, 46° to 60°. We went to Glennallen and I marched with the Legionnaires in the 4th of July parade. I and Joe passed out little flags to the children. The Lions Club had a salmon bake with all the trimmings. Sylvia won a drawing for a "spinning" yard ornament. After supper went over to Henry and Sally's and saw a video he had made by lowering a flashlight and his video camera down his 6" well casing. It showed why the pump was stuck. Hartman had dropped the wires to the pump into the casing. He fished with halibut hooks catching the wire and we got 6l ft of it out. Hooked it again but broke off and we gave up for the night.

Thursday, July 5, 2001—cloudy and rainy, 43° to 51°. Didn't do much today. We went to American Legion mtg. in Glennallen. Took Bart and George along. Saw a bull moose cross the highway ½ mile east of Tolsona Lake.

Friday, July 6, 2001—rain, 44° to 50°. We went to Glennallen on senior van. Shopping and lunch at Caribou. Good Food. Went to Allen and Roxanne's to supper. Tom and Kim were there. Note: Sent order for binoculars.

Saturday, July 7, 2001—cleared up towards evening, 42° to 62°. Worked some on the box and other jobs. Ralph Fuson phoned. Roma is doing well after operation.

Sunday, July 8, 2001—breezy both from east and west, 42° to 52°. Partly cloudy for a few hours to clouding over this evening. Finished the hinges and hasps on the box. Checked camper for leaks and found a small one. Pulled some weeds and yellow willow. Cleaned a little of the M1 stock.

Monday, July 9, 2001—some rain, some sun, 42° to 62°. Sylvia mowed the lawn. The throttle cable sheath was broken and had to be repaired. My boots from Cabela's came. Wrote a couple letters.

Tuesday, July 10, 2001—mostly sunny, 40° to 64°. Up early and went for a walk. Mailed letters and went over to Henry's just as the guys started to run cement. Took a nap. Got shooting gear ready. Took M1 to big gravel pit to shoot some M2 Ball ammo and sight rifle for it. Sight does not hold a zero. Rats! I will have to disassemble it and see what is wrong. Came home and cleaned rifle. Took nap. Got some trout fishing gear ready. Ate supper and went to Ian Mailly's. We went fishing in Ryan Lake using his canoe and 12 volt Min-kota trolling motor. We caught four fish. He measured my largest at 16". The rest were stocked this year. We saw a loon, gulls, and ducks. Kahren and two grandsons came there to fish. Some other people also. Got car ready to go to Wasilla tomorrow.

Wednesday, July 11, 2001—mostly cloudy and showers, 44° to 63°. Left 7:00 AM. We went to Palmer to ask about well drilling. Then to Wasilla, Sylvia had blood drawn to check for any prescription effects on her liver. On to Anchorage, and Home Depot. I picked up four, 5-gallon pails of log oil. three are stains (not what I wanted), but they were stacked in the same pile. Went to GI Joe's got WWII canteen cover, cup and a mess kit and a dummy grenade nostalgia memorabilia. Went to Costco to get hearing aid adjusted. Groceries. Then back to Palmer more groceries and home and unloaded before 7:00 PM.

Thursday, July 12, 2001—partly cloudy, some showers in area, 46° to 61°. Steve Donaldson stopped when I was walking and offered to fish halibut for us by proxy. I said sure. Later when he got to work at Fish & Game he called to say Larry St. Amand had 25 red and 2 king salmon for us at Fish & Game in Glennallen. We ran in and picked them up. Back home about 12:45. They were already filleted. I took the skin off and removed the ribs after Sylvia deslimed them. She then vacuum-sealed them. We got done just before 5:00 PM. Everything was washed and clean. Steve stopped by for Larry's cooler after supper. Then I burned trash and took the skins and ribs and dumped them for the ravens. Washed that bucket and finished for the night. Good feeling having all the salmon in freezer. Allen, Roxanne visited in evening.

Friday, July 13, 2001—mostly cloudy and light showers, 44° to 59°. We went to Glennallen. Shopping, post office and lunch. Did some adjustment of M1 sights. Put some things away, small jobs. Beverly phoned.

Saturday, July 14, 2001—mostly cloudy, 44° to 64°. Went for a walk. Then went over to Mark's and then Ed's. Put two coats of urethane on the wood crate. Ran the sandstone sample from Cottonwood Creek through the gold wheel. There were quite a lot of gold valves left in the concentrate. Called Ed and Allen to come and see for themselves. My back is bad tonight.

Sunday, July 15, 2001—very beautiful day, 45° to 73°. Went to gravel pit and shot the M1 and cleaned it when back home. Put away gold wheel and dried the cons. Lost the one and only large flake. Ralph called and then got another call. Our phone was out for a few hours. Put new cutting blade on mower and mowed lawn. Sylvia is cleaning house. I called Marion this evening.

Monday, July 16, 2001—very nice, mostly breezy, 45° to 75°. Went for walk. Put Sylvia's rug upholstery cleaning machine together and got her started using it. Put hinges on the box. Visited Henry's building project. We asked Harold and Rachel to have supper with us. They brought some ripe bananas.

Tuesday, July 17, 2001—mostly sunny, 50° to 73°. Cleaned M1 rifle stock. Put two coats tung oil with tincture of Minwax walnut stain. Called an office in Anchorage about getting a will drawn up. Pulled some weeds and willows.

Wednesday, July 18, 2001—sunny, 52° to 75°. Went for a walk. Put two coats of oil on gunstock. Put roof sealer on camper. Mary and Kari Odden stopped by for five minutes. Sylvia used her new rug cleaner. Helped move furniture and scrubbed the kitchen door. Got ready to go to Anchorage. Strong breeze tonight.

Thursday, July 19, 2001—partly cloudy, 49° to 73°. Lots of bugs. Put more Tung oil on Sylvia's knitting box. Checked M1 operating rod spring, and the free fall of the operating rod. Put the rifle back together. Cut grass from the lawn "edges" with a hand scythe. Cal and grandson Colby visited awhile. Trimmed some scraps from black bear hide. Did some case preparation on some 30-06 brass.

Friday, July 20, 2001—rain early, partly cloudy and breezy, 50° to 70°. We went to Glennallen on senior bus. Lunch and bank. Soon after returning home Ralph Fuson drove in the yard. He and I went to gravel pit and shot service and match ammo in the M1. The match ammo is really more accurate. He had some reloads 30-06 that were under loaded. He then checked his zero of his 243 Winchester. Came home, ate supper, then he went to a fish wheel he will be using tonight.

Saturday, July 21, 2001—very light rain, low cloudy, 51° to 67°. Took Sylvia to Glennallen for breast cancer screening test. Went on to Darrel and Brenda's. They were not home. Two of his dogs had face full of porcupine quills. Worked on M1 barrel, trying to get all the copper out of it. Took my walk this morning and walked down to lake and well this evening. Lots of red squirrels now. Potato plants look good. Raspberries have bloomed. Carrots are short, fat with lots of "roots" on them.

Sunday, July 22, 2001—foggy, cleared off and partly cloudy, 44° to 67°. East breeze switching to west. Mowed some outlying grass. Smashed cans. Went to gravel pit and shot cast bullet loads in M1. Bob R. stopped there checking out the gravel pit. Shot a squirrel with Sylvia's BB fun. Cleaned rifle and loaded some more. Ron Lester, his mother and wife Evelyn, stopped by because we are interested in re-finishing the house and garage logs.

Monday, July 23, 2001—mostly cloudy and a couple of showers, 48° to 66°. Breezy sometimes. Cut some grass, weed and low brush w hand scythe. Truck has antifreeze leak. Can't find it. Went to gravel pit and shot M1. Seated bullets out and shot better groups. Walked over to Henry's. His crew is putting in forms for cement foundation.

Tuesday, July 24, 2001—partly cloudy, 50° to 68°. A few showers in evening. Built a cushion retainer for rocking chair. Stained it. Will put tung oil on it later. Cleaned garage. Cut willows along our lane. Moved gold wheel to storage shed. Burned trash. Visited Allen. Sylvia gave him some pickled salmon.

Wednesday, July 25, 2001—partly cloudy and pretty heavy rain while we were going to Anchorage. Cloudy and foggy early morning, 52° to 69°. Brought home log preservative for house and garage and groceries. Trip went very well. Steve Donaldson stopped by. He needs my fishing license to fish "by proxy" for halibut for us Saturday.

Thursday, July 26, 2001—partly cloudy and one good shower, 50° to 65°. Cleaned up the woodshop. Then Henry J. brought over his pressure washer for me to use for washing and cleaning up our house and garage logs prior to applying the preservative.

Friday, July 27, 2001—partly cloudy w showers moving through, 49° to 67°. Went to Copper Center and the monthly senior meeting on senior van. Pressure washed east end of house.

Saturday, July 28, 2001—cloudy, some showers, 45° to 63°. Finished power washing the house. Got the car gassed and oiled. Mowed the lawn. Got done shortly before rain started. We went to a rib supper at the American Legion Post with Bart and Rosemary. Bart is very short of breath.

Sunday, July 29, 2001—mostly cloudy, 49° to 68°. We have been doing lots of visiting. Nice to get some of that caught up. Marion and Ken walked over our place and down by the lake. In the afternoon we drove over to the Point Lodge at Lake Louise. Visited the Billmans. Had pie and ice cream. Pointed out where our remote parcel is located. Also where my old trap cabin is located. We stopped at the 4 Mile gravel pit on Lake Louise Road and Ken took some video of Tazlina Glacier at the upper end of Tazlina Lake. We saw a trooper investigating a motor home that had driven off the road. It hadn't rolled over. Steve Donaldson stopped in and brought us six fillets from halibut he had caught on Prince William Sound. After I skinned the fillets Sylvia vacuum packed them for the freezer. We'll eat some fresh halibut for supper.

Monday, Tuesday, July 30-31, 2001—mostly cloudy, 48° to 63°. Ken made a lot of effort trying to get reservations to get on a shuttle bus in Denali Park and was finally successful. We will leave tomorrow. Jim Manning came over for a few minutes. Then we took the M1 to the gravel pit. Set up a target and all three of us shot two clips of ammo and had a good time. When we got back home we put the camper on the truck and got it ready for the trip to Denali National Park. Marion treated us to dinner at Eureka Lodge. Back home we had strawberry and rhubarb pie and ice cream and watched TV hunting. Told old hunting stories. We had a good time.

Wednesday, August 1, 2001—cloudy and rainy, 50° to 63°. Finished loading camper. Did some shopping in Glennallen. The construction on Richardson Highway was slow going for 10 miles. Gasoline and lunch at Paxon. The black top on Denali Highway was very good. Then 120 miles of very rough gravel. 15 to 35 miles per hour. We gassed up at Cantwell. Drove onto Denali National Park. Ken bought tour bus tickets for our road trip into the park as far as Eielson Rest Stop. We saw lots of animals: three Dall rams at 30' - 60', grizzly bear at 40 yards, a large bull moose, cow moose with collar, and other moose. Also a good number of caribou and parka squirrels and Dall sheep at a great distance. Back at park headquarters, we decide to go home by way of Wasilla. Did some shopping, more gasoline and get home about 9:30 PM. I am very tired and got to bed after a bite to eat.

Thursday, August 2, 2001—beautiful day with some breeze, 50° to 70°. We serviced the truck, oil-washer fluid, coolant and gas. Propane bottle went empty, switched that. Rested. Then visited Mark, Ed, Henry and his crew Cal, Sam and Ian. Ken and Marion shot my 44 magnum. We looked at guns and spun yarns. Then planned our trip to Valdez.

Friday, August 3, 2001—cloudy and showers here, 48° to 62°. Rain in Valdez. Finished packing for trip to Valdez. A little shopping in Glennallen. Got my moose and sheep reporting cards. Then drove on to Worthington Glacier. There Ken and Marion took pictures. On to Valdez and got gas. Then a spot to camp. Started fishing and caught 16 pink and one silver salmon, about 13 lbs., very nice. Nice to have entered it in salmon derby. Then ate supper after the fish were filleted. Marion and I talked and Ken went on fishing. Catch and release he thinks maybe 20 pinks. It was foggy and raining and the fish were jumping out of the water all over and even up close to the shore. I got tired slept very hard. It did get cool along towards morning.

Saturday, August 4, 2001—here at home, sunny and very nice. Foggy and rain when we got up, 50° to 70°. Quit raining after we drove into Valdez for breakfast. Drove around town and checked out the boat harbor and seven stores. One store I wanted to see was closed on Saturday's. Ken bought a fish shipping box. Then we started for home. Got gas in Glennallen. Got home just as Sylvia was leaving to go find yard sales with a couple ladies. We washed and vacuumed packed Ken's fish and put them in freezer. Unloaded the camper from truck. A little ermine followed us around for a while. Did some housekeeping chores and made supper for Marion and Ken. Did lots of visiting. Beaut of an evening.

Sunday, August 5, 2001—beaut of a day, 46° to 68°. Leveled camper. Put away gear. Phoned Charlie. Loaded canoe in truck. Fishing gear for rainbow trout. One fly rod and two small spinning rods. Drove to Ryan Lake. Marion and Ken fished from canoe. They got 10 trout. I fished in hip boots and got five trout. They cleaned them when we got home. Bart's D6 CAT was stuck in ditch. Ed, Chuck Farmer, myself, and Bart's roomer, Jim got it out.

Monday, August 6, 2001—mostly sunny and smoky, 47° to 70°. Good breakfast of rainbow trout. Then it was pictures and good-byes and Marion and Ken left to see Anchorage and catch a plane for Minnesota. Visited Ed this morning. Prepared the garage for power-washing. Vacuumed the wood shop. Walked over to see the construction at Henry's. Watered raspberries. The new binoculars came, Leupold Wind River 8 x 42.

Tuesday, August 7, 2001—sunny, beaut of a day—no mosquitoes either, 49° to

73°. Power sprayed both ends of garage. Painted some roof sealer on camper. Cleaned M1.

Wednesday, August 8, 2001—mostly sunny after a cloudy morning, 49° to 72°. Smoke in air. Pressure washed both sides of garage and took the washer back to Henry. Mailed out birthday greetings to Dylan and Brittany plus checks and a little compact for Brittany. Went to Brenda and Darrel's and met her mother, and step-dad Rodney and ate supper with them. Stopped by Grizzly Towing and paid transfer for garbage.

Thursday, August 9, 2001—cloudy, sunny late afternoon. Cut a lot of weed with hand scythe. Did some small jobs. Tried to check the zero on the .338 Winchester. Wasn't using a good rest and it didn't go well. Reloaded another box of 20 and will try on Fri the 10th.

Friday, August 10, 2001—cloudy, partly cloudy, 45° to 68°. Went to Glennallen on senior van for lunch and shopping. Back home and loaded truck with shooting gear and drove to Army Trail Gravel Pit to sight in .338 with new reloads. Shoots very well. Other box shoots very well. Gassed truck, loaded Suzuki. Plan to hunt backside of the Syncline mountains and the Horn Mountains on Alfred Creek.

Saturday, August 11, 2001—cloudy, foggy, Squaw Creek morning, 48° to 68°. Alfred Creek partly cloudy rest of day. Got up extra early. Got as far as Eureka and could see Alfred Creek was socked in, so went back home and slept a couple hours. The fog was gone by time I got unloaded. Several hunter on ATV's back in that country today. Hunting sheep, caribou and bears. Saw one group butchering a caribou. A group of 30 ewes, lambs and three immature rams were reported. A group of ten sheep (gender unknown), was suspected of crossing from Syncline Mountains to Horn Mountains. The caribou were cows, calves and a few bulls thinly scattered over the mountains. Lots of parka squirrels. Saw small hen and three ducklings on Alfred Creek. Lots of mocking birds and their nests. Talked to "Bones" care taker of mining equipment on the claims on Alfred Creek. Seems like a nice guy. Drove up Fossil Creek and walked a way also. Got back home before 5:00. Tired. Trip was enough for one day (25 miles).

Sunday, August 12, 2001—mostly sunny and some breeze, 50° to 72°. Hoed the weeds from Kahren's part of garden. Tried to get broken key out of kitchen door lock. Kahren went with us to pick blueberries. We got 4-5 quarts. Loaded some 44 magnum for griz bear protection. Visited Cal and Mary. Cal gave Kahren and me a ride in his model A street rod. Went over to Ron and Evelyn Lester's for brushes and extendable handles.

Monday, August 13, 2001—sunny, very nice, 49° to 76°. We put a cedar stain on the north side of the house. Started preparing the east end of house for stain. After supper we went to Allen and Roxanne's, Reed has whooping cough. Had coffee ice cream and cookies and heard Allen's hunting story. David got a ram on the Syncline Mountains. Allen gave us some meat. Darrel Gerry phoned me back.

Tuesday, August 14, 2001—cloudy, sunny late afternoon, 51° to 76°. Few sprinkles in the morning. Bob Rudbeck borrowed a pipe threader. I borrowed a ladder and hope to get the ladder jacks tomorrow. We put 1-½ gallon of cedar tone stain on house. Watered a tree, raspberries and garden. Really tired tonight.

Wednesday, August 15, 2001—partly cloudy and sunny, nice breeze, no bugs, 50° to 73°. We stained house logs in the morning on west end of house. In afternoon, I stained the tongue and groove east end of house. That took every ounce of strength I had to wield the long heavy brush. Really played out this evening. Hydro Axes cut brush in roadside ditches today.

Thursday, August 16, 2001—cloudy morning, sunny afternoon, 48° to 70°. We put stain on west end of house and the south side too. We are really happy to have house done. Both are really tired tonight.

Friday, August 17, 2001—cloudy, partly cloudy, 52° to 69°. Went to Glennallen. Shopping, bank, lunch yard sale. Got my American Legion Post 27 jacket. Clayton and Ruth midget are visiting this area from Canada, staying in a cabin at Allen and Roxanne's campground. They had a potluck barbeque for them and invited us. Clayton ministered to Mendeltna Chapel years ago.

Saturday, August 18, 2001—rain in night till mid afternoon, 48° to 61°. Worked at putting a new shaft and pulley on the belt-disc sander. Need a new disk pad for it. Sorted scaffold nails then straightened and sharpened those that needed it for building scaffolding for staining the garage.

Sunday, August 19, 2001—cloudy, sunny, cloudy and windy, 45° to 60°. We built scaffolding and stained north end of garage. Kahren brought over two pieces of raspberry short cake. We moved scaffold to south end of garage then stained the east side. Jim M. brought over some cedar kindling. Brittany phoned her thanks for birthday gift. Tried to call her back but her phone was busy. Theresa phoned with her and Earl's medical update.

Monday, August 20, 2001—cloudy, partly cloudy, 47° to 67°. Few drops of rain. We got stain on south end and west side of garage. Tore down scaffolding and returned it to storage. Henry phoned message and I went over there a few minutes. He had already located the electric tin snips.

Tuesday, August 21, 2001—beautiful golden sunrise, a heart stopper, 46° to 67°. Partly cloudy, thunder and showers in afternoon and evening. Burned some trash. Tried to stain the trim on west end of house from on roof with safety rope. Spilled too much stain-not good. Jim M. and Sylvia steadied the ladder and I reached as far as I could with it and called it best I could do. Weighed some rifle brass and bullets for M1 postal match. Hearing aid quit so packaged it for mailing to Anchorage.

Wednesday, August 22, 2001—cloudy, partly cloudy in evening, 47° to 63°. Sanded and painted meter base gray. Put some stain on some trim on house. Smashed cans. Swept north wall of wood shop, plus a lot of other small jobs. Sylvia put primer on front door this evening after supper.

Thursday, August 23, 2001—partly cloudy, little showers going by, 36° to 64°. Went to Alfred Creek gold camp on Suzuki. Met Jim (?) and son Rick. Got permission to "hand" mine on their claims. Report in and any gold found and location. Saw three Dall ewes and three lambs, one was very small. They were licking rocks at the gorge. Allen stopped by, talked about lots of things. He told me where to find a spike fork moose.

Friday, August 24, 2001—partly cloudy and light showers, 44° to 64°. Went to lunch and shopping in Glennallen. Put a primer coat of paint on garage door. Cleaned some rust off a .410 shotgun. Visited Henry in evening. Looked at pictures of Alfred Creek prospect site. Showed him a tape of gold screw at work.

Saturday, August 25, 2001—partly cloudy and couple showers, 45° to 63°. Worked some more on the .410. Fixed a portable light. After lunch we dropped Ron's painting stuff off at Cal's and went blueberry picking a couple miles west of Eureka. Saw a fox "sign post." He had visited it recently leaving scratch marks. Beautiful evening.

Sunday, August 26, 2001—partly cloudy, 36° to 63°. Henry called mid morning and invited me to go with him, Sally and Phil and son named Phil (who is married to Denise), and Henry's daughter, riding ATV down Alfred Creek. On the trail around the gorge, the Phils got ahead of us. Henry spotted three Dall rams on a steep mountain. I got out my telescope. One ram was definitely legal and probably two were. I wanted to head up after them. Henry wanted me to wait and try driving ATV closer. Then Phil and Phil came back and 54-yr-old Phil wanted the big ram in the worst way. He and his son went back the way we had come in to a mountain. They tried to climb with their Suzuki King Quads. The father almost got to the top when his machine reared and over landing across his legs and rolled some more. Luckily he wasn't hurt. They gave up trying for the sheep. We went down stream and talked to "Bones" gold camp caretaker. The boss Jim had opened the trail to lower cabin with a CAT. To get there we crossed the creek many times - fast and deep water. Henry likes to look for fossils. He knows lots of them and where to likely find them. We stopped and picked a few for keepsakes. At Lower Camp, Sally picked berries. Phil and Phil went hunting. Henry and I put his packer sluice in a creek there and ran five buckets of material from the area that "wimpy" used to clean up his concentrates. We saw quite a few nuggets in the gold pan. Will run the concentrate through the gold wheel at home. We returned to Upper Camp Airstrip to a place on the west side of the cr. That Henry wanted to sample again. This had been hydrolized with a monitor in the early days. I filled the buckets and Henry ran them through the sluice box and panned them—not much gold this time. We drove out to the highway, loaded the machines and went to Eureka. Henry bought Dinner. I had a burger. There are lots of good places to prospect. For instance, Lower Camp, the big stump area up stream. Lots of bedrock, holes and gravel bars.

Monday, August 27, 2001—partly cloudy, 36° to 63°. Sylvia went to Alaska State Fair on senior van. I painted the garage door. Washed ATV. Helped Henry transfer heating oil from tank to tank. The seniors got home before dark.

Tuesday, August 28, 2001—cloudy and sprinkles, 43° to 55°. Put fertilizer and lime on lawn. Checked Suzuki over. Cleaned spark plugs on lawn mower. Carried some trash up out of hole. Ralph phoned, he and Jeff may come here to hunt. His knees are bad.

Wednesday, August 29, 2001—cloudy, partly cloudy and some breeze, 43° to 61°. Ralph phoned. They will be hunting caribou on the trail we drove last summer to see the Calif. Gold dredgers. I decided to stay home. Watered garden—really soaked it. Henry and I ran the cons from Alfred Creek through the gold wheel. Some nice pickers and fine gold. Henry had supper with us. Sylvia gave him a quart of cucumber pickles that she canned today.

Thursday, August 30, 2001—cloudy, sunny, 44° to 60°. Took the finish off the stock for the .410. Repaired one snow plow light. Phoned birthday greetings to Theresa. Phoned Darrel G. He can't go goose hunting till later this month.

Friday, August 31, 2001—mostly sunny, 32° to 61°. Worked on .410 shotgun stock. Went to monthly senior meeting at Kluti-Kaah Hall. Mary G. elected President. Did a few small chores when I got home, including trimming up some trees.

Saturday, September 1, 2001—cloudy and rainy, 42° to 56°. Worked on the forearm on the .410 shotgun. Returned Henry's buckets and gave him a carrot.

Our carrots have as many as 12 on one top, quite twisted and deformed. Sylvia canned 14 quarts of carrots. Got a package in the mail from Ken Wilkins containing a WWII canteen and cup, its cover and a pistol belt. Very nice and thoughtful.

Sunday, September 2, 2001—rain all night, fog and low clouds, 41° to 50°. Worked on .410 stock, sanding, staining. Will put a tung oil finish on it. Allen wanted to borrow a For Sale sign.

Monday, September 3, 2001—rain in night, cloudy, fog and rain till noon then clear and sunny, 40° to 51°. Put a coat of tung oil on stock of .410. Repaired stock screw and re-blue it. Ground a screw driver to fit it. Visited Jim and Elaine. Rosemary Bartley was there also. Mary Odden phoned that they will visit late this evening. Ralph phoned with a report on his and Jeff's hunt for caribou—no luck.

Tuesday, September 4, 2001—cloudy, windy, one hr sunny, cloudy gusting winds, 32° to 53°. One coat tung oil on shotgun stock. Jim, Mary, Kari Odden and friend of Kari visited. Loaded up shooting gear for postal match using M1. Got to gravel pit just as wind started blowing, went back home. Put a new turn signal light on snow plow. Started picking up things for winter. Smashed our paint buckets. The winds were just right to take down the winter damaged tree and its mate on the north side of the house. Pulled them over by chaining them to truck. After supper we went to gravel pit and got a few buckets gravel to fill low places in our driveway.

Wednesday, September 5, 2001—rain, partly cloudy, 34° to 47°. Snow on Slide Mountain and Heavenly Ridge and more distant mountains have lots of snow. Put more tung oil on gunstock. Chopped roots and dirt off the roots of the trees I pulled over. Picked up Bart and we went to American Legion mtg. Fred Rungee stopped by but I was at Legion meeting. Ron filled me in on the "turmoil" at CRNA.

Thursday, September 6, 2001—cloudy, clear and very nice in afternoon, 36° to 53°. Cut up the two down trees. Hauled their limbs over to Ed's. Piled the logs up for drying. Still trying to get a good price on airline ticket.

Friday, September 7, 2001—rainy. 36° to 53°. We went to lunch and pay phone bill in Glennallen on senior bus. Sanded and refinished a small place at wall dividing kitchen sink and pantry hall. Chopped roots and pulled over four spruces with the truck on north side of house. Had them limbed and cut into logs in 1-½ hours. Recoil rope on saw is shot.

Saturday, September 8, 2001—sunny, 27° to 55°. Chopped dirt out of tree stump roots. Hauled the wood to a pile. We dug the potatoes, nine 5-gallon buckets from three rows. Beautiful big spuds. Pulled two stumps out of ground. Hauled tree limbs over to Ed's. Gave him, Henry, and Jim some potatoes and lettuce. Carried spuds into basement cool room.

Sunday, September 9, 2001—sunny. Went to Alfred Creek trail head. Took a great mirror refection photo of Gunsight Mountain in a small lake. The trail was in good shape. Went in as far as the lower end of the gorge. Found an egg shaped rock, quartz etc. Saw an eagle hunting at a great height. The main show was the many ewes and lambs around me in every direction. 1/8 mile, ¼ mile, 2 miles, and 4 miles, saw 49 total. Saw no rams for sure but think the 13 large sheep at 4 miles may have been rams. It's great sit in warm sun and watched the ewes and lambs interact as they eat and move from one area to another. Some parka squirrels along the trail also. Washed the clay mud off the machine when I got home. A great day!

Monday, September 10, 2001—sunny, 27° to 55°. Ron and Jeremy Beshaw went with me to Alfred Creek. Met "Bones" at the claims. His real name is Jerry. Visited there a while, they did some prospecting with no luck. We did see and eagle hunting, a hawk, parka squirrel and quite a few sheep today. I drove my pickup all the way to the upper camp.

Tuesday, September 11, 2001—sunny, 28° to 56°. World Trade Center and Pentagon struck by terrorists flying hi-jacked passenger planes. Nation is shocked. I raised our flag at half mast. I cleaned the dirt off the tree stumps and loaded them on snowgo trailer behind the ATV and hauled them to Ed's. Sylvia and I removed the water manifolds at garden and up here at top of hill and readied the line for winter.

Wednesday, September 12, 2001—mostly sunny, 38° to 57°. Filled stump holes with dirt, replaced sections of sod, brought the area as near to grade as I could. Sylvia watered the area after I limed and fertilized. Bev phoned. We talked to Tyler too. Kahren picked cranberries over here. Visited Allen and Roxanne in evening.

Thursday, September 13, 2001—partly cloudy, 31° to 55°. Started to go to Squaw Creek, trail was real muddy. Turned around and went to Alfred Creek. Lots of parka squirrels in trail. Numerous fox droppings. Couple boo (caribou) and one moose track. No sheep so after waiting 2-3 hours, came back out. The tundra has broken loose and slid down some of the steep slopes. Saw two large moose in west start up lake. Washed Suzuki when I got home. After supper I went to gravel pit and got small load to fill in and dress up where I rounded off and took out trees off corner of lawn. Stressed my back and have a spasm in it tonight. Allen helped finish up scattering gravel in lane.

Friday, September 14, 2001—sunny, very nice, 29° to 56°. My back is very sore. Joints all hurt especially my hands and shoulders. We went to Glennallen on senior van. I forgot to take my large envelope containing cast bullet targets for postal match to post office and mail it. Cashed our checks in town. Watered down the patches of DI gravel in our lane then packed it will truck. Gave Henry all the 3" plastic sewer pipe I have.

Saturday, September 15, 2001—sunny and beautiful, 27° to 54°. Tamped ATV tracks out of the DI gravel at our lawn. Serviced car. Tried to call Jeff. Did get to talk to Roma, Ralph was working. Finished cleaning M1. Kahren and Gracie visited. Finished putting the sander together out in woodshop. Both Fran and Nadia phoned.

Sunday, September 16, 2001—nice day, 27° to 55°. Did some small jobs. Removed solenoid from ATV—it tested bad. Switch is also bad. Cleaned up small chain saw. Prepped to get it fixed. Ralph phoned.

Monday, September 17, 2001—partly cloudy and sprinkles, 35° to 56°. We went to Anchorage. Prescription, groceries, ATV repair. .410 shells. Left chain saw to be repaired. Started putting winch switch on. This ATV is wired different than instructions.

Tuesday, September 18, 2001—mostly cloudy and rainy evening, 48° to 58°. Finished installing winch switch. Did some small jobs. Made some alder slabs Sylvia wanted. Ralph called and is here this evening. We drove the highway to mile 120, saw no moose.

Wednesday, September 19, 2001—cloudy and rain here, 47° to 58°. No rain on Squaw Cree Trail where we hunted. Too many hunters at Goober Knob Trailhead for us. Squaw Cree Trail was muddy. Got stuck quite a few times. I was backing out of some hummocks and laid the machine over on its side. Did a leap and roll to get away from it and not get pinned to the ground. Didn't get hurt at all. This happened over on the bench along the Caribou Creek end of the Syncline Mountains. We did see bear poop and tracks. A couple rams on Sheep Mountain and two cow moose along the highway in morning. Ralph checked there this eve and saw a two brow tine each side bull—not legal to shoot. On our way out along Squaw Creek he spotted a spike fork bull moose about ¾ mile away. It seemed to run away when Ralph tried to call it. I got covered by flying mud all day. ATV fenders aren't really wide enough for these tires. We are tired tonight.

Thursday, September 20, 2001—fog, cloudy, partly cloudy, 40° to 50°. Ralph and I went to Mile 122. Saw a three brow tine bull moose 34" - 36" horns—not legal. Stopped by Eureka for gas, pie and coffee. Decided not to go to Squaw Creek and try for the spike for bull. Ralph decided to go back to Jeff's at Kenny Lake and hunt. Washed the Suzuki and my hip boots. Sylvia washed my duck hunting parka. Reloaded some yard sale cartridges Ralph gave me.

Friday, September 21, 2001—foggy, sunny, 31° to 47°. Went to VA in Anchorage. Lab drew blood, will check for thyroid also. Next appointment Jan 25, 2002. Got prescriptions. There wasn't room to bring my chainsaw home from Palmer.

Saturday, September 22, 2001—partly cloudy, little breeze, 32° to 49°. Went to gravel pit at Army Trail. Target practice with M1. Checked zero of .338 Winchester. Patterned the .410 shotgun and found it to shoot to the left too far. Back home cleaned rifle and brass. Failed to figure out how to get .410 shotgun to shoot to center. Cal and Mary are going outside and stopped by to say so long. Allen, Roxanne, Sammy and Reed visited.

Sunday, September 23, 2001—partly cloudy, strong winds in afternoon and evening, 24° to 47°. Loafed a lot. Did a few small things. Steve Wilkins phoned today. Raked birch leaves and made my wrists sore. Asked Henry and Sally is they would like to go out for dinner but they can't go tonight.

Monday, September 24, 2001—mostly cloudy, 34° to 48°. Snow in mountains to south of us. Spread the sand from carrot storage. Cleaned up the garden. Sylvia invited Bob, Kahren, Lisa, Gracie, Jerry and Mo Lietza were here for supper.

Tuesday, September 25, 2001—partly cloudy, 25° to 46°. Bob and Kahren left to go outside. Wrote letter to BCA and one to a M1 shooter, Don Hanks. Moved the homemade hi banker to under the roof overhang on garage. Joints are sore today.

Wednesday, September 26, 2001—partly cloudy, beaut of a day. We put floor wax on house and garage roof. I "Johnson's waxed" the contact surfaces of the three upstairs opening windows. Sylvia mowed the lawn. I started it for her and put gasoline preservative in mower gas tank. Went trout fishing in Ryan Lake. Hooked and lost one. Found tape measure and cigarette lighter. Stopped by Bartley's and got a paper about our senior program abuse by CRNA. We saw a lot of golden eagles migrating east (perhaps to Haines?) to hunt salmon.

Thursday, September 27, 2001—sunny, 23° to 47°. Made a small stand to support a tray that holds binoculars etc. Tried to charge some flashlight batteries, they are bad. Got gear ready to go caribou hunting up on Denali Highway.

Friday, September 28, 2001—partly cloudy, 30° to 50°. Up early. Finished getting gear loaded in truck. Went to BLM in Glennallen and got caribou hunting permits. Had to show ID at door to get in. Drove to Mile 10-12 on Denali Highway and hunted there. Did not get an opportunity to shoot a bull. Quite a few hunters. Probably half of them were in violation of some sort. Very difficult to know the perimeters of the hunt area, especially after leaving the road. Both AK Fish and Wildlife Protection and BLM Ranger were patrolling the area. Confiscated a number of caribou guns, ATV etc. Saw a few people I know. Drove home in dark. Mount Wrangle was back-lit by the moon—beautiful.

Saturday, September 29, 2001—partly cloudy, 27° to 57°. Went with Henry Chris, his son Jody, Ed Tollman, Peggy Sutton to lower camp on Alfred Creek. The creek crossings were manageable. Trail was muddy and sloppy in some places. Icy then dust in dry parts. Saw a wolf track on way in and 14 Dall sheep ewes and lambs. We ran 30 buckets of material through Henry's sluice box. Henry gave Peggy Sutton the best nuggets from the three pans of concentrate and wants me to get the rest of gold out of concentrate and make two vials of gold for Peggy and Ed T. On our way out, we waved so long to "Bones" (Jerry), and saw a group had set up a tent camp on a small creek in a steep ravine. Nice to get home. Allen and Sammy visited in evening.

Sunday, September 30, 2001—sunny and nice, 25° to 48°. The swans got up and flying every once in a while. Even went over on the river. Put away some gear. Washed the Suzuki. Made some copies over at Jim's on copier. Jeff phoned while I was gone. We ask Henry and Sally to dinner out. They drove and we went to KROA and had T-Bone Steak. Mike and Lanette Phillips went to KROA and extended their visit with Henry and Sally and we got to see them also.

Monday, October 1, 2001—partly cloudy and breezy, 31° to 46°. A cow moose and calf walked through our yard. Went to AARP 55 Alive driving class in Glennallen. Jim M. taught and I rode with him. Two swans still here may be all the ducks are gone.

Tuesday, October 2, 2001—sunny, 28° to 46°. Completed the second day of driving class. I drove Jim's car home. He drove school activities bus. Walked down to lake for ducks, none on our side of lake.

Wednesday, October 3, 2001—cloudy. 23° to 39°. Wrote some letters. Saw a spruce hen. No duck on our lake shore. Re-concentrated the gold-black sand from last trip down Alfred Creek. Went to Legion Meeting.

Thursday, October 4, 2001—mostly sunny, windy late afternoon, 31° to 55°. Put winter tires on Molly car and cleaned the windows. Trimmed the plywood cover on one trailer. Henry stopped by for three vials and some of the nicer flakes that we got last Saturday. I went to gravel pit to shoot the M1. Found a cartridge and three empties. Hunted for spruce hens with no luck. Checked the new solenoid on Suzuki and it is dead.

Friday, October 5, 2001—mostly cloudy, breeze some times, 40° to 50°. We went to Glennallen on senior bus. Got ID for Sylvia, application and renewal of concealed pistol permit postmarked at Post Office for me. Had lunch, paid phone bill. Visited Henry and looked at how his Suzuki and winch are wired. Came home and wired mine and it works well. A small flock of ducks resting on our lake tonight.

Saturday, October 6, 2001—sunny and some breeze, 29° to 46°. Walked down to lake. Ducks feeding on south side. Walked back up from well along water line. Smashed cans, burned trash. Took some potatoes over to Henry and Sally. Cleaned on rifle barrel. Sylvia fixed a bear stew supper and asked Brenda and Darrel over.

Sunday, October 7, 2001—snow on ground this morning and melted off, 26° to 40°. Put winter tires on truck. Changed oil and filter. Put new oil in front differential. Loaded Suzuki in truck bed. Went to Tom and Kim Huddleston's for supper, Allen's were there.

Monday, October 8, 2001—skiff snow melted off, 22° to 41°. We left very early and took Suzuki to Anchorage for tune up and new rear brake. We shopped at several stores. Got gas, picked up repaired chain saw. Pretty good trip. Saw sheep high on mountain at Caribou Creek.

Tuesday, October 9, 2001—mostly sunny, 31° to 43°. I straightened the support system for waterline from well. Hauled 20 buckets of gravel to fill in a sink hole and support the blocking. Couple other small jobs.

Wednesday, October 10, 2001—mostly cloudy, 27° to 42°. A family of five swans took off to the east from our lake. Walked to well and got name of a thermal control. Parked snowgo trailer. A squirrel has become trouble, so I set a trap for it. Jim Manning returned some borrowed books. Beverly phoned.

Thursday, October 11, 2001—cloudy, 15° to 35°. Three quarters of our lake is now frozen over. Some snow on mountains to the south. Put prop up posts under front corners of camper. Cleaned some Alfred Creek concentrate. Shot a rabbit and a squirrel with the .410. Squirrel vandalized the arctic entry. We will eat the rabbit.

Friday, October 12, 2001—snowed all night and quit mid afternoon (four inches), 18° to 29°. We went to Glennallen on senior van, had lunch and some shopping. Modified the bird feeder with squirrel protection and a bigger roof. Covered a little place on waterline at garden. Snow weight pushed some lake ice down and melted it. Two thirds of our lake is open.

Saturday, October 13, 2001—partly cloudy, 5° to 24°. Hauled the ashes and garbage to transfer site. Offered Lee Dudley a ride to Wasilla next time we go. Started making a gun barrel rack. The lake is closer to being frozen over. On lone duck is still on it. Mary Odden phoned.

Sunday, October 14, 2001—mostly cloudy, 3° to 24°. Finished and installed the gun barrel rack. The guns look good in it.

Monday, October 15, 2001—partly cloudy. Some wind from west, 13° to 33°. Worked on some Alfred Creek concentrate. Went with Henry to a scenic highway meeting at Sheep Mountain. Checked antifreeze and car and truck. Beverly called to tell us about the party she gave for Tyler's 16th birthday. She was very happy with how it went.

Tuesday, October 16, 2001—sunny, 12° to 32°. Cleaned some more Alfred Creek concentrate, two flakes of gold. Went to gravel pit at Army Trail to check .338 scope, was way off. Got it sighted in again. Started reloading the brass after supper when Allen and Kyle came over to visit. Fred Rungee visited Sylvia when I was target shooting and I missed seeing him.

Wednesday, October 17, 2001—cloudy and light snow all morning, 12° to 28°. Went for a walk. Finish reloading for the .338 magnum. Phoned birthday greetings to Virginia.

Thursday, October 18, 2001—cloudy, one inch of snow fell and snowing yet this evening, 13° to 30°. Did not feel well this morning. Cleaned up the last of Alfred Creek concentrate. Allen visited this afternoon. Put a bear claw necklace together for Beverly.

Friday, October 19, 2001—cloudy, 6" snow, 17° to 29°. Plowed our snow and driveway to school house. Joe Thomas drove the senior bus, supposedly the last trip on this route. Got a migratory bird stamp at Post Office. Allen called. A griz, with tongue hanging out, chased a moose calf past Ron Russell in his own yard. David Johnson saw a cat with a long tail cross highway and go down ravine near west of Brockman's development.

Saturday, October 20, 2001—cloudy and some snow, 5° to 27°. Checked out the strobe light on truck. It has quit. We went to a prime rib dinner at Legion Post. Very good. Bought Darrel and Brenda's dinner also. Ladies Auxiliary raffled off a king size quilt. We gave George (don't know last name) a ride home to Tolsona campground.

Sunday, October 21, 2001—cloudy to south over the mountains and ice field sunny here, 10° to 27°. Plowed some more snow. Packed trail to well. A mink has crossed the lake from south and went west on our lake.

Monday, October 22, 2001—cloudy,13° to 27°. Started making accessory box for the M1. Will have it painted before bedtime.

Tuesday, October 23, 2001—cloudy, 1-1/2" snow. 17° to 26°. Put hinges and latch on the little wood box. Put a jack to support the ATV and relieve the tires over winter. Lid on box warped from latex paint. GRRRR.

Wednesday, October 24, 2001—cloudy, sunny, 8° to 25°. Did a few little things. More overflow on our lake.

Thursday, October 25, 2001—cloudy, 12° to 22°. Brought the shingle cedar kindling into basement. Phoned Dish Network about a new remote control.

Friday, October 26, 2001—cloudy, 12° to 20°. Visited Henry and Sally. Put together two bear claw necklaces for Bev and Theresa. Phoned Ralph.

Saturday, October 27, 2001—cloudy, -5° to 16°. Got a varmint with .410. Dave and Dee Johnson brought some bookcases to be repaired and visited. Allen visited in evening.

Sunday, October 28, 2001—sunny, -3° to 14°. Worked on the bookcases 4 hours.

Monday, October 29, 2001—sunny, 1° to 15°. Worked on the bookcases, 4 hours. Sylvia helped for three hours.

Tuesday, October 30, 2001—sunny, -4° to 15°. Finished the bookcases for the Johnsons.

Wednesday, October 31, 2001—cloudy and snow in evening, -5° to 15°. Worked on a couple micro sluices. Noticed a coyote "mousing" nearer to east end of lake. It also checked out a muskrat push up. Took a cassette player with a rabbit squeal tape and went down to lake shore w.223 Remington bolt gun. Called the female coyote up to 100 yards. One shot knock down its tail was "wringing." Skinned it out and froze the hide.

Thursday, November 1, 2001—sunny, 8° to 24°. Plowed our snow. Worked on "micro sluices." Went to Army Trail gravel pit sighted .223 reloads with different powder and bullet. Stopped by Grizzly Towing. Laura called.

Friday, November 2, 2001—sunny, 9° to 20°. Finished the "micro sluices" for Henry and Bones. We went to the "Harvest" party at Lottie Sparks School. Pot luck. Fun and games.

Saturday, November 3, 2001—cloudy, 11° to 26°. Packaged our dish receiver up and mailed it in for a replacement. Went to four locations and tried to call in varmints. No luck. Saw wolf, coyote, fox, lynx and caribou tracks. Mixed gas for snowgo. Visited Jim and Elaine. Got a couple copies made. We went to a neighborhood pot luck at KROA. Snowing this evening.

Sunday, November 4, 2001—cloudy and some snow, 16° to 25°. Did not do much of anything today.

Monday, November 5, 2001—cloudy and ice fog, 14° to 21°. We went to Glennallen. Paid electric and phone bills. Cashed our checks, did some shopping. Put new fuel filter on snowgo. Looked at headlight on truck. Moved garbage cans. Mailed bear claw necklace to Beverly.

Tuesday, November 6, 2001—cloudy and light snow, 6° to 16°. Made five magnetic devices to remove magnetite from concentrates containing gold. Put the cover on the well. The crossbills came right in for the black oil sunflower seed Sylvia put out today. We ate breakfast with Allen, Roxanne and Reed.

Wednesday, November 7, 2001—ice fog till noon then sunny and bright all day, - 5° to 12° to -10° in evening. Denny Eastman and Bart Bartley visited in morning. Bart stopped by and I went with him to American Legion meeting in Glennallen.

Thursday, November 8, 2001—sunny and a little fog, -14° to 12°. Oiled bolt on .223 interarms. Couldn't increase the trigger pull weight. Grandson Steve phoned with muzzle loader question that I couldn't answer.

Friday, November 9, 2001—fog, cloudy, sunny, -13° to -2°. We pumped water, and burned trash.

Saturday, November 10, 2001—sunny, fog late evening, -13° to 6°. We went to annual skating party for Dan Billman's birthday, at the Point Lodge on Lake Louise. Got to see some people we only see once a year.

Sunday, November 11, 2001—sunny, -14° to 2°. Two more rat pushups on our lake. Lisa and Emily Smayda visited in afternoon.

Monday, November 12, 2001—sunny, -9° to 12°. Lots of frost on trees. We got our flu shots from nurse at school house. I gave Henry a little concentrate sluice and a magnet device to remove magnetite from day concentrate. We had coffee and visited. Denny Eastman has the skis on his Super Cub. Grandson Steve called and asked for some of my .45 caliber cast bullets to put in sabots and shoot in his muzzle loader.

Tuesday, November 13, 2001—sunny, -14° to 2°. Got the package to Steve mailed this morning and put the bullet casting stuff away.

Wednesday, November 14, 2001—sunny then cloudy, -14° to 3°. Turned a piece of birch in lathe so Henry can use it to repair the "horn" for a Victrola. Joe P. delivered gasoline. Denny Eastman went flying. Allen, Roxanne and Reed visited in evening.

Thursday, November 15, 2001—cloudy, -10° to 3°. Put some silicone on a sill log leak

Friday, November 16, 2001—partly cloudy, -13° to -3°. Did some reading. Phoned about a bill in US Senate. Phoned inquiry about status of repair of our dish receiver.

Saturday, November 17, 2001—cloudy and light snow, 4° to 5°. We pumped water. I put a new 100 watt bulb in well.

Sunday, November 18, 2001—sunny, 2-1/2 inches of snow in the night 4° to 19°. I didn't see any of the meteor shower. Plowed our snow. Towards evening went west two miles and tried calling varmints with squealing snowshoe hare tape. Set up facing a "trail" off hi line. Five or so minutes a lynx approached to 40 yards. Sat on its haunches looking at me through some brush. I shot it with .223 and a "blitzer" 50 grain bullet to the throat, dropping it instantly. Tried calling at gravel pit, no luck. Back home Sylvia took pictures. We ate supper. After supper I started skinning the lynx. After a while Allen came over. He helped skin rest of it out. This is a red letter day for me! My first lynx.

Monday, November 19, 2001—mostly sunny, -5° to 20° to 10°. Made some beaver lure for Allen. Gave Denny Eastman lynx and coyote carcass. He brought over a home movie of calling and shooting fox on Kodiak Island. I fleshed and put the lynx skin on a stretcher. Jim, Mary and Kari visited in evening.

Tuesday, November 20, 2001—mostly sunny, -2° to 14°. We pumped water. Watched Den Eatman's fox hunting video. Phoned UPS and dish network, found our lost receiver. Hope they now have it headed our way. Denny came over and picked up the two carcasses. Cal and Mary stopped by on their way home. Reloaded 10 -.223 Remington cartridges with Ralph's coyote load. We saw six caribou bulls come from SE walk on our lake and leave by southwest corner.

Wednesday, November 21, 2001—partly cloudy, 3° to 13°. We went to Palmer and Wasilla shopping. Saw a moose. Got back in good time.

Thursday, November 22, 2001—partly cloudy, -6° to 9°. Loaded a few .30 cast for hunting fur. We phoned Nadia, Paul and Steve. We had Thanksgiving dinner with Jim, Mary and Kari Odden. John, Coleen Axel and Erik Odden were there. Their niece Emily, her husband, Dave, Grace and two other guests were there.

Friday, November 23, 2001—cloudy, two inches of snow, 5° to 19°. Went calling for fur varmints, no luck. Went to Cal's and got a part for my truck. Put in new headlight on truck. 10:00 PM spectacular red northern lights. Streamer from direction overhead spreading to the entire horizon.

Saturday, November 24, 2001—mostly cloudy, some freezing mist in evening, 7° to 18°. Went west varmint calling. No luck. Saw a lynx and a marten track. I carry my best caller in speaker in a plastic 5-gallon pail. After getting back home I built a cover using 3/8" plywood cut in a circle and cut the inside flange off the plastic lid and screwed it to plywood, fits great. We went to dinner at American Legion Post 27. Very good. Alaska Dept Commander and Service officer and two others were there. Crowd was small. Bart drove.

Sunday, November 25, 2001—cloudy and lots of ice fog, 13° to -4°. Jim, Mary and Kari Odden came and got us. We all went to Sam Lightwoods Farm. Sorted away from cow herd a two year old cow. Jim shot it and we skinned, dressed it and hung it there in Sam's building. We stopped at Caribou café and had hamburgers on our way home. Didn't see very many tracks of fur bearers. Did see one set of "eyes" shining in head lights on way home. Ralph phoned.

Monday, November 26, 2001—sunny, -17° to -7°. Went to Oddens and paid for one quarter of the beef. Set up and called for fur, 4 places on Tazlina Hill. One each at RCA site, Little Nelchina, and Allen's wood lot. Saw lynx, fox and a coyote track. No luck calling one in. We pumped water. Fred Rungee had supper with us, brought ice cream and fruit.

Tuesday, November 27, 2001—mostly sunny, -19° to -8°. Dismantled and burned Sylvia's old chair. The satellite receiver came. Supper with Farmers, Odden family were there.

Wednesday, November 28, 2001—sunny, full moon, -23° to -12°. Smashed tin cans for garbage. Jeff called.

Thursday, November 29, 2001—sunny and ice in the air, -16° to 4°. Went fur hunting along Lake Louise Road. No luck. Saw fox and lynx tracks. Two moose feeding. Caribou tracks. Made five tries then it got windy. Came home and charged batteries. Got two traps and six snares ready to go. The brush is getting taller than the moose along Lake Louise Road.

Friday, November 30, 2001—sunny and ice in air, -27° to -9°. Looking forward to setting a few snares tomorrow. Sylvia went to a baby shower for Davida, David and De Johnson's new daughter. Plan to set a few snares for lynx and try calling again.

Saturday, December 1, 2001—sunny, -31° to -21°. Moon is bright too. I didn't set snares or hunt today, too cold. Corky Dimmick stopped by and stayed for supper.

Sunday, December 2, 2001—sunny, -35° to -28°. Read and watched the outdoor channel on TV. Allen phoned and asked us to lunch at Eureka. We got the lunch. There was a snowmobile race on the lake there. We saw a moose cross highway and fox and lynx tracks. Little Reed is sure growing.

Monday, December 3, 2001—partly cloudy, -32° to -12°. In the afternoon, went to old RCA site tried calling-no luck. Set one snare. Pumped water when I got home.

Tuesday, December 4, 2001—cloudy and a half inch of fine snow. Dave and De Johnson picked up their bookcases.

Wednesday, December 5, 2001—partly cloudy, clear, -23° to -7°. Got things ready to go to Glennallen. Bart rode in with us. Paid phone, electric. Did some shopping. Cashed our checks. Went to Legion Post. Cleaned rifles and we brought pizza, cookies and pop for supper for Jay Rella, Bart and Sylvia and me. Post meeting was at 7:00 PM.

Thursday, December 6, 2001—mostly sunny, -38° to -10°. Didn't do much outside. Walked down by lake.

Friday, December 7, 2001—sunny, -30° to -20°. Built a fire in barrel stove.

Burned trash and enough wood to warm the basement. Shoveled snow of the wood shed. Allen and Samantha visited.

Monday, December 8, 2001—sunny, -24° to -16°. We pumped water. The small line was frozen. Heated the coupling with propane torch and switched to bigger line. The lynx walked through our yard last evening. I called the RCA sight, no luck. Lynx walking around there also. Picked up my snare. Prepared Christmas cards for mailing.

Tuesday, December 9, 2001—mostly sunny, -27° to -10°. Waiting for a phone call, I missed going hunting this morning. Watched TV and read. Didn't go hunting in the evening either, but did a little gun stuff.

Wednesday, December 10, 2001—partly cloudy, -20° to -12°. We had breakfast with Allen, Roxanne and Reed. Pat and Patti Landers were there also. Moved my lynx trap. Tried to call in some fur at Little Nelchina and near DOT. No luck. J. Stewart caller battery doesn't hold a charge.

Thursday, December 11, 2001—mostly cloudy, few flakes snow, -17° to -3°. Made calls about Reddins Powder Scale and Measure and to J Stewart about animal caller. Did get a return call. Packaged scale and measurer for PP. Sylvia went to Queens lunch. We went to house warming for Dru and Bruce in evening.

Friday, December 12, 2001—cloudy and light snow, -4° to 5°. We pumped water and shoveled snow up around the well. Went out calling. Caller battery went dead. Called at four places with scotch call, no luck. Nadia will order a new battery, then I will pay her. She'll get it here much faster.

Saturday, December 13, 2001—cloudy and snowy all day, -2° to 10°. Nadia ordered battery for my Johnny Stewart caller. I shoveled lots of snow off camper, canopy, lean to and storage trailer. Took the car and went out calling at three locations with no luck. Not even fresh tracks. Called dish network about credit for service we didn't get last month. Oddens are bringing over ribs from the cow.

Sunday, December 14, 2001—sunny, cloudy, light frost in air, -13° to -10° to -20°. Lynx walked through our yard. Trailed it east and tried to call it at a couple places with no luck. Went with Denny Eastman up Lake Louise Road hunting fur. Didn't see any. He ate supper with us.

Saturday, December 15, 2001—sunny, ice in air, -36° to -30°. Brought in some of that old birch wood to burn. Scott Rollins called and we had a nice visit. They are going good.

Sunday, December 16, 2001—sunny, with sundogs. -37° to -27°. Brought in two little sled loads old birch. David came up and got us to eat Sun dinner with Farmer family. Oddens were there also. Den E phoned, while we were gone, wanted to hunt coyotes. Darrel G. phoned about time for sighting space shuttle and station in southern sky.

Monday, December 17, 2001—sunny, -37° to 29°. We went to Odden's and cut and packaged the two year old heifer. Was lots of work but went pretty good. Sammy helped by labeling packages, Kari and Ellie helped mix sausage spices in ground meat. Drove truck there as the car wouldn't start.

Tuesday, December 18, 2001—mostly sunny, -37° to -27°. Put two sled loads wood in basement. Allen had coffee with me. Called Cabela's about slippery boots. I am to return them.

Wednesday, December 19, 2001—mostly cloudy, -33° to -23°. Put more wood in basement. Put some fish trimmings out for bait. Checked oil and anti-freeze in truck and car. The battery came for wildlife caller. Still doesn't work. We went to Mannings to dinner and played cards.

Thursday, December 20, 2001—cloudy and three inches of snow, -12° to 0°. We pumped water twice. Both tanks are full. Put two sled loads wood in basement. Phoned J.S. – caller has a short or terminals hooked wrong. Need a fuse. Jim Manning brought over two apple turnovers. Sylvia sent cookies back with him.

Friday, December 21, 2001—one more inch of snow, 20° to 23°. Plowed our snow. Electricity went off, fired up Coleman lantern and a candle. Came back on later. We went to the Christmas program at schoolhouse by the student. Very nice. Lots of food and visit with friends. Ordered a hand loop for passenger side of pickup.

Saturday, December 22, 2001—three inches more snow, 20° to 26°, then dropped to 9°. Plowed snow. Brought in two florescent bulbs from woodshop for dining room table. Did a little body repair on truck. Cousin Gladys from Iowa phoned. We went to Glennallen, a little shopping and Christmas party at Legion post. Mary Gilcrease rode in with us. Gave a fellow named George a ride home to Tolsona Creek.

Sunday, December 23, 2001—cloudy, -8° to 10°. Went to church at Mendeltna Chapel. Finger food lunch afterward. I can't get the caller fixed here. The battery charger burns out its fuse. A group of neighbors sang Christmas carols for us this evening.

Monday, December 24, 2001—cloudy and snow flurries, -2° to 7°. Pulled snow off greenhouse roof and a few other places. Theresa phoned. Packaged the wildlife caller for shipment to get repaired. Elaine M. sent over a gift of skin lotion for Sylvia.

Tuesday, December 25, 2001—cloudy and a skiff of snow, 4° to 17°. No lynx in trap. Went to Odden's for Christmas dinner. Very good Norwegian dinner. Israel was there also. Gave Jim one of the portable folding shooting benches that I had built. We called Paul and Steve and Nadia when we got back home.

Wednesday, December 26, 2001—mostly cloudy and south winds, 36° to 22°. Plowed snow. Pumped water. Jim O. brought over meat scraps and trimmings. Darcy's package to us came today. Phoned Johnny Stewart animal callers. They are sending me a new battery charger. I gave Jim a bunch of heavy angle iron.

Thursday, December 27, 2001—it's 15° to 25°. Tom, Lisa, Lauren, Emily Smayda visited for a couple hours. Will visit Billmans then to the Oddens for supper.

Friday, December 28, 2001—temp is 5° to 20°. Called Denny E. Asked him to go varmint calling. Made some set ups with no luck. No new tracks. Jim, the Mendeltna Chapel pastor stopped by while I was out hunting.

Saturday, December 29, 2001—cloudy and fog, 0° to 9°. Didn't do anything till 3:30 PM. Denny Eastman came over and we drove the highway almost to Dimmicks hunting fur. No luck. Saw a road kill caribou. Lots of people out this way on snowgos. Some came in our yard.

Sunday, December 30, 2001—cloudy, -5° to 12°. Called Nadia. She had a gathering for family members at Chuck and her place. Some had already left. Our call was late. We pumped water. Read a lot. Ralph called from Montana again. He needed information on M1 year of manufacture date.

Monday, December 31, 2001—partly cloudy, 5° to 16°. We went to Glennallen. Some shopping, groceries and hand assist to install in pickup for Sylvia and Bart Bartley's convenience. Drove up the road to telecommunications area on Tolsona Ridge. Not a rabbit track or fur track. Some caribou track. We saw 15? Caribou resting on Frank's Lake.

Dall sheep on Slide Mountain

2002—Hunting Dall sheep

Tuesday, January 1, 2002—sunny, cloudy, 2° to 11°. Ron Beshaw and Darrel and Brenda Garry were here. Sylvia fixed a nice dinner. I put a handle assist on door post of pickup to make it easier for Sylvia and Bart to get into pickup.

Wednesday, January 2, 2002—partly cloudy, 5° to 11°. Slept a lot. Charger came for wild life caller.

Thursday, January 3, 2002—partly cloudy, cloudy in evening, -5° to 7°. My powder measure and scale came back from Redding all repaired. Smashed our tin cans and aluminum. Went out calling, didn't see any fresh tracks so I came home.

Friday, January 4, 2002—mostly sunny, -6° to 9°. Pulled lynx trap. Pumped water. Sorted receipts and other small jobs.

Saturday, January 5, 2002—cloudy, one inch of snow, 14° to 17°. Didn't do anything but read today. Electricity was off a few times.

Sunday, January 6, 2002—cloudy, 15° to 25°. Charged old caller battery, flashlights. Read a good book.

Monday, January 7, 2002—mostly cloudy, 10° to 2°. Had breakfast with Allen and Roxanne. Then he and I put the cowhide, bones and trimmings out for a bait station. Had to chain up the pickup to drive through the ditch and over the trail. Both coyote and fox track in area. Beverly phoned this evening.

Tuesday, January 8, 2002—cloudy, windy evening, 3° to 25°. Sylvia went to Queens luncheon. I went over to Mannings and made some copies. Nadia phoned about family genealogy.

Wednesday, January 9, 2002—cloudy, windy, and some snow, 23° to 34°. Sent off to Cabela's for a pair of boots. Heating oil was delivered. Laura and Brittany called. Phoned Darcy and Lee Austin.

Thursday, January 10, 2002—partly cloudy, 14° to 28°. Ordered a hearing aid. We pumped water and removed 150 watt bulb. Went varmint calling. Saw lynx tracks, no luck calling. Jim Miller, Pastor at Mendeltna Chapel called on us this afternoon.

Friday, January 11, 2002—mostly sunny, 0° to 10°. Sylvia was out with Mary G and Rosemary B. all day at Glennallen and Copper Center. I did some research on spotting scopes. Ed Farmer brought his spotter scope over for me to play with a few days. Mary Gilcrease will copy over a tape for me.

Saturday, January 12, 2002—cloudy, light snow, -13° to 4°. Didn't do much.

Sunday, January 13, 2002—sunny, -10° to 0°. We went to church at Mendeltna Chapel. Had supper with Oddens. Mary's brother Dave Looney is visiting a few days. Called Theresa.

Monday, January 14, 2002—mostly sunny, -5° to 24°. We pumped water. Ian Mailly borrowed a pattern for a trapper hat. He will use fur that he trapped.

Tuesday, January 15, 2002—light snow all day, 2". 10° to 25°. We pumped water and I replaced the light bulb in well. Phoned a couple places about tanning costs for lynx and coyote.

Wednesday, January 16, 2002—cloudy and low fog, 10° to 26°. Plowed our snow. Sylvia fixed a king salmon dinner for Jim and Mary, Kari and Dave Looney, Mary's brother. Nice visit and showed them the Kodiak fox hunting video. Laura phoned—baby she is carrying is fine, normal and a girl. We are happy for her and Brad.

Thursday, January 17, 2002—cloudy, freezing mist in afternoon, 11° to 18°. Returned Ed's spotting scope. Went out calling near at bait station. Ravens and coyote and fox have cleaned it all up. Saw tracks of two moose and some rabbits. Reloaded a few .223 with cast bullets. Stiff and sore today.

Friday, January 18, 2002—3-1/2 inches of snow, clearing off about noon, 13° to 24°. Cleaned snow off lean-to's and woodshed overhang. Plowed our snow. Chronographed yesterday's reloads. They were not very accurate at 50 yards. George called. I called Jackie (Bob and Kahren's daughter), she told me Rodney Borders died of cancer.

Saturday, January 19, 2002—mostly cloudy, one inch of snow in evening, 3° to 20°. Boots I ordered from Cabala's came. We went with Bartley's to a Republican dinner for Wayne Anthony Ross whose is campaigning for Governor. On the way home Bart was driving on a very snowy highway and lost control. We were all over the road for a quarter mile, but didn't go in ditch. Gave thanks to God for keeping us in road and for not meeting any traffic.

Sunday, January 20, 2002—cloudy, 11° to 19°. Did not sleep well last night. Did not do anything today but read and play solitaire. Nadia phoned about her work with the genealogy tracing of Wilkins family.

Monday, January 21, 2002—mostly sunny, -10° to 7°. Allen, Roxanne, Reed and Adam B. had breakfast with us and watched hunting fox on Kodiak Island movie. Reloaded a few more .223 Remington.

Tuesday, January 22, 2002—warming, cloudy, -28° to -12°. Didn't do much. Tried to change VA appointment with no luck. Tom and Lisa Smayda visited in afternoon.

Wednesday, January 23, 2002—partly cloudy, -14° to -8°. We pumped water. Put a bracket container on the side of the bucket that I carry the electronic varmint caller in. Smashed our tin cans.

Thursday, January 24, 2002—mostly sunny with sun dogs, -15° to -5°. Brought some fire wood in house. Drew up plan and laid it out on an aluminum sheet, then cut lines and location of holes for a speaker bracket on varmint caller.

Friday, January 25, 2002—sunny, double sun dogs, -27° to -12°. Got up early. Ron Beshaw picked me up in VA car and took me to appointment in VA clinic. Everything okay, X-ray, blood tests, cholesterol, diabetes, and thyroid. Did a little grocery shopping. Trip to Anchorage was uneventful.

Saturday, January 26, 2002—mostly sunny, -35° to -16°. Brought more wood into house. Nadia phoned. We went to dinner at Legion. Visited uneventful trip. Did a little shopping for groceries in Glennallen.

Sunday, January 27, 2002—mostly cloudy. -23° to -7°. Shoveled snow of camper and woodshed roof. Brought in one sled load wood. Read a lot.

Monday, January 28, 2002—light snow all day (one inch), -4° to 11°. Cut out drilled and bent pieces for caller bracket and made mistake. Bev phoned. Ian and Caleb brought a fox fur hat Ian made from Sylvia's pattern. Ian did a good job on it. We had dinner at Manning's. Oddens were there.

Tuesday, January 29, 2002—mostly sunny, west breeze, 0° to 24°. Shoveled snow off roofs. Finished caller bracket. Shot .223 two loads of .223 over the chronograph. We pumped water. Sylvia did laundry and cleaned and waxed the linoleum.

Wednesday, January 30, 2002—cloudy and skiff of snow, 10° to 27°. Went out calling this afternoon. Saw tracks of coyote working its way east. A lynx crossed highway from Manning to our place then it went east. Didn't have any luck calling. Went down on lake and east on snowgo. Saw large coyote tracks. Ralph phoned.

Thursday, January 31, 2002—foggy all day, flurries in evening, 11° to 21°. Jeff called. I called about spotting scopes. We had Jim and Elaine here to dinner. Allen and David visited and had chocolate cake.

Friday, February 1, 2002—mostly cloudy and fog, 6° to 12°. I'm 74 years old today. Oddens called and sang Happy Birthday. Didn't do much else. Went to Allen and Roxanne's for dinner and rhubarb upside down cake. Very good. Kim, Tom, Charlie and Kindra Huddleston were there. Jim, Mary and Kari came over later. We all had a good visit.

Monday, February 2, 2002—sunny, -20° to -2°. We pumped water. Smashed pop cans. Daughter Theresa, and my sister Virginia phoned.

Tuesday, February 3, 2002—cloudy and some fog, -20° to 0°. Didn't do much of anything today.

Wednesday, February 4, 2002—mostly cloudy, -11° to 5°. Put wood in basement. Cleaned snow off wood shop roof. Emptied the chimney clean out of its creosote. Plowed our snow. Bev called "Happy Birthday." Al Taylor died today.

Thursday, February 5, 2002—mostly sunny, cloudy evening, -7° to 11°. Brought in more wood. Wrote a letter to McLellan. Read some. Phoned Weaver. Re: spotting scopes.

Wednesday, February 6, 2002—sunny, cloudy towards evening, -13° to 6°. Fog in places on way home from Glennallen. We cashed our checks and had a sandwich before we went to Legion meeting. Voted on officers for the coming year plus other business. Put more wood in basement.

Thursday, February 7, 2002—cloudy, some fog, snowy in evening, -5° to 4°. We pumped water. Read. Went to Odden's for supper (beef tongue and trimmings).

Friday, February 8, 2002—cloudy, -15° to 5°. Sylvia went with Mary G. and Rosemary Bartly to Glennallen and Copper Center. Phoned Anchor inquiring about a Swift spotting scope.

Saturday, February 9, 2002—mostly sunny and breezy, -5° to 12°. Ate supper with Mannings. Watched some of the Olympics.

Sunday, February 10, 2002—snowing all day (one inch), -7° to 17°. Brief sun in afternoon. Reading Northwest Passage today. Allen and Reed stopped by to tell me location of key to his house. Later Odden's stopped by to tell me the location of their key to house. Both families are going to Hawaii for couple weeks.

Monday, February 11, 2002—cloudy and snowy towards evening, 0° to 24°. Tried to call a scope dealer with no luck. We pumped water. Saw two day old lynx tracks. Called Darcy to give her our support and talked to Lee. Nadia called, Chuck's mother fell two times recently. Watched the Salt Lake Olympics.

Tuesday, February 12, 2002—mostly sunny some fog to south, 8° to 27°. Checked Allen and Jim's places including Allen's campground water pump. Saw quite a few lynx tracks along the highway also a few canine tracks. More moose are feeding about here now. Mary Gilcrease dropped off a card and valentine treat.

Wednesday, February 13, 2002—partly cloudy, snow later afternoon, 0° to 20°. Didn't do anything today. Loraine Hanson phoned.

Thursday, February 14, 2002—mostly cloudy, 13° to 30°. Checked Jim Odden's place. Had to re-stretch wing covers on plane. Wind had loosened them and put a small hole in left one. Ailerons had moved also. House was okay. Allen's house okay. Tarp had blown off his sawmill motor. Put it back on. We went to Eureka for supper. Bev called.

Friday, February 15, 2002—cloudy and snow moving closer from south, 1° to 24°. Cal G. visited a while this morning. Finally got a price for a spotting scope from a store in Anchorage.

Saturday, February 16, 2002—cloudy, mostly sunny afternoon, -4° to 10°. We pumped water. Sent an order for spotting scope. A couple lynx walked through our place. Checked Allen's house. Bart and Sam rode with us to a steak dinner at Legion Post. Ran Sam down to Tazlina Trading Post to do some shopping.

Sunday, February 17, 2002—cloudy and a few flakes snow, -9° to 17°. We don't feel well – probably dampness in air. Phoned Nadia—she re-injured her ankle, and Chuck's mom broke her arm.

Monday, February 18, 2002—sunny, -14° to 13°. Beverly's birthday, we phoned her. Checked Allen's and Oddens house. Evened the Ailerons and the wing covers on Jim's PA12. Cal visited in the morning. Brought in some wood. Allen's dog was here.

Tuesday, February 19, 2002— sunny, beaut day, -14° to 15°. Brought in some wood. Need a good book to read.

Wednesday, February 20, 2002—sunny, very nice, -19° to 9°. We watch the Olympics every evening.

Thursday, February 21, 2002—sunny, -24° to 4°. Went to Glennallen and posted Allen's mail that I forgot to put in box. Got my lynx hide tagged. Checked Allen and Jim's houses. Jeff phoned.

Friday, February 22, 2002—mostly sunny, -23° to 3°. Watched Olympics. Brought in wood. Jeff phoned.

Saturday, February 23, 2002—it's -23° to 13°. Pumped water. Some ice in well. Both bulbs burned out. Allen and Roxanne picked up their mail and visited. Gave us a fresh pineapple.

Sunday, February 24, 2002—sunny, cloudy in evening, -16° to 14°. Went to a meeting regarding starting Copper Basin Shooting Club. Enjoyed the meeting. Hope it is successful. Jim and Mary stopped by with gifts.

Monday, February 25, 2002—partly cloudy, -9° to 13°. Don't feel good today. We pumped water twice. Put two new bulbs in well-tightened two clamps.

Tuesday, February 26, 2002—mostly cloudy, -9° to 32°. Jim, Mary, Kari visited for blueberry's on biscuits and cream and coffee in evening.

Wednesday, February 27, 2002—sunny, cloudy evening, 6° to 29°. Jim flew out at noon for McGrath. Had to turn back at the pass and return to Skewentna. We put a new Venetian blind at dining window.

Thursday, February 28, 2002—sunny, cloudy, sunny, snow shower, 13° to 37°. Snow slid off garage and 2/3 of north side of house. South was already mostly clear. Plowed away some snow at garage and shoved a little at arctic entry. Joints all hurt a lot this morning.

Friday, March 1, 2002—mostly cloudy and snow later in afternoon, 10° to 24°. Brought in some wood. Re-hung the Venetian blind. Mary Odden stopped by to say good-bye. I called Ingersoll-Rand about the recall of my air compressor. Allen visited late in the afternoon. Then we went to Gilcrease's for supper and to play dominoes. Some one left a mailbox key on arctic entry door knob.

Saturday, March 2, 2002—cloudy, windy and snow (four inches), 14° to 27°. Plowed our snow along towards evening. Got car ready for trip to Palmer.

Sunday, March 3, 2002—partly sunny, 13° to 24°. We went to Palmer. Visited Lucky and Mary Beaudoin. Lucky and I went to gun show. I didn't buy anything but he found a rifle scope he liked. We did some shopping and got home about 6:00 PM or a little after. Saw three moose this morning. Jim Odden phoned, arrived in McGrath.

Monday, March 4, 2002—sunny, very nice. Allen stopped by and had coffee with me. Jeff phoned. I Phoned Ralph.

Tuesday, March 5, 2002—sunny and breezy, -15° to 14°. Dimmicks called from Anchorage and asked if I would check their mailbox for John's paycheck. No check there.

Wednesday, March 6, 2002—sunny, -23° to 12°. Got car ready to go to Legion meeting. Cashed our checks at the bank. Bart and Rosemary rode in with us and treated us to malted milks before legion meeting. Sylvia took in a coffee cake. Saw a large coyote trotting in snowgo trail on north side of highway about mile 170. It was quite faded out.

Thursday, March 7, 2002—sunny, -15° to 22°. Called Oddens and found out where house key is located, then went there and checked the house. Picked up two small pieces of OSB along highway. We pumped water twice. Some ice in our line. Nadia called, she has a genealogy manuscript in mail.

Friday, March 8, 2002—sunny, -17° to 20°. Made recall arrangements for air compressor. My spotting scope came today. Will take some getting used to. Sylvia is making pickled fish. Laura called to everything is fine with her pregnancy. Mary Odden phoned. A family they know may be interested in old Boot Lake property.

Saturday, March 9, 2002—sunny and strong breeze, -14° to 16°. Tom Huddleston brought back our plat of Old Boot Lake. His son Charlie was with him. They broke a trail up Slide Mountain to the top.

Sunday, March 10, 2002—sunny, some breeze, -19° to 5°. Got air compressor ready to go. Brought in a box for lynx skin. Made up a "For Sale" card for Old Boot Lake property.

Monday, March 11, 2002—sunny, -22° to 16°. Checked Odden house. Their guest have been there and left four snowgos. Put oil in car. Mr. and Mrs. Jim Miller, Pastor at Mendeltna, picked up my old compressor turned in on the recall of Ingersoll-Rand.

Tuesday, March 12, 2002—sunny, stiff breeze from west, -17° to 15°. Nadia sent us a huge, three-ring book of her compilation of the genealogy lines of both sides of our family. It is beautiful. Sylvia went to Queens luncheon.

Wednesday, March 13, 2002—sunny, -9° to 13°. "Rose" called from Odden's inquiring about our green acres property that is for sale. Her husband calls himself Pilgrim.

Thursday, March 14, 2002—sunny, -20° to 15°. Put wood in basement and shoveled snow off of and from in front of snowgo trailer.

Friday, March 15, 2002—sunny, -17° to 17°. Allen visited in the morning. Sylvia went with Rosemary B. and Mary G to Glennallen, Copper Center and stayed late. Switched fluorescent bulbs again and a few small jobs. Shot a squirrel with the .410.

Saturday, March 16, 2002—sunny, -13° to 20°. Water line frozen. Tried to thaw it out. We went to St. Patrick's Day dinner at Legion Post. We picked up Mary Gilcrease who wanted to go. We had George (last name?) and Sam Weaver riding with us coming home.

Sunday, March 17, 2002—cloudy and skiff of snow, -10° to 22°. Sylvia added more hose. We now have 150 feet of hose trying to get water line thawed with no luck. We went to Bartley's to a St. Patrick Day dinner. Lots of people there. Played some cards. Lynx walked out on our driveway.

Monday, March 18, 2002—sunny, -8° to 29°. Used new spotting scope.

Tuesday, March 19, 2002—sunny, -8° to 29°. Allen, Roxanne, and Reed took us to Eureka for breakfast. Quite a few lynx tracks around. Built a bracket that fits on spotting scope tripod and I will clamp it to shooting bench in order to visual targets. Saw trail of snowgo? over on Heavenly Ridge. Possibly bear or moose?

Wednesday, March 20, 2002—sunny, breeze from east, -10° to 28°. Bob and Kahren Rudbecks arrived at Nelchina. Kahren visited in afternoon and Bob stopped by and borrowed the water hauling tank. Denny Eastman wanted me to store a cross fox, then changed his mind.

Thursday, March 21, 2002—sunny, -8° to 29°. Put a sled load of wood in basement.

Friday, March 22, 2002—sunny, -9° to 30°. Shoveled some snow off our waterline. Being black, the sun will thaw it. Bob Rudbeck brought our water hauling tank back and visited.

Saturday, March 23, 2002—sunny. -6° to 30°. We went to Wasilla, Sylvia to see her doctor. Had lunch and did some shopping while there and then home.

Nice to get home while it is still daylight. Stopped at a yard sale and got an electric dictionary typewriter for $5.00!

Sunday, March 24, 2002—cloudy, -6° to 26°. Shoveled more snow off water line. Then I checked, and the small line is thawed! Cal and Mary Gilcrease were here for supper and we played dominoes and visited. Theresa visited on the phone.

Monday, March 25, 2002—cloudy, snowy to the south, 8° to 34°. Re-glued water pipe in well and hooked up to small line as it is thawed. Glue didn't set up and came apart when we tried to pump. Re-glued it and will let it cure for 24 hours. Bob and Kahren brought over Sylvia's medicine order. She paid them and gave them potatoes and a jar of sauerkraut.

Tuesday, March 26, 2002—cloudy, snow started in afternoon, 19° to 37°. Some grosbeaks at bird feeder, also hairy woodpecker, chickadees, camp robbers, redpoll etc. Attached pump and pipe to waterline. Removed 150 watt bulb and tarp from well cover. We pumped water. Worked on snowgo carburetor jet. Went Cal's and got a bigger jet. Took them pickled salmon and potatoes. Our granddaughter, Laura Behrendt phoned.

Wednesday, March 27, 2002—4" snow, 20° to 36°. Plowed it off. We pumped water. Put different jet in snowgo. Writing letters on typewriter, hunt and peck style.

Thursday, March 28, 2002—sunny, snow at supper time, 10° to 37°. We rode with Cal and Mary to senior monthly meeting in Glennallen. Figured out how to attach ice auger to motor. Visited Allen in evening. Shipped lynx to tanner.

Friday, March 29, 2002—we now have four inches of snow, -3° to 22°. Plowed snow. Practiced on typewriter.

Saturday, March 30, 2002—it's -6° to 23°. Lynx walked west to east across our place down by garden. We pumped water. Allen welded two nuts together for joining the motor to my ice auger. Stayed and visited a while.

Sunday, March 31, 2002—clear, -16° to 24°. We went to pot luck at KROA Mendeltna, maybe 25 people were there. Back home by 5:00 PM. Played some dominoes, Sylvia loves the game. Called Theresa. Nice talking to her.

Monday, April 1, 2002—clear and some breeze, -16° to 22°. Allen and Roxanne were here for breakfast. They brought Reed also. Allen gave me a printer, PC, fax and printer only capable. Need paper to try it out.

Tuesday, April 2, 2002—clear and very nice, -13° to 30°. Did a little walking here at home. Typed, wrote one letter. Measured heating oil and gasoline in their respective tanks. Bev phoned, nice to talk to her.

Wednesday, April 3, 2002—clear, -10° to 28°. Did a little walking. Had gasoline and heating oil delivered. Took Sam, Bart to Legion post meeting. Gave Sam potatoes and dry beans.

Thursday, April 4, 2002—clear, beaut of a day, -10° to 28°. Started making a small shelf. Worked on copy machine and did a little typing. Kahren visited in the afternoon. She and Bob had supper with us.

Friday, April 5, 2002—clear, sunny, -9° to 38°. Went to Glennallen on senior van; lunch, cashed checks at bank, paid electric bill. In the afternoon we took "FOR SALE" signs to Lodges at Lake Louise advertising our Old Boot Lake Property. Visited Billman's a while.

Saturday, April 6, 2002—sunny, -2° to 38°. Worked a little more on the shelf on for telephone stand. Weighed our small propane bottles to determine how many pounds of propane are in them. We pumped water. Jeff Routt and Amy visited in afternoon.

Sunday, April 7, 2002—sunny, some breeze, 2° to 32°. Replaced "FOR SALE" sign at Eureka. Visited Cal and Mary. Gave us wall brackets for a shelf and I got it put up. Mary Odden came to visit and Kahren came along—then Bob stopped by. Gave them blueberry yogurt and coffee. Put Odden's canopy door in the truck. Then Jeff and Amy stopped by and visited awhile. His mother is doing better. We are seeing lots of tracks over on Heavenly Ridge (6 mile). Can't tell if they are bear or moose.

Monday, April 8, 2002—mostly sunny, -8° to 34°. Practiced typing and ran out of ribbon. Sorted out some ice fishing gear. Mary G and Evelyn stopped by to buy earrings (Sylvia makes them). Evelyn may have ribbon for typewriter.

Tuesday, April 9, 2002—mostly cloudy, -3° to 36°. Started getting ice fishing gear ready. Not much to do.

Wednesday, April 10, 2002—partly cloudy, snow showers late afternoon, 3° to 33°. Rode the senior van to Glennallen, had lunch, senior meeting. Got air intake for plumbing system.

Thursday, April 11, 2002—cloudy, ¾ inch of snow, then sunny, 7° to 28°. Over at Mannings, I copied some maps and papers for Sylvia. Put a little wood in house. Made another shelf to put the genealogy Nadia sent us.

Friday, April 12, 2002—sunny, hazy, -12° to 26°. Senior van refused to start, so no trip to Glennallen. Did my exercises and walking. Put some wood in basement. Made a spinner to rewind typewriter tape. Went too fast and broke tape.

Saturday, April 13, 2002—mostly cloudy in afternoon, -10° to 32°. Did exercises and some walking. Tried to call Darcy. Played some dominos with Sylvia. Located my pintle hitch for snowgo.

Sunday, April 14, 2002—partly cloudy, 15° to 37°. Got six inches of fluffy snow last night. Sorted out some old papers to throw away. Plowed our snow and shoveled some more. Saw two ravens fly out of tall spruce west of our house. Maybe nesting? Phoned Darcy.

Monday, April 15, 2002—sunny, 1° to 35°. Put a quart of oil in truck. Mixed two cycle oil and gas for snowgo. We pumped water. Borrowed Jim Odden's snowgo sled. Saw a marsh hawk.

Tuesday, April 16, 2002—sunny, 4° to 37°. We went to Glennallen to check information on land on patent registry. Put up "gun for sale" signs and had lunch. Stopped by Fish & Game for fishing regulations. Pumped up tires on snowgo trailer and loaded snowgo. Glenn Transport delivered my replacement air compressor from Ingersoll-Rand. A couple magpies have been hanging around here.

Wednesday, April 17, 2002—partly cloudy, 13° to 45°. Finished loading gear, and was ready when phone call from "Susan" came that she and her dad were in Glennallen (interested in Old Boot property). We met them at Lake Louise Junction and drove to Mile 11 pull out and parking. Hitched sled to snowgo. They rode sled and I pulled them out to Old Boot Lake and our property. Got stuck a couple of times and machine over heated. She walked up to building site and liked it. They asked lots of questions. Saw tracks of moose, otter, marten, mink, fox, very few rabbit. She will decide yea or nay and give us a call.

Thursday, April 18, 2002—partly cloudy, 16° to 47°. Some fog went down the valley this morning. Put the propane tanks back in the camper. Put lynx and coyote skulls in freezer till I can find something to boil them in. Sanded the ice on east side of garage. Worked some on snowgo. Pumped water. Removed 150 watt bulb from well. Started getting air compressor ready to use. Fred Rungee visited. Ate a light lunch and ice cream and we had a nice visit. Haven't glassed for a long time any animal tracks on Heavenly Ridge.

Friday, April 19, 2002—cloudy, 22° to 48°. We went to Glennallen on senior van for shopping and lunch. Tried to call Nadia with no luck.

215

Saturday, April 20, 2002—sunny, cloudy and snowy in evening, 28° to 48°. Put summer tires on car. Put one pint of ATF in car. We went to dinner at Legion. Mary Gilcrease rode with us. Yearly installation of officers this evening.

Sunday, April 21, 2002—cloudy, eight inches of snow, 20° to 40°. Plowed it off and sun came out. Tightened some hinge nuts overhead on door on garage. Had dinner at Bob and Kahren's.

Monday, April 22, 2002—sunny, 12° to 34°. Had breakfast at Allen and Roxanne's with David and Reed. Didn't do anything today.

Tuesday, April 23, 2002—sunny, 1° to 36°. Didn't spot any wildlife on Heavenly Ridge. Jeff phoned three times. Vern Adlins stopped by. Bob R. got his nice snowgo stuck in ditch. We wished Nadia happy birthday. Sylvia worked on a quilt at Legion Post in Glennallen.

Wednesday, April 24, 2002—sunny, 4° to 41°. Jeff and Amy arrived in morning. After lunch we saw a coyote on our lake. We went down by well and tried to call the coyote in. It answered by didn't come in till after we were back at house and brought its mate along. Watched them for quite a while. Then we went target shooting at gravel pit across from highway camp. They went spotting for bears after supper. Enjoyable day.

Thursday, April 25, 2002—partly cloudy, cloudy in evening, 7° to 43°. Loaded up the snowgo and Jeff and Amy drove their car and me with truck and trailer and went to Allen's old trap line trail. Got Jeff and Amy headed down the trail and I drove his car home. They hunted grizzly. Didn't have any luck. Went north about to Allen's cabin. Saw wolf, fox, marten track, one old bear track. Lost a rear idler from snowgo and found it in trail on way back out to highway. When they got back home we put a new bearing in the idler and reinstalled it on snowgo. Put snowgo away, parked trailer and put truck in garage. They went target shooting. Looks like snow this evening. We all played dominos in evening.

Friday, April 26, 2002—mostly sunny, lots of snow melted, 26° to 49°. Glassed for bears with no luck. Jeff and Amy borrowed the snowgo and hunted grizzly bear with no luck. Jeff and Amy ate early supper and went to his mother's at Kenny Lake. Allen came over in evening and visited.

Saturday, April 27, 2002—sunny, snow melting fast, 23° to 52°. Hung a Venetian blind in bedroom. Did few little things. Jeff and Amy stopped by on way home to Anchorage. Her nose is blistered, sunburned red.

Sunday, April 28, 2002—sunny, snow melting fast, 30° to 57°. Prepared a bogie wheel to go on snowgo. Started Suzuki ATV and some other little jobs. Theresa phoned Happy Birthday to her mother. Found a key out in yard. Getting ready to go to Anchorage.

Monday, April 29, 2002—rain, fog all the way to Anchorage and most of way home, 36° to 57°. Was sunny here when we got home. We went shopping. Checked on plane tickets. Didn't buy any. Ate at the Royal Fork. Got a new ribbon for typewriter. Frances called Sylvia for her birthday. So did Nadia and Rosemary Bartley.

Sunday, April 30, 2002—mostly sunny, cloudy this evening, 36° to 57°. Typed four letters today. Helped Sylvia assemble her quilting frame. Lots more water on the lake. Lots of snow melting off. Water seeps into the ground. Pretty breezy here this evening. Lots of dust blowing from river.

Wednesday, May 1, 2002—partly cloudy, windy, 28° to 41°. We went to lunch on senior van. Paid electric bill. On way home we saw a broken power line and reported it. Went back to Glennallen in evening to Legion Post meeting. Bart Bartley rode with us.

Thursday, May 2, 2002—mostly cloudy, 24° to 44°. Not much melting of the snow today. Didn't do much. Kahren came over to get some potatoes. Read the stories about Oscar Vogel, Charley Mayse, and Slim Carlson that Charlie Trowbridge sent me. Helped Sylvia put her quilting frame together. Walked down to the well and straightened water line support. Put ashes on snow that slid off house roof all winter to speed melting.

Friday, May 3, 2002—sunny, 24° to 42°. Allen visited in morning. Put summer tires on truck and put winter tires in storage. Repaired two bogies on snowgo.

Saturday, May 4, 2002—snow squalls, partly cloudy, 21° to 45°. Put snowgo away for season. Henry phoned. Called Jim Odden. Ralph called.

Sunday, May 5, 2002—partly cloudy, 15° to 45°. Moved the snowplow to its place out of the way for the summer. Went to birthday party for Vern Adkins. Picked up brass at gravel pit.

Monday, May 6, 2002—cloudy, 26° to 47°. Walked. Shoveled some snow from lawn on north side of house. Henry Johnson came over to see a picture of Bob Abel. Kyle Farmer brought us a graduation announcement.

Tuesday, May 7, 2002—cloudy, few spots of sleet, 31° to 41°. Shoveled more snow off lawn. Laura phoned. We packaged the blanket for her expected baby.

Saw a kestrel at a nesting box.

Wednesday, May 8, 2002—mostly sunny, 29° to 52°. Walked around on our place (1 mile). A vole is "marking" its territory on south edge of our lawn. Sylvia went to Queens luncheon. Saw two robins. Beverly phoned.

Thursday, May 9, 2002—partly cloudy, 32° to 49°. Light showers in evening. Walked. Went to gravel pit for target practice. Spotting scope was a help, enjoyed the practice. Saw two mallard hens.

Friday, May 10, 2002—mostly cloudy, 29° to 49°. Rain and snow all night. Four inches of wet snow on the ground this morning. Raining this evening. We went to Glennallen to bank, Post Office, shopping and lunch. Today is our 54th wedding anniversary. Cleaned a rifle.

Saturday, May 11, 2002—snow and rain ceased in mid afternoon, 31° to 50°. Walked. Denny and Joie E. stopped by with grad cards. Manning dropped off a half dozen oranges. Muskrat out on ice. Mallards on lake edge. Allen visited in evening and had ice cream and coffee.

Sunday, May 12, 2002—partly cloudy, 31° to 52°. Walked down to lake, serviced car to go to Anchorage tomorrow. Typed "For Sale" notices for Old Boot Lake property and made copies at Manning's.

Monday, May 13, 2002—mostly sunny, 29° to 60°. We went to Anchorage. Got plants for Legion Post planter boxes. Car repairs. Some groceries, prescriptions, hearing aid repaired, consigned MAX 36 7.5 x 54 rifle at Ammo King. Tried to find a P17 Enfield with no luck. Good trip but tiring. Den Eastman phoned with lead to P17 Enfield rifle.

Tuesday, May 14, 2002—partly cloudy and sprinkles, 31° to 59°. Last night Denny Eastman phoned with a lead to a P17 Enfield rifle. Called the man, bought it over the phone, got directions to his place (135+ miles) and to be there before noon today. It is what I want. He suggested shooting it, which I did, and paid $300.00 for it. We did some shopping, parts, for car and greenhouse plants for Sylvia. Ate lunch and came home. She is tired and took a good nap. Kahren wants radish seeds if Sylvia has any.

Wednesday, May 15, 2002—snow, 31° to 40°. Some rain. We went to Glennallen for lunch and a little shopping on senior van.

Thursday, May 16, 2002—partly cloudy, 31° to 54°. Checked oil in car and gassed it. Spent some time cleaning the rifle barrel. Reloaded some cartridges with cast bullets. Made some loading record copies.

Friday, May 17, 2002—beautiful sunny day and some breeze, 29° to 67°! Mosquitoes are out. We went to Glennallen for lunch and some shopping. Ron brought me a word processor—typewriter. I cleaned it the best I could and tried it out. Got it to print what I had typed on the second try. We went to a graduation party for Kyle at his parents' home. Lots of people we know were there. Ed Farmer saw a black bear on south side of our lake. We saw a flicker at nest box and a rabbit eating grass at shop.

Saturday, May 18, 2002—sunny and some breeze, 32° to 67°. Mosquitoes are out. We went to Copper Center and toured the not-yet-completed new buildings at National Park Service. From there a tour of Copper Center on a bus and to the New Princess Tours Hotel and back to the park visitor center where the Lion's Club served wieners, pop and chips. Back home I hung a screen door, polished some brass I picked up today and practiced using the word processor Ron gave me. Sylvia is busy as a bee planting and caring for plants in the greenhouse.

Sunday, May 19, 2002—sunny and no mosquitoes, 36° to 71°. Fine day. Changed oil and filter on car. Started on transmission but had the wrong gasket. Wrote a letter on word processor. Adjusted brakes on Suzuki. We went to a picnic at Allen and Roxanne's at supper time.

Monday, May 20, 2002—sunny and windy in afternoon, 37° to 72°. Over half the ice went out on our lake. Wrote a letter on the word processor. Walked down to the lake. Went to a last day at school program and a pot luck lunch. Cleaned some more on P17 Enfield barrel. Went to Huddleston's for dinner and watched the "Survivor" TV show. More ducks are on the lake now.

Tuesday, May 21, 2002—sunny, some breeze, 36° to 77°. Wrote Nadia. Laura phoned. Tilled the gardens and took tiller over to Allen for Ellie's garden. Put tire repair from a can in tires on ATV trailer. One tire is cracking. Sylvia planted two rows potatoes. Put bore of the pitted barrel soaking in bore cleaner. The bore is the worst I have ever seen. I took the bolt apart and cleaned it. Our lake ice went out before bedtime.

Wednesday, May 22, 2002—sunny and breezy, 41° to 70°. Saw a kestrel drive a raven from their nesting area. We went to Glennallen. Sylvia got plants to replace those the voles chewed off. I got a gasket set for a tranny pan on car. Back home put on pan and over filled tranny with oil, had to remove some of it. Bev phoned.

Thursday, May 23, 2002—sunny and breeze, 45° to 73°. Cleaned up ramp and blocking. Moved some sand and gravel with wheelbarrow. Loaded garbage cans. Allen called—grizzly one mile east of Eureka. Loaded gun, binocular, spotting scope, and ran down there. Looked up and down along highway where bear was supposedly seen with no luck. Talked to two ATV riders who had seen a bull moose but no bears. Came home and then went to Grizzly Towing to get transfer site gate key. He actually saw the bear at the camping pull off on North Side, two miles east. After supper Sylvia had an excellent idea for making room for the word processor. We moved dining room table 90°. Brought up an unused homebuilt table from the basement. Altered it to make knee room and settled the word processor there. Looks great. Reloaded some .30-.06 cast bullets. Then we played some dominos for relaxation.

Friday, May 24, 2002—some breeze, 42° to 83? We went to Glennallen. Paid electric bill, got stamps, groceries and lunch. Back home I did some more modifications to legs and top—new plywood on the word processor table. Then put two coats of paint on it. We went to prime rib steak dinner at Post 27 Legion. There were nine caribou bulls swimming in our lake. They acted undecided and finally turned back to the south side and left.

Saturday, May 25, 2002—sunny, breezy, 44° to 78°. Put new windshield washer pump on car and it didn't work. We went to Legion Post to be part of an Honor Guard at a memorial service for a Legion member (wore a black cap, shirt, pants and shoes). Went to two yard sales. Bart rode home with us. Kids are playing at diving raft on lake.

Sunday, May 26, 2002—sunny and breezy, 48° to 84°. Sprayed a grassy weedy area. Honor Guard drill again today, this time for those who have fallen in service to our country. Loaded up shooting gear and went to gravel pit to shoot. Mark and his son Luke (who got a .410 single shotgun for his tenth birthday) drove in and Luke shot his new gun a few times. After they left, I tried the pit shooting cast bullets after though cleaning. It shot very badly. I then shot some jacket match bullets and got a 3-3/4" group. In the afternoon, I did some research for a Mr. Sean Hite about gun stuff, plus some for me and got some written down and organized. Checked the fuses in the car. A two or three year old griz has recently been in the gravel pit.

Monday, May 27, 2002—partly cloudy, 46° to 69°. We spent the day participating in the Memorial Day ceremonies conducted by Legion Post #27 Glennallen. We went to two services, had lunch and went to Copper Center and did two more. I was color bearer this year, also put new flags on the graves of military men buried at Copper Center. Sylvia helped put spruce bows decorated with poppies on graves.

Tuesday, May 28, 2002—mostly cloudy and sprinkles, windy, 43° to 63°. Went to Legion Post and cleaned the rifles. Reloaded 20 cast bullets to fire lap the pit barrel. Sylvia got lots done today.

Wednesday, May 29, 2002—cloudy with rain in late afternoon, 41° to 61°. We went to Glennallen for lunch on senior van. Seeded grass on the two bare spots on north side of house. Cleaned on rifle barrel and typed some notes for PI7 book.

Thursday, May 30, 2002—rainy, fog over by river, 41° to 58°. We went to Glennallen to monthly senior meeting. Worked on cleaning that rifle.

Friday, May 31, 2002—rainy, 40° to 56°. Went to lunch at Glennallen. Yard sale. I think the gun is pretty clean. Nadia called, will send me some floppy discs for the word processor. A guy came by looking for horns.

Saturday, June 1, 2002—sunny and strong breeze, 40° to 60°. Took Sylvia to Tazlina to Jo Child's yard sale. She got a cardboard box full of thread. Stopped by another yard sale and got shirts and a jacket. Then three T-shirts at store in Glennallen. Saw a sharp-tail grouse near highway west of Glennallen. Went to gravel pit and fire lapped the P17 rifle. It shot better afterward. Will clean and polish the bore now.

Sunday, June 2, 2002—partly cloudy and windy, 36° to 62°. Went to gravel pit. Gave up shooting cast bullet. Got one fair group with jacketed bullets. Ralph called me and we talked about how to get this rifle to shoot.

Monday, June 3, 2002—partly cloudy and windy, 36° to 60°. Went to gravel pit and shot the rifle. Got two good groups. Visited Henry, he wants me to rebuild old Victrola horn. I offered to trade our 500-gallon fuel tank for his 300-gallon tank.

Tuesday, June 4, 2002—partly cloudy, 35° to 64°. Saw a rabbit in the yard. Changed front sights on P17 Enfield. Worked on windshield washer on car. Chopped weeds in rhubarb. Put together a double outlet extension cord for word-processor. Walked down and checked well.

Wednesday, June 5, 2002—cloudy and rain, 40° to 60°. Went to Glennallen and ate. Cashed checks, went to post office. The in evening we took Rosemary and Bart with us to Legion meeting in Glennallen. Ron took the two planters of pansies Sylvia raised to the Legion and placed them on the front of building.

Thursday, June 6, 2002—rained in night and most of morning, 39° to 55°. Some sun in afternoon. Walked, then put up Venetian blind in west window upstairs. Practiced on word processor, using its file system.

Friday, June 7, 2002—partly cloudy and sunny with a breeze, 38° to 62°. We went to Glennallen. Sylvia planted red, white and blue pansies around flag poles at American Legion Post #27 in town. Went to lumberyard and hardware store, and ate lunch. Tested a new load in the .308 win, was not impressed. Reloaded more with different powder, plus some .30 br.

Saturday, June 8, 2002—partly cloudy and winds to 36 mph from south then from east, 37° to 62°. Coming back from mailbox a cow moose burst out of trees along the lane not 20 feet from me. She turned and went east on north side of garage, trailing two red calves. That was a shot of adrenaline! Aired up the ATV trailer tires and trying to find leaks or how long they will stay up.

Sunday, June 9, 2002—partly cloudy, 37° to 63°. We went to a birthday part for Gracie Niki Niki at Bob Rudbeck's. Some other people there also. Went shooting at gravel pit.

Monday, June 10, 2002—partly cloudy, threatened rain, 37° to 64°. Didn't practice my shooting. Denny Eastman asked me to go sucker spearing with him in a creek running by Wolverine Lodge on Lake Louise. A few were in there and Denny speared six of them. I cut their heads off and carried them in a plastic bag. I built a small box like structure on shooting bench to serve as a support for the spotting scope. Saw a big-body bull moose with small horns along Lake Louise Road.

Tuesday, June 11, 2002—partly cloudy with light breeze, 38° to 62°. Did some practice shooting this morning. Put a new fuel filter and air cleaner on the car. Cleaned PCV on car.

Wednesday, June 12, 2002—partly cloudy with light breeze, 38° to 65°. Mosquitoes were bad at gravel pit this evening. We went to Glennallen. Paid phone bill. Sylvia got some Pepsi and watered flowers at Legion Post. Went to gravel pit to shoot and David Kyle Farmer came to sight their .338 in. It was 3" high at 100 yards. Went back this evening after seating .308 with cast bullets deeper. Got it sighted in (I hope) and chronographed this load. Beautiful evening.

Thursday, June 13, 2002—partly cloudy to cloudy and a sprinkle, 42° to 70°. We went to Glennallen and had our eyes tested. I have cataracts, more so in left eye. Will probably need an operation within five years. Dr. pulled an eye lash out that had been irritating Sylvia. I made a dentist appointment. We had lunch. Swadged taper some cast bullets and reloaded some for .30 br.

Friday, June 14, 2002—rain in night, partly cloudy today, 43° to 70°. We went to Glennallen on senior van. Lunch a little shopping, post office, put up land for sale signs. Went to gravel pit to shoot and Karen Mailly and 8-9 kids were there catching pollywogs and playing on a sand bank. After they left I did a little shooting. Got the car ready to go to Anchorage. Made out shopping list.

Saturday, June 15, 2002—sunny, 43° to 73°. Up 6:00 AM. Left for Anchorage about 6:30. Got a motor powered brush cutter and a small home type copy machine, groceries and sundrie things. Visited with Jeff, Amy and her son John Paul and daughter Chelsie. That was good. We got back home 6:45 PM. Unloaded the car. Ate a sandwich, had cup of coffee. Assembled the copier and made three copies right away. Wrote a letter to cousin Gladys. It's a beautiful evening out there.

Sunday, June 16, 2002—sunny and breezy, 68° to 78°. Put away garden tiller. Installed a fan in the greenhouse for Sylvia. Reloaded some .308 win cast bullets. Kahren visited. Nadia called Father's Day greetings.

Monday, June 17, 2002—partly sunny and shower in evening, 53° to 77°? I went to Anchorage and exchanged the trimmer I brought home by mistake Saturday. Today I got a brush cutter/trimmer. Also two pair of denim overalls, some oil, spark plugs and wires and a windshield washer for car and a watermelon for Sylvia. Denny Eastman asked to borrow our water hauling tank.

Tuesday, June 18, 2002—partly cloudy with showers, two minutes of hail in morning, 48° to 67°. Put the brush cutter together, mixed gas and oil for it. It runs good and cuts brush up to ½ inch in diameter. Fired two of my cast bullet targets and neither one is good enough to submit. Loaned Denny Eastman's water hauling tank and a pump.

Wednesday, June 19, 2002—cloudy, numerous showers all day, 47° to 57°. We went to lunch on senior van. Sylvia then joined neighborhood event going to Kenny Lake to a greenhouse sale.

Thursday, June 20, 2002—partly cloudy, 38° to 62°. Some showers in the mountains. to south. I went to gravel pit and shot moly-coated bullets in the pit. Then followed with cast bullets. Was home a short time and in drove Jeff, Amy, John and Chelsie. Visited and went on to camp down at Kenny Lake. I put a new windshield washer on car. Then put a new distributor cap, rotor, spark plugs and wires on the car. Boy am I bushed this evening. Kahren stopped by to visit. Sylvia bought some raspberry plants yesterday and we planted them this morning.

Friday, June 21, 2002—partly cloudy, 40° to 64°. Worked a little on the car, ran a water line to raspberries east of house. Checked on Charlie Trowbridge's storage shed. Cut out old canes and tied new growth of raspberries down in garden. Reloaded 80 cartridges with moly-coated bullets in hopes "moly" will fill rifle barrel pits. Allen Farmer visited. Cut some more brush.

Saturday, June 22, 2002—sunny, 43° to 73°. Cut down more brush south of house. Dug out the opening to pump the septic tank. Got ready for John and Mary McLellan from Maine to visit us. Had a nice visit. Theresa called with their news. We went to dinner at Legion post. Rode in with Bart.

Sunday, June 23, 2002—partly cloudy, 44° to 65°. We went for a drive, to The Point, Lake Louise; Dan and Patti. Then to Copper Basin Shooting Club meeting. Sylvia reminded them they would need toilet facilities. Then stopped by John and Mary McLellan at Northern Lights campground and visited a little while. From there to Darrel and Brenda's and then home.

Monday, June 24, 2002—mostly sunny, 42° to 71°. Burned two tanks of gas in the brush cutter. Hauled garden tiller to garden to those parts needing it. The cow moose and calf came through yard between house and garage. I hollered at Sylvia to come and see them. Cow had a diagonal patch of hair 5" - 6" wide by 30 inches long gone from over her right side ribs. There was a much smaller strip of hair gone also. She has lost one calf, probably to a griz. She must have tried to defend the calves. Cleaned some on the P17 Enfield. Kahren and Bob visited a few minutes. Kahren gave us a cucumber.

Tuesday, June 25, 2002—cloudy and rainy, clearing in evening, 44° to 66°. Got up early and went to Glennallen. Got my teeth cleaned. Picked up my new glasses. Sylvia watered flowers at Legion Post. We went to lunch. Filled out a drug discount application to send to Eli Lilly and Company. Windy evening.

Wednesday, June 26, 2002—partly cloudy, windy in evening, 38° to 71°. Went to Glennallen lunch and water flowers. Went target shooting this afternoon. Mailed application to join Alaska Competitive Shooters Organization.

Thursday, June 27, 2002—partly cloudy, 43° to 63°. Truck came to pump out septic tank. Worked on waterline. David Farmer helped by dipping buckets of sand out of our well. He is good help.

Friday, June 28, 2002—couple of showers and partly cloudy with breeze, 45° to 74°. Sylvia went with Kahren to Anchorage for three days. I went to Glennallen to Post Office, lunch and hardware store then left my jacket and the cover for septic tank riser for pumping the tank. Fred Rungee visited. He bought ice cream, cake and broccoli. I cut down some more cottonwood.

Saturday, June 29, 2002—partly cloudy and beautiful, 46° to 74°. Whacked the weeds along the road to garden and on the west end of garden. Made four tall tent poles for the 10' x 10' camping tarp. Received answer and a cap from Remington in response to my letter about the primer problem.

Sunday, June 30, 2002—mostly sunny, clouding over in evening, 47° to 70°. Went to gravel pit to try some new reloads. Got the best groups so far. Then fired 10 shots at offhand practice and did pretty good. Somebody has had a party in pit and did some shooting. Picked up 16 .223 Remington - 2, 300 savage and 10, 44 magnum. Cut some alder roots that have gone out into the garden. Didn't get all of them. Sylvia and Kahren got back from Anchorage okay. Strong breeze this evening.

Monday, July 1, 2002—partly cloudy, dark clouds north of Slide Mountain, 47° to 66°. Went shooting at gravel pit. Got some good groups. Tightened the loose screws on the roof of house and garage. Measured the heating fuel and gasoline. Visited Cal and Mary in evening. Strong breeze down on the lake.

Tuesday, July 2, 2002—partly cloudy, strong wind from west this afternoon, 44° to 68°. Bob Rudbeck gave me two, 4" PVC couplings this morning. I used them putting a stand pipe and plug on the septic tank. Found where the large waterline pulled apart last winter. Sylvia helped me pull it together. Cut out a couple target boards. Started fixing the suitcase Sylvia bought at yard sale.

Wednesday, July 3, 2002—nice day, rain at bedtime, 45° to 68°. We went to Glennallen. Hardware store, bank, light bill and lunch and shopping. Fixed handle on Sylvia's suitcase. We went back to Glennallen to Legion Post meeting.

Thursday, July 4, 2002—raining, 44° to 67°. We got ready and went to Bartley's. Rode with them to Glennallen. Helped the post get ready for the Fourth of July parade. Sylvia was one of the ladies who were sewing on their float. She enjoyed decorating the float and participating in the parade. Afterwards we went to the salmon bake at the ball field. Rode home with Denny and Joey Eastman. Ralph and Roma had just driven in from Fairbanks. We visited for awhile then Ralph and I went to gravel pit for three hours and shot rifles and chronographed different loads, bullets etc. They brought lots of goodies and we had a great supper, watermelon and all. Played a few hands of dominoes and lots of visiting.

Friday, July 5, 2002—quite cloudy, 40° to 62°. We all went to Glennallen and Roma bought some material for sewing. Then we went to Eureka for lunch. Ralph and I went to gravel pit to evaluate his lightweight 30-06 sporter. Just couldn't get consistent good groups. He wants it to shoot sheep at 400 yards. We did a little relieving of forend pressure to no avail. I gave him a shooting bench and made an attachment to mount his spotting scope to the bench. This was a good day. Theresa called again tonight. Earl is out of the hospital. Flickers and kestrels hatched out a few days ago.

Saturday, July 6, 2002—mostly sunny, 45° to 72°. Up early. Corrected a mistake on the spotting scope holder that I made for Ralph's shooting bench. Then he forgot to take it when he and Roma left. I cut some more brush. Took a nap, as that job really wears me out. Straightened up some in garage and storage shed. Burned trash. Straightened out the .30-06 brass. Prepped a little on some .30 br brass. Played some dominoes and read some.

Sunday, July 7, 2002—partly cloudy, 44° to 70°. We went to church services Allen and Roxanne hosted at their place here on the lake and the pot luck afterward. Then we went to Copper Basin Shooting Club meeting at the Brown Bear Rhode House in Glennallen to plan the turkey shoot and BBQ. We got home at 5:00 PM.

Monday, July 8, 2002—sunny, 54° to 79°. Went shooting the .338 Winchester + 30 br. Someone has burned Allen's shooting bench in the gravel pit. Cut some more brush, got pretty sweaty doing it. Modified my best shoot pedestal. Cutting-welding-drilling and tapping. Welder started easily. Very warm today.

Tuesday, July 9, 2002—mostly sunny, 45° to 75°. A shower in evening. Cut more brush. Visited Ed Farmer. Rested. Answered called VA and Jay G. Got a card from Peter and Delaine Achermann their daughter Denise passed away. We are saddened. Sylvia sewed me a neat recoil absorbing pad.

Wednesday, July 10, 2002—sunny, cloudy and showers in our valley, 46° to 74°. We went to Glennallen to bank, lunch, store. Back at home, I cut more Aspen with a Swede saw. Laura phoned.

Thursday, July 11, 2002—partly cloudy and rain late afternoon, 50° to 74°. Target practice at gravel pit. Gave Ed some boat trailer parts. Called Henry. Water is unusually low on Alfred Creek. Their trip was very nice. Someone is conducting tours using large swamp buggies. I cut more brush on our south hillside. The ducks are up and circling the house this evening. Flickers and kestrels working hard every day to feed their offspring.

Friday, July 12, 2002—raining night, 49° to 69°. Partly cloudy. Went to Anchorage for appointment with Ferral at VA. Took blood to monitor prescriptions. "Alfa," a woman from Kenny Lake drove the "senior's van". She is a different kind of driver. I have lost 8 lbs since January.

Saturday, July 13, 2002—rain in night, partly cloudy today. 48° to 70°. Fooled around reloading, prepping brass. Jeff phoned several times about a 03A3 he found at gun show in Anchorage. Looked for some car parts at Cal's with no luck. Saw Allen at Cal's.

Sunday, July 14, 2002—partly cloudy, 48° to 74°. Cleaned three rifles. Cut grass and weeds around and near the green house. We went to Copper Basin Shooting Club meeting to firm up plans for the turkey shoot next Sunday. Jeff phoned after we got home. They had been out shooting.

Monday, July 15, 2002—partly cloudy, 45° to 76°. Whacked more weeds and brush. Went target shooting with P17 Enfield and .30BR. Put ten, 5-gallon buckets crushed rock around the well.

Tuesday, July 16, 2002—partly cloudy, 49° to 84°. Threatening rain. Cut more brush. Went down to get rhubarb from Roxanne. Mary Odden, Kari and friend Troy visited and showered in evening.

Wednesday, July 17, 2002—partly cloudy, threatening rain, 47° to 82°. We went to lunch in Glennallen. Stopped by Ruth Taylor's garage shop sale. Cut more brush. Went to Denny and Joey's and visited a while this evening. Got letter from Vanessa.

Thursday, July 18, 2002—some rain showers in morning prevented Denny from flying, then he got to smoking fish, 50° to 74°. I carved a birch spoon. Then cut down more brush and "whacked" more weeds and grass. Took some pickled salmon over to Henry. Wrote up an ad to sell our remote parcel on a web site.

Friday, July 19, 2002—cloudy in morning, very nice later, 50° to 74°. Went with Denny Eastman in his Super Cub. He flew me by our land on Old Boot Lake. I took pictures of our property. Then we went to Jan Lake, put a canoe in the lake. We caught some rainbow trout and land locked salmon. Then flew back to our home lake. Some mother ducks have lots of little ones with them. We saw a few swans from the air, no signets. We went to Legion social evening and dinner with Rosemary and Bart. We picked up John Dimmick who was hitch hiking and took him home. Sylvia picked up two, 1-gallon jars of pickled dill for Joey Eastman. She needs the glass jars.

Saturday, July 20, 2002—mostly sunny, 49° to 70°. Whacked more weeds. Went shooting at gravel pit. Got dredge ready to go to Albert Creek. Laura called with update on Maggie. Saw cow moose with calf track in gravel pit. Sylvia saw an eagle water soaked in our lake from chasing baby ducks. One old duck hen had so many ducklings they couldn't be counted. Sylvia watered lawn, plants and pumped for the house.

Sunday, July 21, 2002—partly cloudy, light fog on the lake early this morning,

39° to 71°. We went to Copper Basin Shooting Clubs' turkey shoot at their shooting range just north of Gulkana airport. I helped by preparing some targets for shooting events. I didn't have a rifle along that was compatible with any of their events and did not shoot. I did help a young man in understanding the sights on his P17 Enfield. Sylvia helped at the food table. It was a nice learning experience. We stopped by Darrel and Brenda's on our way home. Really nice evening.

Monday, July 22, 2002—pretty cloudy some of time and some sprinkles later in the afternoon on Alfred Creek, 43° to 76°. Picked up Cal Gilcrease and drove over Ballanger Pass and down Alfred Creek to Upper Camp. "Bones," Ed, Chuck and Chuck Jr. and another guy were there. Gave a gold clean up sluice to "Bones," and a magnetic device for picking up dry black sand from gold concentrate to both Bones and Jim. We saw 27 ewes and lamb Dall sheep at Mineral Licks near the upper part of the canyon Alfred Creek goes through. Saw one eagle. We found no place to dredge. We did some sample panning on Alfred and Fossil Creeks. Trail was dry, creeks were low, quite rocky though and had to drive very slow and "save" the old pickup as best I could. It was rougher for Cal as I had the steering wheel to hang on to.

Tuesday, July 23, 2002—sunny, windy in evening, 48° to 75°. Fired up chain saw and cut some larger brush. Worked putting a section of water line to grade. Cleaned up a heavy aluminum tube. Put away the dredge with a disappointed heart. Serviced the car and truck.

Wednesday, July 24, 2002—cloudy and showers, all night and today, 51° to 70°. We went to Glennallen. Paid telephone and electric for a month ahead. Had lunch. Back home I got off a couple letters.

Thursday, July 25, 2002—partly cloudy, 48° to 71°. Wrote a letter to granddaughter, Vanessa. Tilled the garden. Pulled weeds and tree roots growing out into the garden. Stressed my back loading the tiller into ATV trailer. Scraped the dried mashed grass from under the deck of lawn mower. Turned over the blade. It was upside down. Spent a lot of time writing up our air flight itinerary.

Friday, July 26, 2002—mostly cloudy and windy, 44° to 62°. We went to lunch, shopping in Glennallen on the senior van. My back is very bad after stressing it loading the tiller in ATV trailer. Denny Eastman stopped by to borrow the water tank.

Saturday, July 27, 2002—mostly cloudy and some showers, 42° to 61°. The little kestrels started coming out of the nest boxes. We thought they had left already. Very interesting to watch them. Spent all day repairing the shipping breakage

Sylvia's spinning wheel incurred when she brought it over here from Slovenia a few years ago. Had to drill holes and insert a dowel to repair one part. Had partial success welding a steel part. Didn't have enough and "fresh" rod of size needed. Finished with "J B" weld. Bathroom lavatory sink fell apart and we had to clean that all up. Made some wood parts for Sylvia's crafts.

Sunday, July 28, 2002—cloudy and showers, 43° to 55°. The young kestrels, we have seen two, are still in the area of the nest box. Parents are feeding them. Worked some more on the spinning wheel. When I fixed the broken part, I got it turned 90º. Bummer. Too bad I hadn't seen it before it was broken. Cleaned up the parts from lavatory sink drain. Expect to buy all new parts. Denny brought back the water tank. Swabbed some rifle barrels.

Monday, July 29, 2002—Cloudy, light shower, 44° to 58°. Cut more brush, pulled more weeds. Reworked the spinning wheel, got it right now. Reloaded some 30-06. Called Nadia, didn't answer. Laura phoned.

Tuesday, July 30, 2002—partly cloudy, nice, 42° to 72°. Did some small chores. Reloaded more 30-06 cast bullets. This time Nadia called. Typed up our itinerary.

Wednesday, July 31, 2002—partly cloudy and breezy, 45° to 69°. Senior van is broken down. We drove in to Glennallen ourselves because we needed repairs for the vanity sink. Found them at Second Lumber yard. Had lunch at Caribou café and came home. Someone put some D1 gravel out by highway and spread it. I did some raking on it to even it out, then put the repair kit on the vanity sink.

Thursday, August 1, 2002—sunny, sometimes breezy, 41° to 78°. Went to gravel pit to shoot cast bullet postal match and took wrong rifle. Went back with right rifle in afternoon. It did okay for me. While we were eating supper one of the little kestrels landed in a tree 40' from our window and proceeded to dismantle a vole and devour it. It then actually lounged on the tree limb for quite some time. A little later, its two siblings showed up at same tree.

Friday, August 2, 2002—sunny and breezy, 37° to 78°. Put up a rack for tent poles and boat oars. Went to gravel pit. Shot some FM JBT reloads for accuracy. Very good. Then practiced off hand M1 shooting using cast bullets. This went well for a 75 year old man with cataracts in both eyes. Lots of rifle cleaning. Gathered clothes up for trip outside. Jeff called. They plan to camp in the gravel pit.

Saturday, August 3, 2002—sunny, with breeze, 45° to 82°. Went to gravel pit to sight in .338 Winchester Jeff, Amy Kitten, Chelsie, Jarret, John Paul and

Shobbie were camped there. Jeff was frying pancakes. Amy and some of the kids were shooting .22 pistol and rifle target practice. We set up shooting bench and target stand. Shot .338 from 200 yards, could not get the scope to shoot to the same zero. Then shot two of Jeff's rifles. The one had a sticky chamber, this we polished when back to my place. They stopped by for a while in late afternoon. After they left, then we went to Harold and Rachel Dimmick's for supper and visit. I put another scope on the .338.

Sunday, August 4, 2002—sunny and breezy, 54° to 85°. Went to gravel pit to sight in .338. Couldn't get scope zeroed. Came home and loaded more cartridges. Cleaned the rifle. We will leave our car at Chris Woods while gone to Minnesota. Dan Billman will drive up to and from the airport. Bob and Kahren visited a while, Kahren brought over another cucumber. I took a bunch of guns down to Allen's for safe keeping while we are gone. We had a good visit about numerous subjects. Nice evening.

Monday, August 5, 2002—partly cloudy and breezy, 50° to 80°. Went to gravel pit and got the .338 sighted in. Had a heck of time, but better than yesterday. Made several trip related calls today. Sanded my loafer shoes and made repairs with "shoe goo." Waterproofed my hunting boots. Kahren came over again in late afternoon.

Tuesday, August 6, 2002—cooler here, 20°. We loaded the car and went to Palmer, cashed our checks. Went on to Anchorage. Filled Sylvia's prescriptions. Went to Ammo King and discovered my French M367.5x54 had been sold. Took a while to get paid. Went back to Peter's Creek to Chris Wood's home, parked and waited for Dan Billman to come home from work. A next door neighbor phoned city police of our presence there and they came and checked us out. This took maybe an hour (they were just doing their job). Finally they left. Dan came home and we went to Royal Fork for dinner, then Dan drove us all around and through Lake Hood Seaport and landing field, looking at all the planes. Then we went to the air terminal. We passed security OK and then flight was on time. We got to Seattle on time.

Wednesday, August 7, 2002—cool and overcast here. We followed the directions for taking the shuttle bus from Alaska Airline to Northwest Air, though uncertain and apprehensive. This was not helped by some of the airport personnel. Caught the flight to Minneapolis with a few minutes to spare. Flight was on time. Theresa, Earl, Darcy, Jason, Dylan, Devin and Lee met us at the baggage pickup. Nadia came an hour later and drove us out to Rogers MN to Laura and Brad's house. Brittany was also there to greet us. Had a nice visit, pizza and snacks, sandwich to eat. Got to hold Maggie. We are tired after this 27 hour day. Their house is very nice.

Thursday, August 8, 2002—rain in night, 70's, saw five geese fly over. We went to Wal-Mart. Couldn't get film developed. Did a little shopping. Got dominoes for Brittany and played some games with her. Stopped at a second hand store. Did not find a book that I wanted. Brad gets home 3:30 PM. Had a fine dinner. Watched WWII Midway Pacific battle on TV.

Friday, August 9, 2002—partly cloudy in evening, 70s. Brittany and "Shelby" her dog and I went for a walk to the elementary school playground nearby and spent some time there. Shelby is fat and got tired. We would stop walking and give her a chance to rest. Baby Maggie is so good, it is fun to be around her. Laura fixed a great supper. We then watched the movie "Twister," very good! Laura, Brittany and Sylvia went shopping for material for finishing an afghan they started.

Saturday, August 10, 2002—partly cloudy, 70s. Went for a good walk. Played with great granddaughter Maggie. She coos and smiles. After lunch Brad mowed his lawn and trimmed it. We watched the movie "Pearl Harbor," very good movie. Went for a short walk after supper and finished the movie.

Sunday, August 11, 2002—cloudy in the evening, 70s. We all went to Brad and Laura's church to see Margaret Faith "Maggie" baptized. Great grandparents (Sylvia and I) and her father's parents and extended family were there also and at the reception at Brad and Laura's home afterward. Darrell Breider and wife from New Mexico were there. We left early to stay with Nadia and Chuck a few days. Our first time in their new home. It is nice. Fresh corn and tomatoes at every dinner. Phoned Paul Norris, Independence IA. We plan to stop there on our way to Cedar Rapids.

Monday, August 12, 2002—cloudy, partly cloudy 10-15 mph wind, 70s cloudy. We had lunch at Chuck's parents place (Charles Sr. and Lucille Kasun) in Stillwater. Enjoyed our visit. Did a little shopping. Read the newspaper. Packed a bag for trip to Iowa and Illinois. Replaced battery in camera. I have an ear infection. Put a battery in the flight light I bought for Sylvia.

Tuesday, August 13, 2002—70s. Left at 6:00 AM for Iowa. Got to Paul Norris's close to noon. He took us out to lunch. We had a great time reminiscing and visiting. I last saw Paul in 1977. He and his new wife have a beautiful home. She was assisting another lady getting an eye exam. The corn and beans look very good in Minnesota and Iowa. Both Paul's sons (Richard and Bob) farm. We got slightly lost in Cedar Rapids before we found Virginia and Don's place. Visited a while then they took us out to a Mexican supper. After eating they drove us around Cedar Rapids, looking at flowering gardens, schools, golf courses etc. Virginia treated us to pecan pie, then more visiting, pictures of places in Europe and experiences there.

Wednesday, August 14, 2002—some breeze, 80°. Cousin Lester and Ruth Shickel got here about 11:30 AM and brought Harold and Cousin Gladys Schmidt and Cousin Audrey and her husband, John Kooeyman, We visited and Virginia served a great pot luck lunch. Then more visiting. They all left about 5:30 PM. Then Virginia, Don, Nadia, Sylvia and I enjoyed a quiet visit on the deck, watching wrens, robins etc. Earlier in the morning there was a buck deer on the lawn. A little later there was a wild turkey hen that spent quite some time on the edge of the trees in full view.

Thursday, August 15, 2002—20 mph wind and sunny, 84°. Early breakfast with Virginia and Don. Took Highway 218 to US 80 and east to Joliet IL. Found Sylvia's sister, Fran's place. Her son John (our nephew) was there. He set out a fine lunch of meats, bread, cheese and wine. A neighbor lady brought over a newborn kitten. Tried to call Brittany birthday greetings – phone was busy.

Friday, August 16, 2002—partly cloudy, shower in the night, 86°. John came over and took us all to the Botanical Gardens, 385 acres here in Chicago. So many varieties and plantings of trees, shrubs, ornamentals, flowers of many kinds, gardening, displays and on and on. We walked miles looking at all of this, including miniature trains. John bought our lunch and paid our way into the model train exhibit. We went to his house and rested about 1-½ hours, then met his wife, Sandy at a pizza house for an excellent dinner. Then we went on to another place for dessert and to listen to a male singer (very Sinatra-like) and three-member band playing 1920-1940s music. Got back to Fran's house about 9:00 PM

Saturday, August 17, 2002—sunny and windy, 80's. Gusts pushed the car (Saturn) around on the road, after we left Fran's at 8:05 AM. Made the trip back to the Twin Cities and Nadia's house and unloaded the car around 4:00 PM. Chuck was glad to see Nadia back home.

Sunday, August 18, 2002—sunny, nice day, 71°. Up early. Nadia and Chuck took us to Beverly's. Nadia and Chuck left. We had "brunch" with Bev and her boyfriend, Rich. Visited all day. BLT for supper, apple pie and ice cream. Watched a couple movies and read Sunday paper.

Monday, August 19, 2002—sunny, 70°. Walked over to Lyndale Avenue to a billiard store and asked if they had an interest in a "Doctor Pepper" billiard table light (it is in Alaska). They want a picture of it. Got shampoo at K-Mart. Showered and read some.

Tuesday, August 20, 2002—partly cloudy, light shower in evening, 69°. Tyler came over to Bev's to stay with us while we are here. He, Rich and I went to grocery store where Bev was shopping for a birthday party for Vanessa. Scott, Earl, Theresa, Darcy and her boy's Dylan and Devin came. We had lots of fun and visiting, eating a good supper. The little boys are live wires! As the evening wore on they began to get acquainted with Sylvia and me. We were called Grandpa and Grandma before they left.

Wednesday, August 21, 2002—three inches rain in night, lots of lightening strikes close by, 77°. Tyler has a car and took Rich and me with him to MN DMV. Then he bought belts for his cars motor. I got a hair brush, newspaper, and gum. Beverly, Tyler, Rich and I played Monopoly and put the finish touches on the afghan that she is doing for Brittany.

Thursday, August 22, 2002—mostly cloudy, 72°. Rich, Tyler and I went to K-Mart and got a small set of wrenches to put belts on his car motor. Some bolts were metric so we couldn't complete the job. Later Tyler took Sylvia and me to K-Mart for a little shopping and we walked home for exercise. We took Bev, Rich and Tyler to supper at Country Buffet. Watched a movie and went to bed.

Friday, August 23, 2002—mostly cloudy, 70's. Went to Bev's place of employment. Went to Wal-Mart, bought a billfold. Picked up developed pictures. Helped Rich put a light in a hutch. The switch gave Rich a shock. Bev, Tyler, and Rich gave me a book. We gave Bev her pick of the pictures.

Saturday, August 24, 2002—partly cloudy, 70's. Nadia and Chuck picked us up at 8:00 AM and drove us to Paul and Ruth's at Staples. We all had lunch. They will drive back by way of Milaca to look at a "Saturn" car they are interested in. Steve was at work helping a tire company move its inventory to a new building in Motley. He got home in the afternoon. We watched the "Railroad Days" parade as it passed the house. Steve's girlfriend Lisa and her family were out on the lawn to see parade. Steve told bear baiting stories while he ate his sandwich supper.

Sunday, August 25, 2002—sunny, 80s. Went with Steve to his bait station near Moose Lake. Bears have been into two of his stations, but not the third one. Paul fried a huge pile of northern pike for supper. Called Allen Farmer in Alaska, our place is okay. Shortly after we left it froze at Allen's but did not hurt our garden.

Monday, August 26, 2002—sunny and muggy, 80s, 100% humidity. Walked uptown and brought back a pie, cake and ice cream. Took a shower. Peter Achermann came over and took us out to their farm. We visited, then Peter and Delaine showed us around their house (especially the rustic furniture their daughter Denise had built), Delaine's knitting business, and the grounds around the buildings. Their daughter Melanie has horses and a new colt. Gave us a great lunch. We saw sandhill cranes in a field on way home. Steve worked late and went to Wadena to pick up his mounted deer head.

Tuesday, August 27, 2002—sunny, humid, 80°. Went out to Rollins' place with Scott. Saw their latest accomplishment, machinery, colt, crops, Andy's 4 x 4 trooper vehicle. They have bought more land. Saw lots of deer stands. Marvin and Jan Feakes were there also. Allen gave us some sweet corn and they brought us back to Paul's. Ruth had a turkey dinner cooked. Tried to call Ralph F. Called Eva Adams and also Harry and Neva McCoy.

Wednesday, August 28, 2002—cloudy, partly cloudy and rain in evening, 80°. Lorraine Hanson picked us up at 10:00 AM. Visited Eva Adams then went to lunch. Then went for a drive to Wahoo Valley and back down highway 64 to see Al Eckes. Then to see her daughter Phyllis's new home. Then back to Paul's. Walked up town looking for books. Steve and Lisa took us out to supper at Aldrich. Visited Harry and Neva McCoy (who is recovering from second back surgery in Staples hospital).

Thursday, August 29, 2002—cloudy, sunny, 78°. 100% humidity. Went up town a couple times, grocery and newspaper. Peter and Delaine picked us up and we went and saw their son Mike's place. Had a hamburger in Pillager, came back by the north way to Staples and south toward Browerville and looked at two "Pole Barn" houses. Interesting concept. Paul has jury duty. Steve is still moving tires to Motley. Ralph phoned in the morning.

Friday, August 30, 2002—cloudy, sunny, cloudy, 67° to 80°. Walked up town got some groceries. We walked to a garage sale. Paul got home very late from jury duty. Steve left after supper. He was going to the State Fair and Cabela's in Owatonna. Today is Theresa's birthday!

Saturday, August 31, 2002—partly cloudy and strong breeze, 78°. Theresa and Earl came about noon. Visited with Paul and Ruth for an hour or more. Then we went with them to Brainerd and they got groceries for the weekend. Then we drove east on #18 to Nokay Lake Road and North to Twin Oaks Resort. Got settled in, visited, took pictures, watched great-grandkids play. Larry Austin came by. Don and Evelyn Caughey (Earl's folks) came over and we had a good visit. They stayed awhile after supper. Nice to see them. Shortly after dark, a yellow jacket from off of Darcy's pop bottle, got in her mouth and it stung her throat. This distressed her greatly. After things settled down, we went to bed.

Sunday, September 1, 2002—mostly cloudy, some rain and sprinkles, 63° to 73°. Lots of thunder and lightning. It was a fun day playing with Dylan and Devin, reading to Dylan. Lee and Jason went to scrounge up fire wood. Later went 4-wheeling in the new van of Darcy's. Took pictures and sat around campfire in evening. Mother and I went to bed early after a steak supper.

Monday, September 2, 2002—cloudy and light rain, 60° to 70°. We got up 7:00 AM, waited till after 9:00 AM when all were up but Jason and Lee. We played with Dylan and Devin. Had a bite to eat. We finally got both vehicles loaded and left about 11:30 AM from the cabins. Went to Earl's folks and visited for two hours and took pix. Then drove the back tar roads to Elk River and then Highway 10 to 694 to the turn off to Nadia and Chuck's. Chuck has bought a 1995 Saturn station wagon with 235,000 miles. Looks good, he got it for a real good price. Then Theresa and Earl went home and watched a movie in evening.

Tuesday, September 3, 2002—mostly sunny, 57° to 74°. We went to Stillwater Target store and Nadia got her Iowa, Chicago pix. She gave Chuck's folks some tomatoes. We visited there for a while. Called Bev, Laura, Theresa and Ken Wilkins this evening. Did a little planning on the web site to sell our remote parcel.

Wednesday, September 4, 2002—sunny, 60s. Up early, showered and Nadia drove us to airport. We took an earlier flight to Sea-Tac. Had a little trouble finding where Alaska Air was but managed okay. At Anchorage we ran into Jim, Mary, Kari Odden and got to talk 10-15 minutes. Dan picked us up at curb side. Went to Costco. Sylvia got her prescriptions filled and some groceries. We then went to Royal Fork for dinner. Then out to Peter's Creek. Transferred our stuff to our car and started for home. Stopped in Palmer "Carrs," for a few things. Saw a red fox on the highway east of Sutton. Got home 11:30 PM.

Thursday, September 5, 2002—cloudy, 44° to 59°. Saw Allen and Roxanne. Picked up my guns. Denny E. introduced me to Gary Bates. Henry Johnson came over to visit. Went to Bob Rudbeck's watched Gary Bates home movie on calling moose. Allen came over and we went road hunting moose. Saw a cow and large heifer calf mile 134. Had peach pie at his place.

Friday, September 6, 2002—cloudy, rain in night and rain in evening, 44° to 56°. We went to Glennallen on senior van. Post Office, bank, paid propane bill at Fischers fuel, and had lunch. Copied my journal written on our trip over into this book. Paid lots of subscriptions etc. Ralph phoned. Will be out to work on water line and he, Jeff and I plan on doing some hunting.

Saturday, September 7, 2002—rain till 5:00 PM then sunny, 40° to 51°. Burned some trash. Did a few things getting settled in again. Jim Manning visited. Went down to garden and pulled weeds. Denny Eastman came over and we talked about moose hunting. Charlie Trowbridge phoned. He plans on attending the funeral for Harold Dimmick. Granddaughter Laura called and visited awhile.

Sunday, September 8, 2002—foggy, then partly cloudy, 33° to 56°. Reloaded some .338 cartridges. Went to Tazlina and talked to some folks about plowing snow for them. Wanted to shoot to the same point of impact but both gravel pits had people in them. Picked up six pieces 30-06 brass. Darrel and Brenda visited. Had a good time. Mowed our lawn. It was tall and wet. After supper, went to gravel pit—rifle and load went to same point of impact. Just got home and Allen called and ask me to go with him hunting this evening. We rode his new Polaris 4 x 4—liked it. Didn't see any moose on that trail but we saw four moose along the road. Not legal.

Monday, September 9, 2002—foggy and cloudy and rains, 33° to 56°. We went to Wasilla. Went on into Anchorage to the Lutheran church to attend the funeral for Harold Dimmick. Saw some people we knew. It was a nice service. I brought Rachel's mail into town for her. Charlie Trowbridge was there and had dinner with us at the Royal Fork. Ralph and Jeff were here when we got home. Ralph had started laying out heat wires for waterline thaw. Allen came over also and we all talked hunting stories.

Tuesday, September 10, 2002—partly cloudy, some fog, 33° to 53°. Ralph, Jeff and I went to Squaw Creek Trailhead, unloaded the two 4-wheelers, Ralph pulling a trailer. We saw moose and a very large grizzly track in the trail going down to the cabin (five mile on). No one using the cabin so we put our gear in it and went hunting. Saw two rams on a mountain. Went on down the trail and up steep trail of a bench and down bench. Parked machines and took off walking up a mountain. Climbed up it quite a ways. Jeff went looking for the rams and couldn't find any. Guess I got us on wrong part of the mountain. Did see ewes and lambs. Went back to cabin, hunting as we went along. Jeff and Ralph went moose hunting and I fixed some supper. Got to bed a little late, lots of fun today. Jeff gave me a neat camo vest and jacket!

Wednesday, September 11, 2002—partly cloudy, about 33° to 53°. Jeff found one legal bull moose and two other ones and a small cow. They are too far west to pack down to the trail to get to cabin. Ralph and I went north along Squaw Creek hunting as we went. Got way down, close to Alfred Creek. I got tired of getting jerked and thrown around on the ATV and suggested turning around and going back. We made several stands trying to call moose in, with no luck. In trying to cross one mud hole in trail I laid the ATV almost over on its side, the rut kept it from going on over into the mud and water. Jeff saw a small griz chasing a moose cow. Maybe five seconds behind the cow, running with its nose to ground, a silvery griz. He couldn't get a good shot so didn't shoot.

Thursday, September 12, 2002—lots of fog early in morning, clearing later, about

33° to 53°. We went hunting of course. Saw fresh moose and bear tracks. Then back to cabin for breakfast. Jeff needs to go back to Anchorage. We packed up all our gear and pumped up two of Ralph's tires. I swept out the cabin with a spruce bow. The trip out to the truck was good. Loaded up and started for home. Stopped by Eureka and bought us hamburgers. Back home we unpacked and rebuilt the mounting bracket on Ralph's ATV that holds his gun boot on. Sylvia has three pies baked! Jeff leaves for Anchorage and Amy. Ralph and I drive from here to Lake Louise Junction back to mile 119 Glenn Highway. Then east to Bartley's, then west to mile, mile 137 then east back home. Sylvia's supper had been done a while. It was very good as was the cherry pie. Then Allen came over in his new camo bibs - nice! We talk hunting bears especially. Allen wants me to go with him "calling" grizzly bears tomorrow, but I have to go with Ralph to start fish wheel and by some plumbing parts for heat tape in water line.

Friday, September 13, 2002—most cloudy, 36° to 48°. Saw small moose calf near Sam's. Ralph and I went to Glennallen. Talked to Bureau of Land Management supervisor about a trespass cabin that we use some times. It took a while but we did make our argument as to the desirability of leaving the cabin place. Then, Mechanics Warehouse, got a spark plug for Suzuki. Then sent postal money order to CMP for rifle and ammo. He bought gas. We went to lunch. He bought fish lure and knife and line and beer for use of fish wheel. Went to see Ken Kramer about wheel. Then went to wheel and put it in operation. Went to MP Cty Richardson Highway and he fished for silver salmon with no luck. Another fisherman caught limit of three fish. Went back to fish wheel and Thad caught small red salmon. We saw Ken Kramer just as he reached the Glenn Highway and talked a couple minutes. We watched for legal moose all way home with no luck. Ralph went back out on the road looking for a moose. Jeff and Amy came out and saw a cow and calf about ¾ mile west of Nelchina and called Ralph's attention to them. Then they all came here and Sylvia fixed supper for Ralph and me as Jeff and Amy had already eaten. We looked at catalogs and reloading book and visited till late. Sylvia rode senior van to Glennallen. Paid gas bill. Had lunch. Back home she picked 2/3 bucket of real nice cranberries. Studied up on the new Federal BLM map for hunting areas.

Saturday, September 14, 2002—partly cloudy, cloudy, windy most of day, 40° to 53°. We road hunted east to Lake Louise Junction. Saw a moose calf at Sam's. Saw Dale and Heidi, so we stopped and visited a while. Came on home and ate breakfast. Jeff and Amy didn't eat with us and went on to his mothers. We went to the fish wheel. There were four fish in the box. Took pictures. Came home. Someone got a moose across the highway from Frank Zimbicki old place. Ralph packaged the fish. Allen came over to show us the rifle he got from his brother. Very nice! Then we had lunch. Took a nap. Ralph went to check the fish wheel and hunt the road. Sylvia and I dug our potatoes. A rain seems to be coming this way.

Sunday, September 15, 2002—cloudy, partly cloudy, 39° to 54°. We road hunted and went to fish wheel at Tazlina. Saw two cow moose and three calves. 19 fish in the box on wheel. We cut off heads and gutted them and stopped in Glennallen and had breakfast. Back home we filleted the fish. Four for Sylvia and me. Put new spark plug in ATV. Helped Ralph clean up after filleting. He wanted to go up the trail to top of Slide Mt. It is pretty rough. Up on top we glassed the country. Didn't see any bears or moose, but what a magnificent view! While there Bruce Dickerson stopped by on his way down the mountain and visited a while. We went back down and to home. Ralph loaded up his gear, had supper with us and went to Anchorage for next wks work. Allen Farmer came over and we drove the highway. Saw one moose calf.

Monday, September 16, 2002—sprinkles, partly cloudy, 40° to 58°. Told Ed F. where the bulls were. Looked for moose sign in the wood lot one mile west. No sign there. A cow track out by highway. Took a nap. Tried calling moose at sand pit. The orphan baby moose is working its way west and is now at old RCA site. Saw a yearling, 16 mo old cow moose one mile east of here. Jeff called he has an ATV to use.

Tuesday, September 17, 2002—cloudy and low fog clearing in afternoon, 36° to 52°. Windy. Went to trailhead and over Ballanger Pass. Jim was repairing some bad places on the trail to his claim (camp). We talked a little while. Saw 20 or more ewe and lambs – no rams. Sheep were very high and scattered out. A moose calf was struck and killed one mile west. I saw a vehicle parked at site. They butchered it and took off. I didn't know what was going on at the time. It had been called in and someone drove out from Glennallen who was on road kill list—too late. This evening I discovered that I had lost the cover for my gun boot today. My fault for not fastening the bottom pin. Saw a muskrat run across road.

Wednesday, September 18, 2002—cloudy, rainy, partly cloudy, cloudy and hail, 32° to 51°. Checked moosey places close to home with no luck. Went to Glennallen on senior van. Bought a federal migratory bird stamp and flashlight batteries to replace those Ralph gave me. Added oil to truck motor. Put in gas. Noticed oil leak under the Suzuki. Too much oil in motor. Gasoline may have leaked through motor. Changed oil and will shut off gas at tank when not driving it.

Thursday, September 19, 2002—couple showers, mostly cloudy, 56° to 48°. Went east to Army Trail gravel pit—found a wheel for a trailer. Then went west to gun sight then back east on highway. Saw a large cow at bottom of mile 133 hill. Did a few things at home. Hunted the ridge one mile east on south side highway. No luck. Checked out gravel pit and came on home. After supper got ready and drove out to highway—met Allen. Talked a while and drove west. Met Ralph at mile 133.5. We hunted together for a few miles and came on home.

Friday, September 20, 2002—snowed all night (at least six inches, probably more) 28° to 40°. Sun came out later in the afternoon and melted lots of it. Ralph and I drove the highway most all day road hunting, even went down Oil Well Road. Allen F. stopped by a couple times. We saw a cow and calf moose. Hope Allen got one. It was a good day anyhow. Beautiful moon tonight. Joey E. and Dan, Emily came over after dark to pick tomatoes and pull the plants she has in Sylvia's greenhouse. Jeff Routt's niece's husband Duane delivered the ATV Jeff bought to our place this evening.

Saturday, September 21, 2002—sunny, 23° to 48°. Ralph installed a heating tape in our 1-1/2" water line today. Then left for Wasilla. It went pretty good. Lots of trips up and down the hill with both the Suzuki and the pickup. We drained the small water line lateral lines. I washed the Suzuki. The white sox were very bad today. Bob R. borrowed our water tank to haul water for Joey E. Dennis is hunting moose. Jerry R and Bob came by when Ralph was wiring power to the heat tapes and had to find out what was going on. Theresa called.

Sunday, September 22, 2002—sunny, 21° to 46°. Hauled our garbage. Moved some wood so we could park Jeff's Honda ATV in a better spot. Pulled some small trees out by roots to widen our lane. Sharpened chain saw. Bob R. bought back the water tank.

Monday, September 23, 2002—sunny, 21° to 52°. Beaut day. Chopped and cut root of a medium spruce along our lane, then chained it to the truck and pulled it over. Trimmed it and cut it into stove blocks and small logs. It was rotten low to ground. Sighted the .338 in at 100 yards. Bob and Kahren visited an hour at noon. Drained the radiator on car and added almost a gallon of antifreeze. Left message with Darrel G and he called back about BLM caribou situation. Called Steve Donaldson who was discouraging about caribou numbers in that area.

Tuesday, September 24, 2002—mostly cloudy, windy in evening, 32° to 51°. Spent five hours trying to get the two rear lights to work on the truck. A wire was broken off slightly inside of a rubber plug and hard to see. Put antifreeze in the car. Visited Allen in evening, helped unload some building materials.

Wednesday, September 25, 2002—rain in night, partly cloudy and sunny in afternoon, 38° to 55°. We went to Glennallen for lunch on senior van. Staked the raspberry plants for winter.

Thursday, September 26, 2002—cloudy, rain, partly cloudy, 33° to 54°. Loaded ATV and outfit. Went to Denali Highway and hunted caribou with no luck. Saw a couple hundred animals, some very nice bulls but none ventured on BLM land where my permits were valid. Enjoyed hunting. Met BLM Ranger, Ron Nelson. He worked for BLM (I assume). Worked in Kodiak Alaska for 10 years. In his youth he rode bucking horses and bulls. Montana champ one year. Likes to hunt sheep.

Friday, September 27, 2002—partly cloudy, 33° to 50°. Went to Glennallen on senior van. Got Stop Leak for car and rear light bulbs for truck and lunch. Sylvia mowed lawn. I leveled potato rows and found 10-12 potatoes. Washed lawn mower. Started a shooting bench for Jeff.

Saturday, September 28, 2002—partly cloudy and very nice, 34° to 52°. There is a leak in at one of the heating tape entrances into the waterline. Changed oil in truck. Worked on a shooting bench for Jeff. Jim Manning borrowed a "come along." Ron B. had carburetor trouble and called to ask why.

Sunday, September 29, 2002—frost, 29° to 48°. Partly cloudy. Worked on a shooting bench for Jeff. Put leak sealer in car radiator. Went to Copper River Road House and had hamburgers after the Copper Basin Shooting Club Meeting.

Monday, September 30, 2002—cloudy, 32° to 42°. Rain at Glennallen and north to Fairbanks. Saw two young moose cow and two spruce hens on my way to hunt caribou on BLM land along the Richardson Highway. Found a place a trapper sets for wolves. Saw a few small bands of caribou. Each band had a couple meat bulls running with cows and calves. Saw a very small fork horn caribou bull in a large gravel pit. It seemed to be looking for its mother. Ran up close to me and gave bleating like calls or grunts. Didn't want to shoot even though it was a legal bull. Most caribou were killed by shooting across the highway. I could never get a chance at one legally, so didn't get one.

Tuesday, October 1, 2002—wet snow started in night, slowed up by mid afternoon, 32° to 40°. Lots of it melted. Snowing pretty good this evening. Electric power was off about 5:00 AM for five or more hours. Started a fire in wood stove for heat. Put away and cleaned up some hunt gear. Carried wood into house. Straightened out a corner of wood shed. Burned some trash. No ducks close enough to shoot from shore.

Wednesday, October 2, 2002—more wet snow, 32° to 40°. Some sun in the afternoon. Cooler this evening. We went to Glennallen, lunch and shopping. Back home I worked on shooting bench for Jeff. Put studded winter tires on car. Denny E. brought water tank back and visited a few minutes. Wants to give us some moose meat and use our garage to cut up his moose meat. Then we went to Legion meeting at post in Glennallen.

Thursday, October 3, 2002—mostly cloudy, 17° to 35°. Put a wheel barrow load of wood in garage and built a fire Denny Eastman. Put three loads in basement. Swept out garage and got it ready to cut meat. Built a fire in woodshop. Went over to Mannings and got a small roll of carpet. Cut out two pieces of carpet for Jeff and Ralph's shooting benches. Glued one on Jeff's bench. Lifted the front of his ATV up to check the wheels out. Made a stalk on some waterfowl on our lake but swans were mixed in with them and I didn't shoot. We are going to Manning for dinner.

Friday, October 4, 2002—cloudy, 1/4" snow, sunny afternoon, 25° to 34°. We went to Glennallen on senior van. Cashed our checks and had lunch. I am keeping fires going in wood shop and garage.

Saturday, October 5, 2002—cloudy and snow late afternoon, 24° to 36°. Heard swans flying east so high I could not see them. Jeff, Amy, John Paul, Chelsie and Shobbie came out from Anchorage. We visited. Amy got her new .308 win Ruger SS carbine-like rifle sighted in. Denny and Joey E are cutting up two moose in our garage. Sylvia helped them a lot. I helped a little. Sylvia fixed a bunch of steak and we had sandwiches for lunch (all ten of us) and carrot cake for dessert. Ralph got almost all the heat tape wiring done and the water leak at one place fixed. We contact cemented a piece of rug on the shooting bench I had built for him.

Sunday, October 6, 2002—sunny! 27° to 40°. Ralph finished the wiring of heat cable in water line. Denny E and Joey, their son, John and daughter Emily, Sylvia and I finished cutting up the two moose about 6:50 PM. I sure got tired this afternoon. Sure is nice to have all the meat Denny and Joey gave us.

Monday, October 7, 2002—sunny and breeze from southwest, 24° to 45°. No ducks in reach of shotgun on lake. Sylvia cleaned up the moose ribs and packaged them. I cleaned Denny's plywood, put things we have been using back in their place. Shoveled the snow away that slid off the south house roof.

Tuesday, October 8, 2002—cloudy, snow shower in afternoon, 39° to 29°. Did a whole slew of small jobs. Walked down to lake twice, no ducks.

Wednesday, October 9, 2002—sunny, 20° to 37°. Went to Glennallen on senior van, had lunch, and mailed a package to Ralph. Couldn't find a seal to fit our threshold. Dyed a pair of shoes. Put a stronger snap on a belt. Walked down to lake, no ducks in range.

Thursday, October 10, 2002—cloudy, 11° to 33°. Our lake froze over. We went to Reyne Brockman and talked to her about web sites and e-bay in regards to selling our remote parcel. She suggested a realtor. I called and talked to one who might be interested. One didn't call back. We pumped water this evening. The breaker for the heat tape may have failed. Walked over to Allen's. He has south, east and part of the north wall studs framed up on the sill of the building that he wants.

Friday, October 11, 2002—mostly cloudy, some sun in afternoon, 25° to 41°. We went to Glennallen on senior van, lunch and got a water line fitting. Re-did the waterline from pump out of well to main water line. My REM 03A3 rifle came from CMP (order took 28 days). Cleaned the grease cosmoline from it. The bore appears excellent.

Saturday, October 12, 2002—cloudy, partly cloudy, rain in night, 30° to 42°. Started cleaning cosmoline off the O3A3 early morning. Took a lot of time. Wanted to see how it shoots. The striker spring is too weak to activate the primers. Got all set up to shoot at gravel pit, and then found this out. Enjoyed working on it.

Sunday, October 13, 2002—cloudy, 29° to 42°. Worked on well. Ran some more brush's and patches down the rifle barrel. Pulled out a clump of willows. Magpies and camp robbers eat on the moose scraps all day. Jim and Elaine were here to dinner this evening.

Monday, October 14, 2002—cloudy, partly cloudy, 27° to 47°. Phoned CMP Armorer. He will send me a spring and firing pin for 03A3. Cleaned some more on it's barrel and bolt. Cut out two rugs for Sylvia and two shooting bench rugs. Counted my traps. Got car ready to go to Anchorage tomorrow. Went over to Ed Farmer and visited a while.

Tuesday, October 15, 2002—cloudy, snow, rain here, 27° to 41°. Rain in Palmer and Anchorage. Last 50-60 miles on way home was sloppy border line slippery. Went to Lowe Hardware, VA for prescription, gasoline, lunch (Royal Fork), Costco, Wal-Mart, Wasilla Carrs, Palmer and made withdrawal from bank and headed home. Took us 20 minutes to unload and put all the purchases away. All and all a good trip to town. Didn't get black oil sunflower bird seed and some pork sausage.

Wednesday, October 16, 2002—cloudy, partly cloudy, 29° to 42°. We went to lunch in Glennallen. Sylvia got some cardboard. We got dinner tickets to the Friends of NRA dinner. Put up the new light over the reloading bench. Found a piece of plastic pipe for Sylvia to roll up her craft table cover. New parts came for the 03A3 rifle. It now fires cartridges properly.

Thursday, October 17, 2002—cloudy and started snow in afternoon, 18° to 34°. Loaded up shooting gear, went to gravel pit. Another vehicle parked there. Went to pit at Army Trail. Found a few pieces of brass. Had some success zeroing rifle with cast bullet reloads. Rifle will not fire M2 ball ammo. Very disappointed. Shot a squirrel.

Friday, October 18, 2002—cloudy, one inch of snow, 25° to 34°. Worked on 03A3 stock. Switched to a sporter barrel on Remington 700. using .308 cal. Went to gravel pit. Sighted it in. It shot three different loads into same small group. Very happy with results.

Saturday, October 19, 2002—cloudy and rainy, 28° to 34°. We went to Legion Post. I was part of the honor guard for Loren St. Amand funeral. Then killed time till the post's monthly Sat. night dinner. Had planned on Clarence Catledge checking the headspace on the 03A3 but didn't work out today. There were a couple bad vehicle accidents, one at mile 171 the other one fairly near there.

Sunday, October 20, 2002—mostly sunny with breeze, 35° to 50°. Ralph came out to our place. We tried to determine the head space on the 03A3. Whiled doing so I showed Ralph how loose the action was in the stock. Right away he suggested the looseness was keeping the bolt from completely closing and not letting the firing pin fall far enough. Now the rifle shoots fine. We went to gravel pit and shot offhand at plastic pop bottles. Lots of fun and good practice. Then he put in a double breaker and each heating tape is separate now. It should work. We got his supper at Eureka. We visited Cal and Mary for a little while. Their son Philip and his wife Kim live there now.

Monday, October 21, 2002—mostly sunny, windy sometimes, 30° to 45°. Went to Legion Post in Glennallen and cleaned rifles. Paid the propane bill and mailed a package to McLellans. Had lunch and came home. Put a different scope on a rifle and went to gravel pit and sighted it in. Back home I cleaned it. Raked some gravel level. Put a washer under the tang on the 03A3 and leveled up the receiver in the stock. Also carved the bolt handle notch a little deeper.

Tuesday, October 22, 2002—mostly sunny and windy in afternoon, 20° to 42°. Walked over to Allen shop and to mailbox then Ed's shop. No one around. Went out after lunch. Started burning the brush and limbs trimmed off the trees I cut down along the lane. Just a pile of coals and ashes tonight.

Wednesday, October 23, 2002—mostly sunny, 39° to 50°. Earthquake woke us up 3:30 AM. 6.2 epicenter near Delta Junction. Went right back to sleep.

Went to Glennallen a little shopping and lunch. Went to gravel pit to try cast bullets in the 03A3. It shows promise. Lost the bolt that secures the band for bayonet lugs and found it.

Thursday, October 24, 2002—very nice, partly cloudy, 37° to 47°. Jeff Routt drove out from Anchorage to go with me to look for a bull caribou on Federal Land on Richardson Highway and Denali Highway. Driving my truck we saw a cow and calf caribou while on way to Glennallen. We didn't see any game of any kind in area we wanted to hunt. We talked to a man on an ATV who lives on the Denali Highway. He had shot a silver fox today. Nice! We stopped by the rifle range and picked up some brass. We got back home here just at full dark. Jeff is fun to do something like this trip with. He now has a 2-½ - 3 hour trip back to Anchorage.

Friday, October 25, 2002—partly cloudy, cloudy by evening, 35° to 45°. Went to Glennallen. Paid electric bill and mailed our absentee votes. Had lunch. Found a temporary bolt to hold the bayonet lug band on the 03A3. Walked over to Allen's new shop. He has at least ¾ of rafters up. The warmth and wind is taking the ice off our lake. This morning swans with lots of signets started landing on our lake. Now total 47.

Saturday, October 26, 2002—mostly cloudy, 27° to 37°. Up early. Gathered materials and built two plywood target stands for Ellie Farmer for her part in a carnival at high school. Reloaded .30-06 for fowling shots. We rode to a "Friends of NRA" banquet and auction at Glennallen with Bart and Rosemary. Called Theresa.

Sunday, October 27, 2002—mostly sunny, 27° to 37°. Cleaned the ashes out of the stoves. Shoveled up the ashes from burning brush and spread it in the small garden up here by house. Loaded shooting gear. Went to gravel pit to chronograph and test some loads using H4895. Groups (3) were not good. I forgot to take cleaning rod along. Quit and came home. Cleaned and polished some 44 magnum brass. Freed a cross bill that got trapped in garage. Broke my right heel.

Monday, October 28, 2002—cloudy and light snow, 21° to 32°. Took it easy on my right foot all day. Denny E hauled himself a load of water.

Tuesday, October 28, 2002—cloudy, some rain, 29° to 40°. Went to Allen and Roxanne's for lunch. Jim O. came over to weld up his snowplow. The inside right front door on the car quit working. Jim, Mary and Kari visited in evening. Jim brought along a tool to remove window cranks from car doors.

Wednesday, October 30, 2002—very little sun, 29° to 42°. We rode the van to

Glennallen for lunch. Saw a beautiful mature wolf two miles east of Tolsona Creek. Removed inside of door panel on right front of car. Went to Cal's and took a repair door latch off an old car there and put it on our car here at home.

Thursday, October 31, 2002—foggy till 1:00 PM, then sunny turning cloudy about 4:00 PM, 28° to 41°. Cast bullets till 12:30 PM. 250-30 cal. for target practice. Went to gravel pit finishing shooting some loads for development. This rifle needs lots of work on the stock. Oil removal, glass bedding and refinishing. Front sight blade needs replacing. Two neighborhood girls and one boy have showed up for treats, Samantha, Kindra and Adam.

Friday, November 1, 2002—some light snow morning and evening, 28° to 35°. We went to Glennallen shopping and lunch. Saw a young cow caribou and café. Cast some more .30 cal 180 GR bullets. Then mounted snowplow on truck and moved snowgo trailer out where I can hook up to it if I want in the winter. Beverly phoned.

Saturday, November 2, 2002—fog, cloudy, fog, 30° to 35°. Disassembled the 03A3. Applied oven cleaner to remove dirt, grease, old finish and oil. Washed it, and then steamed the dents with a wet tag and hot iron. Took most of the day. Had to make a tool for the stock cross bolts.

A 7.9 EARTHQUAKE SHAKES THE AREA

Sunday, November 3, 2002—fog, cloudy, fog and snow in evening, 26° to 32°. We had a 7.9 earthquake at 1:12 PM lasting three minutes of shaking, tapering off and two after shocks and small tremor's for three hours. It was a lot more damaging in lots of other places. Buildings, road, power etc. I worked on the 03A3 stock getting it ready for refinishing. Allen, Roxanne, Samantha, Reed visited in evening.

Monday, November 4, 2002—foggy, cloudy, foggy, 27° to 33°. Wrote up a plan on bedding 03A3 rifle stock. Cast about 250 bullets. Cal stopped by with pictures of a wood bank someone wants me to make. Denny E. borrowed our water tank. Visited when he brought it back. Nadia, Laura and Beverly phoned about the earthquake yesterday.

Tuesday, November 5, 2002—foggy here, 27° to 41°. Went to Wasilla. Some light rain on the way. We couldn't find the pork sausage we wanted. Got some black oil sunflower bird seed and did some other shopping. I forgot (not on my list) to get a woodshop light fixture. We went to get flu shots. They wanted to know among other things, the names of my parents (Why do they need that at my age? It's silly). I didn't finish filling out the questionnaire and we left without our shots.

Wednesday, November 6, 2002—cloudy, 29° to 39°. Some snow, rain showers. We went to Glennallen, a little shopping and lunch. Finished getting the rifle action stock ready then I glass bedded it.

Thursday, November 7, 2002—sunny, 23° to 35°. Worked with the rifle all morning. Barrel came out of stock easily. Had to fill some voids in glass bedding. Then didn't get barrel pulled down deep enough in stock and had to sand and re-glass late in evening. Wrote four letters and did some phone calls and other paper work.

Friday, November 8, 2002—cloudy, snow showers some places, 21° to 31°. We went to Glennallen. Paid fuel oil bill. Went to Post Office box and went shopping, had lunch. Stopped by the Brown Bear to pick up my door prize, a NRA-ILA brass buckle. Rifle is now glass bedded.

Saturday, November 9, 2002—mostly cloudy, 20° to 32°. Went to gravel pit to test rifle. It seems to be shooting about 35% better. Coyote is still leaving droppings in the pit. Loaded up 50 cartridges with a different powder. We went to supper at Billman's Hanger. He has roof on and drywall. Doorways have plastic for now. Jim Odden was there also.

Sunday, November 10, 2002—cloudy and freezing mist, 20° to 24°. Slippery outside. Did a few small things. Reloaded grounds of match bullets to test the accuracy of the rifle. Allen visited for an hour in late afternoon.

Monday, November 11, 2002—cloudy, 16° to 24°. On the way to gravel pit to shoot targets I saw a goodly number of caribou crossing highway going south. Some targets were good. Some were very large. The more I shot, the worse the targets. The barrel became very fouled even though I brushed one stroke for every shot. Denny E stopped by and did some offhand shooting and shot my rifle a few times. It was too cold (18°) and the ProChrono refused to give me the feet per second of the shots.

Tuesday, November 12, 2002—mostly cloudy, ice fog in the morning, 16° to 22°. Wrote to Brownells about the brown dye. Sorted and weighed the 30-180 GR cast bullets. Made a display box for Sylvia's earrings. Jeff phoned.

Wednesday, November 13, 2002—foggy, mostly clear, a sun dog was out in afternoon, 7° to 20°. We went to lunch in Glennallen. I had to use acetylene torch and heat a reducer to get off the water hauling tank. Denny E helped with wrenches. He is getting a plastic tank from Tom H. Went with Denny to Tom's place to get the tank loaded on Denny's truck. Lubed 100 bullets and swadged them. Allen visited in evening.

Thursday, November 14, 2002–ice fog and cloudy, 11° to 20°. Snow to south of us. Saw a coyote hunting mice in grass along lake and checking out the rat pushups. Couldn't get a shot off at it from up here. It didn't come in to the caller either. Went to Allen's campground and talked to a man about our remote parcel. He doesn't have money enough and it too remote. Charged the "caller." Started reloading some more for 03A3.

Friday, November 15, 2002–low, cloudy and ice fog, 10° to 23°. Went to Glennallen shopping and lunch. Went to gravel pit to shoot 03A3. Saw quite a few caribou today. Beverly phoned. I Called Jeff about powder reloading–to bring me some.

Saturday, November 16, 2002–fog all day, 5° to 19°. Denny and Joie visited about noon, came to borrow water tank. Brought over some moose wieners. Then Jeff, Amy, Chelsie, Jarret and Shobbie visited. We ate wieners and hamburgers, chips, cookies. Then Jeff, Amy and I went varmint calling. Used one of the tapes Jeff gave me. No luck. But we did find a dead caribou with a fox eating on it, but it ran away. Jeff brought out a can of gunpowder I ask him to get. We took Mary G with us to Thanksgiving dinner at Legion Post. Tough, foggy driving getting there. Got better by the time we came home.

Sunday, November 17, 2002–low clouds, 1/4" frost, 11° to 15°. Don't feel well today. Rearranged the Alaska drawing for child's bank. Real estate agent called. Evelyn and Mary and Dusty came over to shop Sylvia's crafts.

Monday, November 18, 2002–partly sunny, 0° to 10°. Don't feel well. Cleaned rifle. Reloaded a few. Nurse stopped by and gave us our flu shots. Denny brought my hole saw back and had a piece of peach pie with us.

Tuesday, November 19, 2002–partly cloudy, -5° to -15°. Went to Anchorage on VA Van. Saw my new doctor, his name is Dr. Acab Quier. Gave me an exam and declared that I am in good health for a man almost 75 years old. He thought my heel would heal up by itself. "Nick" did a little shopping for me while I was with the Dr. On the way home a full moon was coming up behind a snowy mountain. Its redness was shining on, and being reflected off the bottom of the overhead clouds. Very beautiful.

Wednesday, November 20, 2002–partly cloudy, 6° to 22°. Went to Glennallen for lunch and Post office box. To gravel pit to test a powder–got one very good target. Lots of caribou have been using the pit. Went to Mannings and copied targets to shoot at.

Thursday, November 21, 2002—cloudy, 9° to 18°. Cut out and put together four wooden banks. My heel sure hurts tonight. Worked six hours.

Friday, November 22, 2002—cloudy, fog, 3/4" snow, 13° to 32°. We went to Glennallen and paid electric bill, had lunch. We saw caribou on the way in. Then a nice bunch on our lake in the afternoon. An ermine wanted to get in our arctic entry. I worked a couple hours on the banks. Allen stopped by with some goodies and visited an hour or so.

Saturday, November 23, 2002—cloudy, windy and rain last night, less windy today, 32° to 41°. Got three coats of finish on the banks. Cast 50 pure lead bullets and 150 lead 20-tin 1 part. Jim Manning visited quite a while this morning.

Sunday, November 24, 2002—mostly cloudy and some windy, 22° to 37°. Cleaned on rifle barrel. Reloaded some of the newly cast bullets. Put the banks together. We went to Darrel and Brenda's for Thanksgiving dinner, prime rib. Had a good visit, and Brenda's cooking was excellent, as usual.

Monday, November 25, 2002—we had 3" snow by early afternoon, then turned foggy, 19° to 34°. Started the snowgo. Went down to well, covered it with tarp. Stopped by Allen's new shop. Sent seller's contract to Bert, real estate agent. Reloading info to Ralph. Joe and Lois Thomas stopped by with turkeys for Thanksgiving for us, Bartley's, Mannings, and Gilcrease's.

Tuesday, November 26, 2002—we had at least six inches of snow on ground this morning, 24° to 36°. I plowed our snow, went to Dick Anthony's near Tazlina Lodge and plowed that snow. Boxed the Alaska banks for mailing.

Wednesday, November 27, 2002—we had six inches or more of snow, 32° to 35°. VA van didn't go to Anchorage. We went to lunch and bank in Glennallen. I plowed our snow, got stuck once. Broke one lift cable just before I was to go east to plow for Dick Anthony's. Our electricity has been off since 7:00 AM this morning, snow is dragging down the wires and shorting the line out. We have a wood fire in the basement and we are burning a Coleman lantern for light and playing dominoes for entertainment. Called Theresa. She had exploratory operation yesterday. Didn't find out much. Electricity came on about 9:30 PM.

Thursday, November 28, 2002—partly cloudy, 12° to 29°. Cleaned snow off the car. Shoveled some snow. Changed flashlight batteries. Worked on Coleman stove. We went to Tom and Kim Huddleston's Copper Center Lodge for a Thanksgiving dinner. Some people we knew, and some were strangers. Highway was icy but not bad time driving conditions.

Friday, November 29, 2002—cloudy, 3" snow, 22° to 34°. Fixed the lift cable for snow plow. Tried it out here at home then went to Dick Anthony's and plowed there. Some trees were bent over and touching the ground with wt. of snow. Had to shake them off in order to plow snow off to the side. Plowed a drive into Odden's and also at Bartley's. Repaired the left plow wing. It's lightly raining tonight. Tired this evening. Brenda was "T" boned by a semi at her driveway. She was badly hurt and we worry about her condition.

Saturday, November 30, 2002—cloudy, 32° to 35° to 27° this evening. Lots, of icy places around here. Shoveled the snow off the woodshed. Plowed some more snow. Took the old Coleman lantern apart and cleaned it up. Tested it for operating properly. Its fuel is really old and didn't burn brightly. Nadia called. Nice to visit with her. Got a letter from Paul, he shot a deer with his T/C and used one of the 300 grain cast bullets that I had loaded up for his use.

Sunday, December 1, 2002—partly cloudy, fog, 8° to 19°. Sunrise 10:03. Rested all day. Finished a couple letters.

Monday, December 2, 2002—cloudy and foggy all day, 16° to 20°. Cleaned ice off side windows of car and took tarp off windows. Then we went to Glennallen to get the new "lift" cable for snow plow. Had lunch and bought postage stamps.

Tuesday, December 3, 2002—cloudy and some fog, 16° to 19°. Didn't do much. Stayed off my foot a lot. Brenda is improving at Providence Hospital. Talked to Darrel and offered the use of our car. Talked to Brenda in the afternoon for a little while.

Wednesday, December 4, 2002—mostly cloudy, light rain near Glennallen, 15° to 23°. We went to bank, flower shop and lunch. Shot three targets here at home. We each bought a raffle ticket from oldest Brockman boy.

Thursday, December 5, 2002—cloudy and fog moved in this afternoon, 13° to 21°. Nadia's package came (fruit cake she had made). Cast more bullets of lead 20 parts tin 1 part. Melted and fluxed and cast into ingots 14 lbs of lead. Burned our trash. Denny E. came over about supper time and ate with us. We had a good visit, guns, hunting and fishing etc.

Friday, December 6, 2002—cloudy and foggy, 11° to 19°. We went to shop at Glennallen on senior van and had lunch there. Did some target practice. Phoned Nadia, and Brittany. Sylvia has everything ready for the bazaar tomorrow.

Saturday, December 7, 2002—cloudy and 2-½" snow in Glennallen, 8° to 15°.

We took crafts Sylvia has been making to the Christmas Bazaar where she had a table. She recouped $309.00 of the money she had spent on craft supplies. We stopped at the Brown Bear Roadhouse for a hamburger on the way home. It snowed about half way home from Glennallen.

Sunday, December 8, 2002—cloudy, sun poked through for a little while, 13° to 18°. Shoveled snow off camper roof. Cast about 200 .30 caliber bullets. Theresa phoned. Samantha came up and bought two of Sylvia's throw pillows for her mother's Christmas present. She had the Mailly twins with her.

Monday, December 9, 2002—cloudy, 9° to 18°. We are thinking about bidding on a pickup CVTA telephone co-op has up for bid. Went to Odden's and talked to Jim about that model pickup. Pulled snow off arctic entry roof and the greenhouse. Put some oil in the car. Jeff phoned twice. He is laid off for the winter. The A303 barrel is clean and pristine now. Put rifle back together.

Tuesday, December 10, 2002—cloudy, partly cloudy, 0° to 12°. Packed snow on the trail down to well with snowgo. Did a little target practice. Reloaded a few. Allen visited and had supper with us.

Wednesday, December 11, 2002—cloudy, 10° to 16°. Jim Odden picked me up at 8:00 AM and we went to Valdez to look at a pickup that is up for bid. We took it for a trial drive. Jim driving, it seemed okay. I drove it back to town and it missed as through starving for fuel or "brain box" out of whack. I did not submit a bid on it. Boy the snow covered mountains. were beautiful with some sun shining through holes in clouds. We did a lot of visiting. I enjoyed the day.

Thursday, December 12, 2002—cloudy, 5° to 19°. Put Lee powder measure together and made a wood stand for it. Tried to cast some bullets with new Lee 150 grain .30 cal mold. Didn't get factory oil out of it and had poor luck. Called parts house and they suggested things to check out on truck in Valdez. Cal G. stopped by this afternoon and he knew quite a bit about that model truck. Jim O. called back. Denny E. called back and offered to go to Valdez tomorrow.

Friday, December 13, 2002—partly cloudy, 6° to 13°. Denny E. came over and we went to Valdez in his Subaru car. I submitted a bid of $3,712.01 on a 91 4 x 4 Chevy. The only bid submitted! If I would have known, could have saved $200.00. Oh well. It seems to be a good truck, needs a couple parts and service. Icy road. We drove at 45 miles per hour. Everything went well, enjoyable day.

Saturday, December 14, 2002—cloudy, skiff snow, 2° to 11°. Did a couple small things on the "new to us," truck. Made out some Christmas cards. We went to the grand opening of Mendeltna Cr Lodge. Smayda's were there from Palmer,

Dawson's from Lake Louise, Jim, Mary Odden and friends from Kenny Lake and lots of other people.

Sunday, December 15, 2002—partly cloudy, 0° to 10°. We went to the Christmas program and services at Mendeltna Chapel. The highway is really slick. Ralph and Jeff phoned. Jim brought me wheel rims that may fit our truck! He and Mary visited quite a while.

Monday, December 16, 2002—cloudy, skiff snow, 0° to 9°. Jim's wheels do not fit the truck. I greased the front end joints on truck and changed the air filter. It was very dirty. Joints were dry!

Tuesday, December 17, 2002—cloudy, -7° to 3°. I went to Loren Russels' and bought four wheels to fit the 91 Chevy. He wanted to take a tire off one rim then he brought it here. Charlie T. phoned. They would like to visit us 27th, 28th, 29th, Smayda's also. Greased the drive shafts, checked the antifreeze. Test fit wheels to this truck. One wheel is not right. Moved Molly car and removed tools etc. Pretty sore tonight. Phillip Gilcrease brought us some bread, bananas etc. Joe V brought Lactaid milk and a coffee cake. Jeff phoned that he wouldn't be coming out.

Wednesday, December 18, 2002—mostly partly cloudy, -10° to 1°. I went to Glennallen and got thermostat, oil, filter, oil sending unit (which is wrong one) for the truck. Sylvia went to Queens luncheon at Peg Virgin's. Back at home I put in the new thermostat, oil and oil filter. Just as I finished Darrel and Brenda drove in the yard. Brenda looks good, though still in pain, on crutches but made it up our steps. Rested on our couch. Had a light supper with us. Sylvia gave her the pick of her crafts to give for Christmas presents. She was running low on energy and wanted to go home.

Thursday, December 19, 2002—cloudy to foggy, -7° to 3°. Loren ph- will bring over rims to make four of a kind. Worked on truck some more. I just can't find the oil sending sensor. Mark B brought me some repair manuals in hopes they will help. Jim Odden came over this evening and found the sensor and got it off the truck. A big relief for me. I'm really tired tonight. We found that the distributor cap and rotor should be replaced.

Friday, December 20, 2002—cloudy, foggy sometimes with lots of frost, 0° to 5°. Up early. Removed a spark plug from truck for number for new set. We went to Glennallen. Applied for title and license for our new truck. Bought an oil pressure sensor and spark plugs and distributor and rotor. Put on the oil sensor and distributor and rotor when we got home. I'm keeping a fire going in the barrel stove in the garage most of the time. Granddaughter Laura phoned this afternoon.

Saturday, December 21, 2002—partly cloudy, -10° to 1°. Finished installing spark plugs. Checked oil in rear differential and the transmission. Denny E came over and I gave him some glycerin and trapping lures. We went to the Legion Post Christmas dinner and gift exchange.

Sunday, December 22, 2002—mostly cloudy, -10° to 2°. Disabled the back up beeper on the truck. Moved the hand-strap farther fore ward to make it easier for Sylvia to get into the cab. Checked the fluid in the transfer case. Allen, Roxanne and Reed visited. Neighborhood Christmas carolers sang for us. Dan and Patti Billman stopped by. Ralph phoned.

Monday, December 23, 2002—cloudy, some fog in the afternoon, -2° to 6°. Loren traded three rims for three rims so I now have four that are compatible. Put a new hydraulic hose on snowplow. Brushed and wiped off the rims Loren brought. Cal stopped by with a Christmas card and goodies. When I went out to get the mail, I went on over to wish Ed and Sandy Merry Christmas. We talked thread sealing compounds and trucks. Called Gerrys.

Tuesday, December 24, 2002—pretty nice day, 0° to 13°. Made a plan to install a gun rack behind the pickup seat. Sewed up some tears in seat covers. In the afternoon we went to Jim and Mary Odden's for Christmas dinner. Kari was there as well as Nygell and Ann (from Kenny Lake, I think).

Wednesday, December 25, 2002—cloudy, light snow in the afternoon, 7° to 11°. Installed a gun rack behind the seat in the new truck. Lowered the spare tire and re-inflated it and returned it under the bed of pickup. Put more wood in garage. Put gas in the GMC plow truck. Sylvia fixed a Cornish hen for Christmas dinner.

Thursday, December 26, 2002—cloudy, frost in the air sometimes, -3° to 7°. We did some things to get ready for expected company. Fired up the barrel stove in basement as we are warming the upstairs.

Friday, December 27, 2002—cloudy, -5° to +5°. Put two wheelbarrow loads of wood in basement. Fired up snowgo, looked in well and put in a 100 watt to thaw a layer of ice. Shoveled snow up around the well. Charlie T and family arrived before 7:00 PM. Played a couple card games with Paul and Cora.

Saturday, December 28, 2002—fog, partly cloudy, -26° to -18°. Started the snowgo and Charlie gave the kids rides. They did some sliding on the hill but snow wasn't the best. Also some skiing. Then we all got ready and went to the Point Lodge on Lake Louise. Dan and Patti had some guest. Tom, Lisa, Lauren, and Emily Smayda, Jim, Mary, Kari Odden and Elli Farmer came. They played music, skied on Billman's hill, sledded also. We visited. Patti fixed a good dinner and sent some extra home with us. They made homemade ice cream. Some took a sauna.

Sunday, December 29, 2002—mostly cloudy, -20° to -10°. Every body slept late. Charlie and Paul played "go fish" card game. Then I started snowgo and they drove it around and went over to Henry and Sally's. When they came back here, we played some cards. Our waterline is frozen. Charlie offered to help. We went down and checked it. The bulb I had just put in well was burnt out. Replaced that. Water comes out of open spigot in well but does not go up the line. Will have to try again tomorrow. We then ate supper and they went to Odden's to pick up Kari and visit there, then will drive to Palmer and stay with Tom and Lisa Smayda overnight.

Monday, December 30, 2002—cloudy and skiff of snow, -22° to -2°. Made an effort to find where our waterline is frozen. Used two hairdryers to thaw out the line down near the well. Then discovered that the line was not being thawed by the heat tape. Something must be wrong with the "breaker." Sure made a lot of trips up and down the hill on the snowgo. I couldn't have walked that far. Our electric power is going out every once in a while this evening. Called Ralph and ask about tire sizes for the 91 truck. Also about the heat tape and breaker. I am to call him back tomorrow for some more answers. Called Jim O and ask for page number for tire rpm at 55 mph.

Tuesday, December 31, 2002—cloudy morning, clearing to sunny and a sun dog on each side of the sun, -8° to 5°. We tried to pump water with no luck. There has to be ice plugging the line somewhere. Made several calls to Ralph in Fairbanks. Mark Brockman came over and tested the voltage and proclaimed it okay. I'll work on it again tomorrow.

Earthquake damaged road.

Several moose from the air, one looks up at the plane.

2003—A buffalo hunt and two family reunions

Wednesday, January 1, 2003—partly cloudy, -20° to -12°. Worked on well trying to find out why the waterline thaw tape is not working. Had no good luck. Finally gave up. Phoned Ralph numerous times, he is at a loss also. Jim O. came over in evening, picked up his tires and wheels. Gave him a rim for his car hauling trailer.

Thursday, January 2, 2003—mostly cloudy, -20° to -12°. Saw a moose over on the south side of our lake. Called around getting price quotes on tires for pickup. Started organizing service information on the 91 Chevy. Did some other paper work. Tried to pump water on auxiliary line but I broke the line in the well. Tried to glue it down at well but it was too cold and it didn't hold. Brought it in house and did it.

Friday, January 3, 2003—partly cloudy, -11° to 1°. Went to Glennallen on senior van to bank, car part, electric bill, groceries, and lunch. Put repaired pipe in well and pumped water. The serpentine belt I brought home is too large. Did a bunch of paper work on truck. Saw a moose at east end of lake.

Saturday, January 4, 2003—cloudy, two inches of snow and still coming down, -13° to 23°. The top broke out of one tree. We pumped water twice today, tanks are full. Played dominoes, read and wrote some more on a letter. Sorted out some keys.

Sunday, January 5, 2003—cloudy, three to four more inches of snow, 12° all day. We went to Glennallen. Mrs. Reichman wanted a beaded pin for a gift for her mother. Then we went to Brenda and Darrel's. Make, Rob, Robert, Samantha, Ron, Lisa, Gracie & ? were there as a party for Brenda. Looked at the tires Darrel had to sell and decided they were not aggressive enough tread. Went to the Copper Basin Shooting Club meeting. Snowed going to and coming from Glennallen.

Monday, January 6, 2003—10° to 12° dropping to -3°. Plowed some of our snow then went to Dick Anthony's and plowed their snow. Came home and finished plowing here. Finished letter to McLellans. Put wheel rims and cooler in bed of pickup. Jeff and I called back and forth about tires. We plan to go to Anchorage tomorrow.

Tuesday, January 7, 2003—partly cloudy, -16° to -3°. Left home 7:00 AM for Anchorage. Met Jeff and Amy at Sam's Club (Penland) at 11:10. Only three tires there so we went to Diamond Sam's Club and bought four tires and they mounted, balanced and put them on our truck while we ate lunch at a nearby Royal Fork. Said thanks and so long to Jeff and went to (DeBarr) Costco and shopped. Got home 6:20 PM. Saw two moose today. Phoned Jeff and let him know we got home okay. We are pleased with these tires, good traction. Hope they wear a long time.

Wednesday, January 8, 2003—partly cloudy, -20° to -1°. Went to Glennallen to lunch, exchanged the serpentine belt and two keys made. Put the belt on when I got home. Rode back to town with Bart to Legion meeting. We saw a few moose along the highway today.

Thursday, January 9, 2003—partly cloudy, -6° to 6°. Did a few small jobs. Shoveled snow off a trailer and two storage sheds and lean-to. Lowered the air pressure in the new tires to 50 lbs. Studied some more on the maintenance of the new (to us) pick up. We treated Odden family to pizza at Mendeltna Creek Lodge ("New owners" + Mabel). We had a nice visit.

Friday, January 10, 2003—sunny, -1° to 9°. Went to Glennallen, shopping and lunch. Visited Allen and Roxanne in evening. Granddaughter, Laura B. phoned.

Saturday, January 11, 2003—sunny, -2° to 12°. Left before daylight, drove west hoping to see a fox. No such luck. Snowmobiler traffic got heavy near Eureka. Put summer tires in Molly car and summer tires for blue Chevy in tire shed. Electricity went out about 5:00 PM and came on about 8:45. Built a fire in woodstove and light a Coleman lantern. Our cook stove doesn't need electricity.

Sunday, January 12, 2003—fog, sunny, -2° to 8°. Got the battery in the car charged. Did a few little things. We pumped water again today. Sylvia's sister Frances phoned. Kahren Rudbeck called.

Monday, January 13, 2003—mostly sunny, 1° to 15°. Beautiful sky full of "mare's tails". Raked snow off a lean-to. Watched part of "Centennial" video series. "Bert," real estate sales phoned with question on the Boot Lake property. She has an interested client.

Tuesday, January 14, 2003—foggy, light and misty rain, 8° to 12°. I drove and Denny E. and I went up Lake Louis Road hunting ptarmigan. Saw a few. He missed one and shot one. It fell 75 yards off road. He marked the spot and directed me walking out to pick up the bird. We had breakfast at Mendeltna. I went down to Allen's to see his progress on the new shop. Jim and Mary O. visited late evening.

Wednesday, January 15, 2003—very low clouds and light snow, 10° to 5°. We went to lunch in Glennallen. Saw a marten cross the road at about Mile 177.

256

Thursday, January 16, 2003—sunny, -13° to -4°. A moose walked through our place east to west. Browsed on birch tree at our house and willows along the driveway. Didn't do much today. Ron called that he was sick and wouldn't drive tomorrow.

Friday, January 17, 2003—mostly cloudy, -12° to 3°. Read some. Watched a movie.

Saturday, January 18, 2003—sunny, 8° to 14°. Full moon, early morning lighting, late moonlight and the light before the sun gets up over the mountains are very striking. Denny was up flying in his plane. He borrowed my lynx stretcher last night. We took Ron's "Centennial" video tapes to Mary and Cal's for them to watch.

Sunday, January 19, 2003—cloudy and some fog, 1° to 16°. We pumped water. I need to pack the trail to the well. Knocked snow off the waterline down at lower end. Am disappointed that I didn't go to gun show in Wasilla. Sammy came up to our house to ask us to dinner and borrow two eggs. Gave her the eggs. Dinner was great. Jim and Mary and Kari Odden were there also.

Monday, January 20, 2003—sunny, 7° to 15°. We saw a yellow plane flying low over the river. Birds spent a lot of time feeding here today. We pulled the refrigerator away from the wall. Vacuumed the lint and dirt and washed it and the floor. Have a problem with the bathroom light also. Sent order for ejector and upper band screw.

Tuesday, January 21, 2003—mostly clear, 0° to 10°. Allen needed a piece of one inch PVC pipe. I needed a light switch for bathroom. That fixture and switch gave me trouble, but got it fixed. Worked on lavatory faucet. Need a new "O" ring. Measured heating oil and gasoline tanks and ordered fuel. Phoned CVEA that a small tree was leaning on the lower power line.

Wednesday, January 22, 2003—partly cloudy, 4° to 12°. Went to Glennallen. Lunch and faucet washer. Fixed faucet when I got home. Cal and Mary stopped by for a few minutes.

Thursday, January 23, 2003—sunny, -10° to 7°. Shot a limb off a tree with the 10-gauge shotgun. 12-gauge wouldn't do it. Fresh moose and spruce hen tracks here today. Checked the power line here for trees too close to wires. Burned trash. Denny was out flying again today.

Friday, January 24, 2003—partly cloudy, -18° to -3°. Went to Glennallen. Paid gasoline bill. Sylvia shopped and we had lunch. Then went back in towards evening and visited Brenda and Darrel. Then went to dinner and socializing at the Legion Post. Saw several moose and a ptarmigan today. Possibly a wolf.

Saturday, January 25, 2003—mostly sunny, -16° to -2°. Jeff, Amy, John Paul, Chelsie, stopped by and took me with them to Kenny Lake. Saw Jeff's mother and his brother Russ. Then met Vic and Billy at a pull off on the Edgerton Highway overlooking the Copper River. Billy has a permit to kill a buffalo. Jeff spotted one about 3-4 mile away south on river bluff. We drove back a couple miles to a homestead that let Jeff, Vic and Billy walk over to river bluff and glass. There was quite a few buffalo with nice bulls to be seen from this new position. Then back to Jeff's mother's house to visit, target practice for a while, then started home. We saw several moose today. Near Frank Zimbicki's old place Jeff saw a fox in the ditch. We drove up there and parked. He started calling to fox. After five minutes or so the fox was seen looking at us. It was mostly hidden, but was a black with some reddish on its shoulders. Before I could get kneeled down to shoot it spooked and left the area. Didn't see anything more to call. Did see another moose on way home.

Sunday, January 26, 2003—partly cloudy, -18° to -3°. Sylvia feels better and I don't feel well. We pumped water. Discovered the light bulb was burned out in the well and replaced it. Packed the trail down to well.

Monday, January 27, 2003—partly cloudy, -19° to -5°. Allen drove Roxanne, Reed, Sylvia and I to Eureka where we got him a birthday breakfast a day late. Denny E. phoned to borrow our water hauling tank. Cleaned the snow and ice off it. Then he borrowed Allen's and didn't need ours. Finished reading "Crusoe of Lonesome Lake."

Tuesday, January 28, 2003—partly cloudy, -12° to 5°. Checked Oddens place, water plants and ran hot water down the drain. Went to DOT gravel pit and tried varmint calling with no luck. Went with Jim M. to ARP's TV receive signal—sending installation on Tolsona Ridge. In checking things over I noticed the sending unit was on Channel 1, where as the receiver was on Channel 2, which is correct. Switching to Channel 2 on sending resulted in a picture/voice being sent out. While traveling to and from the site, Jim and I visited.

Wednesday, January 29, 2003—low clouds, -4° to 16°. We went to Glennallen. Lunch, shopping and Post Office. Jeff phoned a couple times. We called Theresa. She was in recovery #2. Her legs were numb yet. We will call again later. Laura phoned, she is concerned about our real estate agent's non-performance.

Thursday, January 30, 2003—cloudy and a skiff of snow, 9° to 19°. Wrote a letter. Tried to call the real estate agent again with no luck. We went to senior's monthly meeting. Mary Gilcrease needed a ride home with us. Got to wish Cal "Happy Birthday," his is tomorrow. Called Theresa this morning before she left the hospital. She was walking okay.

Friday, January 31, 2003—cloudy, 5° to 14°. Foggy at Glennallen. We went to Glennallen to lunch and some shopping. Saw three moose out near and crossing the highway. Finally got a hold of our real estate agent. Our answering machine isn't working, needs to be reprogrammed. I tried to do it but was not successful.

Saturday, February 1, 2003—foggy, cloudy, 7° to 16°. Checked Odden's place. Saw a "baldy" bull caribou there. Allen came over to wish me Happy Birthday. Ralph came just before Allen left. Ralph works in Anchorage now. We visited and had light lunch. Then we went out to road hunt ptarmigan and call varmints. Took my pickup so Ralph could try it out. He likes it. We didn't have any luck hunting. Sylvia fixed a good supper with the steak Ralph brought.

Sunday, February 2, 2003—partly cloudy, 10° to 25°. Some fog in morning. Ralph (drove my pick-up) and I left before daylight to hunt ptarmigan or varmints on the Lake Louise Road with no luck. Came home ate breakfast. Jeff got here and ate with us. Then he drove and we went to Tolsona dump hunting ptarmigan and varmints with no luck. Back home we shot pistols for awhile. We went to gravel pit and shot Jeff's new 17 caliber rimfire. That was fun and it is accurate also. Then Ralph drove and we went up Lake Louise Road hunted for ptarmigan and varmints with no luck. But we did see (I spotted) three caribou lying down just off the road. Jeff spotted a moose calf. Back home Jeff reprogrammed our answering machine then we ate a good supper of Ralph's steak and Sylvia's cooking. Then the guys headed out for Wasilla and Anchorage.

Monday, February 3, 2003—mostly cloudy, 7° to 27°. Put some things away. Did a little reloading. Wrote some letters. Saw tracks of smaller caribou in our lane. Burned trash.

Tuesday, February 4, 2003—partly cloudy, 20° to 40°. Shoveled and raked snow off camper, woodshop, woodshed and east side of garage. Plowed the snow away from the buildings. Snow slide off house roof. We cut the ham Ralph gave us into three pieces and put it in zip locks and froze it. Had to put air in the plow truck left front tire.

Wednesday, February 5, 2003—cloudy, windy, mist sometimes, 36° to 40°. Waited here at home till 12:30 before Bert the agent phoned. She will drop us and wants a Joe Russo to take over. Sylvia went to Glennallen shopping and lunch. Checked Odden's house. Fog and mist settled in and I decided not to go to Legion Post meeting in Glennallen.

Thursday, February 6, 2003—cloudy, 17° to 32°. Tried to cast some bullets with new Lee mould with poor luck. We went to Allen and Roxanne to supper and a good visit.

Friday, February 7, 2003—cloudy, 8° to 26°. Highway was pretty slippery but better in Glennallen. We went there on the senior van. Had lunch, mailed a package, cashed a check at bank. Sylvia shopped for slacks at a second hand store. Got some "bell bottoms," that cut and sewed into straight legs. Back at home I tried casting with the Lee mould and got it doing a lot better.

Saturday, February 8, 2003—partly cloudy, cloudy and snow in evening, 12° to 28°. Cast more 150 gr .30 cal bullets. Lubed and put gas checks on the best of them.

Sunday, February 9, 2003—partly cloudy and some fog, 11° to 27°. We had one inch of light snow. Large arch in the fog to the north. Must have been caused by the sun shining from the south. Saw this on the way to Odden's to ck. their house. Packaged some cast bullets for Jeff.

Monday, February 10, 2003—mostly cloudy, damp and cold, 18° to 30°. Cast 150 grain .30 cal bullets using linotype. Excellent bullets with very few rejects. Put on gas checks sized and lubed them. Wrote a short hunting story to send in to the "Fouling Shot CB Journal" magazine.

Tuesday, February 11, 2003—partly cloudy, 15° to 30°. Load up some of new cast bullets. They shot pretty well. Burned a stack of catalogs.

Wednesday, February 12, 2003—cloudy, 15° to 29°. We went to Glennallen shopping and lunch. Did some load development shooting with .30 -150 grain cast bullets then reloaded more.

Thursday, February 13, 2003—partly cloudy, 9° to 22°. We pumped water. Did some reloading and shooting. Checked Odden's house. George Perkins is back, to house sit now. Real Estate agent did not phone today.

Friday, February 14, 2003—cloudy and foggy here, 3° to 20°. We went to Glennallen shopping and lunch. Smashed some aluminum cans. Tried with no success to hook up "the headlights are on," buzzer to the blue truck.

Saturday, February 15, 2003—sunny, cloudy, and skiff of snow, 8° to 15°. Did some target shooting and cleaned rifle. We visited Darrel and Brenda and went to Legion Post dinner. I agreed to be Vice Commander this next year.

Sunday, February 16, 2003—foggy and partly cloudy, -9° to 10°. Joe Russo R. E. agent showed up about 12:30 PM. Talked a little, then we went up Lake Louise Road to 11 Mile where trail starts to our Old Boot Lake property. We put up a sign that property out that was for sale and his name and phone number.

Monday, February 17, 2003—partly cloudy, -14° to 6°. Cleaning on the 10-gauge sizing and lubing some .30 caliber. Studied map of parcels near ours on Old Boot Lake.

Tuesday, February 18, 2003—light snow, frost all day, -10° to 10°. Still cleaning on 10-gauge boxed cast bullets. Worked on powder measure and three moulds. Allen visited a little while Sylvia invited Mannings over to dinner. We played dominos.

Wednesday, February 19, 2003—cloudy all day, -8° to 11°. We went to Glennallen lunch and shopping. Still cleaning on 10-gauge.

Thursday, February 20, 2003—sunny, -15° to 5°. We pumped water. Cleaned on 10-gauge. Burned paper. Put coffee grounds on compost. Jeff called.

Friday, February 21, 2003—partly cloudy, -10° to 12°. Went to Glennallen shopping and lunch. Got a repair manual for 91 blue truck. We saw a few moose. We went up Lake Louise Road, put another arrow on Real Estate sign and put up two "land for sale" notices.

Saturday, February 22, 2003—sunny, -10° to 14°. Cleaned on shot gun barrel again today. Swept snow off car and truck. Read a lot. Jeff phoned a couple of times.

Sunday, February 23, 2003—mostly cloudy, 7° to 22°. We went to Eureka and got a Sunday paper hoping to see the ad for our remote parcel, but no such thing. Visited Gilcrease's on our way home. Called Laura, then Paul and Ruth. Corky Dimmick and "Wayne," stopped by and had a little lunch with us.

Monday, February 24, 2003—foggy to partly cloudy later, 9° to 38°. We pumped water. Some thing may have gotten a spruce hen from the looks of feather I saw. Installed a buzzer that indicates when the lights are on and the switch is off on the blue truck.

Tuesday, February 25, 2003—mostly cloudy, 12° to 34°. R E Joe sent maps for me to draw the trail to Old Boot Lake on. Burned trash. Put up a board to organize all the keys for locks.

Wednesday, February 26, 2003—mostly cloudy, 11° to 33°. Went to Glennallen shopping, Post Office, and lunch.

Thursday, February 27, 2003—mostly sunny, 10° to 34°. Highway had some ice on it. We went to senior meeting in Glennallen. Called Lisa Smayda, we can stay overnight there if we go to town.

Friday, February 28, 2003—mostly sunny, 12° to 37°. We went to Anchorage. Got Sylvia's prescriptions, groceries and reloading supplies. She found a neat "Alaska Caribou" fleece blanket at Wal-Mart and bought it. We stayed overnight with Lisa and Tom Smayda's. Tom was gone but returned later that night. Had a good visit with Lisa.

Saturday, March 1, 2003—nice, beautiful, sunny day, 12° to 37°. Had breakfast with Tom and Lisa. Stopped by "Shucks" and got a couple oil filters, then went to the gun show. Saw some people that I know. Had fun walking up and down the rows of tables looking at all kinds of shooting paraphernalia. Sylvia bought a moose horn pin with a "bear print" on it. I got four neat gunsmithing books and one about a renowned "wildcatter" Harry Donaldson. A white hooded camouflage parka and a brass replica of an Indian head. Bought it for Jeff Routt. We left early. Shopped at Carr's. Got home 4:30 PM. Unloaded the results of our shopping. Put truck in garage and drained it oil while it was still hot. Put on a new oil filter and new synthetic oil. Will be tired by bedtime.

Sunday, March 2, 2003—very nice day, 17° to 34°. Rested a lot. Then went to Glennallen to dinner with Brenda and Darrel. We had a call from Ruth while we were gone. Darrel gave me a book and some magazines.

Monday, March 3, 2003—very nice day, 18° to 40°. Did quite a few small jobs. Called Paul then later and talked to Ruth. Fred Rungee stopped by. He brought angel food cake, strawberries and fruit. We sent some blueberries, rhubarb, moose sausage and bread with him.

Tuesday, March 4, 2003—pretty nice, a little windy, 19° to 34°. Went down to Allen's. Went with him to haul water to a rental cabin. He dropped off frozen rhubarb to Mary Gilcrease. Cal showed us the car he is restoring. We pumped water. Got a letter from Nadia. Packaged a book to send to Ralph.

Wednesday, March 5, 2003—sunny, 10° to 25°. We went to Glennallen. Mailed a book to Ralph. Cashed our checks. Then went back for a Legion post meeting. Did some calling to find a barrel for the pitted Enfield rifle.

Thursday, March 6, 2003—sunny, some breeze, -10° to 21°. Wrote Nadia. Phoned Paul and one gunsmith, OH and Theresa also.

Friday, March 7, 2003—sunny, -9° to 20°. Went to Glennallen to lunch and mailed a manila envelope to Nadia.

Saturday, March 8, 2003—sunny, -6° to 18°. Read a lot. Mary Odden stopped by and visited quite a while. Later Kari O and Ellie Farmer visited also. Theresa called to ask her mother about doing some "beading." Electricity went off this evening.

Sunday, March 9, 2003—sunny, breezy tonight, -15° to 20°. We pumped water. I read "Gunsmith Kinks #1" all day, very good, I enjoy it.

Monday, March 10, 2003—sunny, -11° to 12°. We pumped water. Chopped some bird food. Read a lot. Put the spotting scope on Heavenly Ridge. Saw another set of tracks and probably snowgo tracks up on top of ridge.

Tuesday, March 11, 2003—sunny, -20° to 19°. Ran a lot of hot water down the drains today. Did lots of reading.

Wednesday, March 12, 2003—sunny and windy between here and Glennallen, -20° to 8°. We had lunch there and visited with friends. Tried to confirm my VA appointment and learned I don't have one.

Thursday, March 13, 2003—thin cloudy and windy -19° to -10°. Winds from north and east blew a wind row of spruce cone along the south side of our driveway. We went over to Brockmans and Reyne sent a fax for us. I'm running hot water down our drains these days. Did some reading. Bev phoned in the evening. High winds damaged Palmer, Wasilla, and Anchorage.

Friday, March 14, 2003—partly cloudy, breezy, -28° to 0°. Went to Glennallen, lunch and shopping. Repaired the electrical light fixture in the bathroom. Burned the trash.

Saturday, March 15, 2003—thin cloudy, -13° to 20°. Called around trying to find a good barrel for the P17 Enfield. We went to St Patrick's Day dinner at Legion Post. The installation of this year's officers followed the dinner. I am Vice Commander. Our truck is making a noise that seems to come from the transmission. After we got home I went over to Ed Farmer and had him listen to it. He thinks it is the bearing on the front shaft.

Sunday, March 16, 2003—mostly sunny, 0° to 24°. Read a lot. Went under the blue truck and checked oil level in transmission. It is low. Talked to Ed. We pumped water. A small boreal owl is hunting little birds at the feeder.

Monday, March 17, 2003—sunny, very nice, 0° to 30°. Started putting penetrating oil on bolt on truck preparatory to overhauling the tranny. Took pix of "Molly." Started her and plow truck. Got a package from Darcy and family.

Tuesday, March 18, 2003—sunny and light breeze, -6° to 30°. Allen visited quite awhile this morning We pumped water to house.

Wednesday, March 19, 2003—sunny, 0° to 38°. Drove blue Chevy into Pharmigan Services in Glennallen for repair. Estimate is $1500.00 - 1700.00. Returned book to library and had lunch. Saw a moose on way home. Talked to Jeff and called Ralph and talked to him. They feel bad about truck breaking down. Sylvia and Ron saw a coyote near Sam's place.

Thursday, March 20, 2003—sunny, thin clouds, 0° to 30°. Called John and okay'd repair of truck transmission. I vacuumed the downstairs. Visited Ed and Sandy. Beverly called.

Friday, March 21, 2003—sunny, 6° to 32°. Went to Glennallen, lunch and a little shopping. Went to Allen and Roxanne's to supper and a good visit. Jim Manning wanted us to support the CVEA plea to the legislature for funding.

Saturday, March 22, 2003—sunny and breezy, 7° to 26°. Been watching a lot of "Operation Iraq Freedom." Darrel and Brenda were here to supper. Philip Gilcrease stopped by with bread and fruit.

Sunday, March 23, 2003—sunny, breeze from east, 0° to 29°. Did some walking. Moved car and plowed snow from that spot. Denny E. visited in evening.

Monday, March 24, 2003—partly cloudy, skiff snow, 0° to 27°. We pumped water.

Tuesday, March 25, 2003—sunny, 13° to 33°. The local boreal owl spent quite some time in trees near bird feeder. Took extra bananas to Farmer's. Cleaned a rifle.

Wednesday, March 26, 2003—partly cloudy, 2° to 33°. Some fog in the morning. Went to Glennallen. Lunch then helped set up the Legion Post for the seniors monthly meeting tomorrow.

Thursday, March 27, 2003—sunny and clouding over this evening, 10° to 35°. Did some walking. Put some ATF in the car tranny. Shot a box of .22's practicing. Jeff called.

Friday, March 29, 2003—one inch snow in night, sunny then clouded up this afternoon and evening, 17° to 36°. We went to Glennallen again today. Post office, shopping and lunch. Darcy wrote and sent a calling card.

Saturday, March 30, 2003—mostly cloudy with a few flakes falling some times, 18° to 34°. We pumped water. Wrote a letter. Called Darcy. She is so nice to talk to. Hard worker.

Sunday, March 31, 2003—sunny and windy, 10° to 25°. Did some practice shooting with 22 caliber. Watched the war on TV, history channel also. Read some. Jeff called.

Tuesday, April 1, 2003—sunny, 12° to 24°. A boreal owl returned to perch near the bird feeder. Visited with Ed Farmer. Wrote some letters and made a phone call.

Wednesday, April 2, 2003—sunny, -12° to 24°. Went to Glennallen. Went to Pharmigan Services, paid John for transmission and installing it in the 91 blue pickup. Had lunch and came home. FedEx delivered a check. Bart called and asked me to ride with him to Legion mtg. Got home 9:30 PM.

Thursday, April 3, 2003—sunny, -5° to 30°. Tried to switch the winter tires on blue truck to summer tires. The lug nuts were too tight. Couldn't get the left front off, so I put the winter tire back on the right side so truck would drive correctly. Hate to drive it on bare paving with studded tires on. We pumped water today. Bev phoned.

Friday, April 4, 2003—sunny, -6° to 29°. Went to Glennallen. Paid phone bill, had lunch. Sylvia met the school bus and Samantha stayed here for a little while till her Daddy got off work and he stopped by and visited a little also. I put WD 40 on the lug nuts on blue truck also.

Saturday, April 5, 2003—sunny, -6° to 31°. Managed to get lug nuts loose. Used 30" of leverage. Summer tires are on truck. Back is sore. Talked to grandson Steve in Minnesota.

Sunday, April 6, 2003—mostly clouded over with skiff of snow, 2° to 30°. Laura called to tell us about their NM trip. We went to Glennallen but I had the date of Copper Basin Gun Club meeting wrong. Cal and Mary G visited in late afternoon. Ralph called.

Monday, April 7, 2003—sunny, 14° to 34°. We pumped water. I reattached a part of the garage opener that had come loose. We spread coffee grounds and ashes on snow drifts and ice where we walk-sun will then melt snow and ice faster. Called US Dept of State regarding the renewal of Sylvia's passport. A hairy woodpecker has been showing up here.

Tuesday, April 8, 2003—sunny, 2° to 35°. Went to Dr. in Wasilla for Sylvia's yearly exam. Then went to Anchorage and got pix taken for her new passport. Did some shopping I found a rifle barrel in Palmer to try out on a rifle.

Wednesday, April 9, 2003—sunny, breezy late afternoon, 8° to 41°. Went to Glennallen. Sylvia went to a party the ladies give for her birthday. Tried to call Marion, then he called me, it's his birthday. Denny E. visited this afternoon said he wanted to buy our Goldscrew machine. Put away the snowgo for the summer.

Thursday, April 10, 2003—partly cloudy, 13° to 44°. Scattered some ashes on snow pile on south side of house. Trimmed some branches from a couple trees. Put hub caps back on truck. Don't feel good.

Friday, April 11, 2003—sunny, 17° to 47°. Went to Glennallen and shopped and mailed Sylvia's passport in for renewal and lunch. Couple of the ladies sure took a lot of time on way home. One driver of a car, weaving all over the hill. The owl is seen pretty often. Charlie Trowbridge phoned.

Saturday, April 12, 2003—thin cloudy, 22° to 51°. Sighted .22 rim fire in this morning. Some other small jobs. Helped Cal time his sports car. Siphoned eleven gallons of gas out of the tank on the car.

Sunday, April 13, 2003—mostly cloudy, starting to rain this evening, 28° to 51°. Was really tired all day. Jeff and Ralph phoned. Drove a couple miles east and picked up a large discarded cardboard box. Fired up the Suzuki this evening. Snowing hard 8:20 PM.

Monday, April 14, 2003—we got 8" snow, settled to 6", 27° to 43°. Plowed our snow. Called and told "Roar Rifle Works" that their rifle barrel isn't the one I want.

Tuesday, April 15, 2003—cloudy, 12° to 38°. Pushed some snow away from our driveway with snowplow. Shot a squirrel. A white winged male cross bill flew into a window and died. We put it on the bird feeder to see if the owl takes it.

Wednesday, April 16, 2003—thin cloudy, mostly sunny, 17° to 47°. Snow shrunk down a lot. The owl didn't take the little bird carcass. Sylvia felt sick most of day. Didn't do much but exercise a little today. Saw with spotting scope, some tracks on Heavenly Ridge. Charlie phoned, truck was sold.

Thursday, April 17, 2003—thin clouds and breezy, 18° to 43°. Put ashes on the snow that slid off house roof. Put three tie downs for loads in the blue pickup box. Baked ginger snaps cookies. Expected Ralph to be here today.

Friday, April 18, 2003—sunny, snow is melting, 16° to 45°. Went to lunch, Glennallen. Gave a check to Elaine Manning for support MS 4 mile Wheelchair. We saw two swans on our lake.

Saturday, April 19, 2003—sunny, 21° to 49°. Jeff, Amy, John Paul and Chelsie came out this afternoon. We gave Jeff a bronze savage plaque. He gave me a pair of spring break up boots. We fooled around with his 4-wheeler for awhile. They left and we went to a ham supper at the Legion Post. Some college students gave a sign language demo.

Sunday, April 20, 2003—Easter. Thin clouds, 18° to 49°. Started cleaning up some of the winter damaged trees. Called some of the kids. Allen and Reed brought us two slices cheese cake.

Monday, April 21, 2003—partly cloudy and windy, 29° to 46°. Cleaned us some more damaged trees. Sharpened bow saw and two axes. Laura phoned with what she found out about selling properties and tax responsibilities.

Tuesday, April 22, 2003—mostly cloudy, 28° to 46°. Burned the trimmings from the tree tops. Raked some ruts smooth. Checked the well. Roxanne gave us some romaine lettuce.

Wednesday, April 23, 2003—mostly sunny, 27° to 53°. Snow going fast. Called Nadia as this is her birthday. We went on bus to Glennallen shopping and lunch. I sighted in my .338 magnum.

Thursday, April 24, 2003—sunny and some breeze, 29° to 55°. Put ashes on lower garden and the remaining snow on the lawn. Put some oil in Suzuki. Glued a wood folding chair rung.

Friday, April 25, 2003—sunny and very nice, 28° to 58°. Worked a little on the blue truck. Still can't locate the "lost" folding chair. Sylvia went to Glennallen.

Saturday, April 26, 2003—sunny and light breeze, a beaut of a day, 28° to 61°. Drove up Lake Louise Road. Checked the "For Sale" sign, cut some brush from in front of it. Went to Allen's for biscuits and gravy. Raked some yard. Burned a lot of spruce cones and yard debris.

Sunday, April 27, 2003—sunny and some breeze, 30° to 63°. Finished burning the lawn rakings and spruce cones. Cleaned up the Chevy Malibu. Vacuumed and washed it. Removed studded tires, put summer tires on. Lots more snow melted.

Monday, April 28, 2003—thin clouds, mostly sunny, 29° to 64°. Went to Glennallen and had John Fillman listen to noise in the blue truck. He thinks it is the alternator. Had lunch and came home. Worked a little on the car to ready it for sale.

Tuesday, April 29, 2003—cloudy, then sunny with breeze, 37° to 57°. Carried and spread wood ashes. Shoveled ½ snow pile on north side of house. Asked Ed Farmer to haul us some fill material. Henry came along and we all visited. It's Sylvia's birthday. Went to Eureka for supper and they were closed, so we went to Sheep Mountain. They were closed too. Drove back and went to Mendeltna Lodge and ate there. 90 Mile trip to eat supper—nothing stops us.

Wednesday, April 30, 2003—sunny and very nice, 28° to 57°. Went to Glennallen for lunch on the senior's van. I was gone a little over five hours! I finished shoveling the snow away from north side of house. Being in the shade it melts slowly and injures the grass. I re-epoxied the rearview mirror on to the inside of windshield.

Thursday, May 1, 2003—sunny, 24° to 55°. Raked some lawn and spruce cones. Transplanted some raspberries. Ed Farmer hauled in 8 loads of fill material in the low place east of the house. I gave him a "Gladiron" and a couple lengths of air hose for his truck. Put For Sale Signs on car and moved it out to the road. A hairy woodpecker stopped by here today.

Friday, May 2, 2003—sunny and breezy, 28° to 57°. Sylvia is a little better but not good enough to go on the senior van. I was too stiff and sore to go myself. Did do a little raking in of the fill that Ed brought yesterday.

Saturday, May 3, 2003—sunny and breezy, 26° to 53°. Took garbage to transfer site. Washed blue truck. Checked the truck alternator. Bearing is bad. Cleaned some tar off it.

Sunday, May 4, 2003—sunny and windy from east, 20° to 53°. Didn't do much today, Moved a few wheelbarrows of fill material to low places. Lorraine Hanson called and told us her son Randy is in a coma from a motorcycle accident. She doesn't expect him to recover.

Monday, May 5, 2003—partly cloudy and windy, 25° to 55°. Trimmed the three trees SVEA cut down last winter. Took sign adhesive off blue truck with scraper and WI 40—hard work. Pulley bearing on the alternator is worn out. Removed the alternator. Allen and Samantha visited in evening. Ralph phoned. Son

Paul phoned.

Tuesday, May 6, 2003—mostly sunny, a few small showers and snow rain drifted by, 27° to 50°. We went to Glennallen, lunch, shopping and cash checks. I tried to replace the bad bearing on the alternator and cracked that end of the frame. Called Jeff. Went to gravel pit with old plow truck and graded up a place for shooting bench. Jeff called and talked to Sylvia and invited us to he and Amy's wedding, May 17th. Couldn't get a safe shot at the rabbit.

Wednesday, May 7, 2003—sunny, 27° to 53°. Cut up the trimmed trees and stacked it in wood shed. Darrel and Brenda came out. Brenda put a perm in Sylvia's hair. Some large ducks (mallard and spoon bill) on our lake, more ice has melted.

Thursday, May 8, 2003—partly cloudy, 30° to 60°. Split and stacked some blocks of wood. Cleaned up some trimmed limbs. Raked a little lawn. More ice melted from lake. Some bohemian wax wings stopped by today.

Friday, May 9, 2003—partly cloudy and very windy, 35° to 56°. Went to Glennallen. Lunch and bought alternator for blue truck. Put it on the truck. Walked down to well. Picked up some moose "nuggets" for Sylvia's craft projects.

Saturday, May 10, 2003—partly cloud, very windy. Our 55th Wedding Anniversary. 30° to 50°. We went to Copper Basin Shooting Club Turkey shoot at rifle range north of Glennallen. We got there two hrs. early. Helped a little with getting things ready. The shoot started afternoon. We watched for awhile then started for home. Stopped by Legion Post and bought some baked goods. Had a late lunch at Caribou Café. Drove around in a gravel pit looking for fired brass. Sylvia found a rock she liked. Allen and Roxanne brought fresh strawberries. Marlboro might have seen a black bear on highway.

Sunday, May 11, 2003—cloudy, 30° to 53°. Mostly snow showers. Big flakes in evening. Mother's Day. Made chocolate covered cherries for her. Toyo stove quit, built a wood fire in heater in basement. Reloaded a few practice cartridges for the 03A3. Allen visited a while – give me a bear report. Snow flaked were silver dollar size.

Monday, May 12, 2003—mostly cloudy, some snow flurries, 31° to 49°. Lots of snow is gone now. Wind blows it all different directions. We went down to lower road and got seven buckets of dirt from our pile there. Put out some ant poison. Worked on heating stove. Visited Jim M. greenhouse stove wouldn't light this evening. The sediment bowl at the fuel tank was full of water so changed the filter. Heavy snow storm 10:00 PM – barely see across the lake.

Tuesday, May 13, 2003—mostly sunny, 31° to 53°. Cloudy and rain across the river south in evening. We went to Glennallen. Lunch and a little shopping. Did some more raking in the yard. Allen brought some black dirt for Sylvia. Robbie is floating a bunch of sand bags to the Old Beaver Dam to raise the lake level. The Rudbecks were helping him this evening. Note: Lake ice went out during the night.

Wednesday, May 14, 2003—snowing this morning early, 31° to 49°. Then some rain and snow showers. Sylvia went to the Queens lunch. I visited Denny E. over at Bob Rudbecks shop. About a couple gun control bills being considered at AK legislation. Didn't do much of anything today. Samantha asked Sylvia to sponsor her in the MS walk Saturday. The goldeneye duck are flying around looking for nesting sites. I raked some tractor tracks level.

Thursday, May 15, 2003—partly cloudy, showers of snow and hail, 32° to 53°. Replaced a blown fuse in blue truck. Took Denny E. with me and drove up Lake Louis Road. Saw 6-7 moose. Shot 3 porcupines, one got away. Our real estate sign is OK. We had a good visit while driving along. Snow in evening.

Friday, May 16, 2003—mostly cloudy, several showers of hail like rain and snow, 33° to 51°. We went to Glennallen for lunch. Got things ready to go to Anchorage.

Saturday, May 17, 2003—low clouds near the Eureka Summit, 33° to 52°. We went to Anchorage. Did some shopping. Then killed a few hours as Jeff Routt and Amy's wedding was to be at 9:00 PM. Forgot to check on Jeff's phone number and couldn't reach him for an update. We did find the church. The preacher was 1-½ hrs late. After the ceremony, Ralph, Roma, Sylvia and I went for a late bite to eat. Then Sylvia and I went for home. Got there about 2:30 AM Sunday! Tired.

Sunday, May 18, 2003—sunny and breezy, 31° to 55°. Did a few little things but rested mostly. Sylvia took a couple naps. Bob and Kahren came over to visit. Kahren's dog Amigo died! She is taking it hard. Then we went to Allen Farmers to supper. Allen got home late from a fishing trip with Denny E. Supper was god. Tracy, Roxanne sister stopped there while we were there.

Monday, May 19, 2003—beautiful day with a breeze, 30° to 59°. Cleaned PCV on blue truck. Painted a brake pedal. Put some stop leak stuff in one tire on ATV trailer. Added some grease to its wheel bearings. Made a bunch of phone call: Bev, Darcy, Paul, and Lorraine Hanson.

Tuesday, May 20, 2003—sunny and some breeze, 30° to 59°. Went to

Glennallen to lunch, got a part for the blue truck. Put part on at home. Denny E. hosted a fish fry at Mendeltna Lodge. Lots of neighbors were there. When we went to leave I didn't notice Joey E. had parked behind me and caught my bumper on her bumper and knocked out her turn signal lens. Damn! We saw quite a few caribou along the highway. Al Smith had friend kill a cinnamon color black bear doing damage on his front porch.

Wednesday, May 21, 2003—sunny and breeze, 30° to 61°. Haze is from wild fires in Russia. Looked at possibility of working on the Suzuki oil seal that is leaking. Worked on the driver side floor mat in blue track. Hope I have it repaired. Raked some spruce cones. Visited with Denny E. out by mailbox. Fred Rungee stopped by this evening bearing gifts of ice cream, grapes and books.

Thursday, May 22, 2003—hazy summer and breeze, 30° to 61°. Smoothed the last of the gravel. Repair of blue truck floor mat looks good. Tilled the upper garden. Went to gravel pit target shooting. Did pretty good. My back is really bad.

Friday, May 23, 2003—mostly cloudy, some showers in the distance, 38° to 56°. Went to Glennallen paid electric bill, shopped, PO office, lunch. Forgot Sylvia's groceries on the bus. Called Ron and he brought hem back from 13 miles down the road. Nice of him. Windy this evening. Ralph called to advise us of his plans. Expects to be here towards evening on Saturday.

Saturday, May 24, 2003—some rain showers in the night, 36° to 53°. Went to gravel pit to target practice. Rained. Did a few things here. Jeff, Amy and six kids stopped by for a couple hours. Gave them cake and watermelon. They went on to his mother's at Kenny Lake. We had just eaten our supper and Ralph and Roma drove in from Fairbanks in their new 1 ton Chevy pickup. Very nice! Sylvia fixed some supper for them. They brought lots of groceries of all kinds. I drove us up the Lake Louise Road. Only saw one porcupine. My reload wouldn't chamber the cartridge so I told Ralph to nail it with his 9mm. Got to bed late.

Sunday, May 25, 2003—rainy. After breakfast, Ralph and I went to gravel pit and shot the .44 magnum. Then lunch. Then he drove his truck. We went to pullout at Mile 120 Glenn Highway. looking for a bear or porcupine. No luck. Back home we shot my .22 auto over the ProChrono. Ralph could shoot it really good. After supper we went to Mile 120 again with no luck. We did dig some flowers for Roma in a gravel pit and at our place. We have had root beer floats two nights in a row. The big flock of ducks on our lake flew out during the night. Very few left now. Saw 7 caribou bull on the east side of Nelchina River. River is running high with brown muddy water.

Monday, May 26, 2003—very nice day but breezy, 36° to 61°. We went to Legion post to participate in Memorial Day Services. Ralph and Roma stopped by the post and services on their way back to Fairbanks and home. Sylvia didn't feel like going to Copper Center and wanted to go home and rest. I cleaned some guns this evening. Roma called when they reached home.

Tuesday, May 27, 2003—very nice, good breeze, 35° to 61°. Went to Glennallen. Built a frame to support a plastic cover over two rows of beans in the garden.

Wednesday, May 28, 2003—sunny with nice breeze, 33° to 68°. Limed and tilled the garden. Sylvia put on fertilizer, raked and planted it. I went to Glennallen and cleaned the Legion Post rifles. Visited Darrel and Brenda and went to a Legion meeting to plan a party for Jay and Rella Gandy who are leaving for Utah. Bart Bartly rode home with me.

Thursday, May 29, 2003—beaut of a day, 42° to 69°. Checked ants at well. Sprayed grass. Cleaned spark plug on lawn mower. Ordered airplane tickets. Bev phoned. Kahren was here couple time. Sylvia is getting her work all done. Called real estate agent.

Friday, May 30, 2003—nice day, 46° to 67°. Went to lunch in Glennallen on senior bus. Pulled out an old piece of fallen tree that interfered with snow plowing. Sylvia went to Anchorage with ladies.

Saturday, May 31, 2003—nice all day, then cloudy, 37° to 67°. Showers and very windy in the evening. Renovated the compost bin. Measured braces for garden gate support. Cleaned a gun and put two back together. Showers didn't amount to much but the wind blew from every direction.

Sunday, June 1, 2003—sunny and windy, 33° to 59°. Drove ATV down to Charlie T. storage building and checked it over. Lubed the latch mechanism on tailgate of blue truck. Pulled a tree root out along the driveway. Started "Molly" car and ran it for a few minutes. Sylvia got back from Anchorage in early afternoon.

Monday, June 2, 2003—partly cloudy with showers moving through, 35° to 61°. Hooked up the summer waterlines. Set two new posts and braces for the garden gate. Tired today. Kahren visited, has broken a front tooth off. David Farmer tried out one of their remote controls on our dish receiver and it didn't work. Saw a cow moose over on the south side of our lake. She went by our front window at 9:00 PM. This moose has a white spot on her right rib cage.

Tuesday, June 3, 2003—sunny, 38° to 64°. A few showers went by, none here.

We went to Glennallen to bank and lunch. Denny E. asked me to go sucker spearing with him at Lake Louise. We saw a young bull moose along Lake Louise Road. Saw some suckers but no luck spearing. Some grayling were feeding where the creek empties into the lake. I shot two porcupines along Lake Louise Road.

Wednesday, June 4, 2003—mostly sunny, looks rainy this evening, 33° to 69°. Chopped out an old spruce stump. Denny E and I went sucker spearing. He got one. I got lunch at Wolverine Lodge. Chopped out two more stumps. Put lime and fertilizer on the lawn. We took a box of goodies to Brenda and Darrel. Then went to monthly meeting. Sylvia went to the auxiliary meeting. Got back home in time for the late evening news.

Thursday, June 5, 2003—partly cloudy, cloudy and windy in evening, 45° to 68°. Went to gravel pit for target practice. Saw black bear tracks. Visited with Ed Farmer a few minutes. Did a little shooting at home and cleaned two guns.

Friday, June 6, 2003—partly cloudy, 42° to 63°. Lunch in Glennallen then went with Ed Knoebel to help represent the Legion Post at a memorial service for Bill Etchells at Kenny Lake. Then Ed brought me home. After supper Sylvia and I visited Dan and Patti Billman at Lake Louise. Sam Weaver was there too, had a great visit.

Saturday, June 7, 2003—mostly cloudy, rain and snow in night, 33° to 62°. Sylvia doesn't think here plants outside got hurt. Visited Allen Farmer. Did some small jobs. Washed and wire brushed the winter wheels for blue truck.

Sunday, June 8, 2003—partly cloudy, nice day, 34° to 65°. I now have five blue truck wheels ready to paint. Went to Cal and Mary's to visit. Gave him an "on the floor" shifter kit for automatic transmission. A duck is nesting in a box in the tree on way to outhouse.

Monday, June 9, 2003—mostly sunny, tiny shower, 42° to 71°. Put a primer coat of paint on five truck rims. Sharpened pruning shears for Sylvia. Loaded some subsonic 30-06 loads. They were average accuracy.

Tuesday, June 10, 2003—beaut of a day, 46° to 75°. Marion W. called. We went to Glennallen. I got paint to do the truck rims. Painted five of them. Sylvia helped.

Wednesday, June 11, 2003—Sunny and cloudy in evening, rains going by and thunder is heard, 50° to 76°. Jacked up the blue truck and worked all day washing, sanding and painting on its 4 wheels. Sylvia went to Queens luncheon.

Thursday, June 12, 2003—sunny, clouding in evening, 48° to 77°. Finished painting truck rims and put them on truck. Put water seal on both porch steps on house. Repaired hip boots and floor mat for truck. Listened to the seniors sponsored auction on radio.

Friday, June 13, 2003—sunny with breeze, 40° to 73°. Went to Glennallen lunch, bank, and Post Office. Mailed Macarthy newspapers to Oddens. Paid for the articles I bought on the auction. Father's Day present, Sylvia treated to breakfast at Eureka.

Saturday, June 14, 2003—mostly cloudy, 41° to 62°. Some showers lasted one hour. Washed blue truck. Cleaned some tar speaks off it. Took a nap. Jeff called. Cleaned and sewed up a gun case I got at yard sale this morning. Jeff, Amy, John Paul and Chelsie drove out. Brought KFC. Sylvia had roasted some turkey. We all ate together then we aired up his ATV tires. They washed it and took rides for a while then went to fish and camp out. Nadia called Father's Day greeting.

Sunday, June 15, 2003—mostly cloudy with several rains, 71° to 62°. I got Jeff's air cleaner off and washed. He and family camped at gravel pit last night. We all did some more cleaning on it. Then they rode it a couple hours. Sylvia cooked up a breakfast with their fixings. It started raining again and they went to Anchorage. Jeff gave me a camo fanny pack. Theresa called and wished me a Happy Father's Day and filled us in on the news from down that way.

Monday, June 16, 2003—partly cloudy and some breeze, 43° to 64°. Mosquitoes are bad in protected places. Scrubbed inside cab of blue pickup. Cleaned the windshield and side windows. Did a few other small jobs. Cow moose and baby calf left tracks in our yard.

Tuesday, June 17, 2003—sunny, cloudy. We went to Glennallen to lunch. Went to Bob and Kahren's for mallard duck and goose legs and gizzards. Played a game of cards (garbage).

Wednesday, June 18, 2003—partly cloudy, rainy afternoon. Repaired the bullet stop. Chronographed two rifles—three loads. The ducks sure fly a lot when it rains. Sylvia served the first of this year's cucumbers. Very mild and tasty.

Thursday, June 19, 2003—cloudy, rain in afternoon and evening, 46° to 60°. Checked duck nests, both in use. Transplanted some poppies. Visited Henry Johnson. Sylvia fixed some fresh zucchini. Found the paint number for the blue truck. Jeff called. Got a new barrel for rifle.

Friday, June 20, 2003—cloudy and rain showers all night and day, 47° to 60°.

Seems to be still soaking into soil. We went to Glennallen, lunch and to DMV office. Walked down to lake. Read a lot.

Saturday, June 21, 2003—cloudy and some showers, 46° to 65°. Walked down and up the hill. Did a few little jobs. Did some target practice with some "squib" loads in the 03A3. We went to the dinner at Legion post in honor of Jay and Rella Gandy who are moving to Utah.

Sunday, June 22, 2003—sunny and breezy, 44° to 72°. Short more squib loads. Walked down to well. Saw mother duck and 9 new little ones. Went to Bob and Kahren's for an ice cream social. Most of neighborhood was there. Ralph phoned.

Monday, June 23, 2003—mostly sunny, 46° to 68°. Went to Wasilla and Palmer. Got some cash out of bank for our trip. Couldn't find the shoes I wanted. Did some other shopping.

Tuesday, June 24, 2003—mostly sunny and quite windy, 36° to 65°. We went to Glennallen for lunch and I got a wrench for fuel filter. Did some odd jobs around here, walked down to the lake. Saw quite a flock of ducks, over on other side of lake.

Wednesday, June 25, 2003—partly cloudy and windy, 45° to 69°. Chopped out some tree roots in our driveway. Reloaded some squib loads. Wrote two letters and filled out a VA form. Sylvia thought the Legion meeting was this evening. We drove to Glennallen for nothing. Drat it!

Thursday, June 26, 2003—partly cloudy and windy, 37° to 65°. Seeded grass in a few thin spots in the lawn. Wrote two letters. Did some target practice and cleaned the guns. Laura phoned.

Friday, June 27, 2003—partly cloudy, windy sometimes, 38° to 67°. We went to Glennallen lunch and a little shopping. Checked, walked to well and reloaded for 30 br. Called Charlie Trowbridge.

Saturday, June 28, 2003—mostly sunny with light showers coming from the west, 42° to 72°. Saw the moose cow with the white spot on her rib cage this morning. She has lost her calf. Ed Farmer brought me four loader buckets of nice gravel and clay material fill in along the driveway. Allen F visited for a while this afternoon. I've been working on the new fill. Went to gravel pit target shooting this morning.

Sunday, June 29, 2003—sunny with good breeze, 48° to 77°. Compacted the new material along the driveway. Got the gas weed whacker out and used it for awhile. Young people played on the lake. Pretty tired today. Rested twice.

Monday, June 30, 2003—mostly sunny, some breeze, 52° to 79°. Went target shooting at gravel pit. Whacked the weeds on west side of garden then all the way around it. Sweaty work. Trimmed bear and hair for trip outside. Bob R. called asking particulars about our realtor. A forest fire is on Tazlina River Bluff south, about 4 ½ mile, Ed Knobels' at Glennallen.

Tuesday, July 1, 2003—mostly sunny and some breeze, 52° to 78°. We went to Glennallen lunch and a little shopping. Picked up state hunting regulations. Went to BLM to find out ownership of land at Rainy Creek and Delta River. Cleaned up RCBS reloading press that was given to me. Took Sylvia over to Ed's to visit his mother here from Virginia.

Wednesday, July 2, 2003—mostly cloudy, nice rain in night. 49° to 76°. Visited Ed Farmer with a plan to help him lift trailer ramp. Visited Jim Manning to get Gary Ennon's address. Worked a while at reloading beach. We went early to Glennallen in order to cash checks a 5:00 PM bank and then wait till 6:45 PM to get in Legion post for monthly mtg.

Thursday, July 3, 2003—partly cloudy, with frequent showers, 44° to 60°. Worked a little on our lane. Put out some ant poison. Jeff called. Son Paul wrote us about his hospital visit to Randy Hanson after the motorcycle accident—sad business. A griz sow with two cubs has killed a cow moose in Odden's yard.

Friday, July 4, 2003—sunny, very nice, 43° to 73°. We went to Glennallen to Legion post to assist the post with entries in the 4th of July parade. This went off very good. We stayed in town for the Lion's Club Salmon Bake. Stopped by Army Trail gravel pit, sure enough, Jeff, Amy and kids were there. They followed to our place. Aired up their ATV tires and they went for a long ride to school house area. Sylvia forgot to open her greenhouse to fresh air, it got too hot, things in there are badly hurt. Amy and Jeff brought out steak and we barbequed it tonight. Had a fine time. Denny Eastman came over and borrowed my pipe threader. Bob Rudbeck came over with him. Jeff and Amy went to gravel pit to tent camp this night.

Saturday, July 5, 2003—sunny, very nice, 47° to 74°. Mid morning Jeff, Amy, John Paul, and Chelsie showed up and cooked breakfast out in the garage. I took guns down to Allen's for safekeeping while we go "outside." Jeff and I removed the whole rear off his Honda ATV. It needs lots of bearings, seals etc. They left about 8:00 PM. Will fish at the creek at Tahneta. I gave each of the kids a diamond willow walking stick and played Frisbee for a while with them.

Sunday, July 6, 2003—sunny, thunder showers started 4:00 PM, 49° to 76°. Got things ready so we could leave on our trip to Minnesota. Jeff called. Took garbage to transfer site. About 8:30 PM Ron Beshaw informed me Glenn Highway would be closed 1:00 AM to 7:00 AM for construction at Caribou Creek. I quickly took a shower, dressed and threw suitcases in blue truck, took off for Anchorage. Got past Caribou Creek with time to spare. Had to park at a Carr's store in order to get a few cat naps—very tired.

Monday, July 7, 2003—up at 4:00 AM. Found a working man's open café at 6:00 AM. Had breakfast. Drove across town, found Faye Walton's home. Parked there, she saw us about 8:00 AM and invited us in. Parked the truck on west side of her house. Visited with here till 11:00 AM, had a good time. Called a cab and went to airport. Had a couple little snags but got through airport security OK. Our flight left 1:05 PM on time. Flew at 37,000 ft visibility was pretty good till Yukon Territory. More clouds there and Alberta. We arrived ahead of schedule. Vanessa and Scott met us and took us to Beverly's. Darcy brought Theresa and Dylan and Devin. We all had a good visit.

Tuesday, July 8, 2003—very nice, 75°. Bev, Rich and I walked to K-Mart and a couple other stores in morning. Visited and read. Tyler came over after work and a soccer game. Had late supper here at his mothers. Theresa phoned a couple times.

Wednesday, July 9, 2003—cooler, 68°. Tried to rain in evening, storm to west. Loafed all day. Beverly organized Sylvia's address book. I managed to reach Ken Wilkins on the phone and made plans for the 22nd this month. Tyler came over this evening to visit. Laura and Theresa called. Sylvia called Frances.

Thursday, July 10, 2003—some rainy and mostly cloudy, 68°. Bev went to work today. Rich went to his mother's to fix a lock, went to Dr. also. Got more calls today. Just before dark three helicopters were intensely flying this area.

Friday, July 11, 2003—Cloudy, a shower, some sun, 70°. Cut a couple sticks for Bev's tomatoes. Tyler picked us up 3:00 PM. Went to optometrist eye exam, showed no change in prescription, no cataracts. Went to Wal-Mart and shopped getting sox and pair of shoes. We took Bev, Tyler and Rich out to supper. Sylvia got Tyler a shirt. We had a nice evening here at Bev's.

Saturday, July 12, 2003—sunny, 78°. Earl and Theresa came to Bev's and took us to Darcy's for the day. Earl and I fixed a leaking faucet. He hung a bathroom door also. We played hide and seek with Dylan and Devin, Earl and I went to look at camper that had been given him. His brother Butch brought his girlfriend and his folks, Don and Evelyn. Butch is taking the camper to Brainerd. Jason and Darcy fixed a great B-B Que. By the time we got back to

Bev's we were really tired.

Sunday, July 13, 2003—sunny, 79°. Rich went somewhere. We visited with Bev, read Sunday paper. Tyler came over and took us to several places shopping. Back home to Bev's. She started supper. I took a shower. Rich showed up. We watched a movie.

Monday, July 14, 2003—mostly cloudy, one hard rain, cloudy and a shower, 75°. Tyler drove. Went to pawn shop and Rich signed for Tyler to pawn a musical drum. Then we went to a nice gun shop. Back to Bev's then Scott came and got Sylvia and I, Bev and Rich. He took us to his and Vanessa's home. Barbequed steak and chicken breast. Very good supper. Met Adam and Megan there. They are friends of Scott and Vanessa. We passed by a lake on way back to Bev's, just at dark. The fog was starting to settle in. Skeeters were small, vicious. We forgot to take pictures.

Tuesday, July 15, 2003—mostly sunny, 77°. Nadia came here to Bev's as we will be staying at her place a week or so. Sylvia stopped at a shoe store, at Office Max for her and Nadia. Sweet corn, ham and mac and cheese for supper. Watched a movie. A few gun shots after we went to bed.

Wednesday, July 16, 2003. No entry.

Thursday, July 17, 2003—mostly cloudy, 84°. Nadia took us to a place were Sylvia got two pair glasses. We did some shopping and rib eye steaks for supper. Visited Chuck's mother.

Friday, July 18, 2003—80s. Chuck and Nadia took us over to see Charles— Chuck's dad. Had a nice visit. Later Chuck took me with him when he shopped at Fleet Farm store. I'm having trouble with this phone card when I try to call to Alaska (Ralph and Jeff).

Saturday, July 19, 2003—sunny, 90°. We got up 5:20 AM. Got ready for the trip to Hampton, Iowa and the Wilkins family reunion. We get to Hampton about 10:15 AM. The pavilion is air conditioned. Very nice. About 60 attended. Virginia, Don, Marion and Rae, Bev, Nadia, Theresa, Earl, Darcy, Jason, Dylan, Devin, lots of cousins. Looked at ton of pictures. Lots of people were identified in the pictures. Lots of genealogy was exchanged, wrapped it up in late afternoon. Then put tables and chairs away and swept the floor. Nadia had rooms reserved at a local motel. We all registered and paid for our rooms. Then took in the Franklin County fair. Had an enjoyable time there. Chuck got his picture taken a few times in fun poses.

Sunday, July 20, 2003—partly cloudy, 90°. Slept well here in motel in Hampton.

Ate breakfast at restaurant. Drove down 35W to Gilbert, Iowa. Nevada being close I suggested getting pictures of the house Marion was born in. Some difficulty with new roads but I was able to find it. Renter granted permission to take pictures. The house had been recently painted. Talked to owner's son. Paid Nadia extra money for phone use. We got to church in Gilbert early enough. People came fairly fast then. Maybe 30-40 showed up. Pot luck lunch, very good. Gladys led the meeting of the Sawtell cousins. Marion and Rae from Texas, Michael Dolson of Alaska, Mary Helland, cousin of Minnesota. Virginia and Don, Les and Ruth Shickel, Audrey and John Kooeyman, Nadia and Chuck, Theresa, Earl, Darcy, Jason, Dylan, Devin. Lois Carlson (Sawtell) two of Shickel daughters and families and list goes on. We left for Minneapolis at 3:15 arrived 6:45. Drove pretty much straight through, no rest-exercise stops.

Monday, July 21, 2003—mostly sunny, 80°. We went to a bookstore. Killed time before leaving for Motley so as to not arrive too early. Anyway we got to Paul's in Staples, visited, had good supper and visited. I called Ralph & Jeff. Jeff told of sow griz tearing the face and eyes off a man. Ruth bought a small motor home. Steve used his fiancé's dad's wrecker to get it home.

Tuesday, July 22, 2003—sunny, 80°. Up early, visit with Paul before he goes to work. Steve had already left. Walked uptown. Looked for books, bullet moulds. Very sore and stiff. Got to visit with Steve after supper.

Wednesday, July 23, 2003—partly cloudy, 80°. Visited with Paul before he left for work. Sylvia called Lorraine Hanson. We went with her (saw a deer) to Al Eckes, Harry, Neva McCoy, Don Sirucek wasn't there. Lots of activity here in evening.

Thursday, July 24, 2003—sunny and windy, 80°. Walked to grocery store twice. Read a lot. Bev left a message to call Ken W. Did that and she called in the eve also. Too windy to fish tonight.

Friday, July 25, 2003—sunny and windy, 80s. Walked to grocery store. Walked north a few blocks. Called Pete Achermann. He and Franz came and got us, took us out to their place. Saw Delaine. Visited then brought us to Paul's. Paul, Steve and I went target shooting in evening.

Saturday, July 26, 2003—sunny, 80s. No one is working today. We all hung out here. I sorted out a box of old papers. Found a lot of things we wanted, dating back to 1948. Papers for both Sylvia and I. We took Paul, Ruth, Steven and his girlfriend Lisa out to supper in Motley. Ate ice cream and watch TV afterwards. Mike Achermann called and wants to see us tomorrow about 11:00 AM.

Sunday, July 27, 2003—sunny, 80s to 60s. Got up late, showered. Ruth got a

Sunday paper, read that. Mike A. came over about 1:00 AM. We went with him to his place in Motley. Wife, Marsha and three grandkids were there. Peter and More Achermann's showed up. Mike birthday was yesterday. He goes to Antarctica to work in a couple weeks. She teaches school in Texas. Laura came to Paul's about 12:30 PM. We loaded our stuff in her car. Had lunch in Motley. Drove out to our old farm. No one there. I left some papers relating to barn equip. that I had installed years ago. Then we drove down to Rogers, Minnesota. Brad was there with Brittany and Maggie. Later Laura made a great dinner. Real quiet here.

Monday, July 28, 2003—sunny, 60s to 80s. We went produce shopping. Stopped by a place selling prefab homes. Looked at four models. Brad got home early and mowed his lawn. I had pulled some weeds, grass from near house. We did lots of visiting. Brad and Laura bought us a new camera to replace our broken one. Wonderful of them.

Tuesday, July 29, 2003—sunny, 60°s to 90°. Read and visited. Went for a walk. Laura looked up Story County Iowa recorders office on computer. Found a dozen Bartines live there. No way to tell which one owns the farm I was born on. She looked up the lowest priced properties that might suit our need. Too bad we can't buy right now. Theresa wants us to come there Fri noon. Laura fixed excellent supper and pecan pie. Brad and I visited. We all watched TV after supper.

Wednesday, July 30, 2003—sunny, 60° to 87°. Went for a walk. Took pix of Brit and Maggie. Played domino's with Brit. Sylvia babysat Maggie when Laura got ultrasound that told her and Brad the baby was a boy. They suggested an Italian restaurant and we took them to dinner. It was very good.

Thursday, July 31, 2003—60° to 80°. Went for a walk, checked out a garage sale and the footings for a new house being built. Brad came home from work about 11:00 AM, no more work (stuccoing) for today. Rain with wind about supper time. Some hail in it. Brad barbequed some really good steaks for supper.

Friday, August 1, 2003—mostly sunny, 60s to 80s. Got ready to go to Theresa's. Laura, Sylvia, Brit and Maggie went to neighbor's garage sale. Theresa and Earl picked us up. We had a light lunch on the way to their friend Don Bulfer. We visited there all afternoon. Then on to their house. Darcy, Dylan, Devin, and Jason came over. Earl and Theresa fixed a barbeque picnic out in the yard. Watched the kids play and visited. After eating, Earl went back over to Don's to help haul some chairs.

Saturday, August 2, 2003—partly cloudy and one light shower, 60° to 80°. We went for a walk. Got things ready for picnic at Darcy's while Earl had four new tires put on the van. Went over to see Darcy, Jason, and their sons, Dylan and Devin. Lee and his friend Josh, Jason's little brother Jake and girlfriend Jackie came there also to barbeque. They had lots to eat then a marshmallow roast in fire ring in evening. Back at Earl and Theresa's we watched an interesting PBS Canadian show and had ice cream.

Sunday, August 3, 2003—mostly sunny, 50s to 80°. We went to "Jakes" bar and grill where Jason works for an excellent breakfast. Theresa, Earl, Darcy, Dillon and Devon were there. Also Lee A, we picked him up. Then back to Darcy's, then on way back to Earl and Theresa's place. Saw some salvage aluminum. Went back after unloading a salvage grill and hauled salvage gutters to Earl and Theresa's. Ordered pizza for supper. Later Darcy stopped by.

Monday, August 4, 2003—foggy in the morning, 60° to 80°. Nice day. Earl and I went to sell his aluminum. Then we drove the alleys two times and gathered more scrap. He gave me a brass tea kettle and candle holder. It was fun. Theresa fixed steak for supper. We packed up and Earl and Theresa drove us over to Nadia's. Some small boys are harassing an old woman next door to Nadia and Chuck by throwing rocks and walnuts at her house. What a shame.

Tuesday, August 5, 2003—mostly cloudy morning, 70° to 84°. We went to get some things to preserve some old papers of importance to Sylvia especially. Chuck and I went to Fleet Farm store for stakes, rope and ties to protect pumpkin plant. Did some grocery shopping for king size shrimp Chuck grilled for our supper. Watched history channel.

Wednesday, August 6, 2003—up early, 70° Minneapolis, to 70° Anchorage. Nadia took us to airport early. No problem with airport security. Long wait for our flight, which was very good. Sylvia visited with an elderly lady from Wisconsin. Got our luggage then Patterson Street was under construction and we had to walk from where I paid off the taxi, then climbed the rear lot fence at Faye Walton's. Visited with her for a while. Then went to Costco and got groceries and gas in truck. Saw Sandy Farmer, Missy and hubby at Caribou Creek construction. Visited and gave her a couple copper and brass nick-nacks. Got home before midnight. Found motor on our house water system running. No clue as to how long this has been going on. Worked on it but went to bed. Did listen to messages on phone recorder.

Thursday, August 7, 2003—sunny, 55° to 75°. Lots of Sylvia's flowers died for lack of water. The berries on raspberry canes dried up. Her upper garden is in poor shape as well as the green house. The lower garden looks good. Kahren has some rows planted there. Fixed and primed the house water pressure pump. Pulled weeds and did some small jobs. Read our mail and did the necessary business. Called real estate agents. "Burt" wants to sell Old Boot property but doesn't tend to business. A lady from Denver Colorado wants to buy that land in the worst way. Hope she doesn't get discouraged and loses interest.

Friday, August 8, 2003—sunny and smoky from Siberia, 50° to 80°. Paid some bills and subscriptions. Went to Glennallen to bank, shopping and sheep moose harvest tickets and lunch. Had a helluva time keeping the lawn mower running. Managed to get lawn mowed. Went to Allen's and got my rifles.

Saturday, August 9, 2003—sunny, 50° to 80s. Ralph came down from Fairbanks. I got some gear together, readied the Suzuki and we went to Alfred Creek. Set up his new tent, really nice. I realized I had forgotten my sleeping pad and bag and only had the wool blanket from the truck for a cover. We did lots of glassing for Dall sheep with no luck. Did see two moose. Went to bed late. It was quite cold there 30°s. I got too cold by morning. Ralph brought a propane cooking stove in and warmed the tent. I got some sleep.

Sunday, August 10, 2003—sunny with a breeze, 30°s to 70°s. Bugs can be bad. We found six sheep in the Horn Mountains. Couldn't tell for certain their sex as our spotting scopes resolution was not adequate at that distance. We saw two hunters that had climbed to the peaks above the sheep. Did not see them kill one. The men surely were in good shape to climb and walk those mountains all day. Quite a few caribou hunters here, but no kills that we know of. It looks bleak for any sheep hunting for us. Ralph is rightfully concerned that it will be too cold for me here tonight. We loaded our outfit up, went out to trucks. Stopped by Eureka for a hamburger on way phone. Sylvia made sauerkraut today.

Monday, August 11, 2003—partly cloudy and sprinkles, 48° to 80°. Put fertilizer on lawn. Talked to Susie Zurbrugg, Denver, Colorado about remote parcel. Jose Russo called about progress in selling the parcel. Hoed and pulled weeds in the entire lower garden. Ralph left for home after breakfast. Put away some more gear. Am trying to get caught up on reading material.

Tuesday, August 12, 2003—partly cloudy, 47° to 69°. Visited Ed Farmer. Split a stump. We went blueberry picking at about MP 126 and got five quarts. Sylvia is making pies this evening.

Wednesday, August 13, 2003—partly cloudy, 43° to 64°. Pulled cabbage root and leaves and removed from garden. Dug out old raspberry plants and threw dirt up hill in garden. Started cleaning up the brush in east garden fence. Rearranged laundry gray water line. Called some of the kids. An eagle attempted catching ducks on lake.

Thursday, August 14, 2003—Cloudy and some rain showers, 48° to 61°. Rested today. Didn't feel well. Reloaded some 30-06 cast bullets. Put gas checks on and lubed some cast bullets. Laura called. Allen brought Sammy, Reed and ice cream over and visited.

Friday, August 15, 2003—partly cloudy, rain in Glennallen, 47° to 66°. We went there to shop and have lunch. Went to gravel pit for rifle practice and load experiment-development. Found a 4" ten foot sewer pipe in road ditch. Now that we are here our lawn is greening up.

Saturday, August 16, 2003—partly cloudy and windy in the afternoon, 43° to 65°. Neighbors had a yard sale out by highway. Jeff and Amy got here about 12:30. We worked on his ATV. He went to Tazlina Lodge and got his three kids, neighbor kids with ATV's and motorcycles were here and went over by school house riding their machines.

Sunday, August 17, 2003—partly cloudy and afternoon showers, 43° to 63°. Chopped willows out of garden fence. Mowed lawn. Sylvia defrosted freezers, cleaned and organized them. I reload some practice rounds.

Monday, August 18, 2003—partly cloudy, 43° to 62°. Showers on both sides of our place. Whacked some brush down. Re-mowed the grass to pick up the dry clippings and put it around the raspberries. Allen visited quite a while this evening.

Tuesday, August 19, 2003—mostly sunny after fog in early morning, 30° to 61°. We went to Glennallen shopping and lunch. "Hot" sandwich really burned up my guts. Went shooting in the afternoon. Sam Weaver came over after hearing shots in gravel pit. Visited a while then we went mushroom hunting and found some shaggy mane's. Sylvia cooked some for supper. She is making pickles.

Wednesday, August 20, 2003—partly cloudy, cloudy afternoon and evening, 44° to 64°. Did a lot of small jobs, car, and house water pressure amongst others. Signed counter offer on Old Boot Lake today. Will put it in mail tomorrow. Theresa phoned. Had procedure done. Some raspberries ripening.

Thursday, August 21, 2003—mostly cloudy with rain and hail this afternoon, 40° to 60°. Reloaded .06 cast bullet loads. Took garbage to transfer site dismantled an old lawn mower for its aluminum. Jerry Snow and Henry Johnson came to look at our car for sale. Sent counter offer back to Joe Russo.

Friday, August 22, 2003—partly cloudy, 42° to 61°. Showers in sight in the afternoon. We went to Glennallen. Lunch shopping and rummage sale at the Legion Post for seniors. Finished up stripping an old lawn mower. Guess Jeff is on his way out here. Charlie T. wasn't home when I called. Got some books at rummage sale.

Saturday, August 23, 2003—partly cloudy, 39° to 63°. Jeff stayed overnight. We got up early. Got our gear ready, had breakfast, loaded machines on truck and trailer and went to trailhead at 11 mile. Lake Louise Road. Unloaded here and went east 4 miles parked ATV's and walked to Old Boot Lake. There we re-flagged the property lines of our 37 acres there. Stopped by Oddens cabin and showed it to Jeff. Saw a fish rise on the lake. Bear tracks moose boo and wolf also. Saw an arctic loon fishing. Drove back out to road, loaded up and came home. Ate a sandwich for supper put gear away and Jeff left for town and home.

Sunday, August 24, 2003—woke up to rain which quit in couple hours, 45° to 63°. Charlie T. phone and talked a long time. After lunch I went out and rebuilt the garage man door jamb. Finished a while before supper. Cloudy and rainy evening.

Monday, August 25, 2003—mostly cloudy, 43° to 60°. Washed truck. Went shooting at gravel pit. Sorted our tire shed. Found my two spindles for a trailer I'm building. Some of road crew helped me with a bent spindle. Sylvia sewed and I put up a new tarp for front of tire shed. Tired tonight. Sylvia brought up a four pound rutabaga.

Tuesday, August 26, 2003—mostly cloudy, 43° to 57°. Went to Glennallen lunch and shopping. Wasn't able to get oil seals for ATV trailer. A call to them with a better description of the car these spindles came from helped them find the right seals. Started gathering up parts to put on trailer. Dave Johnson stopped by to borrow the Suzuki shop manual. Was interested in our block and tile chimneys. I asked for his story of his Dall sheep hunt with his oldest son Colton. Very interesting even though they weren't successful in getting a Dall sheep, they had a good hunt.

Wednesday, August 27, 2003—mostly cloudy, 34° to 56°. Worked on ATV trailer all day. Got the axel and tongue welded. Cut and fit spindles to axel and bolted them on. Some cutting, welding and grinding. A goose has adopted Rudbecks lawn down on lake.

Thursday, August 28, 2003—partly cloudy, 39° to 60°. Worked on ATV trailer all day. Finished the frame and primer painted the bottom and wheel rims. Friends of Bob and Kahren visited and gave Sylvia some yarn. Bob borrowed four pounds of brown sugar. Rudbecks have sold their place and will subdivide.

Friday, August 29, 2003—partly sunny, rain in evening, 36° to 59°. Went to Glennallen lunch and shopping. Dan Billman called: a mountain goat was up on a shallow ledge on a steep wall in the 150 mile gravel pit. Went to see and photographed it. Painted on the ATV trailer. Got the oil seals for it. Saw Dan, Patti and Jason at Billman hanger. Picked up Sam and took him to his place.

Saturday, August 30, 2003—cloudy and rain in afternoon and evening, 37° to 54°. Worked on ATV trailer. Painting, oil seals. Some odd jobs. Kahren brought over a coat for me and yarn for Sylvia. Jeff worked on his Honda ATV in PM mounting parts and welding on it. Ate supper with us and staying the night.

Sunday, August 31, 2003—rained all night pretty hard, 40° to 49°. Finally quit in early afternoon. Jeff took all of us to breakfast at Eureka. Mounted wheels to trailer. One was canted quite a bit. Started making cutting out bottom and side for its box. He got some scrap plywood from Jerry Rudbeck. He parked his ATV and removed the wheels. I suggested washing them before taking them to get the new tires mounted.

Monday, September 1, 2003—cloudy and cleared quite a bit today and was nice, 40° to 57°. I got the trailer wheels trued up to frame so it will trail good. Cut out the plywood pieces for bottom and side and painted them with primer. Sylvia and I went to gravel pit to look for mushrooms with no luck.

Tuesday, September 2, 2003—partly cloudy, showers east of us to and including Glennallen, 43° to 59°. We had lunch there and mailed letters. Painted the plywood for Jeff's ATV trailer brown and some small jobs.

Wednesday, September 3, 2003—mostly sunny after early morning fog, 35° to 58°. Adjusted right wheel bearings on trailer. Did some touch up painting. Visited Jim, Mary and Lois Odden (Jim's mother) and had lunch with them. Took Jeff's tires to Glennallen to get them mounted and found the rear tires rims were 1" too big. They are Yamaha, not Honda. We had a couple hours to kill before the monthly Legion business meeting. It went well. Saw a 28" to 30" horned bull moose at mile 180.

Thursday, September 4, 2003—partly cloudy and very nice, 36° to 59°. Had coffee with Oddens. Painted a little on Jeff's ATV trailer. Cleaned ashes out of stove in garage.

Friday, September 5, 2003—sunny and beautiful, 39° to 59°. Real estate agent didn't return our call. Went to Glennallen. Jeff's tires were not mounted. Had lunch. Got home real late. Straightened up the garage. Walked down to well. Allen had a bowl of soup with us.

Saturday, September 6, 2003—sunny, great! 30° to 60°. Started on a seat for the (mine) ATV trailer to haul the two women in to our remote parcel. Talked to her this evening, she plans on being here Thursday. Jeff came out with Amy and kids. He went 13 miles to see his kids, came back and we worked maybe five hours on his ATV trailer - got lots done.

Sunday, September 7, 2003—sunny and beautiful, 31° to 59°. We drove to mile 115 looking for the two bulls and cow Jeff saw with no luck. We were about an hour late. We did see two other cows and a calf. Rigged my ATV trailer to haul people. Painted a little on Jeff's trailer. Cal and Mary visited for awhile. She wants Sylvia to sew on three shirts for Bar. Some airplane activity today. The moon came up "blood red" about 9:30 this evening. Beautiful.

Monday, September 8, 2003—partly cloudy and a shower and sprinkle out north of Eureka, 35° to 60°. Up at 5:00 AM, picked up Allen and drove to 115 ¾ mile. A cow, calf and a spike fork were there. Saw a big bull in far distance. Didn't shoot, was in doubt about the spike fork being legal. Later ask a wildlife protection officer who was staying in Allen's rental cabin; he said that configuration was legal. He told us of some moose bulls. We went home, regrouped, picked up Ed and went to trailhead for going to Monument Mt. Went in 6 miles on our ATVs to look for them. After some time, spotted a cow and two spike fork bulls. Watched a silver shoulder light colored grizzly bear eat blueberries from ¾ mile away. Allen walked over to the moose spike forks and let them leave the area without shooting them. Went back to gravel pit trailhead. I had left my lights on truck and battery was down. Allen gave me a jump. He spotted another spike fork near Dimmicks. After supper and washing ATV and trailer talked to Joe Russo about Old Boot Lake property and Burt Dozark's handling of the sale. I drove Allen back to mile 115 ¾ just at dark but the moose didn't come out. Jeff and Ralph both phoned.

Tuesday, September 9, 2003—sunny, very nice, 38° to 58°. Went to Glennallen picked up Jeff's ATV wheels and tires. Also a tube of silicone II to protect our hands from ATV trailer side board splinters. Put his wheels on his machine when I got home. Put two more irons and all the screw eyes on the trailer.

Wednesday, September 10, 2003—mostly sunny and a short shower, 30° to 59°. Got Suzuki and trailer ready for the trip to Old Boot Lake tomorrow. Started getting gear ready to go hunting. Sylvia and I drove to mile 115 and saw one cow moose. Sylvia vacuumed and waxed the floors and washed most of the house windows on the inside. Charlie T. phoned for Jerry Gerald Rudbeck address and phone number.

Thursday, September 11, 2003—sunny and partly cloudy in afternoon, 38° to 60°. Got ATV and trailer loaded and waited for the two Colorado ladies to arrive. Susie is interested in our remote parcel. Dianne is her friend. The trail was pretty darn good. The ladies rode on the seat I built into the trailer. There was moose, caribou and wolf tracks. No loon this time. We walked the perimeter of our land, ate a lunch at the #3 corner. I used my buck knife to open a package of raisins. Distracted by all the questions and talking, I didn't put it back in its holster, and left it there. Damn! We got back out to Lake Louise Road about 6:30 PM. I showed them an old cabin. Susie then told me that she would have to talk it over with her husband (Henry?). At this I was kind of expecting by the way she had been talking, I don't really expect her to buy the land. Both Ralph and Jeff called tonight. Allen and Ed got a big bull where we were hunting. Gave us some meat and liver from it.

Friday, September 12, 2003—partly cloudy, then rain moved in this evening, 39° to 60°. Went to Glennallen, lunch and shopping. Cashed a check at bank. Dug the potatoes when we got home. Very good size and yield. Biggest one was 2-¼ lbs. Gathered up more hunting gear. Allen stopped by. Dale R. and a guy by the name of Rob stopped. They were going moose hunting. Sylvia baked two pies for hunting trip.

Saturday, September 13, 2003—cloudy and rain, snow on Slide and Heavenly Ridge. Worked at organizing and loading gear till about 2:00 PM. Jeff came mid morning. He had things to do also. Ralph drove 300 miles down from Fairbanks. When everything was ready we left for Squaw Creek Trailhead. Jeff got gas at Eureka. Soon as we got there we sent Jeff on ahead to claim the 5 mile cabin if no one is there. Ralph loaded his trailer and we took off also. Trail was mostly good but Ralph did high center in one mud hole and had to winch out. Jeff beat a group of three to TAE cabin. We got settled in and Ralph cooked steak sandwiches. Sylvia had baked two pies! Peach and blueberry.

Sunday, September 14, 2003—froze ice this morning, sunny. About 20° To 40s? Up early. Went hunting, Jeff went south; Ralph and I went north along Squaw Creek Trail. Saw a kestrel chasing a small bird. I came back to cabin. Jeff went north and saw a cow moose and calf. We ate breakfast then went north. My machine is having trany-clutch trouble. Jeff and I came back to cabin. He crossed the creek and went SW to look at some moose he spotted this morning. Ralph is looking to the north. My back is really bad. Jeff came back didn't see any moose. He and I went to see Ralph H. He had left his ATV and was walking and hunting. Got too dark to spot moose.

    I went down to Squaw Creek for a bucket of water and they came in after a little while. It looks like it will get pretty cold tonight. Jeff saw a red fox at the cabin here. Ralph has been doing all the cooking.

Monday, September 15, 2003—sunny, possibly 0° to 40°. Ralph and I walked west and called but saw no moose. Jeff went east and spotted for moose. Back to camp for breakfast 10:00 AM. Ralph took off for Wasilla for oil and filters for the Suzukis, kerosene for the heater in cabin, sox, propane stove and tanks.

A heavy pair mitts for me, a gift! He got back awhile before supper. Jeff walked back over to the moose he had found before. The bull isn't legal. Saw another cow and four sheep. Some hunters saw a silver wolf way up on Sheep Mountain. It did some howling. They saw two moose cows and a calf. I cut brush from near Jeff and Ralph's ATV's so they had more room to park. Did the dishes and cleaned the cabin. It's cool in here already this evening.

Tuesday, September 16, 2003—pretty cold in morning, still clear...see Mars every night. Same drill, Jeff goes south to hill so he can try to see moose (legal bull) in an area he expects them to be – no luck. Ralph and I walk North with no luck – no moose. Saw Ravens flying as to feed. Back to camp and eat a late breakfast. Ralph and Jeff go south. I clean up around here then walk up to and across trail and east up a creek there. Climb a steep, 61' bank, hit a game trail and walk a ways. Great view from here but no legal game. Sheep are on Sheep Mountain. Ralph changed the oil and filter on his ATV. I came down off the hill before dark. We had our usual late supper. Jeff saw two cows and a calf moose.

Wednesday, September 17, 2003—warmer this morning though still freezing water and mud holes. Clouded over in afternoon and evening. Creeks are getting icy. Ralph and I saw a wolf track in trail and scat with moose hair. Also a small bit of fresh berry bear pooh. Had breakfast and they decided to hunt moose over towards Caribou Creek. We got nearly there and Jeff became concerned as his ATV is running rich. We did get to look over an old cabin belonging to a Squaw Creek miner. Turned around and started back. Jeff did want to try for sheep and didn't want to go up on a high lookout to glass for bull moose. Parked for an hour or so in trail, then he wanted to go pack to cabin as it was getting about time to glass a hill he has been watching. Ate a light lunch and he took off. Ralph crossed the cr. and is taking a ride south on the trail over there. Distance unknown. Jeff sliced the wolf turd in ½ with his hunting knife to see the moose hair inside it. The ravens flew in the same direction again today. Come to find out Jeff went with Ralph. Went 1 ½ south and walked a ways up the mountainside. Saw bear pooh and area looked well used by moose. Called to and to a response by a cow moose. We had a good supper. They had the last of Sylvia's peach pie and I made s-mores, (gram crackers, marshmallows and Hershey bars).

Thursday, September 18, 2003—fairly warm this morning, not so cold, ice froze. Went south and across the cr. towards where Jeff has been hunting. I saw a moose cow and calf and two moose higher on mountain. No shooting came back to cabin and breakfast. Ralph and my ATV front wheels were frozen and wouldn't turn. They thawed out in sun later. I took an ATV trail west and north across Squaw Creek. Got clear up the mountain to the first "break". Followed the edge of it south to the end of it. Stopped there and trimmed a broken toenail. Lots of blueberries. They are soft but good. Then walked down off the mountain. Paced the distance between the two trails 70 paces, then 70 paces to cr. and about 120 yards on up to cabin. Ralph and I went hunting towards evening. Heard four shots and came back. Didn't think it was Jeff, but it was. He got a legal moose and brought in the heart.

Friday, September 19, 2003—froze again this morning. Water got inside the ATV front wheel drums and they won't turn till the sun shines on them for awhile. Ralph and Jeff drove their machines and trailer to base of the where hill Jeff killed his bull last evening. I walked to the site. We cut the bull into four quarters, removed the head and the 50" horns from it. They skidded the meat down to the ATV's and to haul to the trailers. They heard a cow and a bull moose and tried to call them in. Got close but no sighting. Did call in a hunter though went back to the cabin and Ralph cooked up fresh moose heart—very good. They took a "snoozer." I sat in the sun soaking it up. Jeff had to go to Anchorage so we packed up and went back to trailhead and loaded our outfits on the trailers. Had to cut brush off a loading ramp to get Ralph loaded up. Came home here, sorted gear, put some away. We hung up the four quarters in the garage. Jeff went to Anchorage and we had sandwiches for supper and a piece of pie.

Saturday, September 20, 2003—snowed in night and most all the day. Ralph and I got up early and road hunted. Saw a cow moose in gravel pit at DOT. Went again in evening. Saw a cow and calf west of Eureka acting like maybe coming in heat. We stopped to look for a bull but no luck. Ralph called like a cow and the cow came back and looked at him from 30'. I washed mud of Suzuki and put it in shed. Put away camping gear. Ralph organized his camp gear and put it in his pickup canopy. Jeff, Amy and John Paul came from Anchorage to cut up their moose meat. Ralph, Sylvia and I helped. Jeff left a front quarter for us and rear quarter for Ralph. Johnny? Ralph's cousin visited Ralph a few minutes this morning. Allen Farmer came over to see moose meat and horns. Sylvia went to ladies lunch for Lauri (Wikle) Rich. Dick Anthony called to ask me to plow his snow.

Sunday, September 21, 2003—got more snow late afternoon, 28° to 41°. Ralph had breakfast with us, loaded his gear and headed for Fairbanks. Sylvia and I cut up and packaged the front quarter Jeff gave us. Still have to grind the hamburger meat. It's been hectic around here for a while. Allen visited and grandson Steve phoned and talked 45 minutes. Still swans on lake and some ducks. We are going to Evelyn and Ronnie's to borrow meat grinder.

Monday, September 22, 2003—cloudy, sunny, 28° to 41°. Ground hamburger, packaged it and in the freezer. Did some preparing for winter. Cleaned ATV front brake. "Monty" a dog ran off with my moose shoulder blade. The ermine and camp robbers are picking the bones clean.

Tuesday, September 23, 2003—sunny, 13° to 38°. Some lakes starting to freeze over. Some ducks and swans are using our lake. Went to Glennallen. Put away some camp gear. Returned meat grinder. Saw Corky Dimmick. Kahren dropped by with magazines and ask for a copy of "how to choose a puppy."

Wednesday, September 24, 2003—cloudy with snow showers, 26° to 46°. Starting out for Old Boot Lake to look for my knife. I ran into more snow covering the brush. Not wanting to put up with that mess, I turned around at Mile 6 and came back home. Drained the oil from old blue and put in clean new oil. Moved Jeff's trailer, put away some camping gear. Swept garage. Counted 23 swans on lake. Sent spotting scope to be repaired. Bob and Kahren came by on their way out for the winter.

Thursday, September 25, 2003—cloudy and rain towards evening, 30° to 40°. Moved car from "sale" spot out by highway. Moved plow truck and let it run for awhile. Leveled potato rows. Disconnected summer watering lines. Put away more hunting gear. Dave Johnson brought my Suzuki shop manual back. Ice left our lake.

Friday, September 26, 2003—sunny and beautiful, 25° to 50°. Went to Glennallen. Forgot to get an oil filter. Lunch, shopping, and pay light bill. Went to gravel pit. Some one on a dirt bike has torn up most every square foot of it. Checked the .338 magnum zero. The fall I took when hunting caused it to be 1" to right. Shoots excellent now. Appears people moving into Rudbeck's place now.

Saturday, September 27, 2003—sunny, 26° to 44°. Went to 11 mile trailhead on Lake Louise Road and unloaded ATV and went to our land on Old Boot Lake. Saw large bear tracks and lynx tracks then throttle froze or frosted up. Stopped, and the motor heat thawed it out. Saw fox, wolf, otter, moose, one set extra large. Walked to our land and to survey post #3. There I picked up the knife I left there Sept. 11th. Rested and walked back to ATV and drove to trailhead, loaded up ATV. Checked out a gravel pit and picked up 102 .223 Remington brass. Picked up a battery and I'm trying to recharge it. Tired tonight. Glad to retrieve the knife, a gift from Nadia. It was a beautiful day.

Sunday, September 28, 2003—cloudy, sprinkles here, rain on Heavenly Ridge, 30° to 42°. Tried to get the light with chainsaw to run for several hours with no luck. Finally cut up the stove wood with old heavy saw. Wore out this evening.

Monday, September 29, 2003—mostly cloudy. 35° to 58°. We went north of Glennallen to hunt caribou on BLM land. We were cut off 2-3 times and just missed several other chances. No luck at all. Nice to spend the day hunting together.

Tuesday, September 30, 2003—windy, partly cloudy, 48° to 58°. Up at 5:00 AM. Got to mile 148 at daylight. Saw two caribou till 9:00 PM then no more till 3:00 PM. Tried to cut these off on an old section of road. A fellow and his daughter were dressing out a nice boo there. I did see 5 boo out, no bull and thick trees. On way back to truck saw two more boo but no chance to identify or shoot. Saw where someone had dressed out a bear.

Wednesday, October 1, 2003—mostly sunny and very windy in the afternoon, 48° to 64°. Washed blue truck, ATV trailer, and my hip boots. Put air in Jeff's ATV trailer tires. Moved Molly car. Swept garage and mowed the lawn. Sunrise this morning with wind sculptured red pink clouds and gold sun rays breaking through seemed touched by God. Observed a swan fly cross ways of a very strong wind straight as an arrow. I kind of over did the work today.

Thursday, October 2, 2003—partly cloudy, 45° to 60°. Did not do much today. Went to supper at Darrel and Brenda's. Lisa, Reed and Gracie were there. Then to Legion meeting. It went pretty well.

Friday, October 3, 2003—rainy, quit in the afternoon, 37° to 50° Looked for the lost stapler and Jeff's knives. Got truck ready to go to Anchorage. Swans are uneasy. They get up and fly and return etc.

Saturday, October 4, 2003—mostly sunny, 26° to 45°. Got up early and went to Wasilla for groceries, vitamins, blinds for living room, oil filter and Anchorage shopping. Had lunch. Jeff helped carry things in the house. Allen asked me to come down for banana pudding and coffee. Sylvia didn't feel well, so she didn't go. Allen told me where a large black bear hangs out.

Sunday, October 5, 2003—rain, partly sunny, 30° to 46°. Rested a lot today. Went to CBSC meeting. Steve called and will call back. Called Nadia.

Monday, October 6, 2003—partly cloudy, 36° to 46°. Put winter tires on old blue. Put oil filter on it. Took six saw logs over to Allen's. He showed me some photo albums.

Tuesday, October 7, 2003—34° to 44°. Went to Glennallen. Lunch, bank and tried to get a "chime module" warning lights on devise for old blue. Allen brought over the lumber that he sawed out of the logs I took over there. I stickered it when I stacked it into the lean-to. Went to Mile 118 to look for the big black bear seen feeding there but no luck.

Wednesday, October 8, 2003—partly cloudy, cloudy, 25° to 42°. Worked a lot on our pressure water system. Need new part in the pump. Had unleaded gasoline delivered. Sylvia went to lunch with the ladies. Allen reports caribou crossing east to west at Mile 10 Lake Louise Road. Beautiful bulls among them with snow-white capes. Slight amount of ice on our lake this morning.

Thursday, October 9, 2003—cloudy, clearing in the afternoon, 33° to 43°. Worked on water pump. Took it apart, cleaned it, put it back together. It only pumps 40-pound pressure but that is satisfactory. Did some other small jobs. Saw a large flock of about 130 swans flying east. Beautiful. Nice evening too.

Friday, October 10, 2003—sunny, 24° to 41°. Water pump still giving me trouble. We went to Glennallen, lunch, Post Office, NAPA, and grocery store. Put Stabil in ATV and jacked it off its tires. Did a couple other jobs.

Saturday, October 11, 2003—sunny, 16° to 37°. Plumbing at water pump had several leaks. Spent half a day working on that. Denny E. brought over one fitting I needed. Needs new parts to be like new. Put a bulb in well and a tarp cover over well. Half of our lake is frozen over. Some melted today. No water fowl in sight on lake. Chopped out a small stump along driveway.

Sunday, October 12, 2003—sunny and very nice, 18° to 38°. Pump has no leaks today. Put tools away. Clean some on wood shop. Saw some geese fly up our lake. Sally called with Bud's new address for mail. Kahren called – they got the 2 yr-old-lab. Cal and Mary Gilcrease stopped by to say good-bye for the winter. They are going to Arkansas—had supper with us.

Monday, October 13, 2003—sunny, 13° to 35°. A small part of west end of our lake is still open.

Tuesday, October 14, 2003—cloudy, 14° to 29°. We went to Glennallen. Lunch and shopping. Went down to lake, chopped a small hole to test ice thickness—one inch.

Wednesday, October 15, 2003—sunny, 13° to 36°. We went to Palmer, Wasilla, Anchorage shopping. Water pump parts, groceries amongst other things. Was a nice day to do it. I did get quite tired. Managed to get most everything we needed.

Thursday, October 16, 2003—sunny, 12° to 38°. We put plastic "shrink" windows on the upstairs, inside window frames. I burned some old canvas water hoses. The northern lights were outstanding this evening. A halo is around the moon. Neighbor to the east came over to see what the smoke was all about.

Friday, October 17, 2003—sunny, 8° to 32°. Cleaned up the ash pile and the ashes in burn barrel. Cleaned clamps and pieces of hose off the fittings. Straightened up that area. Saw caribou tracks at our lake. Ice is now three inches thick. Checked Charlie's storage building and picked up three aluminum cans.

Saturday, October 18, 2003—sunny, cloudy and a few snow flurries, 9° to 32°. Cleaned up and buried the last of ashes. Cut some stump and roots into firewood. Cleaned up the mess. Walked down to lake and out on the ice to a "white thing" I saw (a piece of frosted ice). We went to supper at the Legion Post. Missed Jeff and family. Funeral for Harold Schmidt (my cousin Gladys' husband who was burned in an accident in a welding accident at his farm in Iowa).

Sunday, October 19, 2003—cloudy and snow flurries to south of us, 18° to 33°. We scrubbed and cleaned both water storage tanks in basement. Both leak now a little. We expected this. Walked down to lake. Reloaded some .308 cartridges to hunt caribou. Called Nadia, she wasn't able go to the funeral for Harold Schmidt. Sylvia heard and saw then called to my attention 100 - 150 swans flying east.

Monday, October 20, 2003—sunny, 12° to 36°. Burned trash, smashed cans. Gassed truck. Went to gravel pit to sight in .308 Winchester. Hunting loads. The ProChrono batteries were low so didn't get any FPS stats. Got rifle sighted in easily and both the cast bullet and jacketed shot to nearly the same group and quite accurate. Some of the parts for the water pump came, short one. Got hunting gear ready for winter caribou season opening tomorrow.

Tuesday, October 21, 2003—sunny, 16° to 35°. Drove to Bureau of Land Management hunt area on Richardson Highway. Ron Nelson, conservation officer, told me the caribou for the most part have left the area. I hunted for four hours and saw little or no sign. I did find a bear baiting station east a mile of Mile 152 Richardson Highway.

Wednesday, October 22, 2003—snow flurry, sunny, 11° to 30°. Started clearing off the bench in garage. Epoxied a fitting on the larger water tank. Clean and oiled guns.

Thursday, October 23, 2003—cloudy with clouds lowering in evening, 20° to 30°. Put up both new Venetian blinds at picture window. Hurt my left knee again. Wrote my brother, Marion. Bill Buck of Colorado called about our 37 acres.

Friday, October 24, 2003—partly cloudy, 21° to 36°. We went to Glennallen. Lunch and shopping. My knee is really bad. Oiled some guns.

Saturday, October 25, 2003—1-1/2 inches of snow last night, 28° to 39°. It settled and melted quite a lot. A fox? was exploring here last night. My knees are sore, left one especially. Jeff called with news of things there. We called Vanessa and also Laura.

Sunday, October 26, 2003—mostly cloudy, 17° to 38°. Knee is bad. Didn't do anything today. Tom Smayda called. He and Lisa came out and visited and had supper with us. They brought some fresh produce. We had a good visit.

Monday, October 27, 2003—cloudy, 17° to 37°. Knee is better. Read most of the day. Sylvia pumped water into the upper tank and found it leaks in a new place.

Tuesday, October 28, 2003—sunny, 27° to 32°. Great northern lights for several nights now. Supposedly due to sun bursts going on at this time. We went to Glennallen. Lunch and shopping, and pick up package at Post Office (spotting scope). Knee is about like it was yesterday. Nadia called.

Wednesday, October 29, 2003—mostly sunny, 0° to 23°. Theresa called shortly after 6:00 PM. She is in hospital with breathing problems on oxygen and they are using a nebulizer to help with breathing. Called the other kids to get them rallied around in support of Theresa. My knee is better. Sylvia talked with Theresa this evening.

Thursday, October 30, 2003—partly cloudy, 7° to 26°. Called Theresa and talked with her. Called Laura also. Joe Russo called and has an inquiry about our 37 acres. Walked down and checked on the well. Lot's of tracks. Pretty sure one set was a young lynx. Shot a revolver and started cleaning it.

Friday, October 31, 2003—partly cloudy, 6° to 30°. Went shopping and lunch in Glennallen. Didn't do much today. Called Theresa and she called us a couple of times. She is getting better. Some neighborhood kids showed up trick or treating. Finished cleaning and oiling the revolver.

Saturday, November 1, 2003—beautiful sunrise, 7° to 25°. Wrote some letters. Walked down to lake. Called Theresa. Bev called. Nadia called. I'm reading a book. Allen visited.

Sunday, November 2, 2003—cloudy, foggy, skiff frozen wet snow, 24° to 34°. Put some more silicone on water tank and couple little jobs. Walked down to lake and back. Ralph phoned.

Monday, November 3, 2003—cloudy and snow flurries, 25° to 31°. We pumped water, walked down to well. Cleaned up a 5-gallon bucket. We went to breakfast Allen and Roxanne's. Called Theresa. She went home from hospital. Did a few small jobs. Al Plisous was included in a film clip of bears and pepper spray on the Anchorage News TV.

Tuesday, November 4, 2003—low cloudy, fog on each side, 23° to 28°. Fox walked through the yard. We are putting out some bird feed. Did some small jobs. Called Theresa, her recovery is not fast. Jeff called a couple times. He went to the shooting range.

Wednesday, November 5, 2003—fog, low clouds, 23° to 32°. Jeff called, won't be coming out. Took the heat exchanger off the Toyo Heater and washed the carbon out of it. Marvin came over to ask the use of our mailbox as his has been knocked down.

Thursday, November 6, 2003—fog, low clouds and skiffs of snow, 24° to 28°. Worked on the pump in the house all day. Took it apart three times. Finally got all the bugs out. Still have to regulate the pressure switch.

Friday, November 7, 2003—cloudy, 12° to 25°. The pressure switch worked after I lowered the pressure in the pressure tank bladder. Put a 100 watt bulb in the well. Jim Miller, preacher at Mendeltna Church visited a while this afternoon. Couldn't reach Theresa this evening.

Saturday, November 8, 2003—cloudy, started snowing about 4:00 PM, 15° to 34°. Called Theresa - she is better. Made a wire mesh bird feeder for tallow for the birds. Had to hang it high to keep Ellie's dog "Morty" from getting it. Tried a net bag but the ermine climbed the tree and robbed tallow out through a hole!

Sunday, November 9, 2003—partly cloudy, 20° to 32°. Read a lot. Called Theresa. Had to work on two supports on the lower end of the water line. Got is all straight again. Felt pretty bad this morning.

Monday, November 10, 2003—partly cloudy, 5° to 23°. Didn't do much today. The fox came back. The birds are using the tallow feeder a lot.

Tuesday, November 11, 2003—Fog, low clouds, fog, light snow all day, 9° to 14°. Reworked the bird feeder. Read and some TV. Fox had been here. Sylvia put out more bird seed.

Wednesday, November 12, 2003—mostly cloudy, 7° to 17°. We had 3" snow. Plowed our driveway and to house. Charged the battery on plow truck, put gas and Heet. Found a board for the end of our bed. Did some small jobs. Jim Odden called and visited quite a while.

Thursday, November 13, 2003—partly cloudy and light snow sometimes, 6° to 18°. Made a board for the foot of our bed and varithaned it. Installed it on the bed.

Friday, November 14, 2003—low clouds and light snow, 4° to 10°. Charged battery on the plow truck and put charger on the car. Called and got appointment to see my doctor. Bob Rudbeck called for info on Medicare insurance.

Saturday, November 15, 2003—cloudy and skiff snow, sunny and sundogs, 6° to - 5°. Loaded gear in truck and went to Mile 152 Richardson Highway and started hunting caribou. Saw a red fox in a big gravel pit. No chance for a shot. Drove to all the places to see caribou with out much luck. Saw 6 that others had gotten. Saw boo in the distance. About 4:00 PM saw seven cross highway. Got ahead of them and ready to shoot but none were a bull. Close to 6:00 PM when I got home.

Sunday, November 16, 2003—cloudy and ice in the air, -20° to -3°. Didn't do much today. Jeff stopped by a few minutes. Called Steve. He and Paul haven't gotten a deer yet.

Monday, November 17, 2003—nice day, -14° to 2°. Went to VA clinic for a doctor visit and yearly exam. Harry Termin drove the VA van. TO Brooks went in also. My exam went okay. Took four blood samples for testing. Did a little shopping. Had dinner in Palmer. A cow moose ran out in front of us (in the dark). Harry got the van stopped in time.

Tuesday, November 18, 2003—sunny, cloudy afternoon, -23° to -7°. Went to Glennallen. Paid fuel oil bill. Sylvia shopped and cashed her check. Lunch. Put up for sale sign on Sparks billboard.

Wednesday, November 19, 2003—cloudy to foggy, -23° to -6°. Tried to fix a balky zipper. Burned paper. Walked down and checked the well.

Thursday, November 20, 2003—cloudy, -13° to -3°. Read a lot today.

Friday, November 21, 2003—2" snow in the morning, -7° to +14°. We went to Glennallen shopping and lunch. Sylvia cut my hair and I cut hers.

Saturday, November 22, 2003—snowing hard when we got up, 0° to 24°. Quit mid morning and cleared up. Plowed our snow and went to Dick Anthony's and plowed the snow there. Rested awhile, then we went to the Legion Thanksgiving dinner. Stopped by Ron Beshaw's on the way and Sylvia gave him a pumpkin pie.

Sunday, November 23, 2003—skiff of snow and cloudy, -5° to 12°. Read a lot. Got up late. Watched fox hunting.

Monday, November 24, 2003—snowed three inches, then mostly cloudy, sun in afternoon, 5° to 13°. Went to Evelyn Lester's and plowed their snow. Philip rode with me, then went over to Cal and Mary's and plowed there also.

Tuesday, November 25, 2003—cloudy and 1-½ inches of snow, 7° to 14°. We went to Glennallen. Lunch and shopping. Allen and Roxanne asked us to come down for coffee which we did. Sylvia gave Sammy and Reed her knitted mitts. The really liked them.

Wednesday, November 26, 2003—cloudy and light snow, -3° to 6°. We pumped water and had ice in line. Ran hot water back down to well and pumped again. Snowgo would not start. Walking up hill in ten inches of snow was a job.

Thursday, November 27, 2003—partly cloudy, -25° to -10°. Did some small chores. Sylvia baked a turkey which we took to Darrel and Brenda Gerry's. They had three friends there for Thanksgiving dinner. Theresa called. We called Bev and Paul with no luck.

Friday, November 28, 2003—cloudy and some light snow, -13° to 7°. Read a lot. Watched some TV. Started little Adam Brockman's snowgo for him. Plowed snow down to water line crossing the lower road. Plowed driveway and around buildings.

Saturday, November 29, 2003—sunny, -13° to 4°. Walked down the hill and back. Read and watched TV.

Sunday, November 30, 2003—cloudy, some breeze and light snow all day (1-3/4 inches), -10° to 7°. Didn't do much of anything except sweep snow off the arctic entry steps.

Monday, December 1, 2003—skiff of snow, sunny, cloudy, -5° to 8°. Ordered four News channels from DISH network. Went to Dick Anthony's and plowed the snow there.

Tuesday, December 2, 2003—sunny, -7° to -2° to -15°. We went to Glennallen shopping. Cash checks and lunch. Shoveled snow up around the well. Tried and failed to get snowgo started.

Wednesday, December 3, 2003—cloudy with fine snow, -25° to -7°. Pulled the snowgo over to garage and Sylvia helped me get it into the garage. Will heat garage and find out why it doesn't start.

Thursday, December 4, 2003—mostly sunny, -10° to 12°. Gave the snowgo a tune up. Spark plugs cleaned and gapped, adjusted the choke cable. Drained carburetor. Repaired cracks in the windshield.

Friday, December 5, 2003—sunny, -13° to -1°. We pumped water. Bulb in well had burned out and warning bulb had jiggled loose in its socket. Got that all fixed and packed the trail with snowgo. Discovered plow truck right rear tire was flat. Checked with soapy water. The only leak must be at the valve core. Testing pressure overnight. Jeff, Amy, John Paul and Chelsie were in afternoon. They sighted in Amy's new rifle. Accurate too. Jeff and family saw 100 caribou 2 miles east of Eureka.

Saturday, December 6, 2003—sunny, -18° to -8°. Sylvia went with Elaine to the Christmas bazaar in Glennallen. I copied a rifle article for Jeff and Amy.

Sunday, December 7, 2003—sunny, -20° to -11°. Put the wheel and tire back on plow truck. Talked to Nadia and Beverly. Allen came up and got us to have lasagna with them. Had a nice visit.

Monday, December 8, 2003—sunny, cloudy in afternoon, -19° to -8°. Jeff came out late in AM and we went varmint hunting. Saw lots of wolf tracks along Lake Louise Road. Some fox and ptarmigan tracks as well as moose and caribou. We didn't call anything in. We even tried at the Tolsona dump. Back home Sylvia put on supper then Jeff wanted me to go with him to inquire some lots for sale around here.

Tuesday, December 9, 2003—partly cloudy and breezy some times, -10° to 28°. Went to Glennallen to bank and lunch. Saw fresh fox and lynx tracks. Wrote some Christmas cards.

Wednesday, December 10, 2003—cloudy and skiff of snow, 11° to 21°. Wrote some Christmas cards. We pumped water. Adjusted pilot jet on snowgo. Shoved snow off camper and one trailer.

Thursday, December 11, 2003—cloudy, 9° to 16°. Wrote more Christmas and birthday cards.

Friday, December 12, 2003—mostly cloudy, -5° to +2°. Went to Glennallen shopping and lunch. Put bucket of coffee grounds on lower garden. Snowgo started.

Saturday, December 13, 2003—partly cloudy, -10° to 1°. Very foggy across the river sometimes. Made out Christmas cards most of the day. Made a lot of calls trying to reach Eva Adams in St. Cloud Hospital then when call went through she was too sedated to understand. Was able to reach Larry Adams at his home this evening. His mother, our old friend Eva, is battling cancer.

Sunday, December 14, 2003—cloudy and lots of fog, -12° to 5°. Nadia called at 3:00 AM to alert us to the capture of Saddam Hussein. We celebrated with a dish of ice cream. Then went back to bed for awhile. I still got up pretty early. Finished most of the Christmas cards. Harry and Neva McCoy called about Eva Adams. Walked down to lake and back. New neighbor walked through our place since we pumped water. Ralph phoned and visited quite a while.

Monday, December 15, 2003—partly cloudy, 2° to 12°. Cleaned snow off some roofs. Plowed some snow. Didn't sleep very well last night. Went to Manning to supper. Jim Miller and daughter Rita were there later.

Tuesday, December 16, 2003—partly cloudy to cloudy and light snow in the afternoon, -7° to 5°. Went to Glennallen, dropped off trapping magazines to Jim Millers. Lunch and shopping in town.

Wednesday, December 17, 2003—cloudy and skiff snow, -3° to 4°. Toyo stove is acting up. Can find the problem. Heating with wood. Went to American Legion meeting – Glennallen.

Thursday, December 18, 2003—sunny, -10° to 3°. We pumped water. Wrote letters. Fred Rungee stopped by with grapefruit and eggplant. Laura and Brad's baby boy was born today about 8:30.

Friday, December 19, 2003—it's -10° - 12° to 15°. Went shopping Glennallen. Lunch. Nadia called and we called Laura. Baby's name is Joseph Bradley. Heating stove is still giving me trouble. We got a Christmas goodie box in the mail from Nadia.

Saturday, December 20, 2003—mostly cloud and snowed one inch in afternoon, two inches overnight. Plowed our snow. We went to Christmas party and dinner at Legion Post.

Sunday, December 21, 2003—foggy with snow in afternoon, 0° to 15°. I didn't go to gun show in Palmer. Found a mistake in programming the Toyo Stove. Corrected that. Called Laura with new prepaid card and misread one number. This gave me a lot of grief. Henry Johnson came over programmed our phone to "speed dial."

Monday, December 22, 2003—Lots of snow in night (about ten inches total), 10° to 22°. Plowed our snow and mailboxes, and some at driveway for Mendeltna Chapel. Plowed out Dick Anthony's. Shoveled some here at home.

Tuesday, December 23, 2003—partly sunny, fog and snow in south mountains, 0° to 10°. Went to Glennallen, lunch shopping. Saw cow moose and calf. Sylvia saw another moose. She gave Ron a pumpkin pie. Worked on some .30-30 brass. A nice Christmas package came from Vanessa and Scott.

Wednesday, December 24, 2003—about one inch of fluffy snow fell, 4° to 10°. Fooled with heating stove. Jim M. came over and looked at it also. Somewhat of a mystery. Allen and Reed brought over a lot of goodies and visited. Reed played dominoes with Sylvia. Jeff and I talked a few times.

Thursday, December 25, 2003—cloudy and fine snow, quite often today, 1° to 6°. Plowed our snow. Oil heater still won't work. Tried to call Vanessa. Allen got called out to plow snow on highway. Had prime rib dinner at Allen and Roxanne's.

Friday, December 26, 2003—partly cloudy and sun dogs out, -7° to -0° to -15°. We went to Glennallen to lunch and shopping. Saw a moose cow. Put four small sled loads of wood in basement. Called Nadia and Paul. Couldn't get a hold of some others.

Saturday, December 27, 2003—partly cloudy, spectacular sun dogs, -27° to -20°. Oil heater still doesn't work so we heat with wood. Christmas card mailed to Paul Norris came back.

Sunday, December 28, 2003—mostly clear, -32° to -19°. Nadia called. Susie and Henry Zurbrugg from Colorado stopped by this afternoon for a few minutes. Cleaned snow off garbage hole. Ermine is using it too. Brought in more firewood. The plow truck tire went flat again.

Monday, December 29, 2003—cloudy, -26° to 24°. We pumped water. Tough walking down and up the hill. Tried to pack trail with snowgo, it didn't run good and had helluva time getting it up to garage. Removed flat and bought it into house to thaw out. Put more wood in basement.

Tuesday, December 30, 2003—cloudy and light snow, 18° to 24°. Went to Glennallen. Jim's repair couldn't find a leak in the tire that goes flat, so brought it back home and put it back on plow truck. Had lunch and a little shopping.

Wednesday, December 31, 2003—mostly cloudy, four inches of snow, 15° to 5°. Went to Tazlina and plowed Anthony's driveway and yard. Plowed out our place. Pulled snow off south side of wood shop, lean to and woodshed overhang. Backed into storage shed and damaged it. Called Jeff about the year manufacture of Marlin. He went to gun shop and looked it up and called back. Beverly called and we had a long visit.

Sylvia in her garden

2004—Selling the remote parcel at Old Boot Lake

Thursday, January 1, 2004—temperature was -25° to -15°. We went with Denny Eastman and his family to Eureka for brunch. Lots of were neighbors there. We met Joe and Melanie, our new neighbors. Put more wood in basement.

Friday, January 2, 2004—still very cold, -27° to -9°. Put more wood in basement. Jeff called. Laurie won't be stopping by till Sunday. Jim M. came over and checked oil burner again. Decided to loan us a stove while he finds out what is the matter with this one. Laura called. Maggie ran into a wall, raising a knot on her forehead. Brad took her to hospital. She will be okay from that, but Laura says Maggie's speech and learning is not developing at a normal rate. Laura is worried about this. We tried to be supportive and assured her of our love.

Saturday, January 3, 2004—sunny, -16° to 6°. We took our heater out and Jim put his loaner in for us to use while ours is being repaired. We pumped water. The bulb that heats the well was burned out and I had to make two trips up and down the hill. Someone left a coffee cake on our pantry window sill.

Sunday, January 4, 2004—sunny, -19° to -6°. Prepared a notebook on the 30-30 Marlin. Laurie dropped off the 30-30 about 6:30 PM. It looks better than Jeff described it.

Monday, January 5, 2004—sunny, -21° to -9°. Cleaned the 30-30 and at 25 yards shot it to check its function, which was okay. Told Jeff how it performed.

Tuesday, January 6, 2004—sunny with sun dogs, -23° to 1°. Went to Glennallen. Quite windy there. Shopping, bank and lunch. Found a hood for a front sight on 30-30 in my gun parts drawer. Bart rode with me to Legion meeting.

Wednesday, January 7, 2004—cloudy, fog, snow on mountains, -16° to -4°. Read a lot. Shoveled snow off woodshed, camper trailer, brown trailer, and storage shed.

Thursday, January 8, 2004—cloudy and skiff of snow in afternoon, -30° to -15°. Pulled more snow off roofs and car, still some left. Cleaned the cartridge tube and spring, and J-B lapped the 30-30 barrel.

Friday, January 9, 2004—partly cloudy, skiff of snow, -20° to -8°. Pulled more snow off roofs. Shoveled some up around arctic entry. Read a lot. Jeff called.

Saturday, January 10, 2004—sunny, -9° to 10°. We pumped water. Carried garbage out, trash to burn barrel. Shoveled snow. Put charger on car battery. Sylvia fixed a dinner and had Allen, Roxanne, Samantha, and Reed up to eat with us.

Sunday, January 11, 2004—mostly sunny, -17° to 10°. Read a lot. Reloaded 45, 30-30 cartridges. Sylvia talked to Lorraine Hanson.

Monday, January 12, 2004—mostly sunny, -10° to 8°. Plowed our driveway. Put air in a front tire and tightened the nut on two valve stems. Straightened the door frame on the storage shed. Tried but couldn't find the plans for building a bullet lube mould. Laura called. The four people who came to evaluate Maggie's learning capacity were quite negative. Here we sincerely hope and pray it isn't that bad. Called Nadia for her input. Called Charlie T. and Jeff and Amy Routt who all have experience along this line. Ask these folks to call Laura and relate their experiences for what they are worth.

Tuesday, January 13, 2004—cloudy and 2 ½" snow, 5° to 10°. Went to Glennallen to shop and lunch. Laura called, she feels a little better, and expressed gratitude for the support that Jeff and Amy gave when they called and told her of their experiences with situations like Maggie's.

Wednesday, January 14, 2004—sunny with sun dogs, 2° to -25°. Plowed snow for Dick Anthony.

Thursday, January 15, 2004—we went to lunch, then I cleaned the Legion Post rifles. Then went to Darrel and Brenda's to visit and dinner. Got back home 7:30 PM. A vehicle had struck a moose about mile 159. The wrecker was lifting the moose when we went by.

Friday, January 16, 2004—sunny, -35° to -25°. Went to Glennallen shopping and lunch.

Saturday, January 17, 2004—it's -38° to -28°. Read a lot. Doing rifle and cast bullet research for correspondence with a couple gun editors for magazines.

Sunday, January 18, 2004—sunny, -42° to -34°. Did some writing. Plugged in the truck to warm it up for starting. Got ourselves ready and went to a memorial service for Jack Chamberlain at Mendeltna.

Monday, January 19, 2004—sunny to cloudy and light snow in evening, -43° to -20°. Walked down to well to make sure the light bulb was still heating it. Saw where two spruce hens had slept over night lots of ermine tracks, one small mink climbed up on well cover. A moose had laid in the trail for a while. David Farmer brought Jacobi Kiser here this evening. Jacobi is in the Marines and is serving in Iraq. His folks live near here.

Tuesday, January 20, 2004—sunny with clouds in afternoon and skiffs of snow, -7° to 7°. Had a long talk with Laura and a second call about Riley Patterson. We pumped water. Then I did some target practice with the 30-30. Listened to the President's State of the Union speech. Charlie T. called and we had a good visit.

Wednesday, January 21, 2004—partly cloudy, -2° to 11°. Three young guys from "Rural Cap" came here at our request to show us how to save on electricity. Mainly putting in energy saving bulbs. I looked through old "Alaska" magazine looking for articles by Oscar Vogel and Charlie Maise. Found a couple other interesting stories.

Thursday, January 22, 2004—partly cloudy, 2° to 22°. Worked almost all day sorting old Alaska magazines and looking up authors that I am researching.

Friday, January 23, 2004—sunny, 6° to 22°. Went to Glennallen, lunch and shopping.

Saturday, January 24, 2004—sunny, -20° to 0°. Dropped off four tires at Darrel's. Helped Legion Post Commander Joe Roche with a funeral for a native veteran at Copper Center.

Sunday, January 25, 2004—sunny, -23° to -8°. Put battery charger on truck. Read a lot. Wrote letters.

Monday, January 26, 2004—sunny, -27° to -12°. Allen's birthday. Asked us to biscuits and gravy but we had already eaten. Came and got us for coffee. Put more wood in basement.

Tuesday, January 27, 2004—sunny and cloudy, -37° to -20°. Went to Glennallen lunch and shopping. Put more wood in basement.

Wednesday, January 28, 2004—partly cloudy, -25° to 11°. Put more wood in basement. Reloaded a few cartridges. Called Larry Adams. Eva is much better. Paul and Steve called and talked a long time.

Thursday, January 29, 2004—sunny, -25° to -16°. Put wood in basement, smashed tin cans. Plowed snow for Ken Nell.

Friday, January 30, 2004—sunny, -41° to -22°. -51° to Glennallen. Lots of activities shutdown. Put in more wood in basement. Didn't go to Glennallen. Nadia sent birthday card.

Saturday, January 31, 2004—sunny, cloudy, -37° to -14°. Put in more wood.

Read a lot. Sylvia made strawberry and peach jam. Nadia called.

Sunday, February 1, 2004—sunny, clouds south over the ice field, -21° to -6°. Virginia called, Frances and Theresa too. We pumped water this afternoon. Sorted some Alaska magazines.

Monday, February 2, 2004—sunny, -22° to -20°. Allen, Roxanne, Sammy, Reed and the two Eastman grandsons were here for biscuits and gravy breakfast. Didn't do much today.

Tuesday, February 3, 2004—foggy, partly cloudy, -19° to 1°. Went to Glennallen for lunch. Beverly called. Cleaned ashes from barrel stove in basement.

Wednesday, February 4, 2004—cloudy, partly cloudy, then snow flurries, -11° to 12°. We pumped water. Did some target shooting. Went to Legion meeting at post this evening. Saw a moose in the ditch.

Thursday, February 5, 2004—cloudy, snow in night and most all day, five or more inches, 7° to 20°. Vanessa called that they have named the baby Liam, it is a boy. Called Laura. Maggie has a broken collar bone. She slipped off the bed and hit her shoulder on the floor. I cleaned the 30-30 rifle. Little birds swarmed after seeds today.

Friday, February 6, 2004—cloudy to clear, 17° to 10°. Up early. Plowed some of our snow. Put a new bulb in the well. Got ready and went to Glennallen. Lunch, bank, shopping, and Post Office. Senior bus quit on us so they rented a van from Jim Sparks. Jeff called.

Saturday, February 7, 2004—sunny, -2° to 18°. Finished plowing our snow. Plowed Manning's driveway. Pulled some snow off a couple roofs. Fooled around with starting snowgo with no luck. Checked its compression, it is okay. Jeff, Dale and John Paul visited. Darrel and Brenda Gerry had supper with us.

Sunday, February 8, 2004—windy with snow, sunny, cloudy, 2° to 34°. Did some target shooting, mostly cast bullets. Theresa and Nadia both phoned. Got some things ready for trip to Wasilla.

Monday, February 9, 2004—sunny, 4° to 14°. We went to Palmer and Wasilla. Sylvia had a doctor appointment. Lots of running around, shopping. Got my drivers license renewed. Saw four moose near the road. Got a new glass top for coffee percolator.

Tuesday, February 10, 2004—snow in night and all day, some huge flakes, 4° to 31°. About 16" so far. Plowed our here at home. Jim Manning had two vehicles stuck. Went over there and helped him. They had to get Elaine from van into the house in a wheelchair. Jane has been staying there and helped also. Snow this deep is a trial. Pushed our snow back as far as I could. Reloaded some 30-30 cartridges. Read some. Charlie T. called and would like to stay a couple days this weekend.

Wednesday, February 11, 2004—partly cloudy, 23° to 33°. Plowed snow at Bartley's and Anthony's. Got stuck once and had to jack up rear wheels to get chains on. Did some target shooting with the 30-30.

Thursday, February 12, 2004—cloudy and fog south of river, 2° to 24°. Rhynell called and wanted some snow plowed. I plowed Sam's parking place while on way home. Shoveled a path out to bird feeder. Bill Buck of Colorado called with the dates he will be here to look at Old Boot Lake property. I'm mailing a couple books on log cabin building for him to look at. Elli Farmer came over to pick up a video tape. We gave her graduation present ($) early to help her with expenses for a volleyball trip to Australia.

Friday, February 13, 2004—foggy, sunny in the afternoon, 13° to 23°. We went to Glennallen, lunch, and shopping. Left a can of starting fluid at store. Sure needed it when I got home. Put a new needle jet in snowgo carburetor. It still won't start. Took fuel pump off and cleaned it. Shoved snow off camper and a trailer. Snow was over crotch deep at the camper. Called Joe Russo. Tired tonight.

Saturday, February 14, 2004—cloudy, 14° to 26°. Worked on snowgo, slept (tired). Put two wheel barrow loads of wood in basement. Got a bed ready for Charlie and Paul and heated the upstairs. We had a good visit. They got here 4:30 PM. After supper they snow shoed over to their storage shed. We played Paul's favorite card game. Charlie and I visited till 11:30.

Sunday, February 15, 2004—sunny, 2° to 22°. Charlie and Paul broke a trail to the storage shed on their property. Stored two windows and covered a trailer with a tarp. While using my snow rake to clear the roof it broke. I worked on snowgo and got it running. Broke the trail down to our well. Charlie and Paul went riding on the snowgo. Got stuck a couple of times. We plan to reload some cartridges for Charlie this evening.

Monday, February 16, 2004—foggy to clear, very nice, -5° to 14°. Played card game "Zoomania" with Paul. Two moose tore down our raspberries and ate them. The snowgo didn't want to start this afternoon. Finally got it running and Charlie took Paul for a ride. Charlie reloaded some cartridges for one of his rifles. They left about 3:30 PM. Dick Anthony called, thanked me for my snow plowing at their cabin.

Tuesday, February 17, 2004—foggy, cloudy, -9° to 4°. Two moose came back to see if they missed anything to eat in the raspberry patch. We went to Glennallen for lunch and a little shopping.

Wednesday, February 18, 2004—sunny, -15° to 7°. Smashed tin and aluminum cans. Shoveled some snow. David Farmer visited in afternoon. Looking for a tank for fuel oil. Gave him a plastic one.

Thursday, February 19, 2004—cloudy and skiff of snow, -8 to 15°. Rebuilt the snow rake, took three hours.

Friday, February 20, 2004—sunny, 1° to 22°. Went to Glennallen, paid propane bill, and had lunch. Shoveled snow off woodshed and raked it off wood shop. Then plowed that snow into berm pile. Put a new bulb in well for heat.

Saturday, February 21, 2004—sunny, skiff of snow last night, 9° to 27°. Did some target practice with the 30-30. Couple good groups. Started the snowgo, adjusted the choke. Drove it to garden and dumped a bucket of coffee grounds. Allen stopped by just as we were getting ready to go to a Legion Post dinner.

Sunday, February 22, 2004—Sunny, snow slid off south side house roof, 15° to 30°. Cleaned 30-30 and polished its bore and trued up the muzzle. Sorted out some mounts to put on it. Jeff called. Has been back to Sportsman's Warehouse and is excited.

Monday, February 23, 2004—sunny, 11° to 30°. Worked on a deep rear sight on the 30-30. This went slowly. Finally came up with a plan and got part of it done. Pulled a small part of the snow off north side of house roof and shoveled it over to the side.

Tuesday, February 24, 2004—sunny, 10° to 26°. My back was very bad when I got up this morning. We went to Glennallen on senior van for lunch and a little shopping. Put a chunk of fat out for the birds. Did some more practice with 30-30 and cast bullets. Ellie's dog, Monty was here last night. Saw a moose, also three caribou, one set lynx tracks, one fox track and one marten track.

Wednesday, February 25, 2004—sunny, 10° to 28°. Saw a spruce hen track here today. The birds really scarf down the food at their feeder. Did a few little jobs. Wrote my brother Jerry. Tried some target practice, quit to clean the barrel. Beverly called and we had a long talk.

Thursday, February 26, 2004—Cloudy and light snow, -3° to 20°. We were tired today. I did shoot the remainder of the 30-30 cartridges I had reloaded.

Friday, February 27, 2004—Cloudy, then snow showers starting in afternoon, 10° to 22°. We went to lunch in Glennallen and mailed pictures to all four of our kids. Felt a faint earthquake. Cleaned the 30-30 again.

Saturday, February 28, 2004—3" snow last night, sunny, 7° to 24°, Plowed our snow. Shoveled off top of garbage pit and carried out garbage. Reloaded some 30-30s. Jeff, Amy, John Paul and Chelsie stopped by for awhile. Sylvia had made strawberry rhubarb pie. We all had pie and ice cream. Jeff brought me out a scope mounting base to fit the Marlin 30-30. I gave him some Leupold bases.

Sunday, February 29, 2004—cloudy, 0° to 23°. Changed out the light bulb in the well. Snowgo fuel line siphoned out all the gas in the tank. Started working on the 03A3 rifle rear sight. I am converting it to fit the Marlin 30-30. Made a dovetail steel part to fill in the bottom of it. Will drill the holes to attach it tomorrow.

Monday, March 1, 2004—cloudy, 2° to 25°. Worked on modifying an 03A3 rear sight to fit on a Marlin 336. Looks good. Will try it, hopefully tomorrow. Jim Manning visited then came over later with our repaired stove and we loaded his stove that we had used in the interim.

Tuesday, March 2, 2004—light snow last night and all day, 10° to 23°. Went to Glennallen. Cashed our checks, some shopping and lunch.

Wednesday, March 3, 2004—cloudy and light snow all day, 15° to 26°. Built a fire in wood shop and am reworking the mounting holes in the rifle sight. Picked up Bar and went to Legion Post monthly meeting. Got a call from "Sportsman's Warehouse," in Anchorage. I have "won" a cap in the drawing there.

Thursday, March 4, 2004—cloudy and 1/2" snow, 8° to 24°. Worked on rifle sight, made a mistake and have to do part of it over. Ames Company, manufacturer of my snow rake sent me a replacement for the one that broke. Nadia called. Tried to call Charlie and Jeff both.

Friday, March 5, 2004—sunny, 3° to 23°. We went to Glennallen. Lunch, bank and Post Office and shopping. Reloaded some and finished putting rear sight on 30-30. Got truck ready to go to Palmer, Wasilla, and Anchorage.

Saturday, March 6, 2004—partly cloudy, -5° to 18°. We went to Palmer. Met Jeff and John Paul at the gun show. Got some powder and brass and looked at a lot of guns. Went to Wasilla Wal-Mart for a little shopping. Then to Jeff and Amy's. They took us to Sportsman's Warehouse. What a neat place. Got some powder and elk sausage and a cap I won in a drawing. Back at their place Jeff made a spaghetti dinner—very good. We stayed at their place overnight.

Sunday, March 7, 2004—it's warmer here in Anchorage, 10°. Had a good breakfast with the Routt family. Then shopped at Costco and Fred Meyer and went home—glad to be here. Unloaded and put away all the groceries and slept real well.

Monday, March 8, 2004—sunny, -5° to 15°. Cow moose and calf were laying along north side of house this morning. Took pix. Did some reading. Allen called and invited us down to supper this evening. Very good supper and lots of visiting all their kids are at home right now.

Tuesday, March 9, 2004—it's -10° to 23°, mostly sunny, cloudy and light snow late afternoon. We went to Glennallen to lunch and post office. Carol Gregoroff rode in also. Has a sprained ankle and knee. I am reading six of Jeff's "collectable" reloading books. Very interesting.

Wednesday, March 10, 2004—sunny, 8° to 38°. Did a lot of small jobs. Put new bulb in well for hear. Found a leak in snowgo fuel line and fixed it. Mixed more fuel. Assembled new garage broom. Shoot some targets. Reloaded more cartridges. Changed front sight on 30-30. Lisa Billman stopped by and gave Sylvia some flowers.

Thursday, March 11, 2004—sunny, 12° to 32°. Wrote lots of letters. Called grandson Lee birthday wishes. Tried to call Darcy. Shot targets and reloaded more to shoot tomorrow. Jim and Elaine are to be here to supper this evening. Allen packed snow on our lake for a landing strip for Denny Eastman's airplane on skis.

Friday, March 12, 2004—sunny, cloudy in evening, 3° to 30°. We went to Glennallen for lunch. Grizzly Towing spent unknown hours trying to pull a pick up out of a ditch along road. Did more target practice. Still sick with this sinus head cold.

Saturday, March 13, 2004—sunny, 3° to 28°. Built a wood fire this morning. Pretty sick with a runny nose, sore throat, bronchial tubes, headache. Rested quite a bit, two naps. Did go out and shoot some targets. Tried to call Bev, Theresa, Darcy. Theresa and Earl called back. Read some books. Luckily Sylvia didn't get as sick as I did. Saw two bald bull caribou and one young cow.

Sunday, March 14, 2004—partly cloudy, -3° to 32°. Still have this runny nose, head cold. Read a lot. Started preparing the next batch of 30-30 cartridges.

Monday, March 15, 2004—mostly sunny, 5° to 34°. Reloaded and shot more cast bullets. Groups were smaller. Made a hoop of sorts to hold the garbage bag open and easier use.

Tuesday, March 16, 2004—sunny, 13° to 32°. Too sick to go to Glennallen today. Measured fuel in gas and heating oil tanks. Prepared some more brass to load.

Wednesday, March 17, 2004—sunny, 4° to 28°. Still sick. Put gas checks on some bullets and annealed some brass. Burned our trash. Jim forgot to shut his garage and Elaine asked me to come over and close it.

Thursday, March 18, 2004—cloudy and windy, 14° to 17° to 7°. Found a "warm" dead spruce hen along our lane early this morning. Still sick with this head cold. Now Sylvia has it. She ran the sewing machine needle through the end of her forefinger.

Friday, March 19, 2004—sunny, -10° to 13°. We are still sick. Didn't go to Glennallen today. Sylvia stayed in bed most of the day. I took a couple naps. I reclaimed 200 30 caliber gas checks from cast bullets. Made a swage from a steel drill bit to reshape the GC cups. Called Jeff and he found a box of GC in Anchorage. Will send them out Sunday.

Saturday, March 20, 2004—sunny, -21° to 13°. Charlie T. called. We still have this crud. We stayed home and didn't go to the supper at Legion Post. Jim Manning asked me to switch stoves for Elaine if one quits while he is gone. Denny E. took off in his plane this evening.

Sunday, March 21, 2004—sunny, -16° to 32°. Denny was flying his plane again today. Washed the dirt off my skids. Charlie T. and two friends stopped in on their way to Delta Junction to hunt buffalo. Charlie brought a dozen yellow roses to Sylvia. Also a big sack of oranges. He bought my no-wax skis. We had a good visit. Allen F. brought us two pieces blackberry pie and ice cream. Wow!

Monday, March 22, 2004—sunny, 2° to 42°. Caribou were moving east on the south side of our lake. We saw quite a few but didn't total a count. They consisted of both bulls and cows. We are still sick. Allen brought us chicken soup and hot bread for lunch. Did some more target practice.

Tuesday, March 23, 2004—sunny and some breeze, 9° to 41°. Saw a few caribou go east on our lake. Reloaded and shot more 30-30 cartridges. 2/3 of snow on North side of house slide off the roof and I plowed it over to the west. Installed the lights left on buzzer in the blue pickup. Grandson Lee called.

Wednesday, March 24, 2004—sunny, 16° to 40°. Saw no caribou. Reload more 30-30s for target practice. Lee called again planning his trip up here. Beverly called while was plowing the snow that slid off garage roof away to a snow pile. Using the spotting scope I saw a trail of something big and heavy over on Heavenly Ridge. Nadia called and visited.

Thursday, March 25, 2004—partly cloudy, 3/4" snow, 12° to 28°. Wrote letters. Some little jobs and got ready to cast some bullets. Lee called again. He has arranged time for his vacation and will come to Alaska. Charlie arrived 11:00 PM and we visited about the hunt till 1:00 AM.

Friday, March 26, 2004—mostly cloudy, 1° to 18°. More visiting. Sylvia went to Glennallen on senior van. We gave Charlie one of our TVs which has trouble holding the signal. Charlie and I switched TVs on dish receiver and he programmed them. Put the Magnavox in its box, carried it out to his car. Charlie went skiing before supper. He partially stripped his Savage 250-3000 and we looked it all over and then he oiled it. Looks like snow this evening.

Saturday, March 27, 2004—partly cloudy, -4° to 22°. Charlie had toast and coffee with me and headed for Homer and home. Rested some. Took a couple naps. The crud still hangs on. Switched scopes on the .338 Winchester, misplaced and hunted for the scope base that fits the marlin 30-30. Found it in the wood shop right where I left it. A red squirrel came to bird feeder three times today.

Sunday, March 28, 2004—mostly thin clouds, -4° to 32°. Really tired this morning. Slept extra. Took peep sight off the Marlin and put a scope on it. Reloaded some cast bullets and sighted in the scope. Shot some excellent groups. Brad Behrendt called and thanked us for the little boost with his truck. Jeff called and talked reloading. The snowbirds are back.

Monday, March 29, 2004—sunny and breezy, 2" now in night, 9° to 32°. Plowed our snow. Cast some 150 grain 30 cal bullets. Allen came over. Brought Sylvia a roasted chicken. We visited and ate ice cream and cookie. I lubed some bullets and reloaded 25 30-30's. Fred Rungee visited and brought a sack of oranges and ice cream.

Tuesday, March 30, 2004—skiff of snow, mostly sunny and strong winds in the afternoon, -4° to 25°. We went to Glennallen for lunch, paid electric bill and a little shopping. Put gas checks on some cast bullets and lubed them. A large flock of snow buntings are feeding on sunflower seeds outside our picture window! Gross beaks, red poll feed there also.

Wednesday, March 31, 2004—sunny, -14° to 19°. Worked on senior care application. Did a few small jobs. Put gas checks and lube on some cast bullets. Sure is a big flock of snow buntings that keep showing up here to eat the sunflower seeds.

Thursday April 1, 2004—sunny, -18° to 20°. Saw three caribou going west today. There are even more snow buntings coming for sunflower seeds. Cast more bullets and put gas checks and lube on them. Worked over another mould for use tomorrow.

Friday, April 2, 2004—we got four inches of snow, 1° to 28°. Went to Glennallen and mailed Sylvia's package of baby blanket and sock "monkey" to Vanessa. The road was really slick with some vehicles in the ditch. The meal wasn't so good. I plowed our snow and reloaded some more cartridges. No snow buntings here today.

Saturday, April 3, 2004—cloudy, sunny, cloudy, 14° to 43°. Did some target practice. Plowed snow at Anthony's cabin. Stopped by Sam Weaver's but he wasn't home. Cleaned the 30-30. Jeff called.

Sunday, April 4, 2004—sunny to cloudy and windy in early evening, 8° to 43°. Chronographed some 30-30 loads. Cast more bullets. Put GC and lubed them. Really tired this evening. Looked the mountains over with spotting scope. Only saw a couple small avalanches. Boo were on the lake.

Monday, April 5, 2004—partly cloudy to cloudy and windy, 24° to 44°. Put a new knob on lid for mailbox. Repaired a fur stretcher. Shot some targets and reloaded more cartridges. We went to a steak dinner at Allen and Roxanne's. Had a good visit. Pulled more snow off north side of house roof.

Tuesday, April 6, 2004—partly cloudy, 27° to 49°. Went to Glennallen. Bank, shopping, and lunch. Substitute driver rode with us on way home. Kim is her name, I believe. Tested a new load for the 30-30 this afternoon. All snow has slid of house roof. Had to shovel some away from house. It appears there is seismic exploration just west of Glennallen Mile 177.

Wednesday, April 7, 2004—mostly sunny, 30° to 50°. Checked fluids in truck. Repaired snow plow turn signal. Adjusted choke on snow go. Put a new light bulb in well. Went to Legion meeting at post. Rode in with Bart and Rosemary.

Thursday, April 8, 2004—mostly cloudy, some sun, 23° to 44°. Took winter tires off old blue and put summer tires on. Repaired the left turn signal on plow truck yesterday and mounted it back on today. Took air compressor out of the basement and to the garage and used it while changing wheels and tires on old blue. I've been watching the mountains to the south for sign of bears with no luck. I did see a bald eagle that was hunting. The snow bunting ceased coming here for seeds.

Friday, April 9, 2004—mostly sunny, 29° to 45°. Went to Glennallen for lunch. Repair came for Lyman bullet luber. Installed part and tried it out on some cast bullets. Okay! Some packed snow softened up and I plowed it off to the side. Joints hurt tonight. Called my brother Marion and wished him Happy Birthday.

Saturday, April 10, 2004—sunny, 17° to 44°. Started working on some fur stretchers. Patti Billman invited us over to dinner this evening. Her two sisters, John Wood and two son's and grandkids and Betty (Great grandmother) were there. Had a nice visit and excellent prime rib in dinner. Sylvia saw one eagle on the way to Lake Louise.

Sunday, April 11, 2004—sunny, 10° to 40°. Sylvia counted 85 caribou going east on our lake this morning. Thirteen returned going west but scared into going south towards the river. We got Sylvia's sewing machine fixed. It had a loose set screw. Allen and Roxanne had us over to dinner, ham and all the goodies. Sylvia took a pan of yams.

Monday, April 12, 2004—sunny, 19° to 44°. Made one mink stretcher. Switched bulbs in the well. Stored the snowgo for the summer. Jim Manning brought some of their left over flower seeds.

Tuesday, April 13, 2004—sunny, 19° to 47°. Five caribou went west on our lake. Loaded some 30-06 and shot them. Reloaded the cases and cleaned the rifle. Didn't feel well this morning. Sylvia started getting the greenhouse ready. Temp reached 95° in there today!

Wednesday, April 14, 2004—sunny, 23° to 45°. Lots of caribou crossing the lake today. Two male robins were in yard as we were eating supper. Pushed the snow back from south side of our lane. A heavy angle iron broke on the plow. Worked very hard and got it repaired. Had to weld it. The welder started throwing oil all over. Managed to finish the job—lucky. Very tired and back really hurts. Sylvia fixed some fish that Charlie left here—good eating.

Thursday, April 15, 2004—partly cloudy, 18° to 47°. Not so many caribou on the lake today. Glassed Heavenly Ridge but saw nothing new. Shot the P17 Enfield with good results. Reloaded more and cleaned the rifle. Steve phoned. We had a good and long visit. I may sell my Browning 10-gauge to him.

Friday, April 16, 2004—Snowed here, melted on highway, 20° to 40°. We went to Wasilla. (Sylvia had a doctor appointment.) We went on to Anchorage, had lunch and then shopped Sportsman's Warehouse, Lowe's Hardware, filled with gasoline and got groceries at Costco's. Stopped at Fred Meyer (new store) and shopped there on our way through Palmer. Sure glad to get home safe and sound. We thanked the Lord for that.

Saturday, April 17, 2004—Snowed all night and half the day (four inches), 30° to 47°. Lots of it melted off today. Started writing a letter. The word processor space bar has quit. Plowed snow from yard and driveway. Allen and Reed brought over a baked chicken. Took a nap. We went to a dinner at Legion Post. Sam Weaver rode home with us. Theresa phoned.

Sunday, April 18, 2004—foggy then sunny with breeze, 20° to 45°. Wrote some letters. Shot the P17 Enfield. Got good groups and cleaned it. Started reloading the empties. Called Larry Adams. His mother, Eva is recovering well. Saw a huge flock of swans flying west. Saw a robin. Lots of snow melted today.

Monday, April 19, 2004—partly cloudy to snow showers, 18° to 44°. Did some more rifle load development before it warmed up and got muddy. It went pretty well. Took a three layer chocolate cake down to Allen Farmer family. Glassed the mountains. Two swans were back on our lake. Sylvia made three peach pies. Sam W called—he saw a small grizzly track at Slide Mountain Trailhead.

Tuesday, April 20, 2004—snow melted off today, 27° to 44°. Sun came out this afternoon. We went to Glennallen lunch. Worked on a fur stretcher and reloaded cast bullets.

Wednesday, April 21, 2004—bright sunny, 17° to 47°. A bunch of caribou came uphill and went past the greenhouse just to the west. Two swans are setting on the lake ice. Shot the P17 Enfield. Did ok. Tried to scrape hard pack snow off our driveway. Visited Henry and Sally.

Thursday, April 22, 2004—cloudy, 30° to 44°. We went to Wasilla (Sylvia had another doctor appointment.) We did some shopping for the garden and greenhouse. I got an oil filter for the truck. The round trip was uneventful. Picked up onion sets for Sam Weaver.

Friday, April 23, 2004—cloudy and snow squalls, clear later in the afternoon, 27° to 46°. We went to Glennallen. Sylvia traded rolls of pennies for cash. Did some shopping. Had lunch. Back at home did more load development on the P17 Enfield. Reloaded 25 cartridges for P17 Enfield. Scraped off more hard pack snow from our driveway as it softens.

Saturday, April 24, 2004—partly cloudy with one snow squall, 28° to 48°. Shot the P17 Enfield again today. Raked some gravel in our driveway. Jacked up the left front wheel on the car. Worked on the snowgo choke. Worked on a stretcher for fox skins. Finished it and put two coats of varithane on it. We had Darrel and Brenda here to dinner and had a good visit.

Sunday, April 25, 2004—Snowed till mid afternoon, 29° to 49°. Worked on the fur stretchers for the Miller boy. Sawed to size and planed some lumber dry. It is so wet it warps when I try to make stretcher of it. We went to a small party, supper that Elaine and Jim put on at Allen and Roxanne's.

Monday, April 26, 2004—partly cloudy, 32° to 50°. Prepared snowgo for storage. Couldn't get plug out of old blue's tranny to ck. the oil. Did a lot of small jobs. Supper time Allen and Reed brought over a picture of the 80 wolves that McMahan got this winter. Cleaned a rifle for Jim Manning. Saw some winter swans, two eagles and two ravens are eating something on top of lake ice. Liam was born today to Granddaughter Vanessa and husband, Scott Beckett.

Tuesday, April 27, 2004—cloudy all day, 30° to 50°. We went to Glennallen to lunch. I am keeping a fire going in woodshop. Drying some boards. Eagles are still hanging around. Read all evening. Had a couple of phone calls.

Wednesday, April 28, 2004—cloudy, very little sun, 23° to 48°. Keeping a fire in woodshop to dry lumber. Did a bunch of small jobs. Joe brought heating oil and unleaded gas. Tried to cast some bullets but the mould was working poorly. Wrote a couple letters.

Thursday, April 29, 2004—cloudy, sunny, 29° to 53°. Sylvia's Birthday! Mary and Cal Gilcrease brought her gifts and a decorated cake. Visited quite awhile and had a bite of lunch with us. They just got back from Arkansas. I put ashes on the snow on the garden. Worked on fur stretchers. Got two made. Put two coats of varithane on them. Took Sylvia to Eureka for supper. Looks like Ed Farmer has an airplane at his shop. Eagles still feed on the lake ice. Sylvia got a few birthday phone calls.

Friday, April 30, 2004—sunny, cloudy, 31° to 54°. Put another coat of varithane on the fur stretchers. We went to Glennallen for lunch. Back home I assembled the stretchers. Straightened the chimney pipe in the greenhouse. Tried to cast some bullets and couldn't get good ones so I quit. Allen and Roxanne had us down for clam chowder. She had made a cake for Sylvia's birthday.

Saturday, May 1, 2004—sunny with some breezes, 35° to 59°. Eagles still occupy part of lake. One flew by dining room window. Cast a couple hundred bullets using two moulds at same time. Sylvia washed outside windows of house. Picked up some bullets out a snow berm. Removed gas checks from them. Jeff, Amy and John Paul stopped by. Jarret (his son) got to take his ATV for the day. Henry and (Sam who picked up his onion sets) were here. Henry wanted a picture of Sylvia and me. We called Nadia. Plants are in the greenhouse overnight.

Sunday, May 2, 2004—rain, clearing somewhat in the afternoon, 38° to 58°. Jeff, Amy and John Paul got here just in time for breakfast this morning. I fooled around with some subsonic loads that would be quieter for pesky squirrels. Some water is standing on the lake ice. Bald eagle flew by a couple times today.

Monday, May 3, 2004—30° to 57° here, and 64° in Palmer-Wasilla. Took Sylvia to her doctor for removal of more stitches. We had a lunch and shopping at Wal-Mart and Carr's for groceries. Some construction is going on at Caribou Creek. Sylvia saw some sheep on Sheep Mountain.

Tuesday, May 4, 2004—sunny, 30° to 62°. Shoveled snow pile from yard on north side of house. Visited Ed and looked at the plane he recently bought. Picked up bullets from snow berm and removed gas checks. Got things ready to clean Legion Post rifles. I saw a couple snowshoe hares.

Wednesday, May 5, 2004—sunny, cloudy in evening, 30° to 69°. We drove up Lake Louise Road to mile 11 trail to our property. Has lots of snow. Saw some pintail, mallard, teal and golden eye ducks. Caribou tracks. Went to Glennallen for lunch. Cashed checks. Cleaned rifles at Legion Post. Went to shooting range and picked up some brass. Snow and ice melted off of lawn on north side of house. Went to monthly Legion meeting. Bart Bartley rode home with us to his place.

Thursday, May 6, 2004—cloudy, sunny, partly cloudy, 30° to 68°. Did some small chores. Took the .338 to gravel pit to sight in a four power scope on it. Went well. Picked up more cast bullets out of melting snow. Put up screen door. Jim and Caleb Miller came over for the fur stretcher I made for them. Started cleaning the .338 Winchester.

Friday, May 7, 2004—partly cloudy. 43° to 70°. Very nice. Finished cleaning the .338 did a few small jobs. Rosemary and Mary C. visited Sylvia. Got Molly the car ready and put her up for sale out at the road. Reloaded 20 cartridges for .338 Winchester.

Saturday, May 8, 2004—sunny and some breeze, 39° to 69°. Went to gravel pit at Army Trail, to sight in .338. It shoots erratically. Did pick up 14 pieces of brass. Hooked up water lines to gardens and green house. Picked up some spruce cones from lawn. The yellow jackets have claimed the lumber lean to. Lots of gull and eagle activity on our lake.

Sunday, May 9, 2004—sunny, partly cloudy, cloudy, 35° to 55°. Cal bought our "Molly" car. Came and got it in the afternoon. Cleaned on .338 Winchester rifle barrel. Gave Sylvia a Mother's Day card and took her to Eureka for a prime rib dinner. Our lake is starting to open up. Swans have water to swim in.

Monday, May 10, 2004—partly cloudy to cloudy, 34° to 63°. Reloaded more .338, and remounted the scope and went to gravel pit. Got scope sighted in and shot some good groups. The eagle is hanging out at our lake a lot. Goldeneye ducks are flying in search of nesting places. The lake opened up more today.

Tuesday, May 11, 2004—cloudy, light rain, sunny, 40° to 60°. Lots more of our lake is open. Ducks flying, swans, eagles and large gulls, robins, kestrels etc. Walked down to well. Later walked down to garden trying to find her garden sprinklers. She found them in a bucket on top of upright freezer. Put fertilizer and lime on lawn. Sylvia started watering the lawn. Grass is greening up. Cleaned the .338 Winchester. Cleaning was easier today. Henry Johnson called and talked quite a while.

Wednesday, May 12, 2004—cloudy, to clear and sunny, 36° to 60°. Went shooting the 30 br at gravel pit. Didn't do well. Didn't bring right front rest. Got back lunch time. Then Henry came over, took pictures of us and our place. He asked me to go with him and watch how to e-mail pictures. Spent several hrs over there. Came home watched the news. Ate supper and loaded more 30 br cartridges and recorded today's targets and results. The kestrels are mating. Lots of ducks here. The ice is almost gone. Allen and Samantha visited this evening.

Thursday, May 13, 2004—sunny, 35° to 66°. Went to Army Trail gravel pit. This went fair with the 30 br. Today the .338 Win again shot erratically. Bummer. Back at home, had lunch Sylvia wanted bathroom vanity stained. That had a couple problems, but got it done, needs finish coat tomorrow. Seeded grass on a small area of lawn. Lake ice is out.

Friday, May 14, 2004—sunny, 38° to 68°. Went to lunch in Glennallen. Did some shopping. Gave the notice of the sale of "Molly" car to DMV office. Saw a caribou along highway. Put some polyurethane on bathroom vanity. Started the Suzuki 4 x 4. Raked some dead grass off the lawn. Marvin Obermiller visited a little while. Switched scopes on the .338 Winchester magazine.

    A fire started southeast of Glennallen near Hoover radiator this afternoon. Out of control at 7:00 PM. Big tanker planes with retardant, etc. flying out from Palmer and Fairbanks. Fire crews coming from all over.

Dispatcher requesting fire investigator to come yet this evening.

Saturday, May 15, 2004—sunny, windy afternoon, 38° to 68°. Went to gravel pit with the Weaver scope on .338 and it shot really well. Yea!! Burned trash at home. Put hand pump in barrel of gasoline and filled the truck. Vanity doors are too wet yet. Cal and Mary ask us to ride with them to a dinner at Legion Post. New officers were installed. Good steak dinner. We saw a thin cow moose browsing on willows in ditch.

Sunday, May 16, 2004—mostly sunny and windy afternoon, 32° to 64°. Checked our well. Spoke to our new neighbor who bought Rudbecks place. Put air in snowgo trailer and Suzuki. Vacuumed woodshop. Put polyurethane on bath vanity again. We were playing dominoes just before supper time when Sylvia thought she saw two caribou on south side of our lake running hard. I turned to look and exclaimed "Those are bears!" A Toklat grizzly, sow and large cub ran along the lake then turned off on a trail going over towards the river. Called Allen and he saw bears also. About 11:00 PM the bears came from the east again.

Monday, May 17, 2004—partly cloudy and breezy, 31° to 65°. I went to their place and talked to David in the afternoon. Worked on the upper garden. Walked a mile. Straightened the wall-roof of the lumber lean to. Parked plow truck for summer. Made a liner for the wood shop stove. Cal stopped by to tell me about a silver tip grizzly walking by their living room window and leaving by walking south on the trail.

Tuesday, May 18, 2004—partly cloudy and breezy in afternoon and evening, 37° to 65°. We went to Glennallen for lunch. Visited with friends, Jay and Rella, who now live in Utah. Did a little shopping. Tilled both gardens. Had to repair throttle cable on tiller. Its reverse belt broke also. Finished job anyhow. Typed up yogurt receipt for Sylvia and made copies for other ladies. Jim Manning came over and asked about trails for a ride out in the mountains.

Wednesday, May 19, 2004—partly cloudy and good breeze, 38° to 66°. Chopped some tree roots out of small garden. Put another coat of polyurethane on the vanity doors. Painted a stand for the woodshop stove. Joe Russo has another buyer for the remote parcel. We went to graduation exercise in Glennallen. Ellie Farmer graduated as Valedictorian. We are proud of her. Afterwards we visited Darrel and Brenda and got to see their motor home. We saw five caribou bulls on way home tonight.

Thursday, May 20, 2004—partly cloudy with breeze, 40° to 65°. Cleaned corner of woodshop. Put a liner in its stove and repaired damper. Put polyurethane on part of vanity door. Put different belt on tiller reverse and oiled two idlers.

Mary and Kari Odden visited in afternoon. Sylvia got lower garden mostly planted.

Friday, May 21, 2004—partly cloudy, 33° to 70°. We went to lunch and shopping in Glennallen. Sylvia worked in garden when we got back and I made a repair on the storage shed. Ate a bite of supper and went to visit Cal and Mary. Stopped by Henry Johnson's place on our way home. He showed us how to scan and view pictures on a computer.

Saturday, May 22, 2004—cloudy, partly cloudy and breezy, 37° to 71°. Worked a lot of the day on repairing the storage shed door. I'm almost done. Allen visited an hour and Dale Routt about an hour. He showed his hunt in which he killed a 10-½ Kodiak grizzly. Very good movie. He gave me some 30-06 cartridges. Sylvia finished planting garden and cleaned the bathroom in anticipation of guests from Colorado. I have lots of splinters in my hands from the old plywood shed door.

Sunday, May 23, 2004—cloudy, sprinkles, rain in afternoon and evening, 37° to 63°. Put more polyurethane on bathroom vanity. Walked a mile and half. Rested. We went to a party for Ellie (graduation). All were close friends. Visited. Lots of good food. Called Nadia. Talked to Chuck a while.

Monday, May 24, 2004—cloudy and rain most all day, 35° to 55°. Tried to walk a mile but a bone in my left foot hurt too badly. Started the Suzuki and moved the snowgo trailer out of the yard and to its place out back. Repairing and painted the plywood carrying case for my ice auger. Sylvia is still cleaning house. It looks great.

Tuesday, May 25, 2004—cloudy and some showers, 38° to 55°. We went to Glennallen for lunch shopping. Paid propane and electric bills. Denny Eastman visited, asked about Tyone Creek and tributaries. Wants to buy one claim on Bukia Creek for $5000. Went to Allen's and welded two eye bolts and put them on truck bed. Made signs to guide the Colorado guys to our place. Put away the ice auger in its repaired case. Bill Buck called in the evening asking about weather gear, use of Odden's cabin, fishing, food, gifts etc. Just at bedtime I saw a moose swimming from the north side of the west end of our lake. When it reached the south side it walked east a ways and swam in a zigzag back to the north side and out of sight, possibly exiting near our boat landing. This could have been a maneuver to evade a grizzly. They do this especially at calving time. I waterproofed my good boots and repaired my buck knife holster.

Wednesday, May 26, 2004—cloudy and showers, 41° to 57°. Started cutting brush on our property lines here at home. Put another ballast on the fluorescent light in woodshop. We went to dinner with Darrel and Brenda who drove their motor home to Mendeltna campground and ask us to have pizza with them.

Thursday, May 27, 2004—partly cloudy, hard rain in night with light shower today, 41° to 64°. Got my gear ready for trip out to Old Boot Lake tomorrow. Bob and Kahren visited us this morning. Just as they were leaving Bud and Gary Swecker (from Motley Minnesota) drove in. They stayed a half hour or so. Told us Bob Mick (used to be our neighbor and friend) committed suicide and other news from our old Minnesota community where we once lived. Bill Buck and Tim Witehead arrived about 6:30 PM. They are from near Boulder Colorado. 8500' elevation. We visited three hours and they went to bed.

Friday, May 28, 2004—rain in night, cloudy and clearing later, 41° to 54°. Bill and Tim had breakfast with us, they brought eggs and ham. Then we loaded our gear. Bill got in with me and Tim followed in their rented car. We drove to the trailhead at Mile 11 Lake Louise Road. Unloaded Suzuki and they loaded their two large packs on it. I led the way and they walked. Several times they had to help me keep the ATV from upsetting. The rain and "hail" had the trail running water. They got to see griz, wolf and moose tracks. Bill found ½ of a moose calf hoof. Parked the ATV and walked the .6 tenths mile as a crow flies to our property on Old Boot Lake. Then pictures and video tape. Bill taped everything about the property. Went to Odden's cabin first. Ate our lunch then walked the survey lines. When we got close to monument #1 we turned off on a likely looking place to locate a trail back to the Seismic trail and the Suzuki. They followed me to the First Creek and made sure that I got across it safely. When I got to the pickup I loaded ATV and started home. Stopped in a gravel pit and found quite a few .223 Remington brass. Unloaded things when I got home. Boy am I tired. Note: At about 1-¼ miles from Lake Louise Road I saw a pair of "Taverner's" Canadian geese.

Saturday, May 29, 2004—cloudy, partly cloudy, cloudy, 37° to 61°. We didn't participate in memorial services at Legion Post in Glennallen because we were involved in selling our remote parcel. Did some small things here. Had phone calls. Jeff and his family came. He borrowed some tools to service his new to him Jeep Cherokee. Later Bill Buck and Tim Whitehead stopped by. They enjoyed Old Boot Lake. Saw grayling. Located a building sight and standing dead spruce to cut for cabin logs and lumber. They walked all the way around the lake today. Their packs got heavy before they got out to the Lake Louise Road. He thinks his wife will approve purchasing the property and will let us know Wednesday. Allen told me the location of a grizzly bear. I drove up to the gravel pit Jeff and family are camping in and told them of the bear in case they wanted to hunt it.

I then went to the gravel pit I usually shoot in because Allen said he and David would be shooting David's new rifle. Allen left soon after I got there.

David and I got his rifle sighted in, and then I took him home. He then had to show me his new Yamaha 660 ATV. It's really nice. Laura called today and talked to Sylvia for awhile and then me. She has a heavy burden, we wish it was easier for her.

Sunday, May 30, 2004—sunny, 38° to 63°. Our washing machine has been broke down. Today was my first free time to try to fix it. I had salvaged spare parts in the past for just such an emergency. Switched out one of the controls. Put things back in their position and it is washing clothes as I write this. Tried to call all the kids. We wanted to share the latest news. Bill Buck called to say his wife concurs with his judgment and to buy our remote parcel. Yea! Nadia called back and we got to tell her. Mowed our lawn. Sylvia took a much needed nap. Allen and Reed came up and asked us to have supper with them. Cal and Mary were there also. Lots of hunting stories were told by Cal and Allen.

Monday, May 31, 2004—sunny, cloudy, 43° to 66°. Rain in night and looking raining now again. Built a fastener on the gun boot. Sorted cartridge brass. Restacked some wood. Re-attached a tarp over one opening on a lean to. A moose cow and calf walked through our yard. Checked the fluid in the transmission on the truck. Grandson Steve called and we talked for over an hour. Grandson Lee called to tell us his time of arrival and flight number this next Wednesday. Theresa called and talked for about an hour. Jeff called a couple times.

Tuesday, June 1, 2004—partly cloudy with sprinkles, 41° to 62°. We went to Glennallen for lunch. Learned that the new senior van is in Anchorage. We are getting ready to go to Anchorage and pick up grandson Lee at the airport. The nesting robins are busy catching bugs in the lawn to feed their broods in the nest. Laura called today to talk about the care of Maggie and how it is going. Joe Russo called this evening to tell me it may take four weeks to get the sale of our remote parcel closed!

Wednesday, June 2, 2004—partly cloudy, 40° to 61°. It rain some of the time on the way to Wasilla. Did a little shopping there, went on to Anchorage and more shopping getting everything on our list. Then we went to the International Airport, met Lee when his flight arrived. Went to Royal for to eat then to Wal-Mart in Wasilla for Lee. On the way to our place he took lots of pictures. I spotted a cow moose and he got a picture of it. Unloaded groceries here at home. We are all tired tonight.

Thursday, June 3, 2004—mostly sunny, 34° to 60°. Went to Herb Simons and Lee got his fishing license. Put a new wheel and tire on the wheelbarrow. Filled the grease gun and little jobs. Practiced with my fly rod. After supper Lee and I went to Ryan Lake. Put in the canoe and paddled to some rising fish. We caught six rainbows. Stopped by the Grizzly Country Store. We cleaned the fish when we got home. Boy am I tired.

Friday, June 4, 2004—sunny, 34° to 41°. We went to Buffalo Lake fishing for rainbows. Caught three. Saw an arctic loon and a large gull. That lake was very low. Cleaned the fish. Took my spinning reel apart and lubed it. Located another anchor. Showed Lee a kestrel that is nesting here. Saw some large scoter ducks on our lake. I am tired tonight. Beautiful evening.

Saturday, June 5, 2004—mostly sunny, breezy, smoke in air, high cloudy in the afternoon and evening, 47° to 75°. Went to Cash Creek to fish for grayling with no luck. I found a small spinner. Talked to Denny Eastman. Came back home. Lee went four wheeling on the Suzuki, 17 miles. Rigged up saw horse so Lee could barbeque steaks for supper. Got some prospecting gear gathered together. We plan to go to Alfred Creek.

Sunday, June 6, 2004—partly cloudy and sprinkles on Alfred Creek, 50° to 79°. We loaded our gear in old pickup and went to Alfred Creek. Had to leave pickup and walk to Fossil Creek. This spring's run off must have been a doozie! Creek looks lots different with much sign of high water. We tried in several areas to find gold. A few small specks were all we saw. Finally quit and came home at 7:00 PM. We saw parka squirrels, caribou bulls, a moose and seven swans on Tahneta Lake. Lee got lots of pictures.

Monday, June 7, 2004—cloudy and rain till noon or so, then slowly clearing, 51° to 69°. We cancelled our fishing plans. Real Estate Joe called to tell us the buyer of our remote parcel has signed the papers. Lee and I did some service work on the old plow truck. He saw a crack in a weld on the plow attachment bracket.

Tuesday, June 8, 2004—rained quite a bit here today, 45° to 65°. We went to lunch at Glennallen. Then to Copper Center to fish the Klutina River at Copper Center, with no luck. Went to Gulkana. No one was fishing there. Stopped at shooting range and picked up some brass and boxes. Stopped at Darrel and Brenda's. Had coffee and visit. Gave me some brass and bug dope. Came home and ate supper and went to Bartley's on Snowshoe Lake. Fished for grayling. I caught one on a Meps spinner. Lee couldn't get one to hit his flies. Ralph called talked fishing a little while then said "Oh Conner!" and said he would call later. I think this was his grandson in Montana, maybe had hurt himself.

Wednesday, June 9, 2004—cloudy, partly cloudy, 43° to 63°. Denny E. called to offer Lee the chance to go with him to a couple lakes to fish. Lee jumped at the offer. They were gone over two hours and saw a bull moose and caught some nice big rainbows. I did some paper work for VA prescriptions. Joe Russo called, remote parcel sale papers are ready for our signatures. Bill Buck called to tell us he had signed papers and would not be up here to start the building of a cabin. We called son Paul his birthday greetings. Talked to grandson Steve also.

Thursday, June 10, 2004—cloudy, rain in night and most all day, 41° to 59°. We rested most all day. Joe Russo advised us the Real Estate closing on the remote parcel will be about the end of June! Took Lee to Lake Louise and the creek in back of Wolverine Lodge. There we asked permission and fished for grayling, catching them on both flies and spinners. We only caught enough for one meal. Lee bought us soft drinks at the Lodge. We got home, cleaned the fish and it was almost 12:30 AM.

Friday, June 11, 2004—mostly sunny, 38° to 57°. Loafed a lot. Put away the fishing gear. Watched the farewell services for President Ronald Regan. A bald eagle is actively hunting ducks here at our lake. Gave Lee a book on how to tie flies for fishing. Lee and I straightened the top of cook stove and added a stiffener.

Saturday, June 12, 2004—partly cloudy, 37° to 67°. We took Lee in to catch his plane back to Minneapolis. Sylvia gave him a diamond willow carving and I drilled it and made a base for a lamp for him to assemble when he gets home. We did some shopping. Took Lee to lunch at Royal Fork. Traffic seemed to be lighter than usual today. Lee saw a duck in one of the nest boxes this morning.

Sunday, June 13, 2004—partly cloudy, rain in night, 41° to 69°. Sprayed some weeds and grass. Sprayed some carpenter ants. Jim Manning and his grandson came over. They had Allen's ATV stuck on the trail starting up Slide Mountain. Jim's ATV blew a fuse and wouldn't run. They asked me to get the stuck machine out so they could pull the broke down ATV home. Everything went well. Sylvia mowed the grass today. Bob Rudbeck visited. Put some gasoline in truck. Racked some more dead grass out of the lawn.

Monday, June 14, 2004—sunny, 46° to 72°. Did some small jobs. Worked on the canoe paddles. Epoxied a split in one. Got several letters ready to mail tomorrow.

Tuesday, June 15, 2004—partly cloudy, 44° to 71°. We went to Glennallen for lunch, Post Office, and bank. Ron drove us to his place to see the new senior bus. Cut brush in our east side survey line. Fooled around with the old sprayer with no luck. Worked on canoe paddles. Joe Russo sent us the earnest money receipt and agreement to purchase papers for Old Boot Lake property.

Wednesday, June 16, 2004—partly cloudy to cloudy and windy in the afternoon,

45° to 67°. Piled some brush that I had cut in the east line of our property. Mailed the purchase agreement papers back to Joe Russo. Did some small jobs. Pulled some 5/8" steel cable out of the brush. Worked on two canoe paddles and put varithane them and a pair of wood-babish snow shoes. Mary Gilcrease gave Sylvia some roses. Evelyn was with her.

Thursday, June 17, 2004—mostly sunny with some wind, 47° to 78°. Finally put the last coat of polyurethane on the two canoe paddles and the snowshoes. Bob and Kahren came over late in the afternoon. A rabbit ran across our yard. I think some young kestrels are flying about.

Friday, June 18, 2004—sunny, 54° to 80°. Went to Glennallen for lunch, shopping. Finished polyurethaning the third canoe paddle. Went for a walk. Philip Gilcrease stopped by to answer questions about my word processor. It is not practicable to repair. Saw fresh moose tracks here. Lots of young robins are flying around here.

Saturday, June 19, 2004—sunny with good breeze, 53° to 80s. Repaired a cardboard box for the word processor monitor. Loaded rifle cleaning gear in truck, plus Sylvia's pot luck dish for Legion Post picnic. Went to Glennallen and cleaned the post rifles. Went over to the ball field for a picnic of barbequed chicken and hamburgers. About 16 people showed up. Bob Rudbeck whispered in Sylvia's ear that a wealthy man with means was looking for a place to buy around here (because we plan to sell our main property in the future).

Sunday, June 20, 2004—sunny with breezes, 62° to 85°. We went to church at campground on Lake Louise. There was a potluck picnic afterwards. Small crowd today. Refilled old blue's gas tank with measured gallons. It gets 22.35 miles per gallon. Didn't do much else. Bob and Kahren came over and asked if it would be okay for Matt to come over and talk about buying our place. Visited a while and went home. Nadia and Laura both called today for Father's Day and Grandpa's Day. Nadia and Chuck have bought a home near Laura and Brad and have put their place up for sale. Rosemary Bartley called and asked if this Matt person could come over in the morning to see us. Sylvia told them yes.

Monday, June 21, 2004—sunny with breezes, 52° to 84°. We hustled around here this morning. Did small jobs making house and yard neat. Matt and Marla? came with Rosemary Bartley to look at our place. He said he liked the place and when told him what we wanted, he asked if we might take less. I didn't say no or yes but offered to include a number of items he might be interested in. They are going back to Michigan and will call us with a decision. Called Patti Billman for the name of her lawyer.

Tuesday, June 22, 2004—sunny and strong breezes, 60° to 84°. We went to Glennallen to lunch. I forgot to take adds to post to sell the pickup camper and the canopy. Did my walk. Made several phone calls regarding sale of our home. Came up with what seems to be a workable plan.

Wednesday, June 23, 2004—sunny with strong breeze, 51° to 83°. Took a walk, then started sanding on the 30-30 rifle stock. We still haven't heard from the title company when the closing will be. Denny E. caught a 53" king salmon yesterday. Sylvia waters the lawn and garden a lot of the time. It's hot and dry here. Raised some dents in the rifle stock with steam.

Thursday, June 24, 2004—sunny, 57° to 86°. Got one coat varithane on rifle stock after filling a few dents. Cleaned the tubular magazine. Roxanne told us about the days leading up to her step-grandfather's death. Frank had cancer of the throat. Ed Farmer brought me two small buckets of gravel to fill a small place along our lane. Suzie and Henry Brugg from Colorado stopped by on their way to their piece of Alaska out by McCarthy.

Friday, June 25, 2004—sunny, 57° to 87°. Went to Glennallen for lunch. Put up "for sale" signs to sell the pick up camper and over-cab camper. Still putting coats of varithane on the rifle stock. Put a coat on the 20-gauge stock. Went for a walk. Title company called and made an appointment for Monday morning in Anchorage. Saw a cow moose and two calves a half mile east of here. Sylvia is in Anchorage.

Saturday, June 26, 2004—sunny and some breeze, 57° to 91°. Up at 5:15 breakfast and went to gravel pit for some clay with sand to cover the coarse gravel recently put in a narrow place on our driveway. Transplanted some poppies. Cut some weeds. Did a little work on fun stocks. Allen visited over two hours. Got a letter from Marion, Jerry is quite sick. Really hot today.

Sunday, June 27, 2004—so smoky the sun was hidden a lot today, 59° to 83°. Only occasionally showing a red orb. Couldn't get going on the typewriter today. Washed old blue and washed the batteries in both trucks. Sure having a time getting the finish on the gunstocks smooth. Made three laps on my walk. Checked the truck for the trip tomorrow. Sylvia gave Samantha seeds for a small garden.

Monday, June 28, 2004—cloudy and smoky here, 57° to 77°. We went to Anchorage (no smoke there) to title co office and signed the sale closing papers on the remote parcel. It will still be about 10 days before we see a check then our bank will hold for a period of time. The greenhouse was too hot for the sweet corn again this year. It is kaput.

Tuesday, June 29, 2004—mostly cloudy and smoky, 52° to 79°. Called and visited with Virginia quite a while. Talked to Joe Roche. Moved some old berm material along the driveway in order to fill in some lower places. Studied some of houses for sale that Nadia sent us info on. Did my walk. Pulled some weeds. Visited Ed Farmer. Put the 30-30 back together. Read the closing papers for Old Boot Lake property.

Wednesday, June 30, 2004—sunrise was bright red rays coming in under and through the smoke, which remained thick all day, 51° to 74°. We could see as far as the river. We run the air purifier some times to improve the air we breathe. I made a one numeral mistake when I wrote down my SS # on the form for reporting our land sale to IRS. Called and left a message at the title office. Moved more of the old berm material. Most of it is in place now. Kahren was here. Two Brockman boys were here asking us to come to their garage sale. Bob R brought a list of items to be auctioned for seniors benefit.

Thursday, July 1, 2004—very smoky all day once again, 44° to 71°. Finished placing the material from the old dozed berms along part of the driveway. Virginia called with the news that Jerry is getting stronger. Moved three wheelbarrow loads gravel this afternoon. Got two plat maps read to send to Bill Bucks and photos to send to Lee. These are of his visit and things we done together.

Friday, July 2, 2004—still smoky but better all day, it is getting thicker this evening, 50° to 75°. We went to lunch in Glennallen. Paid electric bill. Sent two packages. Back home Sylvia hilled the potatoes and I mowed the lawn and scattered the clipping on the sand fill just east of the house.

Saturday, July 3, 2004—hard rain and lots of lightning in the night, 50° to 75°. Small shower this morning. Burned our trash. Seeded a little grass along driveway. Neighborhood kids had a yard sale today. The old "lights on" vehicle buzzer tested okay. Reassembled the 20-gauge double barrel. Sunny with smoke this evening. Cleaned out the pickup cab over camper. Leveled it with the jacks.

Sunday, July 4, 2004—partly cloudy, 52° to 72°. We went to 4th of July parade in Glennallen. Rosemary Bartley rode with us. I drove a WW2 weapons carrier and towed a 105 Howitzer cannon. Had a rider who gave out candy and flags. Joe and I walked the rifle he marched with back to the post when the parade was over. I took Sylvia and Rosemary back to the ball field. The Chamber of Commerce had a salmon bake going. It was excellent salmon. Cooked both traditional and Cajun. After eating we dropped Rosemary off at their place on our way home. It is warm and sunny this evening.

Monday, July 5, 2004—rain in night, rain and showers all day, 49° to 55°. Read some. Took a nap. Went to Darrel and Brenda's to visit and supper. Met an ambulance on way home. Picked up some brass in gravel pit but it is Berdan primed and no good to me.

Tuesday, July 6, 2004—morning sprinkles, 47° to 72°. Lee Adler came out and did an appraisal on our property. Cleaned up the wood shop. On the way down to the lake a kestrel flew all around me making a call to get my attention. There must be young ones just off the nest near by. Skimmed our well water. The lake is quite high. Two aspen have fallen across the trail on the property line between Gerry Rudbeck and us. A really nice evening out there. We got a phone call that Rosemary Bartley is in hospital—touch and go right now. Bart is at Anna Marie's home.

Wednesday, July 7, 2004—beaut of a day with evening showers, 49° to 79°. Wrote letters all morning. Sylvia went to luncheon with the ladies. I took my walk and a nap. We went to Legion meeting this evening.

Thursday, July 8, 2004—partly cloudy, 54° to 74°. Rained in middle of night. Made two trips hauling 12 five gallon buckets of gravel and clay. Put it in a low place in our driveway. Lee Adler has finished his appraisal of our place. My left knee was quite bad this morning.

Friday, July 9, 2004—rain in night and a shower in the afternoon, 51° to 68°. Joe R. called, the check from title company won't be here for a week or so. We went to Glennallen to lunch and cashed our checks. Joe Goodlataw called and wants to look at our pickup camper. Charlie T. hasn't called yet. Joe Roche called and asked us to have dinner with them at Tolsona Lodge Sunday evening.

Saturday, July 10, 2004—a shower, mostly partly cloudy, 42° to 76°. Composed an article for the Cast Bullet Journal and typed it up. Hauled more gravel. Some to support the new fill in the driveway and some to fill and stabilize a fill near the woodshop. Nadia called and visited a while.

Sunday, July 11, 2004—mostly sunny, 44° to 83°. Did lots of walking. Some reading. Took a nap in the afternoon. Got ready to meet Joe and Teresa Roche at Tolsona Lodge. They treated us to dinner tonight. We had a good get to know each other visit. I stopped by the gravel pit on the way home for a small jag of fill for a low place here. Checked on the Zimbicki's property for them.

Monday, July 12, 2004—partly cloudy and light breeze, 48° to 84°. I unloaded the gravel pit fill in a low place. Then we went up Lake Louise Road and removed the Old Boot Lake "For Sale" signs from four places. Visited with Patti Billman who suggested trying eBay to sell our house and gave us some information. I loaded some more fill material on the way by the gravel pit. Unloaded it after lunch. The head light reminder (buzzer) some how got it's magnet corrupted by metal particles. Got it cleaned and it now works okay. Got a letter from my brother Jerry.

Tuesday, July 13, 2004—sunny, 53° to 85°. Wrote letters to my brother Jerry and my sister Virginia. We went to lunch in the new senior van and mailed the letters. Visited with Henry Johnson about eBay etc. He gave me a nice fossil. Heard of a pilot nearby who is looking for property on a lake. He is a pilot. Haven't learned his name yet.

Wednesday, July 14, 2004—the sun was almost hidden by the forest fire smoke, 51° to 82°. Did a little service work on the blue truck. Cleaned up the signs we used selling the remote parcel. They had pitch on them. Jim and Elaine Manning visited. Called my brother Marion.

Thursday, July 15, 2004—very smoky today, 50° to 79°. Did my walk early. Did some letter writing and phone calls after the check came in payment for Old Boot Lake property. Kahren visited a couple times. She brought us two rainbow trout. Elaine M. dropped off a muskmelon. I've started writing a description of our place to possibly put it up for sale on eBay.

Friday, July 16, 2004—some smoke and sunny, 50° to 80°. Went to Glennallen for lunch. Shopping. Postmaster notarized our signatures on letter to TCF bank. Wrote some more on description of our home. We may try selling on eBay because this property is so unique. Whacked some weeds. The string got hung up in the spool.

Saturday, July 17, 2004—partly cloudy and some breeze, 50° to 70°. Sometimes the mosquitoes were persistent. Did my walk. Went to gravel pit to shoot and found campers still in sack. Went back home and ran a tank of gas through the weed wacker. Went back to gravel pit. Those guys were up but still there. Went back home and whacked more weeds. I mowed grass and weed on the west in front of the garden, down the hill and on to the boat landing. Looks lots better.

Sunday, July 18, 2004—partly cloudy and stiff breeze this afternoon, 50° to 72°. Sore and stiff today. Cast some bullets and put gas checks on some of them and lubed and tapered them. Allen and Reed visited this evening. Tried to get pictures of kestrels flying.

Monday, July 19, 2004—partly cloudy and some breeze, 49° to 81°. Went to gravel pit for some target practice. Got one good group. Finished tapering and lubing the cast bullets. Johnny Goodlataw called about the pickup camper then didn't show up. We went to Allen and Roxanne's at the campground for supper—very good. Samantha had just lost a baby tooth. Reed was his usual happy-go-lucky self.

Tuesday, July 20, 2004—partly cloudy to cloudy and more smoke today, 53° to 72°. Wrote some more on a letter. We went to Glennallen for lunch and a little shopping. Whacked some small willows and bigger weeds. That job sure plays me out. Mary O. phoned and talked quite a while. Brenda visit also. Sylvia went over to see the Rudbecks.

Wednesday, July 21, 2004—cloudy, partly cloudy and windy in the evening, 48° to 71°. Went to gravel pit target shooting. Did fair. Renye is going on vacation and can't make a "Home for Sale" sign until after she gets back in 17 days. Cleaned my P90 auto loader. Will reload some more 30 br. My brother Marion phoned. Nice to talk.

Thursday, July 22, 2004—partly cloudy and windy in the afternoon, 47° to 67°. Went to pit for a shooting session. Did a few small jobs. Started on a threshold for front door. Stepping down off the woodshop porch I turned my ankle. Fell on my right side. I heard and felt a rib crack. I did get the parts made for the threshold and a plan for putting it down.

Friday, July 23, 2004— raining when I got up, 48° to 71°. So I quick ran out to the burn barrel and light the trash. Partly cloudy rest of the day. We went to lunch and some shopping. Worked on the threshold at front door. Finished it a little after suppertime. New potatoes and peas for supper. Took pictures of Sylvia and her garden and sunflowers which have seeds setting on it now! Kahren brought us a couple salmon out of a fish wheel. Jeff, Amy, John Paul and Chelsie stopped by on their way to camp for the weekend.

Saturday, July 24, 2004—partly cloudy and windy sometimes, 44° to 70°. Did my walking. Burned a tank of gas in weed whacker. Pulled some weed and hoed five rows in big garden. Nadia returned my call. I was down at lower garden. After lunch we went to Tazlina Hill gravel pit. Jeff Routt, Amy and her kids and Jeff's kids were riding dirt bikes and ATVs. Jeff was shooting his big new SW 500 revolver. He also shot a model 98 Mauser. It was capable of excellent groups. It was a reworked Model 95 with a straight bolt.

Sunday, July 25, 2004—shower in night and partly cloudy and strong breeze in evening, 47° to 71°. Trimmed some limbs off some trees between house and the well to make it easier to see the low well temp warning light when it comes on. Pulled some weeds and carried off some cut brush. Wrote a couple letters and a description of our place to use when and if we try to sell it on eBay. Allen, Roxanne, Samantha, and Reed came over to visit before dark. Ralph and Jeff both called. Jeff left two bikes stored here.

Monday, July 26, 2004—shower early, then breezy. Got windy in the afternoon and evening, 42° to 64°. Called an attorney about how to handle sale of purchase. Ordered our septic tank to be pumped. Trimmed more limbs off trees in order to see light at the well better. Will have to take a ladder down there to reach some higher ones. Reloaded some .308 Win to use up the last little bit of the "Benchmark" powder.

Tuesday, July 27, 2004—partly cloudy and breezy, then really windy in the afternoon and evening, 47° to 62°. Went to Glennallen. Shopping lunch and I lowered the price of our pickup camper that we have up on "For Sale" bulletin board. Went shooting at gravel pit. The loaded cartridges too long for the .308 Winchester. Two guys driving a really old pickup came in the pit looking for a road to drive back into the bush. When asked, they said they were unfamiliar with conditions in Alaska. Entered the results of target practice in the log book for that rifle.

Wednesday, July 28, 2004—mostly cloudy and a few showers, 49° to 66°. Sylvia went to Glennallen with a car load of neighborhood ladies to mobile breast X-ray. They had lunch in Copper Center. I put an extension on the tree trimmer and took off higher limbs in order to see the bulb at the well. Trimmed the front door jam some so the door doesn't rub on it. Reloaded some .308 Winchester, sorted some brass and organized some of it. Fred Rungee stopped by with goodies and a visit.

Thursday, July 29, 2004—partly cloudy and a few showers, 43° to 69°. We went to the senior's picnic at Tazlina River wayside. Bob Peters grilled hot dogs and hamburgers, ladies brought salads and baked goodies. We knew most of the people there and had a good time. We stopped by Gerry's but motor home was gone and no one there. Saw a big truck tire along the highway and told Robbie Farmer about it in case his dad could use it. Robbie came over and reprogrammed our VCR so it will record and play tapes. Jeff called and wants to leave the motorcycles here another week. I reworked some .308 W brass tonight.

Friday, July 30, 2004—partly cloudy and scattered showers, 47° to 67°. Went to Glennallen, lunch, post office and pay light bill. Straightened up a "paper mess" here where I sit. Dropped off a wedding gift for Ian and Heather Mailly. Saw Ralph Fuson for a couple minutes in town.

Saturday, July 31, 2004—partly cloudy and light showers, 48° to 72°. Went to gravel pit to shoot. A small motor home was parked there, so I came back home. A sneeze last night re-broke my partially healed ribs. Are troubling today. Whacked some more small willow brush. Went to pit after lunch. Motor home was long gone. Shot two different loads in the .308 Winchester with sporter barrel. While it was cooling down I target practiced with the .357 magnum. Got back home just as Sylvia was making supper. Boy the spinach was good! Shortly after supper, Bob Rudbeck brought over a sign that he used when selling his house and gave it to us. Brockman's signs will put a new picture of our house on it and we'll put it out at the mailboxes. Entered results of today shooting in .308 record book. Cleaned rifle and some brass.

Sunday, August 1, 2004—partly cloudy and smoky cool west wind, 48° to 63°. Sylvia made deviled eggs for the potluck picnic after church services at Allen and Roxanne's campground. Nice service and a good time. We phoned Brittany and congratulated her on #1 showing (riding in a horse show). Wrote some letters.

Monday, August 2, 2004—partly cloudy, 45° to 71°. Whacked more brush and sharpened the cutter. Ran water into garbage pit to wet the wood ashes and help them rust the tin cans. A board on front door pulled away from the frame. We glued and clamped it and put in a number of long screws to hold it in place. Hope it works. Put a few screws in the front steps also. Ran into one of the clamp pipe ends and knocked my glassed off and skinned my nose. Lucky— could have been my eye.

Tuesday, August 3, 2004—partly cloudy, 38° to 78°. Light fog drifting east and off our lake early this morning. Finished putting screws in front door. Removed the clamps. Went to Glennallen. Lunch, bank, etc. The paint we had for front door didn't look good so we will have to get some in town. I vacuumed the insulation in the well. Whacked a bunch of willows in the area down by the well. We visited Mannings and Cal and Mary Gilcrease.

Wednesday, August 4, 2004—partly cloudy and some breeze, 42° to 73°. Gave Ed Farmer a heli-coil repair kit. Washed blue pick-up windshield. Moved plow truck in a shadier place. Sanded some areas of front door so it fits better in preparation to painting it. We went to Legion Post monthly business meeting. Saw Kyten and ? riding horse and ATV and spending time at KRO Lodge.

Thursday, August 5, 2004—sunny and hot, 50° to 79°. It was hard to get out of bed this morning, but I got going. Went to Anchorage. Visited Rosemary Bartley at the hospital extended care facility. The last stroke left her in bad shape. She had made some improvement. It is sad to see her in such circumstances. Sylvia is especially moved to see Rosemary in such a condition. Bob and Kahren brought over four fresh peaches and borrowed our carpet cleaning machine. Charlie Trowbridge called with questions about his land and about hunting.

Friday, August 6, 2004—sunny, 50° to 83°. Went to Glennallen to bank, telephone coop and lunch. The bus sure is uncomfortable to ride in considering it is new. Shot a squirrel this morning. Did my walk around our place four times. Kahren brought Sylvia's rug cleaning machine back.

Saturday, August 7, 2004—sunny with breeze, 53° to 84°. Charlie and I walked over to and around his place and property line and location of a driveway. Went to gravel pit and he sighted in his .338. His last group was very good, three shot in less than one inch. After supper he wanted to visit Allen. Looked at the sawmill and cabin buildings in progress. Then Denny Eastman came along on his ATV and they visited awhile. Charlie stopped by Henry's on the way home to visit a while.

Sunday, August 8, 2004—sunny, 55° to 83°. Charlie and Mike Sheldon went to Charlie's property. I started making Plexiglas screen guards for front door screen. Charlie, Sylvia and I visited most of the afternoon. Nadia called, Theresa called. We went to Darrel and Brenda's for supper. Checked the two gravel pits for brass. Kyle, David and Robbie followed us into the west pit. It had a tree across the road. They pulled the tree out of the way. Beautiful evening.

Monday, August 9, 2004—partly cloudy, 48° to 80°. Did my walk. Made a package for Charlie's shaving kit and mailed it to him. Sent a description of our place to Nadia for use in placing an ad on eBay to sell our house. Put the screen guards on the front screen door. We had our septic tank pumped today. Jeff, Amy, John Paul, and Chelsie stopped by a few minutes. Jeff is quite pumped about having a cabin on his 20 acres in Kenny Lake at his mothers. Quite a lot of smoke coming from the east.

Tuesday, August 10, 2004—partly cloudy and smoky, 49° to 82°. Went to Glennallen to Post Office and lunch. I started working on the Winchester rifle dealer promotional pictures. Put sod on a bare spot in the lawn at the septic tank pump out place.

Wednesday, August 11, 2004—partly cloudy, cloudy and windy sometimes, 50° to 80°. Thunder in distance. Sylvia went to Queen's luncheon. I felt real bad this morning and not good all day. Went to gravel pit, four 6-44 magnum brass. Did a few piddling things. Denny and Joie Eastman visited for a while this evening.

Thursday, August 12, 2004—partly cloudy-smoky here again, 51° to 74°. Walked down to lake (Junker's dog was barking) Checked well. Raked out big truck tracks. Whacked some brush.

Friday, August 13, 2004—partly cloudy and some breeze, 50° to 74°. We went to Glennallen to lunch. Cleaned some on plaque backing for commemorative rifle pictures. A squirrel is cutting green spruce cones that land in lawn. Picked them up and out of there.

Saturday, August 14, 2004—partly cloudy and quite smoky, 48° to 79°. Couple people sold small stuff off trailers out by the highway. Sylvia got some stuff. She got two pair heavy gloves from the neighborhood Vender kids. Visited with some neighbors. I don't feel well today. Took a short nap. Cemented the commemorative rifle pictures on heavy pressed board. Darrel and Brenda are camping at Tolsona grounds.

Sunday, August 15, 2004—very smoky all day, couldn't see the sky at anytime, 48° to 77°. Smell is strong. Eyes burn. Cannot see individual trees across the lake. Spent most all day on the rifle pictures. Washing, cleaning excessive glue and putting "hangers" on them. Shot the "cone cutting squirrel" with a Mexican "quiet" 22 caliber powderless cartridge. Nadia and Laura both called. Both excited about a new plan to get us down there sooner.

Monday, August 16, 2004—very smoky, 46° to 80°. Went over to Henry's. Looked at pictures of our place he had. He then took more pictures of our place and faxed them to Reyne to use on a roadside ad for sale of our place. Met Don? from Kentucky at Henry's place. Smokey air is hard on nose, throat and eyes. Reyne thinks it will take a couple days to make the sign.

Tuesday, August 17, 2004—smoky, 47° to 84°. Jim Odden is at his home here and came over to visit for 1 ½ hr. Did some walking but it made my knees worse. Rested a couple times in between planning how to mount the "House For Sale" sign on our US Mailbox supports.

Wednesday, August 18, 2004—smoky, 50° to 83°. Worked on supports for the "House For Sale" sign to put out at the road. We went to a picnic with Brenda, Darrel and three little kids of friends of theirs, at Tolsona Wilderness campground. Very smoky tonight. Did too much hack sawing of steel today and sprained my right wrist. Knees are giving me a lot of trouble.

Thursday, August 19, 2004—smoky and cooler today, 48° to 75°. My left knee is better today. Did some small jobs. Gave Reyne B. some cucumbers. Come to find out her computer wouldn't accept e-mail from Henry and she had not got the pictures to make out house for sale sign. Bob and Kahren R. came over, they needed a spark plug for their chainsaw. Wrote a letter to a Cast Bullet Association director in regards to an article I submitted for publication. Allen Farmer came over and visited 2-3 hours this evening.

Friday, August 20, 2004—some showers in night, partly cloudy and cooler, 57° to 65°. Very light shower in the afternoon. We went to Glennallen. Post office, shopping, lunch. Burned our trash in barrel. Dug and pulled out an old birch stump and burning the driest portions of it. Sammy and two Mailly girls came over to pull weeds in the garden for Sylvia. We don't have weeds. Sylvia gave them some cauliflower and showed them the seeds that are developing on the potato plants. I have the darndest throbbing pain in the side of my left big toe, due I guess to the toe nail problem there. Put some better gravel on a bad place in the lane. Washed the truck windshield. Tended the burn barrel.

Saturday, August 21, 2004—mostly sunny and somewhat smoky, 47° to 79°. Hauled more gravel and put it in place. Kept the burn barrel going all day. Pulled some pig weed. Checked on the well. Sylvia checked in with Reyne several times today but due to one thing or another she wasn't able to get the sign finished for us. Called my cousin Gladys and asked how the sale of remote property should be handled when reporting our income tax return. Called Nadia and talked with her about houses and options for us there in Minnesota. Mary O visited this evening and played her first checkers game and seemed to enjoy herself.

Sunday, August 22, 2004—smoky with fog then smoky, thinning by evening, 47° to 77°. Hauled more gravel for our lane. Brockmans got our sign done and we put it up. Sylvia and I got it up by ourselves. Went to Henry's and had him email pix to Nadia. Burn barrel smoldered all day. Watered the compost pile. Sylvia washed house windows. Mary O. borrowed our hand sickle. Ralph called.

Monday, August 23, 2004—sunny, some smoke and breeze, 44° to 75°. Did some small jobs. Sylvia is cleaning and waxing in house and waters lawn and garden.

Tuesday, August 24, 2004—sunny, smoky breezy with clouds and rain in evening, 43° to 75°. We went to Glennallen. Light bill, Post Office and got the perma-chink for house and garage. Hung a window blind. We had an earthquake. Center was 29 miles NE Valdez, 27 miles SE Nelchina – 17 miles deep – 5.7 magnitude.

Wednesday, August 25, 2004—mostly cloudy and real smoky sometimes, 43° to 63°. Snugged down the roofing screws on the lower ends of the house and garage. Nadia got our property up on eBay today. Went to Henry's to see it. Looks excellent to me. Squirrels keep showing up. Got another one. Rained a little and looks like rain this evening.

Thursday, August 26, 2004—some light rain and cloudy clearing somewhat later in day, 44° to 59°. Sam Weaver is putting the perma-chink on the house logs. I did odd jobs around here. Allen brought us a side of caribou ribs. Nadia called. Our web site has 240 hits -40 or so we know of. Rest are potential buyers. Mary Odden dropped us some nectarines and brought the hand sickle back and visited.

Friday, August 27, 2004—nice sunny day and some breeze, 43° to 65°. There was hundreds of yellow jackets in the birch tree here at corner of house. Most have been after nectar or something. Sam got more perm-chink on the house logs. I re-glued 2 stiles on the kitchen cabinets. Refinished some worn places on the cabinets and the "island." Wire brushed creosote stains off the chimney in the basement. Took Sam to Grizzly Store for a little shopping this evening. Peter Heino was at store also. He gave me more magazines. Warren Obermeir visited in the evening.

Saturday, August 28, 2004—nice and sunny, 43° to 65°. Sam finished chinking the house and started the garage. A ladder slipped out from under him and he bruised his ankles. I rebuilt the wood that holds the house roof ladder on the roof when cleaning the chimney. Reset the Oakum chinking on the garage and some odd jobs. Visited Dan and Patti Billman in the evening.

Sunday, August 29, 2004—light shower and sunny, 46° to 66°. Did some small jobs. Rested. Kahren borrowed a spotting scope stand. Ralph called. Theresa called.

Monday, August 30, 2004—nice day, 38° to 65°. Went to Glennallen, had lunch and to dentist office and had my teeth cleaned. Picked up my moose and sheep permits. Did a little shopping for Sam and us. Sam put more perma-chink on garage logs. Got some crushed rock for the well. Quite smoky all day and tonight. Henry came over needing 4-½" elbow pipe fittings and I had them for him. He gave a gallon of perma-chink.

Tuesday, August 31, 2004—partly cloudy, 40° to 65°. Picked up Sam at his place and he got all the perma-chink here on. We need a gallon or so more. Wash the empty baskets. Henry got two documents e-mailed to a prospective buyer for us. Allen brought over some fresh ripe pears and peaches. I saw a young spruce hen today. Allen told me where a spike fork is hanging out. Nadia called a couple times. Charlie T. also. Called Theresa and wished her happy 50th birthday.

Wednesday, September 1, 2004—partly cloudy, 40° to 62°. Removed camper anchors from 80 GMC pickup. Rebuilt two steel fence posts. Cleaned up around garage. We visited Brenda and Darrel. Went to American Legion Post monthly meeting.

Thursday, September 2, 2004–cloudy and some showers, 41° to 56°. Visited with Henry Johnson and then Ed Farmer. After lunch I started wiring a good fan to mount on the green house. Then started making the frame to support the fan. Charlie came by after Mike Shelton got a driveway built for him. I went with Charlie and Mike to Eureka. They ate dinner and I had a piece of pie. We all told stories and had a good time.

Friday, September 3, 2004–light rain most all day, 37° to 47°. Built a frame to mount the exhaust fan on the greenhouse. Charlie came back at noon and after lunch we mounted it on east end of greenhouse. Tested it and it works ok. Then we went over to Charlie's new driveway on his property. Cut some posts. Dug the holes with my post hole digger auger and rigged him a pole gate. He went to Odden's after supper to play music at a festival.

Saturday, September 4, 2004–partly cloudy and breezy, 34° to 51°. Four swans on lake. Helped Charlie reload some cartridges. The he and Mike Shelton went down to Oddens to play music. Jim Manning is doing a yard sale out at highway. Visited with him. Some guy's borrowed pickup broke down at Mannings drive. Some other people were there. Darrel and Brenda brought a Toyo heater for Jim to fix and we got to visit Darrel. Didn't want to stay for supper. I sharpened my cartridge trimmer. Son Paul called from his friend Steve's place and visited quite some time. Joe Junker has been flying in meat from Moose Camp.

Sunday, September 5, 2004–partly cloudy, 31° to 54°. Frost on lower garden. Charlie reloaded more rifle cartridges. After lunch he went home. Did a few small jobs and took a short nap. Then went to the music festival at Odden's. Went over to Dan and Patti's. Dan showed us the Stinson "Junior" plane built in 1933 that he just bought. Tom and Lisa Smayda came over and we all visited in Dan and Pattie's hanger.

Monday, September 6, 2004–sunny and light breeze, 29° to 53°. Started planning the installation of the thermostat for the green house exhaust fan. Took out the fan we have been using. Painted the two steel posts that I repaired. Visited with Jim M. Darrel G. called to tell us of having a grizzly break out one of their windows in the house last night. Darrel hasn't slept since. He bought batteries so his flashlight will work if bear comes back tonight. Called Ralph. He plans to come here next weekend.

Tuesday, September 7, 2004–sunny, 22° to 53°. We went to Glennallen lunch, post office, shopping bank. This bus is a very rough ride. We dug the potatoes when we got back home. Two rows yielded 240 lbs. Went walking after weighing potatoes. I weigh 176 dressed with heavy boots on. Sure a beaut of an evening.

Wednesday, September 8, 2004—sunny, 24° to 58°. Worked a little on the thermostat for greenhouse. Carried old potato stalks and kohlrabi roots out of garden. Leveled the dirt in the potato rows. Carried the spuds down into the basement after Sylvia hosed them off. Brenda called—no sign of more bear trouble—yet.

Thursday, September 9, 2004—sunny, 26° to 58°. Stated on mounting the green house thermostat. Took our portable fan apart and put it back in its box. Nadia called—a prospect wants pix of inside of our house. Henry came over and took the photos. The guy's computer rejected the email. Henry will try tomorrow. We went to Allen and Roxanne for dinner. Bob and Kahren were there. Jacobi Kiser is back from Iraq and has finished his five year enlistment in the Marines. I am reading the book "Some Bears Kill." It is very good. A guy called and asked me about the camper we have for sale.

Friday, September 10, 2004—sunny, 27° to 55°. We went to Glennallen and got the perma-chink to finish chinking the garage. Had lunch, Post Office. Henry got the house pix sent to a man in Oregon. A man and woman saw our house for sale sign and asked Don (staying at Henry's) for direction to our place. They walked in and looked all around and called this evening and asked lots of questions. We were in Glennallen when they stopped by.

Saturday, September 11, 2004—sunny and a little breeze, 28° to 56°. Cleaned out some of basement. Went and got Sam to come and finish chinking the garage. Charles Burt came and bought our camper. Brought his employer later to haul it home. Kestrels were back today for a little while. Worked some on the mounting of thermostat in greenhouse.

Sunday, September 12, 2004—partly cloudy, 28° to 54°. We are working at cleaning up around here. Sylvia in the basement and I'm in garage. Jeff and Ralph called. Ralph is trying to get a bull moose he saw on the way here. Allen and Reed visited. David shot a bull moose. Charlie T. called and talked for over an hour.

Monday, September 13, 2004—cloudy and sprinkles, 30° to 50°. Returned a book to Kahren R. We burned a lot of old cardboard boxes. The basement is all cleaned now. In the afternoon, I worked at wiring the thermostat in the greenhouse. Jeff called. He can't get off work to hunt.

Tuesday, September 14, 2004—sunny, 24° to 47°. Went to Glennallen. Took down my camper for sale. Sylvia cashed her SS check. We had lunch. Harry and Judy Termin are back from their trip. Gathered up my aluminum and loaded it on pickup. Henry gave me 12 plastic bags of aluminum cans. We had Bob and Kahren R. here to supper. They are leaving tomorrow.

Wednesday, September 15, 2004—partly cloudy, 26° to 45°. We went to Palmer, Wasilla, and Anchorage. Went to bank, got groceries, and title company. Sold aluminum and alum cans and a little bit copper and brass. Visited Rosemary Bartley at Providence Extended Care. She is better but is far from being independent. Her left side is still paralyzed. We saw a cow moose and twin calves. Very tired when we got home and unloaded groceries. Left the bathroom medicine chest in truck tonight.

Thursday, September 16, 2004—mostly cloudy, 25° to 41°. Wired the greenhouse fan. Burned some more trash. Showed our place to Will Renou who works for BLM here in Glennallen. He said he would call and give us an answer.

Friday, September 17, 2004—snow in night and early morning, then melted, 27° to 38°. Went to Glennallen. Got RV antifreeze and lunch. Did a couple small jobs at home. Jeff and Theresa called. Road and gravel pit hunted morning and evening. Saw nothing.

Saturday, September 18, 2004—sunny, clouded over in the evening, 22° to 44°. Back was very bad today. Ralph stopped by this morning. He wired the greenhouse thermostat for us. Helped gather the sunflower seed heads. After lunch we went to Squaw Creek to hunt moose. I cut some brush out of north survey line here at home. Went to gravel pit but no sign of moose so I came back home.

Sunday, September 19, 2004—cloudy, 21° to 40°. Jeff, Amy, John Paul and Chelsie were here till mid afternoon. Had a nice visit. Went to a trail near Little Nelchina River and glassed for moose up on shoulder of Slide Mountain Didn't see any. Then they went back to town. Allen and Roxanne ask us to have supper with them. It was very good and we had a nice visit.

Monday, September 20, 2004—cloudy, fog, and light rain clearing off in the afternoon, 32° to 48°. Started to install light bar for medicine cabinet and ran into a problem with wiring. Ralph was to be here by noon. At 12 o'clock I loaded ATV and went to find him. He had stopped at Eureka for lunch. He looked at bathroom wiring and suggested putting in another switch for the light bar.

Tuesday, September 21, 2004—mostly cloudy, a shower and snow on top of Slide Mountain, 33° to 49°. Went to Glennallen. Got some electrical stuff to wire the medicine cabinet. Got it put on the wall when we got home. Some swans are still on the lake. Called Denny E. and visited a while.

Wednesday, September 22, 2004—partly cloudy and couple showers, 29° to 47°. Didn't do much today. Harry and Judy Termin visit a little while.

Thursday, September 23, 2004—cloudy and rain, snow that melted, 28° to 41°. Sorted and burned junk. Serviced truck. Water line winterized. Pulled sunflower stalks. Put them on compost pile. The people from Willow called and ask to look at our place tomorrow. Borrowed Allen's device to fill propane bottles.

Friday, September 24, 2004—partly cloudy, 24° to 38°. Worked at cleaning up the place. Sigrud and Dieter (from Willow) came to see our place. They have a beautiful home in a subdivision and want to move and get away from noise and covenants. Must sell theirs to buy ours. They like our place.

Saturday, September 25, 2004—cloudy, 21° to 38°. Snowed here most of day, (four to six inches). Swans are gone. I burned brush, slash and stumps in the lower road. Really looks nice around there. We went to a prime rib dinner at Legion post, very good. Allen and Reed visited.

Sunday, September 26, 2004—cloudy, sunny, breezy afternoon, 29° to 47°. Wrote letters. Shoveled ashes out of middle of lower road. Rested. Jeff stopped by for a few minutes. My brother Jerry is to get out of hospital today.

Monday, September 27, 2004—cloudy, sunny afternoon, 25° to 40°. Put snow plow on truck. Dumped burn barrel in pit. Filled propane bottles. Started making a wood box to store the ProChrono in plus some small jobs.

Tuesday, September 28, 2004—cloudy, some more snow then mid afternoon, it snowed hard, 15° to 33°. We went to Glennallen. Paid electric and propane bills, Post Office, and shopping. Lunch. Made the lid for ProChrono box and put a coat of stain on it. A guy called to ask if we would rent our home to him. Told him no at this time.

Wednesday, September 29, 2004—cloudy, snow, (three inches), 21° to 31°. Packed the snow where I plow with the plow truck. Hope it freezes and keeps the plow from digging down into the gravel. Finished the box for the ProChrono. Put plastic over the windows on the inside upstairs. Nadia called to tell us they got moved into their new home at last.

Thursday, September 30, 2004—cloudy and some rain in afternoon, 27° to 40°. Went to Glennallen to lunch and AARP's 55 Alive driving class. Ron told me the caribou are crossing the Denali highway at Hungry Hollow by the thousands yesterday.

Friday, October 1, 2004—sunny, 30° to 40°. Went to 55 Alive class. Bought a breaker for greenhouse but isn't correct one. Sorted some old papers to destroy.

Saturday, October 2, 2004—cloudy and snow most all day, 25° to 30°. Didn't do much today. Ralph called to tell me that Dale's friend Bart, a well known hunter and wildlife authority appears to have ran into trouble on a lone hunting trip out of Whitehorse Yukon Territory. Dale and others went to look for him.

Sunday, October 3, 2004—cloudy, snow and melting snow, 27° to 41°. Partially clearing in evening. The people who called did not show up. Perhaps due to bad weather. Called Nadia. She got our phone card extended. Went for a walk. The yellow ribbons on the birch tree were getting tight so I loosened them. Jeff called a couple times. The Mounties won't let Dale and friends go out to Bart's campsite until tomorrow. The bow and bugle were found leaning on a tree.

Just got another call from Jeff. Heidi told him the Mounties have found Bart. It appears a griz grabbed him from behind and killed him so quickly he didn't know what hit him. Dale and friends left Whitehorse at 11:00 AM today in their vehicle.

Monday, October 4, 2004—mostly cloudy, 27° to 40°. Jim and Mary Odden visited for an hour or so. Did some work on garage attic floor. Burned some trash, some cleaning up. Brought some toilet paper that was in the garage attic into the arctic entry. Forgot to call in a prescription and notify vehicle insurance that I had attended 55 Alive class. Went to gravel pit and returned Allen's propane accessory.

Tuesday, October 5, 2004—cloudy, some fog with rain in sight, 25° to 45°. Went to Glennallen. Kermit (Lee) Dudley rode senior bus for first time. Went to bank, lunch and got a can of urethane insulation. We sealed the joint between the arctic entry floor and the house. Our lake thawed out a little today. We saw lots of caribou between Mile 170 -178. It was really nice to see them. Sylvia sure got excited to see them.

Wednesday, October 6, 2004—Rain most all day and into night, 32° to 38°. Fifty to sixty swans on our lake ice resting. Later more swans and five Canadians joined them. The older birds get up and circle and call to the signets coaxing them to join them. Signets must be tired and still rest here tonight with the mature birds. Five spruce hens walked through front yard. Took pix of them also. Worked at upholstering one of dining room chairs. Preacher Jim Miller visited a half hour just before we left to go to Legion Post meeting this evening.

We drove in snow and rain to get there. A speeding (80 MPH?) passed us, 29 miles later it was in the ditch awaiting a wrecker to pull them out.

Thursday, October 7, 2004—cloudy and rain with snow in it sometimes, 33° to 42°. We got Sylvia's chair finished today. The swan's left in the night. Spruce hens were in yard again. A magpie has showed recently.

Friday, October 8, 2004—cloudy with a little rain, 32° to 36°. We went to Glennallen. Lunch and shopping. Started reupholstering another chair. Saw more caribou along the highway today.

Saturday, October 9, 2004—cloudy, an inch of snow melted to a half inch today, 25° to 35°. Woke up tired. Rested most all day. Organized the electric circuit record on out breaker panel here in the house. We invited Joe and Teresa Roche to dinner at the Copper Center Lodge. We saw some caribou between here and Glennallen. Stopped by Glennallen Building Supply and ordered two breakers. Ralph and Jeff called.

Sunday, October 10, 2004—cloudy, 29° to 40°. We worked at re-upholstering the chairs. We cut out more components and starting putting one seat together. Our lake thawed out a little. There are a few ducks out there. An eagle tries to get them—we don't know how often it is successful.

Monday, October 11, 2004—cloudy, 27° to 37°. Henry couldn
T go out for breakfast. We worked on chairs. Sylvia got tired and took a nap in the afternoon. I took an Aleve and kept going. Sure would like to get them done. Shot a squirrel today. It thought I hadn't noticed it.

Tuesday, October 12, 2004—cloudy, 26° to 36°. Light snow in evening. We went to Glennallen. Lunch and couldn't find staples that fit my new staple gun. Grrrrr. We dismantled the upholstery on the last two chairs. Covered one chair this afternoon. Joe Roche called me with information he has found out about the 10 meals that got carried away from the last Legion supper. Eleven swans and two ducks flew off our lake this morn. Sylvia put out left over salmon for the little birds.

Wednesday, October 13, 2004—partly cloudy after 2-1/2" snow last night, 32° to 42°. We finished the chairs with exception of one little job. We are tired. Sylvia made a batch of doughnuts this evening. Tried to call Steve Wilkins, but no one answered. More of our lake froze over. There is still a few ducks on our lake.

Thursday, October 14, 2004—mostly cloudy, a little rain last night, 26° to 41°. Made a cup holder for use in truck. Went to gravel pit and cut into firewood a tree that strong winds had blown down. It was quite green yet. Split and stacked the bigger pieces. Henry stopped by. Nadia called and ask if we were considering lowering the price of our home. Forty people are watching it everyday.

Friday, October 15, 2004—mostly sunny, low clouds in late afternoon and evening, 27° to 43°. Went to Glennallen. Saw caribou groups going and coming. Lunch, shopping. Cut down a dead spruce tree and cut into firewood and burned the slash. A few ducks on open third of our lake.

Saturday, October 16, 2004—partly cloudy, 29° to 40°. Went out after lunch and cut seven dead spruce trees up into firewood and put it in the woodshed. Steve W. called and visited quite a long time. We got an inquiry on our home from Ben Comptin? He has a home in Wasilla.

Sunday, October 17, 2004—mostly sunny here, foggy in Palmer, 25° to 36°. We went to Palmer to shop and go to gun show. Jeff, Amy, John Paul and Chelsie were at gun show and we had a good time. Sylvia got to see some sheep on mountain at Caribou Creek. There are muskrat pushups on Tahneta Lake. I bought a $4.00 sling for my Garand rifle.

Monday, October 18, 2004—partly cloudy, 9° to 32°. Our lake is now frozen over. We gave Mabel at Mendeltna Lodge 28 Pizza boxes that we won't be using. We got our flu shots today. Henry gave me some slab wood and a birch tree. I got quite a bit of it cut up today. Put some in basement. Split all the large birch blocks and stacked them in woodshed. Sure stiff and sore tonight.

Tuesday, October 19, 2004—skiff of snow, 19° to 29°. Went to Glennallen. Lunch and a little shopping. Cut up some more slabs at Henry's. Put most of it in basement. We saw caribou along highway and five spruce hens in our yard, picking up gravel near the garage.

Wednesday, October 20, 2004—cloudy and damp. Called birthday greetings to Virginia (it was the 19th). Cut and stacked more wood. Boxed the Alaska Trapper magazines. A man is to come get them tomorrow. Gathered up some caribou hunting gear.

Thursday, October 21, 2004—mostly cloudy, 15° to 29°. Got up at 4:00 AM and was ready to go caribou hunting with Denny E and Dennis G. They got here shortly after 5:00 AM. Went to the federal lands along Richardson Highway and Denali Highway looking for caribou. We had no luck. We did see a few tracks of boo, wolf, fox, porcupine and saw feeding ptarmigan and one spruce hen and two moose cows feeding. Dennis tried calling with his rabbit call. Got interest from eagles and a boreal owl. Ate breakfast at Paxson Lodge. Someone ran off the road a couple miles east of here. The man we expected to pick up The Alaska Trapper magazines did not show up.

Friday, October 22, 2004—sunny, 12° to 28°. Voted by absentee ballot. Had lunch. Hardware store can't find the electrical breakers I need. We saw a couple hunters dressing out caribou in the road ditch. We asked Henry and Sally to have dinner with us. They drove us to Copper Center Lodge and we had a good steak and visit. We stopped by to see her son Chris and his wife Suzie and their new garage. Coming home was uneventful which is good considering all the caribou along highway.

Saturday, October 23, 2004—partly cloudy, 9° to 22. Rested a lot today. We bought tickets to Friends of NRA dinner at Brown Bear Road House yesterday and invited Denny and Joey to go to Glennallen tonight. Denny drove. We had a very good prime rib dinner. We didn't win anything in the drawings. Denny won a cap and Joey won three Bianchi pistol belts.

Sunday, October 24, 2004—partly cloudy and skiff snow this morning, 17° to 31°. Felt real bad when I got up. Went out and got some dead and down trees up from the big hole west of the house. Put some dry wood in basement and wet went in wood shed. Fritz (don't know his last name), a vet and senior who lives at Tazlina had a stroke last Thursday evening. It appears to be a serious one. We are sorry to hear this news. Beverly called to tell us everything is well with her. She gave us Tyler's phone number and we called him. He is doing great, working and going to college.

Monday, October 25, 2004—partly cloudy, cloudy, 13° to 34°. Stacked wood in basement. Went down to Allen Farmer's. David and Kyle cut up some slabs and helped me load up the truck. Very nice of them. Here at home I off loaded it into the wheel barrow and pushed it around the house to wood chute and pitched it into the basement. While I loaded the next wheel barrow load Sylvia stacked the slabs. She kept up with me and we got the job done in jig time. Took a little rest then showered, dressed and went to Oddens to dinner. Mary's brother cliff and his wife were there from Oregon. Mary had fixed a really good meal. We had a good visit.

Tuesday, October 26, 2004—mostly cloudy, 21° to 31°. Went to Glennallen shopping and lunch. Learned that "Fritz" died late yesterday. Denny E. showed up at restaurant. Saw a lost dog along highway. Headed towards Glennallen. Check on well. Everything okay. Chopped a hole in our lake. Ice is four inches thick. Checked a duck nesting box. It is fairly clean, a little down and egg shells. Cut up some more wood and put it in basement.

Wednesday, October 27, 2004—partly cloudy, 23° to 35°. We did not get the

344

forecast. Started typing a letter and made so many mistakes I quit and went outside and started the snowgo. When I wanted to hook up the sled I discovered one nylon skeg had two broken rivets. Fixed that and hauled the wood stacked down by lake up here to wood shed and stacked it. Measured the oil in heating oil tank. Sylvia made popcorn balls and "pumpkin cookies" to give to trick-or-treaters at Halloween. I took two cookies and two pieces of lemon bars to Jim and Elaine and visited quite a while.

Thursday, October 28, 2004—mostly cloudy, 17° to 32°. Wrote letters. Visited Marvin. J.R. is renter. Jeff called. I fire the wood stove most every morning.

Friday, October 29, 2004—cloudy, 22° to 32°. 1+ inches snow over night. Snowed most of today. We have three plus inches now. We went to Glennallen. Shopping, lunch. I put up three traps for sale fliers. We saw two caribou near Mendeltna Chapel. Called Denny E., Jeremy B., Denny E. about caribou hunting. Jeff R. called couple times.

Saturday, October 30, 2004—cloudy, 18° to 28°. We have about four inches snow now. Got my gear together and went with Denny E. up the Richardson Highway caribou hunting. We saw three or four near here, but few tracks and no caribou. We did see an owl and a beautiful red fox. Had a roll and Pepsi at Meyers Lake Road House. Very few hunters out. Denny has been seeing a lost dog near mile 181 Glenn Highway. We saw it again this evening. He caught it and put it in the car. Went back to Glennallen and called the phone number on the lost dog poster. Met the owners in front of Brown Bear Road House and they took the dog. We got home just before dark.

Sunday, October 31, 2004—cloudy, some more fluffy snow, 20° to 10°. Slept late. Put the burn barrel in wheelbarrow and pushed it to our trash hole and dumped the ashes. Disassembled an 8mm Mauser cartridge that I found. Its primer had not fired. Put in a new primer and reassembled it. Dan and Patti Billman stopped by with cardboard moving boxes for us from Lisa Billman. Called Nadia about travel fare I found in paper. Oh! Yes, Billmans brought the news that Red "Loyd" Walton has passed away. They gave me "Reds" hearing aid. Trick-or-treaters showed up in their costumes and got popcorn balls and cookies shaped like pumpkins.

Monday, November 1, 2004—mostly cloudy, two inches of snow, 2° to 17°. Plowed our lane this afternoon. Lots of caribou crossing our lake. Joe and Melanie's dog barked at them. Allen had two friends with tags who opted to not shoot as they had other things to do and Jacobi didn't shoot because none of bulls had large enough horns. Nadia hasn't found economical plane tickets yet. Allen and Roxanne had us there for a good supper. Even came and got us and brought us home.

Tuesday, November 2, 2004—cloudy, four inches more snow, -4° to 10°. Went to Glennallen. Paid electric bill and had lunch. A few hunters along the highway. A few caribou are crossing our lake. Yesterday a 58 year old man was picked up on the Nelchina River area near us. He had been out two nights without fire. We are watching vote results tonight. Tried to find cheap plane tickets with no luck

Wednesday, November 3, 2004—snowed nine inches overnight, 3° to 31°. Plowed our snow, got tired. Backed into one of the lean-tos and broke some boards just as I was finishing up. We are glad George Bush is re-elected. We don't trust the far left Kerry. I went to Bartley's and took Bart to the Legion Post monthly meeting. It went quite well. Walt our commander does a very good job. I don't care much for driving these winter roads. Saw some caribou tracks. I worry that they might run out in front of the truck.

Thursday, November 4, 2004—partly cloudy, 12° to 23°. Looking snowy this evening. A few caribou walking up and down the lake all day. Sylvia put out some of her sunflower seed. Some little sparrow-like birds came to eat it. A camp robber swooped in grabbed a sparrow, pecked it in the head and flew off to eat it at its leisure. Denny E. brought a couple 1948-50 magazines for me to read. Called Nadia to tell her it looked unlikely we would come down for the holidays.

Friday, November 5, 2004—cloudy mostly, 0° to 12°. Went to Glennallen. Bank, Post Office, lunch shopping and Bureau of Land Management. Gave Ron another batch of birch seed that the birds dropped out of the tree. Shoveled snow off woodshed roof and some along shed front.

Saturday, November 6, 2004—mostly cloudy, -18° to -5°. Didn't do much all day. Went to Glennallen and had dinner with Joe and Teresa Roche at Brown Bear Road House. Saw some caribou on way there, out on lake.

Sunday, November 7, 2004—mostly cloudy here some sun east of us, -10° to 1°. We went to Sun dinner at Darrel and Brenda's. Robin Herdan and family and son Ron, also Reed and Lisa were there also. We saw caribou from highway both coming and going from Glennallen and a marten in highway ditch hunting. Ron Beshaw called and told us Bill Horvath died at the Glennallen clinic. Our CO alarm was going off.

Monday, November 8, 2004—partly cloudy, -11° to 6°. Jim M. came over to look at our Toyo stove and why it leaked CO. A gasket at the igniter was worn out. He gave me another one. He asked if we could pick up their mail three days this week. I mixed oil and gas for the snowgo. Got it started and had to put isopropyl alcohol in the gas. Drove it down to the lake to break my usual trail. Found a lot of overflow on the ice at our boat landing. Squeezed the throttle wide open. Parked in woodshed. Had to roll it on its side so I could dig and scrape the freezing mushy snow and water from the track and wheels. Warren Obermeyer came over to visit this afternoon.

Tuesday, November 9, 2004—cloudy, windy, east of here, -6° to 10°. Went to Glennallen. Did some shopping and had lunch. Put license sticker on blue truck. Put out heating oil conditioner at fuel tank. Called VA for appointment. Saw caribou here at home and along highway between here and Glennallen.

Wednesday, November 10, 2004—cloudy, partly cloudy, 10° to 40°. The heavy snow forecast did not materialize. Shoveled some snow. Plowed, some snow slid off house roof and half the garage roof. We had heating oil delivered. A few dozen caribou crossed our lake to the east. Allen called and told me he saw two grey wolves west of his driveway. Amy got me an appointment at VA clinic in Anchorage. She works in that office.

Thursday, November 11, 2004—cloudy, 19° to 34°. Saw 12 caribou on our lake. Did a few little jobs. Would have been a good day to have gone caribou hunting. Veteran's Day today.

Friday, November 12, 2004—some light snow, 18° to 28°. Went to Glennallen and got a fax sent to VA clinic in Anchorage. Had lunch also. Sylvia went to Queens Thanksgiving lunch. Saw two caribou bulls, one was pretty nice. Saw a helicopter parked at Jerry Lee's hanger. Might be on F & G animal coloring job?

Saturday, November 13, 2004—some fog on and off today, 25° to 28°. Walked down to lake. Checked well and ice on lake. Very few caribou on lake today. Darren Tehaven of Kansas City sent a letter and asked for info and wants pix. Henry is sending photos via email. We went to Odden's for supper. Very good. Dan and Patti were there. Nice visit and Jim, Mary and Kari played a couple pieces of music. Kari has a brand new brass fiddle.

Sunday, November 14, 2004—16° most all day 13° this evening. We emptied the two water storage tanks in to buckets and the drain. Carried the iron contaminated water out to the garbage pit. Put silicone sealer on a couple leaky places. Talked to Steve Wilkins about his deer hunting this gun season. Also Theresa and Earl. He got four deer. Theresa got to spend some time with her grandson Zachery today. Jeff called this evening. Allen called and invited us to breakfast in the morning.

Monday, November 15, 2004—foggy morning, cloudy, 8° to 16° to 8°. Went to

Roxanne and Allen's for breakfast. We put silicone on the places that looked as though water had leaked from the two storage tanks. Later in the afternoon we put them in position and pumped some water in them. Will pump more after the silicone has cured, 24 hours. Saw seven caribou on our lake. Jim O. called. He is ready to go caribou hunting tomorrow. I must get my gear ready tonight to go with him.

Tuesday, November 16, 2004—cloudy and clearing, 10° to 16° to 1°. Went to Jim's. Piled my hunting gear in his pickup. He has hooked to a trailer with snowgo and sled on it. On the way to Glennallen we came upon three bulls out on highway. Jim managed to get slowed down and bulls went into ditch. Two bulls had shed their horns and one still had one horn yet. We went north from Glennallen on Richardson Highway and started hunting at Mile 149 little or no sign till about Mile 163-164. Lots of kills in that area but only two bulls were seen. We saw one of these but safety conditions were such we wouldn't even think of shooting. Jim went out on his snowgo twice with no luck. He did see two fox and two marten tracks. We left at dark. Stopped by PWS College to get a grocery list from Mary O and wound up being there for an hour. Stopped at Brown Bear Roadhouse for hamburgers. We were barely in bed when the CO alarm went off. Sylvia opened the doors for fresh air. We got the Toyo stove shut off and I built a fire in barrel stove in the basement. I got sick in middle of night, felt like throwing up. Sylvia took my blood pressure 116 over 63.

Wednesday, November 17, 2004—sunny with fog in area, 0° to 8°. I haven't felt well all day. I didn't participate with Legion Post in the memorial service for Cy Neely. In the afternoon, I took the Toyo stove front off to see where the CO is coming from. Jim Manning came over to look at it and suggested a new gasket. I also put a different screw in that holds the heat exchanger in place. We are testing it now.

Thursday, November 18, 2004—cloudy, frosty, light snow, -5° to 15°. Went for a walk. Didn't feel good much of the day.

Friday, November 19, 2004—mostly cloudy, skiff of snow, 1° to 28°. Pete and Sis ? took us to Anchorage in VA van. Me for my annual exam. No change from last year. Won't know about blood tests for a while. While I was seeing my doctor, they took Sylvia to Costco's to shop prescriptions and groceries. Costco overcharged her, found the error and left a message on our phone. We will be reimbursed. Tired tonight.

Saturday, November 20, 2004—partly cloudy, 7° to 25° mostly 16°. Costco is returning Sylvia's money as they shouldn't have charged her anything. Loaded up almost all of my traps and took them to a young man in Glennallen who is just starting to learn trapping. We picked up Bart and took him with us to

Legion Post social supper of Red King crab, shrimp, and halibut. Very good dinner and everyone seemed to have an exceptionally good time this evening. Charlie T phoned and talked over an hour. "Pete" Aquila called to check on us and Sylvia's pharmacy overcharge.

Sunday, November 21, 2004—sunny, cloudy in evening, 6° to 22°. Wrote letters this morning. Walked down to well and checked the light bulb. Heard shooting on both ends of our lake. Likely Tier II caribou hunters. About 4:30 PM, Allen, Roxanne, Samantha and Reed visited. David stopped by for a few minutes. Sylvia put on a quick supper that was good.

Monday, November 22, 2004—partly cloudy and low clouds moving along Heavenly Ridge, 0° to 12°. It felt raw out there. Wrote more letters. Did some research on Ruger No. 1 and No. 3's. Smashed our empty tin cans and put them and the garbage in the pit. Went for a walk. We didn't see any caribou today. Nadia called: A person whose name is the same as a well-known Iraqi town has inquired about our house!

Tuesday, November 23, 2004—mostly cloudy, 6° to 19°. We went to Glennallen to lunch and shopping. Stopped by BLM to ask about my taking help along to hunt caribou. We saw a few caribou at different locations. I wrote up instructions for fire lapping rifle barrels and made copies. Jim Manning brought over a CO detector to test with ours.

Wednesday, November 24, 2004—mostly cloudy, some quite low, half inch of snow, 8° to 12°. Kept a wood fire going and heated the upstairs. Made phone call about next year's vehicle insurance policy. Reloaded some 30 caliber fire lapping cartridges. Made a bore mop to use J-B compound in fire lapping. Cleaned some more around the wood pile in the basement. Talked to Henry about lots of things and thanked him again for all his computer help.

Thursday, November 25, 2004—cloudy, fog, partly cloudy, 1° to 16°. Charlie, Beth, Charlie Jr., Cora, and Paul got here about noon—a few minutes apart in two cars. Cora and Paul went sliding on our hill. Rest of us visited. About 2:00 PM, we went to Odden's but not before charging the battery on our truck. It was run down. Met Dave, Mel and their baby Solomon (Mary O's nephew and family). Jim's niece Amy and her family and more people Nigul for one, Ellie and Reed Farmer. We had a great dinner and topped it off with homemade ice cream. They played music. We came home early.

Friday, November 26, 2004—partly cloudy, nice day, 0° to 12°. My back is really sore. Didn't do any work. Played some games: Paul, Cora, Charlie, Sylvia and I. They (Charlie and Paul) went skiing for quite a while this morning. We all went to Odden's to visit and supper. Some were making lefse. Sylvia helped with that. Dan and Patti Billman came over after supper for a couple of hours. A car was pulled over to side of the road. We stopped. They were ok, only covering their car radiator.

Saturday, November 27, 2004—3° to 21°. After breakfast I went out and started the snowgo for Paul and Cora to drive. They must have run it three hours or so and had fun. Jeff stopped by and left a rifle for me to shoot cast bullets with. Along towards evening went to Odden's again. Tom and Lisa Smayda were there from Palmer as well as the folks that were there last night. A lady and three girls that we didn't know came later. Billmans gave us a "For Sale by Owner" sign and some video cassettes. We saw some caribou on the lake.

Sunday, November 28, 2004—snow in night ending about noon, leaving twelve inches behind, 16° to 34°. Charlie and family got their gear loaded in their van. Had breakfast with us. I fired up the plow truck and opened a lane out to highway for them. Plowed Mannings main driveway and all our snow. Pulled snow off lean-to's and shoveled quite a bit. Did some small jobs. My right shoulder is nearly useless. Saw a marten over at Mannings.

Monday, November 29, 2004—mostly sunny, moon was beautiful, 6° to 14°. Snow settled to 9 1/2". State snowplow has thrown snow on our "House for Sale" sign and leaned it over. We got another call on the house. This one from Minnesota. Worked on making 8mm Mauser cartridge cases and readying them for reloading.

Tuesday, November 30, 2004—most cloudy with some sun, 4° to 20°. Fog between here and Glennallen. Went there for lunch on senior bus. Back home I took our "Lake Home for Sale" sign down from our mailbox support beam. We put it in the basement to thaw the snow that was plastered on it off. State snow plows sling it with great force when they plow the highway. Tried to start the snowgo with no luck. Filled the blue truck with gas. Did a bunch of phone calls. The bulb that heats our well burned out at 10:15 PM. I got dressed, put flashlight and new 100 watt bulb. Grabbed the scoop shovel and waded the snow down to the well. Shoved the snow off the well cover. Opened door, put in the new bulb. Closed well up and walked back up the hill to house. Time lapse 25 min! I am tired. Not too bad for almost 77 yrs old.

Wednesday, December 1, 2004—mostly cloudy, 9° to 32°. Spitting snow here and rain in Glennallen. We went there to lunch and to clean Post #27 rifles. Took rifle "Anzio" to rifle range and shot 25 blank cartridges. They all fired. I found unburned flakes of powder on face of the bolt. Perhaps this was cause of misfires. Stayed at post until the monthly meeting. Commander Walt conducted and directed an excellent even-handed meeting and got some important issues resolved. We were tired when we got home. Sylvia made sandwiches for the people at the post as supper time. She had bought two packages of cookies for people to munch on.

Thursday, December 2, 2004—cloudy and light snow all day (one inch), 18° to 28°. Returned Manning's CO detector to them. Reloaded some of the brass I picked up at the shooting range yesterday. We saw three caribou on our lake today. Steve called to tell us he had killed a doe deer using a bullet that I had cast. He was using his muzzle loading rifle. He has it butchered out and the meat in the freezer.

Friday, December 3, 2004—snow in night and almost all day, (seven and a half inches total),16° to 24°. Plow truck battery was dead this morning. Put battery charger on it. Went to Glennallen for lunch, bank and some shopping. Ron drove. We saw a semi and trailer in the ditch at around Mile 150. It was out and gone when we went past that location on way home. I plowed our snow and Manning's driveway. Couldn't get the snowgo motor to run good so I didn't get the latest snow packed on the trail to well and back up to the house. Sylvia has lost her Alaska ID card. Will have to get a replacement.

Saturday, December 4, 2004—partly cloudy, 10° to -2° this evening. Shot some bore lapping loads in the P17 Enfield. Also did some target practice with 357 magnum. Snowgo started easily and I packed the snow on trail down to well and back. Shoveled some snow too. Reload some cast loads to shoot tomorrow. Went to Glennallen and had dinner with Joe and Teresa Roche.

Sunday, December 5, 2004—partly cloudy and fog in area, -23° to -13°. Slept late. Read some. Sewed a different elastic on a pair of long johns. We went to a meeting of the Copper Basin Shooting Club. Only 8 members attended, that is discouraging. We saw a caribou that had been hit by a vehicle. A moose was browsing along the trees and brush at highway ditch.

Monday, December 6, 2004—mostly cloudy with fog in area, -18° to -7°. My package did not come today. Shoveled snow off woodshed roof. Added kerosene to the gun cleaner "Ed's Red." Checked bore on P17 Enfield. It is clean. Checked the neck thickness on the 8MM cases that I have from 30-06 cases. It is okay. Carried the full coffee ground bucket down to the lower garden.

Tuesday, December 7, 2004—cloudy, -12° to -2°. Saw a "sundog" peeking through this afternoon. Went to Glennallen. DMV office was closed when we were there. Lunch was good today. My package didn't come today. I shot the P17 Enfield today trying to fire lap its barrel and tested it for any improvement. Jim M. dropped off our capital credit check from CVEA. He will bring a loaner stove and try to find out why ours is not working correctly. I plan to reload some more cartridges for testing the P17 barrel.

Wednesday, December 8, 2004—partly cloudy, -14° to -5°. Spruce hen was back in same spruce tree. My package didn't come so I called Charlie T. My things were back ordered and were finally sent December 2nd. Did a lot of reading. We had some extra food and dropped it off at Preacher Jim Millers. Went to a special American Legion Post meeting and got some issues and business settled. Northern lights were beautiful.

Thursday, December 9, 2004—partly cloudy, sundogs in the afternoon, -25° to -13°. We saw a few caribou on our lake. They appeared to be after something deep in snow on the lake. Checked the voltage of plow truck battery. Cleared the trail to bird feeder. Jim O. called to tell me Mary's brother, Dave Looney and the crew he serves with, landing their Black Hawk helicopter on the Odden airstrip. I got to meet the five-man crew of which Dave Looney is a member. We put together blankets, clothes, cups and plates to give to Geney (sp?) Linley whose house burned with all her belongings.

Friday, December 10, 2004—partly cloudy and sun dogs, -24° to -11°. We went to Glennallen to bank, lunch, Post Office, DMV for Sylvia's new ID card and dropped off our gifts at Legion Post for Geney Lindley. The package containing my bullet mould, gas checks and sizing kit came today. I prepped the mould for use. We saw a nice bunch of caribou on Frank Zimbicki's lake. I called to Brooks and told him of the location. He said he would try to get one of them. Jim and Mary O. visited this evening.

Saturday, December 11, 2004—cloudy and skiff of snow, -21° to -4°. Built a fire in garage stove. Set up bullet casting equipment. After a little trial and error I got the new bullet mould to put out good looking bullet and cast about 120. Lubed them with Lee's lube.

Sunday, December 12, 2004—cloudy and 4" snow, -18° to 7°. Plowed our snow in the afternoon. Took garbage out. Did some exercises. Reloaded 20 8MM cartridges with yesterday's cast bullets. I am pushing the snow as far back as I can and piling it high.

Monday, December 13, 2004—Very low clouds and 1" snow in night, -1° to 20°. Tried out the newly cast 8 MM bullets. I need a better target in order to shoot in poor light conditions. The P17 Enfield shot the best ever since I fire lapped the barrel. Did some small jobs. Around here. Called Charlie to get the total cost of my mould order and mailed payment to him. He called back in the late afternoon with suggestions from a friend of his regarding our troubles with our Toyo heater. Ralph Fuson called with news from up his way.

Tuesday, December 14, 2004—partly cloudy, cloudy evening, -11° to 10°. Went to Glennallen for lunch and shopping. Saw quite a few caribou from Tolsona Creek and east. Some on our lake and going east. Knocked snow out of a couple trees. Plowed Manning's driveway. Shot the 8MM Mauser some more and got best targets yet. Reloaded more 8 MM Mauser with different powder.

Wednesday, December 15, 2004—mostly cloudy, 0° to 13°. Tried a new load in the 8MM. Wasn't quite as good as yesterday, but okay. Pulled two feet of snow off the greenhouse roof. Quite a job for an old duffer. I don't feel well. Just couldn't get started on writing the Christmas cards. Brenda called. Jim M. couldn't come over to work on the heating stove.

Thursday, December 16, 2004—mostly cloudy, 5° to 24°. Wrote some Christmas cards. Cast 150 bullets this afternoon. Then dismantled the Toyo stove enough to get the heat exchanger out. Took it to basement drain and washed it out with hot soapy water. Filled it with more water and we could see two places where it was leaking. Jim M. brought over a box that fits it for me to use to mail the exchanger to Homer, Alaska to have the leaks welded shut. After all that the bulb in the well burned out and I had to walk down there and put in a new bulb. It is a tough walk. Saw more caribou today. Lubed the cast bullets with Lee lube.

Friday, December 17, 2004—quite a bit of sun, 2° to 10°. Went to Glennallen shopping, Post Office, lunch. Saw caribou and moose from highway. Got most of the Christmas cards in mail. Mailed heat exchanger. (Called PO Wed 29th they want me to wait till Jan 5th then call back).

Saturday, December 18, 2004—two inches of snow and mostly cloudy, -20° to 25°. I lubed the 8 MM after sizing in the lee sizer. Shoveled snow, then plowed our place out. Packed the trail to well and back with snowgo. Our grandson Joe was one year old today. We took Bart with us to the Christmas dinner at Legion Post. He bought our dinners.

Sunday, December 19, 2004—mostly low cloudy, 19° -26° -20°. Shot both the PI7 and 8MM. Got a really great target, five shots 0.416 at 100 yards, center to center. Cleaned snow off pickup canopy stored out back. A bunch of small jobs. Spent lots of time on the phone to rest of our family.

Monday, December 20, 2004—cloudy, 3 1/2" snow, 20° to 15°. Reloaded some 8MM. Sorted some cast lube bullets. Plowed our snow. Talked to a guy from Kentucky interested in our place. Laura called. Jim, Mary and Kari were here to chili supper. They brought rhubarb pie and Christmas cookies.

Tuesday, December 21, 2004—cloudy, half inch of snow, 11° to 6°. We went to

Glennallen shopping and lunch. Target shooting 8 MM. Reloaded 25 more rounds. Allen visited. He gave me some ¼" copper tubing. Beverly called.

Wednesday, December 22, 2004—cloudy, one inch of light snow, 7° to 30°. Didn't feel well and did not do much. Marvin Obermeyer visited. Vanessa, Theresa and Jeff called. Dan Pearman from Kentucky called and wants to see our place.

Thursday, December 23, 2004—cloudy and snowing after dark, 25° to 21°. Worked on a propane device to anneal cartridge cases. John Brivogel stopped by and visited three hours. He is a smart, informed man with excellent memory. A group (15+) sang Christmas carols for us. We gave them Christmas cookies. We had candles in ice containers on the arctic entry steps.

Friday, December 24, 2004—snowing, clearing in the afternoon, 5° to -13°. Plowed our snow and Manning's driveway. Shoveled snow off storage shed and trailer roofs. Found some fittings for case annealer. Still need one coupling. We went to Odden's for a Christmas evening dinner. Allen, Roxanne, Ellie, Sammy and Reed were there this evening. They had another friend there.

Saturday, December 25, 2004—mostly sunny, -26° to -13°. Theresa called with Christmas wishes. We called Beverly. Vanessa, Liam and Tyler will visit her. That old raspberry eating moose came back today. Pawed down through the snow and ate on the raspberry plants. Cut up a small piece of broken birch tree with Swede saw and carried it into basement. Jeff called. Read a lot. I am so tired, slept two to three hours today.

Sunday, December 26, 2004—cloudy, -21° to -1°. Put a couple wheelbarrow loads of wood in basement. Wheelbarrow tire was low and I had to air it up. Jeff and Shobbie stopped by mid afternoon. Jeff wanted to get to town before dark. Didn't stay long. Left 16 hunting videos for me to watch. We did not do any shooting.

Monday, December 27, 2004—cloudy with three and a half inches of snow last night and one and a half coming down lightly today, 0° to 9°. Worked on my annealer and couldn't get the flame to come in properly. Joe Phillips delivered propane this afternoon and had coco and conversation with us. I plowed our snow. Allen F borrowed a hydraulic hose for his plow. Put a wheel barrow of wood in the basement. More caribou going east on our lake. Lots of birds at feeder.

Tuesday, December 28, 2004—mostly cloudy, one and a half inches of snow in the night, 3° to 9°. Sun rays shown through clouds on mountains with unusually beautiful colors. We went to Glennallen shopping and lunch. Saw quite a few caribou along the highway. Tried to start the snowgo to pack the trail to well and it wouldn't run good. Plowed our snow, then the bulb burned out at the well and I had to walk down, replace the bulb, and of course walk back up—with several rest stops. Bev called with some good news. We know two people who are in the area of the huge tsunami.

Wednesday, December 29, 2004—partly cloudy and some wind, -20° to -9°. Calf moose walked through our yard. Put more wood in basement. Shoveled snow off wood shed roof. Post Office says wait a week and call again about package I sent to Homer. Talked to Nadia and Theresa.

Thursday, December 30, 2004—mostly sunny, -25° to -15°. The old cow moose was browsing on our raspberries before the sun came up. I took some pictures of her. Put some more wood in the basement. Jeff called this afternoon. Jim and Mary Odden visited and we played dominoes. They seemed to enjoy the game. We had pumpkin pie and ice cream.

Friday, December 31, 2004—partly cloudy, -21° to -4°. Rested, took a couple naps. Managed to get snowgo started and packed the trail down to well. There is overflow on the lake ice—hidden by the deep snow. Shoveled some snow. Took garbage to our dump. Moose has started eating on the pile of discarded garden plants at the lower garden. Allen's boy put out an ice fishing tip up just at dark. Bev called twice. Jeff did too.

Norman Wilkins panning with friends. Photo courtesy of Henry Johnson, Nelchina Lodge.

2005—Leaving Alaska

Saturday, January 1, 2005—cloudy. -10° to -3°. Saw 23 caribou going east on our lake and one moose walked over to south side of the lake. Denny and Joey Eastman brought us the sugar that Oddens had picked up for us in Anchorage and visited a while. Before they left Jeff, Amy, John Paul and Chelsie came. The Routt family stayed and had roast turkey with us. Jeff brought the can of powder that I needed. We called Laura and Brad and Earl, Theresa and Beverly. I don't feel well today.

Sunday, January 2, 2005—cloudy, sunny, partly cloudy. -8° to 6°. Wrote letter to four people. Put two wheel barrow loads wood in basement. Reloaded a few 8MM. Copied some targets. Played dominoes with Sylvia.

Monday, January 3, 2005—mostly cloudy with some sun. -7° to 24°. Saw cow and calf moose when I took letters to mail box. I did some target shooting. Reloaded a few 8 MM Mauser.

Tuesday, January 4, 2005—cloudy, skiff of snow in the afternoon. 19° to 32°. We went to Glennallen. Lunch, bank, shopping and Post Office. Saw three moose along roads. Icy parking lots in town very dangerous to walk on. Did target shooting again. Then cast more 8MM bullets, sorted and lubed them. Beverly called and talked a long time. We liked that. Charlie Trowbridge called the "lost" package has been in Homer Post Office all this time!!

Wednesday, January 5, 2005—partly cloudy, 1 inch of snow on ground. 6° to 20°. Charlie phoned – heat exchanger is welded and is in the mail. Reloaded some more 8 MM Mauser and shot 20 of them. Put some wood in basement. Went to Legion Post business meeting. Theresa called. She is going to have some medical tests done. Lots of traffic both coming and going in Glennallen.

Thursday, January 6, 2005—mostly sunny. 5° to 12°. Shot two targets and reloaded some more. Rested a lot today. Bill Buck called. He needs a stove for the cabin he plans to build on Old Boot Lake. I talked to Allen F. about a stove he has.

Friday, January 7, 2005—mostly sunny. 22° to 37°. Some unique light colors and cloud shapes today. Went to Glennallen, bank, grocery, Post Office and lunch. We saw caribou and moose along hwy. Did target shooting in the afternoon. Then installed the repaired heat exchanger in Toyo stove. Bev phoned again tonight. We talked a lot. Mannings left for NC – son-in-law died. I'm to pick up mail.

Saturday, January 8, 2005—partly cloudy and some breeze. 20° to 30°. Pushed the snow back along our lane. Shot some more 8mm x 57 practice targets. Dan Pearman called. He will be coming a week later than planned. Oddens have some kind of flue bug. Jeff called.

Sunday, January 9, 2005—sunny. 10° to 20°. Some people stopped in wanting directions to Botley Creek. They are interested in buying Clair White's cabin on Botley Cr. I told them our place is for sale. Also, we went to Brenda and Darrel's for dinner. Got back home shortly after dark at 5:30 PM.

Monday, January 10, 2005—mostly sunny. -15° to -5°. Phoned for heating oil and prepared the oil treatment – measured the amount. Did some small things on my list. Ron Beshaw stopped in and showed us the handmade wedding rings he is taking to China where his sweetie lives. He met her on computer.

Tuesday, January 11, 2005—sunny. -33° to -23°. We went to Glennallen shopping, Post Office and lunch. Just got back home an hour or so. I was making a cover for basement drain. George Campbell and Heika? drove in. George wanted help with a road kill bull moose (butchering and hauling it to Glennallen and home). I got back home from that job just before 7:00 PM.

Wednesday, January 12, 2005—sunny. -43° to -33°. I finished the basement floor drain cover. Put some high temperature silicone sealer on the heating stove igniter. We had a fuel delivery of 100 gallons today. Stove still emits about 44-48 PPM CO while operating on "high." I built a fire in barrel stove in basement so we could go to sleep safely. The stove shifted to "low," and the CO level dropped to 0. Beverly called to talk. Jim O. called to see how the heating stove was doing.

Thursday, January 13, 2005—cloudy and skiff of snow. -42° to -20°. Took out garbage, smashed the tin cans. Put some wood in basement. Heater is running on low and not putting out so much CO. Sylvia is organizing the pantry.

Friday, January 14, 2005—cloudy and light fine grain snow most all day. -11° to -6°. We went to Glennallen. Shopping and lunch. Saw moose and calf at nearby school house. Al Smith is not plowing his driveway. I parked our truck near house. We ran a hose from hot water heater out to truck and hosed the moose blood and stomach juices out of the truck bed. I walked down to well and checked that everything was OK there.

Saturday, January 15, 2005—cloudy and 1" snow in night. -6° to 2°. Partly cloudy in the middle of day. Visited Ed F. this morning when I went out for the mail. Put some wood in basement. We still have CO coming from the Toyo oil burner. Aired up the wheel barrow tire again. I wanted to go to gun show in

Wasilla but didn't feel like going.

Sunday, January 16, 2005—mostly cloudy and one inch of snow. -7° to 5°. We got up early and went shopping at Wasilla Wal-Mart. Then to gun show. Didn't sell my gun or find the exact one I want. Stopped by Carr's grocery on our way home. We were glad to get home. Sylvia took a nap after supper. Jeff called.

Monday, January 17, 2005—some light fluffy snow, partly cloudy. -24° to -12°. We were tired today. Only salvaged a good heavy 22" zipper for a coat. Allen and Roxanne had us to a smoked-baked turkey dinner. Jim Miller and oldest son stopped there later. We had a good visit. Got back home and had a message on phone from Dan Pearman. Will call him in the morning.

Tuesday, January 18, 2005—mostly sunny. -37° to -16°. Went to Glennallen, Post Office and lunch. Saw a moose and 5 caribou along the hwy. Called Jim Miller. He asked to be called if I saw caribou along highway. He has a proxy hunt permit for an aunt. Called Toyo heater technician about the CO our stove is putting out. He urged me to quit using the stove until it emits no CO. We burn wood again. Called Nadia. She is sick, so is Chuck. Dan – from Kentucky. I called him with Henry's phone number. Jeff found two rifles I would like to have but they cost too much. Couldn't fix the shower valve - still leaks.

Wednesday, January 19, 2005—partly cloudy. 37° to 18°. Put a big wheel barrow load of wood in basement. Carried the air compressor up from basement to wheelbarrow. Pushed it to plow truck and pumped up the right rear tire then put it back in basement. Sylvia is cleaning house. We owed Jim Odden $9.00 for sugar. I went there and paid him and gave him a five quart bucket of ice cream. When I got back the light bulb in the well was burned out so I went down and replaced it with a good one.

Thursday, January 20, 2005—partly cloudy. -21° to -6°. Plowed what little snow we had. Went down to Allen's and looked over the stove Bill Buck may be interested in. Drew a picture of it and measurements. Allen had hot caramel brownies fresh out of the oven. Wrote a letter to Bill Buck. Put three wheel barrow loads of wood in basement. We saw 6 caribou cross our lake west to east. Straightened up some of my reloading things upstairs.

Wednesday, January 21, 2005—mostly cloudy. -7° to 10°. Sylvia went to Glennallen. I waited here at home in case Jim Luce would show up to look at our place. Swept basement floor. Rigged up a string and vents to dry the inside of a pair of rubber gloves. Jim and Elaine Manning returned home from NC. Their son-in-law David died of a heart attack.

Thursday, January 22, 2005—partly cloudy. 0° to 10°. The little birds are at the feeder. Dan Pearman got here this morning. Visited a lot today. Showed him the house and property. He had lunch with us. He went over to Henry's and got a room at the motel and went for a drive looking at the country. We had him here to supper and visited more this evening.

Friday, January 23, 2005—mostly cloudy. 2° to 11°. Dan was over here before I got up. He never gets tired of looking at the view from out our picture window. He loves this place. He will pay us our asking price. He asked me to throw in my Suzuki ATV which we agreed to do. We studied the For Sale by Owner packet the title company gave us. Finished the owner's disclosure notice. He went for a long drive this afternoon. A moose walked by the house during the night. We managed to get calls through to Nadia and Theresa.

Saturday, January 24, 2005—partly cloudy. -7° to 11°. We got up at 6:00 AM. Dan was here shortly after. We had a light breakfast and went to Wasilla in our own vehicles. At First American Title we were shown in to the escrow officer Patty Gebauer. She made sure all our "for sale by owner" papers were in order and helped us come to a fair agreement on the terms of the sale of our home to Dan and his partners. We need a survey, as built to complete our obligation to the sale contract. Dan then took us to a late breakfast. After which we went to Anchorage to get Sylvia's prescriptions filled and little shopping and gas for the truck. Dan had some gift shopping for his family and a plane to catch and return to Kentucky. We hand an uneventful trip returning home in early evening.

Sunday, January 25, 2005—partly cloudy. -7° to 6°. Went to Glennallen to lunch. Back home. Spent a lot of time on the phone trying to find a surveyor. Talked to Chad Wilson in hopes he can land the job of appraising our place for the lending bank for the buyers. Repaired the guide for a kitchen drawer. Laura called about our sale. We called Beverly and had a good talk.

Monday, January 26, 2005—very beautiful day. -9° to 10°. Jim C. and friend Stan came to see books and magazines I have for sale but they were too new for him. Sorted and burned some of them. Brenda and Darrel were here to supper. Allen called us to eat with them but too late.

Tuesday, January 27, 2005—sunny day. -15° to -5°. Our surveyor says we will have to add that small 1/17 of acre that AK State DOT gave back to us, due to realignment of the hwy. Sylvia's four spruce hens come to eat out of the same tree every day. She watches them from the kitchen window. We had supper with Jim and Mary Odden.

Wednesday, January 28, 2005—sunny. -20° to -5°. My shoulder is very sore. Calls to and from surveyor, Henry and Bev.

Thursday, January 29, 2005—sunny. -25° to -3°. Didn't sleep well last night. Denny Eastman stopped by and picked a couple magazines. He had left for me to read. He didn't stay long. I put on snowshoes. Took aluminum scoop shovel and went to two survey monuments and shoveled the snow from around them so the surveyor can readily find them when he comes to do the as/built survey.

Friday, January 30, 2005—partly cloudy, cloudy and snowing late afternoon and evening. -15° to 6°. Put more wood in basement. Split two large pieces. Brought the right rear wheel and tire in house. When it warmed up, I changed valve cores and I hope I have cured it from leaking air. Smashed some pop cans. Worked on Federal Income tax.

Saturday, January 31, 2005—sunny, cloudy. 2° to 9° to 0°. We got 3 1/2" snow last night. Got up real early. Wrote a letter and got a sympathy card ready for Shirley Legenre. Took a nap. Ate breakfast and plowed our snow and Mannings driveway. Put more wood in basement. Finished reading the book "Walk Softly with Me," by Sharon McLeod-Everete who was raised 20 odd miles east of here. Dan Pearman called. He is working on getting a mortgage to buy our place.

Tuesday, February 1, 2005—sunny. -30° to -10°. Went to Glennallen to Post Office and shopping and lunch. Allen came over and broke trail to #1 property monument with his new snow machine. This will make it easier for the surveyor to do his job. Allen helped carry wood over to discuss repairing our Toyo stove. They had a piece of my birthday cake that Sylvia made and some ice cream. The Jim Odden came over to look over the welder and cutting torch. He is interested in buying the torch and I'm giving him the welder. Theresa called Happy Birthday greetings. So did Fran Collins and Reed Farmer and Brenda. Jeff called to tell me of buying two more rifles.

Wednesday, February 2, 2005—sunny. -30° to -10°. Put more wood in basement. Had to pump up the wheel barrow tire. Brother Marion called. He had got my most recent letter and wished Happy Birthday. Jim M. believes he had our Toyo Stove repaired and brought it over. I will attach the fuel line tomorrow. We had to rush off to Legion and auxiliary meeting in Glennallen. It's a long trip especially in this temperature. Told the guys no office position for me as we sold our place and planned to leave Alaska. Joe Virgin called and offered his regrets that we would be leaving.

Thursday, February 3, 2005—sunny. -34° to -14°. Charlie T. called just after lunch and talked quite awhile. Shortly after that Jack Phillips drove in to do as/built survey of our place as required in the sale agreement. He got it done easily this afternoon in spite of the cold. I got our Toyo stove hooked up and it seems to run OK. It tended to leak at the fuel line. I hope I got it tight enough. The four spruce hens are still feeding on spruce needle in the trees on east side of house. Jim Miller visited this morning—I gave him a fleshing beam for fox-coyote etc. This evening I called Jack and ask about the small piece of land the state gave back to us due to hwy realignment – he had not done anything about it. I must call the title co tomorrow.

Friday, February 4, 2005—sunny. -33° to -18°. Went to Glennallen. Lunch, shopping and cash checks at bank. Saw a moose today. Bev called and we had a long talk. The birds flock to the feeder. I worked on bathtub-shower.

Saturday, February 5, 2005—sunny. -36° to -19°. Went to Manning's and congratulating them on their 50th wedding anniversary. Slept a lot today. Took garbage to the pit. Spruce hens still feeding in the spruce trees.

Sunday, February 6, 2005—sunny, cloudy and 1" snow in evening. -31° to -5°. Rested quite a bit today. Sylvia fixed a dinner and we took it over to Mannings. Elaine is wheel chair bound so it is too hard for them to come here to a dinner. They taught us a new domino game called chicken foot.

Monday, February 7, 2005—partly cloudy. -13° to 7°. Called the title co. They wanted me to send by fax a letter of vacation to a small piece of land that went back to us from realignment of the hwy. Henry couldn't do it so Reyne Brockman did it. Dug the burn barrel out of snow and burned some trash.

Tuesday, February 8, 2005—light snow 2", cloudy. -23° to 21. Went to Glennallen bank. Post Office, shopping and lunch. Saw 5 caribou. Jim O came over and loaded up my welder- need front crankcase seal and my acetylene-oxygen torch. An Anchorage lady called and asked about our home for sale. Told her of the pending sale and its contingencies. She wants one of our fliers. Gave some specifics over the phone.

Wednesday, February 9, 2005—skiff of snow. 6° to 31°. Sylvia went to Queen's lunch. Waited for a call from title company. Did not come. Bill Buck called. Started snowgo and packed the trail to well. Checked the bulb in well. Took a bucket of coffee grounds down to garden. Plowed our lane and area around house and garage. Put isopro in gas tank of plow truck. Saw 2 caribou on our lake.

Thursday, February 10, 2005—mostly cloudy. 13° to 25°. We ask Harry and Sally to have breakfast at Eureka with us. They drove their car. Denny E. was eating breakfast when we got there. We just got started home and saw a great many ptarmigan on both sides of the hwy and some birds were picking up gravel from the roadway. Really neat to see them. A pick up hit and killed one bird. I picked it up and brought it home to eat. I sorted the manuals in the notebook those that will stay with the house went in a large notebook. Did some exercises. Nadia called. Jim O. called ask us to supper tomorrow night.

Friday, February 11, 2005—cloudy and 1/2" snow – breezy. 7° to 18°. Went to Glennallen to income tax service, PO shopping and bank and lunch. Went to Jim and Mary Odden's for a great supper. Met Joe and Dianna ?. Nice people to visit with. Jim and I went over to Billman's hanger to pick up some moving box's that their daughter Lisa gave us.

Saturday, February 12, 2005—sunny. -10° to 7°. Warren Obermier visited in the morning. Shot a pesky squirrel this afternoon. Reading "The Lynx Point People." My back is real bad.

Sunday, February 13, 2005—partly cloudy. -20° to -2°. Read a lot. Called Jeff. Talked to Amy also. Took trash to burn barrel. Sylvia went to a birthday party for Sandy Farmer, 50 yrs old. Called and left a message for Bev.

Monday, February 14, 2005—partly cloudy, cloudy. -15° to 20°. Cow and calf moose walked through our yard and out the lane. Studied papers regarding sale of our home. Looks snowy tonight. Ron Beshaw stopped by on his way home from his trip to China. He showed us lots of photos and told us how it went. The woman he went to meet got cold feet and backed out. Her family introduced him to another 31 year old woman. They hit it off. He went on a 28 hour one way bus trip with her to meet her family.

Tuesday, February 15, 2005—partly cloudy, 2" snow in night. -18° to 30°. Went to Glennallen shopping and lunch. Put a new bath tub diverter spout on tub. Plowed our snow, Manning's driveway. Packed trail down to well. Cleaned snow off gas bulk tank. Went to Allen's for dinner. Oddens showed up later and we all visited. Bev called and talked to Mom for a long time, that was nice. Jeff called a couple of times. My brother Jerry wrote us a letter.

Wednesday, February 16, 2005—cloudy down to ground at mid afternoon. 0° to 16°. Tinkered with the bathtub diverter and got it to screw on one more pipe thread. Slept and read a lot. Called Jeff and left a message for Charlie T. Sylvia's spruce hens have been absent for a week or so.

Thursday, February 17, 2005—sunny, beaut of a day. 0° to 18°. Took garbage to the pit. Exercises. Jeff called. We played some "chicken foot" dominoes.

Friday, February 18, 2005—very low clouds. 9° to 18°. Went to Glennallen. Lunch and shopping. The gas exploration is progressing. They are hauling snow and water and building what is called a winter road. Dan Pearman called. He hasn't heard yea or nay from their loan application to buy our home. Had a call regarding purchasing our Polaris LT snowgo. May come to see it tomorrow.

Saturday, February 19 2005—cloudy, skiff snow, sunny. 9° to 24°. Burned trash. Removed my tools from snowgo. Called Lisa Smayda with our condolences for loss of her dad. Took Bartley with us to Mexican dinner and installation of American Legion Post 27 officer for 2005. Stopped by a couple of over the road truckers and inquired about hauling our household goods to Minn. Didn't have much luck for sure. Stopped at Brown Bear and talked to Doug about giving my shooting magazines for door prizes at the shooting club Wild Game Feed and Auction.

Sunday, February 20, 2005—cloudy, sunny. 12° to 23°. Read some. Took a nap. We invited Dan and Patti Billman and Jim and Mary and Kari Odden here to supper. We had a really nice visit. Mike Airhart called to say he was interested in moving our household goods.

Monday, February 21, 2005—sunny. 10° to 25°. Estimated cubic feet of some things we will be moving to Minn. Cleaned ashes out of barrel stove in basement. Cow moose walked by on south side of house. Took pix. Called Nadia, Laura, didn't reach Beverly.

Tuesday, February 22, 2005—cloudy and one inch snow. 6° to 26°. Went to Glennallen. Lunch, flower shop and post office. Saw a couple moose. Put up the plow truck and snowgo for sale at a couple places.

Wednesday, February 23, 2005—sunny. 6° to 25°. Pulled some snow off the south end of garage roof and off the water hauling tank. Shoveled the snow off to one side. Sorted papers to be burned. Felt tired today. Called FedEx about shipping guns. Called Paul and Steve about receiving of the funds. F16 jets flew over us at very low altitude.

Thursday, February 24, 2005—sunny. 7° to 28°. The cow moose walked all over our place last night and today. Went to Eureka for breakfast. Put up a for sale flier on snowgo and snowplow and truck. Saw Allen and Dave there. Jim Odden visited - he is going back to work at McGraff. Rounded up some shipping I have around here. Estimated some more of my stuff in cubic feet.

Friday, February 25, 2005—sunny, partly cloudy. 10° to 22°. Went to Glennallen shopping and lunch. Dug up the blue bucket. The pile of dirt at garage hole wasn't frozen so hard but what I was able to get enough sand to fill the hole. The bucket left. We packaged Sylvia's quilting frame.

Saturday, February 26, 2005—cloudy and 1 1/2" snow. 9° to 26°. Decided on what to do with the blue bucket. Found a box in garage attic that was big enough to pack a quilt rack, the quilting hoop and the spinning wheel in and packed them. Located some other boxes.

Sunday, February 27, 2005—got 1 1/2" snow, then sunny. 16° to 24°. Wrote a letter and fixed a birthday card to Lee, Austen and Zach. Plowed our snow and Manning's. Tied up the spark plug wires on plow truck. Burned trash. Shoveled some snow. Sylvia fixed a stew and asked Allen, Roxanne, David and Heather (fiancé) Samantha, Reed over for supper. I put on a video movie (Calling Bears) after supper.

Monday, February 28, 2005—cloudy and 1 1/2" snow. 15° to 28°. Plowed our snow. Cleaned two drawers at the sink. Sorted good stuff from junk. Had Henry listen to plow truck motor. He thinks it has a bad plug or plug wire. Dan, the buyer of our place sent Henry an email saying it looks good that the sale will go through in 4-5 weeks.

Tuesday, March 1, 2005—cloudy, sunny, cloudy. 12° to 26°. Went to Glennallen shopping and lunch. Changed spark plugs on plow truck. The old ones were hard to get out. Put anti-seize on threads of the plug I put in. Tightened the valve cover bolts and changed air cleaner. Burned some trash. Fired up the snowgo and packed the trail down to the well. Saw a cow moose and calf down by and on the lake. They went from our place to Joe Junkers. A guy named "Don" called and inquired about buying the snowgo.

Wednesday, March 2, 2005—sunny, clouded in eve and light snow after dark. 2° to 25°. Helped Sylvia pack her best dishes in boxes. Changed oil and filter on plow truck. Shoveled snow off garbage pit. Took a shower and picked up Bart and went to Legion Post monthly business mtg. Got some Oreo cookies for the guys. Bart and I told yarns to and from Glennallen. Mannings got back this evening and picked up their mail.

Thursday, March 3, 2005—cloudy. 10° to 27°. Packaged our coin collection to be sent to Nadia. Prepared my .338 Winchester magnum for sale, hopefully before we leave for Minnesota. Helped Jim M. get his van closer to his garage.

Friday, March 4, 2005—fog, cloudy, skiff snow. 12° to 26°. Went to Glennallen. Coin collection sent to Nadia. Sold gas barrel to Chris Rhodes. Joe Virgin looked plow truck over and will bring it up at a church board mtg. Alerted Nadia to expect a package.

Saturday, March 5, 2005—3/4" snow in night, foggy morning. 15° to 34°. Went to gun show in Palmer. Got to see some people I know including Bart Bartly and Jeff, Amy, John Paul and Chelsie. Walked a lot. Had 3 inquiries on guns I had for sale but no takers. Bought 2 WW II rifle slings and one of them lacks the latch necessary for it to work. Talked to people about buying some of our books. Saw a moose and a bald eagle. Matanuska River is starting to open up.

Sunday, March 6, 2005—sunny, cloudy evening. 2° to 21°. Lots of pretty birds at the feeder eating the sunflower seeds Sylvia raised. Plowed the snow out by the woodshed. Shoveled the snow out of pickup box and made a path so we can get the summer set of tires that will go with the plow truck. Joe Virgin called to tell me the Mendeltna Chapel will buy our plow truck. Cleaned the junk out of it. Jim M. came over and tested and found the Toyo exhaust fan (spare) is well with "specks." Ed Farmer was flying his totally restored airplane the last two days.

Monday, March 7, 2005—sunny and very nice. 8° to 34°. Boxed up some reloading things. It is hard to find boxes that are a good fit. Burned some trash. Shoveled some snow. Started getting crates ready to pack rifles in. Called Henry and told him Mendeltna Chapel wanted the plow truck. Jeff called a couple times. We went to Manning for a supper of chicken soup and BLT's.

Tuesday, March 8, 2005—partly cloudy and breezy in evening. 15° to 42°. Went to Glennallen, lunch, bank and lumberyard. Called title office for info on our property sale. They called "Countrywide," the financier for the people buying our place. Then a Gordon Alington called me. They want our place appraised and if satisfied will finance it for the buyers. He likes the borrowers. They seem to be well qualified. Snow slide off house roof, had to shovel some of it out of our walkway. I pulled some snow off the east side of garage and pushed it off to the north. Don? Called and ask if I still had the Polaris long track for sale yet.

Wednesday, March 9, 2005—partly cloudy and cloudy and snow flurry in the afternoon. 13° to 42°. Loaded summer tires in plow truck. Pushed some snow away from snowgo trailer. Shoveled snow off of it and pulled it out in the open. Burned some trash. Joe Virgin brought a check to pay for the plow truck and drove it away. A spruce hen rested by garage door. When I tried to get a picture it ran towards me, hopped in the air and flew to a spruce tree that they like to eat needles from.

Thursday, March 10, 2005—mostly cloudy, 1/2" snow and flurries all day. 19° to 38°. Fiddled with garage door remote after we got back from breakfast at Eureka. Wrote letters.

Friday, March 11, 2005—3" snow over night. 24° to 41°. Cloudy and clearing in the afternoon. Sylvia went to queen's luncheon. I went to Glennallen to post office, lunch and left a number of shopping bag w/dozens of gun related magazines. Worked a couple hours cleaning out the storage shed. Burned lots of trash.

Saturday, March 12, 2005—partly cloudy. 18° to 42°. Did some more organizing and cleaning up preparing to move. I did not feel well. Sam Weaver stopped by and visited a couple hours. A guy came by to look at the snowmobile but doesn't have the money to buy it. We went to the wild game feed at the Brown Bear Road House. Put on by Copper Basin Shooting Club. We took a crock pot on sauerkraut for the pot luck and a car top carrier for a canoe and donated it for auction to raise club revenue.

Sunday, March 13, 2005—sunny, started snowing 5:00 PM. 25° to 45°. Spruce hen feed on a spruce tree in front yard. I am cleaning the woodshop and garage and worked all day. Burned lots of scrap wood and junk. Put a lot of kindling in wood shed. Allen brought up some peach muffins that Sammy had baked. Very good! Called Theresa.

Monday, March 14, 2005—3" snow in night, cloudy morning, then sunny. 18° to 40°. Worked at clearing up wood shop and garage. Burned lots of trash. Cast some 8 x 57 Mauser bullets for Jeff. Bev called this evening to talk to me.

Tuesday, March 15, 2005—mostly sunny. 4° to 33°. Went to Glennallen, lunch and shopping. Measured and made a list of some lumber to sell. Started packing some bullet casting things. Put gas checks on sized and lubed some 8 x 57 Mauser cast bullets. Changed out some light bulbs. Walked down to well twice. Appraiser from Fairbanks Jim Williams called – he will be here 3/24/05 to do our place for "Countrywide."

Wednesday, March 16, 2005—sunny. 1° to 35°. Made dividers for Sylvia's canned cranberry boxes. Burned lots of trash after moving the burn barrel near the garbage hole. Cleaned some more on garage and attic. Packed some reloading gear. Very tired tonight.

Thursday, March 17, 2005—sunny. 1° to 33°. Made a box for Christmas decorations that Sylvia handmade. We hope they survive the trip to Minn. I got four boxes of reloading gear packed to move. Warren Obermiller visited a couple times.

Friday, March 18, 2005—sunny. -2° to 34°. Went to Glennallen lunch and shopping. We packed more box's in anticipation of moving. Our work goes slow. Sylvia canned another batch of cranberry sauce. I have to remake some of the box's to fit the things we have to put in them. Gave Ron a stove, strainer and rugs.

Saturday, March 19, 2005—sunny. -0° to 37°. Remodeled some cardboard boxes. Made a cardboard tube to put a take down frame in that Nadia had given Sylvia. Loaded a stove in the truck. Got ready and we picked up Bart. Went to a corned beef and cabbage dinner at Legion Post. Very few people showed up.

Sunday, March 20, 2005—sunny turning cloudy in the afternoon, 15° to 24° to 8°. Sylvia worked at packing craft things and sewing material, blankets while I was packing reloading stuff. Burned some old books and magazines. Dan Billman called. Sylvia called her sister Frances.

Monday, March 21, 2005— -2° to 20°. Went to Glennallen to dentist. X-ray some teeth and evaluate what needs to be done to them. Took books and movies to Darrel and Brenda. They gave us some donuts. Went to John Kunik – he was busy. Talked to Kevin about filing income tax. Nadia and Laura called, the package got there. Dan Pearman's lender called to see if the appraiser had an appointment with us (yes). Got some more things packed to move.

Tuesday, March 22, 2005—partly cloudy. 1° to 24°. Went to Glennallen. Lunch and shopping. Got some more cardboard boxes. Pack some more boxes. Cleaned up some upstairs. Burned some trash.

Wednesday, March 23, 2005—sunny and light breeze. 10° to 36°. We burned a lot of trash. Cleaned the house. Straightened garage and woodshop, swept floor and the storage shed. Saw Ed Farmer out at mailbox and visited a little while. Gordon A. "Countrywide" called for info regarding sale of our place. Said he would expedite the matter when he gets the appraisal at his office.

Thursday, March 24, 2005—clear and some breeze. 2° to 35°. We have house etc. ready for appraiser to show up at 11:00 AM. He called to change the appointment to 5:00 PM. Then about 4:30 PM called again and ask to come here at 9:00 AM tomorrow. Of course we agreed. We rested today. That in itself was good for us. I did very little else.

Friday, March 25, 2005—partly cloudy. 7° to 34°. Jim Williams – appraiser from Fairbanks and for Countrywide came to do his job. Seemed like a nice guy. Later Charlie T. and son Paul visited in the afternoon and had supper and more nice visiting in evening. Then they went to Mary Oddens for the night.

Saturday, March 26, 2005—partly cloudy. 13° to 38°. Charlie and Paul came over. He gave me a crate. Tom and Lisa Smyada visited most of day. Gave Tom a couple books and Lisa two gallon jars. Played dominoes and cards with Paul.

Mary O. came over to visit. Charlie did some small jobs for me. Very helpful.

Sunday, March 27, 2005—snow, sun, snow 2". 19° to 37°. Called Theresa. Charlie stopped in with flyer he had typed. He bought the ATV trailer. Jeff Routt picked up his rifle and video tapes. I packed winter gear. Went to Allen and Roxanne's to an Easter dinner. Visited with them and some guests.

Monday, March 28, 2005—2" more snow. 16° to 34°. Packed some more boxes. Laura called.

Tuesday, March 29, 2005—mostly sunny. 6° to 28°. Went to Glennallen. Checked on income tax progress. Post Office, shopping and lunch. Packed some more stuff. Preacher Jim Miller stopped by to visit a while. Got truck ready to go to Anchorage tomorrow. Mary O. and Kari brought over the list of things we have for sale that she printed up and made copies of.

Wednesday, March 30, 2005—partly cloudy. -4° to 33°. Went to Palmer-Wasilla and Anchorage. Got lots done but we couldn't get Sylvia's prescriptions refilled – she has to see her doctor first. Saw a bald eagle. We got back about 4:15 PM. We got a fire proof safe, computerized. Took me over an hour to figure out how to lock and unlock it.

Thursday, March 31, 2005—cloudy, sunny, a little breeze and very nice. 17° to 39°. Packed three rifles. Started on four rifle crates by resetting the nails and painted them. Have a small fire in wood shop to help dry the paint. Dan Pearman called to say the closing for our place will be April 29. We talked quite awhile. He offered to pay the repair that the Suzuki needs. Beverly called. Nadia called to tell us Chuck's dad passed away. So far 65.5" snow.

Friday, April 1, 2005—sunny with light snow shower. 8° to 40°. Went to Glennallen to income tax preparer. Sylvia got some cardboard boxes. We went to lunch and paid the electric bill. She packed three boxes of material and I worked on the wooden boxes to ship guns in.

Saturday, April 2, 2005—put hasps on the four wood boxes. Packed the scroll saw for Theresa. Repack the nice box with the three longest rifles. The military boxes are 5 ½ shorter. Theresa called a couple times.

Sunday, April 3, 2005—sunny. Tried to start snowgo with no luck. Pulled it out from behind the Suzuki with a come-a-long. Hurt my back rolling the Suzuki back a few feet so I could charge its dead battery. Dan and Patty Billman stopped in and we had a nice visit. I gave Patty a cutting board set I had made. After they went home I started the Suzuki and drove it up near the house and inflated its tires. Then pulled a garden hose out that was on the hot water heater and hosed the Suzuki down so it will be clean as I'm taking it into Anchorage to have an oil leak fixed. I loaded it on the truck. Rudbecks called and Jeff called.

Monday, April 4, 2005—sunny. 1° to 37°. Went to Wasilla to Sylvia's doctor. Also to Anchorage and left Suzuki at dealer to repair an oil leak. Due to misunderstanding I drove back from Wasilla thinking the Suzuki would be fixed – wrong trip for nothing. Sylvia did see two moose. Had a good meal at Windbreak Café of skillet prime rib.

Tuesday, April 5, 2005—mostly sunny, cloudy evening. 14° to 42°. Did a little more packing. Started the snowgo and checked the well. Pulled the tarp off the well and burned it as it was worn out. Allen visited in evening. Had several phone calls today.

Wednesday, April 6, 2005—cloudy, sunny. 22° to 43°. Snow settled and melted a lot. We worked hard at packing our stuff that will go with us. I'm having a hard time getting the guns into the crates as they are about 2" shorter than the guns. The trucker we have been talking to about hauling our stuff stopped by. He can back in on our lane to house. He tells me customs will want $75.00 per gun to go through Canada!!! I told him I would check out shipping by container to Tacoma WA and onto Mpls and let him know.

Thursday, April 7, 2005—sunny and some breeze. 20° to 42°. Worked at packing more stuff. Burned things we don't need. Mike Roscovious was reading our electric meter and visited awhile. I had told him I would give him some cast bullets.

Friday, April 8, 2005—mostly sunny and some breeze. 10° to 43°. Went to Glennallen, lunch, bank, Post Office, groceries. Lots of ph calls. Worked at sorting and packing boxes and burning trash. Brenda and Darrel brought us a spaghetti dinner. They are interested in some of the things we will be selling at garage sale.

Saturday, April 9, 2005—sunny. 11° to 44°. Tried to call Marion – he returned my call later. Today is his 72nd birthday. Put a new bulb in the light in the well. Boxed more stuff. Worked in the wood shop on some things. We sure get tired. Reed and Brett of the moving company stopped in to estimate the size of container we will need for moving our household goods.

Sunday, April 10, 2005—cloudy, sunny all day, cloudy in evening. 13° to 45°. Put varithane on 6 wood clothes hangers. Made garage sale signs. Jim and Mary Odden visited for an hour. Ron Beshaw and Rich Lampe visited 2 hrs in morning. Sylvia canned 12 pints of cranberry sauce. Baked a cake. I burned 6 arm loads of trash and made a lid and padding for berry jars.

Monday, April 11, 2005—Cloudy, sunny, it snowed in Heavenly Ridge till noon. 24° to 45°. Sylvia canned cranberries, blueberries and rose hip - current jelly all day. I worked on moving stuff phone calls. Darrel and Brenda came for the Polaris snowgo and snowgo trailer. We ask them to have pizza at Mendeltna then they wouldn't let us pay for dinner! Stopped at Jerry Snows and picked up a lot of sacked aluminum cans. He was glad to see them go.

Tuesday, April 12, 2005—mostly sunny. 28° to 43°. Did very little packing. Shoveled a lot of snow off of and in front of a two wheel trailer with four log chains I was able to reach the truck. Got it ¾ the way out of deep snow and had to shovel more snow out of the way. Got it out then. Sure couldn't sell it back in the deep snow. Went over to Henry's. He gave me 6 small plastic bags of aluminum cans. Must have over 200 lbs now. Keven had our income taxes done and I wrote a check for $176. Put stamps on envelope, ready for mail box. Sylvia is still canning berries. We went to Glennallen, shopping, cardboard boxes and lunch. Sylvia saw an eagle. Allen, Roxanne, and Reed visited for awhile.

Wednesday, April 13, 2005—sunny. 13° to 43°. We boxed the last of the canning of blueberries, cranberries and sauces and jam jelly. Worked on getting garage ready for moving sale. Prepared the aluminum cans and sacked them. Loaded them and some copper and aluminum in pickup. Burned more trash. We are getting tired. Joe Roche called as soon as he got back from Florida and North Carolina.

Thursday, April 14, 2005—sunny. 11° to 47°. We took the aluminum cans and copper to recycling place in Anchorage. Ate Royal Fork chicken for lunch, much to Sylvia's delight. Visited Rosemary Bartley in extended care. This was a bad day for her and she asked us to leave after a few minutes. Tried to find a box big enough for my bison head mount with no luck. Picked up the Suzuki ATV and brought it home. Nice day for the trip.

Arranged saw horse and plywood sheets in the garage to display things we sell in the moving sale.

Friday, April 15, 2005—breeze in evening. 13° to 42°. Went to Glennallen shopping and lunch. Put our moving sale on the Glennallen radio. Only got one box. Worked in garage getting it ready for the moving sale tomorrow. Ray Kiser, his wife and son Jacobi came and bought the lathe planer, skill saw worm drive and 61 pieces of diamond willow. After supper I worked on direction sale signs.

Saturday, April 16, 2005—some breezy from south. 9° to 41°. We put up the signs about 9:00 AM. Before long we had lots of people here all wanted to be waited on. It was quite hectic for awhile. We got ride of quite a lot of stuff. It was a good day. We visited with lots of people. Ron Baker from Delta Jct. stopped in with a lady. Gave me the latest news of his family and people from that area. Ron Beshaw barely got started working at his new job at a gold mine when he had an attack of kidney stone. Will be ok when it is passed.

Sunday, April 17, 2005—sunny and beautiful. 10° to 45°. Put up the signs about 10:00 AM. We had quite a few stop in, didn't sell much large stuff. Put out more things. Very tired tonight – both of us.

Monday, April 18, 2005—partly cloudy. 17° to 43°. A cold wind blew in from the mountains and Tazlina Lake. We had a pretty good day with the moving sale. Got a compliment on our highway signs on the sale. Rhynell Hoffman came over this evening to see what we had to sell. We filled her car clear full with stuff. She had coffee and a bowl of ice cream with us. Bev called.

Tuesday, April 19, 2005—cloudy, sunny. 19° to 50°. Worked hard at sorting trash from moving sale items. Sold near 600 today. Sylvia went to Glennallen and put up for sale fliers. Did some shopping. Jeff Routt's sister Mary bought our lawn mower and dredge.

Wednesday, April 20, 2005—partly cloudy and westerly breeze. 21° to 51°. Worked hard at getting more things out to sell. The people seem to come in spurts. Sylvia got a little rest after lunch. We had a pretty good day – got lots done too.

Thursday, April 21, 2005—\cloudy, sunny, cloudy. 30° to 52°. People started coming about 9:30 AM. We did quite well today. Dan Pearman called. He will be here for the closing on the sale of our home Apr. 29th.

Friday, April 22, 2005—Cloudy, sunny, snow is going fast. 31° to 54°. Sylvia went to Glennallen and put up new sale flyers. We had fewer buyers but did OK. It is very tiring to have lots of people around all day. But is must be done. I ask Allen to scrape the slush off our driveway. Sylvia gave him two quarts sauerkraut and other stuff. He also gave me a couple big cardboard boxes. Lots of water on top of lake ice. Went to Henry's - he showed me Dick Proenneke movie of his wilderness life.

Saturday, April 23, 2005—sunny. 26° to 54°. Boxed up AK geographic periodicals. Got things ready. Opened the place up for moving sales. We did fair. Duane picked up the gold screw. Walt paid me for the Winchester model 70. We went to a dinner at Legion Post. Saw two bunches of caribou while driving home. Mary and her hubby Cal Bowman came and picked up the water hauling tank.

Sunday, April 24, 2005—sunny. 33° to 54°. Boxed more books. Tended the moving sale. It was slow and increased to 5 cars and trucks at one time!! Rhynell has bought lots of stuff and will buy all we have left. Cleaned out the storage trailer.

Monday, April 25, 2005—sunny. 26° to 56°. Filled some more boxes. Carried more things out to sell. Tried to take it easy today. Didn't put our moving sale signs. Gave Denny E. two Army sleeping bags. Both Marvin and Allen visited. Gave Allen some moving sale things. The kestrels are mating now.

Tuesday, April 26, 2005—sunny. 28° to 60°. Made a "crate" for a mirror Sylvia wants to keep. Had a couple customers – we didn't have moving sale signs up. I'm tired tonight.

Wednesday, April 27, 2005—sunny. 35° to 62°. We ran moving sale again today. Sales went good. Finished mirror crate and started one for the buffalo mount. Some old friends stopped by. Rhynell continues to haul things away. Such a nice beautiful day.

Thursday, April 28, 2005—sunny and windy in the evening. 35° to 65°. We did well with moving sale – got a few buck for things we don't need. Worked on the box – crate for buffalo head. Dan Pearman called. He was at motel out of Palmer. He said Genie was trying to get insurance on this home so it would qualify for a loan. He will be here late tomorrow evening.

Friday, April 29, 2005—Happy Birthday Sylvia. 33° to 63°. She did not feel well and went back to bed this morning. She felt better in the afternoon. We had lots of phone calls. Dan Pearman got insurance on the property including liability. This held up the closing and delayed it till next week? We had the moving sale going on this afternoon. Just a small amount of sales. Denney E. told me of seeing a black bear on Slide Mt. I got the buffalo head and sheep horns crated.

Saturday, April 30, 2005—sunny and some breeze. 34° to 64°. We ask Dan and William to have breakfast at Eureka with us. Harry and Judy Termin arrived there a minute after we parked and ate with us. We had a good visit. 5-6 cars to buy from our moving sale even though all our signs were down. Allen and Roxanne, Samantha and Reed visited as well as Denny, Jo Eastman and Marvin Overmiller among others. Dan and William ate supper with us. Played a card game and a domino game with William. Dan, Sylvia and I discussed how we would handle the change of possession when the time came.

Sunday, May 1, 2005—sunny and some breeze. 33° to 64°. Looks to be snowing on the ice field to the south. Switched the summer tires on the truck. Did some odd jobs. Put out moving sale signs about 1:00 PM. Sold a few dollars worth. Went to Mendeltna for pizza. Dan and Sue William joined us.

Monday, May 2, 2005—sunny. 32° to 57°. We did small jobs till Dan and William got here about 11:00 AM. We walked him through the maintenance and operation of our house. Took some pictures. Hot dogs for lunch and they left for Wasilla, Anchorage and the airport to catch a plane back to Kentucky. I put out moving sale signs. Made a couple sales. Darrel Gerry was on their computer looking for airfares and found Sun Country offering one way fare to Mpls for $111.-!! This morning I called Nadia to buy two fares for Sylvia and me good for 5/20/05.

Tuesday, May 3, 2005—sunny. 27° to 53°. More clouds and a little rain in late afternoon. Went to Glennallen. Advised both electric and phone companies that we were moving. Went to Post Office, bank, groceries and radio station. Had lunch. Back home I ran the Suzuki over to Henry's. He will attempt to install a new oil seal. I cleaned the garage and put more books out for sale. Laura called this evening.

Wednesday, May 4, 2005—partly cloudy. 32° to 55°. Rain and hailed here in early evening. Jim Barnes and Rhynell hauled four loads of lumber, roofing and steel to Rhynell. We loaded culverts, wire fencing, lumber on Marvin Obermiller's long trailer to go to her place. Jim loaded the crate and belt pulley attachment for a 7U D4 CAT in my truck. Art and Bonnie Wikle visited and helped with some loading of Marvin's trailer. We okay'd the ordering of a "container" for our household goods. It is to be here May 18th. Went to monthly Legion business meeting. John Kunik had closed shop early so I couldn't leave the belt pulley attachment there.

Thursday, May 5, 2005—Marvin, Jim and Rhynell all got here about 9:00 AM and Marvin pulled his loaded trailer to their place. We got ready to go to Glennallen to have lunch with Joe and Theresa Roche. Enjoyed the lunch and visit with them. Then dropped the belt pulley attachment off at John Kunik's machine shop. Stopped by Darrel and Brenda's for a couple of hours. Back home we had a light supper and went to Allen and Roxanne's. We gave Kyle a large box of Louie Lamoure paper backs and Allen planed the knife cut off 2 of Sylvia's cutting boards.

Friday, May 6, 2005—nice day. 28° to 59°. Went to Glennallen. Paid phone bill, shopping and lunch. Cleaned up trash and burned. Henry had the Suzuki back together and drove it over here and I took him back home. Henry got some books and brought Sam over to pick out some for him. I gave Marvin four 50 gal drums so he could haul diesel home for his truck. He hauled a load of stuff to Rhynell's for us. Gordon called to tell us there will be another delay in closing our home sale.

Saturday, May 7, 2005—sunny and breeze. 33° to 69°. Packed a few boxes. Got all the boxes and plastic from attic over the garage. Packed a big box with caribou horns and water fowl hunting gear. Melanie Junker got all of Sylvia's greenhouse supplies and cleaned all the trash out. I burned the trash. Ralph and Roma got here late afternoon. Visited and we went to Eureka for dinner. Back home we visited then Ralph and I went to gravel pit. Shot pistols at pop bottles and had a great time.

Sunday, May 8, 2005—sunny and a nice breeze. 40° to 67°. Ralph and Roma Fuson came down from Fairbanks. Brought a lot of food. We loafed around on the lawn. I gave him a lot of ammo and other stuff including a frozen coyote pelt. Picked up more cast bullets from a melting snow berm. Walked down to the well. Read. Adjusted some supports for the TGI under the waterline. Carried coffee grounds down to garden. Drained the last of the gasoline from the storage tank.

Monday, May 9, 2005—sunny and some breeze. 38° to 70°. Put together a large wooden box for Sylvia's Hauser. Started one for tools. Filled some ammo boxes this morning Burned some ammo. Emptied burn barrel. Gordon of Countrywide called and wanted proof in form of pictures of the smoke detectors and the drop pipe from the water heater pop off valve. Over half of the ice on the lake went out today. Two swans and some ducks are now seen using the water. Mary and Kari O. came and took digital photos to send to Gordon. Marvin came over to see if there was anything he could do for us.

Tuesday, May 10, 2005—sunny and light breeze. 32° to 67°. Today is our 57th wedding anniversary. Sylvia went to Glennallen on errands shopping and lunch. I worked on a heavy duty crate. In the afternoon, I sorted fishing gear and prepped it for moving. The washing machine quit for Sylvia that affected two cycles which lead me to think belt trouble. Sure enough the drive belt needed adjustment and it then worked OK. Yea! There is only 1/6 of our lake with rotten candle ice on it. Ducks are flying and courting.

Wednesday, May 11, 2005—sunny with strong breeze from the south. 34° to 69°. The rest of lake ice went out early this morning. Got some more packaging done. Lots of telephone time back and forth with Dan's lender, the people who are going to move our things to Minnesota, also Dan Pearman. Plus Jim Barnes – he drove the pickup about 4 miles, turned around and came back. Made me an offer of $4500.00. We didn't have a deal. He had Rhynell with him. They stayed a couple hours. I got to take the beer sign over to Henry's and it was time to get ready to go to Allen and Roxanne's for a BBQ hamburger supper. Mary and Kari O were there too. Visited quite a while. There is a bad forest fire at Renn Lake area.

Thursday, May 12, 2005—cloudy, with good breeze sometimes. 37° to 57°. Filled more boxes. Pulled some nails and started taking the safety screws out of some furniture. Rhynell got some more stuff and gave us another check. I hauled the bladder, 6 electric motors and some fertilizer-lime to her place. Pulled a winter broken birch tree over and filled the hole, cut trunk into manageable lengths and put them in wood shop. Started burning the stump. Tired tonight. Sylvia is feeling better this evening.

Friday, May 13, 2005—Cloudy and very light showers, cleared up before noon. 34° to 64°. Got lots boxed today. Lots of company. Allen brought lunch. Very nice. D. Billman stopped by and I gave him the ramp for the trailer he bought. Marvin stopped by. Rhynell hauled multiple loads of scrap steel etc.

Saturday, May 14, 2005—pretty nice day. 36° to 62°. Rhynell hauled some more stuff. Dan and Mary O came over and got his trailer ramp and she took Charlie T ATV trailer to store for him. I brought 80+ coffee cans from lower garden and smashed them and put them in garbage pit. Worked at packing job. Allen came over for bolts and steel but too late.

Sunday, May 15, 2005—Woke up to rain, we got 3/4", it quit early afternoon. 36° to 48°. Rich Lampe came to look at some blank ammo. Offered 30. I let him have it for that as I can't send it on the boat. We burned lots of cardboard today and boxed quit a bit of stuff. Upstairs is close to finished. Fred Rungee stopped by on the way to Labrador for the summer. He left gifts as usual. We will miss him.

Monday, May 16, 2005—Rain 1/2" and froze 1/4" ice. Went to Wasilla for shopping and signed the papers completing the sale of our home to Dan Pearman and two of his friends. Then went to Eagle River and using a map Dan Billman drew, found his and Patti's home. We were there only a short time and Patti came home and not long after Dan came home from work. We had a good visit and a very good steak dinner. More visiting and ice cream and off to bed and a good nights sleep. They live on a lake. It is pretty there and quiet.

Tuesday, May 17, 2005—Breezy, cloudy morning and partly cloudy afternoon. 33° to 61°. Changed oil in pickup. Packed more stuff. Rhynell hauled away several car loads. Darrel and Brenda stopped by. We gave them a lot of frozen food and lots of other things. Went to Allen and Roxanne for a pot luck and cook out. Quite a few families from the neighborhood were there to wish us well on this next adventure in our life. It is after 11:00 PM as I write this. Mary O and Kari O stopped by on their way home and helped us take our bed apart so it can be loaded on the container tomorrow morning. They really got after it! Jeff Routt called wanting to know when we would get to Anchorage. Jim O. called and talked awhile.

Wednesday, May 18, 2005—mostly sunny. 38° to 62°. The movers came after 8:00 AM and started wrapping furniture, carrying boxes out into the yard. About 10:00 AM the tractor trailer showed up and promptly drove out in the wet sand and got very stuck. Finally they allowed me to call Ed Farmer to come and pull them out, which he did. Then the driver went out near Hwy - turned around and backed in to be loaded. This worked well. These guys work very fast. We had a helluva time packing some boxes and answering questions about what all was to be loaded consequently some things failed to get loaded on the trailer. Mostly not very important stuff. Finally they left, we spent hours burning last of clothes etc, junk papers and such. Roxanne, Melody did the hardest part of washing and cleaning the house. Sylvia helped and got quite tired. Mary O. vacuumed the garage attic and other work which helped a lot. Sam helped a lot today. Then Darrel and Brenda showed up and finished out the day. Brenda made a pizza supper, then we all worked some more. Emotions ran high when Allen, Roxanne left to go home. We gave hug and heartfelt thanks to everyone who helped so much today. Sammy and Reed came to visit and say good-bye. Shortly thereafter David and Heather were here and another emotional good-bye. They plan to get married. We did a few small chores and went to bed at 11:30 PM.

Thursday, May 19, 2005—mostly sunny. Up early and packing like mad. Burning more trash. People came to get their things or to take things to store for folks who couldn't get here for themselves. The moving gang really worked fast. The semi drive drove off into the sandy fill near the septic line. Ed Farmer came over and pulled it out on solid land. The driver backed out to end of our lane turned around and back in like he should have in the first place and they loaded our stuff into a 45 foot trailer. Then loaded the pickup in the trailer and chocked it good and they were gone. Then we found some things that got missed in the hullabaloo and we have to pack that into two boxes of 70# each. Showered and Darrel and Brenda drove us to Palmer where we cashed-traded small bill for one hundreds and closed our account out at the bank. Shopped for money belts. Tried to sell caribou horns with no luck. Ate supper at North Slope Restaurant. Went to Jeff and Amy's. They drove us over to see the new to them home they are buying.

We watched a couple hunting movies and visited. Mother and I counted our money (cash) and put it in money belts for traveling tomorrow.

Friday, May 20, 2005—up early. We all went to McDonald's for breakfast. Then Jeff drove us to airport, helped load our heavy luggage on a car and said good-by and went to work. We had no trouble getting checked in for our flight. It left a little late. Nadia met us. Collected our baggage and had a little problem with the rear door latch but Chuck knew how to fix that. Got the grand tour of their new place. Had some pizza and were ready to go to bed. Been another hectic day.

Saturday, May 21, 2005—pretty nice day though windy all morning. We went to "Target" for some shopping and to green house. Nadia for garden and flower plants. Sylvia got Nadia a nice flower planting.

Sunday, May 22, 2005—back here I helped Nadia clean up some spilled black dirt. When Chuck got back from taking his mother to lunch I helped him with some small jobs in garage and he showed me what he wanted done in the storage shed to prepare it for our things when they get here. Chuck cooks a very good sirloin steak, sweet corn and bread dinner this eve. We can't seem to reach any of the rest of the family – except for Laura.

Monday, May 23, 2005—sunny and nice. Laura came over with Joey and Maggie. We went driving. Saw a for sale house, we didn't care for it. Drove around some more with no luck. Back at Nadia's had a sandwich and started cleaning and organizing the storage shed. Had a heck of a time getting their bicycles hung off the floor. When Chuck came home from work he said it would have been OK to have hung them upside down by the wheel rims. Darn!

Tuesday, May 24, 2005—71°. Nadia had the day off. Went to eye Dr. for tests. Ordered two pair glasses. Went to Fleet Farm and got a pair jeans. Didn't do much. I am stiff from yesterday. Dan Pearman called while we were out and he wasn't in when I called him.

Wednesday, May 25, 2005—Rain all day. Helped Chuck install pipe and shutoff for watering plants from on the deck off the kitchen. When Nadia got off work we went north to a couple towns looking (drive by) at homes for sale. All were too pricey for us. We bought supper at a Chinese buffet and gas for their car. Theresa called in evening.

Thursday, May 26, 2005—Re-arranged the bicycle hook hangers. Chuck and I put the trailer under the deck and hooked up a hose to water plants. Nadia got me started on email lessons.

Friday, May 27, 2005—went with Chuck looking for a riding lawn mower for him and a dock to unload our pickup out of the semi-trailer when it gets here with our stuff. In the afternoon, we went to visit his mother. Nadia downloaded some more properties for us to consider. So many are small lots or high priced.

Saturday, May 28, 2005—Went to St Cloud. Looked at lots of houses, priced high or unsuitable for us. Went to Milaca. Found one that was interesting but couldn't see it today. Later in the evening we learned more about it and circumstances. The caution flags are up. We get to see it about noon tomorrow. Then we will go to Little Falls – Royalton and look at more houses. Chuck got pretty tired today and went to bed early.

Sunday, May 29, 2005—Went to Milaca to look at a house – didn't like it or a few others. Went to Randall. Saw outside of a beautiful brick home. Just loved it but out of our price range. Just before we got to Little Falls we saw a few house and one may be the one for us. Large garden spot for Sylvia. Large four stall garage. Real nice older home. We're not able to see house interior. Looked at a lot of houses in Little Falls and rejected most for price, lot size, location etc. Pretty tired when we got back to Nadia and Chuck's. Long day of driving for Nadia.

Monday, May 30, 2005—Chuck, Nadia, Sylvia, Brad and I put up a "Cabana" on their deck. I help Chuck bury some chicken wire in their gardening area in an effort to keep moles from burrowing in that area. We made plans to go back to Little Falls to look at a house we may be interested in.

Tuesday, May 31, 2005—Chuck drove us to Little Falls. After lunch we met "Roxanne" realtor who has the listing of a house we are interested in. The house has a large yard and will accommodate a garden for Sylvia. It has a four car garage. The house has lots of small rooms but can be made to work for us. Some modifications and repair have to be done. Sylvia likes it and thinks it will work for us and it is in our price range. When Nadia got home we went to Costco's and got prime rib eye steaks and a special bread for Chuck. We set up a meeting to sign a purchase agreement tomorrow. We had a message on phone that semi-trailer was in Mpls with our household belongings as is our pickup truck. These got here 7-10 days early.

Wednesday, June 1, 2005—went to Becker Minnesota. Met the realtor Roxanne. We signed a purchase agreement and made a $500.00 earnest money down payment on a house on outskirts of Little Falls, Minnesota. Afterward we had lunch and came back to Dayton. There was a flurry of phone calls involving the counter offer and our acceptance then more calls trying to get the trailer with our household goods out of the rail yard. We had hoped to escape loading and unloading it twice. Beverly, Theresa and Vanessa called today.

Thursday, June 2, 2005—got a cashier's check at the bank to pay for the inspection of the house we plan to buy. Made several calls regarding the inspection. Went to Nadia's place of employment. Realty agent faxed purchase agreement price change that we had to initial and fax back to her. Chuck fixed shrimp shish kabobs for dinner. Spent a nice evening out on the deck.

Friday, June 3, 2005—mowed lawn. Pruned tree. Serviced mower. Small job or two. Got a surprise delivery of semi trailer with our pickup and household goods in late afternoon. A towing co with flat bed truck came and unloaded the pickup from trailer and let truck down on tarmac. All went well. Cost $100. The battery connection was corroded and had to be wire brushed before I could start the truck. We unloaded the winter tires and some stuff that used to be in storage shed at Nelchina. Looks like rain tonight. The truck driver parked the trailer in the driveway so that Nadia and Chuck can get their vehicles in and out. He sure seemed like a nice guy.

Saturday, June 4, 2005—there was a big #3 birthday for Great granddaughter, Maggie here at Nadia and Chucks. Darrel Breider from New Mexico was here with new wife. Nice party. Sylvia, Brad, Chuck and I unloaded over ½ of our household goods. After the party guests left, filled about ½ Chuck's garage. Steve called with news of their new house.

Sunday, June 5, 2005—Sylvia and I unloaded most of the smaller boxes before noon. Later Tyler, Beverly, Theresa, Sylvia and I finished the unloading in between showers. We then had pizza and brownies - cake. It was nice working on a job that needed doing with the girls. Nadia has a right foot in bad shape.

Monday, June 6, 2005—Sylvia and I went to the bank to cash a couple small checks. Got some gas and picked up some lumber for a grape arbor for Nadia and Chuck. I put together a composter so she can compost table scraps etc. She brought home the Minnesota DOT driver license study book she got off the Internet.

Tuesday, June 7, 2005—94° in the afternoon. Got my little post hole digger out and assembled. Chuck didn't think we needed to use it. We got the supports built for the grape arbor when he got home this afternoon. The place he chose for one of the posts happened to be close to a buried TV cable, but we missed it. Then we quite for the day--too hot. Called some old friends from around Leader, Minnesota. (The farm we had before we went to Alaska was 8.5 miles north of Motley, and about five miles south of the little town of Leader.) It is nice to reconnect.

Wednesday, June 8, 2005—Lots of rain last night. 88° in the afternoon. When Chuck came home from work we finished putting up the grape arbor. Sylvia helped also. Called Joe Roche. I have a headache tonight. Tried to call Allen Farmer with no luck.

Thursday, June 9, 2005—nice day. 80s. Laura, Maggie, and Joey came over and we went garage-saling. Sylvia got a pair of shoes and a telephone and recorder. I got a shovel handle and a garden rake. Back then to Nadia and Chucks. Nadia was at work and Chuck went to see his mother. The grass dried off pretty good by noon so I mowed the lawn here. Took a couple hours. Called Larry Adams and Henry and Roxanne Farmer. Did some reading. We don't care for air conditioning – at least at these temps. It feels so cold to us.

Friday, June 10, 2005—lightening and rain in night and to mid-morning. Went to get my eye glasses in Roseville, Minnesota. One pair lightweight with grey tint in sunshine. Both are bifocal. Then to Laura and Brads. Nadia and us babysat Maggie and Joey while Laura and Brad took a break and went to lunch. We had toasted cheese sandwiches and coffee with them when they got back to house. Got wieners on way home. Sylvia and Nadia are making rhubarb upside down cake. Called realtor Roxanne – she says sewer passed its test. Water quality test results not back yet.

Saturday, June 11, 2005—rained hard and tornados-though not near us. Temp is in the 80s, Chuck brought a small charcoal broiler home and asked me to assemble it. He then used it to do hamburgers for supper.

Sunday, June 12, 2005—beautiful day, 80s. Visited Laura, Maggie and Joey. Brad was with his dad on a job in St Cloud. Did some shopping, came back to Nadia's. Then went back over to Brad and Laura for chicken fried steak dinner. Played some more with the kids mostly watching the antics that they go through while playing.

Monday, June 13, 2005—Mostly cloudy & rain, some heavy and tornado alerts all over mid Minnesota and in the 80s. My left knee is sore. Didn't do much today. Got a note from Rhynell with check. Also FFG realtor called – the water test of well on the property we intend to buy was satisfactory. Nadia developed some neat pix of the place at Little Falls. Went to Fleet Farm store in Anoka and did a little shopping.

Tuesday, June 14, 2005—quite cloudy. 70°. Went with Chuck to Menard's building supplies. He got a light fixture and some product to remove engine oil from the asphalt in front of the garage. When I finished with the asphalt I helped a little bit with the light though not much. Looked for our coffee pot with no luck. Made a couple calls to AK. Thanked Rhynell for check and letter and Dan Pearman who is staying in the house he bought from us. Learned Sam Weaver had to kill a black bear that got into his food and was hanging out around Sam's cabin.

Wednesday, June 15, 2005—mostly sunny. 70°. We went with Chuck to Menards. He did some shopping. Sylvia looked for a lamp globe. My knee is real bad. Helped Chuck put up new outside house lights. Nadia, Sylvia and I went to Lee Austen's GED graduation exercises. His sister and family, mother and his girl friend and some other friends were there also. Chuck showed me how to change out water line filters.

Thursday, June 16, 2005—sunny. 75°. Went yard-saling. Sylvia bought a couple dressers. Laura got a small table for her kids. My leg gave me a lot of trouble. Did some small things here.

Friday, June 17, 2005—sunny. 85°. Sylvia and Nadia went to Laura's. I helped with some of Chucks projects. Sylvia and Nadia helped put down a black plastic material to discourage weeds. Chuck could only find six bags of mulch that was on sale to put on the black stuff. We started building a work bench he wants in his garage.

Saturday, June 18, 2005—sunny. 85°. Went to several places in this area. Mostly Nadia and Chuck shopping. Back here we put more mulch in their garden. Then we worked at building a work bench for the garage. Got it done and a vice mounted on it. Nadia and Sylvia spent a lot of time over at Laura and Brads. Got some great pix of Maggie and Joey. Nadia printed and sent pix of our new house to Henry, Marion, Jim O and Gerry's.

Sunday, June 19, 2005—80s.

Monday, June 20, 2005—80s. Stormy day, wind and rain.

Tuesday, June 21, 2005—sunny. 85° +. Swept up some of storm trash. Mowed most of lawn.

Wednesday, June 22, 2005—High 80s - Low 90s. Went to Fleet Farm to buy a lawn mower - they had none in stock. Got a pair of jeans and some groceries at Cub store at supper time. Roxanne (realtor) called asking if we would back out of our contact to buy the house in Little Falls. Seems the sellers lost his job and can't get a loan to build a new house. As we were talking this new development she called back to say that the sellers on talking it over some more themselves had decided they would rescind their request. Sooo it looks like the closing will still go on as scheduled 6/30. Sure had us shook up for a few minutes. Helped Chuck with a few of his jobs around here.

Thursday, June 23, 2005—very breezy. 99°. Mowed the rest of the lawn. Chuck was gone most all the day. I called four insurance agents for quotes to insure our house we are buying. That took 5-6 hrs out of the middle of the day.

Friday, June 24, 2005–Shower in night, sunny day. 82°. Went grocery shopping and garage-saling. Wrote a check to CVEA for electricity in Glennallen. Filled out some change of address postal cards. Nadia's flowers and garden stuff is growing by leaps and bounds.

Saturday, June 25, 2005–some windy. 80°. Helped Chuck with some of his projects. Got a heavy duty pair of drive on vehicle ramp at a yard sale. Henry J. phoned – not long after Bill Buck called with a report on progress building cabin on Old Boot Lake. Sure hit me hard emotionally. I miss Alaska.

Sunday, June 26, 2005–some wind. 85°. Nadia put on a party for the Red Hat Club. Sylvia participated. Laura and Brit came also. Brit is staying the night. I went over to Brads and repaired our dresser and chest of drawers and got to see Maggie and Joey. Called Bev and Steve.

Monday, June 27, 2005–Showers. 90° +. Went to Brad and Laura's. Baby sat Joey while his folks took his sister to an autism class. Went to Menards for a couple of sheets plywood and 3 2x4's. Got a new skill saw with a laser beam.

Tuesday, June 28, 2005–cloudy, sunny evening. 70s. Chuck left. Sylvia and I build 2' high addition to pickup box with the plywood and 2 x 4's we got yesterday. Decided on the house insurance agent. Ask Crow Wing Power to keep the electricity service at our new home. Mowed the lawn after supper.

Wednesday, June 29, 2005–couple showers. 80s. Helped Chuck fix a door. Went to bank and got cashier's check to pay for house and house insurance. Shopped for a tarp, rope, bungee "Spider" for Chuck to secure things on his trailer. Went to Fleet Farm and picked up our new Husqvarna lawn mower with Honda motor. Did that at evening "rush hour."

Thursday, June 30, 2005–70s. Loaded our pickup and Chuck and Nadia's car and trailer. Went to the place we are buying. The people there were still moving out. Went to Little Falls and filled up on gas. Called Roxanne that we would meet her for the "walk through" of the property. Me, those people went to the title office. Closing was conducted by a young lady with a tattoo between her buns! The closing went good. Then we unloaded our vehicles and went back to Nadia and Chucks and loaded vehicles for a trip to our new place.

Friday, July 1, 2005–hauled a load to our place and unloaded in garage and some in house. Went back to Nadia's and loaded our truck for an early start tomorrow.

Saturday, July 2, 2005–left early for our place. Not much holiday traffic this morn. Got here just before 9:00 AM. Brad got here soon after with his load. Laura, Maggie and Joey came for a short visit. Then Darcy, Dylan and Devin came. Darcy took Sylvia in to Little Falls for some grocery shopping. Vanessa, Scott, Liam, Beverly, Theresa came. The girls helped Sylvia and Scott, Brad, and Chuck helped me. We got a lot of stuff in the house and the garage. Got the bed assembled. We like the water here for both drinking and showers. There is a nice breeze blowing through here. Tried to call Paul and Steve with no luck. Very good day with family and working together and having laughs and fun with the kids.

Sunday, July 3, 2005—rain in night. Bev and I went to Dayton. Nadia and Chuck's and got four of mother's cabinets and her **sea hauser** and some miscellaneous small stuff. We got back here 12:15 PM. Sylvia and Theresa put wieners, buns, pork and beans etc on for lunch just about the time Steve, Lisa, Ruth and Paul got here. We wrestled the cabinets into place and sorted and carried a lot of boxes of stuff into house and opened even more out in the garage looking for my battery power screw driver. The damn drains are very slow in the house. The bath tub had 30" old rotten hair that I pulled out of its drain. Someone has made a serious mistake when they installed the house drainage system. Don't know yet what to do about it. We hooked up the 12 volt, 5" TV for temporality entertainment. Called Jim and Elaine Manning.

Monday, July 4, 2005—sunny, breezy, cool this morn. After breakfast, Beverly, Theresa, Sylvia and I went to Wal-Mart shopping for things we need to get settled in here. Then to a grocery store called Coburn's. Later went back to Wal-Mart for some more items. Took the lawn mower out of its box. Put in gas and it started right up. I mowed some of the lawn. It is fun to do things and have the girls helping.

Tuesday, July 5, 2005—sunny, small showers. Went to Morrison Co court house and got homestead status tax on our place. Did some more shopping. Changed out the main door lock. We are having septic system failure. Did a lot of small jobs. Bev and Theresa went back to Minneapolis. Sure great to have them here.

Wednesday, July 6, 2005—sunny and some breeze. 56° to 87°. Mowed most of lawn. Did some small jobs. Started fixing the paneling in laundry room. Cut below soil surface a small dead tree. The septic system is very slow. Sylvia painted a small dresser for her spices and has it in the kitchen. Ordered the Sunday paper.

Thursday, July 7, 2005—sunny and some breeze. 57° to 93°. Finish mowing lawn. Fooled around with sewer. Called Roxanne again. She referred me to a plumber who is to come 7/8/05, Craig ? from Baxter. Installed a dish for DISH network. The receiver quit while he was programming it. Another one is to be here in 4-5 days. We leveled Sylvia's cook stove, it was way off. Got two doors to shut better now. Someone came and took the For Sale sign away. Met Jim Ckhon who lives to south of us.

Friday, July 8, 2005—mostly sunny, some breeze. 82° to 94°. Moved more books in on porch. Mailman brought our old mail box Henry mailed to us. Did some small jobs. Uncovered the inspection pipes on the septic tank. Could not find any obstructions there. Plumber came in late afternoon. Couldn't find the blockage location. He did cut out poorly installed pipe and rebuilt it correctly.

Saturday, July 9, 2005—sunny and some wind this PM. 80°'s to 90°'s. We drove down to the recycling center 3 mi from us. Went to Wal-Mart shopping for house things. Nadia and Chuck drove up with some more of our things and gave us some things they don't use. Worked on the drain pipes to septic tank without much luck. We have very sore throats.

Sunday, July 10, 2005—sunny and some wind. 80°'s to 98°'s. Hunted through boxes for copier outlet cord with no luck. Sorted some boxes upstairs. Worked on plumbing again today. Helped it a little bit. Called my brother Jerry.

Monday, July 11, 2005—mostly sunny and breezy. 82° to 96°. Checked the septic vent pipe. Got six more boxes in the house. Spend a lot of time "hunting for things." UPS delivered our dish network receiver. Too complicated for me to do.

Tuesday, July 12, 2005—cloudy, sometimes and a light shower in the afternoon, 70° to 90°. Worked on toilet stool and installing a shut off valve in the water line. Made four trips to Wal-Mart and one trip to hardware store. Two young men from Krolls Plumbing were here a couple hours. They got a 2" diameter drawer pull out of the stool. Grandson-in-law Brad Behrendt brought an air conditioner that he, Laura, Nadia and Chuck had gone together and bought for us. He installed it and got our dish receiver hooked up to TV and putting out a great picture. He is a fine young man and he and Laura sure have a nice family.

Wednesday, July 13, 2005—sunny. 72° to 96°. I replaced the wet and rotted plywood from around the bathroom stool. Plus some other little things. Went to Archer's Lumber for four 2 x 4 x 8' and the plywood. We had lots of calls today. Called Paul. He seemed to be getting better. We see the cottontail rabbits most every day. Sylvia got stung on the head by a wasp yesterday.

Thursday, July 14, 2005—sunny and hazy. 67° to 98°. Went into town and got some "blueboard" to cover the sewer pipe from house to sewer tank. Got some adhesive to put the linoleum back down under the bathroom stool. Sylvia wanted some Pepsi. Also Marion called to say they would be here July 23rd to visit us. Called Ruth and got a report on how Paul is doing. Got his correct phone number and called him and visited awhile.

Friday, July 15, 2005—hazy and light shower after supper. 67° to 101°. Burned paper for five hours. Took the plywood box off pickup and put a primer coat of paint on it. Carried numerous buckets of water to the aspen saplings in the yard. A guy delivered our garbage can today. Ruth and Steve stopped in on their way home from visiting Paul in the Vet's hospital in St. Cloud. They visited for awhile.

Saturday, July 16, 2005—very hot again today. 72° to 101°. I put a blue finish on the plywood box for pickup. Sweat runs down my arms and off the ends of my fingers and falls on the paint as I work. I tied more bundles of packing material today. Got almost all of it burned up. Did some other small jobs. It was a very hot day. Sylvia is better and got some of her work done.

Sunday, July 17, 2005—hot and really windy in the afternoon. 70° to 101° +. Burned more paper cardboard and some plywood from the dog pen. Moved some things around and brought some house things in. Slowly garage looks better. Drilled holes in the bottom of 5-gallon buckets that the tomatoes are in. The heat has wilted them badly. Allen Farmer family called with a long visit as did Charlie Trowbridge. Found the misplaced screw eye and finished the plywood box for truck.

Monday, July 18, 2005—mostly cloudy and quite windy. 71° to 86°. Went in to town to grocery shop and Wal-Mart for a dehumidifier, garden hose, and broom. "Rock" representing Mid Minnesota Ins. looked the house and garage over. He doesn't like the wood stove at all. So I suggested we would try to get a new furnace in the house and put old one in the garage. We moved the freezer to another location in basement. Got the new dehumidifier installed and working. Rearranged some boxes. Nadia called as did Beverly. Trying to clean the bathroom basin drain.

Tuesday, July 19, 2005—cloudy, sunny and windy. 48° to 94°. Mowed about half the lawn and tweaked my knee. Got plenty hot. We put up blinds on three windows this afternoon. Ruth and Steve went to St Cloud and brought Paul and stopped by. Visited on their way home. Steve gave us a can of wasp spray. Same kind as he uses on the job.

Wednesday, July 20, 2005—1/2" rain in night and sunny day. 70° to 90°. Hunted really hard for gun lock key and lever for 30-30 with no luck. Finished mowing our lawn. My knee is really bad. Insurance agent was here. I had to sign a wood stove waiver. The AC and dehumidifier work good. Called some guys about furnace and chimneys. Called Norman Hanson and got some names. Visited about his folks and home place, Leader etc. Talked to Nadia also. Theresa called.

Thursday, July 21, 2005—sunny. 66° to 88°. Worked on one of the door jambs. Tried again to find the missing gun lock keys with no luck. Found the lever for the Marlin 30-30. Oiled it and a couple others. My knee is really bad, back also. Maybe from walking so crooked. Our lawn is too dry. The plums are still hard and are falling to the ground.

Friday, July 22, 2005—sunny. 62° to 94°. Pulled some weeds and grass. We have some sandburs here. Did a few little things. My knee and hip are quite sore. Went in to town and shopped for a lunch when Marion, Ray, Ken and Julie get here. We expect Laura, Brad, Paul, Ruth and Steve to be here also.

Saturday, July 23, 2005—mostly cloudy. 64° to 84°. Some rain in morning. Brad and Laura gave us four deck chairs and a table and brought them here for us! They also gave us a nice dining table. We sure needed one. This was very nice of them to do. Marion, Rae, Ken, Julie, Jessica and Courtney Wilkins visited us in afternoon. Marion and Rae from Texas are visiting son Ken and family for a few days. We sure had a good time with our visitors today. Lots of reminiscing and visiting etc.

Sunday, July 24, 2005—mostly sunny. 70° to 88°. My back, left hip, leg muscles and knee are giving me a lot of hurts. Didn't do much today but rest. Tried to call Paul with no luck.

Monday, July 25, 2005—cloudy most all day and rain about 3:00 PM that soaked in an inch. 76° to 70° to 63°. Took it pretty easy all day. Did some small jobs. Pulled garbage container on wheels out to road to be picked up. Moved the east rain gutter discharge so it won't run over to garage. Shoveled some dirt into a hole in the lawn that their dogs had dug.

Tuesday, July 26, 2005—partly cloudy and sunny. 66° to 77°. Went to the Department of Motor Vehicles and asked about driver test for license. I need my birth certificate. Did a little shopping at a couple stores. Rested after lunch. Pulled some 2 x 4's out of the dog kennel and put pick up box sides on truck. Sylvia mowed the grass from over the septic lines.

Wednesday, July 27, 2005—partly cloudy. 47° to 70°. Went to Laura and Brad's. Got to spend some time with Maggie and Joey. Laura helped load two pieces of Sylvia's furniture as Brad was working. Then we went to Nadia and Chucks. He helped load the rest of the things we had stored there. Nadia was at work. When I opened the last big box I found the keys and important family papers that we have been looking for weeks now. Got the truck unloaded and the side off and stored away. Dan Pearman returned my call and we had a good visit.

Thursday, July 28, 2005—shower in night, partly cloudy today. 60° to 85°. Passed my written test for a Minnesota driver's license. Did a little shopping. Pulled some weeds out of lawn. My back and left leg is a lot better. Sylvia cooked the zucchini from Nadia's garden – very good.

Friday, July 29, 2005—sunny. 52° to 80s. Pulled more of the weeds with white blossoms. Went to motor vehicles and got our pickup titled and licensed here in Minnesota. We went out to the Morrison County fair. Saw the judging of the Holstein heifers. Most all the cattle looked really good. This was emotional for me (remembering the farm and the day we sold off the cattle). They had some old as well as new tractors and machinery. Hogs, sheep, goats, horse, rabbis, crops and vegetables. We got our lunch at the 4H food concession. Put the new license plates on truck. Mike Olsen, his wife, and two little daughters came over to visit lake this afternoon. They live just across the road. They brought potatoes, cucumbers and an onion fresh from their garden. They are really nice people.

Saturday, July 30, 2005—mostly sunny. 65° to 88°. Pulled more weeds. Rerouted the oil line to the furnace. We rearranged our bedroom and made room for Sylvia's dresser and chest of drawers.

Sunday, July 31, 2005—sunny with a breeze. 64° to 90s. Nadia drove up here this morning. We had a good time and nice visit. She brought rhubarb plants that we divided into 6 sets and planted them under the eve of west side of garage roof. Nadia brought a stainless steel pot (large) for Sylvia. I pulled some nails, screws and staples from rafters and wall studs in garage. It had been supporting a plastic ceiling.

Monday, August 1, 2005—sunny and sultry. 70° to 100°. Went to Little Falls and opened a checking account at the bank. Went to Fleet Supply and Coburn's grocery for shopping. Put new "o" rings in kitchen sink faucets and stopped a dripping leak. Re-attached the front license plate on the truck. Louis has pneumonia, expected to get well.

Tuesday, August 2, 2005—sunny and hot. 74° to 90°. Took Sylvia in to a hairdresser for a perm (curly). Went to Post Office and mailed keys to Dan Pearman. Too hot to work so didn't do much. Neighbor Mike's two little daughters brought cucumbers and string beans fresh from the garden. Very nice of them.

Wednesday, August 3, 2005—some rain along towards morning, mostly sunny today. 70° to 91°. Called a clinic and got Sylvia an appointment with a Dr. Called Minnesota University for <u>info</u> on musty basement. Did some measuring to locate septic line and for rain gutter on west side of house. After lunch we went to clinic and Sylvia met her new doctor who gave her the prescriptions that she needs. This went good. Went to Wal-Mart pharmacy to fill them. They were out of one medicine and have to order it in. Stopped by UBC lumber to ask about rain gutter and drywall and insulation for garage. Went seven miles east on Highway 27 to "Shooting Sports" to get some powder to reload some cartridges.

Thursday, August 4, 2005—nice shower in the night. 60° to 85°. Did some small jobs. Removed the chimney on south side of garage. It was a little tricky but got it down without needing a ladder. Mowed a little grass. Just before bed time I watered the small trees and flowers at the well and north end of house.

Friday, August 5, 2005—nice breeze. 50° to 85°. Started digging up the septic line from house to tank. Got it done by lunch time. Put concrete block supports under it in hopes it will stay on grade. It had sagged about 2" and had two big hunks of congealed fat along with other stuff stuck to inside of pipe. Got it very clean. Then covered it with some till, the 2" x 24" x 13' of blue board and covered it with the rest of fill dirt. Actually things went quite well. Sylvia helped a lot that was nice.

Saturday, August 6, 2005—clear and some breeze. 58° to 95°. Did some small jobs. We started dismantling the kennel. Sylvia wants to plant her grapevine on part of it. Ralf called and talked quite awhile. Watered the small trees and some flowers and ran out of water before I got done. Another disappointment. Saw a kill deer bird today. Sylvia took us out for dinner this evening. She picked a prescription at Wal-Mart and did a little shopping.

Sunday, August 7, 2005—partly cloudy and a little breeze. 64° to 92°. We worked some more dismantling the kennel wire. Got done. Leveled 40% of pen area, sprayed a small nest of wasps.

Monday, August 8, 2005—partly cloudy, windy sometimes. 72° to 89°. A dog got into Mike Olson's garbage. Sylvia and I re-sacked it as Olson's were gone for the day. Finished leveling the kennel pen. Dug up and reset one of the big posts, cut to length one steel pipes to match the other one. This will be Sylvia's grape arbor. She will paint it. Closed the hole in garage wall that used to be for the stove pipe. Did a couple other small jobs. Nadia got our social security checks sent to this address (Sylvia) and mine to our checking account in this bank. We went out at 9:00 PM (88°) and sanded the rust off the two pieces of 1" pipe for Sylvia's grape arbor.

Tuesday, August 9, 2005—rain in night and very windy. 65° to 87°. Maybe 1" rain. We are grateful for rain. Went in to town and got parts for rain gutter. Looked at some pickups – priced too high for me. Did some shopping and came home and worked on rain gutter. Put siding over the hole in garage wall. Went over to Paul Peterson's, father of "Jeff" who wants to earn some money at odd jobs, like lawn mowing. I seem to hurt my knee every time I mow lawn. After supper we visited Mike Olson and family. They gave us fresh cabbage, green beans, cucumbers and an onion. There are young cottontail rabbits in the yard every morning.

Wednesday, August 10, 2005—partly cloudy. 57° to 88°. Went to Staples. Visited with Paul. Took him to lunch. Then visited Eva Adams at Care Center. She has decided not to undergo more surgery – cancer must be returning again. She looks good and carries a good conversation. Then visited Lorraine Hanson. She was full of news. Then went to see Al Eckes near Leader. Went back to Paul's place. After while Ruth got home from work and after a bit we all went over to Steve and Lisa's home they recently bought. They have freshly painted the inside. It looks nice. Steve fixed a spaghetti supper. Lisa was shopping. Had a nice visit and good eats. We got back home shortly after 9:00 PM – tired.

Thursday, August 11, 2005—mostly cloudy, some light showers. 57° to 82°. Went to Archer Lumber and got some 2 x 4 studs and drywall and etc. Got eight gallons of paint and a ladder from Wal-Mart. We started cleaning the storage and utility room in basement. Sylvia vacuumed it, then started caulking around the bath rub. Called around for some gravel. The real young cottontail rabbits sure aren't afraid of us.

Friday, August 12, 2005—mostly sunny, heavy dew; it dried off by noon. 62° to 84°. Jeff Peterson, a neighbor kid mowed our lawn this afternoon. Sylvia and I sprayed the furnace room with Clorox and water mix hoping to kill the mold spores. I added another light fixture in that room and started on an adding an outlet. Really tired tonight. Beverly plans on coming to Little Falls on the bus in the morning. Scott Rollins just called; he and Andy will visit us tomorrow morning.

Saturday, August 13, 2005—sunny and cooler. 53° to 74°. Beverly caught a bus to Little Falls. We picked her up a little after 10:00 AM. We were back home a short while when Scott and Andy Rollins was knocking at our door. We had a lot of visiting in order to get caught up. Sylvia made brownies and chicken noodle soup. Sure had a good time. After they left, went to Little Falls. Sylvia and Bev did grocery shopping and I got some needed electrical stuff. Then the ladies started painting the cement walls of furnace room. I wired in another outlet for the freezer and helped with the painting and cleaned up the roller and brush etc afterward. The job looks better all the time as it dries. We are pleased with this day.

Sunday, August 14, 2005—sunny. 46° to 84°. We three worked at getting the drywall up in the furnace room. We only have a half sheet left to be finished. Ran into lots of problems but hung in there and persevered. Beverly was a big help and fun to have around.

Monday, August 15, 2005—mostly sunny. 52° to 88°. We finished putting sheet rock up. Beverly and Sylvia started painting the floor of the furnace room. Two gallons of paint was soon gone and they sent me after another gallon. I brought home wrong paint. Took it back and got another one which was also wrong but we used it anyway. Bev and I carried a rug up out of the basement and put it in the garage. We took Beverly in to the bus stop in town so she could get home this evening. Hated to see her leave. The two little neighbor girls brought over fresh green beans.

Tuesday, August 16, 2005—Sunny then about 5:30 we got a pretty good shower that we really needed. 58° to 93°. Worked on the shut off valve on the heating oil tank. Had to get some packing cord to fix it. Went to dentist who cleaned and determined three teeth needed filled. We repaired and painted blue the deck chairs and table. Sylvia found 6 ripe tomatoes today!

Wednesday, August 17, 2005—2 1/2" rain in night, sunny today. 63° to 86°. Ask Jeff to come over and we put up rain gutter on west side of kitchen. Sylvia painted 2nd coat on deck chairs and table. Worked, removed lazy Susan from kitchen cabinet. We got a delivery of heating oil today. Kahren R. asked us to give Meloney Junker our movers name and phone #.

Thursday, August 18, 2005—we got some pretty good showers today and some sunshine also. 66° to 78°. Went to town and got some things for the drawers from the kitchen cabinets. Got them repaired and Sylvia put a coat of white enamel on them. We had fresh tomatoes and string beans thanks to Olson family.

Friday, August 19, 2005—some morning showers and sunny afternoon. 62° to 84°. Started on the drywall in furnace room. It went pretty good. We carried the deck chair and table out of garage to deck. Went to Little Falls and took some drawer guides back - they wouldn't work on these drawers. Made arrangements for delivery of gravel for driveway and black dirt for garden. Sylvia thinks she saw a monarch butterfly.

Saturday, August 20, 2005—couple showers in the early morning, then sunny. 54° to 80°. Started pulling staples from bottom of the rafters in the garage. We measured and staked the garden spot. Brad Bursey brought us 12 yards of black dirt and unloaded it in that spot. Jeff came over and helped shovel and level the dirt. Would have been a big job for me to do alone.

Sunday, August 21, 2005—heavy dew again this morning, sunny and some breeze. 51° to 77°. Sanded the drywall and put the last coat of mud on it. Wrote some letters and sent payment for ins. to AARP. Did some small things. Jeff mowed the grass that grows on top of the septic drain field. Jeff borrowed our lawn mower to cut grass for some woman with a broken leg. Was gone 3 hours. Sylvia and I measured our property size 150' x 250', ¾ acre. Jeff and his sister walked over and visited awhile. We ate supper out on the deck this evening. Ralph called. I called an ad about RR ties.

Monday, August 22, 2005—sunny, very nice. 46° to 77°. Sanded the drywall in furnace room. Then we painted it white. Shortly after that Brad Bursey brought us 5 yards of Class 5 material for the low places in our driveway. Called Jeff and he came over to help spread the class 5. Went over to his home and got a hand cart to move material needed out at the end of the driveway. After low places were level I packed it with pickup truck. Did some other little thing. Called Paul and Allen Rollins. We expect to go visit them tomorrow. Sylvia spent the afternoon scrubbing kitchen cabinets.

Tuesday, August 23, 2005—sunny. 47° to 80°. Up early and went to Motley. Pick up Paul and went to Rollins family. Saw 6 sand hill cranes on the way. After visiting awhile, had coffee cake, we went on a tour of the most west of their deer hunting stands. Then Allen picked some sweet corn and we had a great lunch and more dessert. Then Allen took me out to look at some more deer stands. We used a couple Honda 3 wheelers.

Back at their shooting range we participated in some more rifle and pistol shooting. Great fun shooting clay pigeons too! Always something going on there. Richard ?, Lillian's uncle was there. They invited me to hunt on their place this deer season.

Then we went to Larry Adams place. Gwen was at the hair dressers. We had a good hour visiting with Larry about old times and catching up on the news. Went back to Paul's place in Staples. Ruth was home from work. We visited a while and talked about finishing the inside of our garage and if Paul could help us. He said he could.

Then we headed for Motley and looked at some railroad ties. They were poor quality and priced high. On the way home we turned west from Randal and went about seven miles west and north to Ron Frey's farm. He had good RR ties and we bought 14 for $100 - stopped at grocery store in Little Falls for some meat and stuff. It's been a full day with lots accomplished.

Wednesday, August 24, 2005—mostly sunny, cloudy evening, pretty good breeze. 56° to 81°. We had Jeff come over and help unload and place the RR ties.

They were clumsy and heavy to ___ any thing with. But we got them placed. After lunch, shoveled and leveled some more gravel and later put screws in the rain gutter down spout and anchored it with a cement block. Then shoveled more of the garden black dirt out toward the outer edge of the garden.

Thursday, August 25, 2005—quite cloudy today. 66° to 80°. Went into town to dentist and had two fillings on upper left teeth. Shortly after getting home, Jerry and Mo Litza from St Cloud stopped in. Had lunch and talked almost all afternoon. Sylvia got 2/3rds of her upper kitchen cupboards painted with a first coat. I didn't get much of anything accomplished.

Friday, August 26, 2005—lots of rain fell in the night (I do not have a measurement), lots of lightning. 63° to 82°. While the low places still had water in them I shoveled gravel in them to fill them up. Later in the afternoon they were dry enough that I drove the truck back and forth over them and packed them down. It looks very good. I pulled the last of the paper staples out of the bottoms of the garage rafters. Made a material list for finishing inside of garage.

Saturday, August 27, 2005—sunny. 54° to 80°. Fixed the garden rake. The rake was loose on the handle. Used liquid steel. We went to Nadia and Chucks. Looked at all the work Chuck has been doing and Nadia's garden, flowers, lawn etc. All have great color and growth. Then rode with them to Darcy and Jason Wood's wedding. About 100 people present. Nice ceremony. Got to visit with lots of family and the food was very good. We got home 9:00 PM. Saw lots of giant Canadian honkers.

Sunday, August 28, 2005—nice day. Did a few things then went to an auction in town in hopes of getting a snow blower. The auction dragged on and on. Finally we left for Staples as Paul had called that he was ready to work. We didn't stay long in Staples. Stopped at a pizza place in Little Falls for supper.

Monday, August 29, 2005—another nice day. Didn't sleep well, got up late. Paul and I put the side boards on the pickup and went to Menard's lumber in St Cloud and bought plywood, paint, etc to finish the inside of our garage. Got home mid afternoon. Off loaded the purchases and got a prime coat on some of plywood. Then he went up on our roof and took down a TV antenna. We visited for awhile out on the south deck. That was nice.

Tuesday, August 30, 2005—beautiful day. Paul and I went to Menards in St Paul and got more materials for the garage. Got back home and unloaded materials. Sylvia replanted her aloe-vera plant. I got Jeff to mow our lawn. Sylvia and Paul painted some more plywood sheets. I prepared some stuff for putting up the ceiling vapor barrier. Sylvia worked hard all day so we went to KFC for supper, Wal-Mart for shopping and Coburn's for a few groceries.

Wednesday, August 31, 2005—cloudy all morning after a heavy dew. 50°'s to 80°. Some sprinkles in the afternoon when Paul and I were wiring for some light fixtures. Got some lumber and plywood clips, light fixtures. Stopped by a construction site and was given some cast off pieces of lumber. We had another bat in the house last night. I caught it and we killed a darn cricket. Paul called my attention to a sand hill crane trying to fly into the wind. We saw a lot of eagles circling near the highway near Royalton yesterday. The dove's come to the water hole across the road from us. Made two saw horses today.

Thursday, September 1, 2005—very windy. 50°s to 70s. Sylvia has been picking up fallen plums every day or so. Went to dentist and got the last cavity filled. Picked up two more drawer guides and some nails. We checked out some shingles on garage. Put more vapor barrier on garage ceiling and got three 4 x 8 plywood sheets put on. Moved a lot of reloading things into basement. Jeff R. called with a report of things in Alaska.

Friday, September 2, 2005—sunny and nice. 50°'s to 70°'s. Beverly came in to Little Falls about 10:00 AM. Paul and I had already been to a construction site and no one was there to ask about scrap lumber. Picked up Bev and went to Wal-Mart and Coburn's shopping. Back home we worked on the garage getting more vapor barrier stapled to the bottom of the rafters. Had to disconnect the door openers. That went good. We got more plywood screwed to the rafters. Put a primer coat on some more plywood before supper and another coat after supper. Henry Johnson called. He has a new web site. He has a picture of me on the site.

Saturday, September 3, 2005—mostly cloudy all day, very dark wildly shaped clouds preceded rain about 11:00 AM. 50° to 70°. Chuck and Nadia drove up from Dayton with a bed for our guest room. We had a nice visit and a good noon meal. Paul, Bev, Sylvia and I got a little work done in the morning and some more in PM. Then went to Little Falls for some shopping. We built a 4' x 8' platform, 23" high to better help us drive the screws to hold the plywood to the bottom of rafters for a ceiling.

Sunday, September 4, 2005—sunny, very nice day. 60°'s to 80°'s. We got more plywood on the ceiling plus the opening in ceiling for a stairs, the last of vapor barrier on the ceiling. Everything went pretty good today. Sylvia picked a lot of plums off the ground this evening. Paul saw a cotton tail rabbit. Bev is moving all the time helping with everything around the place. My sister Virginia called and visited quite a while.

Monday, September 5, 2005—Cloudy, then thunder, lightening for quite some time, then rain and pretty hard for a short while, quit before supper time. 60°'s to 70°'s. We four put up a lot of plywood on the ceiling today. All went pretty good. We quit early to take showers and to supper in Little Falls then to Jefferson bus line stop for bus service. Bev got on the bus a little after 6:00 PM to go home. She sure helped a lot here. We did some shopping at Wal-Mart. Came home and put primer on eight sheets of plywood.

Tuesday, September 6, 2005—cloudy and turning sunny with a good breeze. 60°'s to 80°'s. The house flies and mosquitoes are pests. Sylvia put a second coat of white on 8 sheets of plywood. Paul did the wiring of outlets on west side of garage and more light fixtures including a pull chain up in the attic. We got the narrow strip along the west side screwed to the rafters.

The corn field across the road is chopped for silage. Sylvia went out and put 2nd coat of paint on the seven plywood sheets. She won't allow me to do it - would let me clean up though.

Wednesday, September 7, 2005—partly cloudy. 60°'s to 80°'s. Went to town for more paint and some groceries. None of us feel good today. Worked too hard yesterday. Sylvia painted 17 sheets plywood. I painted 6 and Paul 3. Paul and I mounted the propane furnace on the ceiling of the garage. Boy was it hot up in the attic when were bolting it up there. Went back to town in evening and got more paint, some fly sticker strip and light bulbs. Paul had a bee sit on his finger for the longest time. You could see it run its tongue out seemingly to taste Paul's skin. It did this a lot.

Thursday, September 8, 2005—cloudy, partly cloudy and some breeze. 60° to 84°. House fly and mosquitoes bad sometimes. We ran wire to propane furnace then installed the folding stairs to the garage attic. Then ran a string of outlets on the east side of the garage. Sprayed Sylvia's garden with round up to kill the grass. She painted 8 sheets of plywood, fixed three meals and did some laundry.

Friday, September 9, 2005—cloudy and high humidity, sunny, then cloudy and very muggy. 66° to 82°. Went to Little Falls. Forgot my billfold and had to go home to get it. Got some 2 x 4's. Came home and worked on garage. Paul got the heater wired in and helped me finish roughing in two windows in south end of garage. Sylvia finished painting the last of plywood sheets. I got some insulating in the south wall. Jeff Peterson came and mowed our lawn. Beverly and Tyler got here after 800 PM. They want to help on the garage. We had a gab session, ice cream, pop and cookies then went out to the garage for show and tell.

Saturday, September 10, 2005—sunny. 68° to 90°. Paul, Tyler, Bev, Sylvia and I got a lot done today. The ceiling is covered and part of south wall. Paul got even more wiring done. Tyler is a good worker. Bev is on the ball and a real spark plug on and off the job. We sure enjoyed their company and help. We took some breaks to rest and talk, especially after Sylvia's turkey supper. We sat around out on the deck enjoying the evening breeze and its coolness. We watched a little TV just before bed time.

Sunday, September 11, 2005—most sunny. 75° to 85°. We got ½ east side insulated. Vapor barrier and plywood by noon. At lunch, Ruth and friend Mary came to take Paul home. Paid Paul for his help. Shortly after, Beverly and Tyler went home. Sure quiet now. We insulated vapor barrier and plywood on the little bit there is of the north end where the doors are. Then Mike Olson offered to till our garden. His tiller had a belt start slipping so he took it home and brought a power cultivator and finished the job. Jeff and his sister stopped by while the cultivating was going on. A monarch butterfly was here both in the morning and afternoon - must be their migration time. Saw what appeared to be tame geese get up from a harvested corn field and fly off. Also some ducks.

Monday, September 12, 2005—several pretty hard rains. 68° to 74°. Did some wiring in the garage. A gas co. man names Jim came to make an estimate to supply propane and hook up the garage furnace. We took our lawn clippings to the composting place. Shopped for things we need. Went to several stores. Back home we put vapor barrier plastic on 20' of garage east side and got five sheets of plywood nailed to the studs.

Tuesday, September 13, 2005—Lots of rain in night and some in the morning. 57° to 74°. I have a virus infection of my ear and could not stand for several hours this morning. I feel much better this evening. Did get a couple hours of light work later in the afternoon. Called Nadia and Theresa.

Wednesday, September 14, 2005—very nice day. 45° to 74°. Went to town and got more needed stuff for the garage. Sylvia and I rebuilt the power conduit as it comes in to breaker box, then we insulated 8' of wall in that area and covered it with vapor barrier and 2 sheets of plywood. We are pleased with all we accomplished today. Saw 5 geese landing in the field on the farm across the road, undoubtedly they will feed on waste corn.

Thursday, September 15, 2005—nice day. 65° to 82°. We had just started work on garage when we heard some gun shots and a flock of geese got up off the harvested corn field across the road. I have an outlet circuit that isn't carrying a charge and can't find the reason why. We got all the insulation in the last wall, the vapor barrier is up and only three sheets and one small narrow piece to put on yet. Spent an awful lot of time on the electric problem. Had to run in to town to get more nails. Lots of phone calls this evening.

Friday, September 16, 2005—partly cloudy. 62° to 82°. Saw 3-4 flocks of geese.

They feed on the harvested fields. I got the electric problem in garage fixed. Some of it has to be put back together. I had to remove two sheets of plywood to run a new outlet circuit. We finished the inside walls of garage. Sylvia painted a number of ceiling panels. Giving us again a grey looking white, we are perplexed as to why. Slept poorly last night with the electric problems on my mind. Worked to nearly 9:00 PM to make up for it.

Saturday, September 17, 2005—some light rain and partly cloudy. 58° to 72°. The geese are spending time in the field west of us! Some white geese in with the Canadians. I installed a motion detector light the fore part of the day. Then finished nailing on some more plywood. Two 1/3 sheets left to nail. Swept up and cleaned up the floor in the garage. Jeff mowed our lawn. I visited Mike Olson for a little while.

Sunday, September 18, 2005—sunny. 53° to 80°. Helped straighten up the house. Worked a little on garage. Went to grocery store in the morning. Peter and Delaine Achermann came about 1:00 PM. We had a real good visit. Sylvia put a light lunch on the table and cake and ice cream. They brought us four big containers of ripe tomatoes!! Theresa and Earl brought his parents, Don and Evelyn and they visited a couple hours. They are 89 and 87 yrs old. We went into town in evening to get some canning jars for the tomatoes. We were sitting out on deck after dark when we heard geese talking. Shortly they flew by right over our plum trees.

Monday, September 19, 2005—had a couple showers. 50°'s to 80°'s. Worked on the electrical wiring. Believe it is finished. Started building a retainer around the stairs opening to garage attic. After supper Roar Hartold came to discuss insulating garage attic. He doesn't like blowing insulation, suggested rolls of fiberglass. He will do it for $200 or we can do it our self. Roar is interesting to visit with. Earl wanted to spend the evening with his nephew and brother. The nephew is going to Iraq.

Tuesday, September 20, 2005—heavy dew, sunny day. 57° to 87°. We tried to caulk the cracks between the plywood sheets on garage ceilings. It is too difficult for us. I wasn't feeling good either. Put up a window blind at the kitchen sink that Sylvia has wanted for awhile. Earl visited a while when he came to pick up Theresa. I did some adjustments to the motion detector lights thus increasing the period of time they stay on after being activated. The geese are still feeding in the field across the road.

Wednesday, September 21, 2005—real nice day. 52° to 87°. We left early for St Cloud. Went to Menards for insulation, paint, furring strips and some small stuff all for the garage. Tried to find Jerry and Mo's place but no luck. Got home 1:00 PM and worked all afternoon. Theresa and Earl stopped by, she had left some things here. They had his folks with them and were going to a dinner in LF for the nephew – grandson who is a reservist who will soon be shipping out to Iraq. The gopher is giving me a bad time. Tried to hose him out with water but no luck.

Thursday, September 22, 2005—sunny. 56° to 71°. Moved a bunch of box's to ease getting the insulation to the attic ladder. We decided to have Roar place the insulation in the attic. I paid the taxes on the property today. Got some more paint. Sylvia painted some more white in basement and some trim. Just after lunch, Mike Achermann called and came to visit. He leaves to work at a station in Antarctica. We are still trying to drown the gopher.

Friday, September 23, 2005—sunny, breezy but switching directions. 40° to 72°. We worked on the furring strips. I sanded and Sylvia put a prime coat on them. We did 60 of them. Measured the house windows. She wants shutters for 9 of them. We stack the furring strips, strap them together and put weights on them, trying to keep them straight while they dry. Neighborhood lady borrowed some of Sylvia's canning equipment today. Later her two little girls brought over a pint of home canned pears. So far it appears our water treatment has worked on Mr. Gopher.

Saturday, September 24, 2005—cloudy and rain in the afternoon. 54° to 67°. Finished preparing furring strips for painting. Sylvia put the primer coat on them. Later in the afternoon she put thin finish coat on 41 of them. I got some preparation done for putting trim up. Drew up plan for the two south windows. Burned some trash. No sign of activity by the gopher. Nadia called. Sylvia called Francis.

Sunday, September 25, 2005—Cloudy and rain in night, showers all day, sometimes a hard rain. 54° to 64°. We worked on garage. Sylvia finished painting the batting strips. Then she helped me in putting them on the plywood joints.

Monday, September 26, 2005—cloudy and cleared and beautiful day. 40° to 73°. We got quite a lot done in the garage today. Pickup off the ground some old dog pen plywood and leaned it against the dog shed to dry before getting rid of it. Hope to burn some dry weeds this evening. Haven't seen any geese today.

Tuesday, September 27, 2005—sunny with a breeze, beautiful day. 47° to 80°. Last nights grass pile burned down pretty good. Sylvia painted the exposed screen and nail heads and smudges on the bats and plywood on the ceilings and walls of garage. Got some of the stuff we work with sorted and organized. Went to town for supper and got paint, camera film, shoes for Sylvia etc at Wal-Mart. Nadia called a couple times about our arranging a river boat trip on the St Croix

River.

Wednesday, September 28, 2005—light rain in the night, cloudy morning and sunny afternoon. 40° to 64°. Went to a garage sale – they wanted too much for a snow blower. Later we went to St Cloud. Got some shutters for house and 20 more furring strips for the garage. Had lunch and stopped by Jerry and Mo Lizza's. They have a beautiful fully furnished home with an "Alaska room" which has lots of ivory and art and trophy's from Alaska. Visited quite a while and drove on home. I sanded the furring strips and Sylvia put a primer coat on them. After supper she painted them and I prepared rebate application to Johns Mansville insulation company.

Thursday, September 29, 2005—Frost on everything this morning. 33° to 66°. Put a few more strips on the garage plywood. Then Jim from home furnace co. came to check out and prepare our furnace for the winter. After he left, we went to a garage sale and a moving sale. Looked at snow blowers and garden tillers. Got back home and it was cold and called Jim. He came and checked furnace motor and it is kaput. Darrel and Brenda called and talked a long time at our supper time, mid afternoon their time. Had a good visit and got lots of news. We took the air conditioner out of house window.

Friday, September 30, 2005—partly cloudy, beautiful day. 48° to 80°. Saw large flock of barn pigeons landing to feed in the corn field across the road from us. Some crows were harassing them. Probably trying chase the pigeons away from feeding there. Jim the furnace man brought a motor and installed and the furnace seems to be OK now.

I built an enclosure around the opening for the garage attic. After lunch, Sylvia helped and we started trimming out the east and west windows in the garage. Got quite a bit done. After supper I went out and finished them.

Saturday, October 1, 2005—plenty warm today. 47° to 83°. Roar Hartold from Norway came to place the insulation in garage. Maybe jammed it a little too close together as we are 18 bats short of finishing the job. I started dismantling the section of old counter that is left in garage. Worked at leveling the dirt in garden. Shoveled some gravel into some low places in the driveway and area in front of the house. We loaded the springs and bed frame that goes back to Nadia and Chuck in the truck. Jeff Peterson stopped by, he has a new chocolate lab and some one gave him a lawn mower. Roxanne and Allen Farmer called and we had a long visit.

Sunday, October 2, 2005—cloudy then nice. 60° to 80°. Went to Nadia and Chuck's unloaded the bed springs. Went to Menard's in Anoka and got some lumber and four more 47" shutters for the house and 18 bats of insulation. Went back to Nadia's and we all got in Chuck's car and went to Stillwater on St Croix River. I wanted for a couple years to take Sylvia on a river boat ride. So we asked Nadia and Chuck to go with us. Shortly after we arrived at the boat docks we went up the river a nice little distance. Watching all things interesting in lime stone formations, eagles, sea gulls etc. They gave us a real nice chicken and roast beef meal on the boat (buffet style). Saw some sailboats out on the river. Also saw countless geese all along the highways today and in the towns and cities. Went with Chuck to see his mother Lucille. Back at their place we got in the old pickup, headed home, reaching there about 7:30 in evening.

Monday, October 3, 2005—cloudy, partly cloudy, cloudy and a light shower after supper. 64° to 73°. Looked like rain so I hurried around and finished leveling the dirt in the garden and mowed the grass on the septic drain field. Got the two new furring strips sanded. One needed extra work. Washed two windows in garage. Roar came and finished placing the insulation in the garage attic. His estimate of insulation we needed was one bundle too many. He gave me a threshold and some caulking for the garage man door. I got started on installing it. Found a short in wiring of one door opener and fixed it.

Tuesday, October 4, 2005—rain in night and most of today. 50° to 60°. Mississippi River was running strong. Went to bank. Groceries, post office and put ad in paper to sell wood stove. Shopped at Wal-Mart too. Finished the electrical work in garage. Raining so hard water is running every where.

Wednesday, October 5, 2005—rain in night, 5" in last 24 hrs. 53° to 58°. Went to yard sale and got a book case. Had to do a little repair. It has been in a wreck or something. We managed to get it down into the basement. Assembled the wheel barrow. Refilled some low spots in the driveway.

Thursday, October 6, 2005—cloudy and partly cloudy. 43° to 51°. Went to St. Cloud. Closed our account there. Went to Menards for more insulation, five 1" x 8" x 8" select boards and some rain gutter for garage. Back home we then went to bank and opened an account there. Then to a garage sale but the table saw was already sold. When we got home, changed clothes, called over to Jeff's to come and help us put the insulation in the two attics on the house. I drove him home afterward. He showed me his new chocolate colored lab. It is 8 months old. Nice looking dog. Called and told Nadia about the bank account switch. Charlie Trowbridge called. We talked over an hour. I forgot to ask how Cora's health is.

Friday, October 7, 2005—mostly sunny. 27° to 58°. Put a false floor over the stairs to the basement in order to do some ceiling painting. It is a suspended ceiling. Took the panels out to garage. Sylvia painted them with a primer coat today. Called a garage sale and they had not sold two single beds and Sylvia wants them. Gave $50 for them. Traffic was heavy and doing 70+ mph when we went to get the beds. We are tired tonight.

Saturday, October 8, 2005—sunny, frost and cool till noon, breezy afternoon. 33° to 58°. Roar Harold came to put Sylvia's shutters on the house and didn't charge us for labor. Very nice of him. The shutters add some pazazz to the house. Sylvia is very pleased with them. Roar gave me some nails, screws and a bit to drill the holes in the cement floor for a door threshold. After lunch we put up the rain gutter over the man door of garage. Sylvia put a coat of paint on the house entry way to basement (The ceiling blocks). I trued up the man door jam and screwed it to the frame. Drilled holes in the cement to take the threshold. Later Jeff Peterson asked me to take him into Little Falls and pick up a friend of his who wanted to visit Jeff this evening. On the way I stopped at hardware store and got the three "blue" screws that I needed for the threshold. While I was on that errand someone called asking about the heating stove (wood) that we have for sale in the newspaper.

Sunday, October 9, 2005—sunny, heavy dew. 37° to 63°. Randy from Lake Alexander got here about 7:00 AM to load up our wood burning stove. It was a tussle as the darn thing is sure heavy. Lots of calls for it. A few snow blower calls. Might have bought one from Brainerd but the guy didn't bring it down when he came to Little Falls. I got a new threshold put in the man door of garage. Sylvia painted the wood on the windows in the garage. The ceiling panels for the south entry got dry and we put them up. They look nice now. Some shooting on the farm across the road.

Monday, October 10, 2005—sunny, frosty morning. 33° to 68°. We bought a nice table saw from a lady a couple miles from here. It was all Sylvia and I wanted to get it unloaded off the truck. Worked on it a little. Needs a new pulley on the saw. Sylvia washed the east side of the garage. It was very dirty. Looks great now. When Jeff got home from school he and I went into LF. I needed a pulley for the table saw. Then we went to the city composting place and got a nice load shoveled on the pickup. Drove home, backed up to our garden plot shoveled it over ¼ of the garden. Stopped by the neighbor who owns the farm across the road from us and got permission to hunt small game on his place.

Tuesday, October 11, 2005—frost, sunny. 34° to 68°. Raked the compost that we hauled in yesterday. Buried a PVC drain pipe for the east side of house rain gutter. Fiddled around with the table saw. Its motor sure is noisy. Then school bus went by - Jeff is home. Went over and picked him up. Went to hunting license station and got my hunting licenses and tags. Ask about Jeff going along hunting without a license. They didn't think he could but to call DNR. We then went to compost yard and shoveled a load on the pickup. Drove home and unloaded it and took Jeff home. After supper I burned trash, cardboard boxes and the dead limbs that I trimmed off a plum tree.

Wednesday, October 12, 2005—cloudy all day, rain in the late afternoon. 52° to 60°. Burned some more cardboard and trashy wood. Fiddled around with the table saw. It tripped the circuit breaker once.

Thursday, October 13, 2005—cloudy to partly cloudy in the afternoon. 52° to 60°. "Bob" came to look at setting a propane tank and hook up for garage. Did some small jobs like sacking the ashes in the fire pit. Saw lots of geese flying today. Ducks were using the ponds across the road. When Jeff got out of school we went after a load of compost. That makes three; one more will cover the garden.

Friday, October 14, 2005—partly cloudy and windy all afternoon. 45° to 70°. Raked some of garden and moved some compost to SW corner. Washed the box on truck and went to a moving sale. Sylvia bought the sofa she hoped to get. It was some difficult to get it into the house. These doors are quite narrow but we persevered and got it into place. Moved a lot of furniture around. Put another single bed frame together. Fooled around with the table saw. It keeps tripping the breaker. When Jeff got home from school we went to the compost yard and loaded the truck. This load is the fourth and last one. Hosed out the truck bed for the second time today.

Saturday, October 15, 2005—sunny. 35° to 72°. Picked pieces of wood, rocks and plastic out of the compost we put on the garden. Did a little servicing on truck. Touched up some caulking at man door on garage. Swept garage. Readjusted the motion detector light and visited with Paul for awhile. Plan to have birthday dinner with them tomorrow, Steve's birthday dinner.

Sunday, October 16, 2005—sunny and sometime windy. 32° to 69°. Went to Staples for a dinner for Steve's birthday at his folks, Paul and Ruth. Got to catch up on visiting. We got groceries at Little Falls. Steve gave us some venison wieners, breakfast sausage and polish sausage. Fiddled around with motion detector this morning. Heard someone shoot off a .22 this morning.

Monday, October 17, 2005—beautiful day, windy though. 50° to 68°. We went to Randall to Evens Implement and bought a snow blower and a garden tiller. After lunch we took the table saw motor to a repair shop in town. Then shopping at Wal-Mart and gassed truck and filled a small container. The road ditch here at home made a good place to unload the tiller and snow blower. I took Jeff with me hunting ducks on the little ponds across the road. Didn't see any. Came home, watched TV hunting and shooting shows. Ate supper and went back to ponds. Seven ducks circled 3-4 times then two came in and landed. I didn't shoot hoping the rest would come in. Then these two crew nervous and left. I still didn't shoot because I didn't want to scare them. Sylvia has company coming tomorrow. Lorraine Hanson is having someone drive her down here from Staples.

Tuesday, October 18, 2005—partly cloudy, breezy to windy all day. 42° to 78°. Picked some trash off the garden plot. Lorraine Hanson and Al Eckes spent the afternoon visiting us. I put up a tennis ball on a monofilament line hung from the garage ceiling hung in a manor to touch the truck windshield when it is in the garage far enough to close the overhead door behind the truck. Also put covers on a bunch of outlets. After supper went across the road hunting ducks till sunset. No ducks but did see a feral tom cat. My sister Virginia's birthday is tomorrow, so I called her this evening in case her and Don might be gone tomorrow. Turns out they are planning on going to a dentist in Mexico.

Wednesday, October 19, 2005—mostly sunny. 41° to 67°. George and ? from the propane co-op came to install a 500 gal tank and hook-ups for the propane furnace in the garage. I think they did a good job and very reasonable. We went to town for shopping. Wasn't able to get the electric motor. Went back later and got the electric motor for the table saw and couple more things. Installed the motor on the saw. Strung thermostat wire from the garage heater. Got the garden tiller out to garden and tried it out. We took pictures of each other running it. It seems to do a good job of chopping and mixing the dirt. I went across the road to the ponds to hunt duck but a guy was already there. He had one duck, a mallard drake.

Thursday, October 20, 2005—thin fog here. 32° to 63°. We decided to go to the Leader area today. Achermann's had a funeral to attend. Harry McCoy was hauling manure. We drove the roads looking at the places that people we used to know, used to live in. Al and Lillian Rollins were to be home about 1:00 PM and were there. Scott and Darlene had been to Little Falls for a tractor part and were back home. Andy was home. They are selling this year's calf crop tomorrow. I sighted in one rifle. We had a good visit. Got back too late to go duck hunting.

Friday, October 21, 2005—cloudy till 4:00 PM, partly cloudy. 40° to 50°. Put a weather strip on bottom of door that goes out on porch. Got the thermostat wired in for the heater in garage. Hunted up some more duck hunting gear. Jeff was here this afternoon. It looks like we will have to find a different place to duck hunt. The owner is putting shelled corn out for his tame water fowl. I tilled the garden again this evening.

Saturday, October 22, 2005—29° to 52°. Tried to figure out what to do with the furnace room. Picked a few little rocks and trash from our garden. Took a nap. Made four push sticks for use on the table saw. Wrote a newsy letter on what we have been doing and mailed copies to 8 addresses. Nadia and Brittany were coming to our place but the brakes went out on her car. It was a scary thing to happen but no accident.

Sunday, October 23, 2005—turned into a really nice day. 39° to 54°. Did lots small jobs. Like caulking, finished the "pushers" for the table saw, sacked the ashes from the fire pit. Pried 48 studs out of one winter snow tire. Cleaned up the lawn mower. Gathered up the garbage and pulled the container out to the road to be picked up tomorrow morning. Heard a number of .22 caliber shots in late afternoon. Checked the .30-30 and found I had not tightened the scope in its mounts. Theresa called this afternoon.

Monday, October 24, 2005—warmed up in the afternoon. 37° to 53°. Pulled 48 more studs out of a tire. Found my box of animal and water fowl calls. Moved a double shelf storage and fastened it to basement wall. Sanded the rough parts and Sylvia put a primer coat on them. We prepared the freezer for a coat of primer. She did that while I took a broken spindle out of the banister at head of basement stairs. Drilled it for a dowel and glued the two pieces together and put it back in its place in the banister. Then pulled 20 more studs out of a tire. Sylvia dropped her eyeglasses and broke them.

Tuesday, October 25, 2005—foggy then sunny. 26° to 58°. We went to Menards in St Cloud. Returned some insulation and cashed in a rebate credit. We got some building materials and came home with more money than we went there with!! Got home, had a little lunch and got a whole lot of things done around here. I now have studs pulled from two truck tires.

Wednesday, October 26, 2005—light fog clearing off and got quite warm in the afternoon. 29° to 62°. Sylvia got a lot of painting done in the furnace room. The lid on the deep freezer, two storage racks, some cement block wall and the area under the stair steps. Then did the walls of the basement stairs going up. I got two storage racks built in the garage and we got the plywood cut to size for the racks. Ran out of nails and went to get some. Got Sylvia some Pepsi. Mike Olson tells me I need to cover our septic system with a layer of hay. His two little daughters brought Sylvia a real jack o'lantern.

Thursday, October 27, 2005—nice day, warming up in the afternoon. 27° to 61°. Got the studs out of the last snow tire. 96 studs in each tire, 384 total. Repaired cut out holes in two plywood sheets. Put stabilizer braces on the storage racks then nailed the 2' x 8' shelves on each rack. Then tilled the garden once again. The men splitting wood and loading trucks were at it again today. We are seeing blue jays now. We called Laura and visited for awhile.

Friday, October 28, 2005—sunny and went to town. 36° to 64°. Inquired about shooting range. Grocery shopped. Sylvia got her prescriptions filled. I had the truck lubed. Got a lot of tools and stuff put up on racks. Nadia called – the plan to get here about 7:00 AM tomorrow.

Saturday, October 29, 2005—cloudy and sunny in afternoon. 36° to 69°. Nadia, Brittany and Chuck drove up to visit. Nadia and Chuck got a new van, black and very nice. They brought gifts and Brittany along. We looked new van over and showed them our most recent progress in our efforts on this place. It was nice to have Brittany here. Sylvia fixed a nice lunch and we had a good visit. After they left I got some more organizing of the tools. Called Lorraine and took her up on her offer of a couple nights at her place during deer hunting season.

Sunday, October 30, 2005—rain in night, cloudy and sunny afternoon. 49° to 63°. Took a nap this morning. Caulked leaks where air was coming in around garage, furnace exhaust pipe. More need to be done. Got the east garage door adjusted better. Right front tire on the truck was flat. Put a different valve on it. Picked up the goose lawn decorations.

Monday, October 31, 2005—mostly cloudy all day, very little sunshine. 39° to 52°. Went to town. Stopped by Pap's Sport Shop and paid $11.00 for a senior's membership in Little Falls Rifle and Pistol Club. Just as we left home the door latch broke so I got a new one and some other things at Hardware Hanks. When we left town we went east on #27 about 3 mi and turned south 3 mi turned west on #35 and back home. We saw three rooster pheasants. Put the new lock on the door and had lunch. Did some small stuff for a couple hours. Then Sylvia came out and helped with the new trim for the garage vehicle doors that stops drafts. Only took us an hour and looks great. Did several more small things and went in for coffee. Trick-or-treaters were here before dark and suppertime.

Tuesday, November 1, 2005—cloudy, sprinkle of rain, partly cloudy. 30° to 59°. Spent some time finding a shotgun barrel. Allen Rollins called to talk about the upcoming deer season opener. Sylvia went along and I took a 12 ga. bbl into town to get the choke opened up to modified in order to shoot steel shot. We did a little shopping at Wal-Mart. Then went east on #27 to farm and bought 12 bales of oat straw @ $2.00 each to put on our sewer system. Drove south then east to home. Stacked the straw and covered with a tarp. Checked the winter tires for air pressure and added some air to all four of them. Adjusted the bottom garage door seals. Smashed some pop cans.

Wednesday, November 2, 2005—cloudy, up early and off to St Cloud to my annual check-up. 30° to 67°. First time I've been to the VA Clinic in St Cloud. It is really nice. Appears well organized. We were impressed. My evaluation by Dr. was I am in very good health. My weight with shoes, and fully dressed was 160 lbs. 17 pounds less than last year. We shopped at Menards for a few things for garage. Tarp and spikes for holding the straw in place over the septic system and one 1" x 12" x 8' for a stool for boots in the entry room.

Thursday, November 3, 2005—partly cloudy. 36° to 57°. Worked at adjusting the garage vehicle doors so that when they close and meet the floor it will be even. Gathered up hunting gear for trip north.

Friday, November 4, 2005—frost. We got ready to go to Leader area. Checked the mail and found a letter from England. A precious metals outfit is inquiring about our claims on Nelchina Glacier River. That sure got my attention. We got copies of the letter in the mail to Nadia and Billmans. Called Billmans and discussed this at length. Then off to bank. Sylvia cashed her SS check. Some shopping and up to Staples. Sylvia is staying with Lorraine Hanson and I go to the Rollins's - Scott, Darlene, Andy, Allen and Lillian. They drive me around to their deer hunting stands and give me my choice of a lot of them to hunt from. Then Richard, Tony and son and a couple others who will be hunting here drive in. Lots of hunt talk, eating this evening. I stayed at Allen and Lillian's and slept on their couch.

Saturday, November 5, 2005—frost in morning. Up early. Had a breakfast and I go to my stand and get in it maybe 20 min before legal shooting time. Saw two large deer - to dark tell sex, i.e. horns. Then three smaller does that were too fast for me to shoot. Saw a grey squirrel and a black phase one, also some chickadees. Then I had a shot at a medium-sized doe but was pretty sure I missed. I searched quite an area for it or signs with no luck. Even Scott and Darlene helped look. Later on in the day, Tony's son shot one nice buck that Tony called in. I got to see the effect of calling on a buck deer from my stand. It was impressive the way that deer did a left turn and run to the caller. Shortly before legal shooting would end for the day a fawn jumped the fence. I shot and missed it! It was startled but at a loss at what to do. I knew I was shooting too high. Lowered the cross hairs and killed it. So near dark, after I got the truck there I had to use the lights to fill out the tag paper work. Scott and Darlene came looking for me just as I got the first ½ of it skinned out. In jig time skinning and gutting and in to the meat sacks and we were off to the Rollins place and hung my little button buck up alongside Tony and son's big buck. Then it was a deer tenderloin dinner fit for a king.

Sunday, November 6, 2005—dense fog and quite foggy till noon. Had oatmeal with Allen and coffee. More coffee at Allen and Darlene's. All the other hunters getting ready to hunt. Scott loaded a large round bale for covering our sewer system in back of the pickup. I loaded my deer and went to Staples in the fog. It was slowly thinning out. At Lorraine's I had pie and coffee and we talked for quite awhile. She had given Sylvia a cultivating fork for use in the garden. Went to Paul and Ruth's house and visited. Then remembered the garden fork and went back to get it. After a while we head for LF and home after a little shopping. She got things squared away here and started cleaning and packaging the deer. I got Jeff to help me get the big round bale of hay off the truck. Then helped a little with the packaging of the deer. Jeff had been on a great hunt for pheasants, geese and duck a week ago. After supper, Oddens and Farmers from Nelchina AK phoned us. It was nice to hear their voices. I moved the scope sight on the Remington rifle with .308 with barrel farther to the rear in the mounts so that I can see the cross hairs properly. Put a thermometer in the deep freezer to check it out.

Monday, November 7, 2005—a beautiful day. 38° to 64°. Went to LF and registered the deer I got. Then on to the shooting range. Picked up about 40 pieces of brass and sighted my rifle in after moving the scope in its bases. I was out of ammo so stopped by Wal-Mart and got a box of 20 and Pepsi for Sylvia and some rubber gloves. Cleaned the rifle when I got home. Had a short nap. Sylvia had a nap too - rested after getting the last of the deer meat packaged. We started putting down some straw on the septic system. That went so good we unrolled the big round bale and covered the whole works with plastic tarps and staked it down with 7" spikes. By that time supper had to be made. We had venison back strap steaks. It was very tender and tasty. Sylvia had made butterfly steaks ¼ " thick.

Tuesday, November 8, 2005—cloudy. 32° to 53°. Did a lot of organizing in the garage. Give me more room and things will be much easier to locate when needed. Early in the afternoon, Jerry and Mo Litza drove in. We had a long visit. Sylvia had just made three blueberry pies so we had pie and ice cream. Later son Paul and Ruth drove in had pie and visited quite awhile. Sylvia fixed a deer meat - rice supper. After supper I called up to Rollins. Scott had gotten a huge deer and one smaller. Someone else had also gotten a deer. I gathered up my gear preparatory to going hunting tomorrow. Packed two blueberry pies to take to Rollins.

Wednesday, November 9, 2005—cloud with winds, 15-45 mph gusts. 36° to 53° to 33°. I aborted the deer hunting plan and went to work on stabilizing the straw, hay and tapes on the septic system. Carried out of the garage every suitable thing that would hold the straw, hay and tarps down. Just as it's getting daylight, I called Allen to tell him I wouldn't be coming to hunt. Went to town and got a doe deer permit, gas in the truck and long spikes to hold the tarps down. Wind died down about 4:30 PM. Sylvia and I repair the damage and reorganized the tarps and weighted them down. Put in the longer spikes. Dan called telling us that we have 13 valid claims. This is exciting. I wonder where it will lead?

Thursday, November 10, 2005—nice day. 24° to 40s. On the phone to AK DNR Mining and Waters about the 12 remaining gold claims we have in the Nelchina area. Having already packed my deer hunting gear I left for the farm of Scott and Allen Rollins. Saw a few deer, no shots for me though. Allen got a nice young buck. We got it to the bldg they hang meat in after Scott removed the entrails. A picture photo session followed. It is a nice buck.

Friday, November 11, 2005—went back to the stand I have been using. I saw five deer but no shot for me. I saw lots of grey squirrels, couple little reds and the large black squirrel. Lots of crow activity to the south for awhile. I stayed out there all day. We all exchanged what we did and saw every day.

Saturday, November 12, 2005—up early and we go to our stands. Today I am at a different stand. Soon after it got light enough to see to shoot, I hear shots from the area Darlene is at today. Then see her leave the stand. The doe she shot has jumped the property line fence. Darlene crossed the fence and finds the dead doe a few yards away. She dragged it back to and under the fence and left to get Scott to help with the doe. I walked over there but unsure when they would come back and how they wanted it dressed out and where etc. I went back to my stand. Later they came back and took care of the deer. I saw a pillated wood pecker nearby and watched it for quite some time as it fed on something on the ground. During lunch it started sprinkling and I went back to Rollins place. Had coffee and visited. They gave me the glass pie plates back that Sylvia had sent to them by me filled with Alaska blueberries. Said my goodbyes and went to the township recycling place and said so long to Allen and came on home. Unloaded my hunting gear. Sylvia helped put a lot of the wood that was holding the tarps down on the straw and hay that covers the septic system. It has rained quite a bit. Lots of thunder this evening. Forecast is for more of the same storm and high winds.

Sunday, November 13, 2005—very windy morning, clear and windy most all day. 48° to 39°. Put some weights on the tarps. Last night it rained quite a bit filling low places on the tarp and helping hold it down. Oiled the rifle. Washed a window on garage. Called Dan about our claims. Called Rollins and Steve Wilkins.

Monday, November 14, 2005—windy and cloudy in the morning. 25° to 43°.

Had to rework the septic field hay cover and replace the tarp. 1/2" ice on the puddles. Took summer tires off the truck and put winter tires on. Made a holder for the air compressor hose to keep it up off the floor. Did some small jobs too. Called gun shop – my 12-gauge barrel isn't finished yet - to be honed to modified chore.

Tuesday, November 15, 2005—rain, snow with rain, snow. 36° to 27°. I didn't feel good today. Took Sylvia to get her doctor check up and flu shot. Then to Wal-Mart to get her prescriptions filled and a little shopping. Neighbor laid a string of shelled corn from pond to building to coax his geese to come to the homestead. No luck with that. Now the crows have found the corn and feed on it. The two little neighbor girls brought two chocolate cupcakes decorated like turkeys with corn candy for a "treat" for us. Note: Mailed letter to England.

Wednesday, November 16, 2005—blowing snow, windy, sunny. 24° to 13°. Patrick Cheetham, Tertiary minerals called from England to talk about our Nelchina claims. He talks fast and asked some tough questions. I referred him to Dan. Called and alerted Patti that he would be calling Dan. Worked on a house door latch. After lunch we tackled putting roller slides on five drawers in Sylvia's kitchen. Ran into a number of snags but did get one done. Talked with Nadia about our Nelchina claims. Dan B. returned my call and filled me in on his call he got from Patrick Cheetham, who is interested in our Nelchina claims. We talked at length about our prospecting efforts at Nelchina.

Thursday, November 17, 2005—cloudy and skiff of snow in afternoon. 2° to 21°. We worked on Sylvia's kitchen drawers and got three more on rollers. Nadia called a couple times. The quit claim forms came from Alaska.

Friday, November 18, 2005—partly cloudy to cloudy. 18° to 44°. Some snow melted. Called Billmans - too early. They called back later. I needed info for the Quit Claim Deed. Got the papers filled out and mailed to Chitina recorder's office in Valdez AZ. Spent all afternoon getting slides on one drawer for Sylvia's kitchen cabinets. Only bullheaded perseverance gets some jobs done.

Saturday, November 19, 2005—cloudy, feels raw. 35° to 40°. Saw big ducks circling the pond across the road – didn't land. I fixed a place where the kitchen cabinets and the linoleum meet. Looks much better now. Swept garage floor. Put tools away. Removed the summer windshield washer fluid and put in winter fluid.

Sunday, November 20, 2005—cloudy, partly cloudy and very nice. 31° to 44°. Mounted a new fluorescent light over Sylvia's cook stove. It got to be a project. Looks good and made her happy. Did a few small things.

Monday, November 21, 2005—mostly cloudy. 31° to 39°. Didn't feel much like doing anything today. Did a few little things in the garage. We played dominoes for an hour and half. Nadia called to make plans for Thanksgiving dinner here at our place. Sounds like 19 guests. Saw a flock of 40 geese over head at dusk this evening.

Tuesday, November 22, 2005—mostly cloudy. 27° to 39°. Sylvia did her Thanksgiving shopping. Pap's Sport Shop didn't call me back regarding my shot gun barrel. A wire nut came loose at a light fixture. Fixed that. Sorted screws and nails that were on the rolling table. Cleaned table top off.

Wednesday, November 23, 2005—partly cloudy. 18° to 35°. Went to town to shop and fill gas tank on truck. Wasn't able to get a county plat map or a lights are on buzzer. Did a few things in the garage. "Found" a box of picture frames Sylvia was looking for. We played dominoes a while.

Thursday, November 24, 2005—partly cloudy and windy. 9° to 18°. We went to Brad and Laura's for Thanksgiving dinner with them and Maggie and Joey. The kids are fun to be with and watch their antics. Brittney was there until her dad picked her up and took her to his place. Nadia and Chuck showed up just as we were having pie and we had a nice visit.

Friday, November 25, 2005—cloudy and 1" snow. 9° to 24°. Removed the lumber from on top of the tarps that cover the hay over the septic system. I prepared the mounted buffalo head to be hung on the garage wall. Put new edges on two windshield scrapers. Helped Sylvia get the turkey roaster ready. Larry and Gwen Adams stopped by and visited quite a while. We had a good time. Nadia called - she has found some Nelchina Gold Claim papers and records.

Saturday, November 26, 2005—cloudy. 13° to 30°. Sylvia baked a turkey. All our children, grandchildren (except Laura and her family, who we visited with on Thursday) and grand children were here for a Thanksgiving dinner. My, what a good time we had. After a huge meal (everyone brought pot luck to go with turkey) the men went out in the garage to discuss where to put the gun safe I had in the bed of the pickup. After much discussion pro and con it was decided to put it in the basement. We had some problems but got it there. Then it was pie and ice cream on top of already full stomachs. More play with the grandkids and it was time for everyone to head for home. We are tired tonight.

Sunday, November 27, 2005—foggy with a thin coat of ice that melted about noon. 23° to 39°. Did a few small things and rested a lot today.

Monday, November 28, 2005—raining till 2:00 PM and started again about 5:00 PM. 40° to 34°. Tried to level the garbage truck tracks. Did a few small things. Called Patti Billman about our claims. Nadia told us, Lucille fell and broke her hip.

Tuesday, November 29, 2005—34° to 16° most of day. We have snow and it's windy some times. Shoveled the snow off the deck, one flag pole got bent so I brought the flag in. Started the snow blower and tried it out. It can't hold a candle to my old plow truck. Got a bunch of letters addressed. Sylvia's sister Frances called to tell her that her brother Frank had a leg amputated and went into a coma. Fran then talked a long time.

Wednesday, November 30, 2005—9° to 24°. partly cloudy, sunny, cloudy. Went into town. Checked on my shotgun barrel. Got eight 2 x 4 x 8' at lumber yard. Started building a reloading bench. Sylvia's brother Frank Kolenc (lives in Lokve, Slovenia) has died.

Thursday, December 1, 2005—very little snow, cloudy. 12° to 20°. Worked a while on plans and how to set up my reloading bench and gun cleaning table and also the work bench for garage. I haven't found a missing part for a reloading press. Sylvia is slowly fighting off the crud. She feels better today!

Friday, December 2, 2005—mostly cloudy. 6° to 20°. Hunted through my stuff for the missing part for my reloading press with no luck. Worked on the reloading bench. Talked to Lillian and Allen Rollins. He has congenital heart failure, but is out of hospital now. Lorraine Hanson called – Neva McCoy has had a stroke.

Saturday, December 3, 2005—Cloudy and light snow. 12° to 22° to 5°. Mike Olson asked me to come over and help him with a throttle problem on his ATV. Got it lubed in the cable and working again. He came over later and plowed our driveway. We carried the frame for the reloading bench into the basement and assembled. Needs plywood ends and read panel, drawer and paint. Carried a bunch of cardboard boxes to storage shed. I found the two pieces that were misplaced and go with my RCBS reloading press. A red letter day! Dragged an old mattress out to junk shed.

Sunday, December 4, 2005—mostly cloudy. -2° to 14°. Saw tracks of a small deer in our driveway. Did a little on the reloading bench. Swept snow off the deck. Called Jerry Lizza and got Kahren's phone number, left a message, and Kahren called back. Sylvia and she had a nice visit.

Monday, December 5, 2005—partly cloudy. -3° to 8°. Worked a little on reloading bench. After lunch – took Sylvia in to get a mammogram done at local hospital. Stopped by Pap's Gun Shop but my shotgun barrel wasn't ready. We shopped for groceries at Coburn's. When we got home the lock on the door wouldn't unlock. I finally had to destroy it to get the door open.

Tuesday, December 6, 2005—mostly cloudy with very light snow. -2° to 16°. I have a headache and sinus draining giving me a sore throat. Didn't do anything much today.

Wednesday, December 7, 2005—partly cloudy. 11° to 30°. Pear Harbor Day! We went to St Cloud to have our "Directive for our Health Care" drawn up. This also referred to as a "Living Will." We met with a VA social worker who guided us in this. We visited Jerry and Mo Lizza. After shopping at Menards we went back to Jerry and Mo's. The ladies visited, and we men went to Sportsman Warehouse where I did a little shopping and also another store. After supper here at home I installed new entry locks on the house. Theresa called. She has asthma attack and is in hospital.

Thursday, December 8, 2005—sunny sometimes, very nice. 3° to 31°. We prepared for painting and painted the reloading bench and work bench for the garage. Went into town and picked up my shotgun barrel from Pap's Gun Shop. It took their gunsmith five weeks to ream the full choke out to modified choke. Then over to Wal-Mart for Sylvia's prescriptions and some shopping.

Friday, December 9, 2005—mostly cloudy. 0° to 21°. We went to Peter and Delaine Achermann's North of Leader MN and visited quite awhile. Had a nice lunch. We stopped by Harry McCoy and visited then on to Staples Hospital and visited Neva McCoy and Eva Adams. Stopped by our son Paul's place. He had just got home from work. Gave him copies of our "Living Will Directive." We had supper at a restaurant in Little Falls and then came home. Lots of call on our message phone. Two were to tell us that Bart Bartly had died. Theresa tells us she is home from hospital. She has a number of health problems.

Saturday, December 10, 2005—cloudy all day. 16° to 39°. Lots of phone calls. One lasted 2 ½ hrs. In between ph calls I worked on the reloading bench. Put supports and a shelf in the storage area. Installed the bench part of the glides. We carried in the panel for the bench back side.

Sunday, December 11, 2005—cloudy. 10° to 29°. Worked on loading bench drawers. Finished two of them. Had a heck of a time with the second one. Tired tonight. We didn't get delivery of the Star Tribune Sunday paper.

Monday, December 12, 2005—cloudy, skiff of snow in night. 18° to 36°.
Worked on reloading bench and started on garage work bench. Sylvia did most
of painting. Had to go to Archers (1 mile) for 1 sheet of plywood. Harry
Termin called – he and Judy will visit us tomorrow. Went in to grocery store for
a few things we needed including salt for cement between house and garage.

Tuesday, December 13, 2005—cloudy. 22° to 33°. We met Harry and Judy
Termin at "Perkins" and had breakfast. Then we all went to our house and
showed them our house. Sylvia put a soup and ham sandwich on for lunch.
We got caught up on the Alaska news. Weather report is for 3 days of snow.
Harry wanted to get to Michigan, ahead of the storm and left.

Wednesday, December 14, 2005—Snow in night and all day. 28° to 33°.
Shoveled some snow and used snow blower on some and neighbor Mike Olson
plowed some with his ATV. Cut out styrene blocks to stop loss of heat at
basement windows. Did some other small things including Christmas cards.

Thursday, December 15, 2005—Cloudy and 2+" in snow overnight. 21° to 39°.
Plowed some snow from in front of garage. Shoveled the deck off and the berm
the township plow leaving across our driveway. Took Sylvia to hair dresser to
get a permanent. While she was there I ask two heating contractors for a quote
for a new furnace. Stopped by the newspaper office and got a Morrison Co. plat
book. Went to Co. Assessors office to make sure we had homestead exemption
on our property then went to Wal-Mart for some shopping. I checked out a
portable battery "jumper" there. Got home and Mike Olson had plowed our
drive. Looks good. Sylvia brought home an artificial Christmas tree.

Friday, December 16, 2005—cloudy and 1-2" snow. 23° to 12°. Burned some
packing material from moving. Some newspapers and cardboard boxes. Sylvia
made a pretzel candy with chocolate. Ate too much of it. Cleaned up some
stuff from basement. Found my powder measure and mounted it on reloading
bench. Rearranged some things in garage. Got more Christmas cards ready to
go. Winds gusted enough to blow snow around. Moved some reloading
furniture and carried lots of boxes of books down to the book cases in basement.

Saturday, December 17, 2005—pretty nice day. 11° to 20° to 3°. We went to a
gun show in Brainerd. Saw Allen, Scott and Andy Rollins. Also Richard, Paul
and Al Eckes. Bought a pair dress gloves and a gun list. We then went to
Theresa Parts Store and got repairs for our cook stove. Stopped at Arby's for a
sandwich. Took hwy 210 west a ways turned north to Bob and Kahren
Rudbecks. Visited a while. They gave us two squash, a goose and couple ducks.
Went on west to Staples and visited Paul and Ruth. I stopped at Tru Value
hardware and bought a Yugoslavia Mauser 8MM. We then got pizza for supper

and went home.

Sunday, December 18, 2005—sunny. -6° to 11°. Went to Wal-Mart for a couple gifts for Joey and Maggie. Went to their house in Rogers to celebrate Joey's 2nd birthday. His father Brad's parents, Kay Behrendt and his wife, Marilyn and sisters, Lisa and Katie were there. We had a good time. The six kids all played together very well. We saw a small flock of geese flying out to feed in mid afternoon. Got home and dismantled an old display case. Will use the parts in building a garage work bench.

Monday, December 19, 2005—sunny. -12° to 23°. Started on a table for cleaning guns on. The gas co. came and ran a line to house from supply tank. Left a regulator to be attached to house and service the propane furnace when it is installed. Couldn't get through on the phone to the person that is to help us with deciding who will be providing Sylvia's prescriptions.

Tuesday, December 20, 2005—sunny. 2° to 32°. Put both a primer and a coat of enamel on the frame and legs for the gun cleaning table. Looks good. Did some cleaning of the 8 mm rifle barrel. Everything went good with Allen Rollins hernia operation. Went rabbit hunting after lunch. Only saw one pheasant track; I think it was a hen. Tripped on something in the snow. Fell and plugged the shotgun barrel with snow so I went home.

Wednesday, December 21, 2005—Moderate temps. Worked on frame for cleaning guns and storage. Painted it. Made a shelf to go between the bench top and floor. Sylvia helped me carry it down in to basement. Rearranged gun room. Went grocery shopping.

Thursday, December 22, 2005—Went to rifle range to shoot the 8mm Mauser. Took some getting used to sights. Did get a 3 7/8" group at 100 yards. Sure did a lot of walking back and forth to target. Drove around on some of the roads east of here. Got turned around a couple times but figured out where I went wrong. Cleaned the 8 mm after supper and put away some more reloading things.

Friday, December 23, 2005—partly cloudy, foggy at noon, sunny. 12° to 50°! Returned the signed proposal to home furnace and plumbing to install a propane furnace in our basement. Took a bucket of ice cream over to Mike our neighbor and visited. His brother-in-law Steve stopped by so I got to meet him. Then took a bucket of ice cream over to Jeff Peterson – Christmas gift. Cast some 8 mm lead bullets in the afternoon. Earl dropped Theresa here for the weekend and went on to his parents. Cleaned some more on the 8 mm rifle. Spent a lot of time looking for my shell holders.

Saturday, December 24, 2005—Cloudy, some fog, cloudy. 32° to 39°. Nadia and Chuck got here mid-morning with lots of ham, bread, Danish coffee sweets and other things. Took them around the house to show them what we had been doing. We had a great lunch with lemon and pumpkin pie and ice cream. Lots of visiting and story telling. They left mid afternoon. Sylvia and Theresa took naps. I cleaned on the bore of the Yugo 98 Mauser. Sorted books and took some to basement.

Sunday, December 25, 2005—mostly cloudy. 32° to 36°. Laura, Brad, Maggie and Joey came up from Rogers bringing a breakfast. We had a great time and enjoyed every minute. Showed Brad the progress that's been made with the garage and basement of the house. Laura took a DVD disc home with here and will copy it and send it to Ralph at North Pole, Alaska.

Paul, Ruth, Steve and Lisa came in early afternoon. We had a ham sandwich, salad, dipped snacks, pies etc. till we were stuffed. Then sat around visiting, drinking soft drinks and coffee all afternoon. They all were interested in the progress we have made making this place into a home. Earl came to pick up Theresa and go back to Mpls. Called Allen Rollins and we visited with them till the calling card ran out of time. I put a new champfer on the muzzle of the Yugo 48 Mauser. Started shining up metal but plate on its stock. Gave the bore a few strokes also. The rifle is starting to look better. Sylvia's right shoulder is hurting her.

Monday, December 26, 2005—cloudy. 30° to 35°. Cut and sanded more parts for the work bench in the garage. Made some adjustment on the table saw. Sylvia helped assemble some of lower parts of bench.

Tuesday, December 27, 2005—cloudy and foggy. 31° to 37°. Finished the frame for the work bench. Working on the drawers now. Tired tonight.

Wednesday, December 28, 2005—cloudy, skiff of snow and fog. 31° to 36°. Went to town. At Wal-Mart Sylvia made arrangements to go with Humana's program for prescriptions. I cut out the parts for 3 work bench drawers and Sylvia helped to assemble them. I put on the primer paint coat.

Thursday, December 29, 2005—Cloudy, snow started after dark. 31° to 34°. Put a first coat of grey on the drawers and face of the workbench. Went to Wal-Mart to get a gift for David and Heather. Started prepping some rifle brass.

Friday, December 30, 2005—Snow all night and day, 8". 29° to 31°. Mike tried to clear our snow but ran out of gas. I did it with our blower. Mike and I put chains on his ATV which has a snowblade. Made a blade height adjustment. I reconstructed a cardboard box for David Farmers wedding present. I painted the drawers for the work bench.

Saturday, December 31, 2005–cloudy. 30° to 34° to 24°. Shopping for primers, paint, groceries, etc. Post office was closed. Finish painting the drawers for work bench. Put gas check on and sized 70 8 mm cast bullets. Prepared and reloaded 50 8 mm cartridges. My order for dies and gas check came this morning. Laura sent our DVD back.

Fall, 2009: Norman keeps shooting skills honed at a range in Little Falls, MN.

Epilogue—A poetic encounter with wolves

The following transcript is from an email Norman sent to several friends and family members in 2007 after settling back into life in Minnesota. Still missing his beloved Alaska, Norman found ways to savor and enjoy nature-or perhaps I should say, nature devised ways to find him!

Sunday, October 12, 2007—The Wolves

Sylvia and I had business to do up in Cass County, Minnesota. Sylvia fixed a good breakfast of oatmeal. I put traveling and hunting gear in the car.

After we finished our business, we drove to some county land that is open to hunting. Sylvia set about gathering willow shoots of a size for weaving a basket. I set out to explore the area and perhaps see a squirrel. There are a lot of gray squirrels around there and some are black in color. Plus, there was a chance I might see a grouse. Early on I saw a chickadee, then a sandhill crane that was flying around as if lost from the rest of the flock. An eagle was soaring on the air currents.

After a bit, I came to a field that looked to be growing back a scattering of brush and tall grass. I stood there with my back to heavy brush, wearing blaze orange camo, just soaking up what there was to be seen.

After a few minutes, I noticed two bounding forms about a 150 yards out, coming in my direction. Clumps of willows hindered my view. At about 125 yards, they went behind willows. Shortly, a large wolf with a chunk of what looked like meat, came out in the open. I regretted having forgotten to bring my binoculars. The wolf dropped to its belly and consumed this meat, then rolled around on that area before getting to its feet and going back behind the willows. The other wolf exited out the other side of the willows.

In a little while, I saw three wolves at one time; they seemed to be playing. Then two came out on each side of the willow clump headed directly at me at a trot. They had looked my way several times, but always went back to eating or playing. Perhaps they decided to identify what it was they were looking at. When they got to about 60 yards from me, I touched off the right barrel of my 20 gauge; the shot going over their heads. The two big ones did a sharp 180 and left at a run towards the west. Wolves with a belly full of meat can't run very fast. The other two split off, running to the north a couple hundred yards, then veered off to the east.

The fun being over, I then hunted on my way back to our parking place. Later I got to thinking about all this. I wished I had walked over to what must have been a kill site-but that would have been trespassing on someone else's land.
So long for now,

Norman

Norman and Sylvia Wilkins, Thanksgiving, 2009

About the author and his wife

Norman Wilkins and Slovenia-born Ladislava Kolenc (Sylvia to those who know her) met in postwar Gorizia Italy in 1946, marrying there in 1948. They moved to Iowa where Norman grew up, and farmed in several communities until 1957 when they moved to Motley, Minnesota and built the Tamarack Dell dairy farm. There, they raised their family and farmed until the late 1970s.

Norman had long felt the pull of the north, drawn to the mystique of Alaska—"The Last American Frontier" many said, and once the children were on their own, that desire to go north grew stronger. He made more than one hunting trip to Alaska before the 1978 expedition included in this book, and as the trips unfolded, so did Norman's desire to make Alaska his permanent home—to be a part of the expansive wilderness and yes, explore for gold!

Sylvia was not so enthusiastic in the beginning. (Bear in mind, those first few years they lived in a one-room, 12'x16' plywood cabin with no indoor toilet, no electricity and no running water.) Once, after they settled in Nelchina, Sylvia was asked how she liked Alaska, to which she replied, "I really like the people here, but you can take Alaska and give it back to the Eskimos!"

They *did* find gold in Alaska. They found it in the air, the mountains, the wildlife and especially in the people—the people they worked shoulder to shoulder with and shared their table with; each one weaving an independent piece of the tapestry of everyday life in the '70s, '80s, '90s and until 2005 along the Glenn Highway.

From their log cabin overlooking Scoter Lake at Nelchina, radiating outward to Glennallen, Anchorage, Copper Center, Tok, Palmer, Wasilla, Fairbanks, Denali, Matanuska, Susitna, Valdez, Cordova and other arctic communities, Norman Wilkins recorded daily journal entries throughout the entire 25+ years he and Sylvia spent carving out a life on the Alaskan tundra.

Norman and Sylvia currently live in Minnesota, but a big part of Norman's heart remains in Alaska. I'm proud to call them my parents.

—Nadia Giordana, Cloud 9 Publishing

For more information about the author and his wife,
or to learn where to get additional copies of this book,
go to www.10000daysinalaska.com.

10,000 Days in Alaska by Norman Wilkins
is a three-volume, documentary journal.
To contact the publisher,
email Nadia Giordana

at

iinadia@msn.com

or

nadiagiordana99@gmail.com

Cloud 9 Publishing

Norman Wilkins

www.ingramcontent.com/pod-product-compliance
Lightning Source LLC
Chambersburg PA
CBHW070905100426
42737CB00047B/2611